Turbo Pascal® for Windows™ Bible

Turbo Pascal® for Windows™ Bible

Gary Entsminger

SAMS

A Division of Macmillan Computer Publishing

11711 North College, Carmel, Indiana 46032 USA

For Alison

FIRST EDITION
FIRST PRINTING—1991

International Standard Book Number: 0-672-30212-8
Library of Congress Catalog No.: 91-66924

Publisher
Richard K. Swadley

Publishing Manager
Joseph Wikert

Managing Editor
Neweleen A. Trebnik

Acquisitions Editor
Gregory S. Croy

Development Editor
Paula Northam Grady

Editors
Kezia Endsley
Becky Freeman
Jodi Jensen
Rebecca Whitney

Technical Editor
Jeffrey Hsu

Production
Claudia Bell
Sandy Grieshop
Denny Hager
Audra Hershman
Bob LaRoche
Laurie Lee
Juli Pavey
Howard Peirce
Tad Ringo
Bruce Steed
Mary Beth Wakefield
Lisa Wilson
Phil Worthington
Christine Young

Book Design
Scott Cook
Michele Laseau

Cover Design
Tim Amrhein

Indexer
Johnna VanHoose

Composed in Garamond and MCP Digital by Macmillan Computer Publishing.

Printed in the United States of America

Overview

Contents

III REFERENCES

A ObjectWindows Objects, 405

B ObjectWindows Constants, 499

Introduction

Look out of any window, any morning, any evening, any day.
Robert Hunter

How This Book Is Organized

Welcome to *Turbo Pascal for Windows Bible*, a book that will clear many of the mysteries of Windows programming in Turbo Pascal for Windows style. Windows programming is difficult, but Turbo Pascal for Windows makes the difficulty manageable. In fact, developing Windows applications with Turbo Pascal for Windows is much more fun once you get the hang of it. This bible shows you how to get the hang of it.

Turbo Pascal for Windows Bible consists of three sections:

1. Working With TPW

   An introduction to object-oriented programming and the Turbo Pascal for Windows object library, ObjectWindows, plus the language syntax and other details. This section is loaded with practical examples and is intended to bring you up to Windows application development speed in a hurry.

2. Advanced topics

   This section discusses some of the more complex aspects of Windows application development, such as memory management, dynamic data exchange (DDE), dynamic link libraries (DLL), design considerations, and so on. This section is the one to read and study after you know the basics of object-oriented programming, TPW-style.

3. Reference

   A detailed account of the ObjectWindow object-oriented library, including objects, procedures, records, and constants. The reference also is a complete description of the Windows API functions, a glossary, a reading list, and anything else that is important but does not fit in the first two sections.

Reader, Who Are You?

Although I cannot be sure, I assume that you already know how to program using Turbo Pascal (for DOS). Turbo Pascal for Windows uses similar syntax and many of the same functions and procedures as Turbo Pascal (for DOS). Anything specific to Turbo Pascal for Windows is explained, and any differences between Turbo Pascal for Windows and Turbo Pascal (for DOS) are discussed. If you have never programmed in Turbo Pascal for Windows, but have programmed in a procedural language such as C, C++, or Modula 2, you probably will manage to learn Turbo Pascal for Windows programming. This book makes it easier for you with a general introduction to Turbo Pascal syntax and programming. If you need more details about Turbo Pascal in general (not Windows-specific information), pick up a good Turbo Pascal (for DOS) book, such as Tom Swan's *Mastering Turbo Pascal 6* (Hayden Books) to use as a general Turbo Pascal reference.

If you are already familiar with the Turbo Pascal for Windows integrated development environment (IDE) and editor, you can either glance over or skip the first chapter. Chapter 1 is primarily intended to familiarize you with the preliminaries: how to install Turbo Pascal for Windows, system requirements, how the IDE, compiler, and editor work, and so on. The "real" programming and object-oriented discussions start in Chapter 2.

Conventions in This Book

These conventions have been used throughout the book to increase its readability:

- All program listings; "snippets" of program code; keywords; procedure, function, and method names; types (such as `base` and `derived`); and objects (such as `BasicInterface`, `MainWindow`, `TWindow`, `TApplication`, `BasicApplication`) are in `monospace` type.

- Book titles, along with terms included in the Glossary (on first occurrence in the text), appear in *italics*.
- Units, program names, and library names (ObjectWindows) appear in regular type.

Acknowledgments

I'd like to thank a few folks who have supported, advised, offered suggestions, read the manuscript, provided software, or just plain been helpful to me during the writing of *Turbo Pascal for Windows Bible*: Greg Croy and Paula Northam Grady at Macmillan Computer Publishing; Nan Borenson at Borland International; Phil Davis at the Whitewater Group; Alison Brody; Susan Allen; and Billy Barr at the Rocky Mountain Biological Laboratory.

Trademarks

About the Author

Gary Entsminger is a writer, programmer, and consultant. He was an associate editor for *Micro Cornucopia, (the technical journal)* for five years, and a columnist for Borland's *Turbo Technix* magazine.

He is the author of *The Tao of Objects*, a beginner's guide to object-oriented programming, and his articles have appeared in *Dr. Dobb's Journal*, *Computer Language*, *AI Expert*, *Midnight Engineering*, *AI Week*, and *Neural Network News*. Gary lives in the Elk Mountains of Colorado.

Gary Entsminger
c/o: Rocky Mountain Biological Laboratory
Box 519
Crested Butte, CO 81224

PART ONE

WORKING WITH TPW

1

CHAPTER

GETTING STARTED

In earlier days, the video display was used solely to echo text that the user typed using the keyboard. In a graphical user interface, the video display itself becomes a source of user input.

Charles Petzold

Creating Windows Applications

You can create Windows applications using Turbo Pascal for Windows in three different ways:

1. The easiest way is to use the `WinCrt` unit. This unit enables you to write "standard" Turbo Pascal for Windows applications that use Turbo Pascal (for DOS) functions and procedures, such as `Readln` and `Writeln` in a scrollable window. The `WinCrt` unit also lets you transfer your existing Turbo Pascal code to Windows with the least amount of effort. I describe the `WinCrt` unit in more detail in Chapter 2, "Elements of Application Development," and in the reference section.

2. You also can write Windows applications in the more or less "traditional" way, by creating your own windows and windows classes, and setting up your own message loop. This is the way "C'ers" usually do it, and I briefly describe this method in an example in Chapter 2.

3. The best way to write full-featured, extendable Windows applications is to use the ObjectWindows application framework (or object library).

ObjectWindows uses object-oriented techniques to encapsulate complex Windows behavior and make connections between Windows and your application. If you use ObjectWindows, Windows applications are both easier to write and more efficient. Throughout this book, I use and describe in detail how to use ObjectWindows.

System Requirements and Installation

To run Turbo Pascal for Windows, you need Microsoft Windows, a PC with at least 2M (megabytes) of RAM, and an EGA, VGA, or Hercules video adapter. You also have to run Windows in Standard or 386 Enhanced mode because Turbo Pascal for Windows does not run in Real mode. In addition, if you plan to debug in SVGA (Super Video Graphics Adapter) mode, you must use dual monitors.

To install Turbo Pascal for Windows, use the Install program on the Turbo Pascal for Windows distribution disks. The Turbo Pascal for Windows system and example files on the distribution disks are archived, so Install de-archives them for you, puts them in convenient subdirectories, and automatically creates configuration files for both the command-line compiler and the integrated development environment (IDE).

To run the installation program from drive A, enter:

```
C:\ Win A:Install
```

or, if Windows is active, select the Program Manager's `File/Run` command and enter:

```
A:Install
```

Note: If you are a hands-on kind of person, or have another motive, you can use Unpak.exe to unpack the archived files manually.

After you have completed the installation, add the Turbo Pascal for Windows directories (for example, `C:\TPW; C:\TPW\UTILS`) in the DOS path you specify in AUTOEXEC.BAT. If you do not know how to edit your AUTOEXEC.BAT file, refer to your DOS manuals.

The Turbo Pascal for Windows IDE

Turbo Pascal for Windows is a complete development environment for Microsoft Windows. It consists of an editor, compiler, linker, and debugger in one package. You can edit many source-code files (as a project), compile them, and link them into an executable application without leaving the Turbo Pascal for Windows environment. Figure 1.1 shows the Turbo Pascal for Windows start-up screen.

Most of your visual activity (what you see) occurs in a Turbo Pascal for Windows Edit window. Turbo Pascal for Windows lets you have as many as 32 windows open at a time, provided there is enough memory. Only one window can be active at a time. The active window is the one in which you are working (editing, compiling, and so on).

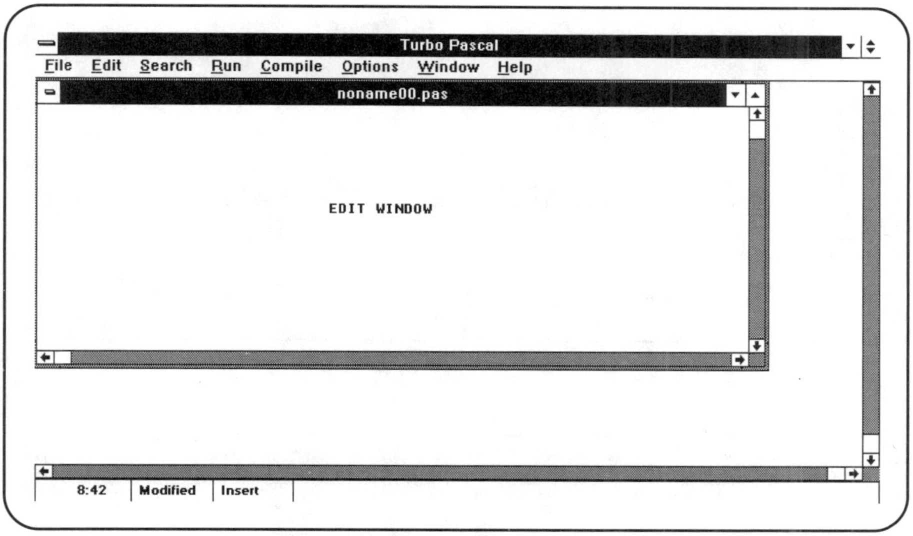

Figure 1.1. *The Turbo Pascal for Windows start-up screen.*

An Edit window consists of

- A title bar
- The Window Control menu box
- Scroll bars
- Minimize and Maximize buttons

Refer to figure 1.2 for a sample Edit window.

In addition to Edit windows, Turbo Pascal for Windows displays various dialog windows in response to user menu selections, errors, and so on. A Replace Text dialog box, for example, appears when you select `Search/Replace Text` from the Main menu, as shown in figure 1.3.

Dialogs (which you will learn much more about in this book) can consist of input boxes, command buttons, and so on. Typically, you check boxes, input text, and specify options; then you click a command button to close the dialog box.

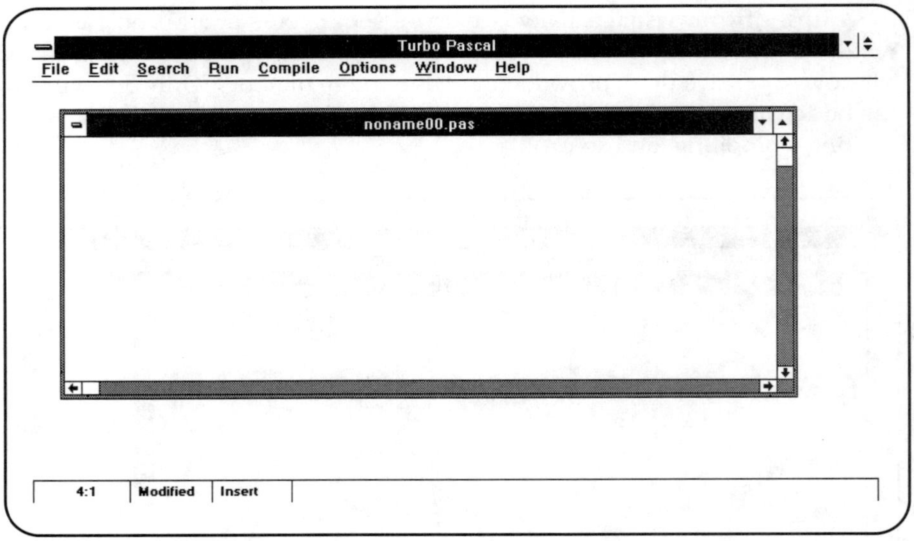

Figure 1.2. An Edit window.

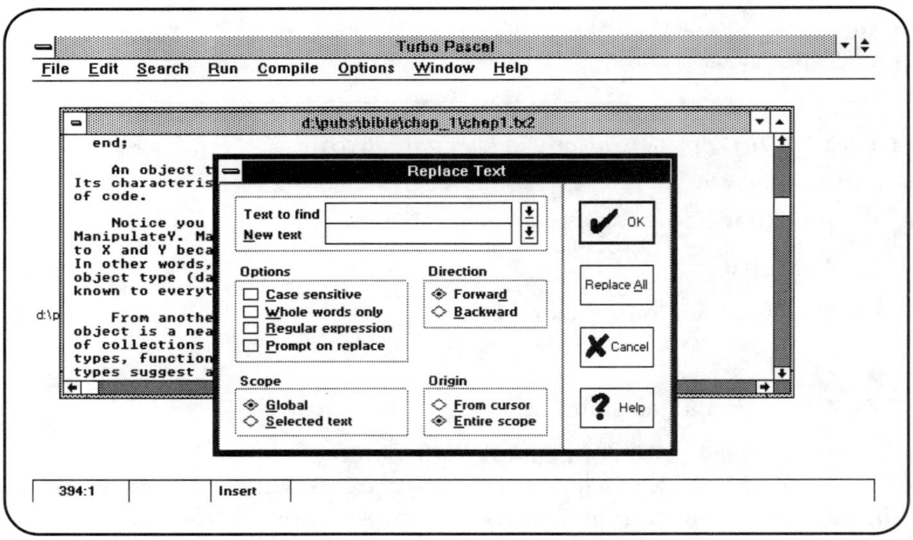

Figure 1.3. A Replace Text dialog box.

Turbo Pascal for Windows IDE Menu Commands

The Turbo Pascal for Windows IDE Menu options are complex and powerful. For your convenience, the menus are separated into

- Desktop control
- Edit window control
- File
- Edit
- Search
- Run
- Compile
- Options
- Window
- Help menus

The Turbo Pascal for Windows Desktop Control Menu

The Turbo Pascal for Windows Control Menu box is on the far left side of the title bar. Click the control menu box once or press Alt-Spacebar to display the menu. The commands grouped in this menu manage the Turbo Pascal for Windows desktop.

Each Edit window and dialog box also has a (similar) Control menu.

The Desktop Control menu commands are

- Restore
- Move
- Size
- Minimize
- Maximize
- Close
- Switch To

Restore

When you select the Restore command from the Desktop Control menu, the Turbo Pascal for Windows desktop window returns to its previous size.

Note: You can use this command only if the Turbo Pascal for Windows desktop window is maximized or minimized.

Move

The Move command moves the desktop window. Use the arrow keys to move the window where you want it and then press Enter. You also can move the window by dragging its title bar. The title bar is the top horizontal bar of a window; it contains the name of the file that is in the window.

Note: You cannot use this command when the desktop is maximized.

Size

You can alter the size of the desktop window with the Size command. Use the cursor arrow keys to move the window borders. Then press Enter when you are satisfied with the window's size.

Note: Size is an available option only when the Turbo Pascal for Windows desktop is not maximized.

Minimize

By selecting the Minimize command, you can turn the Turbo Pascal for Windows desktop into the TPW icon. (An icon represents a window in its minimized state. Applications, such as TPW, can have their own unique icons.)

Note: You can select this command only if the desktop window hasn't been minimized already.

Maximize

If you select the Maximize command, the desktop window fills the entire screen.

Note: You can select this command only if the Turbo Pascal for Windows desktop window has not been maximized already.

Close

The Close command closes the desktop and then unloads Turbo Pascal for Windows from memory. The command is activated in two different ways, depending on the current mode:

- In CUA (command user access) mode, you press Alt-F4 to close the desktop.
- In Alternate mode, you press Alt-X to close the desktop.

You also can click the close box in the upper-left corner to close the window.

If you have modified an Edit window but have not saved the file, a dialog box appears so that you can verify whether you want to save the file before closing.

Switch To

The Switch To command displays the Task List dialog box that you can use to switch from one application to another and to rearrange application windows.

The Edit Window Control Menu

Each Edit window has a Control menu when the window is active. The commands on this menu are similar to those of the Turbo Pascal for Windows Control menu.

These commands are available on the Edit Window Control menu:

- Restore
- Move
- Size
- Minimize
- Maximize
- Close
- Next

Restore

The Restore command returns the Edit window to its default size. If you have minimized or maximized the Edit window, use Restore to return it to its previous (default) size. If you have not minimized or maximized the window, the Restore command is disabled.

Move

Use the Move command to move your Edit window with keyboard keys or by dragging its title bar.

After you select Move, use the arrow keys to move the window. When you're satisfied with the window's new position, press Enter.

Note: You can use Move only when your Edit window isn't maximized.

Size

You can change the size of your Edit window using the keyboard; or, if a window has a Resize corner, you can drag the corner to resize the window.

After selecting Size, use the arrow keys to move the window borders. When you are satisfied, press Enter.

Note: You can use Size only when your Edit window isn't maximized or minimized.

Minimize

Select the Minimize command to shrink your Edit window to an icon on the Turbo Pascal for Windows desktop.

Note: You can select this command only if the window has not been minimized already.

Maximize

The Maximize command enlarges the Edit window so that it fills the Turbo Pascal for Windows desktop.

Note: You can select this command only when the window has not been maximized already.

Close

The Close command closes the Edit window.

You also can double-click the Close box in the upper-left corner to close a window.

If you have modified text in the window and have not saved the text, a dialog box appears that gives you the option of saving the file before you close.

Next

The Next command activates the next open window or icon.

The File Menu

The File menu offers you choices for creating new files, opening and loading existing files, saving files, printing files, and exiting Turbo Pascal for Windows. The File menu commands include the following:

- New
- Open
- Save
- Save As
- Save All
- Print
- Printer Setup
- Exit
- List of closed files

New

New opens a new Edit window with the default name NONAMExx.PAS (the xx stands for a number from 00 to 99), and makes the new Edit window active.

A NONAME file is used as a temporary edit buffer. If you try to save a NONAME file, Turbo Pascal for Windows prompts you to name it before it can be saved.

Open

The Open command displays the File Open dialog box. In this dialog box, you select the file you want to open, as illustrated in figure 1.4.

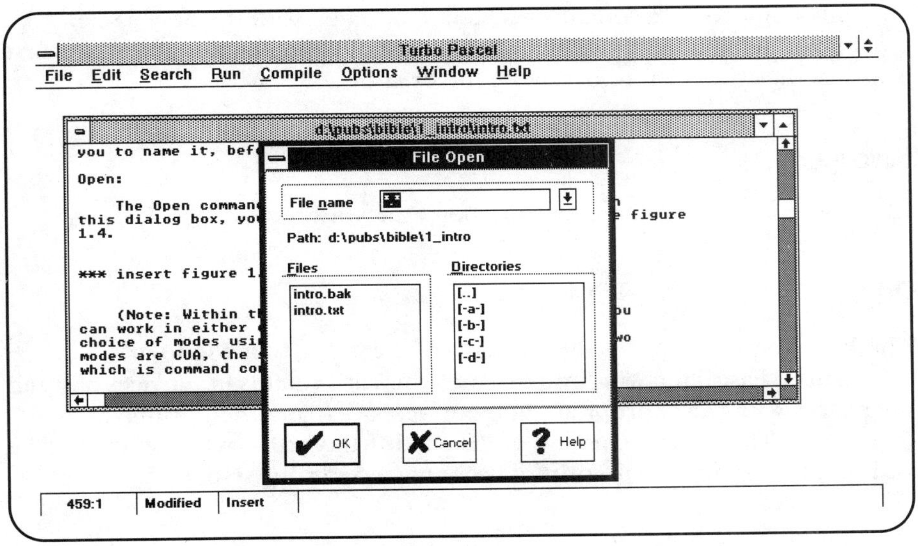

Figure 1.4. The File Open dialog box.

> **Note:** In the Turbo Pascal for Windows Desktop, you can work in either of two edit modes. You specify your choice of modes using the Options/Preferences menu. The two modes are CUA, the standard Windows mode, and Alternate, which is command-compatible with other Borland editors.

In Alternate mode, press F3 to open a file.

Save

The Save command saves to a disk the file in the active Edit window. If the file has a default name (such as NONAME00.PAS), Turbo Pascal for Windows opens the File Save As dialog box so that you can rename the file and save it in a different directory or on a different drive.

If you use an existing file name to name the file, Turbo Pascal for Windows asks whether you want to overwrite the existing file.

If you want to save all modified files, not just the file in the active Edit window, select File/Save All.

In Alternate mode, press F2 to save a file.

Save As

Save As opens the File Save As dialog box, which lets you save the file in the active Edit window under a different name, in a different directory, or on a different drive (see figure 1.5).

All windows that contain this file are updated with the new name.

If you select a file name that already exists, Turbo Pascal for Windows first asks whether you want to overwrite the existing file.

Save All

This command saves all the files in open Edit windows.

Print

The Print command prints the contents of the active Edit window.

Turbo Pascal for Windows expands the Tabs (that is, it replaces any Tab characters with the appropriate number of spaces) and then prints the file.

Note: The Print command is disabled if the active window cannot be printed; for example, if no printer is connected to your system.

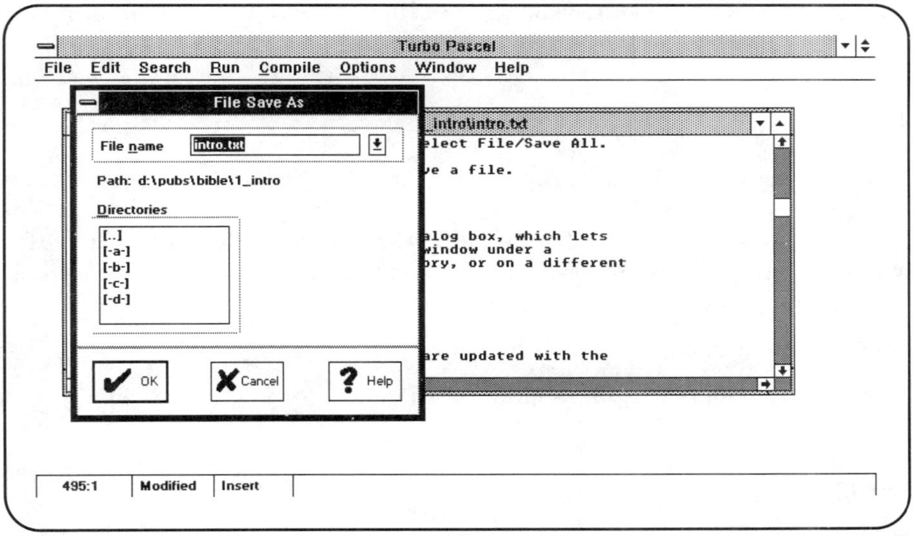

Figure 1.5. *The File Save As dialog box.*

Printer Setup

The Printer Setup command displays a Select Printer dialog box, which lets you select a printer type for Turbo Pascal for Windows (see figure 1.6).

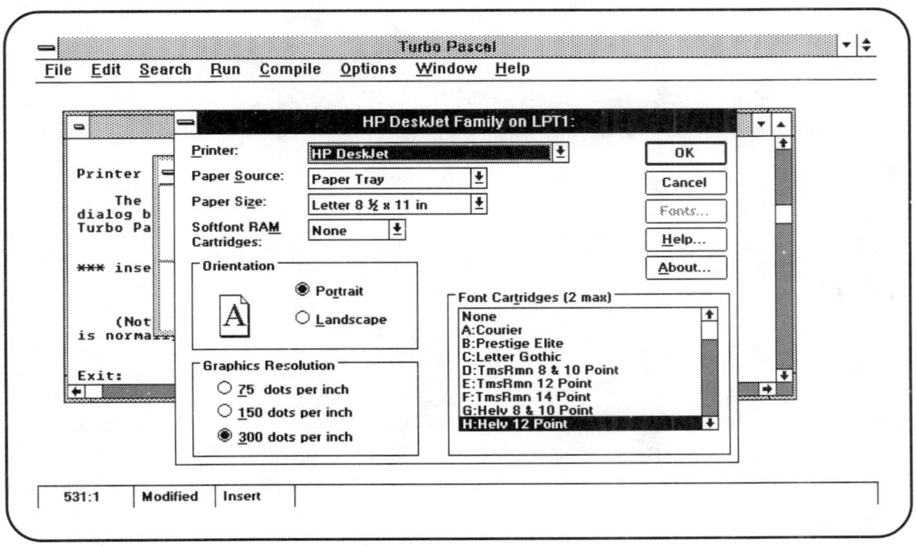

Figure 1.6. *The Select Printer dialog box.*

Note: If you do not want to alter the way your printer is normally configured, you do not have to use Printer Setup.

Exit

The Exit command exits Turbo Pascal for Windows and removes it from memory.

If you have modified a source file without saving it, Turbo Pascal for Windows prompts you to save the file before exiting. The Exit command is mode-dependent:

- In CUA mode, press Alt-F4 to exit.
- In Alternate mode, press Alt-X to exit.

List of Closed Files

This command lists all the files that have been closed since start-up. Select any closed file from the menu to quickly reopen it.

The Edit Menu

The Edit menu includes commands to undo, redo, cut, copy, paste, and clear text in Edit windows.

Also, you can open a `Clipboard` window to view or edit its contents.

The Edit menu commands are

- Undo
- Redo
- Cut
- Copy
- Paste
- Clear

Undo

The Undo command restores the most recent edit or cursor movement.

Undo inserts any characters you deleted, deletes any characters you inserted, replaces any characters you overwrote, and moves your cursor back to the previous position.

If you undo a block operation, the file reappears as it did before you executed the block operation.

If you press Undo more than once, it continues to undo changes as long as it can. However, the Undo command does not change an option setting that affects more than one window.

The Group-Undo option in the Options/Preferences dialog box specifies Undo and Redo behavior.

Redo

Redo reverses the effect of the most recent Undo command. Redo is effective only immediately after an Undo or another Redo.

A series of Redo commands reverses the effects of a series of Undo commands.

Cut

The Cut command removes the selected text from a document in the Edit window and puts the text in the Clipboard.

You can then use Edit/Paste to copy the text to another document or to a different place in the current document.

The text remains selected in the Clipboard until you replace it with other text, so you can paste it many times, in as many files as you want.

Copy

The Copy command does not remove the selected text; it leaves the text intact and places an exact copy of it in the Clipboard.

To paste the copied text into another document, select Edit/Paste. You also can copy text from a Help window:

- Using the keyboard, press Shift and an arrow key to select the text you want to copy.
- Use the mouse to click and drag the text you want to copy.

Paste

The Paste command inserts the selected text from the Clipboard into the active window at the current cursor position.

Clear

The Clear command removes the selected text from the document in the active window, but does not move it to the Clipboard. Thus, you cannot paste "cleared" text in a document as you can when you use Cut or Copy.

Note: Although you cannot paste the cleared text, you can undo the Clear command with Undo.

Clear is handy for deleting text without overwriting the current text in the Clipboard.

The Search Menu

The Search menu includes the commands to search for text and error locations in your files.

The Search menu commands are

- Find
- Replace
- Search Again
- Go to Line Number
- Show Last Compile Error
- Find Error

Find

The Find command displays the Find Text dialog box, which lets you type in the text you want to search for. Several options in this dialog box let you specify the details of the search (see figure 1.7).

Replace

The Replace command displays the Replace Text dialog box, which lets you type in the text you want to search for and the text you want to replace it with (see figure 1.8).

Search Again

The Search Again command repeats the previous Find or Replace command.

The previous settings you made in the Find Text or Replace Text dialog box are in effect when you choose Search Again.

In CUA mode, press F3 to search again.

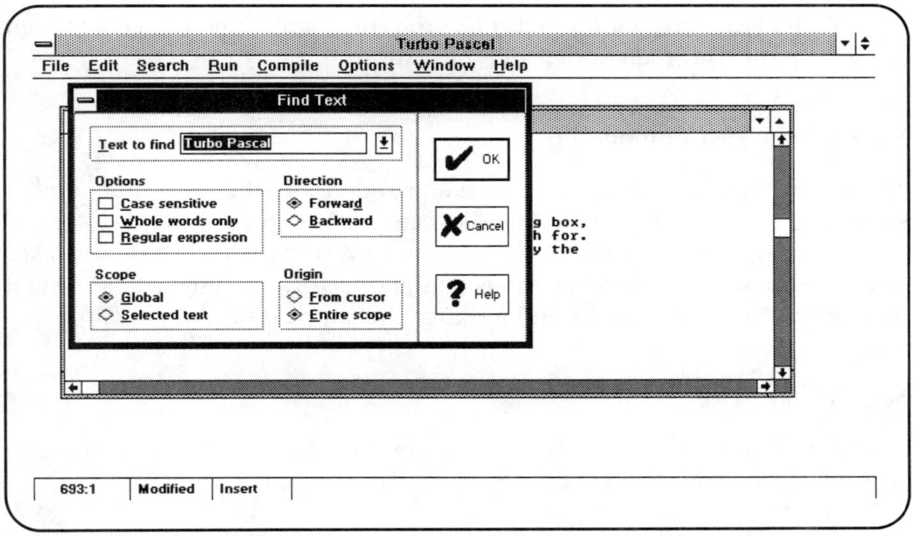

Figure 1.7. The Find Text dialog box.

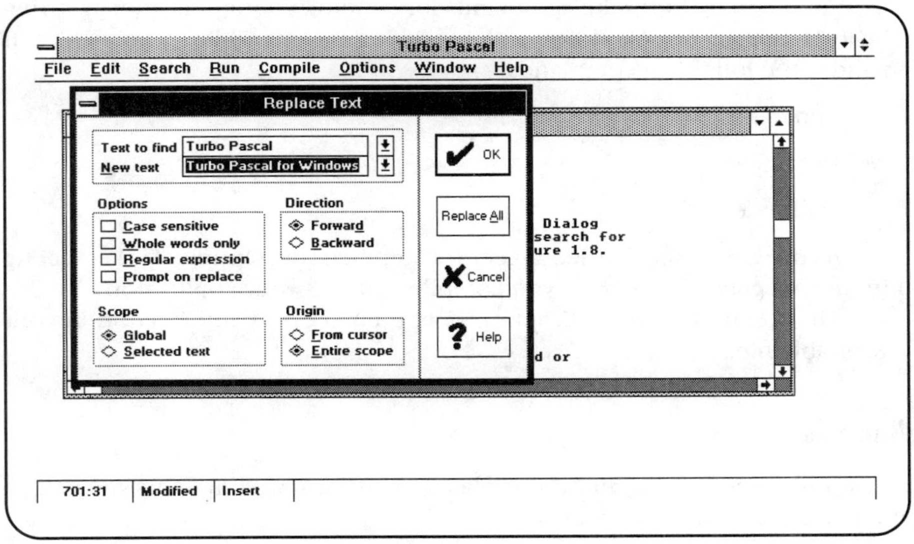

Figure 1.8. The Replace Text dialog box.

Go to Line Number

The Go to Line Number command displays the Go to Line Number dialog box, which prompts you for the line number you want to find.

Turbo Pascal for Windows displays the current line number and column number in the lower-left corner of every Edit window.

Search/Show Last Compile Error

The Search/Show Last Compile Error command locates the previous compiler error. The cursor moves to the line that caused the error.

If the error is not in the active window, Turbo Pascal for Windows makes active the window with the previous compiler error, opening a closed file if necessary. The error number and message then appear on the status bar.

Search/Find Error

The Search/Find Error command brings up the Find Error dialog box, which lets you specify the address of the most recent run-time error.

The Run Menu

The Run menu includes the commands for running your application, starting Turbo Debugger for Windows, and specifying command-line parameters. It includes the following commands:

- Run
- Debugger
- Parameters

If you want to use the debugger on a file, check the Options/Linker/Debug Info in EXE check box before you compile and link your application.

The Debug Info in EXE option puts the necessary information in your executable file.

Run/Run

The Run/Run command runs the application, using any parameters you pass to it through the Run/Parameters command.

If your source code has been modified since the previous compilation, the compiler automatically "does a make" and links your application.

Run/Debugger

The Run/Debugger command starts Turbo Debugger for Windows, and allows you to debug the application.

Turbo Pascal for Windows tells Turbo Debugger for Windows which application to debug.

Check the Options/Linker/Debug Info in the EXE check box before you compile and link your application if you want to use Turbo Debugger to debug it.

The Options/Linker/Debug Info in EXE check box puts the necessary debug information in the executable file.

To get the most from Turbo Debugger's symbolic debugging capabilities, you also should check the Options/Compiler/Debug Information box and the Options/Compiler/Local Symbols box before compiling your application.

Run/Parameters

The Run/Parameters command passes parameters to your application program when you run it as though you were running the application from the Program Manager's File/Run menu.

When you select this command, the Parameters dialog box appears. Your job is to specify the command-line arguments (see figure 1.9).

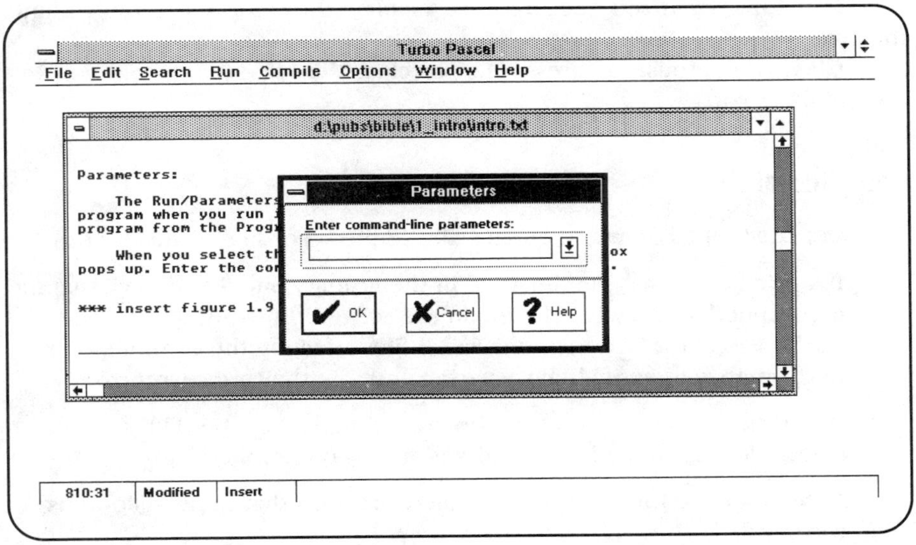

Figure 1.9. The Parameters dialog box.

The Compile Menu

You use the commands on the Compile menu to compile, make, or build your application program.

To use the `Compile` command, you must have a file open in an active window. To use `Make` and `Build`, you must have a primary file defined. Select from these commands:

- Compile
- Make
- Build
- Primary File
- Clear Primary File
- Information

Compile/Compile

The Compile/Compile command compiles the file in the active Edit window.

A Compile Status information box displays the compilation progress and results.

If an error occurred, the status bar displays the error line and highlights the error.

Click your mouse or press a key to clear the message so that you can correct the error.

Compile/Make

The `Compile/Make` command creates a .EXE file according to these rules:

- If a primary file has been named in the Primary File dialog box, that file is compiled. Otherwise, the file in the active Edit window is compiled. Turbo Pascal for Windows checks all files affecting the compiled file's performance to verify that they exist and that they are current.
- If the source file for a unit has been modified since the .TPU (object code) file was created, the modified unit is recompiled.
- If the interface for a unit has changed, any unit that depends on it is recompiled.
- If a unit links in a .OBJ file (external routines), and the .OBJ file is newer than the unit's .TPU file, the unit is recompiled.
- If a unit contains an Include file and the Include file is newer than that unit's .TPU file, the unit is recompiled.
- If the source to a unit (.TPU file) cannot be located, the unit is not compiled.

This option is identical to Compile/Build, except it is conditional. Build rebuilds all files, whether or not they are current.

Compile/Build

The Compile/Build command rebuilds all the components of your application, whether or not they are current.

This option is identical to Compile/Make, except it is unconditional. Make rebuilds only those files that are not current.

The Compile/Build command recompiles all the files included in the primary file.

If you abort a Compile/Build command by pressing Ctrl-Break or receive errors that terminate the build, you can restart the build where it was terminated by selecting Compile/Make.

Compile/Primary File

The Compile/Primary File command displays the Primary File dialog box, which lets you specify which .PAS file will be compiled when you choose Compile/Make or Compile/Build.

Use Compile/Primary File when you are working on an application that uses several unit (.TPU) or Include files. Regardless of the file you are editing, Compile/Make and Compile/Build always operate on your primary file. If you specify another file as a primary file, but want to compile only the file in the active Edit window, choose Compile.

Compile/Clear Primary File

The Compile/Clear Primary File command removes the name of the primary file you specified with the Compile/Primary File command. If a primary file has not been specified, however, the command is disabled.

Compile/Information

The Compile/Information command displays the Compile Information box, the name of your primary file (if you are using one), and the name of the previous file compiled.

Compile Information Box

The Compile Information box lists:

- The name of the primary file (if you are using one)
- The name of the previous file compiled
- The source compiled
- Code size
- Data size

- Stack size
- Local heap size

The Options Menu

The Options menu contains commands for viewing and changing various default settings in Turbo Pascal for Windows. Most of the commands in this menu initiate a dialog box. The commands are

- Compiler
- Linker
- Directories
- Preferences
- Open
- Save
- Save As

Compiler

The Options/Compiler command displays the Compiler Options dialog box, which lets you select the options that determine how your code is compiled (see figure 1.10).

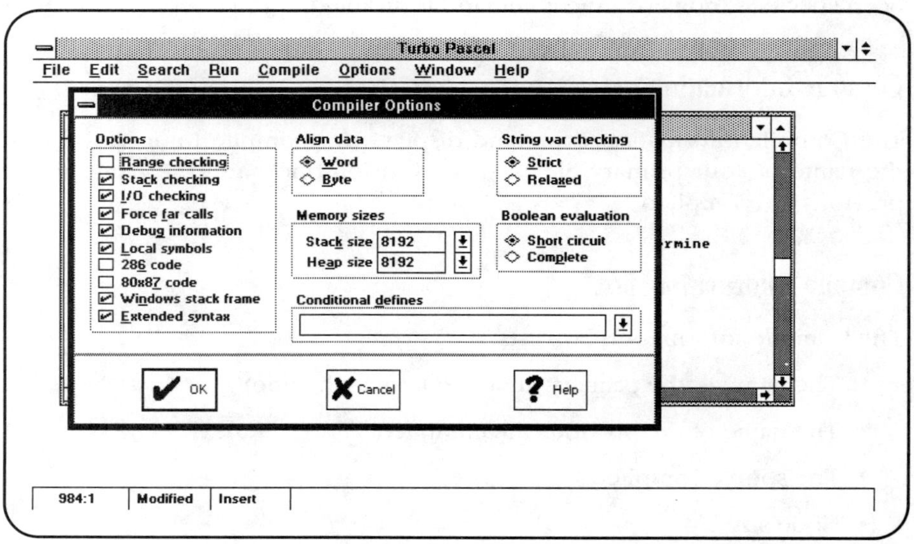

Figure 1.10. *The Compiler Options dialog box.*

Linker

The Options/Linker command displays the Linker Options dialog box, which lets you select the options that determine how your application files are linked, as shown in figure 1.11.

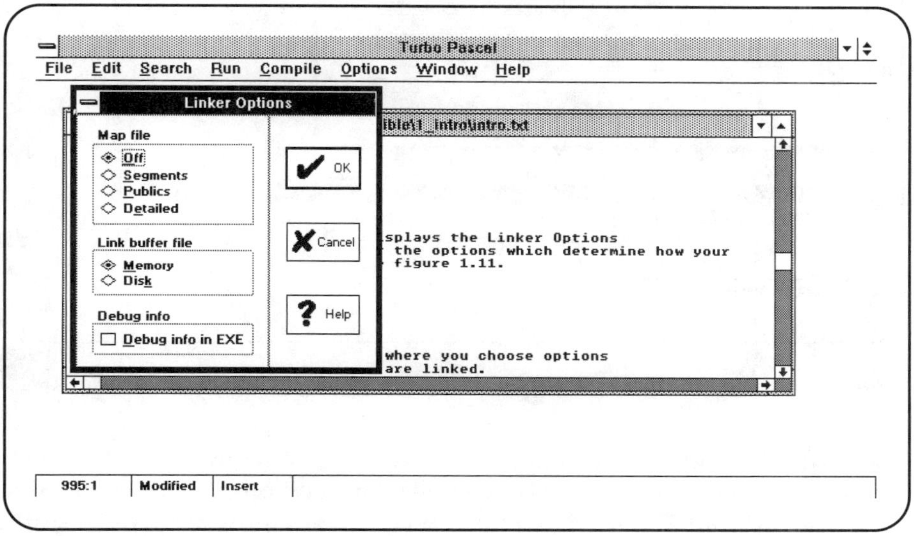

Figure 1.11. The Linker Options dialog box.

Map File options

The Map File options (Off, Segments, Publics, and Detailed) determine the type of map file produced.

Link Buffer File options

The Link Buffer File options (Memory or Disk) specify the location of the link buffer.

Debug Info in EXE option

The Debug Info in EXE option puts debug information in your program's executable file.

Directories

The Directories command opens the Directories dialog box, where you specify the directories you want Turbo Pascal for Windows to use when running and storing your application programs, as illustrated in figure 1.12.

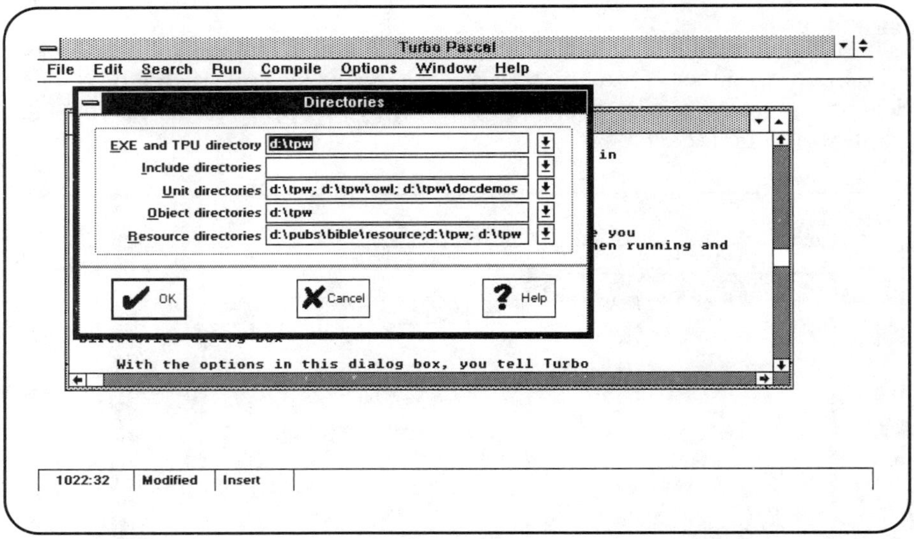

Figure 1.12. *The Directories dialog box.*

With the options in this dialog box, you decide where Turbo Pascal for Windows finds the files it needs to compile, link, and output executable files.

The EXE and TPU Directory input box specifies the directory that stores your .EXE and .TPU (object code) files.

The Include Directories input box specifies the directories that contain your standard Include files.

The Unit Directories input box specifies the directories that contain your Turbo Pascal for Windows unit files.

The Object Directories input box specifies the directories that contain your .OBJ files (assembly language routines).

The Resource Directories input box specifies the directories in which your resource files are kept.

Guidelines for Entering Directory Names

Use the following guidelines when you enter directories in the Options/ Directories input boxes:

- Separate multiple directory path names (if allowed) with a semicolon (;).
- Use a maximum of 127 characters (including white space). White space before and after the semicolon is allowed but not required.
- Relative and absolute path names are allowed, including path names relative to the logged position in drives other than the current one.

For example:

```
C:\ ; D:\TPW
D:\;C:\TPW;D:\TPW
```

Preferences

The Options/Preferences menu command opens the Preferences dialog box, which lets you decide the behavior and physical appearance of the Turbo Pascal for Windows environment (see figure 1.13).

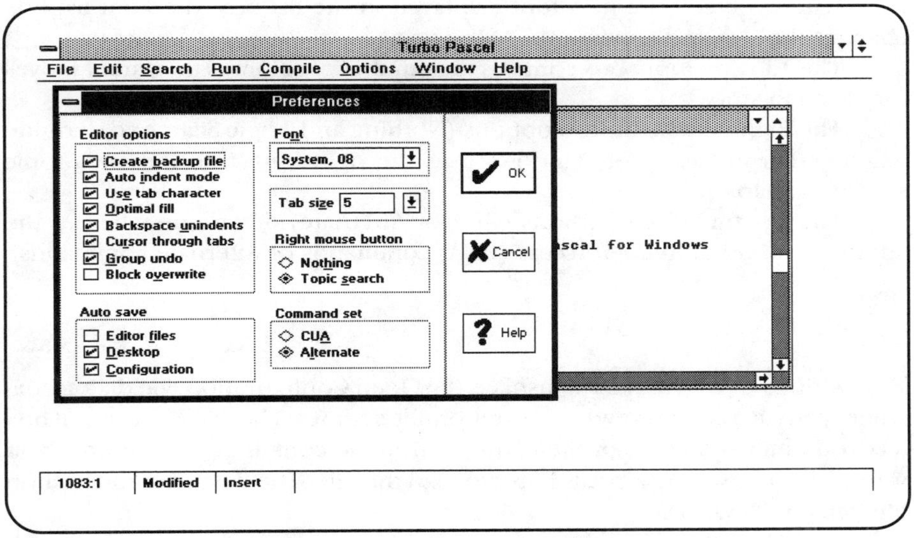

Figure 1.13. *The Preferences dialog box.*

Editor Options

The Editor Options group has several check boxes that control text handling in Edit windows. They are

- Create Backup File
- Auto Indent Mode
- Use Tab Character
- Optimal Fill
- Backspace Unindents

- Cursor through Tabs
- Group Undo
- Block Overwrite

The Auto Save options define when and how often Turbo Pascal for Windows saves your open files, settings, and options. They are

- Editor Files
- Desktop
- Configuration

When you select a new font displayed in the list box, the Font list box changes the size and appearance of the text.

The Tab Size input box controls the number of columns the cursor moves for each tab stop.

The Right Mouse Button options (Nothing and Topic Search) determine whether Turbo Pascal for Windows uses the right button to initiate a topic search in Help.

The Command Set options (CUA or Alternate) determine whether the editor uses Common User Access (CUA) commands or Alternate commands.

Open

The Options/Open command displays the Open Configuration File dialog box, where you can retrieve new configuration-file settings. The File Name input box lets you enter the name of the configuration file containing the settings you want; you choose OK or press Enter to load that file. The default configuration file name is TPW.CFG.

The Files list box lists the names of files in the current directory that match the file-name mask in the File-Name input box.

The Directories list box lets you select a different directory to view. Press Alt-D to place the cursor in this list box.

Save

The Options/Save command saves in the current configuration file the primary file name, the settings you selected with the Options menu, and the desktop setup.

Use Options/Save As to save options to a different configuration file. The name of the current configuration file appears next to the Options/Save command.

- All options and the editor command table are stored in TPW.CFG, the default saved-options file.

- History lists, the desktop state, and breakpoint locations are stored in TPW.INI.

Save As

The Options/Save As command opens the Configuration Save As dialog box, where you enter a new name for your configuration file (see figure 1.14).

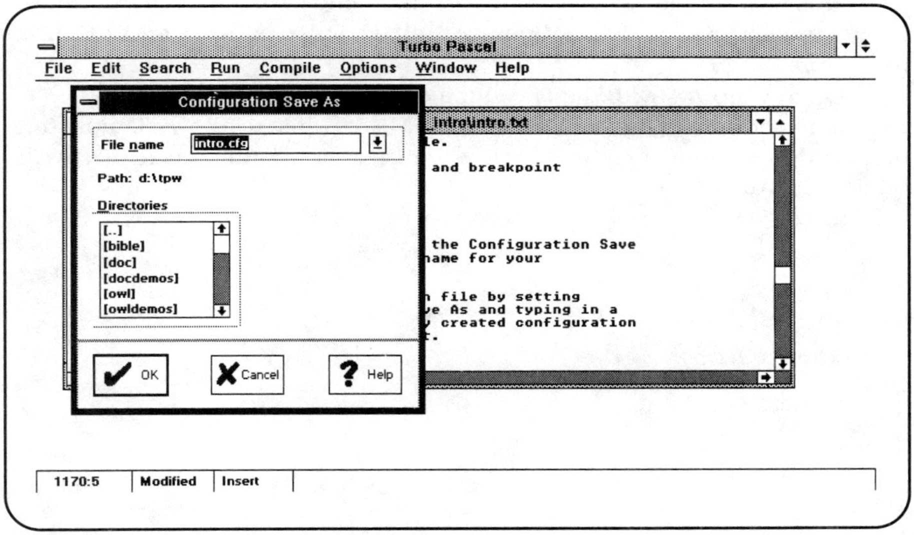

Figure 1.14. The Configuration Save As dialog box.

You can create a new configuration file by setting options and then selecting Options/Save As and entering a new configuration file name. The newly created configuration file is now in effect.

In the File Name input box, enter a new name for the configuration file. Choose OK or press Enter to create a .CFG file with the new name.

If you do not specify a file extension, Turbo Pascal for Windows adds a .CFG extension for you. For example:

```
YOUR becomes YOUR.CFG.
```

A history list is attached to the File Name input box. If the Configuration option is on, settings made to the current configuration file are saved when you exit.

Directories List Box

Use the Directories list box to change to another directory. Press Alt-D to place the cursor in the Directories list box.

The Window Menu

The Window menu has commands for manipulating and opening windows.

Most of the windows you open from this menu have the standard window elements such as scroll bars, Minimize and Maximize buttons, and a Control menu box.

Open windows with the File/Open or File/New commands.

At the bottom of the Window menu is a list of open windows. If more than one window is open, you can switch to another window and make it active by selecting it from the list.

These are the Window menu commands:

- Tile
- Cascade
- Arrange Icons
- Close All

Tile

Choose Window/Tile to tile your open windows. Using this command arranges the windows so that they cover the entire desktop without overlapping one another.

Cascade

Choose Window/Cascade to stack all open Edit windows. Cascade overlaps open windows so that each window is the same size, but part of each underlying window is visible.

Arrange Icons

Select Window/Arrange Icons to rearrange the icons.

Rearranged icons are evenly spaced, beginning at the lower-left corner on the desktop. The open files must be Minimized or this command is disabled.

Close All

Choose Window/Close All to close all open windows on the desktop. If the text was changed since the previous time you saved it, a dialog box warns you to save the file before closing the window. Choose Yes, No, or Cancel.

The Help Menu (Alt-H)

The Help menu provides access to on-line Help, which appears in a special Help window. The Help system provides information about most aspects of the integrated environment and Turbo Pascal for Windows. The following list shows the Help menu commands:

- Index
- Topic Search
- Using Help
- Compiler Directives
- ObjectWindows
- Procedures and Functions
- Reserved Words
- Standard Units
- Turbo Pascal for Windows Language
- Windows API
- About Turbo Pascal for Windows

Index (Shift-F1)

Turbo Pascal for Windows' on-line Help comes with a comprehensive index that summarizes the organization and contents of the Help system. To get into the Help system from the index, select one of the highlighted words or phrases in the index, click it or Tab to it, and then press Enter.

If you don't know how to use a Help system under Windows, choose the Help/Using Help Menu command.

Topic Search (Ctrl-F1)

If you place your cursor on a word (a "token") in the active Edit window and choose Help/Topic Search, a Help window opens with information about that token.

You can set up the Right mouse button (in the Options/Preferences dialog box) to initiate a topic search.

Help provides on-line reference for many elements of the Turbo Pascal for Windows language, including functions and procedures, reserved words, global variables, ObjectWindows, the Windows API, and so on.

Help/Using Help

The Help/Using Help command displays information on how to use Turbo Pascal for Windows' Help system (or any other Help system under Windows).

Compiler Directives

When you choose this menu command, you see an index of compiler directives. Compiler directives control some of Turbo Pascal for Windows' features.

- Some turn compiler features on or off.
- Some specify parameters that affect how your application program is compiled.
- Others control the conditional compilation of your application.

A compiler directive is a comment with a special syntax that you can put anywhere a comment is allowed.

ObjectWindows

When you select this menu command, you see a hierarchy of ObjectWindows types.

Procedures and Functions

When you choose this menu command, you see an index of the Turbo Pascal for Windows library procedures and functions that you can use to develop applications.

Reserved Words

When you select this menu command, you see an index of all the reserved words in the Turbo Pascal for Windows language. Reserved words have special meaning to the compiler. Do not use a reserved word to name your variables, procedures, functions, objects, and so on.

Standard Units

When you select this menu command, you see an index of Turbo Pascal for Windows' standard units. A standard unit is a collection of predefined constants, data types, variables, procedures, and functions. You tell your application program to use only the units it needs.

Turbo Pascal for Windows Language

When you select this menu command, you see a list of the elements that comprise the Turbo Pascal for Windows language.

Windows API

When you select this menu command, you see an index of the constants, styles, messages, types, functions, and procedures that comprise the Windows Application Programming Interface (API). Turbo Pascal for Windows declares all the Windows styles, constants, and types in the `WinTypes` unit. The `WinProcs` unit has all the API procedures and functions.

About Turbo Pascal for Windows

When you select this command, a dialog box appears with copyright and version information.

Press Esc or click OK or Cancel to close the box.

Editor

The Turbo Pascal for Windows editor is a complete programming editor. In almost all cases, you use it to develop all facets of your applications. In addition to being a full-screen, command-rich editor, it is based on Windows' multi-document interface, which you learn how to use in Chapter 7, "Many Windows: A Multi-Document Interface." The multi-document interface enables many files to be open simultaneously. Thus, you can open files for several units and switch between them easily without closing any files—a great feature when you develop large projects.

The Editor Commands

Turbo Pascal for Windows' editor commands are summarized in the following groups of commands:

- Block commands
- Block commands (CUA and Alternate)
- Block commands (Borland style)
- Extending selected blocks
- Other commands
- Cursor-movement commands
- Insert and Delete commands
- More about editor commands
- Miscellaneous keyboard commands

The Block Commands

The following sections describe the block commands.

Copy Block

This command copies a previously selected block to the Clipboard and pastes it to the current cursor position. The original block is unchanged. If no block is selected, nothing happens.

Copy Text

This command copies selected text to the Clipboard. Press Ctrl-Ins to use the command.

Cut Text

This commands cuts selected text to the Clipboard. Press Shift-Del to use the command.

Delete Block

This command deletes a selected block. You can "undelete" a block with Undo. Press Ctrl-Del or Ctrl-KY to use this command.

Move Block

This command moves a previously selected block from its original position to the Clipboard and then pastes it to the cursor position. The block disappears from its original position. If no block is marked, nothing happens. Press Shift-Del to move text to Clipboard and Shift-Ins to paste text in current document.

Paste from Clipboard

This command pastes the contents of the Clipboard to cursor location. Press Shift-Ins to use the command.

Read Block from Disk

This command reads a disk file into the current text at the cursor position exactly as though it was a block. Press Shift-Ctrl-R or Ctrl-KR to use this command.

The text read is then selected as a block. When this command is initiated, you are prompted for the name of the file to read. You can use wildcards to select a file to read, and a directory is displayed. The file specified can be any legal file name.

Write Block to Disk

This command writes a selected block to a file. Press Shift-Ctrl-W or Ctrl-KW to use this command. When you specify this command, Turbo Pascal for Windows prompts you for the name of the file to write to. The file can be given any legal name (the default extension is .PAS). If you prefer to use a file name without an extension, append a period to the end of its name.

Note: If the file specified already exists, a warning is issued before the existing file is overwritten. If no block is selected, nothing happens.

Editor-Command Tables

The tables throughout this section list the editor commands and their function or meaning.

Table 1.1. *The Block commands (CUA and Alternate).*

Movement	*CUA*	*Both*	*Alternate*
Delete block	Ctrl-Del	Ctrl-Del	——
Copy to Clipboard	Ctrl-Ins	Ctrl-Ins	——
Cut to Clipboard	Shift-Del	Shift-Del	——
Paste from Clipboard	Shift-Ins	Shift-Ins	——
Read block from disk	Shift-Ctrl-R	——	Ctrl-KR
Write block to disk	Shift-Ctrl-W	——	Ctrl-KW
Indent block	Shift-Ctrl-I	——	Ctrl-KI
Unindent block	Shift-Ctrl-U	——	Ctrl-KU

Table 1.2. The Block commands (Borland style).

Command	***Keys***	***Function***
Text selection On	Ctrl-KB	Begins the selection of text; text selection ends with copying (Ctrl-KK) or cutting (Ctrl-KV) to the Clipboard, or turning text selection off with Ctrl-KH
Text selection Off	Ctrl-KH	Stops the selection of text, and the selected text becomes unselected
Copy text to Clipboard	Ctrl-KK	Copies the selected text to the Clipboard
Cut text to Clipboard	Ctrl-KV	Cuts the selected text to the Clipboard
Paste from Clipboard	Ctrl-KC	Pastes the contents of the Clipboard into your active Edit window

Extending selected blocks

Movement	***CUA***	***Both***	***Alternate***
Left 1 character	Shift-Left	Shift-Left	—
Right 1 character	Shift-Right	Shift-Right	—
End of line	Shift-End	Shift-End	—
Beginning of line	Shift-Home	Shift-Home	—
Same column, next line	Shift-Down	Shift-Down	—
Same column, previous line	Shift-Up	Shift-Up	—
One page down	Shift-PgDn	Shift-PgDn	—
One page up	Shift-PgUp	Shift-PgUp	—
Left one word	Shift-Ctrl-Left	Shift-Ctrl-Left	—
Right one word	Shift-Ctrl-Right	Shift-Ctrl-Right	—
End of file	Shift-Ctrl-End	Shift-Ctrl-End	Shift-Ctrl-PgDn
Beginning of file	Shift-Ctrl-Home	Shift-Ctrl-Home	Shift-Ctrl-PgUp

> **Note:** Turbo Pascal for Windows' Borland-style block commands work only with the Alternate command set.

Table 1.3. *Commands that extend selected blocks.*

Movement	*CUA*	*Both*	*Alternate*
Left 1 character	Shift-Left	Shift-Left	——
Right 1 character	Shift-Right	Shift-Right	——
End of line	Shift-End	Shift-End	——
Beginning of line	Shift-Home	Shift-Home	——
Same column, next line	Shift-Down	Shift-Down	——
Same column, previous line	Shift-Up	Shift-Up	——
One page down	Shift-PgDn	Shift-PgDn	——
One page up	Shift-PgUp	Shift-PgUp	——
Left one word	Shift-Ctrl-Left	Shift-Ctrl-Left	——
Right one word	Shift-Ctrl-Right	Shift-Ctrl-Right	——
End of file	Shift-Ctrl-End	Shift-Ctrl-End	Shift-Ctrl-PgDn
Beginning of file	Shift-Ctrl-Home	Shift-Ctrl-Home	Shift-Ctrl-PgUp

Table 1.4. *The cursor-movement commands (CUA and Alternate).*

Movement	*CUA*	*Both*	*Alternate*
Character left	Left	Left	Ctrl-S
Character right	Ctrl-Right	Right	Ctrl-D
Word left	Ctrl-Left	Ctrl-Left	Ctrl-A
Scroll down 1 line	Ctrl-Z	Ctrl-Z	Ctrl-Z
Line up	Up	Up	Ctrl-E
Line down	Down	Down	Ctrl-X
Scroll up 1 line	Ctrl-W	Ctrl-W	Ctrl-W
Scroll down 1 line	Ctrl-Z	Ctrl-Z	Ctrl-Z
Page up	PgUp	PgUp	Ctrl-R

continues

Table 1.4. continued

Movement	*CUA*	*Both*	*Alternate*
Page down	PgDn	PgDn	Ctrl-C
Last cursor position	—	—	Ctrl-QP
Beginning of line	Home	Home	Ctrl-QS
End of line	End	End	Ctrl-QD
Top of window	Ctrl-E	—	Ctrl-QE
Bottom of window	Ctrl-X	—	Ctrl-QX
Top of file	Ctrl-Home	Ctrl-Home	Ctrl-QR, Ctrl-PgUp
Bottom of file	Ctrl-End	Ctrl-End	Ctrl-QC, Ctrl-PgDn

Table 1.5. The Insert and Delete commands (CUA and Alternate).

Movement	*CUA*	*Both*	*Alternate*
Delete char	Del	Ctrl-G	—
Delete char to left	Backspace	Backspace	—
Delete line	Ctrl-Y	Ctrl-Y	—
Delete line end	Shift-Ctrl-Y	—	Ctrl-QY
Delete word	—	—	Ctrl-T
Insert line	Ctrl-N	—	Ctrl-N
Insert mode On/Off	Ins	Ins	Ctrl-V

Auto Indent

This command toggles the automatic indenting of successive lines. You also can use Options/Preferences/AutoIndent in the IDE to turn automatic indenting on and off.

Current Compiler Options

Inserts the current compiler-option settings at the head of your active Edit window.

Cursor through Tabs

The arrow keys move the cursor to the middle of tabs when this option is on; otherwise the cursor would jump several columns when it moves over multiple tabs. Ctrl-OR is a toggle.

Find Place Marker

This command finds a maximum of ten place markers (N can be any number in the range zero to nine) in text. Move the cursor to any previously set marker by pressing Ctrl-Q and the marker number.

Open File

Opens an existing file in an Edit window.

Optimal Fill

Optimal Fill begins every line with the minimum number of characters possible, using Tabs and spaces as necessary. This option produces lines with fewer characters.

Save File

This command saves the file and returns to the editor.

Set Place

This command marks a maximum of ten places in text when you press Ctrl-K, followed by a single-marker digit (zero to nine). After marking your location, you can work elsewhere in the file and then return to a marked location by using the Find Place Marker command (be sure to use the same marker number). You can have as many as ten places marked in each window.

Show Last Compile Error

This command highlights the last syntax error that the compiler found during the previous compile. The error message appears on the status bar. If you have already closed that file, Turbo Pascal for Windows reopens it and highlights the error.

Tab Mode

You can specify the use of true Tab characters in the IDE with the Options/Preferences/Use Tab Character option.

Unindent

You can turn Unindent on and off from the IDE with the Options/Preferences/Backspace Unindents option.

Table 1.6. Miscellaneous keyboard commands.

Movement	*CUA*	*Both*	*Alternate*
Autoindent on/off	———	———	Ctrl-OI
Compiler options	———	———	Ctrl-OO
Cursor through Tabs on/off	———	———	Ctrl-OR
Find place marker N	Ctrl-N*	———	Ctrl-Q-N*
Help	F1	F1	———
Help index	Shift-F1	Shift-F1	———
Maximize window	———	———	F5
Open file	———	———	F3
Optimal fill mode on/off	———	———	Ctrl-OF
Pair matching	Alt-[, Alt-]	Ctrl-Q	[, Ctrl-Q]
Save file	———	———	F2, Ctrl-KS
Search	———	———	Ctrl-QF
Search again	F3	F3	———
Search and replace	———	———	Ctrl-QA
Show last compile error	———	———	Ctrl-QW
Set marker	Shift-Ctrl-N*	———	Ctrl-K-N*
Tabs mode on/off	———	———	Ctrl-OT
Topic Help	Ctrl-F1	Ctrl-F1	———
Exit	Alt-F4	———	Alt-X
Undo	Alt-Backspace	Alt-Backspace	———
Unindent mode on/off	———	———	Ctrl-OU
Insert control character	Ctrl-P **	Ctrl-P **	———

** N indicates a number from zero to nine.*

*** To enter a control character, first enter Ctrl-P, and then enter the control character.*

The TPW Command-line Compiler

The Turbo Pascal for Windows command-line compiler (TPCW.EXE) lets you invoke all the functions of the IDE compiler (TPW.EXE) from the DOS command line.

Turbo Pascal for Windows command-line options use this syntax:

```
TPCW   [options]   <file name>   [options]
```

where `[options]` can be one or more options, separated by spaces. You designate the status of the compiler option by specifying a plus (+) or a minus (–) after the option.

- Place a + (or a space) after an option to turn it On.
- Place a – after the option to turn it Off.

Table 1.7. *Compiler options.*

Option	***Meaning***
	Directive options
/$A	Align data
/$B	Boolean evaluation
/$D	Debug information
/$F	Force FAR calls
/$G	Generate 286 instructions
/$I	Input/Output checking
/$L	Local Symbol information
/$N	80x87 Code (numeric coprocessor)
/$R	Range checking
/$S	Stack-overflow checking
/$V	String variable checking
/$W	Windows stack frame
/$X	Extended syntax
	Mode options
/B	Build all
/F	Find error
/L	Link buffer
/M	Make
/Q	Quiet (no IDE equivalent)
	Conditional defines option
/D	Conditional defines

continues

Table 1.7. continued

Option	Meaning
	Debug options
/G	.MAP file
/V	Debug information in EXE option
	Directory options
/E	EXE and TPU directory
/I	Include directories
/O	Object Files directories
/R	Resource directories
/T	Turbo directory
/U	Unit directories

Most of the command-line options have equivalent menu commands.

Table 1.8. Command-line options and their IDE equivalents.

Option	IDE Equivalent
/$A	Options/Compiler/Align data
/$B	Options/Compiler/Boolean evaluation
/$D	Options/Compiler/Debug information
/$F	Options/Compiler/Force far calls
/$G	Options/Compiler/286 code
/$I	Options/Compiler/I/O checking
/$L	Options/Compiler/local symbols
/$M	Options/Compiler/Memory sizes
/$N	Options/Compiler/80x87 code
/$R	Options/Compiler/Range checking
/$S	Options/Compiler/Stack checking
/$V	Options/Compiler/String Variable Checking Options
/$W	Options/Compiler/Windows Stack Frames
/$X	Options/Compiler/Extended Syntax
/B	Compile/Build

Option	IDE Equivalent
/D	Options/Compiler/Conditional Defines
/E	Options/Directories/EXE and TPU Directory
/F	Search/Find Error
/G	Options/Linker/Map File
/I	Options/Compiler/Include Directories
/L	Options/Linker/Link Buffer
/M	Compile/Make
/O	Options/Directories/Object Directories
/Q	(none)
/R	Options/Directories/Resource Directories
/T	(none)
/U	Options/Directories/Unit Directories
/V	Options/Linker/Debug Information in EXE

Onward, Forward, and Upward

Turbo Pascal for Windows is a flexible, powerful application development environment for Microsoft Windows, complete with editor, compiler, debugger, linker, and a powerful library of objects and tools. You don't have to be a Windows or Turbo Pascal expert to use Turbo Pascal for Windows; instead it helps you become the Windows expert.

A Turbo Pascal for Windows application is limited only by your imagination. You can use units and libraries to create large and powerful Windows applications using either the IDE or the command-line compiler.

In the next few hundred pages, I'll show you just how easy and fun it can be to create Windows applications Turbo Pascal style, using the power and flexibility of object-oriented programming techniques. Sound easy? It is. In the next chapter, you will go to it!

2

CHAPTER

ELEMENTS OF APPLICATION DEVELOPMENT

Your Windows program doesn't interact directly with the screen, keyboard, printer, or any other device. Windows does all that, and places the results in an application message queue (in a device-independent fashion).

Lee and Mark Atkinson

If you have programmed in any language, you undoubtedly have your own ideas about how to develop an application, whether it is for Windows or otherwise. To develop an application for Windows, you have to learn how Windows works, but only at an easy level. You also have to prepare your application to run in a Windows window and you have to think (at least somewhat) in terms of events. The beans and rice of a Windows application is what you are used to: code for solving problems—code that manipulates information (or data).

The biggest difference between developing a DOS application and a Windows application is that, with DOS, you are required to create your own user interface (unless you are writing a primitive application or one that does not require an interface). If you are writing a Windows application, you must "connect" to the Windows GUI (graphical user interface), but you do not have to create it. You use the Windows Interface, and you continue to use most of what you already know about programming.

To use a Windows application to solve a problem, you have to

1. Interact with Windows (mostly using ObjectWindows).
2. Get information into the application (the input component).
3. Store information (the data component).
4. Manipulate the information, using procedures, functions, or object methods (the operations component).
5. Get the results (the output component).

These steps are straightforward and probably familiar to you, except for the Windows connection. To connect with Windows, use ObjectWindows, the Turbo Pascal for Windows OOP library. ObjectWindows is an object-oriented library, packaged with Turbo Pascal for Windows, that greatly simplifies Windows applications development by encapsulating (packaging) complex Windows information in a simpler, more easily accessible form.

To handle actions 2 through 5, you structure your application along traditional "structured" programming lines. You use conditional statements (`Ifs`) and loops (`whiles`, `repeats`, and so on). You divide groups of instructions into sections that can be referenced by name (procedures, functions, objects). This again is programming as you probably already know it (whether you program in Pascal or another similarly structured language such as C or C++).

Turbo Pascal for Windows, like Turbo Pascal for DOS, supplies a rich set of data types and built-in operators, controls, procedures, and functions for manipulating information. Turbo Pascal for Windows lets you create large applications by dividing any program (or application) into pieces (units) that can be compiled separately.

The remainder of this chapter briefly covers some of the basic aspects of Turbo Pascal for Windows and its development capabilities. If you already know Turbo Pascal, feel free to skip this section and move on to the next chapter, where you learn how to develop Windows applications using the object-oriented techniques of ObjectWindows. (You will not see any Windows-specific code until the next chapter.) If you want more information about the standard (or built-in) Turbo Pascal for Windows procedures and functions, check out the reference section.

Units

To develop any Turbo Pascal for Windows application, you must use at least one Turbo Pascal for Windows standard unit, but you can use many more units if you have to (either standard ones or units you create).

A *unit* is a collection of constants, data types, variables, procedures, and functions. In a nutshell, a unit is the basis of modular programming in Turbo Pascal for DOS and Turbo Pascal for Windows. You use units to create libraries and to divide large applications into logically related modules.

Turbo Pascal for Windows supplies the following standard units:

Strings
System
`WinCrt`
`WinDOS`
`WinProcs`
`WinTypes`

These standard units (which are stored in TPW.TPL) support your Turbo Pascal for Windows applications in many ways, taking much of the work out of developing applications.

The Strings unit supports a type of character strings called *null-terminated strings*. Null-terminated strings are the type of strings required by the Windows Application Programming Interface (API). (Previously, Turbo Pascal did not support null-terminated strings.)

The System unit (SYSTEM.TPU) is the Turbo Pascal for Windows run-time library. It implements low-level, run-time support routines (procedures and functions) for all the built-in Turbo Pascal for Windows "features," such as file Input/Output, floating point operations, string-handling, and dynamic memory allocation.

All units and programs automatically use the System unit, so you do not have to specify it in a `uses` declaration. (You learn more about the `uses` declaration in this section).

The `WinCrt` unit implements a terminal-like text screen in a window. You do not have to write "Windows-specific" code if your application uses `WinCrt`. In many cases, you can start with Turbo Pascal for Windows quickly by translating existing Turbo Pascal (for DOS) code and using the `WinCrt` screen to "run" it. You will learn how to use `WinCrt` in the next chapter.

The `WinDos` unit implements operating system and file-handling procedures and functions. These procedures and functions are specific to Turbo Pascal and are not defined by standard Pascal.

The `WinProcs` unit defines function and procedure headers for the Windows API. You can access every function in the standard Windows libraries through `WinProcs`. The `WinProcs` and `WinTypes` units both define the Turbo Pascal for Windows implementation of the Windows API.

The `WinTypes` unit defines Turbo Pascal versions of all the types used by the Windows API functions, including simple types and data structures (records, and so on) and all the standard Windows constants, including flags, messages, and styles.

Units are both conceptually and pragmatically important because

- They are precompiled so you can use the functions, procedures, and so on in a unit without recompiling the unit each time you compile another part of your application. Thus, units save time.

- Units also let you break up functionality for separate development, modification, and use. Projects thus can be large and their development and management simplified.

Units are nifty, useful structures that change the way your Turbo Pascal for Windows application code is stored in memory. Consider first how a compiled Turbo Pascal for Windows application (without units) stores itself in memory. It divides itself into four main sections:

1. `Code` segment
2. `Data` segment
3. `Stack` segment
4. Heap

The `code` segment contains the application's procedures, functions, and the main program body of the application. The `data` segment contains the application's global variables and constants. The `stack` segment contains return addresses for the applications' functions and procedures and most of the local variables declared inside functions and procedures. The *heap* contains any variables you create dynamically using the Turbo Pascal for Windows keyword, `New`.

Each section (`code`, `data`, and `stack` segments) can use as much as 64K (kilobytes) of memory, and the heap can grow as large as available memory allows. Figure 2.1 shows a memory map of this scheme.

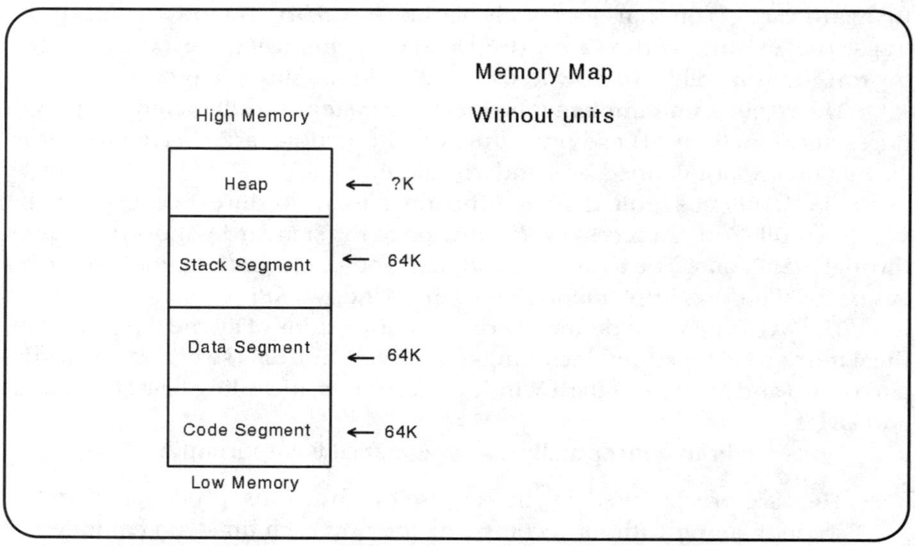

***Figure 2.1.** A memory map of three segments, plus the heap.*

Without units, a compiled Turbo Pascal for Windows application can be about 192K plus the heap (whose size depends on the number of dynamically allocated variables).

In contrast, the procedures and functions in a unit are stored in separate segments apart from the main module. Each unit can use as much as 64K of memory. Thus, an application that uses units can consist of as many of these 64K units as memory (the system's, not yours) allows. Of course, applications that use units can be large. Figure 2.2 shows a memory map of an application segmented into units.

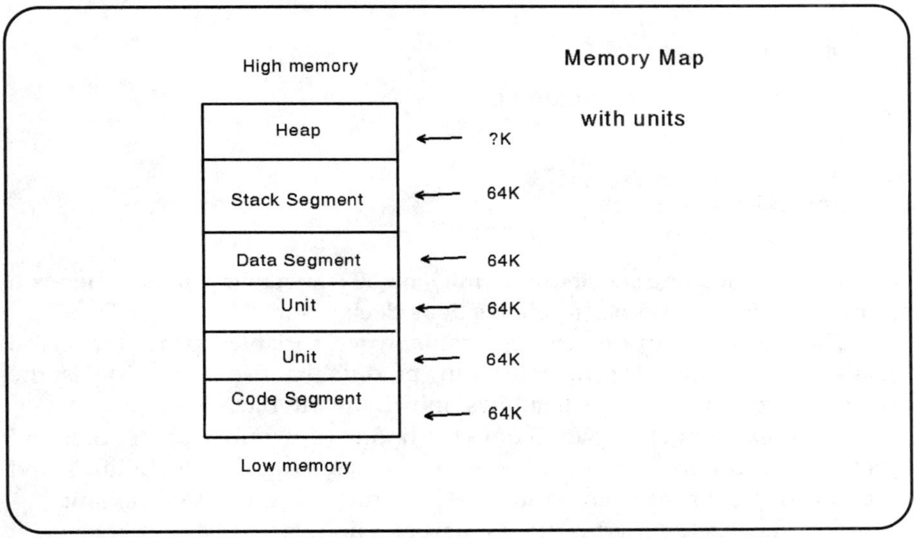

Figure 2.2. A memory map of units.

To use a standard (or precompiled) unit, add a `uses` declaration at the beginning of the `main` module of your application:

```
Program Main;

uses
    WinCrt;

{ .... body here ... }
```

To use more than one unit, separate the units by commas:

```
Program Main;

uses
    WinTypes,
    Strings,
```

```
    WinProcs,
    WObjects;

{ ... body here ... }
```

You use the standard Turbo Pascal for Windows units throughout this book, and they are discussed in more detail as you move along.

Creating your own units is similar to creating the `main` module of an application, with a couple of exceptions:

1. Rather than designate the module as a program, you designate it as a unit:

   ```
   Unit YourUnit;
   ```

2. You also divide the unit into parts:

   Unit heading
   Interface part
   Implementation part
   Initialization part

The unit heading specifies the unit's name (the name you use when you refer to this unit in another module's `Uses` declaration).

The interface part declares constants, types, variables, procedures, and functions that are public (available to any module that uses the unit). List the procedures and functions as headings only in the interface part.

The implementation part defines the bodies of all public procedures and functions. In addition, it declares constants, types, variables, procedures, and functions that are private and, thus, are not available to users of the unit.

The initialization part is the last part of a unit. It consists of either:

- The reserved word `end` (no initialization code)

  or

- A statement part to be executed to initialize the unit

Listing 2.1 shows the layout of a unit.

Listing 2.1. The general layout of a unit.

```
Unit YourUnit;

Interface

{
Use something
here
}
```

```
{
CONST,
TYPE,
VAR
declarations here
}

{
PROCEDURE and
FUNCTION
declarations here
}

Implementation

{
Another
Use
here, if you want it
}

{
Any Private
LABEL,
CONST,
TYPE,
VAR
declarations here
}

{
Procedure and
function
bodies here
}

Begin

{
Initialization statements
}

End.
```

Turbo Pascal for Windows handles units intelligently. For example, if several modules (or units) in an application refer to the same unit, only one copy of that unit—not several—is loaded into memory.

Data Types and Identifiers

Application development begins and ends with variables. Whenever you declare a variable, you must specify its type. The variable type indicates

- The range of values the variable can take
- The operations that can be performed on it

When you specify a type (in a `type` declaration) you specify an identifier that denotes a type.

You use identifiers throughout your application, and a Turbo Pascal for Windows identifier can denote any of the following:

- Constants
- Fields in records
- Functions
- Labels
- Procedures
- Programs
- Types
- Units
- Variables

Identifiers can be any length, but only the first 63 characters are significant (recognized by Turbo Pascal for Windows).

You have to follow a few rules when you use identifiers:

- The first character of an identifier must be a letter.
- The characters that follow the first character must be letters, digits, or underscores (no spaces).
- Identifiers are not case-sensitive.

As this chapter states, applications development begins and ends with variables. Variables must be `typed` in Turbo Pascal. It is helpful to divide these types into six major classes, which are covered next. For more in-depth information about Turbo Pascal for Windows types, consult the Turbo Pascal for Windows manuals.

Qualified Identifiers

When your application declares several instances of the same identifier, you might have to qualify the identifier by specifying a unit identifier to select the correct instance of the identifier.

The combined `Unit.Identifier` specification is called a *qualified identifier*.

For example, the following are qualified identifiers:

`System.Exit` (unit = `System`, identifier = `Exit`)

`Dos.Exec` (unit = `Dos`, identifier = `Exec`)

`Crt.Window` (unit = `Crt`, identifier = `Window`)

You can divide types as follows:

1. Simple types that define ordered sets of values:

   A. Ordinal types, which include:

      Integer types
      Boolean types
      `Char` type
      Enumerated types
      Subrange types

   B. Real types

2. String types that represent a sequence of characters with a dynamic length attribute and a constant size attribute.

3. Structured types that hold more than one value. These include:

      Array types
      Record types
      Object types
      Set types
      File types

4. Pointer types that define a set of values that point to dynamic variables of some type. A dynamic variable is one that is allocated on the heap and manipulated using pointers. Because the heap can be quite large (much larger than a stack allocated in the data segment, which is limited to 64K), dynamic variables also can be quite large.

5. Procedural types that allow procedures and functions to be treated as objects. An object, which you learn much more about throughout this

book, consists of data and the procedures and functions that you use to manipulate that data. For example:

```
AWindow = object
  x1, x2, y1, y2 :Integer;
  procedure minimize;
  procedure maximize;
end;
```

6. Object types are structures that consist of a fixed number of components.

Ordinal Types

Turbo Pascal has nine predefined ordinal types. Five of these integer types denote a specific subset of the whole numbers:

Type	*Range*	*Size*
Shortint	128..127	8-bit
Integer	–32768..32767	16-bit
Longint	–2147483648..2147483647	32-bit
Byte	0.255	8-bit
Word	0.65535	16-bit

The other four predefined ordinal types are the Booleans (`Boolean`, `WordBool`, `LongBool`), and `Char`.

Two other classes of user-defined ordinal types are enumerated types and subrange types.

Three standard functions can be used with all ordinal types:

1. `Ord` (which returns the ordinality of the value). For example:

   `Ord(False) = 0;`

2. `Pred` (which returns the predecessor of the value). For example:

   `Pred(True) = False;`

3. `Succ` (which returns the successor of the value). For example:

   `Succ(True) = False;`

Boolean Types

Turbo Pascal for Windows has three predefined Boolean types: `Boolean`, `WordBool`, and `LongBool`, which are defined as follows:

```
type
Boolean  = (False, True);
WordBool = (False, True);
LongBool = (False, True);
```

These types have the following sizes:

- `Boolean` is byte-sized (8 bits).
- `WordBool` is word-sized (16 bits).
- `LongBool` is `longint`-sized (32 bits).

Because Booleans are enumerated ordinal types, the following relationships exist among Boolean types:

True > False

`Ord(False)` = 0

`Ord(True)` = 1

`Succ(False)` = True

`Pred(True)` = False

Among the "Booleans," `Boolean` is the preferred type and uses the least memory. `WordBool` and `LongBool` exist primarily for compatibility with your applications in the Windows environment.

In an expression, the following relational operators produce results of type `Boolean`:

```
=
<>
>
<
>=
<=
IN
```

For Windows compatibility, Booleans can assume ordinal values other than zero and one. A Boolean expression is considered false when its ordinal value is zero, and true when its ordinal value is nonzero.

Char Type

Use variables of the ordinal type `Char` to store ASCII characters. Write character constants between single quotations, as in the following:

```
'9'
'A'
'L'
'i'
'&'
```

The single quotation character is written as two single quotations within single quotations, like this:

```
''''
```

The `Chr` function converts an integer value into a character with the corresponding ASCII value.

The `Ord` function returns a character's ASCII value.

Enumerated Types

Enumerated types define ordered sets of values by enumerating the identifiers that denote the values. Their ordering is determined by the sequence in which the identifiers are enumerated.

For example:

```
type
Food = (Apple, Kiwi, Peach, Date);
```

In this declaration, `Kiwi` is a constant of type `Food`.

The `Ord` standard function returns the ordinality of an enumerated constant. In this example:

```
Ord(Apple) = 0
Ord(Kiwi)  = 1
Ord(Peach) = 2
Ord(Date)  = 3
```

The identifiers in the type definition become constants of the enumerated type.

The first constant has an ordinality of zero, the second has an ordinality of one, the third an ordinality of two, and so on.

Subrange Types

A subrange type is a range of values from an ordinal type sometimes called the *host type*.

For example:

```
LittleConstant .. BiggerConstant
```

specifies the smallest and largest value in the subrange. In this case, the subrange is from `LittleConstant` to `BiggerConstant`.

Both constants must be of the same ordinal type, and the first constant must be less than or equal to the second constant.

The `$R` compiler directive controls range-checking of subrange types. The following are subrange examples:

```
0..49

-128..127
```

Reals

A real type has a set of values that is a subset of the real numbers, which can be represented in floating-point notation with a fixed number of digits.

A value's floating-point notation normally consists of three values: `M`, `B`, and `E`, such that `M x B E = N` where `B` is always 10, `M` is a rational number, and `E` is an integer in the real type's range.

Turbo Pascal for Windows supplies four predefined real types. Each type has a specific range and precision:

Type	*Range*	*Digits*	*Bytes*
Real	2.9e-39..1.7e38	11-12	6
Single	1.5e-45..3.4e38	7-8	4
Double	5.0e-324..1.7e308	15-16	8
Extended	3.4e-4932..1.1e4932	19-20	10

Note: Turbo Pascal for Windows supports two models of floating-point code generation:

1. Software floating point
2. 80x87 floating point

Use the `$N` compiler directive to switch between the two models.

Strings

A Turbo Pascal string type variable (not a null-terminated string type) is a sequence of characters with a dynamic length, and a constant maximum size between 1 and 255.

If you declare a string without a maximum size, it automatically becomes a size of 255.

String constants are written in quotations; for example:

```
'Windows'

'Bible'
```

Notice that two consecutive single quotations are used to indicate a single quotation in a string.

The following operators can be used with string type values:

```
+
=
<>
<
>
<=
>=
```

Operators compare strings by using the ASCII codes for letters and numbers. For example, the ASCII code for *M* is 77 and *T* is 84. Thus, a string beginning with an *M* is less than one beginning with a *T*. The ASCII code for a lowercase *m*, however, is 109. Thus, an uppercase *T* is less than a lowercase *m*. Keep this in mind when you compare strings.

Structured Types

A structured type can hold more than one value. Structured types are

- Array (types)
- File (types)
- Object (types)
- Record (types)
- Set (types)

If a component type is structured, the resulting structured type has more than one level of structuring and can, in fact, have unlimited levels of structuring (memory permitting). In other words, a structured type can contain other types that are themselves structured. These other types can, in turn, contain more types that also are structured.

The maximum size of any structured type in Turbo Pascal is 65,520 bytes (about 64K). The reserved word `packed` in a structured type's declaration tells the compiler to compress data when it stores the type. *Note:* Turbo Pascal for Windows accepts the reserved word `packed`, but ignores it.

Arrays

An array is a collection of values of the same type. Arrays make data much more manageable.

You declare an array as follows:

```
array [index-type] of element-type
```

The element type can be any type, but the index type must be an ordinal type. You can use several index types if you separate them by commas. Each index type separated by a comma represents a dimension of the array.

For example:

```
type
  CharData = array['A'..'Z'] of Byte;       { 1 Dimension }
  NumList  = array[1..600] of Integer;      { 1 Dimension }
  Matrix   = array[0..21, 0..21] of real;   { 2 Dimensions }
```

Records

A record contains a number of components, or fields, that can be of different types.

A record declaration begins with the keyword `record` and ends with an `end`.

For example:

```
ThisRecord = Record
  Month: 0 .. 12;
  Day  : 1 .. 31;
  Year : Integer;
end;
```

A record also can be variant. In other words, a group of records can have different structures dependent on a condition.

For example:

```
type
  ClassType  = (Num, Dat, Str);

  Date    = record
     D, M, Y: Integer;
end;

Facts = record
  Name: string[10];
```

```
  case Kind: ClassType of
    Num: (N: real);
    Dat: (D: Date);
    Str: (S: string);
end;
```

Depending on whether `Kind` is a `Num`, `Dat`, or `Str`, the `Facts` record contains an `N`, `D`, or `S` data field.

Object Types

An object type is a data structure similar to a record, also containing a fixed number of components. Each component is either a field (which contains data of a particular type) or a method (procedure or function), which "operates" on an object's data.

For example:

```
GenericObject = object
  Field1 : integer;      { Object data }
  Field2 : real;
  ...
  procedure Method1;     { Object behavior }
  procedure Method2;
end;
```

When you declare a field, you specify an identifier that names the fields and their data types. When you declare a method, you specify a procedure, function, constructor, or destructor heading. Here's the scenario in somewhat formal form:

```
Field     = FieldName(s): type;

Method    = procedure MethodName(<parameter(s)>:type);

or = function
          MethodName(<parameter(s)>:type):type;

or = constructor
          MethodName(<parameter(s)>:type
          [;<parameter(s)>: type]); [virtual];

or = destructor
          MethodName[(<parameters>:
          type)];[virtual];
```

An object type can inherit the data and behavior (its components) from another object type. The inheriting object is a descendant, and the object that supplies the data and behavior for inheritance is an ancestor.

The domain of an object type consists of itself and all its descendants.

Sets

Sets define collections of elements of a specific scalar or subrange type. For example, the following are set types:

```
type
  Day = (Sun, Mon, Tue, Wed, Thu, Fri, Sat);
  CharSet = set of Char;
  Digits = set of 0..4;
  Days = set of Day;
  Months = (January, February, March, April, May, June,
            July, August, September, October, November, December);
```

The base type of a set must be an ordinal type with not more than 256 possible values. Thus, the ordinal values of the upper and lower bounds of the base type must be in the range 0..255.

A set constructor, which denotes a set type value, is formed by writing expressions in brackets. Each expression denotes a value of the set.

The bracket notation [ ] denotes the empty set—compatible with all set types.

For example, the following are set constructors:

```
[Mon..Sat]
[1, 3, I + 1 .. J - 1]
['0'..'5', 'A'..'Q', 'd'..'z', '_']
```

Files

A file type consists of a linear sequence of components of some component type, which can be any type except a file type. If you omit the component type, the type denotes an untyped file.

The predefined file type `Text` signifies a file containing characters organized into lines.

For example, the following are `File` type declarations:

```
type
  Employee = record
    ID       : Integer;
    FirstName: string[10];
    LastName : string[20];
    Address  : string[40];
  end;
```

```
EmployeeFile = file of Employee;

NumberFile = file of Real;

SwapFile = file;
```

Pointer Types

A pointer type variable contains the memory address of a dynamic variable of some "specified" base type. In other words, a pointer does not contain a data value; it contains a memory address. A pointer "points to" a unique location in memory. Pointers can point to locations that contain byte values, integers, reals, records, strings, or any other data type.

Pointers are extremely important in object-oriented programming and are used throughout this book. Although you might think that pointers are complicated creatures (rumor has it), they are not. Keep in mind that a pointer holds a memory address, not a data value. You assign data values to the addresses held in the pointer by using the pointer. The pointer is the only way you can get at the data. This procedure sounds a little indirect, but it is important in both object-oriented and Windows programming, and it is discussed in detail throughout the book.

You can assign a value to a pointer variable with:

- The `New` or `GetMem` procedures
- The `@` operator
- The `Ptr` function

The reserved word `nil` denotes a pointer constant that points nowhere.

The predefined type `Pointer` denotes an untyped pointer (a pointer that does not point to any specific type).

For an application to use a pointer, it must first request memory for the type of data the pointer points to. It requests memory by initializing the pointer with `New`:

```
var
    APointer : ^Integer;

begin
    New(APointer);
....
end;
```

In this case, `New` reserves space for an integer value.

You can then store a value at the address pointed to by `APointer`, using a caret after the pointer name:

```
APointer^ := 28;
```

The caret indicates that you do not want the pointer itself (as an address), but the value at the address pointed to by the pointer. This is called *dereferencing* the pointer.

The following are pointer type declarations:

```
type
  BytePtr  = ^Byte;
  WordPtr  = ^Word;
  IdentPtr = ^IdentRec;
  IdentRec = record
    Ident: string[24];
    RefCount: Word;
    Next: IdentPtr;
  end;
```

If you are not used to using pointers, you might wonder why it is worth going to the extra trouble of using them, because pointers are, by their nature, indirect. One good reason to use pointers is that variables pointed to by pointers use memory that is in the heap, not in the `data` segment. The heap is dynamic and can grow as large as it has to (memory permitting). The `data` segment is a fixed size, and variables in the `data` segment are of a fixed size as well.

If you are designing applications such as a database, which has to be flexible about how much memory it eventually uses, pointers add the flexibility. Databases, spreadsheets, and anything else that depends on linked lists, trees, and other dynamic structures rest on pointers.

An array must have precise dimensions, and thus must specify in advance (at compile time) how much memory it uses. Variables addressed through pointers do not have to specify their exact size at compile time. Decisions can be delayed until run-time—a definite plus in many applications.

For example, if one computer system has 8M (megabytes) of memory and another 640K, a database or spreadsheet that uses pointers to allocate memory can utilize the extra memory to create larger data sets on the larger system.

PChar

The predefined type `PChar` denotes a pointer to a null-terminated string.

Declare `PChar` as follows:

```
type
  PChar = ^Char;
```

Turbo Pascal for Windows supports a set of extended syntax rules (controlled by the `$X` compiler directive) to facilitate handling of strings using the `PChar` type.

Procedural Types

Standard Pascal regards procedures and functions strictly as program parts that can be executed through procedure or function calls.

Turbo Pascal and Turbo Pascal for Windows have much broader views of procedures and functions. Through procedural types, Turbo Pascal allows you to treat procedures and functions as objects that can be assigned to variables and passed as parameters.

A procedural type declaration specifies the parameters and, for a function, the result type. The key difference between a procedure and a function is that a procedure does not return a value for the procedure itself. A function always returns a value of some type: integer, real, and so on.

The syntax for a procedural type declaration is exactly the same as that for a procedure or function header, except you omit the identifier after the `procedure` or `function` keyword.

For example:

```
type
  AProc = procedure;
  ASwapProc = procedure(var A, B: Integer);
  AStrProc = procedure(S: String);
  AMathFunc = function(A: Real): Real;
  ADeviceFunc = function(var F: Text): Integer;
  AMinFunc = function(A,B: Real; F: AMathFunc): Real;
```

The parameter names in a procedural type declaration have no effect on the meaning of the declaration.

Turbo Pascal for Windows does not let you declare functions that return procedural type values. A function result value must be a `String`, `Real`, `Integer`, `Char`, `Boolean`, `Pointer`, or a user-defined enumeration.

Turbo Pascal for Windows Reserved Words

Reserved words are words that have fixed meanings in the Turbo Pascal for Windows language. In other words, you cannot redefine reserved words. You must use them as they are.

Turbo Pascal for Windows is not case-sensitive, so you can use upper- or lowercase letters to specify reserved words.

The Turbo Pascal for Windows reserved words are as follows:

```
and            goto              program
asm            if                record
array          implementation    repeat
begin          in                set
case           inline            shl
const          interface         shr
constructor    label             string
destructor     library           then
div            mod               to
do             nil               type
downto         not               unit
else           object            until
end            of                uses
exports        or                var
file           packed            while
for            pointer           with
function       procedure         xor
```

Statements

A statement is one of the following:

- assignment (:=)
- begin..end
- case..of..else..end
- for..to/downto..do
- goto
- if..then..else
- inline(...)
- procedure call
- repeat..until
- while..do
- with..do

Table 2.1 shows the operator precedence for the mathematical, relational, and logical operators in Turbo Pascal for Windows.

Table 2.1. Operator precedence from high to low.

Operators	*Precedence*
@, not	First (high)
*, /, div, mod, and, shl, shr	Second
+, –, or, xor	Third
=, <>, <, >, <=, >=, in	Fourth (low)

assignment (:=)

An assignment operator (:=) assigns the value of an expression to a variable. The variable must be assignment-compatible with the result type of the expression. The variable that is assigned the new value is on the left of the assignment operator. The value its assigned to is on the right.

For example:

```
A := B;     { A is assigned the value B. }

C[I] := C[I] + 1;  { C[I] is assigned the value C{I} + 1 }

LoopR := (I > 0) and (I < 30)  { LoopR is assigned the value that }
                               { results from the evaluation of }
                               { the expression on the right. }
```

begin..end

The `begin...end` constructs serve as statement brackets.

For example:

```
begin
  Statement1;
  Statement2;
  ...
  StatementX;
end;
```

When they are bracketed in this way, any number of consecutive statements can be treated as a single statement. For example:

```
{Compound statement used in an 'if' statement }

if First < Last then
begin
  Temp := First;
  First := Last;
  Last := Temp;
end;
```

case..of..else..end

The case statement consists of an expression (the selector) and a list of statements, each prefixed with a case. For example, a simple case:

```
case AnExpression of
  case: Statement1;
  ...
  case: Statement2;
end;
```

or a case-else:

```
case AnExpression of
  case: Statement1;
 ...
  case: Statement2;
else
  Statement3;
end;
```

A case consists of one or more constants or ranges, separated by commas. The else part is optional. For example:

```
case Ch of
  'A'..'Z', 'a'..'z':  WriteLn('Letter');
  '0'..'9':            WriteLn('Digit');
  '+', '-', '*', '/':  WriteLn('Operator');
else
  WriteLn('A Special character');
end;
```

for..to/downto..do

The for statement causes the statement after do to be executed once for each value in the range first to last.

For example, a for-to:

```
for Var1 := First to Last do
   Statement1;
```

or

```
for Var1 := First to last do
     begin
        Statement1;
        Statement2:
     end;
```

or a for-downto:

```
for Var1 := First downto Last do
  Statement1;
```

The control variable and initial and final values must be ordinal types.

If you use a Downto, the value of the control variable falls in increments of one for each loop.

With downto, the value of the control variable falls in decrements by one for each loop.

For example:

```
{ for ... to, for ... downto }

for I := 1 to ParamCount do
  WriteLn(ParamStr(I);

for I := 1 to 15 do
  for J := 1 to 15 do
  begin
    X := 0;
    for K := 1 to 15 do
     X := X + Matrix1[I,K] * Matrix2[K,J];
    Matrix[I,J] := X;
  end;
```

goto

A goto statement transfers program execution to the statement prefixed by the label referenced in the statement.

For example:

```
goto ALabel
```

The label must be in the same block as the goto statement; you cannot transfer execution out of a procedure or a function.

For example:

```
label 1, 2;
goto 1
    .
    .
    .
1: WriteLn ('Something can happen here');
2: WriteLn ('Something different here');
```

if..then..else

If, then, and else specify the conditions under which a statement is executed.

For example, a simple if-then:

```
if AnExpression then
   Statement1;
```

or

```
if AnExpression then
   begin
      Statement1;
      Statement2;
   end;
```

Or an if-then-else:

```
if AnExpression then
   Statement1
else
   Statement2;
```

If the Boolean expression after the if is true, the statement after then is executed. Otherwise, if there is an else part, the statement after else is executed.

For example:

```
{ 'if' statements }

if (X < Min) or (X > Max) then
   X := 0;
```

```
if ParamCount <> 2 then
begin
  WriteLn('Can not execute the command line');
  Halt(1);
end
else
begin
  ReadFile(ParamStr(1));
  WriteFile(ParamStr(2));
end;
```

inline(...)

`Inline` statements and directives allow you to insert machine-code instructions directly into the code of a main program module or a unit.

For example:

```
inline (data/data/...data)
```

If you use `inline` as a statement, the `inline` data elements are inserted directly in the code.

If you use `inline` as a directive in a procedure or a function declaration, the `inline` data elements are inserted in the code each time the procedure or function is called.

An `inline` data element consists of a constant or a variable identifier, optionally prefixed by a size specifier: `<` or `>`.

A variable identifier can be followed by a `+` or a `-` and a constant that specifies an offset from the variable's address.

An `inline` element generates one byte of code if it is a constant in the range 0..255. Otherwise, it generates one word.

You use the < and > operators to override the automatic size selection:

< means "always generate a byte."
> means "always generate a word."

For example:

```
{ 'inline' statement }

procedure FillWord(var Dest; Count: Word; Data: Word);
begin
  inline(
    $C4/$7E/<Dest/     (* LES   DI,Dest[BP] *)
```

```
    $8B/$4E/<Count/      (* MOV   CX,Count[BP]*)
    $8B/$46/<Data/       (* MOV   AX,Data[BP] *)
    $FC/                 (* CLD               *)
    $F3/$AB);            (* REP   STOSW       *)
end;
```

procedure call

A procedure is a program component that defines a specific action or operation on a variable or group of variables.

For example:

```
procedure identifier;
```

Or, a procedure can have parameters:

```
procedure identifier ( parameters );
```

The procedure heading specifies the identifier for the procedure and the formal parameters, if there are any.

A procedure is activated by a procedure statement. The procedure heading is followed by:

- A declaration part that declares local objects
- The statements between `begin` and `end`, which specify what action occurs when the procedure is called

Rather than specify the declaration and statement parts, a procedure declaration can specify a forward, external, or inline directive.

A forward declaration indicates that a procedure will be defined later (that is, forward) in the code:

```
procedure GetNum (X: Integer); forward
```

An external declaration refers to separately compiled procedures and functions written in assembly language:

```
procedure Copyword (var Source, Dest,Count: Word);external;
```

An inline directive allows you to put machine-code instructions directly into your code:

```
procedure DisableInterrupts; inline ($FA);
```

For example:

```
{ A Procedure Declaration }

  procedure WrStr(X, Y: integer; S: string);
  var
    SaveX, SaveY: Integer;
  begin
    SaveX := X;
    SaveY := Y;
    Writeln(S);
  end;
```

repeat..until

The statements between `repeat` and `until` are executed in sequence until the Boolean expression is true at the *end* of the sequence.

For example:

```
repeat
  Statement1;
  Statement2;
  ...
  StatementN
until AnExpression
```

A `repeat-until` sequence is executed at least once.

For example:

```
{ Repeat Statements }
  repeat Ch := GetChar
  until Ch <> ' ';

  repeat
    Write('Enter a value: ');
    ReadLn(V);
  until (V >= 0) and (V <= '99');
```

while..do

A `while` statement contains an expression that controls the repeated execution of a statement (which can be a compound statement).

For example:

```
while AnExpression do
    Statement1
```

The statement after do is executed repeatedly as long as the Boolean expression is true.

The expression is evaluated before the statement is executed, so if the expression is false at the beginning, the statement is not executed. In other words, there is no certainty that a while-do executes even once.

For example:

```
{ 'while' statements }
  while Ch = ' ' do
    Ch := GetChar;
  while not Eof(InputFile) do  { Eof means End of file }
  begin
    ReadLn(InputFile, Line);
    WriteLn(OutputFile, Line);
    Inc(LineCount);
  end;
```

with..do

The with statement is an alternate method for referencing the fields of a record.

For example:

```
with ARecord do
Statement1;
```

In the statement after do, the fields of one or more record variables can be accessed using only their field identifiers.

For example:

```
{ 'with' statement }

  with Date[C] do
  begin
    Month := 1;
    Year  := Year + 1;
  end;
```

This is equivalent to

```
Date[C].Month := 1;
Date[C].Year  := Date[C].Year + 1;
```

Debugging Turbo Pascal for Windows Applications

Although you probably never make mistakes (ha, ha), you might want to know that if you do, Turbo Pascal for Windows can help. Its help comes in the form of the Turbo Pascal for Windows Debugger.

The Turbo Pascal for Windows Debugger is a powerful tool for debugging Windows applications. It goes a major step or two further than the built-in debugging capabilities of the Turbo Pascal for Windows compiler. The Turbo Pascal for Windows compiler's bug-detecting power focuses on your application code syntax. If you have an unknown identifier or have omitted a necessary semicolon, the compiler finds it. It cannot guarantee more than correct syntax. Your code can survive compiler bug-detection and still crash miserably at run-time. Run-time errors are the domain of another class of bug detectors: "debuggers."

Debuggers help you isolate and correct mistakes that usually are not due to errors in syntax. This is a broad and complex group of errors you can make in the logic of your code, by not accounting for the full range of possible actions of your code, and so on. Debugging, in this realm, is an imperfect "art" at best, and debugging Windows applications is even more imperfect. The key to debugging Windows applications lies in isolating the more likely error-prone areas of your code.

A few simple development tactics help:

1. Code in small fragments. Use object-oriented techniques to keep data and the behavior for manipulating data in objects.

2. Develop objects, units, or other structural blocks one at a time. Make sure that an object or a block works before moving on to other objects or blocks, particularly if these objects and blocks are interrelated.

3. Reduce the number of procedures, functions, and so on, that can manipulate data. If you do not use objects, then use local variables.

These tactics help, but they probably will not eliminate all your bugs. When you discover a bug in your Windows application, call on Turbo Debugger for Windows. In effect, it slows down the execution of an application and lets you examine its specific aspects. You can examine the stack, variable values, CPU registers, Windows messages, and so on.

Turbo Debugger gives you seven main ways to explore your code:

1. Tracing (executing an application one line at a time).

2. Back tracing (stepping backward through the application code one line at a time, and reversing the execution).

3. Stepping (executing the application code one line at a time but "stepping over" any calls to procedures or functions). This way the procedure or function is executed as a block and any values are returned, but you do not "trace" through the procedure or function one line at a time.

4. Viewing (opening a window for viewing the states of various components of the application). These components are the application's variables, break points you set, the stack, a Turbo Debugger log, a data file, a source file, CPU code, memory, registers, numeric processor information, object hierarchies, the application's execution history, and the application's output.

5. Inspecting data structures (such as arrays).

6. Changing (manipulating the application by replacing the current value of a variable with a new value that you specify).

7. Watching application variables (tracking the changing values of variables you specify).

All the Turbo Debugger for Windows features are available in pull-down menus.

The simplest way to use Turbo Debugger for Windows is to load the application you want to debug into a Turbo Pascal for Windows edit window, and then select Debugger from the Turbo Pascal for Windows Run/Debugger menu. Make sure, though, that you select Options/Linker/Debug info into an executable file (.EXE) before you run Turbo Debugger.

The specifics of how you debug your application depend on the kind of application and possible error. In general, you do not want to trace through an entire Windows application. Instead, try to isolate the error as best you can and set break points in likely troubled areas. (You probably are thinking that if you knew where the error was, you would not need the debugger—Yes and No.) If you are developing the application object-by-object or block-by-block, you can at least reduce the bug to that area. Set a break point, and then trace through the application from the break point.

In many situations, making sure that a procedure, function, or method is called, or monitoring a variable's values can locate the bug. Most debug sessions are started by setting break points and adding the variables in those break points using Add Watch. Then you step or trace through the code.

If you get a run-time error that typically looks like this:

```
Runtime error 204 at 0001:004
```

Notice the address (you probably want to write it down), and use the Find Error command on the Turbo Pascal for Windows Search menu to locate the error in your source code (see figure 2.3).

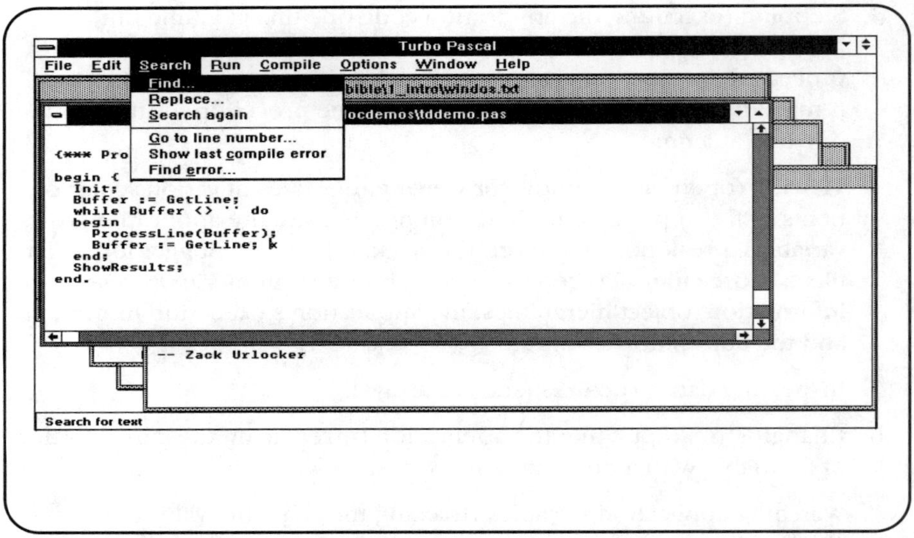

Figure 2.3. The Find error... command in the Search menu.

The Find Error dialog box appears (see figure 2.4).

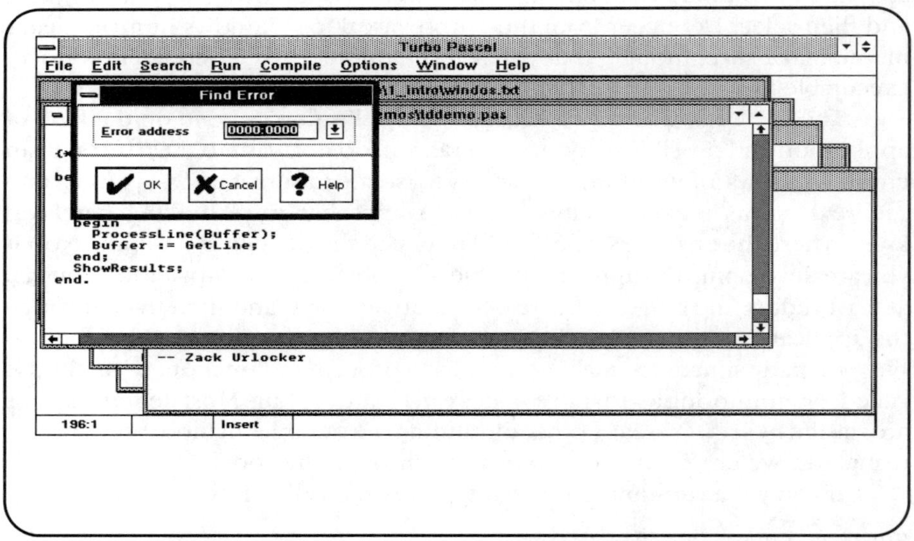

Figure 2.4. Result of selecting the Find error... command.

Enter the address of the error in the Error Address box. Turbo Pascal for Windows then recompiles your code and stops when it reaches the address you specify, highlighting the statement that caused the error.

Then, fix the error (in the edit window) and recompile. Repeat the process if you have to.

Begin..

A Windows application is complex and impressive. In fact, a good way to impress your friends is to tell them how complex a Windows application is and then show them a Windows application you created. If you use Turbo Pascal for Windows, you can impress your friends and develop applications that were beyond the scope of most "good" programmers only one year ago.

Progress, at least of a kind, one has to admit. Sometimes, when I find myself peering through one window or another, I'm not sure whether I should be surprised by the progress.

3

CHAPTER

OBJECTS FOR WINDOWS

So if Windows is the future, how do programmers get there?
The answer is, of course, by using object-oriented programming.
Zack Urlocker

Overture

Turbo Pascal for Windows makes developing a Microsoft Windows (called Windows from now on) application affordable (mentally, I mean). Because Turbo Pascal for Windows is a Windows application (that is, it runs in a Microsoft Windows window), you can write, test, and debug source code in Windows without having to shift between text and graphic modes. This process makes developing Windows applications convenient, efficient, and (believe it or not) enjoyable.

If you're a Turbo Pascal programmer, you already know that you have the niftiest compiler in personal computing. It's fast, has a terrific user interface (IDE), and, starting with version 5.5, has included object-oriented extensions. These extensions are your ticket into the Windows development arena.

In short, Turbo Pascal for Windows is mostly Turbo Pascal plus ObjectWindows, an object-oriented library that encapsulates the complex behaviors of Windows applications in objects. These inheritable, extendable objects handle most of the tedious initialization required before an application can communicate with Windows. If you already know Turbo Pascal, you'll be running Windows applications in minutes by using Turbo Pascal for Windows. You build them out of objects derived from ObjectWindows.

About Turbo Pascal Windows

Until recently, a developer creating a Microsoft Windows application could expect to learn at least 550 functions at a low level and write an application in either assembly language or Microsoft C—a difficult, time-consuming task at best.

The latest version of Borland International's world-class compiler, Turbo Pascal, called Turbo Pascal for Windows, makes Microsoft Windows development much, much easier.

The advantages of this compiler/programming environment are several:

1. Because its core and IDE (integrated development environment) are similar to previous versions of Turbo Pascal, only a short learning investment is required by the million-plus current Turbo Pascal programmers.

2. It abstracts the 550 Windows API (Application Programming Interface) functions to a high level through the use of object-oriented techniques, and thus lets a programmer "inherit" existing Windows functionality (buttons, dialogue windows, menus, and so on) rather than create each window from scratch. Programmers call low-level Windows API functions through a high-level object-oriented unit called "ObjectWindows."

3. It lets a programmer write, compile, run, and debug applications in the Windows environment, without exiting to DOS. No other popular compiler (including Microsoft C and Borland C++) can do this.

4. It includes the Whitewater Resource Compiler, which significantly simplifies the writing of menus, dialogues, controls, and so on.

Figure 3.1 shows Windows, the Turbo Pascal for Windows IDE, and the Whitewater Resource Compiler running together.

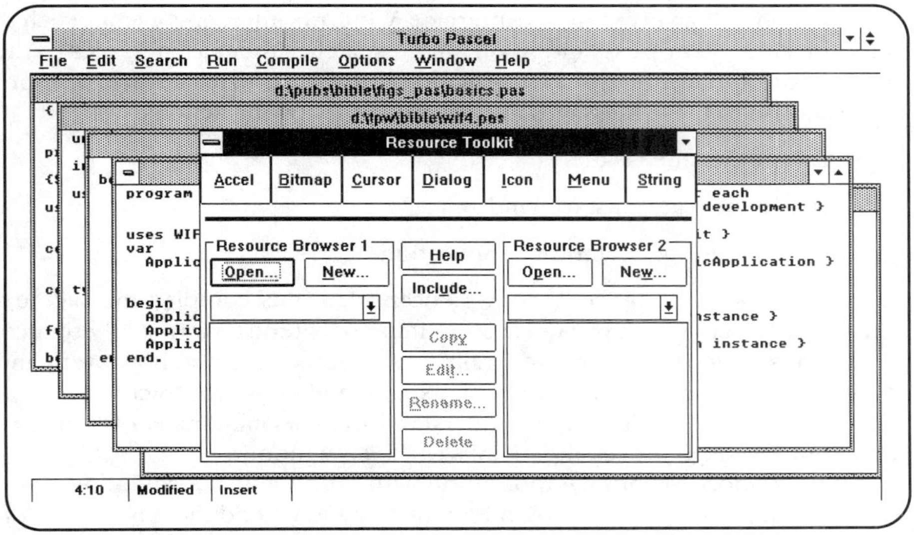

Figure 3.1. Windows, the IDE, and the compiler running together.

Because Turbo Pascal programmers can learn object-oriented programming (OOP, for short) without giving up a language they already know, they get the best of both computing worlds—structured programming and objects. More important, because Turbo Pascal is general-purpose and fast, it's practical for commercial applications. Turbo Pascal for Windows compiles code at the same blazing speed as Turbo Pascal 6.0—on my modestly paced 386SX, running at 16Mhz: 40,000+ lines per minute.

The addition of ObjectWindows to the Turbo Pascal core is the best thing that has happened to Turbo Pascal since units, and Turbo Pascal for Windows is the best thing that has happened to Windows since, well, Windows.

In this book, I guide you through two passes of the Windows development process: 1) a quick and clean pass and 2) a detailed and dirty pass. On the first one, I show you how to build a `BasicInterface` (object) that handles many of your applications. I go quickly, sparing you the details I think you can live without. If you're not a programming whiz, don't worry; you won't have to be. Turbo Pascal for Windows does most of the work. You don't need to know most of the details to create a major application.

On the second pass, I fill in many of the blanks for you aficionados and hackers. This pass includes the fun stuff. Windows, even for a command-line kind of guy like myself, is undeniably a pleasant, fun environment to work in, especially if you think in pictures. Many folks do, so a deeper understanding of optimization techniques, memory management, and other juicy topics can be profitable.

Windows is an event-driven interface. Windows intercepts events, such as a mouse click, a keypress, and so on, and dispatches them as messages to the appropriate application windows. A Windows application makes the appropriate response to these messages to perform the following actions:

- Carry out some task
- Send a message back to Windows
- Send a message to another application

The objects in ObjectWindows encapsulate this complex message exchange in objects, which you use as stock items or extend by way of inheritance.

You should understand generally how objects work and how event and message processing occurs, so I both explain and show you pictures as you move along. You don't have to understand the specific details of Windows event and message processing, thanks to ObjectWindows.

To develop a Windows application with Turbo Pascal for Windows, you use a few objects in the ObjectWindows library and extend them however you need to. The `BasicInterface` I develop in Chapter 4, "Inheriting an Interface," is derived from ObjectWindows and can be easily extended for your specific needs. I'll show you how.

As our interfaces, programming languages, and computing tools become more powerful, they become more complex as well. One path through the complexity is the repackaging of applications in an event-driven architecture like Windows. Not that event-driven architectures aren't complex—they are, but they can be managed easily with OOP techniques.

Objects inherently communicate through messages. When you want an object to do something, you send one of its methods (functions or procedures) a message. The object performs a task (which could entail sending a message to another object). Objects you derive from ObjectWindows also can send and receive messages from Windows. If you're thinking that objects and Windows do things quite alike, you're right, and well on your way to understanding how to write Windows applications with Turbo Pascal for Windows.

Windows is a graphics environment; that's the exceptional reason for using it. Sure, the multitasking and standardized interface and device drivers are wonderful, but you can get those features elsewhere. It's graphics, plus those attributes, that make Windows special.

The applications you develop with Turbo Pascal for Windows pay special attention to graphics. In this book, I pay the same special attention and use many graphics to illustrate what might otherwise be tough to conceptualize. You're good at visualizing, manipulating, learning from images—a big reason you use graphics interfaces.

So, "Nuff said," some hurried hero said. Let's get to it.

Why Does the World Make So Much Sense?

Actually, this question is more than a little debatable.

Why does Turbo Pascal for Windows make so much sense?

That question I tackle in the next hundred or so pages, beginning with general concepts such as events, messages, and objects. I begin with OOP, working toward Windows and the ObjectWindows connection. Turbo Pascal for Windows is another amazing development in the evolution of Turbo Pascal. It is *the* dynamite solution to what was almost an overwhelming programming problem: how to make sense of Microsoft Windows' development.

The Tao of Objects

Chinese philosophers in ancient times expressed a belief in a unifying reality that they called the Tao. To these philosophers, the Tao was a way of understanding that the world was not a static entity, but a dynamic, ever-changing process. The objects that make up the world reflect the dynamic process, because they are ever-changing. I use the phrase "the Tao of objects" to express the dynamic nature of programming problems and the modeling of systems based on "the real world." Because the world is evolving, your programming models of the world must evolve as well. In his introduction to my book, *The Tao of Objects*, Bruce Eckel wrote:

> One difficulty people have when learning object-oriented programming is finding a way to think about it. Often you hear such unhelpful things as "It's easier for someone who doesn't know how to program to learn OOP than for an experienced programmer" or "You need to unlearn what you know." My personal experience hasn't supported this. Although thinking about objects is different from thinking about procedural programming, it's different because you're stepping into a larger world, not because everything you know is wrong. This is especially true with hybrid languages like C++ and Turbo Pascal; you'll see that the ability to create user-defined [object] types isn't such a radical idea, since you use data types so much that you usually don't even think about them. However, it does tend to highlight the limitations of the built-in types and (to my mind) the relative primitiveness of what we've been using as programming languages so far. Once you begin using an object-oriented language, it's hard to go back.

I couldn't agree more with Bruce. If you start with what you know (I assume Turbo Pascal), and add knowledge of OOP and knowledge of Windows, you'll have Windows programming, Turbo Pascal style, down.

You can start with OOP.

Objects and actions compose our world. Objects (the nouns of the grammatical world) have attributes or characteristics. Actions (the verbs of the grammatical world) express behaviors.

A spruce sways. Snow falls. Her eyes open. The application window sends or receives a message. A user responds to a menu. You click a mouse, and so on.

In a program, data are the characteristics of an object. Operations are its behaviors. An object-oriented programming language like Turbo Pascal encapsulates an object's characteristics and its behaviors within a single block of source code. Operations and behaviors are in one place, which makes good sense. It's convenient and safer than having them spread about. Putting together data and the operations to manipulate data is *encapsulation*.

Using OOP techniques, programmers can create their own object types, which the compiler treats just as it does built-in types. You build up complex types from simpler types that share characteristics and behaviors.

This description shouldn't sound all that new to you. Turbo Pascal programmers have been creating new types all along—by collecting variables into records. Objects simply add the functions and procedures to manipulate the data to the package.

So, not unexpectedly, an object type looks much like its data-only counterpart—a record in Pascal. It's just a little more; a record plus the functions and procedures (which OOP calls methods) to manipulate the data fields.

Recall that you declare a record like this:

```
type
record1 = aRecord;
aRecord = record
  ID  : integer;
  Name: string;
  X,Y : integer;
end;
```

Define an object like this:

```
type
anObject = object
  ID  : integer;
  X,Y : integer;
  procedure ManipulateX;
  procedure ManipulateY;
end;
```

A variable of type `anObject` looks like this:

```
var ov: anObject;
```

A pointer looks like this:

```
var op: ^anObject;
op = @ov;
```

X and Y are data fields. ManipulateX and ManipulateY are methods for manipulating the data fields, X and Y.

To access members of an instance (a variable) of an object type, you use the same selection operators you use with records—or a With statement:

```
ov.X := 256;
op^ManipulateX;  { procedure call! }

With ov do
  begin
    X:= 256;
    Y:= 128;
    ManipulateX;
    ManipulateY;
  end;
```

An object type consists of everything that describes it. Its characteristics and behaviors are together in one block of code.

Notice that you don't have to pass X and Y to the methods ManipulateX and ManipulateY. ManipulateX and ManipulateY already have access to X and Y because they both are packaged in the same type. In other words, they share a local scope. Everything in an object type (data fields and methods) is shared and thus known to everything else.

From another perspective, combining data and code in an object is a neat extension of Pascal units. Programs consist of collections of units. Units contain definitions of object types, functions, and variables. So, at one level, object types suggest a way to organize code. There's much more to it than that: it's a more powerful way of thinking about code.

Different objects can share some characteristics and behaviors, while not sharing others. Shared characteristics and behaviors can be collected in a common type called a *base type*. For example: mandolins, guitars, drums, banjos, fiddles, and flutes are all types of musical instruments. They have different specific characteristics, but each has a way of making sound and can be played. The base type, the musical instrument, encapsulates these common characteristics: it creates sound and it can be played.

The act of playing the instrument and the way the instrument sounds differ from instrument to instrument. You pluck the strings of a banjo with your fingers; you blow air into a flute. The vibrations of strings combined with wood creates a guitar sound. The pressure and volume of air produced by your lips and lungs combine with wood or metal to create a flute sound.

In the everyday world, you classify objects into types and extend your knowledge by assigning the attributes you know (from previous object types) to new ones. Using OOP techniques, you create applications in a similar manner, by creating base object types and deriving new object types from them.

Inheritance

Encapsulation is the beginning, and there's much more to OOP than that. How do you modify or extend an object's functionality? If you can help it, you don't go in and muck around the code. This can easily lead to new bugs, and you too often will mess up something that already works.

A better path, after you've defined a new base type, is to build on the base type using inheritance. When a new type (called a *derived type*) inherits from a base type, the new type automatically receives all the characteristics and behaviors of the base type, without "lifting a finger."

You also can assemble a new type of object from a group of existing objects. This process is called *composition*. A woodland community, for example, is composed of trees, herbaceous plants, animals, and the microorganisms that sustain them. Derivation and composition enable you to reuse existing code without introducing new bugs. You can develop applications faster, more efficiently, and more clearly.

In an important sense, object-oriented programming is a way to build family trees (or hierarchies) for data structures. In Turbo Pascal (unlike in some OOP languages) an object can have only one immediate ancestor, or a *single inheritance* (see figure 3.2). (An object can have any number of ancestors, but only one *immediate* ancestor.)

Let's say that you've created a base type:

```
base = object
  X,Y: integer;
  procedure ManipulateX;
  procedure ManipulateY;
end;
```

Now you want to add some specialized functionality to it. Therefore, you create a new type from this base type. You want the derived type to be identical to the base type except to extend the base by adding a method called `RecalculateXandY`.

You create the `derived` type's characteristics by simply inheriting the characteristics from the `base` type.

```
derived = object (base)
  procedure RecalculateXandY;
end;
```

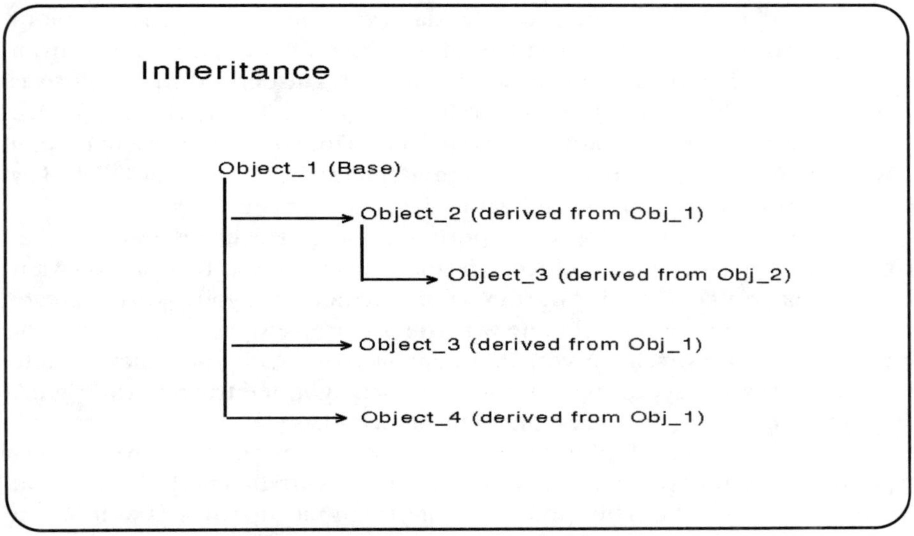

Figure 3.2. *Single inheritance.*

Because `derived` (the new object type) inherits all the data fields and methods of `base` (its ancestor object type), you don't need to redefine `base`'s data fields and methods. You just tell the compiler you want to derive a new type from a base type—the line `derived = object (base)` does the trick—and add the new method.

Now you can use `ManipulateX`, `ManipulateY`, and `RecalculateXandY` with any instance (variable) of type `derived`, just as though all three methods had been defined in `derived`:

```
var
d: derived;

With d do
  begin
    X:= 40;
    Y:= 32;
    ManipulateX;
    RecalculateXandY;
    ManipulateY;
  end;
```

Notice that you don't have to pass the variables `X` and `Y` to any of `derived`'s methods; it inherited access to `X` and `Y` along with `base`'s methods.

Inheritance lets you build complex data types when you need to, without repeating any code. A new object type simply inherits whatever it needs from an ancestor and ignores or revises what it doesn't. The derived type can use as much or as little of its ancestors' code as it wants. The derived type can reimplement (or override) any method it decides to. This reimplementation of base type methods in derived types is fundamental to another of OOP's key concepts, polymorphism, which I get to in a moment.

Inheritance is useful for two important reasons. The first is a simple one: when you're given a working object type that doesn't do exactly what you want (let's say that your neighbor in the next cubicle handed it to you), you can create a new object type from the old one with inheritance, adding characteristics or behaviors to suit yourself. This capability enables you to program quickly, while isolating the existing code (which works—your neighbor is trustworthy, right?) from your new, experimental code (which may not).

The second use of inheritance involves the behavior of derived object types that descend from the same base. When you learn to handle a kayak, you learn something that can be applied to a bicycle or pickup truck as well. When you steer any of these vehicles, you don't have to think about which type of vehicle it is—you steer and the vehicle moves. Because this is true in the world, why shouldn't it be true with programming as well?

Polymorphism

Using polymorphism, you can represent this vehicular system with a base object type called `vehicle` and derived object types called `kayak`, `bicycle`, and `pickup`. The base type contains a generic `steer` method:

```
vehicle = object
    Afield : integer;
    procedure Steer; virtual;
end;
```

and each derived type contains a reimplemented `Steer` method:

```
bicycle = object
    Afield : integer;
    procedure Steer; virtual;
end;
```

Any vehicle can be steered (because `vehicle` contains a `steer` method), but each vehicle can steer itself differently (by overriding the vehicle steer method). Because `vehicle` can respond to a message called `steer`, any type derived from `vehicle` also can accept that message.

Thus, bicycles, kayaks, and pickups can be steered because they're vehicles, but the method each specific type uses when `vehicle` gets the `steer` message can differ. In a nutshell this is polymorphism. You tell the vehicle to steer itself (send it a `steer` message), and the vehicle figures out how to carry out the message.

Why is polymorphism so useful? Because this system (which uses polymorphism) won't have to relearn everything each time it encounters a new type of vehicle. This system applies existing knowledge to new situations. An object-oriented program that steers vehicles doesn't need to be rewritten just because it needs to handle a new type of vehicle. It already knows that any vehicle can respond to the `steer` message and act accordingly (see figure 3.3).

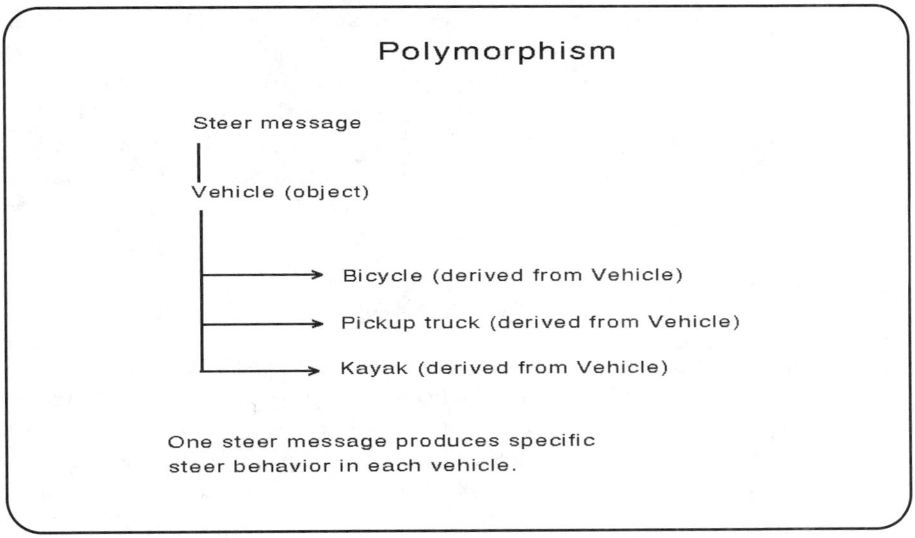

Figure 3.3. *Polymorphism.*

Polymorphism is important because programmers can't know everything about a program or the problem a program needs to solve while developing the program. Programs should be able to change their behaviors in response to new information.

Text editors (or word processors) didn't know about fonts and styles when they were first created; new features had to be added as users became more sophisticated and their needs evolved. The need for programs to change and evolve has been a nemesis of software development since the early days. Change is both expensive and necessary, and the inability to change quickly often leads to programming obsolescence.

Evolution and change must be an integral part of a program. New information might come from understanding a system in a new way or because the problem changes in the real world. Either way, change is inevitable. Polymorphism lets you create extensible programs.

Behaviors such as steering a vehicle or making musical sounds can be common to a group of types but implemented differently for each. The concept is the same, but the implementation details might differ.

Using polymorphism, you can create a system which knows that musical instruments can be played, but not how a particular instrument is played. Specific playing details can come later. The system is extensible because you can add new types of instruments (or vehicles, or whatever) and new ways of playing without redesigning the program.

The capability to create object types is a powerful one indeed, one that fits in well with how people view the world. If you think in terms of types, representing a real-world system as an application (or program) composed of `base` and `derived` types is a natural process. Ideally, the model of a system in a program is a direct mapping of a system from the world. Therefore, as the system in the world changes, it is easier to change the model in the computer.

Messages

Conventional programming systems typically view a program as a collection of functions and procedures. These functions and procedures are the active components of the program; data are passive. When you declare data globally, any function or procedure can access them, thus placing the data at any function's or procedure's mercy. The likelihood of incorrect data manipulation is high.

When you declare data locally (in a procedure), only that procedure can get at the data. The data are safer, but a little too restricted for most tastes. Some flexibility usually is needed, an in-between solution, in which data can be accessed by some restricted number of defined functions and procedures. In object-oriented programming, a method (an object's functions and procedures) is programmed to manipulate only certain data, and data accept manipulation by only certain methods. Manipulation is handled through the sending and receiving of messages (see figure 3.4).

In a procedural program, a program's flow of control is determined by the ordering of procedures and control mechanisms such as `if`, `while`, `switch`, and so on. This ordering implies that you know how to structure the entire program when you create the program. In programs designed to "capture" the essence of a dynamic world, this assumption is unrealistic and cumbersome. The world is evolving, and our ideas and models of the world must adapt to survive. A better alternative captures the design flow in terms of the logical relationships among objects.

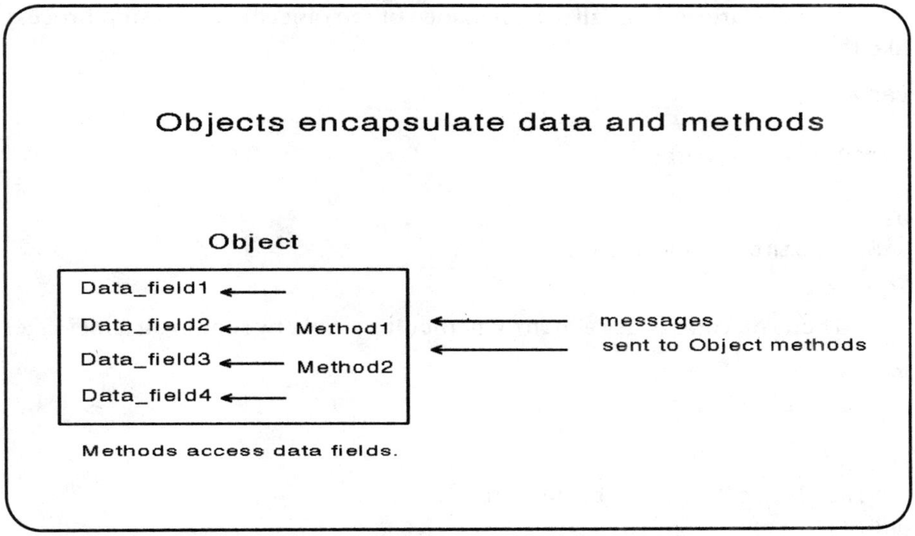

Figure 3.4. *Messages.*

OOP captures these logical relationships in objects, and the flow of control in an object-oriented application is determined by the messages sent to and received from objects. When you send a message, you clarify the communication among the components of a program. Objects respond to the messages sent to them and send messages to other objects.

Messages, not data, move through the system. Rather than "invoke a function on some data" (the procedural approach), you "send a message to an object" (the object-oriented approach).

To send a message to an object, you specify the object and the method you want to invoke.

Suppose that you've declared the following point type:

```
Point = object
   X : integer;
   Y : integer;
   constructor Init(InitX, InitY : integer);
   function IsVisible: integer; { is the point on or off? Return State. }
end;
```

`Point`'s characteristics are its location on-screen (X and Y coordinates). Its behaviors are to construct itself and to report (if it receives a message requesting this information) whether it's visible.

You declare and initialize an instance of the object in a two-step process like this:

```
var

SomePoint : Point;

begin
  SomePoint.Init(23,28);
end;
```

Then you can ask `SomePoint` whether it's visible by sending it a message:

```
var
  Visible : integer;

begin
  Visible := SomePoint.IsVisible;
end;
```

Sending a message means calling an object's method, which manipulates or interprets the type's characteristics.

Static and Dynamic Binding

Each object talked about so far uses statically bound methods. When a method is statically bound (also referred to as *early binding*) the compiler allocates and resolves all references to the method at compile-time. When you call a statically bound method, the compiler determines exactly which method to send a message to at compile-time—an efficient way to search for methods unless you want to use polymorphism.

With polymorphism, you want to send a message to an object and let the object determine which method to use. So, you're asking the compiler to resolve some references at run-time; this process is called *late*, or *dynamic*, *binding*.

To resolve references to methods at run-time, you create virtual methods. To create a virtual method, add the keyword `virtual` to the method in the base object type and include a special procedure called a `constructor` in the object. After a method is declared `virtual` in a base type, this method must be declared `virtual` in all inherited types. To make `AddXandY` a virtual method, for example, you declare it as `virtual` at its earliest and in all subsequent declarations:

```
derived = object(base)
  constructor Init;
  procedure AddXandY; virtual;
end;

anObject2 = object(derived)
  constructor Init;
  procedure AddXandY; virtual;
end;
```

Virtual methods enable derived types to have their own distinct versions of a base type method. You use this thorny (but quite powerful) aspect of object-oriented programming again and again.

Dynamic Style

Most folks who discuss object-oriented programming emphasize only three of its aspects: encapsulation, inheritance, and polymorphism. The Tao of objects, as I've explored it, must also incorporate another important concept: dynamic style or the use of dynamic objects.

Although you can create an instance of a polymorphic object on the stack (without using pointers), it's convenient and helpful to create an instance at run-time by allocating it on the heap, using a pointer. Turbo Pascal manipulates dynamic variables easily and efficiently through the `New` and `Dispose` procedures in Turbo Pascal.

To create an instance of an object type, pass `New` a pointer to the instance of the type to be created:

```
var ShapePointer : ^Shape;

New(ShapePointer);
```

As with records, `New` allocates enough space on the heap for an instance of the pointer's base type, and stores that space's address (in the pointer). When the dynamic variable contains any `virtual` methods, you must use a constructor to initialize the type before sending any messages to the object. You can use `New` to allocate space and initialize the instance of the type in one step, because `New` can take the constructor (`Init`) as a parameter:

```
var
   EllipsePtr : ^Ellipse;

New(EllipsePtr,Init(140,75,50)); { points and radius }
```

Dynamic variables are useful because you can add any number of instances of them at run-time without knowing the exact number of instances at compile-time.

By delaying system-determining decisions until run-time, you allow code to be disconnected from a type's specific details, and the system becomes more flexible. A working system can be modified, adjusted, and so on, long after it's "finished." Instances of new types can be added to the system easily without disrupting it.

Many languages can easily handle small- to medium-size programs, but the real problems begin when the programs get big. Windows applications are big by default. Turbo Pascal (with extensions for separate compilation) enables you to program "in the large." Turbo Pascal for Windows allows you to encapsulate into an object the data and operations needed to handle a window.

Extended Views

It's helpful to think of an object as a little program. An object has its own data (like a program) and an interface for sending and receiving messages. You use programs such as a text editor (an object), which manages its own data (characters and words). Using a keyboard or a mouse, you send the text editor messages such as "append a specific character" or "move back to the previous word."

Each object of your program handles a task. So, an object-oriented program is similar to a multitasking environment. You might use a communication program to send and receive files (data), a database to store it, a spreadsheet to analyze it, and a desktop publishing system to format it. Although you can (in theory at least) write spreadsheets and database systems yourself, you don't have to (nor do you usually want to!); you save time and effort by using programs someone else has written.

When you request some data or action (a report or a recalculation by a spreadsheet, for example) you probably don't want to know the specifics of how the spreadsheet handled the math. You want the results. Creating programs out of objects works similarly. In effect, you "run" objects (just as you "run" programs) that manipulate their data. You may write the code for these objects or you may derive your objects from someone else's.

An object-oriented program saves time and effort by enabling you to reuse existing objects. ObjectWindows is the library of existing objects you use to get to Windows programming. All the objects you need to get started are coded for you. The `BasicInterface` in Chapter 4, "Inheriting an Interface," uses (and extends) these objects. You, in turn, use as much of the `BasicInterface` as you want and extend it for your own purposes.

You communicate with objects by sending them messages. A program, then, consists of objects and the messages you send them (see figure 3.5).

This view is consistent with how you should think about a Windows program. Each application (or program) running in a Windows window is an object that sends and receives messages. When you want a task done, you send a message to an application window (an object), and it completes the task.

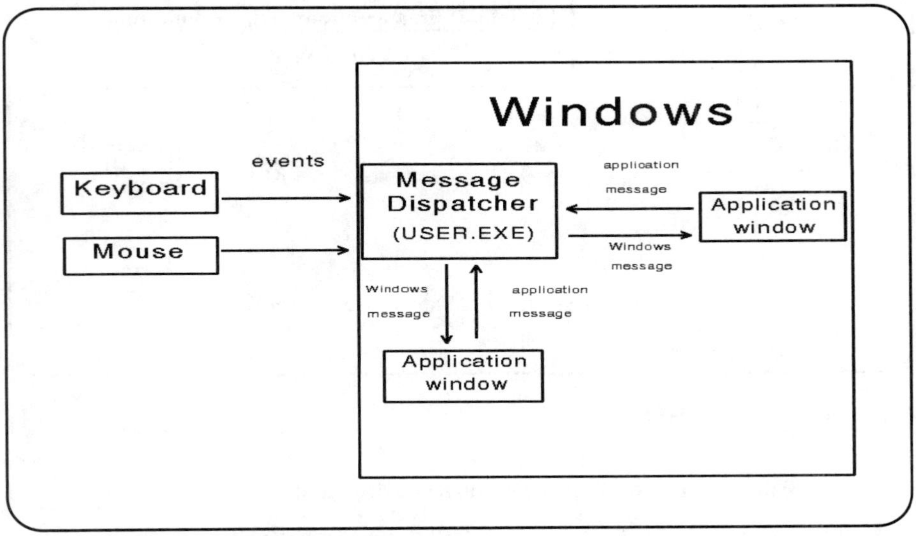

Figure 3.5. Objects and messages.

About Microsoft Windows

Microsoft Windows has become the graphical user interface (or GUI) of choice for a majority of PC users. Certainly, in the next few years, you should expect an explosion of Windows users and programmers. Windows is wonderful, powerful, and complex, but it doesn't have everything yet. Its application lineup still has many positions to fill. Any programmer can benefit by adding Windows skills to her tool kit.

Windows runs in graphics mode on IBM PCs and compatibles. Windows is an interface, not an operating system, so it doesn't replace DOS; instead it works with it. For example, Windows utilizes DOS for file I/O (see figure 3.6).

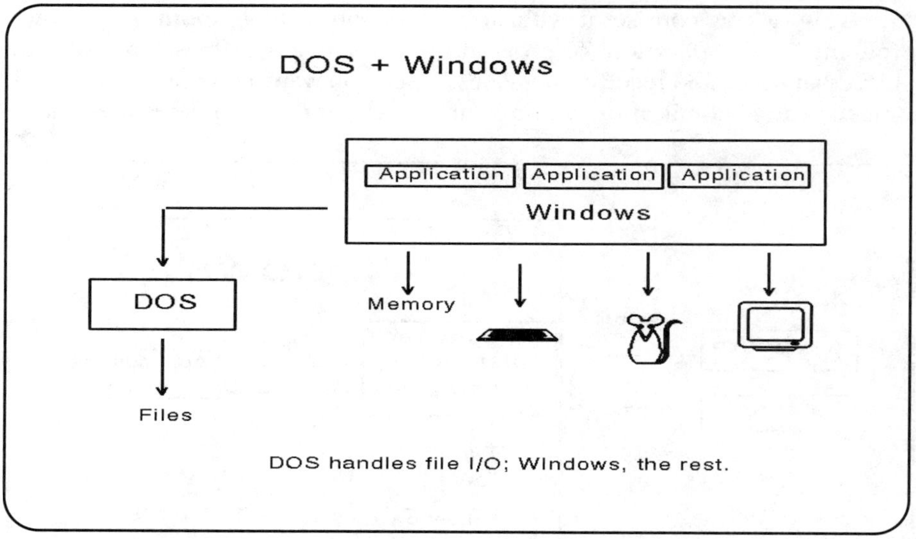

Figure 3.6. DOS plus Windows.

There are many excellent reasons for using Windows:

- Because Windows offers a standard, consistent user interface, users do not have to learn new cues and keystrokes to get up to speed with new applications. Thus, they can run many otherwise dissimilar applications easier because there's less to learn.
- Windows enables you to write device-independent applications. You write generic code that solves the problem, and Windows takes care of running the application with various displays, printing to different kinds of printers, and so on.
- Windows allows applications to talk to each other. Not only can your applications send and receive messages to objects in themselves, but they also can send messages to and receive them from other applications *you didn't even write*. Your application can tap into programs it didn't even know about when the programs were written.
- Windows allows more than one application and more than one instance of an application to run simultaneously. *Note:* More than one application is not using the CPU at the same time although they appear to be running simultaneously; it's a beautiful Windows illusion.
- Windows enables applications to share memory (at least in appearance) by sharing code.

On the down side:

- Windows requires a more powerful computer, more memory, a faster CPU, and a better graphics adapter.
- You, the programmer, must learn your way around an event-driven architecture and learn how to communicate with the Windows management facilities. You have access to a beautiful and powerful interface, but to really use it, you must understand its language. C and C++ programmers generally still must learn hundreds and hundreds of new function calls to make their Windows programs shine. Turbo Pascal for Windows folks can use ObjectWindows and take hundreds of shortcuts.

Windows Structure

The functionality of Windows resides in Windows' Application Programming Interface (or API), contained in three external library modules. These modules are part of the retail version of Windows. Thus, your applications do not create Windows functionality, they simply tap into it.

When you write a Windows application using Turbo Pascal for Windows, your application interacts with (and uses) the modules

- KERNEL.EXE
- GDI.EXE
- USER.EXE

behind the scenes. KERNEL.EXE handles memory and resource management, scheduling, and interaction with DOS. GDI.EXE displays graphics on the screen and printer. USER.EXE handles window management, user input, and communications. You don't need to think of these modules as separate entities when you write your applications. From your application's perspective, they're together—just Windows.

Although a complete Windows application has the .EXE extension (TPW.EXE, for example), the .EXE isn't a typical DOS .EXE file. Because a Windows-compatible compiler attaches some special information to the .EXE file, Windows can recognize and run it. An application designed to run in Windows won't run in DOS without Windows' support, but a DOS application might run in Windows.

In addition to the code the compiler attached to your .EXE (remember: you don't have to worry about it), even the simplest application you write for Windows must meet some other minimal requirements. The application must at least

1. Create a main window.
2. Be able to communicate with Windows.
3. Close the window.
4. Remove the window when it's no longer needed.

Because Turbo Pascal for Windows is Windows-compatible, even without the ObjectWindows library, you can write a Windows-compatible application without ObjectWindows' support.

To write the application, you must handle many details that ObjectWindows usually handles for you. In general, you do not want to bypass ObjectWindows, but because you might, you should take a quick look at the process. If you never bypass ObjectWindows, it helps to appreciate the work ObjectWindows is doing for you "under the table." The code is about 100 lines long (the equivalent C code is about 80). See the complete code in listing 3.1. If you are unfamiliar with the Turbo Pascal for Windows IDE and are not sure how to run a program, review the discussion of the IDE in Chapter 1, "Getting Started."

***Listing 3.1.** Creating a window without ObjectWindows.*

```
{ Basic Windows application written in
  Turbo Pascal without ObjectWindows }

program Basics;

{ $R BASICS }

uses WinTypes,                        { to use Windows API types }
     WinProcs;                        { to use API processes }

const
  AppName = 'Basics';

const                                 { function About is a frill }
  idm_About = 100;                    { but shows basic wm_processing }

function About(Dialog: HWnd; Message, WParam: Word;
  LParam: Longint): Bool; export;
begin
  About := True;
  case Message of                     { basic wm_ processing }
    wm_InitDialog:
      Exit;
```

```
    wm_Command:
      if (WParam = id_Ok) or (WParam = id_Cancel) then
      begin
        EndDialog(Dialog, 1);
        Exit;
      end;
  end;
  About := False;
end;

function WindowProc(Window: HWnd; Message, WParam: Word;
  LParam: Longint): Longint; export;
var
  AboutProc: TFarProc;
begin
  WindowProc := 0;              { intercept messages }
  case Message of               { message responses }
    wm_Command:
      if WParam = idm_About then
      begin
        AboutProc := MakeProcInstance(@About, HInstance);
        DialogBox(HInstance, 'AboutBox', Window, AboutProc);
        FreeProcInstance(AboutProc);
        Exit;
      end;
    wm_Destroy:                 { destroy window }
      begin
        PostQuitMessage(0);
        Exit;
      end;
  end;
  WindowProc := DefWindowProc(Window, Message, WParam, LParam);
end;
                                { create a main window }
procedure WinMain;
var
  Window: HWnd;                 { HWnd is a handle for a window }
  Message: TMsg;                { TMsg is in WinTypes }
const
  WindowClass: TWndClass = (    { register window class }
    style: 0;
    lpfnWndProc: @WindowProc;   { default window info }
    cbClsExtra: 0;
  cbWndExtra: 0;
```

continues

Listing 3.1 continued

```
    hInstance: 0;
    hIcon: 0;
    hCursor: 0;
    hbrBackground: 0;
    lpszMenuName: AppName;
    lpszClassName: AppName);
begin                              { handle multiple instances }
  if HPrevInst = 0 then
  begin
    WindowClass.hInstance := HInstance; { specify icon, cursor, and so on }
    WindowClass.hIcon := LoadIcon(0, idi_Application);
    WindowClass.hCursor := LoadCursor(0, idc_Arrow);
    WindowClass.hbrBackground :=GetStockObject(white_Brush);
    if not RegisterClass(WindowClass) then Halt(255);
  end;
  Window := CreateWindow(          { create main window }
    AppName,
    'Basic Windows w/o ObjectWindows',
    ws_OverlappedWindow,           { default window }
    cw_UseDefault,
    cw_UseDefault,
    cw_UseDefault,
    cw_UseDefault,
    0,
    0,
    HInstance,                     { note the instance }
    nil);
  ShowWindow(Window, CmdShow);     { show the window }
  UpdateWindow(Window);            { update when necessary }
  while GetMessage(Message, 0, 0, 0) do
                                   { run the message loop }
  begin
    TranslateMessage(Message);
    DispatchMessage(Message);
  end;
  Halt(Message.wParam);
end;

begin
  WinMain;                         { create a main window }
end.
```

Figure 3.7 shows the window created by this code.

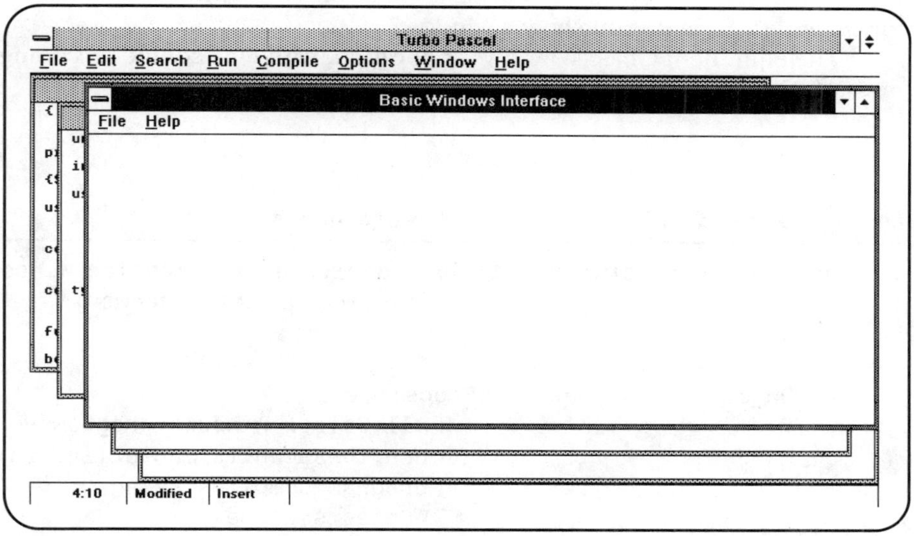

***Figure 3.7.** The created window.*

Several "general" things happen to the application in this code:

- It registers the window class, in the code beginning

  `WindowClass: TWndClass = (.....`

- It creates a main window in the code beginning

  `Window := CreateWindow(....))`

  using stock or default attributes.

- It shows the window `ShowWindow(Window, CmdShow);`.

- It sets up a message loop to process Windows messages:

  ```
  while GetMessage(Message, 0, 0, 0) do
  begin TranslateMessage(Message);
  DispatchMessage(Message); end;.
  ```

- The application halts (`Halt(Message.wParam);`.

- In the beginning it used a `$R` (resource) file `uses $R BASICS`.

This directive makes the compiler link into a resource file. I discuss resources in Chapter 8. For now, if you do not have the *Turbo Pascal for Windows Bible* disk, just link in the GENERIC.RES file that came with your Turbo Pascal for Windows. The file works fine for this example. *Note:* If you are using the IDE, Turbo Pascal for Windows automatically links in any resources specified with `$R`.

It might surprise you that the code in listing 3.1 (despite its many lines) is hiding most of Windows' complexity. What's happening in `CreateWindow`, for example? (How do you show a window?)

The equivalent ObjectWindows application, with ObjectWindows doing most of the work, requires 16 lines (see listing 3.2).

Listing 3.2. Creating a window with `ObjectWindows`.

```
 program BasicObjectWindowsAppl; { derive an application window
                                   using Object windows }


 uses WObjects, WinTypes, WinProcs;
                               { All Object Windows programs
                                 use these units; actually, this
                                 program compiles using
                                 WObjects alone }

 type

           { Derive an application object from TApplication }
           { you must initialize a new main window or you
             get a nil window }
   App1 = object(TApplication)
     procedure InitMainWindow; virtual;
   end;

            { Construct App1's MainWindow object }
 procedure App1.InitMainWindow;
begin                          { window name here }
                               { new gets a pointer to a TWindow }

  MainWindow := New(PWindow, Init(nil, 'Application 1'));

end;

           { Declare an instance of type App1 }
var
  Instance1: App1;

           { Run Instance1 }
begin
```

```
  Instance1.Init('App1');        { init application instance }
  Instance1.Run;                 { message loop }
  Instance1.Done;                { clean up }
end.
```

ObjectWindows gains many lines for you, but more important, it is encapsulating information in objects you do not need to understand in detail. Face it, you can retain only so much information in your brain for quick recall, so why not be spared a few details? Save yourself for the beans and potatoes of your applications.

Why OOP and Windows

Object-oriented programming (OOP) techniques hide program complexity in objects. Object-oriented libraries such as ObjectWindows package these objects. Specifically, ObjectWindows conceals the complexity of the Windows Application Programming Interface (API).

With ObjectWindows, you don't need to understand the Windows API from the bottom up. You don't need to learn and place dozens of function calls to create a window. Instead, you just need to know that predefined object types in ObjectWindows handle it for you. You then use inheritance to extend these objects to make your application special.

I mentioned that another more subtle link between Windows and OOP is that Windows is message-based. Figure 3.8 illustrates this concept.

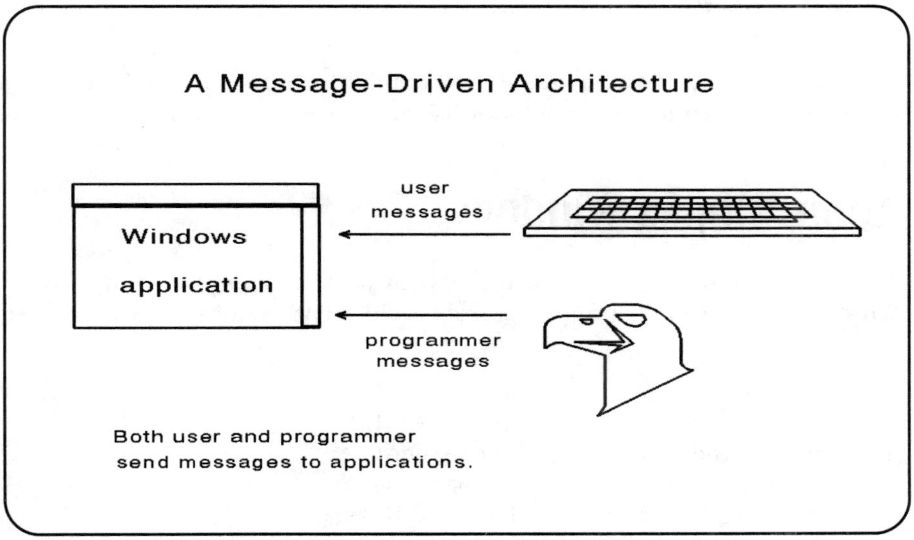

***Figure 3.8.** A message-driven architecture.*

Windows treats user events (clicking the mouse, pressing a key) as messages that must be dispatched to the correct application. The objects you derive using ObjectWindows communicate by responding to the messages they receive from Windows.

Your Windows application is composed of objects that represent the complex user-interface elements of a Windows application. A window is an object. A dialog is an object. An application is an object that sets up the interface to Windows, and so on (see figure 3.9).

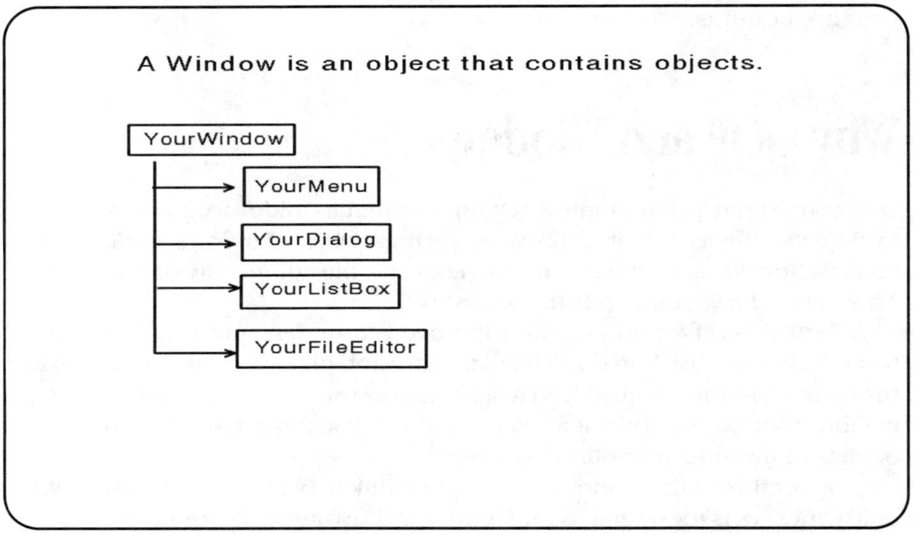

Figure 3.9. *Several objects in one object.*

Because ObjectWindows is so conceptually compatible with Windows, it simplifies the learning of the Windows event-driven operation.

About Object Windows

The power of Windows lies in the 550 or so functions that comprise the Windows API. Recall a few functions from BASICS.PAS, required to set up a basic window:

```
LoadIcon                LoadCursor
GetStockObject          RegisterClass
CreateWindow            ShowWindow
UpdateWindow            GetMessage
TranslateMessage        DispatchMessage
DefWindowProc
```

When a Windows application wants to change its appearance, or respond to user input, it sends a message to a Windows function. Typically, when you write a Windows application without ObjectWindows (in C, for example), you send messages to these Windows functions directly. These messages specify the numerous parameters required of a Windows function, and they handle any other protocol required of the function. The following fragment, for example, sends Windows an API `CreateWindow` message directly:

```
Window := CreateWindow(
    AppName,
    'Your Window Application Name',
    ws_OverlappedWindow,
    cw_UseDefault,
    cw_UseDefault,
    cw_UseDefault,
    cw_UseDefault,
    0,
    0,
    HInstance,
    nil);
```

Notice the complexity of the CreateWindow message, which requires 11 parameters (see figure 3.10). These parameters are, in order, the ClassName, the WindowName, the WindowStyle, the Window's initial height and width (specified here by `cw_UseDefault`), the window's parent (0 here because the window has no parent), a menu (0 here for none), the Instance, and a pointer (nil here) for MDI windows. Simple? No; this is one of the many reasons that you don't create Windows and applications without the help of ObjectWindows.

The equivalent ObjectWindows call looks something like this:

```
MainWindow := New(PtrWindow, Init(nil,
              'Your Window Application Name'));
```

Other ObjectWindows object types manage the message-processing and other behaviors required of a Windows program.

ObjectWindows simplifies the calling of Windows functions by repackaging the API in an object-oriented library. ObjectWindows encapsulates all the Windows information contained in the API. ObjectWindows abstracts the Windows API functions and automates message response. ObjectWindows handles any messages you don't want to handle directly, as shown in figure 3.11.

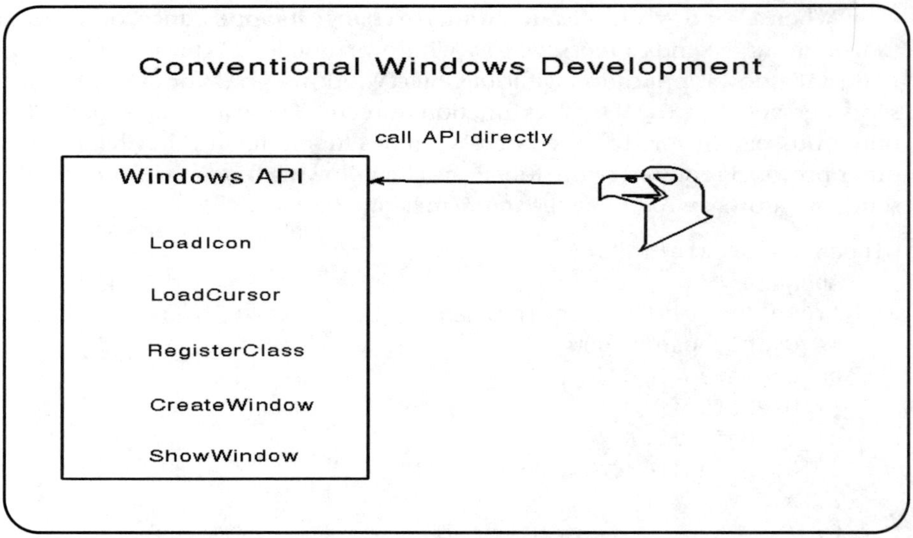

Figure 3.10. *Conventional Windows development.*

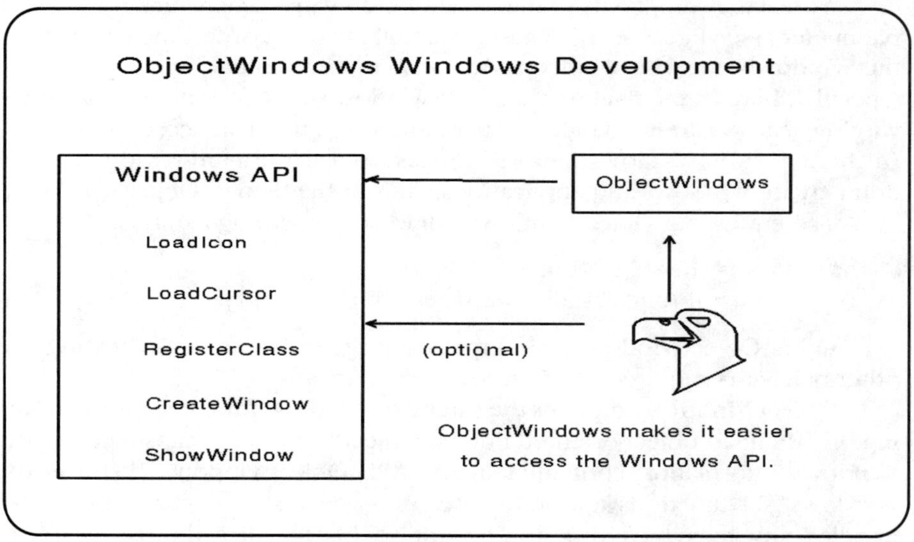

Figure 3.11. *ObjectWindows Windows development.*

By encapsulating the details of Windows in objects, ObjectWindows insulates you from much of Windows' complexity. Most of the parameter passing, setup, and so on occurs under cover in ObjectWindows. You create an instance of an object you need in order to handle a job; the object handles it without your worrying about the details.

You also can think of the ObjectWindows approach as an indirect one. In ObjectWindows are the objects you use to create windows, dialogs, controls, and so on. You should keep in mind that in many cases, ObjectWindows is not actually implementing many of its behaviors itself. Whenever it can, it has Windows do the work. So Windows handles many of the details, another level away from the objects you create. In fact, Windows is responsible for every physical element you see on your computer screen.

Let me explain. ObjectWindows, for example, defines window, dialog, and control objects you can utilize to create applications. ObjectWindows itself does not actually implement windows, dialogs, and so on. It only represents them. ObjectWindows requests Windows to actually create them or remove them from the screen. It supplies only the specific behavior and attributes of the objects.

This distinction might seem confusing, but it's an important one that helps you understand the ObjectWindows approach. The term used by Borland to define ObjectWindows objects is *interface objects*, and the visual elements (what you see on your screen) are called *interface elements*. These two components are connected by way of a Windows handle (see figure 3.12).

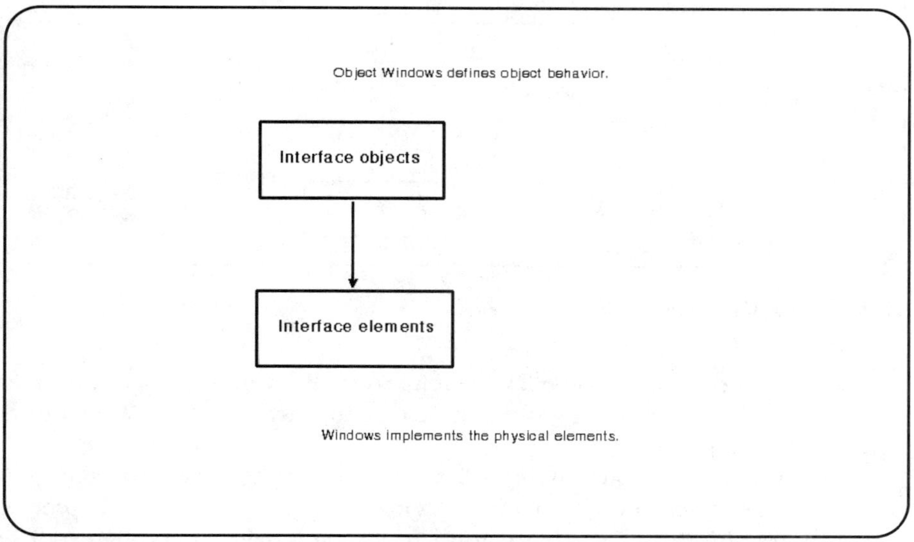

Figure 3.12. *Interface objects versus interface elements.*

When you construct an interface object, ObjectWindows asks Windows to create the corresponding element. Windows creates the element and returns a handle that identifies the element throughout its life. This handle is used any time a Windows function needs to send a message to the element. ObjectWindows stores this handle in a `TWindows` object field called `HWindow`, which you read much more about in the next chapter.

Events, Messages, and Objects

Windows is based on an event-driven architecture. Windows handles all user input (keyboard and mouse) as events, and generates a message corresponding to the event (see figure 3.13).

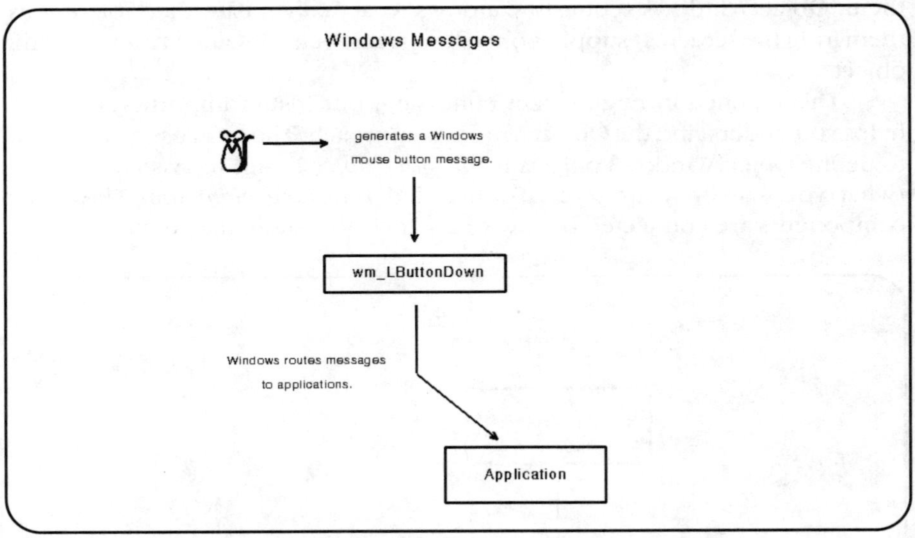

***Figure 3.13.** Windows messages.*

For example, when you click the left mouse button, Windows generates a left-button-down message (`wm_LButtonDown`), where `wm` is a windows message.

When you press a key, Windows generates a `wm_KeyDown` message.

The user's selection of a menu item is also an event. In Chapter 4, "Inheriting an Interface," you learn how to define command-message response methods for responding to menus.

Events trigger Windows messages to objects. When these objects are derived from ObjectWindows, they can easily be taught to respond to Windows messages.

The user also can use the mouse to click various control buttons and select items from a list box (called Control events). ObjectWindows makes it easy for your objects to respond to these events as well (again, more on this in Chapter 4, "Inheriting an Interface").

Windows Messages

There are more than 100 standard Windows messages. Windows sends messages to applications in response to events. The application responds to these messages and acts accordingly. Windows objects respond to incoming Windows messages (see figure 3.14).

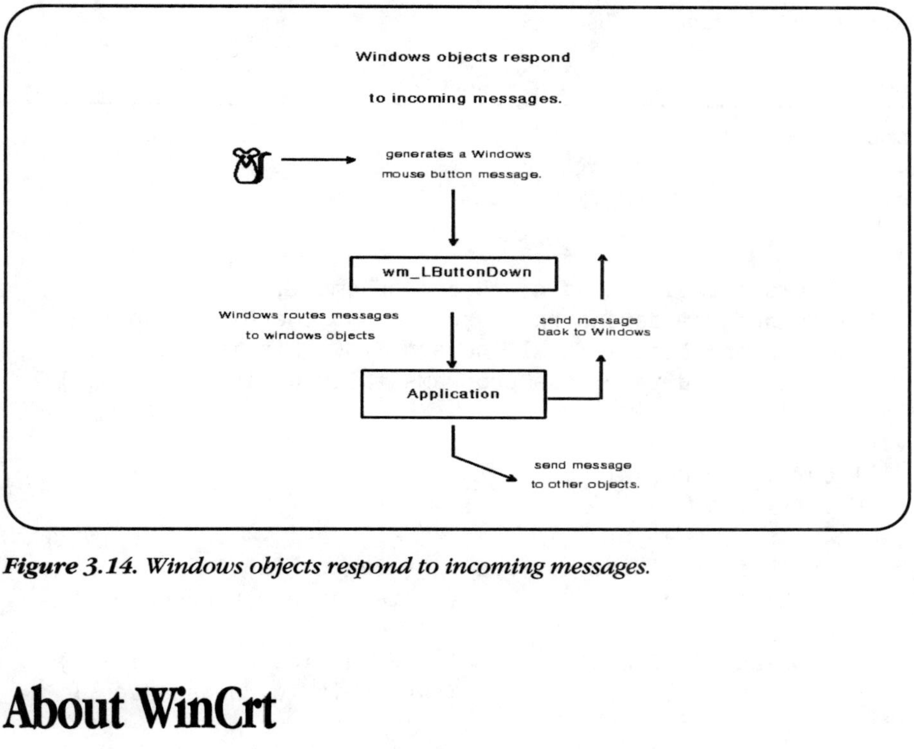

Figure 3.14. *Windows objects respond to incoming messages.*

About WinCrt

Before you get to the heart of Windows programming ObjectWindows-style, I should point out a quick and clean way to get a Turbo Pascal for Windows application up and running in no time at all.

Because Windows doesn't support traditional text-oriented file I/O, when you try to use your existing Turbo Pascal programs to read and write files, you receive a fatal error message.

The way to utilize your existing code and the simplest way to get a simple application running with Turbo Pascal for Windows is to use the `WinCrt` unit. `WinCrt` contains the control logic to emulate a text screen in a window.

The WinCrt unit enables you to run standard Turbo Pascal programs in Windows by adding one line of code: uses WinCrt;. You can't take advantage of complex Windows features, but you can still use old code that's text-based. This feature makes the transition to Windows programming easier.

The following code fragment demonstrates standard Turbo Pascal input and output, using Writeln, Readln. Notice the repeat/until loops that the input and output echo until Input = 'quit'. 'Quit' does not close the Window. The window remains on-screen and is closed just as any Window is by way of the FileMenu (see listing 3.3).

***Listing 3.3.** Using standard Turbo Pascal I/O.*

```
program WindCRTex;

uses
  WinCrt;

  { Allows Writeln, Readln, cursor movement, and so on. }
  { This program demonstrates how to use the WinCrt unit
    to perform "traditional" screen I/O. This is the easiest
    way to build text mode programs that run in a window. }

var
   Input : string[80];
   F : text;
begin
        Assign(F,'wincrtex.pas'); { Basic FILE I/O }
        Reset(F);                { Note: no error checking }
  repeat
        Readln(F,Input);         { Read a line of the file  }
        Write(Input);            { Write it to the screen  }
        Writeln;
        Writeln('What do you say?'); { Interact with user }
        Readln(Input);
        Writeln('Got it... You said ', Input);
  until (Input = 'quit') or EOF(F);
  Close(F);                      { Close the file. }
  DoneWinCrt;                    { Destroys the CRT window   }
end.                             { so that the user doesn't  }
                                 { have to close it manually }
```

When your application doesn't need to use anything more than a single "frill-less" window and is text-based, the WinCrt route is definitely the easiest route to get a Windows application going.

Using `WinCrt` eliminates the need to write specific Windows code—a plus in the short term, but limiting in the long term. To use the many features provided by Windows to their fullest extent, you should go beyond the text-based windowing provided by `WinCrt` to the ObjectWindows library. That's where Turbo Pascal for Windows shines.

Movin' On

That's enough information for an introduction. The next chapter develops a basic application and window interface that I continue to use throughout the book. This `BasicInterface` creates a main window (through inheritance) and attaches dialogs, menus, and controls to it. Use it as the starting point for all your Windows applications (I do).

Windows and objects are a great match: an interface and the tools for easily manipulating that interface. Putting the two together requires a little initial effort (and perhaps) a new programming point of view, but the payoff for a little effort is more than enough compensation.

OOP is a powerful programming technique in the PC arena, and Windows is the most powerful programming environment. Turbo Pascal for Windows (with its ObjectWindows library) links the two in a pleasant, powerful IDE, fit for the princes and princesses of programming like you and me.

4

CHAPTER

INHERITING AN INTERFACE

What the user and applications developer want today is a graphics-oriented user interface, multitasking capability, and hardware independence. Windows has come of age.

William H. Murray, III and
Chris H. Pappas

Object-oriented programming languages (such as Turbo Pascal for Windows) encourage you to change the way you think about developing applications. Using OOP techniques, you can design general (or base) object types, and your applications can inherit characteristics and behaviors from these base types. This inheritance results in your saving significant programming time and effort, because you write only the code that differs from the base type.

ObjectWindows contains enough base types for you to create a complete Windows interface. Objects that create menus for user responses, list boxes for user selections, file dialogs for opening and saving files, and editors for modifying files are a few ObjectWindows base object types that are ready to go right out of the box. Eventually you will use most of the objects in ObjectWindows, so it's worth taking a look at how the objects fit together hierarchically. Figure 4.1 shows the ObjectWindows object hierarchy.

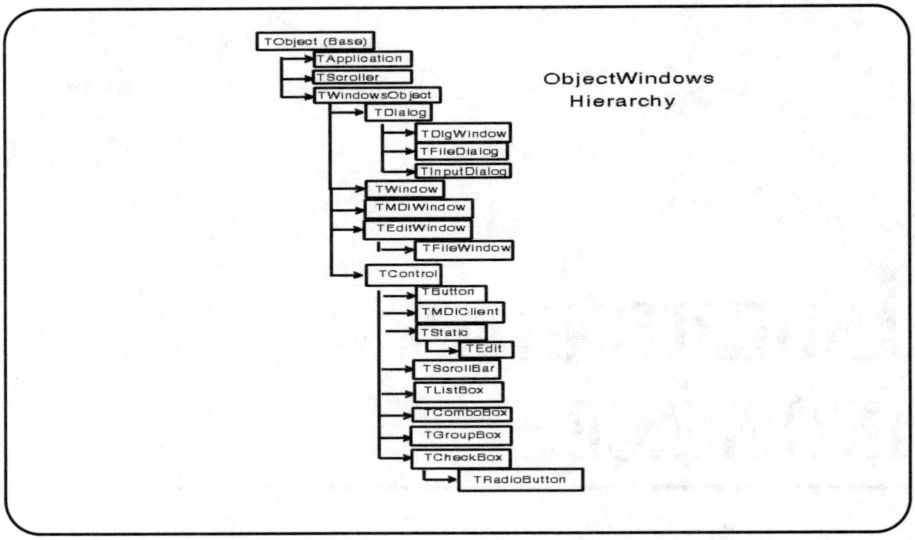

Figure 4.1. *The ObjectWindows hierarchy.*

ObjectWindows is a terrific library: easy to use and well thought out. You do have to specify the behaviors of menus, dialogs, boxes, and so on, but you don't have to specify what they look like or how they operate. Those details all are ready to be inherited by the objects you create using ObjectWindows.

In addition, these behaviors can be defined outside your Turbo Pascal source code as resources (using the Whitewater Resource Toolkit packaged with Turbo Pascal for Windows, which is discussed in Chapter 8, "Resources and Control Objects," and in Reference O, "Object Graphics." You can modify them without necessarily modifying your source code—a definite plus when you develop large or generic applications.

To include a menu, for example, your application

1. Loads a menu from a compiled resource file.
2. Specifies how the application should respond to a user's menu selections.

To include a list box, your application

1. Loads a list box from a resource file.
2. Specifies what should go in the list and how the application should respond to list selections.

To include other resources in your application, you follow a similar procedure.

Any application you create using ObjectWindows starts from two basic objects in the library (`TApplication` and `TWindow`). You derive new applications and windows from these base application and window objects. You don't have to reinvent the application or the window. You expend virtually no energy designing the look and feel of your application's interface. It already looks and feels like any other Windows application. You concentrate, instead, on the details of your specific application, making you, your boss, and your family happy. Because each application you create using `TApplication` and `TWindow` shares the common attributes and behaviors of other Windows applications, both you and your users benefit.

A user learns how to use a general interface (in this case, the Windows GUI), and comes up to speed in new applications much more quickly. You concentrate on the specific aspects of the application, not on how to use the interface. You don't have to rewrite an interface for each application. You reuse an existing one, adding the bells and whistles you need. Everybody wins, especially marketing.

The BasicInterface

It's worth repeating: Windows is a graphical user interface (a GUI). Everything—text, dots, fills, and pictures—are treated by Windows not as ASCII characters (DOS-style), but as pixels turned on and off in a display context (the Windows name for a painting surface). Dealing with pixels rather than characters empowers GUIs, but it also makes them difficult for application programmers.

Every aspect of the applications you develop using Turbo Pascal for Windows and ObjectWindows must deal with pixels. You *can* use the `WinCrt` unit (described in Chapter 3, "Objects for Windows,") for simple text-oriented Windows applications, but for anything complex, your application must translate to pixels. Fortunately, using pixels is only slightly more difficult than using text. Amazing!

In this chapter, you use the OOP concepts discussed in Chapter 2 to create a useful and powerful interface. After you have this `BasicInterface` in your toolbox, you use it as a starting point each time you write a Windows application. It is general enough to use as is and simultaneously customizable. Each time you write a new application you concentrate on its details, and the `BasicInterface` handles communications with Windows.

The `BasicInterface` consists of two big objects derived from `TApplication` and `TWindow`:

1. An application
2. Its main window and the objects that are attached to it

The `BasicInterface` object (I call it `WIF`, for Windows InterFace) handles your application's low-level interactions with Windows, channeling messages back and forth between Windows and the application's main window. The main window, in turn, controls other window objects (such as buttons, menus, scroll bars, and boxes).

For convenience, you keep the `BasicInterface` in a unit (WIF.PAS), which you include in each of your applications. This unit also manages the loading of other basic units and resources required by ObjectWindows—another detail you don't have to be concerned about. I build the `BasicInterface` a component at a time, and show the code to you in pieces. The complete `BasicInterface` code, ready to plug into your applications, is in listing 4.7, at the end of this chapter.

Your applications inherit all the behaviors and characteristics of the `BasicInterface`: communicating with Windows, creating and managing main and child windows, interacting with the user, and so on. You sometimes need to modify the `BasicInterface` a bit (to specify responses to dialogs and menu selections, for example), but for many generic purposes, it works fine as is. Modifying the `BasicInterface` is easy, thanks to OOP techniques. Chapters 5 through 13 show you how to extend the `BasicInterface` to handle many different kinds of problems.

Application and Window Objects

Any Windows application must initiate and maintain a communication link between itself and Windows. Recall from Chapter 3, "Objects for Windows," that to set up the basic machinery required to initialize a main window in Windows and to set up communications between your application and Windows requires about 100 lines of Turbo Pascal for Windows code, if your application sends messages to the Windows API directly. Although you can call the API (Application Programming Interface) directly each time you create an application, you usually don't want to because you can often achieve the same results in far fewer lines using ObjectWindows.

Three units packaged with Turbo Pascal for Windows (WObjects, `WinTypes`, and `WinProcs`) establish the interface between your applications and Windows. WObjects is the ObjectWindows object library. `WinTypes` and `WinProcs` define the Turbo Pascal for Windows function types and processes for sending messages to the Windows API directly.

If your application sends messages to the Windows API only through ObjectWindows, it doesn't need to include the `WinTypes` and `WinProcs` units. The `BasicInterface` sometimes sends messages to the API directly, so it includes all three units. (*Note:* Including these units doesn't incur any extra overhead for the `BasicInterface`. The Turbo Pascal for Windows compiler is smart and compiles only the code actually used by your application.)

The `BasicInterface` consists of two objects (`BasicApplication` and `MainWindow`). The `BasicApplication` "owns" the `MainWindow`, but the two are distinct objects; they're not related hierarchically. Ownership of this type is called an ***instance linkage***.

The `BasicApplication` is derived from the `TApplication` object (in ObjectWindows). The `MainWindow` is derived from the `TWindow` object (in ObjectWindows).

The `TApplication` object in ObjectWindows already knows how to handle all of Windows' initialization for you. The only specific initialization the `BasicApplication` has to handle itself is to create a new `MainWindow` using inheritance (see figure 4.2).

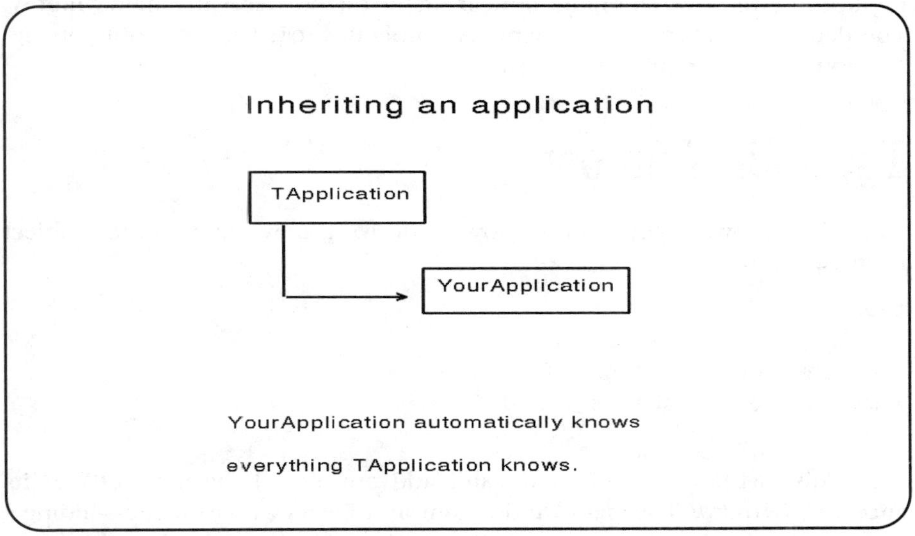

Figure 4.2. Inheriting an application.

Your first order of business in creating the `BasicInterface` is to derive a `BasicApplication` object type from a `TApplication` object:

```
type
  BasicApplication = object(TApplication)
    procedure InitMainWindow; virtual;
  end;
```

The procedure `InitMainWindow` is virtual (thus, its behavior can be overridden), defined originally as a `TApplication` method. Each application derived from `TApplication` should override this method:

```
procedure BasicApplication.InitMainWindow;
begin
    MainWindow := New(PMainWindow, Init(nil,
'BasicInterface'));
end;
```

InitMainWindow "connects" the BasicApplication to its MainWindow, by way of a pointer (PMainWinsdow). The Turbo Pascal for Windows extended syntax for the New procedure enables you to specify the object type you want to create (a MainWindow) and construct it (using Init) in one step.

The MainWindow's default constructor (defined in TWindow) requires two parameters: nil (required for initialization purposes), and a name for the application window. This name appears in the top border of the main window. The default BasicInterface name is simply BasicInterface, but you can (obviously) change this name easily.

The Main Window

The following code shows how to derive a new main window object from TWindow:

```
type

  PMainWindow = ^MainWindow;
  MainWindow  = object(TWindow)
  end;
```

This MainWindow object doesn't add any new behavior (yet!) to its ancestor, TWindow. The main window simply appears with its name—hiding a menu with close, resize, move, and other options when you run the application (see figure 4.3).

This main window (by way of its connection to the BasicApplication) responds automatically to Windows messages (the keyboard, the mouse, and so on) and to user events (menu selections, check boxes, dialogs, and so on). In almost all cases, your application wants to implement some of its own responses to specific Windows messages. No problem. By beginning with a general main window that can handle any Windows message automatically, you have to implement only the responses you want to specify. You add only the behaviors you want to override by adding response methods to the basic main window. More on this in a moment.

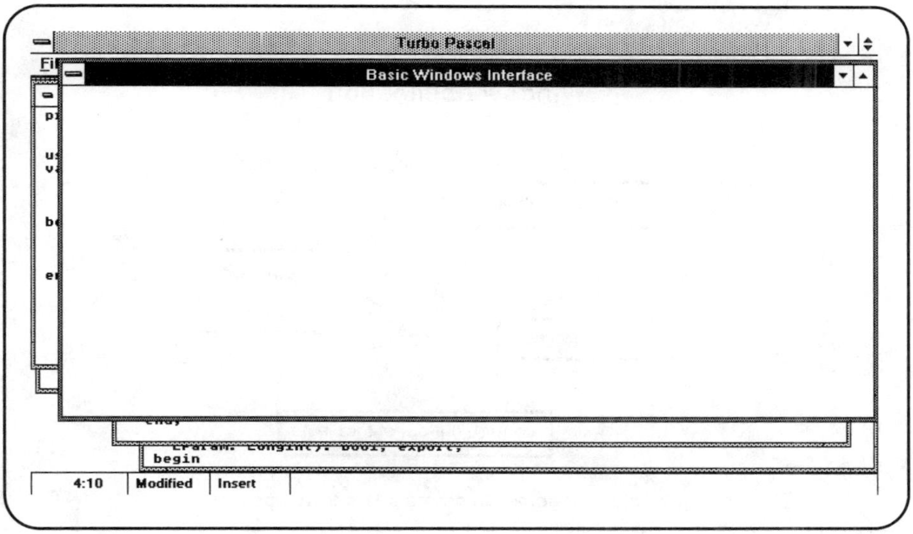

Figure 4.3. *The default window of* `TWindow.Init`.

You can derive most of your applications from the `BasicInterface` developed in this chapter. Your applications that need to have more than one document open at a time can use a variation of the `BasicInterface` set up for you in Chapter 5, "Putting Pictures in Windows." The variation uses a main window as well but calls it a parent window and attaches other windows (called *children*) to it. This many-window system is defined by the multi-document interface (or MDI).

In sum, the `BasicInterface` at its simplest is an application and a main window object, as illustrated by figure 4.4.

To use these two objects:

1. Declare an instance (for example, a variable) of object type `BasicApplication` (but you don't create an instance of `MainWindow`!):

   ```
   var Application1 : BasicApplication;
   ```

2. Construct it:

   ```
   Application1.Init('Application1');
   ```

3. Set it in motion:

   ```
   Application1.Run;
   ```

4. Arrange for it to be destroyed when you finish with it:

   ```
   Application1.Done;
   ```

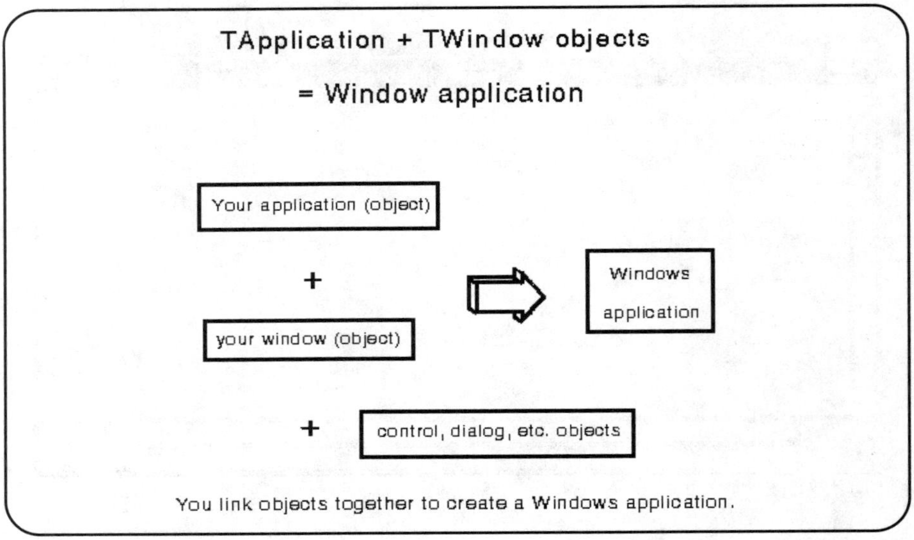

Figure 4.4. Creating a windows application.

Listing 4.1 shows the first phase (preliminary, but workable) of the `BasicInterface` (WIF1.PAS). Listing 4.2 shows a little program you use throughout this chapter to test the `BasicInterface`.

Listing 4.1. The preliminary version of `BasicInterface`.

```
unit WIF1;          { Contains Basic Windows application interface
                      version 1 derived from ObjectWindows }
interface

uses
  WObjects,         { ObjectWindows library of objects }
  WinTypes,         { Windows types:      for accessing the API }
  WinProcs;         { Windows processes: for accessing the API }

type
  BasicApplication = object(TApplication)
                    { Derive an application object }
    procedure InitMainWindow; virtual;  {Init a main window }
  end;

  PMainWindow = ^MainWindow;      { Pointer to a main window }
  MainWindow = object(TWindow)    { Derive a main window }
  end;
```

```
implementation

procedure BasicApplication.InitMainWindow;
begin
  MainWindow := New(PWindow, Init(nil, 'Basic Windows Interface'));
end;

end.
{ end unit }
```

***Listing 4.2.** Testing the* `BasicInterface`.

```
program Test_Interface;         { A generic way to test each
                                  phase of interface development }

uses WIF5;                      { BasicInterface unit }
var
  Application1: BasicApplication;  { An instance of
BasicApplication }
                                   { Run Application1 }
begin
  Application1.Init('BasicInterface');  { init application instance
}
  Application1.Run;                     { Message loop }
  Application1.Done;             { Destroy application instance }
end.                             { End test program }
```

Notice that you don't have to write the `Init`, `Run`, or `Done` methods yourself. The `BasicApplication` object inherited these methods from `TApplication`.

Details

Although you don't need to know how `Init`, `Run`, and `Done` work, you might appreciate a brief explanation of how they handle your application for you.

When you construct the basic application (`Application1.Init`), the Turbo Pascal for Windows compiler checks whether it can send a message to `Application1`'s constructor. `Application1`, in fact, doesn't have its own constructor. It inherited one (from `TApplication`), so the compiler sends the construct message to `TApplication` (the ancestor of `BasicApplication`). *Note:* `Application1` is an instance of the object type (`BasicApplication`), not the object itself.

The TApplication constructor (Init) constructs the BasicApplication. Specifically, it sends a message to its ancestor TObject.Init, the base object type or common ancestor of all ObjectWindows object types. The constructor then sets the ObjectWindows global variable (Application) to @Self, and several of the BasicApplication fields. These fields, like the constructor, were inherited by the BasicApplication from TApplication.

Init sets the BasicApplication Name field to the application name it received in the message (Application1.Init('Name here'). Init then sets to zero both the BasicApplication.HAccTable (for handle to an accelerator table) and BasicApplication.Status fields. Then it initializes the MainWindow and KBHandlerWnd (for keyboard handler window) to nil. Finally, if this is the first instance of the application (there can be more than one instance—more on this later in this chapter), Init sends a message to InitApplication (another default TApplication method) to handle any specific initialization for a first instance of an application.

In other words, whew. There's a lot going on, and you don't have to think about most of it. A BasicApplication is constructed with no effort on your part. In most cases, this automatic construction suffices, but your application can always override this default behavior if it needs to.

Application1.Run, the message loop, is where the action is.

Basically, the Run method (again inherited from TApplication) is the dispatch message loop you saw earlier in the NoFrills.pas code in Chapter 3, "Objects for Windows."

Run sends a message to its MessageLoop method, which processes incoming Windows messages. The MessageLoop works automatically (of course), so again you can ignore the details of its processing of basic Windows messages. You can reimplement this MessageLoop, if you're trying to optimize your application (see Chapter 12, "Sharing Libraries").

Finally, when Application1. receives an end message (from Windows), it sends a message to its destructor (Application1.Done), which destroys the application instance.

It's worth emphasizing that destructors don't destroy object types, they destroy instances (or variables) of the object. Your application can create more than one instance of an object type. Figure 4.5 illustrates this concept, and the following adjustment to the BasicInterface handles multiple instances:

```
procedure BasicApplication.InitMainWindow;
begin
  if FirstApplication then
  MainWindow := New(PMainWindow, Init(nil, 'Basic Windows Interface'))
  else MainWindow := New(PMainWindow, Init(nil,'Additional Instance of BI'));
end;
```

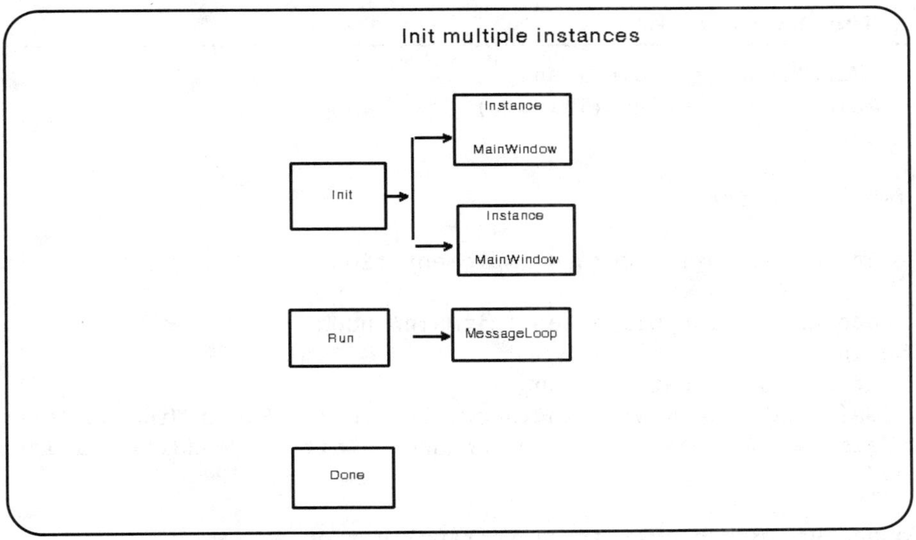

Figure 4.5. *Multiple instances of* `Init`.

Although many, if not most, of your applications need only one instance, some of them will need multiple instances. You should include these adjustments in the `BasicInterface`. Listing 4.3 shows this new state of the `BasicInterface` (`WIF2.PAS`). Throughout this chapter, use the `TEST_WIF.PAS` code in listing 4.2 to test the new versions of the `BasicInterface`.

Listing 4.3. *A revision of* `BasicInterface`.

```
unit WIF2;    { Contains Basic Windows application
                     interface derived from ObjectWindows }
interface

uses
  WObjects,        { ObjectWindows library of objects }
  WinTypes,        { Windows types: for accessing the API }
  WinProcs;        { Windows processes: for accessing the API }

type

  BasicApplication = object(TApplication)
                   { Derive an application object }
    FirstApplication : boolean;
    procedure InitMainWindow; virtual;  { Init a main window }
    procedure InitApplication; virtual;
  end;
```

continues

Listing 4.3. continued

```
  PMainWindow = ^MainWindow;
  MainWindow = object(TWindow)
  end;

implementation

{ BasicApplication method implementation }

procedure BasicApplication.InitMainWindow;
begin
  if FirstApplication then
  MainWindow := New(PMainWindow, Init(nil, 'Basic Windows Interface'))
  else MainWindow := New(PMainWindow, Init(nil,'Additional Instance of BI'));
end;

procedure BasicApplication.InitApplication;
begin
     FirstApplication := True;
end;

end.
```

Window Messages

The `BasicApplication` object (derived from `TApplication`) does many things for you:

- Sets up the interface to Windows (`BasicApplication.Init`)
- Handles the GetMessage-Dispatch Message loop in the (`BasicApplication.Run`)
- Cleans up (`BasicApplication.Done`)

During `Run`'s message loop, messages sent to your application by Windows (called "Windows messages") are processed automatically. Then the `MessageLoop` method sends a message to its sister method, `ProcessAppMsg`, which in turn sends messages to three "translation methods" that get "first crack" at processing Windows messages:

1. `ProcessDlg` handles dialogs without models.
2. `ProcessAccels` handles accelerators.
3. `ProcessMDIAccels` handles accelerators for MDI applications.

This message translation is also happening behind the scenes; and unless you need to optimize, for example, you can ignore this message translation.

There are well over 100 Windows messages, and they all begin with the prefix wm_. They handle everything from keyboard- and mouse-event processing to undoing operations in edit controls, to notifying a window that its size has changed or that a menu item has been selected. Here are a few examples:

* wm_LButtonDown
* wm_RButtonDown
* wm_LButtonUp
* wm_RButtonUp
* wm_MouseMove
* wm_ShowWindow
* wm_Size
* wm_SysCommand

Your application's main window object is responsible for responding to these Windows messages, and it's handled for you automatically by default in a method that MainWindow inherited from TWindow: DefWndProc, which supplies default actions for each Windows message.

In most cases, your application is delighted that DefWndProc is doing the work. It doesn't want to be bothered resizing and showing windows, for example. You don't want to be bothered writing all that code. You're concentrating on the details of your specific application, not on the interface.

Sometimes, though, you want to intercept a Windows message to specify a behavior. For example, say that you want to add your own mouse interface to your application. To respond to user events (such as the mouse and the keyboard), your application intercepts specific Windows messages.

To intercept a Windows message, simply override (redefine) the TWindow methods, which MainWindow inherited, for the message you want your application to respond to—like this:

```
procedure WMLButtonDown(var Msg: TMessage);
        virtual wm_First + wm_LButtonDown;
```

You then implement the method, detailing its behavior:

```
procedure WMLButtonDown(var Msg: TMessage);
begin
    { detail response here }
end;
```

Each time your application's main window receives a wm_LButtonDown message, it responds with whatever behavior is specified in the overridden method. The message won't reach the default behavior for the wm_LButtonDown message specified by DefWndProc.

What about other messages, such as a wm_RButtonDown? Your application window hasn't specifically defined a new response method for them. No problem. You override only the messages you want. You can override one or 50 messages; any message you don't define is passed to DefWindowProc automatically. It's a great system: you inherit all the behavior of an object (TWindow), and override only the behaviors you want to override.

Because mouse events often generate messages your applications want to respond to, you should put them in the BasicInterface. For now, you only implement abstract methods for them that you will implement (override) later.

> **Another Advantage of OOP**
>
> You can define methods for objects and compile them to test the BasicInterface without implementing any of the methods. This "prototype style" is particularly handy for large programming projects.

You can add message-response methods for mouse clicks to the BasicInterface MainWindow object. Listing 4.4 shows the new version of the BasicInterface (WIF3.PAS).

***Listing 4.4.** Version 3 of BasicInterface.*

```
unit WIF3;          { Contains Basic Windows application
                      interface derived from ObjectWindows }
interface

uses
  WObjects,         { ObjectWindows library of objects }
  WinTypes,         { Windows types:   for accessing the API }
  WinProcs;         { Windows processes: for accessing the API }

type

  BasicApplication = object(TApplication)
                    { Derive an application object }
    FirstApplication : boolean;
    procedure InitMainWindow; virtual;    { Init a main window }
    procedure InitApplication; virtual;
  end;

  PMainWindow = ^MainWindow;
  MainWindow = object(TWindow)
```

```
  procedure WMLButtonDown(var Msg: TMessage); virtual
          wm_first + wm_LButtonDown;
  procedure WMLButtonUp(var Msg: TMessage); virtual
          wm_first + wm_LButtonUp;
  procedure WMRButtonDown(var Msg: TMessage); virtual
          wm_first + wm_RButtonDown;
  procedure WMRButtonUp(var Msg: TMessage); virtual
          wm_first + wm_RButtonUp;
  procedure WMMouseMove(var Msg: TMessage); virtual
          wm_first + wm_MouseMove;
  end;

implementation

{ BasicApplication method implementation }

procedure BasicApplication.InitMainWindow;
begin
  if FirstApplication then      { If instance flag is set }
  MainWindow := New(PMainWindow, Init(nil, 'Basic Windows Interface'))
  else MainWindow := New(PMainWindow, Init(nil,'Additional Instance of BI'));
end;

procedure BasicApplication.InitApplication;
begin
     FirstApplication := True; { Set instance flag }
end;

{ Abstract implementation of basic MainWindow Mouse events }

procedure MainWindow.WMLButtonDown(var Msg: TMessage);
begin end;

procedure MainWindow.WMLButtonUp(var Msg: TMessage);
begin end;

procedure MainWindow.WMRButtonDown(var Msg: TMessage);
begin end;

procedure MainWindow.WMRButtonUp(var Msg: TMessage);
begin end;

procedure MainWindow.WMMouseMove(var Msg: TMessage);
begin end;

end.
```

Before abandoning Windows messages temporarily, note that you can define response methods for any Windows message, not just mouse events as I've done here. You probably won't want to do so, however; most of the messages your application handles directly through ObjectWindows.

Display Contexts

Before you add anything else to your `BasicInterface` (dialogs and menus are discussed later in this chapter and in Chapter 5, "Putting Pictures in Windows"), I want to digress a bit and briefly discuss several aspects of Windows programming that text-based Pascal programming hasn't likely prepared you for. The first of these you need to know about is a display context. To draw text or graphics in a window, you use a display context.

A display context is an element (recall the element-object dichotomy) that represents the surface of a window. It's a data structure maintained by the Windows Graphics Device Interface (GDI). Windows associates each display context with a specific display device: the screen, a printer, and so on.

The attributes of a display context determine text color, background color, font, coordinate mapping, and so on. Whether your application is writing text or drawing pictures, it first needs to obtain a handle to a device context. This handle is simply a number that identifies the Windows display context, and is defined in the Windows type, `HDC`, in `WinTypes`.

Windows actually manages all display contexts for applications, but each application must use a Windows display context to display text or pictures (other than in a resource, that is). Because device contexts are memory-intensive, they need to be released as soon your application finishes with them. Windows allows only five display contexts to be active in any single Windows session.

It's a simple matter for your application to use a display context. The following code shows the process:

```
var
  DisplayContext : HDC;
begin
  DisplayContext := GetDC(HWindow);
      { write or draw something }
  ReleaseDC(HWindow);
end;
```

`GetDc` is a Windows API function that actually gets the display context for the interface element designated by the ObjectWindows handle (`HWindow`).

Note also that your applications can't use the standard Turbo Pascal `Read`, `Readln`, `Write`, and `Writeln` procedures to display text. They must use the Windows function `TextPut` to write to a display context:

```
TextOut(DisplayContext,X,Y,S,StrLen(S));
```

where X and Y are the screen coordinates and S is a null-terminated string (required by Windows). I will talk about null-terminated strings in this chapter, in the section called "Pascal and C Strings," and show you how to use display contexts in many examples in later chapters.

Using Resources

Another name for the graphical elements that comprise your Windows application is *resources*. These resources (cursor shape, menus, icons, and so on) are similar in all your applications, so it makes sense to store them in files outside your source code and link them with your source code when you need them. This process eases any modification without affecting your application code. Recall from Chapter 3, "Objects for Windows," that resources are linked in automatically when you use the $R directive. Chapter 8, "Resources and Control Objects," also details the use of resources.

The separation of PAS (Pascal) and RES (Resource) code is a crucial aspect of Windows programming. You write your applications in Pascal (as usual) by deriving applications (using OOP techniques). You build and modify resources with the Whitewater Resource Toolkit (that comes with Turbo Pascal for Windows). Figure 4.6 illustrates this concept.

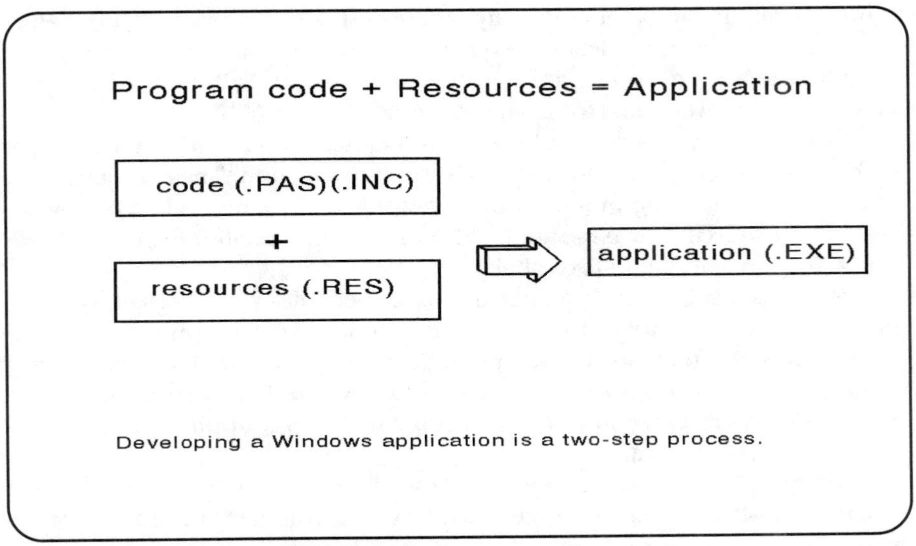

Figure 4.6. Developing a Windows application.

By separating code and resources, you transfer management responsibility for resources from the source code to Windows. Your source code wants to focus on its specifics, not on Windows, so this is neat packaging.

Resources are data characterized by the following types:

- Accelerators
- Bit maps
- Cursors
- Icons
- Dialog boxes
- Menus
- Strings

An accelerator is a key (or combination of keys) that you can use as a shortcut for making menu selections. For example, you can define an accelerator (Shift-Delete, for example) to replace a menu selection (Edit-Cut, for example).

A bit map is a picture, or more specifically, the data representing a picture. It is made up of pixels (dots).

A cursor is the object on-screen that represents the position for the next input. In text-based applications, a cursor is either a block, a line, or something in between. In Windows applications, a cursor is a 32-by-32-pixel bit map. A Windows cursor can be one of many different shapes, and is itself a bit map.

An icon is the graphical screen element that represents your application program's state. You select an icon from the Windows Program Manager's window to run programs, for example. An icon, too, is a bit map.

A dialog box, which is a bit more complicated, is an input screen (or window) for insertion of information in your application. The dialog box can be baritones or contain other Windows graphical elements (called *controls*).

The resource data associated with a dialog box specifies the dialog box's size, screen location, and text labels.

A menu displays application options and enables you to select one. The menu's resource identifies the order and number of these options.

Strings are text displayed by application menus, dialog boxes, error messages, and so on. Strings don't have to be specified as resources, but maintaining them as resources helps keep your specific application code and its visual aspects separate.

Chapter 8, "Resources and Control Objects," details the use of the Resource Toolkit and the Resource Workshop. Until then, the `BasicInterface` loads existing resources that I've already designed and compiled in a `BasicInterface` resource file (`WIF.RES`). It supplies the resources you need for many applications, and saves your having to learn every aspect of Windows programming at once. It's also another example of not reinventing when you don't have to, a sub-theme of *The Tao of Objects*.

Until Chapter 8, "Resources and Control Objects," all the resources you need to use with the `BasicInterface` can be linked into your program using the `$R` compiler directive:

```
$R WIF.RES
```

If you feel you have to know everything at once, skip over to Chapter 8 for resource design details. The complete `WIF.RES` file (created with the Whitewater Resource Toolkit) is on the disk in the back of this book. You don't have to use `WIF.RES` to use the `BasicInterface`, however. Until you get to Chapter 8, just use the `COOKBOOK.RES` resource file packaged with Turbo Pascal for Windows. It does just fine. To include the `COOKBOOK.RES`, use the $R directive:

```
$R Cookbook.res
```

Pascal and C Strings

The Windows API requires that strings be null-terminated, the format used by C. In other words, a string is represented as a sequence of characters terminated by a `NULL (#0)`. Turbo Pascal for Windows stores null-terminated strings as arrays of characters:

```
type
 NTstring = array[0..79] of Char;
```

A null-terminated string in Turbo Pascal for Windows can be as long as 65,535 characters (a limitation imposed by DOS and Windows).

Turbo Pascal stores its standard strings in the "string" type; a length byte followed by a sequence of as many as 255 characters.

```
type
 TPstring = string[80];
```

Because Windows doesn't recognize Turbo Pascal strings, your application must either use null-terminated strings exclusively or convert any Pascal strings to null-terminated before passing them to Windows (to display, for example).

The `strings` unit supplied by Turbo Pascal for Windows provides the conversion functions and a complete manipulation package for handling null-terminated strings.

Some of the functions in the `strings` unit are

- `StrPas`: Converts a null-terminated string to a Turbo Pascal string
- `StrPCopy`: Copies a Turbo Pascal string into a null-terminated string
- `StrPos`: Returns a pointer to the first occurrence of a substring in a null-terminated string (similar to `Pos` for Turbo Pascal strings)
- `StrLower`: Converts a null-terminated string to lowercase

Twenty or so of these functions are in the `strings` unit you need to use if you display strings in Windows. Add this unit to the `BasicInterface`:

```
uses strings
```

A Few Rules

Before you get on with the `BasicInterface`, let's sum up a few "rules" you need to keep in mind when you develop Windows applications.

Your application creates interface objects (using ObjectWindows), but allows Windows to handle the interface elements they represent.

Your application allows Windows to handle memory management (discussed in Chapter 9, "Memory Matters").

Your application must define message-response methods in order to intercept Windows messages (to process mouse events, for example).

Your applications must send a message to Windows GDI functions to draw graphics in a window or print.

Your application uses resources compiled outside your Turbo Pascal source code to implement menus, dialogs, and so on.

Adding Dialogs

Most of your applications use the important resource, a dialog. Dialogs can be modal or modeless.

When Windows displays a modal dialog application, execution in other windows is suspended until the user responds to the dialog. In other words, the user cannot select or use the parent window (the `MainWindow` in the `BasicInterface`) until she clicks on the OK or Cancel option, which destroys the dialog. For DOS users, this situation is similar to using a PAUSE; nothing happens until another key is pressed.

Displaying a dialog that is modeless, on the other hand, doesn't suspend application operation, and thus can be used repeatedly during the life of the application. In other words, the user doesn't have to click a button in the dialog to continue processing in other windows.

For now, add a modal dialog to the `BasicInterface`, because that's the one needed most often. Adding a dialog to an application is basically a two-step process, and a simple one, thanks to ObjectWindows. In short, link a dialog resource to the Pascal application code that requests the dialog through the application's `ExecDialog` method.

Windows actually creates the dialog box (a window) for the application. Your source code just defines its behavior and uses the standard dialog resources packaged with Turbo Pascal for Windows. Thus, most of the work has already been done for you. To use a standard input dialog:

1. Include the STDDLGS unit:

   ```
   uses StdDlgs
   ```

2. Construct and execute the dialog in one step that basically looks like this:

   ```
   var
        Application1 : BasicInterface;

   if Application1^.ExecDialog(New(PInputDialog,
     Init(@Self, '.... then
   { handle dialog results }
   ```

`ExecDialog` creates the dialog's (the interface object's) corresponding element by sending a message to the dialog object's `Execute` method. It checks first, though, to ensure that there's enough memory to create the dialog.

Listing 4.5 (WIF4.PAS) shows the new version of the `BasicInterface` with modal dialog capability. Figure 4.7 shows a screen produced by the code in listing 4.5.

Listing 4.5. *`BasicInterface` with modal dialog capability.*

```
unit WIF4;          { Contains Basic Windows application
                      interface derived from ObjectWindows }
interface

uses
  WObjects,         { ObjectWindows library of objects }
  WinTypes,         { Windows types:   for accessing the API }
  WinProcs,         { Windows processes: for accessing the API }
  Strings,          { Null-terminated strings unit }
  StdDlgs;          { Standard dialogs unit }

type

  BasicApplication = object(TApplication)
```

continues

Listing 4.5. continued

```
                 { Derive an application object }
    FirstApplication : boolean;
    procedure InitMainWindow; virtual;   { Init a main window }
    procedure InitApplication; virtual;
  end;

  PMainWindow = ^MainWindow;
  MainWindow = object(TWindow)
  DisplayContext1 : HDC;       { Handle to a display context }
  ButtonDown : boolean;
  constructor Init(AParent : PWindowsObject; ATitle: PChar);
  procedure WMLButtonDown(var Msg: TMessage); virtual
            wm_first + wm_LButtonDown;
  procedure WMLButtonUp(var Msg: TMessage); virtual
            wm_first + wm_LButtonUp;
  procedure WMRButtonDown(var Msg: TMessage); virtual
            wm_first + wm_RButtonDown;
  procedure WMRButtonUp(var Msg: TMessage); virtual
            wm_first + wm_RButtonUp;
  procedure WMMouseMove(var Msg: TMessage); virtual
            wm_first + wm_MouseMove;
  end;

implementation

{ BasicApplication method implementation }

procedure BasicApplication.InitMainWindow;
begin
  if FirstApplication then
  MainWindow := New(PMainWindow, Init(nil, 'Basic Windows Interface'))
  else MainWindow := New(PMainWindow, Init(nil,'Additional Instance of BI'
end;

procedure BasicApplication.InitApplication;
begin
     FirstApplication := True;
end;

{ New MainWindow constructor }

constructor MainWindow.Init(AParent : PWindowsObject; ATitle : PChar);
begin
```

```
     TWindow.Init(AParent, ATitle);
                  {Send message to ancestor's constructor}
     ButtonDown := False;
end;

{ Abstract implementation of basic MainWindow Mouse events }

procedure MainWindow.WMLButtonDown(var Msg: TMessage);
begin end;

procedure MainWindow.WMLButtonUp(var Msg: TMessage);
begin end;

procedure MainWindow.WMRButtonDown(var Msg: TMessage);
                  { popup dialog if Right Button down }
var
   InputText : array[0..15] of char;
begin
     if not ButtonDown then
     begin
          if Application^.ExecDialog(New(PInputDialog,
          Init(@Self,'Message1','Message2',
          InputText, SizeOf(InputText)))) = id_Ok then
          begin
            { Deal with message here }
          end;
     end;
end;

procedure MainWindow.WMRButtonUp(var Msg: TMessage);
begin end;

procedure MainWindow.WMMouseMove(var Msg: TMessage);
begin end;

end.
```

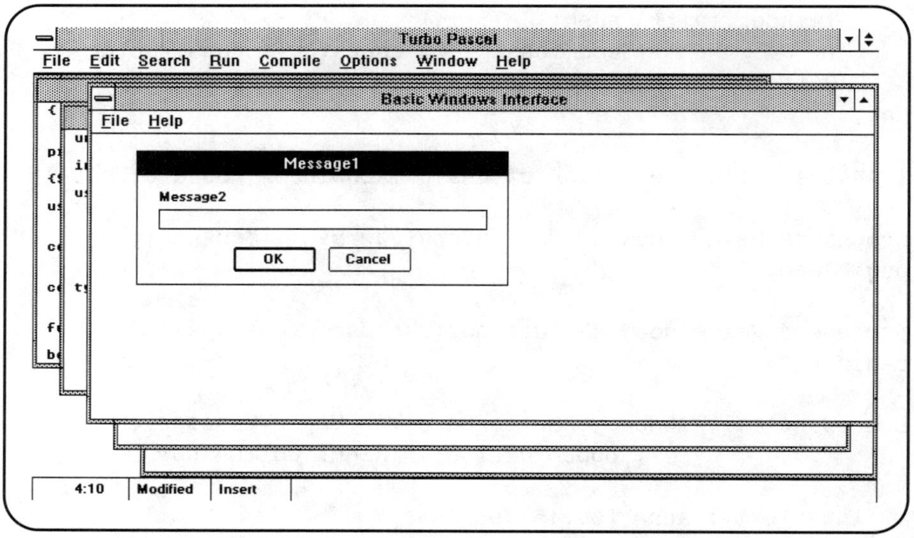

Figure 4.7. A basic Windows interface screen.

Adding a File Dialog

A second type of dialog you use in any of your applications that work with files is the file dialog. As you're no doubt expecting, putting a file dialog in your application is no trouble at all. You just use the one that ObjectWindows provides; it is already complete for many purposes.

To add a file dialog to the `BasicInterface`:

1. Use the `stdlgs` unit (which is already being used in the `BasicInterface`):

   ```
   uses Stdlgs
   ```

2. Include its corresponding resource file (the `BasicInterface` is already using a resource file that handles file dialogs—WIF.RES):

   ```
   $R WIF.RES
   ```

3. Initialize the file dialog and send a message to it in one step (much the way you initialized a modal dialog earlier):

   ```
   if Application1^.ExecDialog(New(PFileDialog,
   Init(@Self,PChar(sd_FileOpen),AFile))) = id_OK then
     begin
       OpenFile(AFile);
     end;
   ```

Figure 4.8 shows a File Open dialog.

The File Open dialog uses a list box to display the files on the current directory. The user can either type the file to open it, or double-click the particular file. The file is then opened with `OpenFile`.

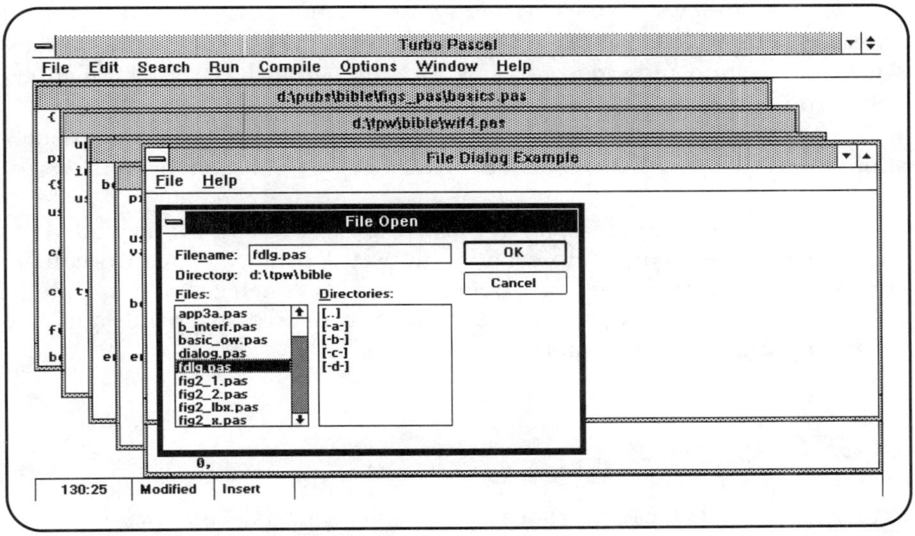

Figure 4.8. *A file dialog example.*

`PFileDialog` is a pointer to the stock dialog defined in ObjectWindows.

Two Kinds of File Dialogs

File dialogs come in two stock forms:

1. One for opening files
2. One for saving files

Specify the one you want in the `name` parameter of the constructor `call`. For an open file:

```
sd_FileOpen
```

For a save file:

```
sd_FileSave
```

Constants

Another aspect of ObjectWindows programming that many programmers working in DOS-based environments often ignore is the use of constants.

ObjectWindows defines numerous constants to represent command messages: button, check box, and radio-button states; errors; child ID messages; notification messages; streams messages; transfer flags; bit-mapped fields; and Windows messages.

The use of constants improves program readability and makes it easier for a program to change in response to changes in subsequent versions of Windows.

The complete `BasicInterface` in listing 4.7 (`WIF.PAS`) at the end of the chapter defines many of the most commonly used constants. You can, of course, comment out the ones that your application doesn't need and add the ones it does. The constant section in the `BasicInterface` serves as a handy template for adding your own constants.

Controls

At this point, the `BasicInterface` uses a simple (almost default) main window (precisely, a main window plus a menu). The main window can be much more complicated, however, by other window objects and controls. For example, you can vary the style, colors, and so on, of the main window and attach various child windows to it. Future examples show you how to add and vary these window objects, which aren't necessary for the `BasicInterface`. For now, however, you should be aware of what controls are and how they're used.

Controls are user interface devices. Table 4.1 shows the controls that ObjectWindows supports.

Table 4.1. Windows controls supported by ObjectWindows.

Control	*Object Type*
Check box	TCheckBox
Combo box	TComboBox
Edit control	TEdit
Group box	TGroupBox
List box	TListBox
MDI client	TMDIClient
Push button	TButton
Radio button	TRadioButton
Scroll bar	TScrollBar
Static control	TStatic

Figure 4.9 shows what a few of these controls look like.

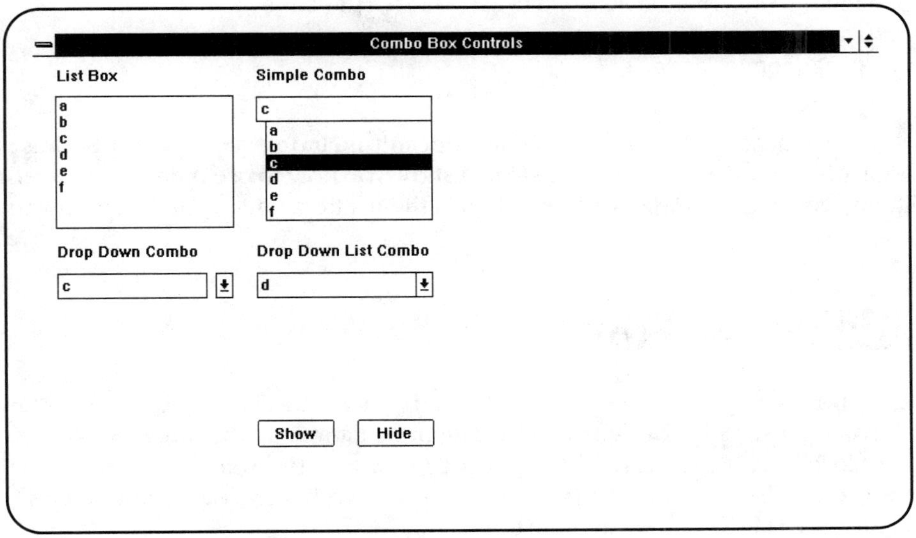

Figure 4.9. Combo box controls.

Creating a control is another two-step process:

1. Construct the control object.
2. Construct its corresponding control element.

Usually, you take both of these steps in the constructor of the parent window. For example, the following fragment constructs a push button:

```
PB1 := New(PButton, Init(@Self, id_PB1,
  'A Button', 30,50,300,19,False);
```

Controls can send messages in response to user events (a user clicking a button, for example). By default, ObjectWindows responds to these messages, if your application doesn't. Usually you want your application to handle the message itself, however. The following fragment shows how your application defines a response method to a button-clicked message:

```
AMainWindow = object(MainWindow)
   PB1 : PButton;
   procedure IDPB1(var Msg: TMessage); virtual id_First +
id_PB1;
   { other methods here }
end;
```

The following fragment implements the IDPB1 method:

```
procedure AMainWindow.IDPB1(var Msg: TMessage);
begin
   { response here }
end;
```

The BasicInterface, as I said, doesn't include every control because controls are fairly specialized. Instead, I show you how to use them as you need them, as you go along. One I use often is the list box, which you learn how to use next.

Adding List Boxes

A list box is a kind of window (it's defined by a rectangle on the screen) that shows the user a list of information. The information can be integers, strings, and so on. The user can click on a list item, and the selected item can be transferred into another variable or can trigger other messages and actions. Figure 4.10 shows an example list box.

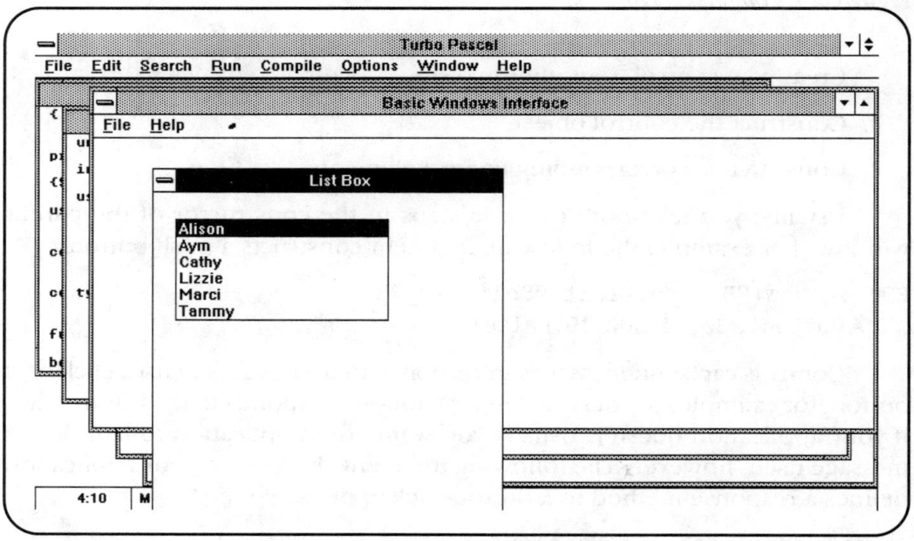

Figure 4.10. A list box example.

Listing 4.6 shows the code required to create the list box displayed in figure 4.10.

Listing 4.6. Code to create a list box.

```
unit LBWind;

interface

uses Strings, WObjects, WinTypes, WinProcs;

const
  id_LB1 = 201;
  id_BN2 = 203;

type

  PListBoxWindow = ^ListBoxWindow;
  ListBoxWindow = object(TWindow)
    LB1: PListBox;
    constructor Init(AParent: PWindowsObject; ATitle: PChar);
    procedure SetupWindow; virtual; { override TWindow's SetUpWindow }
    procedure IDLB1(var Msg: TMessage); virtual id_First + id_LB1;
    procedure IDBN2(var Msg: TMessage); virtual id_First + id_BN2;
  end;

implementation

constructor ListBoxWindow.Init(AParent: PWindowsObject; ATitle: PChar);
begin
  TWindow.Init(AParent, ATitle);
  DisableAutoCreate;
  Attr.Style := ws_PopupWindow or ws_Caption or ws_Visible;
  Attr.X := 100;
  Attr.Y := 100;
  Attr.W := 200;
  Attr.H := 200;
  LB1 := New(PListBox, Init(@Self, id_LB1, 20, 20, 180, 80));
end;

procedure ListBoxWindow.SetupWindow;
begin
  TWindow.SetupWindow;
  { Fill the list box with strings }
  LB1^.AddString('Alison');
  LB1^.AddString('Marci');
  LB1^.AddString('Lizzie');
  LB1^.AddString('Amy');
```

continues

Listing 4.6. continued

```
  LB1^.AddString('Tammy');
  LB1^.AddString('Susan');
  LB1^.SetSelIndex(0);
end;

{ A generic example of doing something with the list box }
procedure ListBoxWindow.IDLB1(var Msg: TMessage);
var
  SelString: array[0..25] of Char;
begin
  if Msg.LParamHi = lbn_DblClk then
  begin
    LB1^.GetSelString(SelString, 25);
  end;
end;

procedure ListBoxWindow.IDBN2(var Msg: TMessage);
begin
  CloseWindow;     { Clean up }
end;

end.
```

`Listbox` is a window object you construct at specific coordinates, with a specific style, after sending a message to the base window object type, `TWindow`, to handle default construction:

```
constructor ListBoxWindow.Init(AParent: PWindowsObject;
ATitle: PChar);
begin

  TWindow.Init(AParent, ATitle);
  DisableAutoCreate;  { So that you can create your own style }
  Attr.Style := ws_PopupWindow or ws_Caption or ws_Visible;
  Attr.X := 100;   Attr.Y := 100;
  Attr.W := 200;   Attr.H := 200;
  LB1 := New(PListBox, Init(@Self, id_LB1, 20, 20, 180, 80));
end;
```

You then set up the list box by adding strings:

```
procedure ListBoxWindow.SetupWindow;
begin
  TWindow.SetupWindow;
  { Fill the list box }
```

```
  LB1^.AddString('Alison');
  LB1^.AddString('Marci');
  ....
end;
```

The example in listing 4.6 loads the strings you want to add to the ListBox from the source code, but a more general approach adds the strings in response to ongoing changes—for example, user input, based on a change in the application itself, or a file fc r examples.

In Chapter 6, "Painting, Collecting, and Streaming," when streams are discussed, the ListBox is used in a more interesting manner.

The ListBoxWindow.IDLB1 method handles mouse double clicks, but at this point, it doesn't do anything useful. It's just a generic example of how you might use it. In Chapter 7, "Many Windows: A Multi-Document Interface," you add a help window to the basic MDI interface that uses the list box window to provide help information.

The ListBoxWindow.IDBN2 method destroys the list box when the user clicks the Close box in the upper-left corner of the list box window:

```
procedure ListBoxWindow.IDBN2(var Msg: TMessage);
begin
  CloseWindow;      { clean up }
end;
```

Message Boxes

Although ObjectWindows does an amazing amount of work for you, sometimes you want to bypass ObjectWindows and send messages to the API directly. You do this by using the WinTypes and WinProcs units in your source code:

```
uses WinTypes, WinProcs
```

The BasicInterface already uses these units, but you still need to include them in any new unit that needs to access them directly.

A particularly helpful example of sending messages to the API is to put a message box on the screen. Figure 4.11 shows a message box that the following fragment (added to the BasicInterface) created:

```
var MessageResponse : integer;
begin
    MessageResponse := MessageBox(HWindow...
end;
```

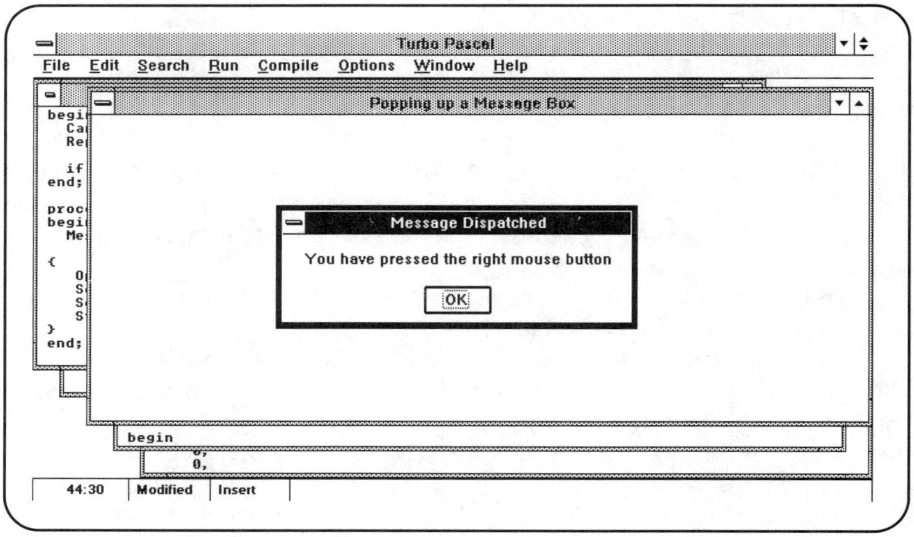

Figure 4.11. Popping up a message box.

Closing an Application

Typically, Windows applications terminate when the user double clicks the control-menu box in the upper-left corner of its main window. When this happens to an application derived from the BasicInterface, a number of messages are sent and received by the BasicApplication and MainWindow before BasicApplication is destroyed by destructor, Done.

For the most part, you can ignore the complex processing that goes on behind the scenes. ObjectWindows does the work again. One addition to the BasicInterface is helpful for double-checking whether the user of your application actually intended to quit. To double-check, reimplement (override) the MainWindow's CanClose method (that it inherited from TWindow). The following code does the trick:

```
function MainWindow.CanClose: Boolean;
var UserResponse;
begin
     CanClose := True;
     UserResponse := MessageBox(HWindow, Message1,Message2,
                     mb_YesNo or mb_IconQuestion);
     if UserResponse = idYes then CanClose := false;
end;
```

Wrapping Up the BasicInterface

That does it for the basics of Windows application programming, Turbo Pascal for Windows style. There's much more to it than can be covered in these two chapters, but the rest is gravy. From here on I talk about varying the interface to handle the multi-document interface (MDI), how to use other objects in the ObjectWindows library, and how to create many different kinds of applications using the `BasicInterface`.

The complete `BasicInterface` consists of

- A basic application
- A main window
- A generic mouse interface
- A menu and other basic resources
- Methods for adding dialogs
- An awareness of device contexts
- A few time-savers such as constant definitions, windows message definitions, inclusion of key units, and so on.

Figure 4.12 shows the complete interface on-screen.

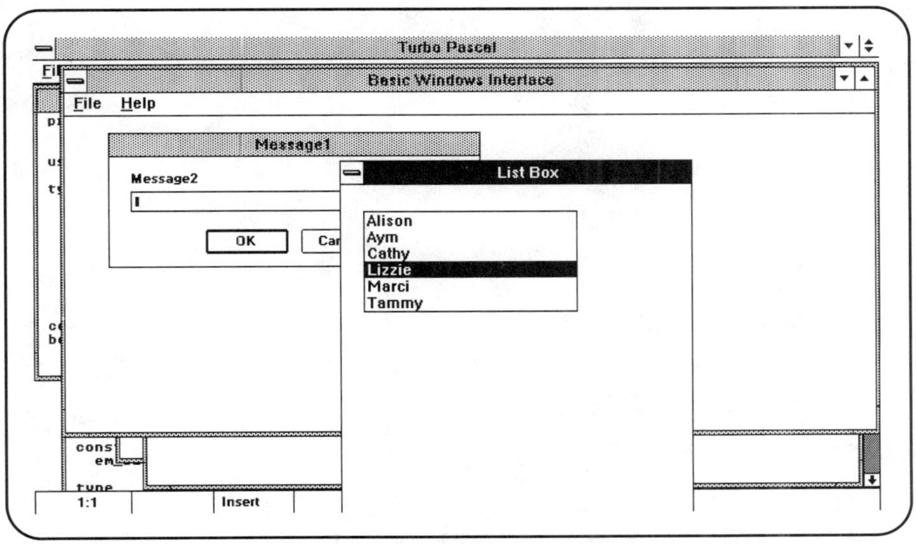

Figure 4.12. The complete interface.

Listing 4.7 (WIF5.PAS) shows the `BasicInterface` on-screen.

Many applications (as I'll show you) can begin with the `BasicInterface`, and with little or no modification, run in Windows. By using a `BasicInterface` derived from ObjectWindows, you can ignore most of the hassles programmers traditionally associate with Windows development. Windows is a powerful environment, and if you use Turbo Pascal for Windows, you don't have to spend months and months coming up to speed in order to write many applications.

Both user and programmer can have a powerful environment to work in without either of them going crazy. Let's hear it for Windows, object-oriented programming, and the language that brings them together: Turbo Pascal for Windows. Who would have thought that programming Windows could be this easy?

Listing 4.7. *Code for the* `BasicInterface` *on-screen.*

```
unit WIF5;          { Contains Basic Windows application
                      interface derived from ObjectWindows }
interface

uses
  WObjects,         { ObjectWindows library of objects }
  WinTypes,         { Windows types:    for accessing the API }
  WinProcs,         { Windows processes: for accessing the API }
  Strings,          { Null-terminated strings unit }
  StdDlgs,          { Standard dialogs unit }
  lbwind;           { List box }

{$R WIF.RES }

const

    cm_New    = 101;
    cm_Open   = 102;
    cm_Save   = 103;
    cm_SaveAs = 104;
    cm_Help   = 901;

    id_LB1    = 201;

type

  BasicApplication = object(TApplication)
                      { Derive an application object }
    FirstApplication : boolean;
    procedure InitMainWindow; virtual;   { Init a main window }
```

```
    procedure InitApplication; virtual;
  end;

  PMainWindow = ^MainWindow;
  MainWindow = object(TWindow)
  DisplayContext1 : HDC;                     { Display Context handle }
  ButtonDown : boolean;                      { Button-down status flag }
  constructor Init(AParent : PWindowsObject; ATitle: PChar);
  procedure WMLButtonDown(var Msg: TMessage); virtual
            wm_first + wm_LButtonDown;
  procedure WMLButtonUp(var Msg: TMessage); virtual
            wm_first + wm_LButtonUp;
  procedure WMRButtonDown(var Msg: TMessage); virtual
            wm_first + wm_RButtonDown;
  procedure WMRButtonUp(var Msg: TMessage); virtual
            wm_first + wm_RButtonUp;
  procedure WMMouseMove(var Msg: TMessage); virtual
            wm_first + wm_MouseMove;
  procedure ListBox(var Msg: TMessage); virtual
            cm_First + cm_Help;
  function  CanClose: Boolean;
end;

implementation

{ BasicApplication method implementation }

procedure BasicApplication.InitMainWindow;
begin
  if FirstApplication then
  MainWindow := New(PMainWindow, Init(nil, 'Basic Windows Interface'))
  else MainWindow := New(PMainWindow, Init(nil,'Additional Instance of BI'));
end;

procedure BasicApplication.InitApplication;
begin
     FirstApplication := True;
end;

{ New MainWindow constructor }

constructor MainWindow.Init(AParent : PWindowsObject; ATitle : PChar);
begin
```

continues

Listing 4.7. continued

```
     TWindow.Init(AParent, ATitle); { Send msg to ancestor's
                                      constructor }
     Attr.Menu  := LoadMenu(HInstance, PChar(100)); { 100 = menu ID }
     ButtonDown := False;             { Set status flag }
end;

{ Abstract implementation of basic MainWindow Mouse events }

procedure MainWindow.WMLButtonDown(var Msg: TMessage);
begin end;

procedure MainWindow.WMLButtonUp(var Msg: TMessage);
begin end;

procedure MainWindow.WMRButtonDown(var Msg: TMessage);
          { popup dialog if Right Button down }
var
   InputText : array[0..15] of char;  { Vary this for input length }
begin
     if not ButtonDown then
     begin
          if Application^.ExecDialog(New(PInputDialog,
          Init(@Self,'Message1','Message2',
          InputText, SizeOf(InputText)))) = id_Ok then
          begin
          { Deal with message here }
          end;
     end;
end;

procedure MainWindow.WMRButtonUp(var Msg: TMessage);
begin end;

procedure MainWindow.WMMouseMove(var Msg: TMessage);
begin end;

procedure MainWindow.ListBox(var Msg: TMessage);
var
  ListBoxWnd: PWindow;
begin
```

```
  ListBoxWnd := New(PListBoxWindow, Init(@Self, 'List Box'));
  Application^.MakeWindow(ListBoxWnd);
end;

function MainWindow.CanClose: Boolean;
var UserResponse;
begin
     CanClose := True;
     UserResponse := MessageBox(HWindow, Message1,Message2,
                     mb_YesNo or mb_IconQuestion);
     if UserResponse = idYes then CanClose := false;
end;

end.
```

5

CHAPTER

PUTTING PICTURES IN WINDOWS

You can no longer think in terms of 25 lines and 80 columns of text.
Charles Petzold

It's worth repeating: Windows is a complex environment, but not a difficult one in which to develop applications if you use Turbo Pascal for Windows and the object-oriented techniques built into ObjectWindows. The `BasicInterface` you developed in Chapter 4, "Inheriting an Interface," encapsulates most of the complex details of Windows programming in two objects: an application and its main window.

A simple way for you to develop new Windows applications is to

1. Derive the new application's interface from the `BasicInterface` (using inheritance).
2. Add the new application's specific behaviors to the derived interface.

Your application can focus on its specific aspects while the `BasicInterface` handles the underlying interface details.

Because Windows is based on an event-driven architecture, it makes sense to think of your applications reacting to events (or even as being events). In other words, an application (an editor, a spreadsheet, or any other task) responds to events it learns about through either Windows (`wm`) or command (`cm`) messages.

An application's response can be a single action (displaying a dialog, a message or list box, and so on), or a series of actions (for example, a task consisting of many functions and procedures). In other words, an application running in a window can behave exactly as it would if it weren't running in a window. Because you allow the `BasicInterface` or ObjectWindows (if you bypass the `BasicInterface` and derive Windows behavior directly) to handle the interface details, your programming chore can be reduced to two steps. These include writing the application (teaching it how to respond to events) and teaching it when to respond to events.

You can teach your application to initiate its behavior by responding to various kinds of events. In Chapter 4, "Inheriting an Interface," for example, you taught the `BasicInterface` to respond in a general way to mouse events. One of the simplest and most useful ways to initiate an application's behavior, however, is to have it respond to a user selecting items from a menu.

In this chapter, I focus on this menu response aspect by deriving from the `BasicInterface` several applications that respond to menu command messages. I begin by showing the basics of this approach, developing applications that simulate general tasks and using display contexts and Windows functions to display graphic images. I finally lead up to a multitasking version of the `BasicInterface`.

I use modeling systems, which are general-purpose, to show you how you can develop your own multitasking system by plugging your applications into this version of the `BasicInterface`.

In each example in this chapter you can associate a menu and its corresponding menu command messages to activate task windows. Menus are an elegant and simple way to allow your users to control a Windows application. In the examples I lead you through, you find the user dynamically creating and destroying task windows at run-time, when your programming effort is long gone.

Menus, IDs, and Messages

Each menu is a resource and also has a resource ID you use to identify the menu. Recall from the `BasicInterface` that you attach a specific menu to a window by

1. Including the menu resource. For example:

   ```
   {$R WIF.RES}
   ```

2. Setting the menu attribute variable for the window you're attaching the menu to:

```
Attr.Menu := LoadMenu(HInstance, PChar(100));
```

Typically, you set the attribute in the window's constructor. For example:

```
constructor ATask.Init(AParent: PWindowsObject; ATitle: PChar);
begin
  TWindow.Init(AParent, ATitle);
  Attr.Style := ws_PopupWindow or ws_Caption or ws_Visible;
  Attr.Menu  := LoadMenu(HInstance, PChar(99));
  (* details here *)
end;
```

When the main window for an application is displayed, it appears with the menu corresponding to `Attr.Menu`'s ID. Optionally, you could use a symbolic identifier to represent the menu, when you set `Attr.Menu`:

```
Attr.Menu := LoadMenu(HInstance, 'Task1 Menu');
```

Whether you use a `PChar` or a symbolic identifier with the `BasicInterface` is up to you. You associate an ID with a menu using the Whitewater Resource Toolkit (see Chapter 8, "Resources and Control Objects," for the details of how to set up a menu and give it a corresponding ID).

You also create the specific selections available in a menu in the resource file and test the menu in the Whitewater Resource Toolkit. However, the responses you want the application to make (in response to menu selections) must be defined in your Turbo Pascal source code. In other words, you specify a resource's attributes (in this case, a menu) in the resource file, but you specify the specific responses an application makes to a menu in the Turbo Pascal source code file. This process opens up the possibility of creating and testing menus before you actually write the application. You can develop the look and feel of your application (prototype it) before you start writing code; a very useful prospect in developing large applications that involve more than one programmer.

When a user selects a menu, the window the menu is attached to receives a Windows command message. Your application then processes the command message by defining a response method for each selection. (*Note:* This is similar to how the `BasicInterface` handles Windows command messages. Also note that Windows command messages are prefixed by `wm_` and menu command messages by `cm_`; they represent entirely different classes of messages.)

A menu command message might look like this, for example:

```
procedure CMNewMethod(var Msg: TMessage); virtual cm_First + 101;
```

where cm_First is a constant (defined by ObjectWindows) designating the beginning of a range of command constants. 101 is the specific Menu ID for this method (CmNewMethod).

For consistency, I use the cm_ prefix to name any method that responds to a command message, so it should be easy to spot these methods within objects.

You can, if you want, use constants to represent these Menu IDs, and substitute the constant for the ID. Again for consistency, I use the same prefix (cm_) to designate any command message constant. For example:

```
const
   cm_New = 101

procedure CMNewMethod(var Msg: TMessage); virtual cm_First + cm_New;
```

The menu I showed you in the BasicInterface (contained in WIF.RES) doesn't do anything. It's there strictly in the abstract to show you what a window with a menu looks like. It is a simple matter to make the menu useful.

To make an application respond to menu selections:

1. Define a constant that corresponds to a menu message ID (in your Turbo Pascal code).
2. Define and implement a method that responds to the menu message (in your Turbo Pascal code).
3. Add the new menu selection option to the menu resource (using the Whitewater Resource Toolkit).

The BasicInterface already handles the application-Windows connection, so you have to concentrate only on how each new application works. Responding to events (menu command messages, mouse, and so forth) is the only Windows-specific aspect you have to worry about at this juncture.

Because each application is associated with its main window, and because I'm leading you up to a mini-multitasking system within Windows (itself a multitasking system), your first response to a menu selection should be the creation of a new window (call it a child window) that contains the application.

In other words, say that your menu option is called "Task1," and the MainWindow's response to the user selecting Task1 is to create a child window that runs the task. Figure 5.1 shows the MainWindow with the Task1 option.

I want to keep the task simple for now. Say, for example, that this task simply outputs some text in its window in response to a menu selection. In barebones notation, the application accomplishes the equivalent of a Write statement without going through the WinCrt unit.

Start with the MainWindow you derived from TWindow in Chapter 4, "Inheriting an Interface," and derive from it a new window object that responds to menu command messages. (Note that you don't have to start with

MainWindow—you can, of course, derive a new window directly from TWindow. MainWindow inherited all TWindow's characteristics and behaviors, and in addition has a characteristic you need: the Display Context. Therefore, you derive the new window from MainWindow.

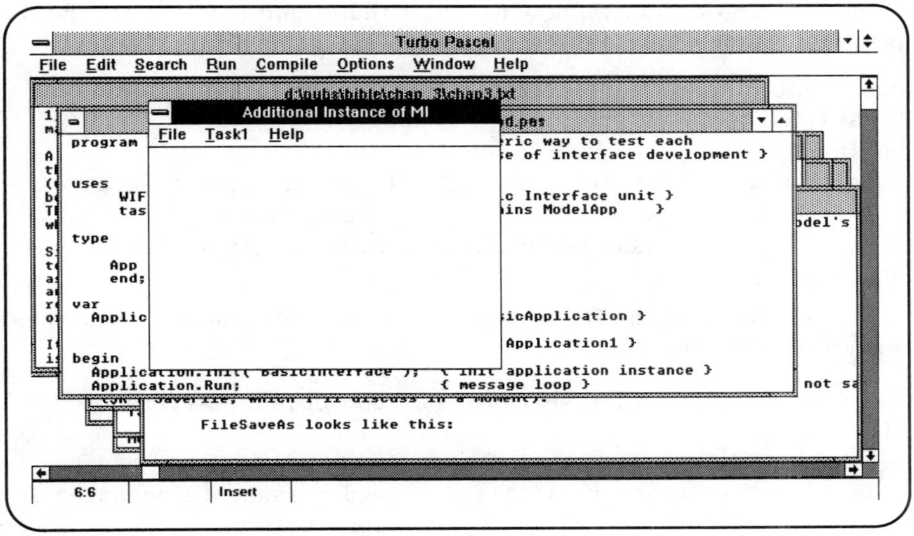

Figure 5.1. MainWindow with the Task1 option.

This new window object, called TaskWindow1, consists of its own constructor and destructor, two data fields to represent screen coordinates, and a method to iterate the task. I call the method by the general name, cm_Iterate, using the cm_ prefix to indicate that it responds to a menu command message. It looks like this:

```
PTask1 = ^Task1;                    { Pointer to this task }
Task1 = object(MainWindow)          { A simple task }
  X, Y : integer;                   { X and Y fields }
  constructor Init(AParent: PWindowsObject; ATitle: PChar);
                                    { New constructor}
  destructor Done; virtual;         { New destructor }
  procedure CMIterate(var Msg: TMessage);
     virtual cm_First + cm_Task1;
end;
```

Notice that I've also defined a pointer to the TaskWindow (object). In general, you always construct a window using the New procedure that requires a pointer to an object, not the object itself.

Because you're implementing a new constructor for TaskWindow, its ancestor's (TWindow) constructor is overridden, and thus not used. However,

TWindow's constructor initiates some behavior you don't want to reimplement. You can send a message to it explicitly within TaskWindow's constructor and have it handle all that initialization for you. Then you can implement the specific behavior you want to add to TaskWindow.

The constructor first sends a message to its ancestor's constructor, implementing a default window for TaskWindow, and then loads a specific menu for TaskWindow by setting the menu attribute field:

```
constructor Task1.Init(AParent: PWindowsObject; ATitle:
PChar);
begin
  TWindow.Init(AParent, ATitle);   { Send a message to ancestor's
                                     constructor }
  Attr.Menu   := LoadMenu(HInstance, PChar(99)); { 99 = menu ID }
end;
```

Alternatively, the Task1 constructor can implement a specific kind and size of window:

```
constructor Task1.Init(AParent: PWindowsObject; ATitle:
PChar);
begin
  TWindow.Init(AParent, ATitle); { Send message to ancestor's
                                   constructor }
  DisableAutoCreate;       { Abort default window creation }
                           { Create a specific window }
  Attr.Style := ws_PopupWindow or ws_Caption or ws_Visible;
  Attr.Menu   := LoadMenu(HInstance, PChar(99)); { 99 = menu ID}
  Attr.X := 100;           { Set window dimensions }
  Attr.Y := 50;
  Attr.W := 300;
  Attr.H := 200;
end;
```

Now implement the task iterate method, which has several responsibilities:

1. It makes sure that any cursor input is sent to the correct window (TaskWindow) regardless of where the mouse is located.
2. It gets a display context for TaskWindow.
3. It decides where to write the text within the window.
4. It writes the text.
5. It releases the captured window and display context:

```
procedure Task1.CMIterate(var Msg: TMessage);
var
   S : array[0.14] of Char;
```

```
begin
   X := Attr.X + 50;
   Y := Attr.Y + 50;
   EndX := X + 50;
   EndY := Y + 50;
   SetCapture(HWindow);             { Certify the window }
   DC := GetDC(HWindow);            { Get a display context }
   TextOut(DC,X,Y,S,SizeOf(S));     { Write something }
   ReleaseCapture;
   ReleaseDC(HWindow,DC);           { Release display context }
end;
```

The display context is the surface of the window you have to specify in order to display text or graphics in a window.

Note also that `S` is a C-style (null-terminated) string, not a Turbo Pascal string. Windows functions always require C-style strings, so if your applications use Turbo Pascal strings, you always need to convert them before you use them with Windows functions. The Turbo Pascal for Windows strings unit contains a rich set of C-style string-conversion and -manipulation functions. Part III, "Reference," details the functions.

Figure 5.2 shows the default `BasicInterface` window created by `TWindow.Init`. Figure 5.3 shows the specific window created by `TaskWindow.Init`. Notice that the title and menu bars are different in the two figures.

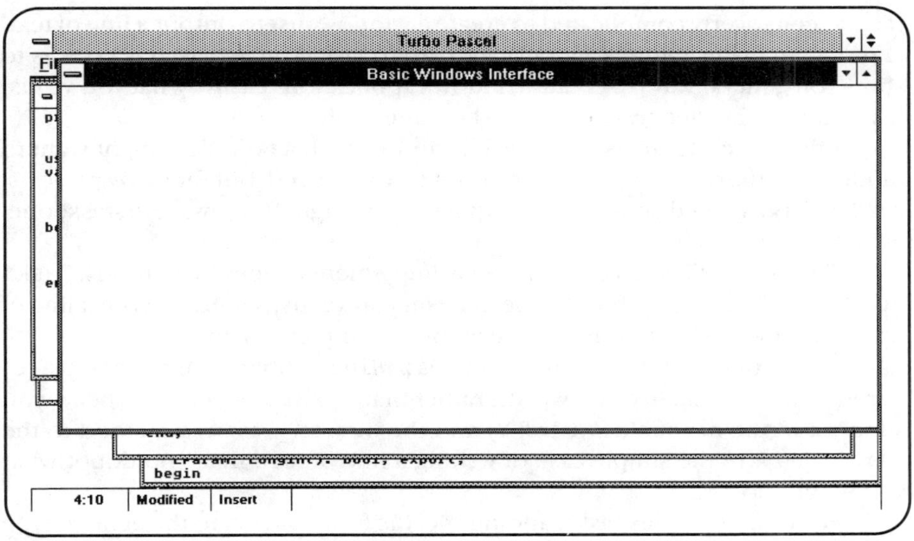

***Figure 5.2.** The default window of* `TWindow.Init`.

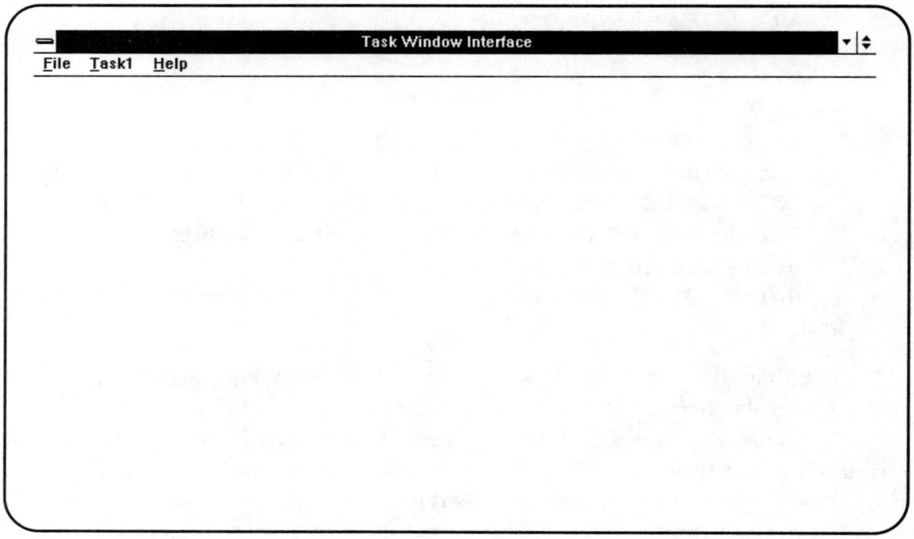

Figure 5.3. *A specific window created by* `TaskWindow.Init`.

Tasks

It may seem overly complicated to create a window just to output a line of text, and of course it is if that's all you ever plan to task. The goal of this book is to show you general ways to create Windows applications easily. What you've just learned is in fact general enough to be quite useful.

I find it helpful to associate each window with a task. You might want to modify this approach as you become more experienced, but for many projects, particularly as you discover your own route through Windows, one-task, one-window works well.

The task itself is an object that may implement dozens of methods. `Task1` just wrote a line of text, but the mechanism you've just set up to write a line of text can serve as a blueprint for much more complex tasking.

You could, of course, remodel the `MainWindow` (in the `BasicInterface`) to reflect a new task. In other words, rather than derive a new `TaskWindow`, you simply add the new fields (`X` and `Y`) and the new `cm_Iterate` method to the `MainWindow`. In the simple case of writing a line of text, that's no doubt what you would do.

For more complex tasks, adding specific functionality to the general type misses entirely the object-oriented approach. It is better to create abstract types and use inheritance to derive new windows, thus enabling task focus on its own specific functionality.

I've designed the `BasicInterface` with this attitude in mind. You use the `BasicInterface` as your general (abstract) connection to Windows and derive a Specific Interface for your new applications or tasks. In this simple two-step process:

1. You derive a new application from the `BasicInterface` Application object and let it know which window it needs to know about and use:

```
TaskApp = object(BasicApplication)      { TaskApp = a kind of
                                          BasicApplication }
   procedure InitMainWindow; virtual; { Init a specific MainWindow }
end;                                    { for the TaskApp }

implementation

procedure TaskApp.InitMainWindow;       { Init a MainWindow for
                                          the Task }
begin
  if FirstApplication then
  MainWindow := New(PTask1, Init(nil, 'Task Window Interface'))
  else MainWindow := New(PTask1, Init(nil,'Additional Instance of TWI'));
end;
```

2. Derive a new `MainWindow` (object) that includes the new task:

```
PTask1 = ^Task1;                 { Pointer to this task }
Task1 = object(MainWindow)
   (* new task methods and fields here *)
end;
```

There's a (perhaps) subtle polymorphic aspect to this process. Notice that the `InitMainWindow` constructs a new window object type through the use of a pointer. Because the window is constructed through a pointer the new window type can be any `TWindow` descendant. The `InitMainWindow` method simply sends the message "construct a window pointed to by the pointer." The functionality of the window can change and `InitMainWindow` is unaffected. It simply sends a general message (see figure 5.4).

The task is set in motion when the `TaskWindow` receives a command message generated by a menu selection.

That is it for the Turbo Pascal side of things. When the menu message matching the constant code is sent, the task is put in motion in its own window. Note that the window has all the basic capability of a `TWindow`; it can be resized, moved, minimized, and so on.

Figure 5.5 shows the task window (and task) created by the code in listing 5.1.

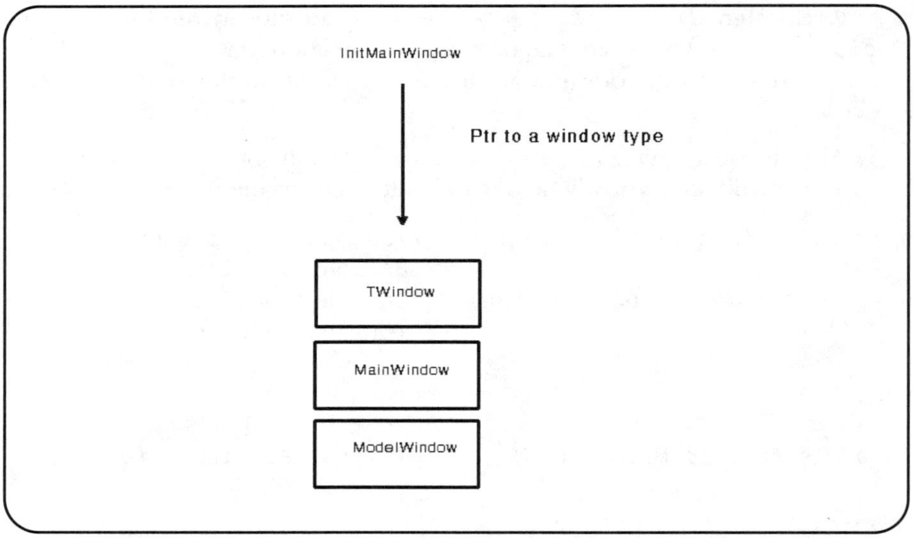

Figure 5.4. A kind of polymorphism.

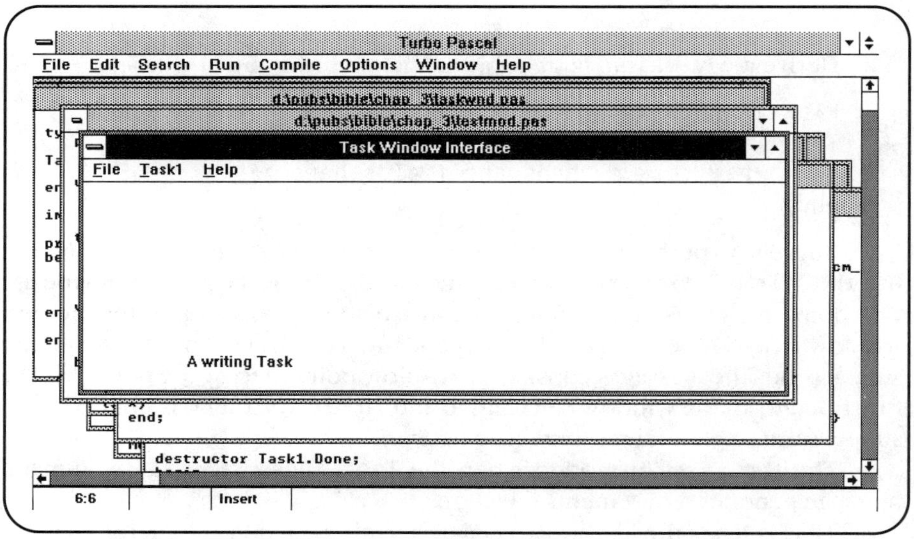

Figure 5.5. The task window (and task) created by listing 5.1.

Listing 5.1. Code to create a task window and task.

```
{ contains two units: Write1, a task,
  and TaskWnd, to set up the task and a test program }

unit Write1;             { A model task }
                         { responds to cm_Task1 (message) }

interface

uses WObjects,           { Units specific to this unit }
   WinTypes,
   WinProcs,
   strings,
   StdDlgs,
   WIF5;                 { BasicInterface : contains MainWindow }
                         {                : BasicApplication }

type

PTask1 = ^Task1;                      { Pointer to this task }
Task1 = object(MainWindow)            { Time Series }
  X, Y : integer;
  constructor Init(AParent: PWindowsObject; ATitle: PChar);
  destructor Done; virtual;           { Clean up }
  procedure cm_Iterate(var Msg: TMessage);
     virtual cm_First + cm_Task1;
end;

implementation

constructor Task1.Init(AParent: PWindowsObject; ATitle:
PChar);
begin
  TWindow.Init(AParent, ATitle);
  DisableAutoCreate;
  Attr.Style := ws_PopupWindow or ws_Caption or ws_Visible;
  Attr.Menu  := LoadMenu(HInstance, PChar(99)); { 99 = menu ID }

  Attr.X := 100;       { Set window dimensions }
  Attr.Y := 50;
  Attr.W := 300;
  Attr.H := 200;
end;
```

continues

Listing 5.1 continued

```
procedure Task1.cm_Iterate(var Msg: TMessage); { Act on menu's
                                                 task1 (cm_) }
begin
   X := Attr.X + 50;
   Y := Attr.Y + 50;
   SetCapture(HWindow);
   DC := GetDC(HWindow);              { Get a display context }
   TextOut(DC,X,Y,'A writing Task',14);  { Write something }
   ReleaseCapture;
   ReleaseDC(HWindow,DC);             { Release display context }
end;

destructor Task1.Done;
begin
   TWindow.Done;                      { Call ancestor's destructor }
end;

end.  { unit Write1 }
```

```
unit TaskWnd;             { Sets up a Task }
                          { Responds to cm_Task1 (message) }
                          { Responds to cm_Task2 (message) }

interface

uses WObjects,            { Units specific to this unit }
   WinTypes,
   WinProcs,
   strings,
   StdDlgs,
   WIF5,                  { BasicInterface unit }

                          { TaskList }
   write1;                { Task 1   }

{$R TASKWND.RES}          { TaskWnd resource }
```

```
type

TaskApp = object(BasicApplication)    { ModelApp = a kind of
                                        BasicApplication }
  procedure InitMainWindow; virtual; { Init a specific MainWindow }
end;

implementation

procedure TaskApp.InitMainWindow;     { Init a model
                                        application window }
begin
  if FirstApplication then
  MainWindow := New(PTask1, Init(nil, 'Task Window Interface'))
  else MainWindow := New(PTask1, Init(nil,'Additional Instance of MI'));
end;

end. { unit TaskWnd }


program Test_Interface;   { A generic way to test each
                            phase of interface development }


uses
   WIF5,                  { BasicInterface unit }
   taskwnd;               { contains this TaskApp }

type

    App = object(TaskApp)
    end;

var
  Application: App;       { An instance of BasicApplication }

                       { Run Application1 }
begin
  Application.Init('TaskInterface');   { init application instance }
  Application.Run;                     { Message loop }
  Application.Done;                    { Destroy application
                                         instance }
end.
```

> **Note:** It's not essential, but it is convenient, to associate one menu with each window. In other words, `Task1` (the window) has an associate menu contained in the `Task1` resource file (TASK1.RES). This association helps you keep your windows and menus from straying too far from each other.

The only detail left out is how to add the menu item. Chapter 8, "Resources and Control Objects," details resource creation, which in the case of adding menu selections, is very simple. In a nutshell, you open the Whitewater Resource Toolkit Menu Editor, open a resource file, add the menu choice, and add its corresponding command code.

Other Windows, Other Tasks

Now that you have a general task window, what about adding more tasks? Easily added. The process is more or less creating a new `CMIterate` method for each task. For example, create a window that displays text and draws a line:

```
procedure Task2.CMIterate(var Msg: TMessage);
begin
   X := Attr.X + 50;     { Line dimensions }
   Y := Attr.Y + 50;
   EndX := X + 50;
   EndY := Y + 50;       { Line dimensions }
   SetCapture(HWindow);
   DC := GetDC(HWindow);
   TextOut(DC,X,Y,'A writing Task',14);
   DrawLine := LineTo(DC,EndX,EndY);
   ReleaseCapture;
   ReleaseDC(HWindow,DC);
end;
```

Model Tasks

You're no doubt noticing that text and graphics can be displayed in a window with similar ease. It's all pixels to a GUI like Windows.

In general, you want to think of your applications performing tasks in response to the messages they receive. The messages can come from menus, the mouse, the keyboard, ports, the application itself, and even other applications. In this next section, I show you how to set up an abstract model task (or simulation) that demonstrates how you create your own specialized tasks. Then

I show you how to multitask by putting several model tasks in windows that can be displayed simultaneously.

In order for you to have a little fun with the tasks I develop here, I discuss modeling in general and then eventually move to one of the hottest topics in modeling: chaos theory.

Modeling

Modeling is a way to encapsulate some part of a system's behavior in terms of the mathematical relationships among variables. One hopes that these variables encapsulate the system's behavior, and you select the variables you think are important in determining changes of state in the system. Then you stand back and watch the system change state.

For example, in a two-dimensional system, with variables X and Y, you might say that the current state of Y is equal to three times the current state of X; or, in mathematical terms, $Y = 3X$. This is a simple linear model, and you can easily visualize how the system changes from state to state: Y is always three times as big as X. Figure 5.6 pictures this system's changing state.

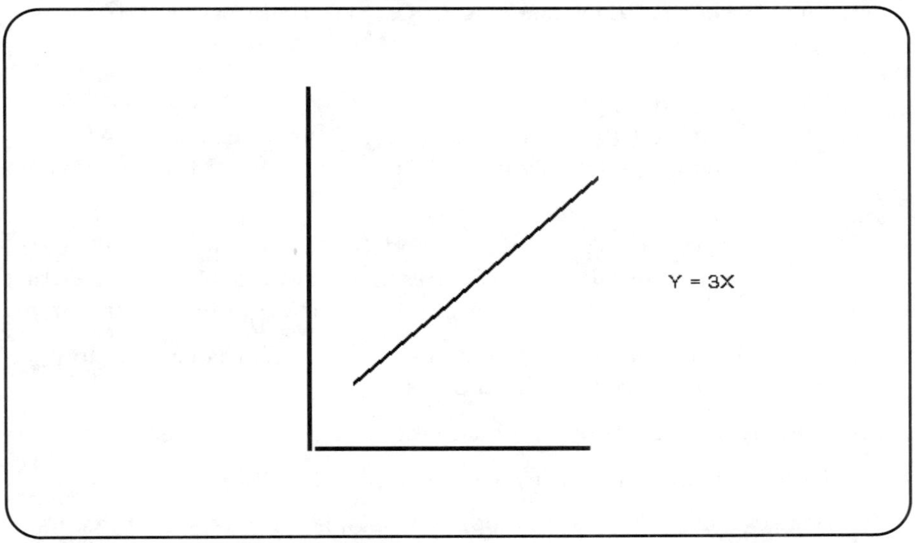

Figure 5.6. *A linear equation.*

To display this system in a window, you can simply graph the values of Y for each increment in X.

To graph these changes of state, the task needs to implement several new data fields to represent screen coordinates, ranges to graph, initial values for variables, and methods for scaling and iterating the task.

Call this task `Model1` and define it this way, as a window derived from `MainWindow`:

```
PModel1 = ^Model1;                   { Pointer to this task }
Model1 = object(MainWindow)          { A Time Series model }
                                     { Task's data fields }
  InitX, InitY :    real;            { Initial points }
  RangeX1, RangeX2, RangeY1, RangeY2 : real;  { Range to view }
  X, Y : integer;                    { Point to plot }
  A, B : real;                       { Factors for this model task }
                                     { Task's methods }
  constructor Init(AParent: PWindowsObject; ATitle: PChar);
  procedure  Scale;                  { Scale point to window }
  procedure  Iterate;                { Iterate model task }
  destructor Done; virtual;          { Clean up }
  procedure CMIterate(var Msg: TMessage);
          virtual cm_First + cm_Task1;
end;
```

You implement the methods in a moment. For now, simply let `App.InitMainWindow` construct a `Model1`:

```
procedure TaskApp.InitMainWindow; { Init a MainWindow for
                                    the Task }
begin
  if FirstApplication then
  MainWindow := New(PModel1, Init(nil, 'Task Window Interface'))
  else MainWindow := New(PModel1, Init(nil,'Additional Instance of TWI')
end;
```

You have another task (this time a model) in a window. Nothing new in this episode, but suppose that you want to set up a more general interface that allows you to multitask several windows at once. This requires two main steps:

1. Another layer of abstraction in the form of an intermediary window that creates the various task windows
2. A slightly more complex command message-response setup

   The intermediary (or setup) window looks like this:

```
PModelWindow = ^ModelWindow;{ModelWnd is a kind of MainWnd }
ModelWindow = object(MainWindow)
  constructor Init(AParent : PWindowsObject; ATitle : PChar);
  procedure CMTask1(var Msg: TMessage); virtual { run task1 }
   cm_First + cm_Task1;
  procedure CMTask2(var Msg: TMessage); virtual { run task2 }
   cm_First + cm_Task2;
end;
```

where CMTask1 and CMTask2 are response methods for menu command messages to construct and iterate each task. Figure 5.7 illustrates this concept.

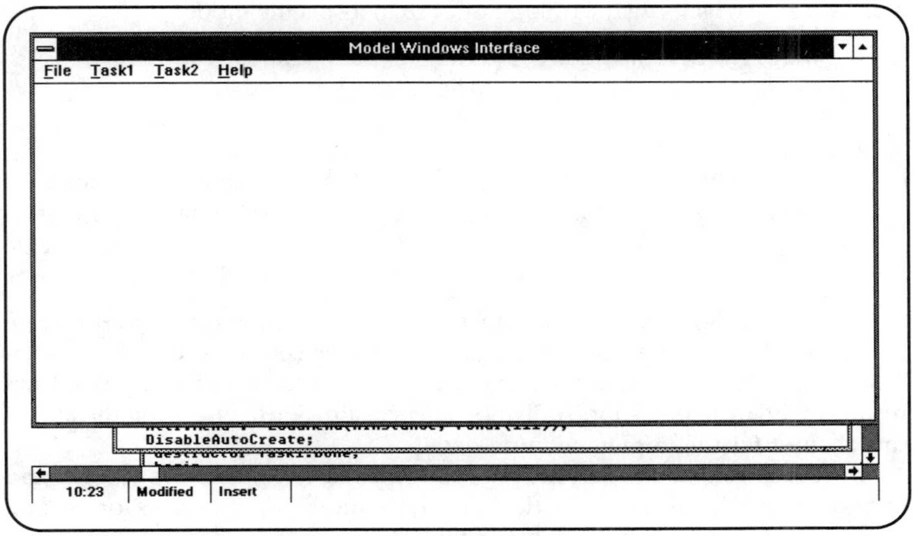

Figure 5.7. *Task1 and Task2 on model windows interface.*

ModelWindow.CMTask1 looks like this:

```
procedure ModelWindow.CMTask1(var Msg: TMessage);
var
   Task1 : PModel1;                   { Pointer to a Task }
begin
   Task1 := New(PModel1, Init(@Self, 'TimeSeries Model'));
   Application^.MakeWindow(Task1);
   Task1^.cm_Iterate;                 { Iterate the task  }
end;
```

Responding to the cm_task1 message, CMTask1 constructs a Model1 window and then iterates the model.

ModelWindow.CMTask2 looks like this:

```
procedure ModelWindow.CMTTask2(var Msg: TMessage);
var
   Task2 : PModel2;                 { Pointer to a Task }
begin
   Task2 := New(PModel2, Init(@Self, 'Henon Attractor'));
   Application^.MakeWindow(Task2);
   Task2^.Iterate;                  { Iterate the task  }
end;
```

Responding to the cm_task2 message, CMTask2 constructs a Model2 window and then iterates the model.

To set this system in motion, have TaskApp.InitMainWindow construct a ModelWindow as its MainWindow rather than a specific model:

```
procedure TaskApp.InitMainWindow;  { Init a MainWindow for
                                      the Task }
begin
  if FirstApplication then
  MainWindow := New(PModelWindow, Init(nil, 'Task Window Interface'))
  else MainWindow := New(PModelWindow, Init(nil,'Additional Instance of TWI'));
end;
```

That's all there is to it.

Note that both Model1 and the ModelWindow can respond to the same command message (cm_Task1). The same goes for Model2 and ModelWindow (cm_Task2). Note also that the same message sent to two different windows results in different behaviors: polymorphism again. See listing 5.3 at the end of this chapter for the implementation details.

If the ModelWindow gets the cm_Task1 message, it constructs a model and iterates it. If the Model1 gets the cm_Task1 message, it iterates only itself (because it has already been constructed!). C-o-o-o-l.

Chaos and Strange Attractors

Now, just for fun and because chaotic models are a fascinating way to explore the world, I discuss some of the theory behind Model2.

In recent years, researchers in various fields that involve dynamics have used computers to model nonlinear systems that exhibit behavior not easily visualized nor understood by just looking at the numbers. The key to understanding many of these systems is to uncover the attractors of the system.

An attractor is, loosely, a state toward which a system evolves. You find attractors in a computer-generated phase (or state) space. In state space, a point represents all the information you know about a system's state, and the space itself is a picture of a system's current state plotted against its next state (see figure 5.8).

The key to understanding the system is to determine what state (or states) the system is evolving toward. Attractors "attract" a system. As the system evolves, the collection of points that represent successive states can either:

1. Settle to one point (a point attractor). See figure 5.9.
2. Repeatedly return to a set of points (a periodic attractor). See figure 5.10.

3. Not return to a well-defined group of points, or return to a strange set of points (see figure 5.11).

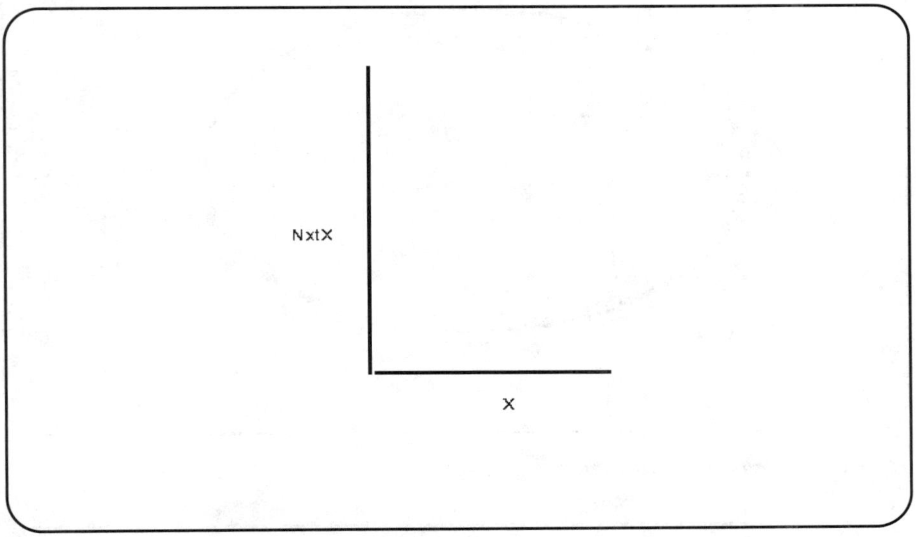

Figure 5.8. *State space.*

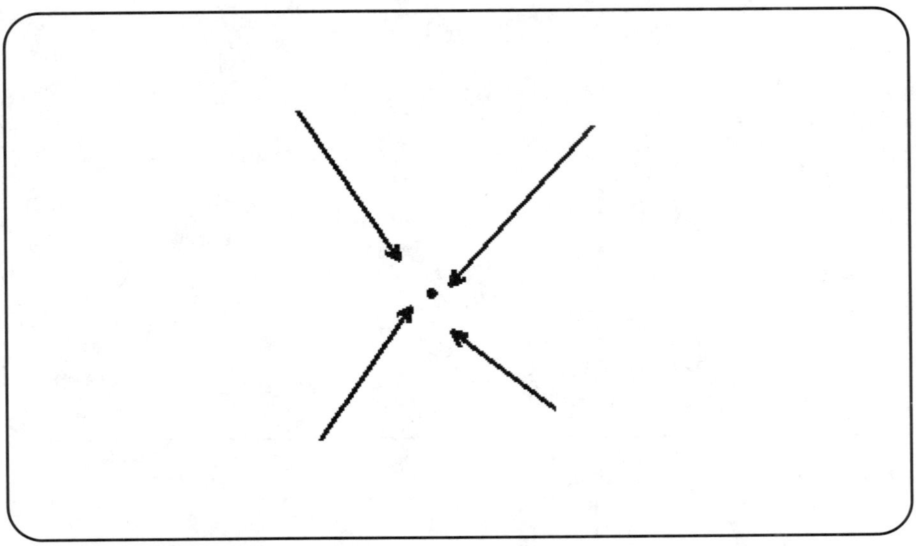

Figure 5.9. *A point attractor.*

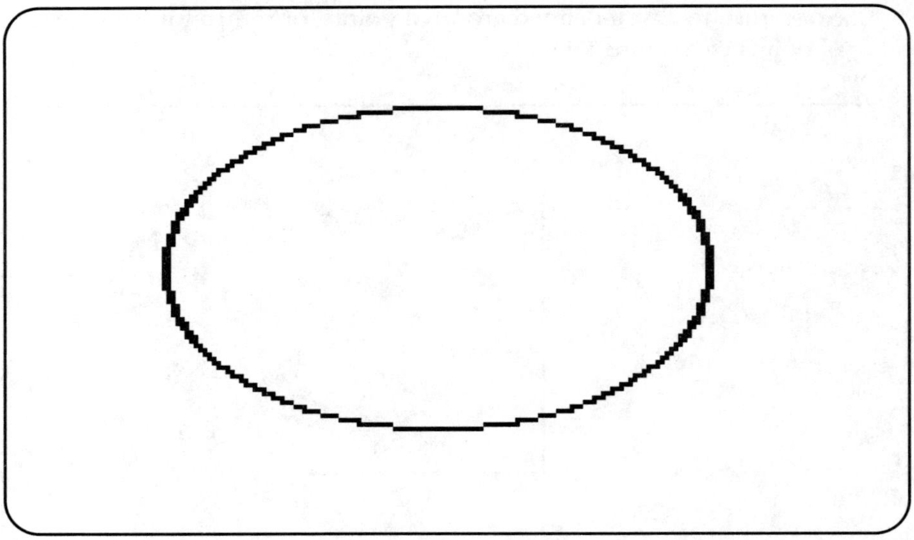

Figure 5.10. *A periodic attractor.*

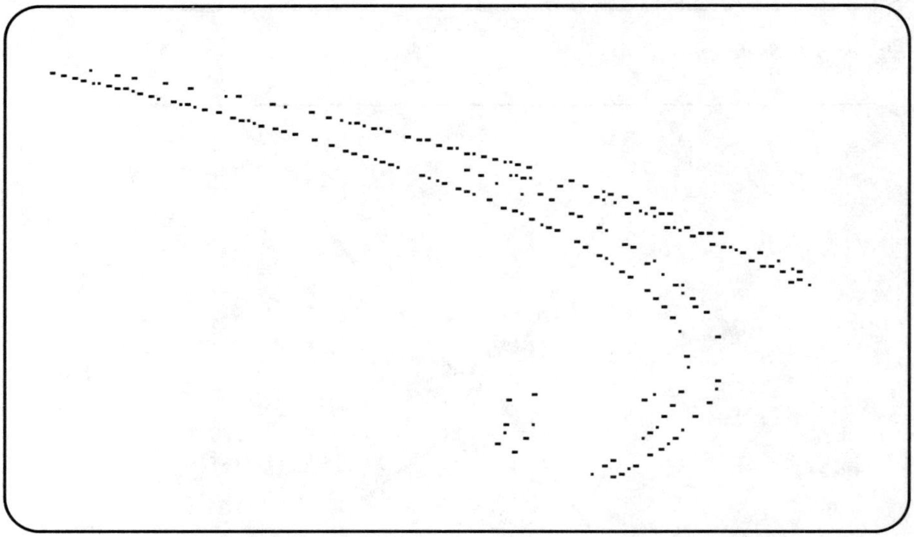

Figure 5.11. *A strange attractor.*

The system evolves as the values of the current state become the initial values of the next state. Each time, before each loop into the next state, the model records or plots the current system's state in phase space.

Modeling systems (like tasking systems in general) are best described with object-oriented techniques for several reasons. It's easy to generalize the characteristics that models have in common. Any model is a type of model, related to other models. From a computing perspective, models share low-level graphics primitives like points. They're all plotted in some kind of space, although differing in how they generate states in that space.

A dynamic system, which a model represents, can be anything

- You can describe by knowing the values of variables
- Whose current state depends on its previous states

The state of the system can be something measured on a continuous scale, something with logical changes (Is it yes? Is it on? Has something happened since you checked last?), and so on.

In a speech-recognition system, one of my favorite examples, each word in the sentence carries some individual weight and affects (and is affected by) all the other words in the sentence.

In a sense one can consider a "sentence" to be a dynamic system that changes state through the addition of words and punctuation marks. Initially a sentence is empty. You add a word (the one word is the new sentence). You add a word (the two words are the new sentence). You add a word (the three words are the new sentence). You add a punctuation mark (three words plus punctuation = new sentence). And so on.

When you speak, words necessarily follow each other. When you write, they follow or displace one another (by replacing or being inserted between words). Each new state represents your attempts to clarify the state of the sentence. (As many of you know, each new state can clarify or confuse—one reason that parsing sentences is so difficult.) *Parsing* is the breaking up of sentences into component parts, usually for grammatical description.

The sentence in its next state is very sensitive to its current state (or condition) and to its previous states.

You might say that "meanings" are the attractors in the dynamic system "sentence." At any state the sentence may have no meaning (an extinction state), one meaning (a stable state), or many meanings (possibly a chaotic state). The meaning of the sentence depends on any number of things—point of view, reading or writing skill, and so on.

Mathematic Attraction

Scientists (in mathematics, physics, engineering, biology, computer science, business, economics, and so on) are trying to understand dynamic systems. Their discoveries have led to at least one agreeable conclusion—anything of interest that changes state is beautifully complex.

Mathematicians and computer scientists try to twist meaning out of complex systems by representing them with equations (or rules), and they visualize the system in pictures.

Some particularly interesting pictures exist in phase (or state) space, where each point holds all the information needed to describe a dynamic system at any one time (or state).

For example, suppose that a system varies (changes state) depending on a variable—such as size or number. Call the variable, X, and call its rate of change, R. Then equations such as

```
Nextx = R * X( * (1-X)
```

can describe the system.

In this case, the numeral `1` represents the system at some maximum state and `0` represents the system at some minimum state. Either extreme state (when `Nextx` = 1 or 0) translates into an infinite state.

The previous equation, the so-called "standard map" or "logistic equation," has been explored for many years by mathematically inclined folks in many fields. They've discovered that it (and presumably the dynamic system it describes) behaves unpredictably. In general, any system you describe with any nonlinear equation or equations behaves unpredictably.

Logistic equations are unpredictable because they're extremely sensitive to initial conditions. Nearby values of `X` in one state may lead to values (of `Nextx`) that are far apart in the next state.

You can complicate matters even more by increasing the number of variables in a system (that is, our representation of a system). For example, these two rules for changes in state

```
Nextx = AX - (1-(Y*Y*Y))     { 2 coupled nonlinear equations }
Nexty = 1 - BY
```

can present an "infinite" number of states (`Nextx` values) responding to infinitely small changes in the condition of the previous state (or `X` value). This infinity of values is the chaotic set for this dynamic system.

You can see this chaos easily by plotting the values of each state (`Nextx`) in time. (The X axis is time. The Y axis is the value of each `X`. See figure 5.12.)

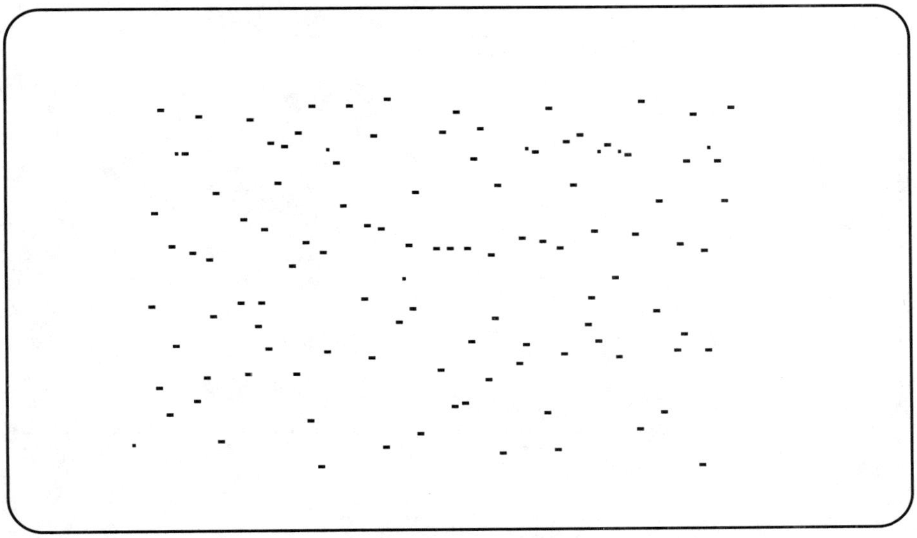

Figure 5.12. *Chaos.*

Order in Chaos

In even the most chaotic systems, there's an intriguing and often surprising order. One way to see this order is in phase space. When you plot values of `Nextx` against values of current `X`, you uncover the attractor for the chaotic set. This attractor occupies the phase space and is composed of all the points in the chaotic set. By mutual agreement it's called "strange." Figure 5.13 shows the strange attractor corresponding to the chaotic set in figure 5.12. Listing 5.2 shows the task code to create this attractor.

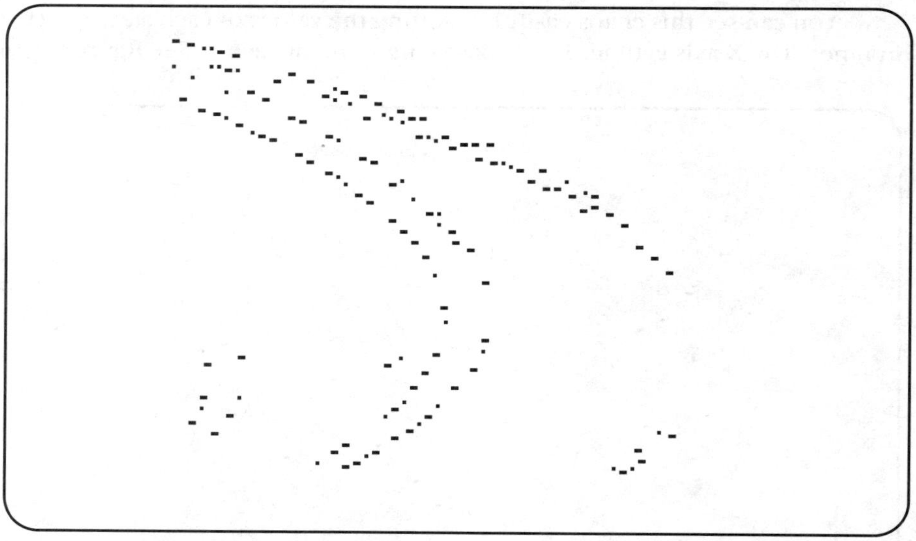

Figure 5.13. Order in chaos.

Listing 5.2. Code to create strange attractor in figure 5.13.

```
unit Attract2;               { Contains Henon Attractor }
                             { Responds to cm_Task2 (message) }

interface

uses WObjects,               { Units specific to this unit }
   WinTypes,
   WinProcs,
   strings,
   StdDlgs,
   WIF5;                     { BasicInterface unit }

{$R ATTRACT2.RES}

const
   cm_ChangeFactor_A   = 303; { ''          '''' ''  ''       }

type

PModel2 = ^Model2;
Model2 = object(MainWindow)                          { Henon Attractor }
```

```
                                               { Model's data fields }
  InitX, InitY :    real;                      { Initial points }
  RangeX1, RangeX2, RangeY1, RangeY2 : real;   { Range to view }
  X, Y : integer;                              { Point to plot }
  A, B : real;                                 { Factors for this model }

                                               { Model's methods }
  constructor Init(AParent: PWindowsObject; ATitle: PChar);
  procedure  Scale;                            { Scale point to window }
  procedure  Iterate;                          { Iterate model }
  destructor Done; virtual;                    { Clean up }
  procedure cm_Iterate(var Msg: TMessage);     { Iterate  }
  virtual cm_First + cm_Task2;
  procedure cm_ChangeFactorA(var Msg: TMessage);
      virtual cm_First + cm_ChangeFactor_A;
end;


implementation

const
   Iterations = 3000;      { Number of iterations }


constructor Model2.Init(AParent: PWindowsObject; ATitle: PChar);
begin
  TWindow.Init(AParent, ATitle);
  Attr.Menu := LoadMenu(HInstance, PChar(102));
  DisableAutoCreate;
  Attr.Style := ws_PopupWindow or ws_Caption or ws_Visible;

  Attr.X := 150;
  Attr.Y := 100;
  Attr.W := 300;
  Attr.H := 200;


  RangeX1 :=  -1.03;          { Set ranges to view }
  RangeX2 :=  1.27;
  RangeY1 :=  -0.3;
  RangeY2 :=  0.45;

  A := 1.4;                   { Set factors }
  B := 0.3;
```

continues

Listing 5.2. continued

```
  InitX := 0.4;
  InitY := 0;

  X := 0;                        { Initial point in space }
  Y := 0;
end;

procedure Model2.cm_Iterate(var Msg: TMessage);
begin
   Iterate;                      { Iterate the model }
end;

procedure Model2.cm_ChangeFactorA(var Msg: TMessage);
var
   InputText: array[0..5] of Char;
   New_A : real;
   ErrorPos : integer;
begin                            { Use dialog to change A factor }
   Str(A,InputText);
   if Application^.ExecDialog(New(PInputDialog,
      Init(@Self,'Factor A','Input a new A Factor:',
      InputText, SizeOf(InputText)))) = id_Ok then
   begin
      Val(InputText,New_A,ErrorPos);
      if ErrorPos = 0 then A := New_A;
   end;
end;

procedure Model2.Scale;
begin                            { Scale point in space to window }
   If (InitX = RangeX1) then     { A little troubleshooting }
     X := Attr.X;
   If (InitX = RangeX2) then
     X := Attr.W;                { And here }
   If (InitX = 0) then
     X := X;
   If (InitX > RangeX1) then
      X := round((InitX - RangeX1)/(RangeX2 - RangeX1) * (Attr.W - Attr.X));
   Y := Attr.H - (round((InitY - RangeY1)/(RangeY2 - RangeY1) * (Attr.H -
Attr.Y)));
end;

destructor Model2.Done;
begin
```

```
    TWindow.Done;                    { Call ancestor's destructor }
end;

procedure Model2.Iterate;
var
  I : integer;
  TempX, TempY : real;

begin
    SetCapture(HWindow);
    DC := GetDC(HWindow);         { Get a display context }
    for I := 1 to Iterations do
    begin
       TempX := InitX;            { Save last state }
       TempY := InitY;            { Save last state }
       InitX := TempY + 1 - (A * TempX * TempX);  { this model }
       InitY := B * TempX;                        { this model }
       Scale;                     { Scale new state to a window }
       TextOut(DC,X,Y,'.',1);     { Draw a point }
    end;
    ReleaseCapture;
    ReleaseDC(HWindow,DC);        { Release Display context }
end;

end.
```

The fractal (or self-similar) nature of the system becomes apparent when you zoom in on any area of the attractor. The deeper you go, the more complex (and detailed) the attractor becomes, and yet the more orderly it seems.

Grand Finale

Listing 5.3 shows the complete code for this multitasking model system, including the specific code for a chaotic model and a strange attractor. Figure 5.14 shows the display produced by this code.

Deriving your own multitasking from this new version of the `BasicInterface` is a simple matter. Although a modeling system might not be at all what you have in mind for your own applications, it's a general one that illustrates how easily you can create a multitasking system within Windows. You simply create or derive your own tasks, define pointers to them, and then construct those windows from the `ModelWindow` (the `MainWindow` for the multitasking system).

Note that I've adopted a useful convention of putting each separate task in its own unit. I don't know about you, but I easily lose track of where I keep objects. So a task per unit in many cases makes good sense to me. Chapter 13, "Designing Windows Applications," talks again about organization in regard to Windows applications. You, of course, decide what works best for you.

Chapter 5, "Putting Pictures In Windows," closes with a reflection: Windows is a multitasking interface, so doesn't it makes sense that you can create your own multitasking system within Windows? ...Yes!

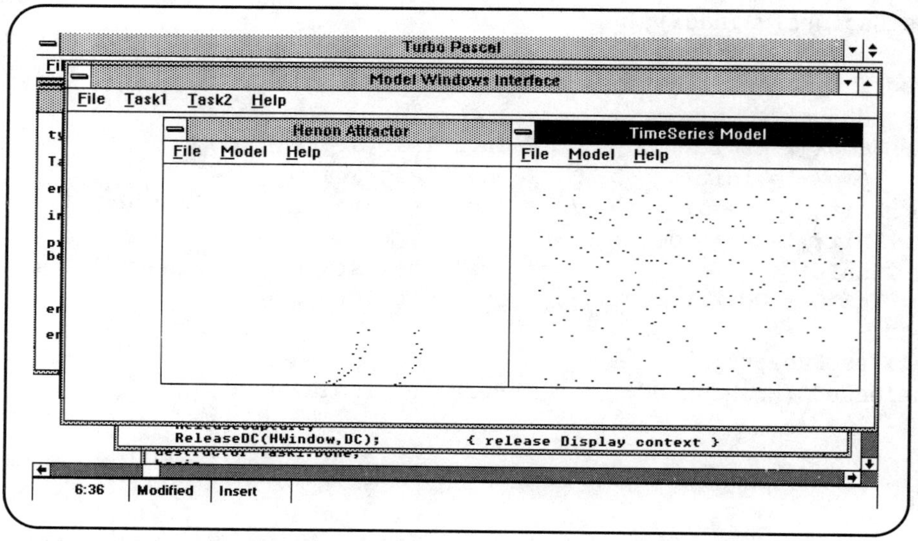

***Figure 5.14.** The results of listing 5.3.*

***Listing 5.3.** Code for a chaotic model and a strange attractor.*

```
{ This listing includes three units: time1
                         attract2
                         modelwnd
                         and a test interface program }

{ Time1 }

unit Time1;              { A model task }
                         { responds to cm_Task1 (message) }

interface
```

```
uses WObjects,          { Units specific to this unit }
   WinTypes,
   WinProcs,
   strings,
   StdDlgs,
   WIF5;                { BasicInterface : contains MainWindow }
                        {                : contains BasicApplication }

{$R TIME1.RES}          { This task's new resources }

type

PModel1 = ^Model1;      { Pointer to this task }
Model1 = object(MainWindow)        { Time Series }

                { Task's data fields }
  InitX, InitY :    real;                     { Initial points }
  RangeX1, RangeX2, RangeY1, RangeY2 : real;  { range to view }
  X, Y : integer;       { Point to plot }
  A, B : real;          { factors for this model task }

                        { Task's methods }
  constructor Init(AParent: PWindowsObject; ATitle: PChar);
  procedure  Scale;     { Scale point to window }
  procedure  Iterate;   { Iterate model task }
  destructor Done; virtual;      { Clean up }
  procedure cm_Iterate(var Msg: TMessage);
      virtual cm_First + cm_Task1;
end;


implementation

const
   Iterations = 3000;  { Number of iterations for this model }


constructor Model1.Init(AParent: PWindowsObject; ATitle:
PChar);
begin
  TWindow.Init(AParent, ATitle);
  Attr.Menu := LoadMenu(HInstance, PChar(111));
  DisableAutoCreate;
  Attr.Style := ws_PopupWindow or ws_Caption or ws_Visible;
```

continues

Listing 5.3. continued

```
  Attr.X := 100;         { Set window dimensions }
  Attr.Y := 50;
  Attr.W := 300;
  Attr.H := 200;

  RangeX1 :=  -1.03;     { Set ranges to view }
  RangeX2 :=  1.27;
  RangeY1 :=  -0.3;
  RangeY2 :=  0.45;

  A := 1.4;              { Set factors }
  B := 0.3;
  InitX := 0.4;
  InitY := 0;

  X := 0;                { Initial point in space }
  Y := 0;
end;


procedure Model1.cm_Iterate(var Msg: TMessage);
begin
   Iterate;              { Iterate the model }
end;

procedure Model1.Scale;
begin                    { Scale point in space to window }
   If (InitX = RangeX1) then        { A little troubleshooting }
     X := Attr.X;
   If (InitX = RangeX2) then
     X := Attr.W;        { And here }
   If (InitX = 0) then
     X := X;
   If (InitX > RangeX1) then
      X := round((InitX - RangeX1)/(RangeX2 - RangeX1) *
           (Attr.W - Attr.X));
      Y := Attr.H - (round((InitY - RangeY1)/(RangeY2 - RangeY1) *
           (Attr.H - Attr.Y)));
end;

destructor Model1.Done;
begin
   TWindow.Done;         { Call ancestor's destructor }
end;
```

```
procedure Model1.Iterate;
var
  I : integer;
  TempX, TempY : real;

begin
   InvalidateRect(HWindow, nil,True);
   SetCapture(HWindow);
   DC := GetDC(HWindow);              { Get a display context }
   for I := 1 to Iterations do
   begin
      TempX := InitX;                 { Save last state }
      TempY := InitY;                 { Save last state }
      InitX := TempY + 1 - (A * TempX * TempX);    {This model }
      InitY := B * TempX;             { This model    }
      Scale;           { Scale new state to a window }
      X := I;
      TextOut(DC,X,Y,'.',1);          { Draw a point }
   end;
   ReleaseCapture;
   ReleaseDC(HWindow,DC);             { Release display context }
end;

end.   { unit time1 }

{ Attract 2 }

unit Attract2;          { Contains Henon Attractor }
                        { Responds to cm_Task2 (message) }

interface

uses WObjects,          { Units specific to this unit }
   WinTypes,
   WinProcs,
   strings,
   StdDlgs,
   WIF5;                { BasicInterface unit }

{$R ATTRACT2.RES}

const
   cm_ChangeFactor_A   = 303;   { ''       '' '' ''  ''       }
```

continues

Listing 5.3. continued

```
type

PModel2 = ^Model2;
Model2 = object(MainWindow)          { Henon Attractor }
                                     { Model's data fields }
  InitX, InitY :   real;             { Initial points }
  RangeX1, RangeX2, RangeY1, RangeY2 : real;  { Range to view }
  X, Y : integer;                    { Point to plot }
  A, B : real;
     { factors for this model }
                                     { Model's methods }
  constructor Init(AParent: PWindowsObject; ATitle: PChar);
  procedure  Scale;                  { Scale point to window }
  procedure  Iterate;                { Iterate model }
  destructor Done; virtual;          { Clean up }
  procedure cm_Iterate(var Msg: TMessage);      { Iterate  }
  virtual cm_First + cm_Task2;
  procedure cm_ChangeFactorA(var Msg: TMessage);
      virtual cm_First + cm_ChangeFactor_A;
end;

implementation

const
   Iterations = 3000;                  { Number of iterations }

constructor Model2.Init(AParent: PWindowsObject; ATitle: PChar);
begin
  TWindow.Init(AParent, ATitle);
  Attr.Menu := LoadMenu(HInstance, PChar(102));
  DisableAutoCreate;
  Attr.Style := ws_PopupWindow or ws_Caption or ws_Visible;

  Attr.X := 150;       { Window dimensions }
  Attr.Y := 100;
  Attr.W := 300;
  Attr.H := 200;

  RangeX1 :=  -1.03;   { Set ranges to view }
  RangeX2 :=  1.27;
  RangeY1 :=  -0.3;
  RangeY2 :=  0.45;

  A := 1.4;            { Set factors }
```

```
  B := 0.3;
  InitX := 0.4;
  InitY := 0;

  X := 0;                { Initial point in space }
  Y := 0;
end;

procedure Model2.cm_Iterate(var Msg: TMessage);
begin
   Iterate;              { Iterate the model }
end;

procedure Model2.cm_ChangeFactorA(var Msg: TMessage);
var
   InputText: array[0..5] of Char;
   New_A : real;
   ErrorPos : integer;
begin                    { Use dialog to change A factor }
   Str(A,InputText);
   if Application^.ExecDialog(New(PInputDialog,
      Init(@Self,'Factor A','Input a new A Factor:',
      InputText, SizeOf(InputText)))) = id_Ok then
   begin
      Val(InputText,New_A,ErrorPos);
      if ErrorPos = 0 then A := New_A;
   end;
end;

procedure Model2.Scale;
begin                    { Scale point in space to window }
   If (InitX = RangeX1) then { A little troubleshooting }
     X := Attr.X;
   If (InitX = RangeX2) then
     X := Attr.W;              { And here }
   If (InitX = 0) then
     X := X;
   If (InitX > RangeX1) then
      X := round((InitX - RangeX1)/(RangeX2 - RangeX1) *
              (Attr.W - Attr.X));
   Y := Attr.H - (round((InitY - RangeY1)/(RangeY2 - RangeY1) *
              (Attr.H - Attr.Y)));
end;
```

continues

Listing 5.3. continued

```
destructor Model2.Done;
begin
   TWindow.Done;       { Call ancestor's destructor }
end;

procedure Model2.Iterate;
var
  I : integer;
  TempX, TempY : real;

begin
   SetCapture(HWindow);
   DC := GetDC(HWindow);             { Get a display context }
   for I := 1 to Iterations do
   begin
      TempX := InitX;                { Save last state }
      TempY := InitY;                { Save last state }
      InitX := TempY + 1 - (A * TempX * TempX); {This model}
      InitY := B * TempX;                       {This model}
      Scale;        { Scale new state to a window }
      TextOut(DC,X,Y,'.',1);         { Draw a point }
   end;
   ReleaseCapture;
   ReleaseDC(HWindow,DC);            { Release Display context }
end;

end. { end unit Attract2 }

{ ModelWnd }

unit ModelWnd;          { Contains a Model Window }
                        { Responds to cm_Task1 (message)}
                        { Responds to cm_Task2 (message) }
interface

uses WObjects,          { Units specific to this unit }
   WinTypes,
   WinProcs,
   strings,
   StdDlgs,
   WIF5,                { BasicInterface unit }

                        { TaskList }
   time1,               { Task 1   }
```

```
   attract2;            { Task 2   }

{$R MODWND2.RES}        { ModelWnd resource }

type

ModelApp = object(BasicApplication)  { ModelApp=a kind
                                       of BasicApplication }
   procedure InitMainWindow; virtual;   { Init a specific
                                          MainWindow }
end;

PModelWindow = ^ModelWindow;          { ModelWnd is a
                                        kind of MainWnd }
ModelWindow = object(MainWindow)
  constructor Init(AParent : PWindowsObject; ATitle :
                   PChar);
  procedure cm_Task1(var Msg: TMessage); virtual  {Run Task1 }
   cm_First + cm_Task1;
  procedure cm_Task2(var Msg: TMessage); virtual  {Run Task2 }
   cm_First + cm_Task2;
end;


implementation


procedure ModelApp.InitMainWindow;     { Init a model
                                         application window }
begin
  if FirstApplication then
  MainWindow := New(PModelWindow, Init(nil, 'Model Windows Interface'))
  else MainWindow := New(PModelWindow, Init(nil,'Additional Instance of MI'));
end;

constructor ModelWindow.Init(AParent : PWindowsObject;
ATitle : PChar);
begin
   TWindow.Init(AParent, ATitle);      { Send message to
                                          ancestor's constructor }
   Attr.Menu  := LoadMenu(HInstance, PChar(99)); { 99 = menu ID }
   ButtonDown := False;                { Set status flag }
end;
procedure ModelWindow.cm_Task1(var Msg: TMessage);
var
```

continues

Listing 5.3. continued

```
   Task1 : PModel1;                        { Pointer to a task }
begin
   Task1 := New(PModel1, Init(@Self, 'TimeSeries Model'));
   Application^.MakeWindow(Task1);
   Task1^.cm_Iterate;                      { Iterate the task  }
end;

procedure ModelWindow.cm_Task2(var Msg: TMessage);
var
   Task2 : PModel2;                        { Pointer to a task }
begin
   Task2 := New(PModel2, Init(@Self, 'Henon Attractor'));
   Application^.MakeWindow(Task2);
   Task2^.Iterate;                         { Iterate the task  }
end;

end.  { unit Modelwnd }

{ Main test program }

program Test_Interface;   { Generic way to test each
                            phase of interface development }


uses
   WIF5,                  { BasicInterface unit }
   modelwnd;              { contains ModelApp,
                            multitasking units  }


type

    App = object(TaskApp)
    end;


var
  Application: App;     { An instance of BasicApplication }

                        { Run Application1 }
begin
  Application.Init('BasicInterface'); { init application instance }
  Application.Run;                         { Message loop }
  Application.Done;     { Destroy application instance }
end.

{ end Main test program }
```

6

CHAPTER

PAINTING, COLLECTING, AND STREAMING

Programming in an object-oriented language consists in dynamically creating a number of objects, according to a pattern which is usually impossible to predict at compile time.

Bertrand Meyer

A significant shortcoming of all the windows discussed so far (including the Main, Task and Model windows derived from `TWindow` in Chapter 4, "Inheriting An Interface," and Chapter 5, "Putting Pictures In Windows") is their tentativeness. In other words, any of the text and graphics displayed in a window can disappear whenever a window is covered by another window (for example, when you switch windows). When a window is subsequently uncovered it needs to have its contents updated (or Painted). Part of the screen has been covered by another window, leaving a window (when uncovered) only partially correct. Dots should have filled both sides of the screen. Figure 6.1 illustrates this point.

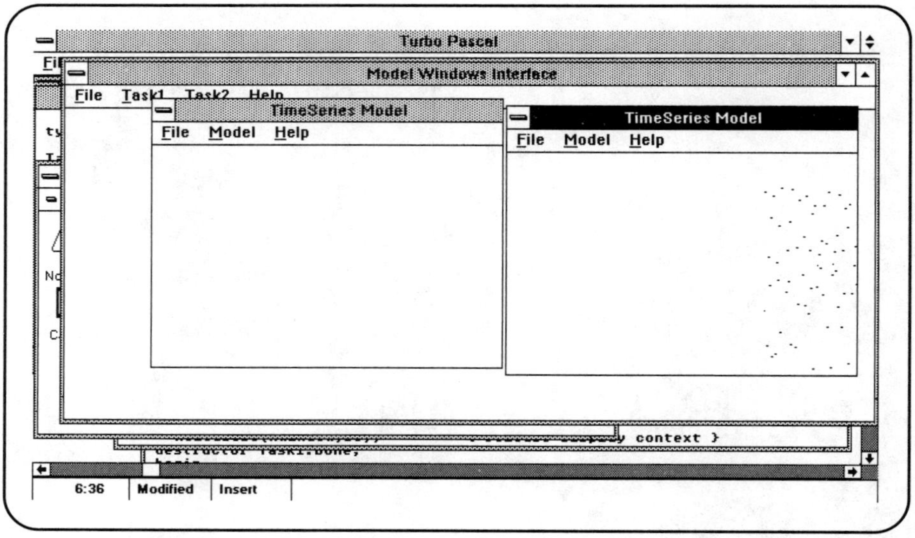

Figure 6.1. *A time series model.*

When a window needs to update its contents, Windows sends it a `Paint` message. It is then the window's responsibility to paint itself because Windows does not keep track of the contents of a window. As you might expect, the mechanics of receiving that message from Windows are handled automatically by `TWindow` and any window you derive from it.

The `TWindow` `Paint` method automatically responds to any `wm_Paint` message, but it does not actually paint the window.

`TWindow.Paint` is abstract, and if you think about it, it is abstract for a good reason; it does not know what is going to be displayed in any of its descendant's windows. Thus, any derived window needs to handle the crucial detail of painting itself.

To paint itself, the window overrides the `TWindow.Paint` method to handle the paint. How it decides to paint itself is entirely up to the window.

Reconsider the multitasking windows from Chapter 5, "Putting Pictures in Windows," and determine how to go about reimplementing a `Paint` method for them. The two models generate points corresponding to calculations, and display each point just after it is calculated.

If the windows containing the model tasks are covered and required to respond to `Paint` messages, they have to recalculate each point to redisplay it—not very efficient. Calculating and displaying point-by-point works fine only if you do not have to consider redisplaying (Painting) the window. You do have to consider this, however, and you need a classier solution.

A good approach (do not hesitate to think of a better one) is to calculate a set of points and store the calculated points where they can be easily retrieved and redisplayed whenever you need them.

The simplest (and a typical Pascal) way to collect items such as points is to store the points in an array. An array, though simple and direct, is a single-type, single-size solution, and OOP offers a more flexible, dynamic, and polymorphic solution—one with most of the details already handled by ObjectWindows.

Typically, if you store data in an array you have to write the code to create and manipulate the array. Simple enough, but still a little more work, most of which you do not need. OOP offers a generic solution: a collection of pointers to objects and the corresponding methods for manipulating the collection.

Polymorphic Collections

The ObjectWindows `TCollection` object is an abstract type and has two significant advantages over arrays: `TCollection` objects can size themselves dynamically at run-time, and they can be polymorphic. Thus, a collection can grow as you need it to, without changing any code. Because it is polymorphic as well, you can put any kind of object (and even non-objects) in it. You can even mix the object types within a single collection!

Because a collection uses nontyped pointers, it does not need to know anything about the objects it's given to process. It just stores them and gives them back; very flexible (see figure 6.2).

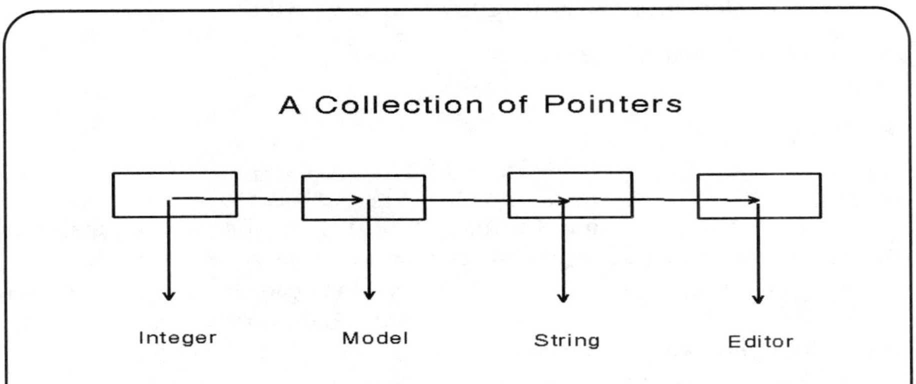

Figure 6.2. *A collection of pointers.*

Because collections are general-purpose, they are useful in many different kinds of situations. One package of methods designed for handling the general type can handle any specific type. Thus, if you use a collection, you do not reinvent data-handling methods each time you change the data type. Bravo, bravo.

Returning to the model tasks of Chapter 5, "Putting Pictures in Windows," what do you need to do to handle the Paint problem? Recall that the model object has fields to define the X and Y screen coordinates where points are displayed and an iterate method for generating points. You can redefine those coordinates as a point object, include that object in the `ModelWindow` object, collect those points rather than display them in the `Iterate` method, and define a `Paint` method for displaying the points when the window receives the `wm_Paint` message.

First, define a `point` (object):

```
APoint = object(TObject)
  X, Y: Integer;
  constructor Init(AX, AY: Integer);
end;
```

Derive the `point` from `TObject`, the base object for all ObjectWindows objects, because any object that uses ObjectWindows' streams must be derived from (or trace its origin to) `TObject`.

Then implement a constructor to create each point:

```
constructor APoint.Init(AX, AY: Integer);
begin
  X := AX;
  Y := AY;
end;
```

You also need to define a pointer to `APoint` because you are going to construct points dynamically (as you need them), using the `New` procedure and `APoint`'s constructor (`Init`). Because a collection already has a method, called `Insert` for inserting items into the collection, you do not even have to worry about adding the point to the collection.

Define a pointer to `APoint`:

```
PtrPoint = ^APoint;
```

Create a collection of points by declaring a variable of type `PCollection` (a predefined pointer to a `TCollection` object), and then dynamically create the `collection` (object):

```
var

 Points : PCollection;

 Points := New(PCollection, Init(1000, 100));
```

where `1000` is the size of the initial `collection` and `100` represents the incremental growth of the `collection`. In other words, you specify an initial size for a `collection`, but the `collection` is not limited to that size; it can grow dynamically by the increment you select. In fact, it can grow to a maximum size of about 16K, memory permitting, with each object requiring 4 bytes (the pointer size).

If there is not enough memory to add elements to the `collection`, the `TCollection` method—`TCollection.Error`—automatically receives a message specifying this not-enough-memory condition. The objects you derive from `TCollection` might want to handle this error themselves. For now, do not worry too much about out-of-memory errors; just leave them until Chapter 9, "Memory Matters," which explores memory and other more complex matters.

Construct and insert a point into the `collection` in a single step:

```
Points^.Insert(New(APoint, Init(X, Y)));
```

Although you are only going to collect points in this `collection`, remember that you can insert (and retrieve) other types of objects in this same `collection` using the same technique.

Collecting Points

Now to change a model task from Chapter 5, "Putting Pictures in Windows":

1. Add the `collection` to the object (see listing 6.1).

Listing 6.1. Adding the collection to the object.

```
PModel1 = ^Model1;                            { Pointer to this task }
Model1 = object(MainWindow)                   { Time series }
                                              { Task's data fields }
  InitX, InitY :    real;                     { Initial points }
  RangeX1, RangeX2, RangeY1, RangeY2 : real;  { Range to view }
  A, B : real;                                { Factors for this model task }
  Points : PCollection;                       { Add the collection }
                                              { Task's methods }
```

continues

Listing 6.1. continued

```
  constructor Init(AParent: PWindowsObject;
             ATitle: PChar);
  procedure  Scale;                     { Scale point to window }
  procedure  Iterate;                   { Iterate model task }
  destructor Done; virtual;             { Clean up }
  procedure cm_Iterate(var Msg: TMessage);
                        virtual cm_First + cm_Task1;
   procedure Paint(PaintDC: HDC;        { Override Paint }
      var PaintInfo: TPaintStruct); virtual;
end;
```

2. You also have to construct the collection and let the model know about it. A good place to handle this detail is in the Model's constructor. See listing 6.2.

Listing 6.2. The Model's constructor.

```
constructor Model1.Init(AParent: PWindowsObject; ATitle: PChar);
begin
  TWindow.Init(AParent, ATitle);
  Attr.Menu := LoadMenu(HInstance, PChar(111));
  DisableAutoCreate;
  Attr.Style := ws_PopupWindow or ws_Caption or ws_Visible;

  Attr.X := 100;            { Set window dimensions }
  Attr.Y := 50;
  Attr.W := 300;
  Attr.H := 200;

  RangeX1 :=  -1.03;        { Set ranges to view }
  RangeX2 :=  1.27;
  RangeY1 :=  -0.3;
  RangeY2 :=  0.45;

  A := 1.4;                 { Set factors }
  B := 0.3;
  InitX := 0.4;
  InitY := 0;
```

```
  X := 0;                { Initial point in space }
  Y := 0;

  Points := New(PCollection, Init(50, 50)); { Construct the collection }
end;
```

3. Then, rather than (or after you) display a point, insert the point in the collection (see listing 6.3).

Listing 6.3. Inserting the point in the collection.

```
procedure Model1.Iterate;
var
  I : integer;
  TempX, TempY : real;

begin
   InvalidateRect(HWindow, nil,True); { Clear screen }
   SetCapture(HWindow);
   DC := GetDC(HWindow);          { Get a display context }
   for I := 1 to Iterations do
   begin
      TempX := InitX;             { Save last state }
      TempY := InitY;             { Save last state }
      InitX := TempY + 1 - (A * TempX * TempX);{ This model }
      InitY := B * TempX;                       { This model }
      Scale;                   { Scale new state to a window }
      X := I;
      TextOut(DC,X,Y,'.',1);      { Draw a point }
      Points^.Insert(New(APoint, Init(X, Y)));
                                  { Insert it in collection }
   end;
   ReleaseCapture;
   ReleaseDC(HWindow,DC);         { Release Display context }
end;
```

4. Then display the collection in the revised `Paint` method using the built-in `TCollection` method, `ForEach` (see listing 6.4).

Listing 6.4. Displaying the collection.

```
procedure Model1.Paint(PaintDC: HDC; var PaintInfo: TPaintStruct);
var
  First: Boolean;              { A where-are-you flag }

   procedure DisplayPoints(P: PAPoint); far;
   begin
       TextOut(PaintDC,P^.X,P^.Y,'.',1);
       First := False;
   end;

begin
  First := True;
  Points^.ForEach(@DisplayPoints);
end;
```

ForEach is one of the many TCollection iterator methods that you can use to traverse and manipulate the collection. FirstThat and LastThat, for example, work much the same way to allow access to specific items in the collection.

Note also that Paint uses a specific display context, called PaintDC. PaintDC is obtained automatically by TWindow (and its descendants) before the Paint message is sent. PaintDC is released automatically after Paint is finished. (Remember that you must release any display context immediately after you are finished with it because it eats up so much memory.)

A collection is an amazingly useful tool, and any collection, as stated earlier, can contain a mixture of objects. Suppose, for example, that you had two objects:

- A point
- A string of text:

```
AString = object(TObject)
   S: array[0..5] of Char;
   constructor Init(AnS: array[0..5] of Char);
 end;
```

You could add them to the same collection and play them back one at a time. Create the new string object with its constructor:

```
constructor Init(AnS: array[0..5] of Char);
```

and insert it:

```
Points^.Insert(New(PtrAStr, Init(S)));
```

Note that it is your responsibility to make sure that you get the correct object back from a `collection`. The previous fragment works, but for illustrative purposes only. In a more complex situation, you probably want some way of identifying the object. If you do plan to use mixed `collections`, you should implement some foolproof plan for recognizing objects in the `collections`. An approach used with success is to add an ID field to each object you want to put in the `collection`. For example:

```
APoint = object(TObject)
  ID : word;
  X, Y: Integer;
  constructor Init(AnID: word AX, AY: Integer);
end;
```

Then when you insert the `point`, you insert its *ID* as well:

```
Id := 100;                        { 100 indicates a point }
Points^.Insert(New(APoint, Init(ID,X,Y)));
```

The same goes for the *`string`*:

```
Id := 102;                        { 102 indicates a string }
Points^.Insert(New(AStr, Init(ID,S)));
```

5. Then traverse the `collection` and get only the items you need—for example, just the points. A revised `Paint` method to handle this scenario might look like listing 6.5.

Listing 6.5. *The revised* `Paint` *method.*

```
procedure Model1.Paint(PaintDC: HDC; var PaintInfo:
TPaintStruct);
var
  First: Boolean;                { A where-are-you flag }

   procedure DisplayPoints(P: PAPoint); far;
   begin
        If P^.ID = 100 then
        begin
         TextOut(PaintDC,P^.X,P^.Y,'.',1);
```

continues

Listing 6.5. continued

```
        First := False;
      end;
  end;

begin
  First := True;
  Points^.ForEach(@DisplayPoints);
end;
```

Streams

The `collections` you have created so far handle the Paint problem beautifully as long as you do not turn off the computer, quit the program, or fall prey to some unforeseen natural disaster, such as a power failure. The problem is that these `collections` exist only in memory. What if you need to preserve the `collection` for another computing session? In other words, how can you `Paint` a window later, after the points are no longer retained in memory?

Answer: by using streams.

A stream is a collection of objects on its way to some device: a file, a port, EMS, and so on. Again, ObjectWindows already has implemented the methods you need to handle streams. Remember, streams are dynamic and polymorphic, so they are capable of handling dynamic and polymorphic collections. You just put objects in a stream and get them back (see figure 6.3).

A stream does not need to know the kind of objects it will see, as long as the objects it sees have been registered as "streamable" objects.

To use a stream, you need to

1. Define a stream registration record for the object you want to make streamable.

2. Register the stream by calling the global procedure `RegisterType` with the specific stream record as its parameter.

Here is how to define a stream record for `Apoint`:

```
const
  RPoint: TStreamRec = (
    ObjType: 500;
    VmtLink: Ofs(TypeOf(APoint)^);
    Load: @Point.Load;
    Store: @Point.Store);
  end;
```

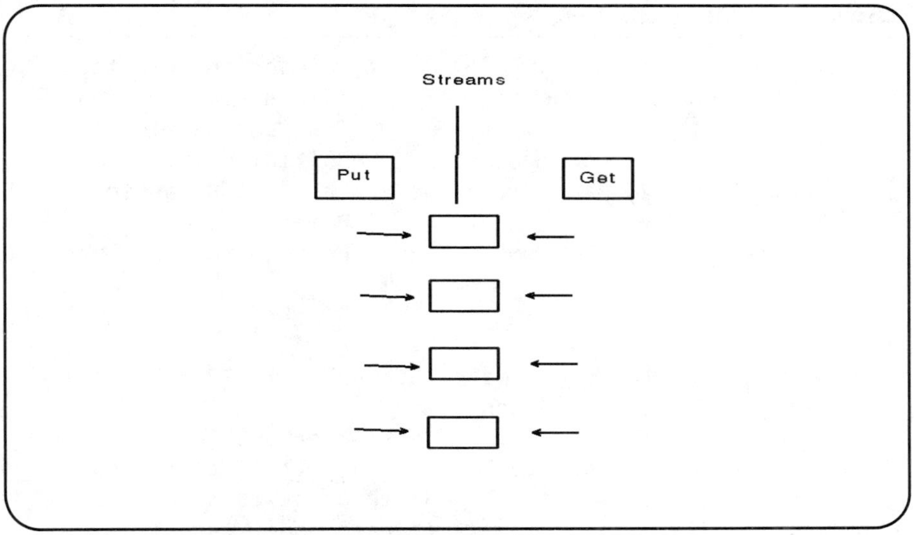

Figure 6.3. Streams.

By convention any stream constant begins with an `R` prefix.

The `ObjType` field is a number (a word type) that you define. ObjectWindows reserves the registration numbers 0 through 99, so your registration numbers can be anything from 100 through 65,535. The choice is yours, and it can be entirely arbitrary, but it is a good idea to maintain a file or library of stream registration numbers to make it easier to keep up with them.

The `VmtLink` field links your object to the Virtual method table (VMT). You simply assign it as the offset to your object type.

The `Load` and `Store` fields hold the addresses of the `Load` and `Store` methods of the object.

After you have constructed the stream registration record, you register the stream. Because all the examples in this chapter put collections in streams, you need to register the collection type as well as the point type, which is in the collection:

```
procedure StreamRegistration;
begin
  RegisterType(RCollection);
  RegisterType(RPoint);
end;
```

Modify the model to include methods for handling the stream (see listing 6.6).

Listing 6.6. Stream handling.

```
PModel1 = ^Model1;                    { Pointer to this task }
Model1 = object(MainWindow)           { Time series }
                                      { Task's data fields }
  InitX, InitY :    real;             { Initial points }
  RangeX1, RangeX2, RangeY1, RangeY2 : real; { Range to view }
  X, Y : integer;                     { Point to plot }
  A, B : real;                        { Factors for this model task }

  Points : PCollection;

  FileName: array[0..fsPathName] of Char;
  IsDirty, IsNewFile: Boolean;
                                { Task's methods }
  constructor Init(AParent: PWindowsObject; ATitle: PChar);
  procedure  Scale;             { Scale point to window }
  procedure  Iterate;           { Iterate model task }
  destructor Done; virtual;     { Clean up }
  procedure cm_Iterate(var Msg: TMessage);
    virtual cm_First + cm_Task1;
  procedure Paint(PaintDC: HDC; var PaintInfo:
   TPaintStruct); virtual;
  procedure LoadFile;
  procedure SaveFile;
end;
```

Define `Point`'s `Load` method to specifically handle the reading of the `X` and `Y` fields. `Read` is an abstract method of `TStream` and must be overridden to load specific objects:

```
constructor Point.Load(var S: TStream);
begin
  S.Read(X, SizeOf(X));
  S.Read(Y, SizeOf(Y));
end;
```

Define the `Store` Method to handle the writing of `Point`'s `X` and `Y` fields. `Write`, like `Read`, is an abstract `TStream` method, which must be overridden by any `TStream` descendant:

```
procedure Point.Store(var S: TStream);
begin
  S.Write(X, SizeOf(X));
  S.Write(Y, SizeOf(Y));
end;
```

Next, add the menu message response methods to the model task. Although you need to create only `FileOpen` and `FileSave` methods (to correspond to loading and saving points to a file), you can expand the model task at this point to include creating a new file (`FileNew`) and saving a file under a different name (`FileSaveAs`). These files make spiffy additions to any window or task that needs to do general file I/O. All these new methods use file dialogs (discussed in Chapter 3, "Objects for Windows") and employ the same stream methods for saving and getting points.

Add these four methods to the model object:

1. `procedure CMFileNew(var Msg: TMessage);`

   `virtual cm_First + cm_New;`

2. `procedure CMFileOpen(var Msg: TMessage);`

   `virtual cm_First + cm_Open;`

3. `procedure CMFileSave(var Msg: TMessage);`

   `virtual cm_First + cm_Save;`

4. `procedure CMFileSaveAs(var Msg: TMessage);`

   `virtual cm_First + cm_SaveAs;`

Again, the `CM` prefix is used to designate that the method responds to menu command messages. That way, it's easier to recognize these response methods.

The menu command messages (`cm_Save`, `cm_SaveAs`, `cm_Open`, and `cm_New`) already have been added to the `BasicInterface` (Chapter 4, "Inheriting an Interface"), so you need to just define and implement the responses.

`FileNew` looks like this:

```
procedure Model1.FileNew(var Msg: TMessage);
begin
  Points^.FreeAll;      { New collection }
  InvalidateRect(HWindow, nil, True); { Clear screen }
  IsDirty := False;     { Unchanged file flag }
  IsNewFile := True;    { New file flag }
end;
```

First `FileNew` deletes and disposes of all the items in the `collection` (using the `TCollection` method `FreeAll`). Then it forces a `Paint` message (`InvalidateRect`), which causes the display to be updated, using the new `Paint` method. Because there are no points to display, it clears the window. Finally, it sets some flags to specify that the file is new (`IsNewFile := True`) and that nothing new has been added to the file (`IsDirty := False`).

`FileOpen` looks like this:

```
procedure Model1.FileOpen(var Msg: TMessage);
begin
  if CanClose then
    if Application^.ExecDialog(New(PFileDialog,
      Init(@Self, PChar(sd_FileOpen),
      StrCopy(FileName, '*.PTS')))) = id_Ok then
      LoadFile;
end;
```

`FileOpen` sends a message (`ExecDialog`) to create a new file dialog object, and then opens the file (`sd_Open`). If all goes well, it loads the file, using the model's `LoadFile` method, which in turn uses the stream facilities you have just set up.

`FileSave` looks like this:

```
procedure Model1.FileSave(var Msg: TMessage);
begin
  if IsNewFile then FileSaveAs(Msg) else SaveFile;
end;
```

`FileSave` simply decides whether it is dealing with a `NewFile`, and if not, saves the file (using `SaveFile`, which is discussed in a moment).

`FileSaveAs` looks like this:

```
procedure Model1.FileSaveAs(var Msg: TMessage);
var
  FileDlg: PFileDialog;
begin
  if IsNewFile then StrCopy(FileName, '');
  if Application^.ExecDialog(New(PFileDialog,
    Init(@Self, PChar(sd_FileSave), FileName))) = id_Ok then
    SaveFile;
end;
```

`FileSaveAs` also sends a message (`ExecDialog`) to create a file dialog, and after it gets a `SaveName`, calls `SaveFile` to actually save the file. `SaveFile` is in listing 6.6.

Now you can `Store` points to a file and `Load` them into the application menu whenever you need to. The code in listing 6.8 at the end of this chapter shows the completely updated model simulation allowing storing and loading from files.

Add `Load` and `Store` Methods to point:

```
  PAPoint = ^APoint;
  APoint = object(TObject)
    X, Y: Integer;
    constructor Init(AX, AY: Integer);
    constructor Load(var S: TStream);
    procedure Store(var S: TStream);
  end;
```

Before you learn how a point (or any object) is put in a stream, note that adding collectable, streamable objects to the model also could be handled a bit differently. You can derive a new model object that only adds the new collectable, streamable details. That model could look like this:

```
PStreamModel1 = ^StreamModel1;     { Pointer to this task }
StreamModel1 = object(Model1)      { Time Series }
                                   { Task's data fields }
  Points : PCollection;
  FileName: array[0..fsPathName] of Char;
  IsDirty, IsNewFile: Boolean;
                                   { Task's methods }
  constructor Init(AParent: PWindowsObject; ATitle: PChar);
  procedure CMIterate(var Msg: TMessage);
            virtual cm_First + cm_Task1;
  procedure Paint(PaintDC: HDC; var PaintInfo:
            TPaintStruct); virtual;
  procedure LoadFile;
  procedure SaveFile;
end;
```

Only the new fields and new or reimplemented methods need to be designated in this new streamable object. The choice of when to derive and when to add to an existing object is a matter of taste and, to a certain extent, a matter of where you draw the general-specific line. Because the "unstreamable" model developed in Chapter 5, "Putting Pictures in Windows," needs stream and collection capability to be general-purpose, add that functionality to it rather than derive new objects to represent 1) a collectable and 2) a streamable version. Throughout your Windows (OOP programming) life, you have to decide how to handle many such decisions.

Putting Points in a Stream

Declare a variable of a stream type descended from `TStream` (either `TDosStream`, `TBufStream`, or `TEmsStream`).

TDosStream implements unbuffered DOS file streams. Its constructor allows you to specify a file access mode (stCreate, stOpenRead, stOpenWrite, and stOpen). Use a TDosStream if you do not have to read and write many small chunks of data.

TBufStream implements buffered DOS file streams. It allows you to specify the size of a buffer, and thus is useful for reading and writing small chunks of data.

TEMSStream implements streams in EMS memory.

In this example, you use TDosStream:

```
var
  TheFile: TDosStream;
```

and initialize it:

```
  TheFile.Init(FileName, stCreate);
```

After the stream is initialized, you can Put to it and Get from it. The following line puts all the points in the collection in the stream:

```
  TheFile.Put(Points);
```

How Put Works

You put objects on a stream and Put does all the work. You do not need to know how Put works, but for the pleasure of it, the underlying workings are covered here.

First the stream takes the VMT pointer from offset 0 of the object (point, in this case) and tries to match it with an object registered with it. If it finds a matching registered object, it writes the stream's registration number to the stream's destination. In this example, the stream's destination is a file, so the first thing it writes to the file is the object's ID number. This step is important because it uses that ID later when it tries to get objects from the stream.

The stream then sends a message to the object's Store method (which you have to define when you define the object), which stores the object itself. Store uses the low-level write procedure for writing the object to the stream. It is best to use the SizeOf function, as you did in storing a point, to make sure that the correct number of bytes are written to the stream:

```
S.Write(X, SizeOf(X));
S.Write(Y, SizeOf(Y));
```

That is all there is to putting an object in a stream. The object does not need to know anything about the stream, just how to load and store itself. The streaming details (like most everything else in the ObjectWindows bag of tricks) are handled for you.

The only other detail you need to take care of is explicitly sending a destructor message to cleanup:

```
TheFile.Done;
```

Because `TheFile` (in this case) is a stream type derived from `TDosStream`, it already has a destructor (`TDosStream.Done`), which takes care of the cleanup automatically. You do not need to reimplement it.

The code in listing 6.7 saves all the points created by `Model1`.

Listing 6.7. *Saving all points created by* `Model1`.

```
procedure Model1.SaveFile;
var
  TheFile: TDosStream;

begin
  TheFile.Init(FileName, stCreate);
  TheFile.Put(Points);
  TheFile.Done;
  IsNewFile := False;
  IsDirty := False;
end;
```

Alternatively, you could have used other streams (`TBufStream`, and so on), and the implementation would have been similar.

Getting Points

Getting points out of a stream is just as simple. You declare variables to represent the collection and the stream:

```
var:

  TempColl: PCollection;
  AFile: TDosStream;
```

Initialize the stream (`AFile`), and specify that you want to open it for reading (using `stOpen`):

```
AFile.Init(FileName, stOpen);
```

Then get the objects:

```
TempColl := PCollection(TheFile.Get);
```

The Get process is the reverse of the Put. First Get retrieves the object's ID number and scans the registered stream types until it finds a matching ID number. The registration record contains the address of the Load method for the object. Get then sends a message to the Load method, which uses the stream's Read method to actually read objects from the file one at a time:

```
S.Read(X, SizeOf(X));
S.Read(Y, SizeOf(Y));
```

Note again that Read relies on the SizeOf function to determine the correct size of the object it needs to read.

Then clean up, by sending a Done message:

```
TheFile.Done;
```

Again, the destructor has already been implemented for you, so you do not have to do anything other than send the Done message to TheFile (a TDosStream).

Listing 6.8 shows the complete code necessary for reading the points stored to the stream earlier. Note again the InvalidateRect procedure, which forces a repaint message to be sent to the object. As discussed earlier, the Paint message (which is now defined for the Model1 object) causes the points to be displayed.

Listing 6.8. Reading points already stored to the stream.

```
procedure Model1.LoadFile;
var
  TempColl: PCollection;
  TheFile: TDosStream;
begin
  TheFile.Init(FileName, stOpen);
  TempColl := PCollection(TheFile.Get);
  TheFile.Done;
  if TempColl <> nil then
  begin
    Dispose(Points, Done);
    Points := TempColl;
    InvalidateRect(HWindow, nil, True);  {forces Paint message}
  end;
  IsDirty := False;
  IsNewFile := False;
end;
```

Putting it all together, listing 6.8 shows how to extend the model task from Chapter 5, “Putting Pictures in Windows,” making it collectable, streamable, and repaintable.

The Sum of Streams

Streams are polymorphic. All a stream needs to know is that it is dealing with an object derived from `TObject`. Thus, you can put different object types in the same stream.

Your programming responsibility is simply to define and register the kinds of objects you want the stream to handle. You can then put objects in the stream and get them back using the methods provided for you in ObjectWindows.

Registering objects, as shown, is a simple matter, almost automatic. Putting and getting objects to and from a stream is almost automatic as well. Your primary programming task is to register objects with a stream and keep an inventory of your registered object records.

Streams and collections are classic cases of potentially difficult programming tasks becoming almost trivial with Turbo Pascal for Windows. (You probably think that Turbo Pascal for Windows has taken most the work out of developing Windows applications. You are right.)

Using the `BasicInterface` and its multitask extensions discussed in Chapter 5, “Putting Pictures in Windows,” you can almost roll into any application problem and add the new behaviors you need for your specific problem. You modify and extend, not reinvent, using OOP techniques.

Windows complexity is encapsulated in ObjectWindows objects, from which you derive your objects, using inheritance. Many of the basic programming problems, such as file I/O and data collecting, have been generalized beautifully, so you use polymorphism to handle them. Streams and collections are excellent examples of how OOP simplifies, yet empowers, programming tasks.

Windows and OOP (Turbo Pascal for Windows-style) are fine examples of how a sophisticated graphics environment and a programming language can both simplify and empower. If you have tried to develop Windows applications using the SDK or even Borland’s C++, you already know this. Turbo Pascal for Windows allows you to avoid many musty levels (see listing 6.9).

***Listing 6.9.** Making a collectable, streamable, and repaintable task.*

```
unit Time3;             { A Model Task }
                        { Responds to cm_Task1 (message) }
                        { Adds streams to Time2 }
interface

uses WObjects,          { Units specific to this unit }
```

continues

Listing 6.9. continued

```
   WinTypes,
   WinProcs,
   strings,
   StdDlgs,
   WinDos,
   WIF5;               { Basic Interface : contains MainWindow }
                       {                 :   BasicApplication }

{$R TIME1.RES}         { This task's new resources }

type

PModel1 = ^Model1;                     { Pointer to this task }
Model1 = object(MainWindow)            { Time Series }
                                       { Task's data fields }
  InitX, InitY :    real               { Initial points }
  RangeX1, RangeX2, RangeY1, RangeY2 : real; { Range to view }
  X, Y : integer;                      { Point to plot }
  A, B : real;                         { Factors for this model task }

  Points : PCollection;

  FileName: array[0..fsPathName] of Char;
  IsDirty, IsNewFile: Boolean;

                                       { Task's methods }
  constructor Init(AParent: PWindowsObject; ATitle: PChar);
  procedure  Scale;                    { Scale point to window }
  procedure  Iterate;                  { Iterate model task }
  destructor Done; virtual;            { Clean up }
  procedure cm_Iterate(var Msg: TMessage);
  virtual cm_First + cm_Task1;

  procedure Paint(PaintDC: HDC; var PaintInfo:
   TPaintStruct); virtual;

  procedure FileNew(var Msg: TMessage);
    virtual cm_First + cm_New;
  procedure FileOpen(var Msg: TMessage);
    virtual cm_First + cm_Open;
  procedure FileSave(var Msg: TMessage);
    virtual cm_First + cm_Save;
```

```
  procedure FileSaveAs(var Msg: TMessage);
    virtual cm_First + cm_SaveAs;
  procedure LoadFile;
  procedure SaveFile;

end;

  PAPoint = ^APoint;
  APoint = object(TObject)
    X, Y: Integer;
    constructor Init(AX, AY: Integer);
    constructor Load(var S: TStream);
    procedure Store(var S: TStream);
  end;

implementation


const
  RAPoint: TStreamRec = (
    ObjType: 500;
    VmtLink: Ofs(TypeOf(APoint)^);
    Load: @APoint.Load;
    Store: @APoint.Store);


procedure StreamRegistration;
begin
  RegisterType(RCollection);
  RegisterType(RAPoint);
end;


constructor APoint.Init(AX, AY: Integer);
begin
  X := AX;
  Y := AY;
end;


const
   Iterations = 3000;      { Number of iterations for this model }
```

continues

Listing 6.9. continued

```
constructor Model1.Init(AParent: PWindowsObject; ATitle: PChar);
begin
  TWindow.Init(AParent, ATitle);
  Attr.Menu := LoadMenu(HInstance, PChar(111));
  DisableAutoCreate;
  Attr.Style := ws_PopupWindow or ws_Caption or ws_Visible;

  Attr.X := 100;              { Set window dimensions }
  Attr.Y := 50;
  Attr.W := 300;
  Attr.H := 200;

  RangeX1 :=  -1.03;          { Set ranges to view }
  RangeX2 :=  1.27;
  RangeY1 :=  -0.3;
  RangeY2 :=  0.45;

  A := 1.4;                   { Set factors }
  B := 0.3;
  InitX := 0.4;
  InitY := 0;

  X := 0;                     { Initial point in space }
  Y := 0;

  Points := New(PCollection, Init(50, 50));

  IsDirty := False;
  IsNewFile := True;
  StreamRegistration;         { Register stream }


end;


procedure Model1.cm_Iterate(var Msg: TMessage);
begin
   Iterate;                   { Iterate the model }
end;

procedure Model1.Scale;
```

```
begin                              { Scale point in space to window }
   If (InitX = RangeX1) then       { A little troubleshooting }
     X := Attr.X;
   If (InitX = RangeX2) then
     X := Attr.W;                  { and here }
   If (InitX = 0) then
     X := X;
   If (InitX > RangeX1) then
      X := round((InitX - RangeX1)/(RangeX2 - RangeX1) *
             (Attr.W - Attr.X));
   Y := Attr.H - (round((InitY - RangeY1)/(RangeY2 - RangeY1) *
            (Attr.H - Attr.Y)));
end;

destructor Model1.Done;
begin

   Dispose(Points,Done);           { Clean up points }
   TWindow.Done;                   { Call ancestor's destructor }
end;

procedure Model1.Iterate;
var
  I : integer;
  TempX, TempY : real;

begin
   InvalidateRect(HWindow, nil,True);
   SetCapture(HWindow);
   DC := GetDC(HWindow);           { Get a display context }
   for I := 1 to Iterations do
   begin
      TempX := InitX;              { Save last state }
      TempY := InitY;              { Save last state }
      InitX := TempY + 1 - (A * TempX * TempX); {This model }
      InitY := B * TempX;                       {This model }
      Scale;                    { Scale new state to a window }
      X := I;
      TextOut(DC,X,Y,'.',1);      { Draw a point }
      Points^.Insert(New(PAPoint, Init(X, Y)));
   end;
```

continues

Listing 6.9. continued

```
   ReleaseCapture;
   ReleaseDC(HWindow,DC);        { Release Display context }
end;


procedure Model1.Paint(PaintDC: HDC; var PaintInfo: TPaintStruct);
var
  First: Boolean;

   procedure DisplayPoints(P: PAPoint); far;
   begin
      TextOut(PaintDC,P^.X,P^.Y,'.',1);
      First := False;
   end;

begin
  First := True;
  Points^.ForEach(@DisplayPoints);
end;


procedure Model1.FileNew(var Msg: TMessage);
begin
  Points^.FreeAll;
  InvalidateRect(HWindow, nil, True);
  IsDirty := False;
  IsNewFile := True;
end;

procedure Model1.FileOpen(var Msg: TMessage);
begin
  if CanClose then
    if Application^.ExecDialog(New(PFileDialog,
      Init(@Self, PChar(sd_FileOpen),
      StrCopy(FileName, '*.PTS')))) = id_Ok then
      LoadFile;
end;

procedure Model1.FileSave(var Msg: TMessage);
begin
  if IsNewFile then FileSaveAs(Msg) else SaveFile;
end;
```

```
procedure Model1.FileSaveAs(var Msg: TMessage);
var
  FileDlg: PFileDialog;
begin
  if IsNewFile then StrCopy(FileName, '');
  if Application^.ExecDialog(New(PFileDialog,
    Init(@Self, PChar(sd_FileSave), FileName))) = id_Ok then
    SaveFile;
end;

procedure Model1.LoadFile;
var
  TempColl: PCollection;
  TheFile: TDosStream;
begin
  TheFile.Init(FileName, stOpen);
  TempColl := PCollection(TheFile.Get);
  TheFile.Done;
  if TempColl <> nil then
  begin
    Dispose(Points, Done);
    Points := TempColl;
    InvalidateRect(HWindow, nil, True); { Forces Paint message }
  end;
  IsDirty := False;
  IsNewFile := False;
end;


procedure Model1.SaveFile;
var
  TheFile: TDosStream;
begin
  TheFile.Init(FileName, stCreate);
  TheFile.Put(Points);
  TheFile.Done;
  IsNewFile := False;
  IsDirty := False;
end;


constructor APoint.Load(var S: TStream);
begin
  S.Read(X, SizeOf(X));
```

continues

Listing 6.9. continued

```
  S.Read(Y, SizeOf(Y));
end;

procedure APoint.Store(var S: TStream);
begin
  S.Write(X, SizeOf(X));
  S.Write(Y, SizeOf(Y));
end;


end. { Unit time3 }
```

PART TWO

ADVANCED TOPICS

7

CHAPTER

MANY WINDOWS: A MULTI-DOCUMENT INTERFACE

It's an inherent property of intelligence that it can jump out of the task which it's performing, and survey what it has done; it is always looking for, and often finding, patterns.

Douglas R. Hofstadter

ObjectWindows supports the Windows Multi-Document Interface (MDI) standard, which allows an application or task to work simultaneously with many open documents. Usually you think of these documents as text, database, or spreadsheet files.

You might think of this as a special kind of multitasking system, similar yet decidedly different from the multitasking version of the `BasicInterface` developed in Chapter 5, "Putting Pictures in Windows." The key difference between the `BasicInterface` and MDI is that MDI makes it easy for a single application window to work with many open files. A good example of this kind of application is a multifile editor, demonstrated later in this chapter.

The `BasicInterface` can have many applications running simultaneously, which means many open files, but it is still primarily a "1 window, 1 task, 1 open file" system. In the `BasicInterface`, one file is open for each window, and each window has its own menu.

In an MDI system, a single menu serves as the control center for several windows at once. The Turbo Pascal IDE and Microsoft Excel are excellent examples of MDI in sophisticated action (see figure 7.1).

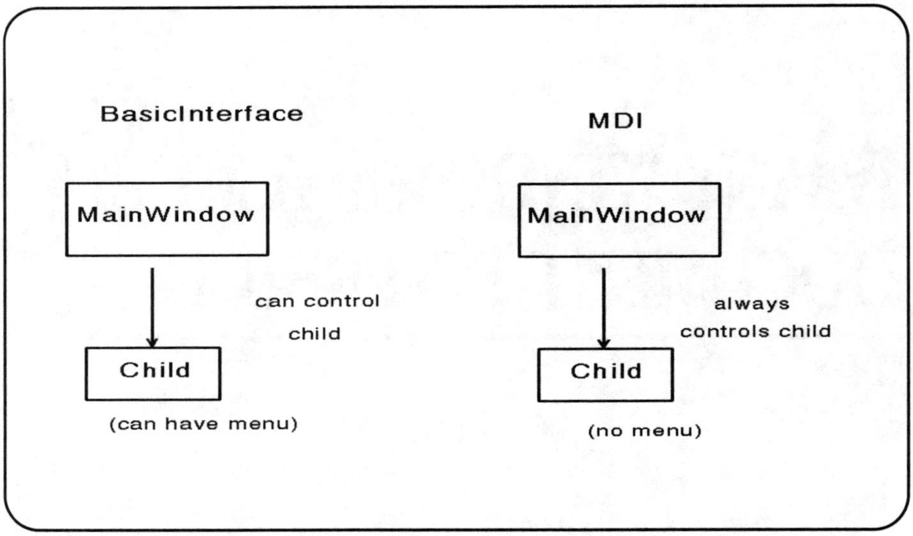

***Figure** 7.1.* `BasicInterface` *versus MDI.*

You can add multidocument capability to the `BasicInterface` by writing more code to handle additional open files, but an easier way is to use an MDI object and derive from it the specific applications you need.

This chapter shows you how to create a Basic `MDI Interface`, which is then used to derive two additional MDI applications.

A Basic MDI Interface

Just as the `BasicInterface` does, the `MDI Interface` consists of two basic objects: an `Application` and a `MainWindow`.

As you might expect, they look similar. The MDI Application object (also derived from `TApplication`) reimplements two methods: `InitMainWindow` and `InitApplication` (see figure 7.2).

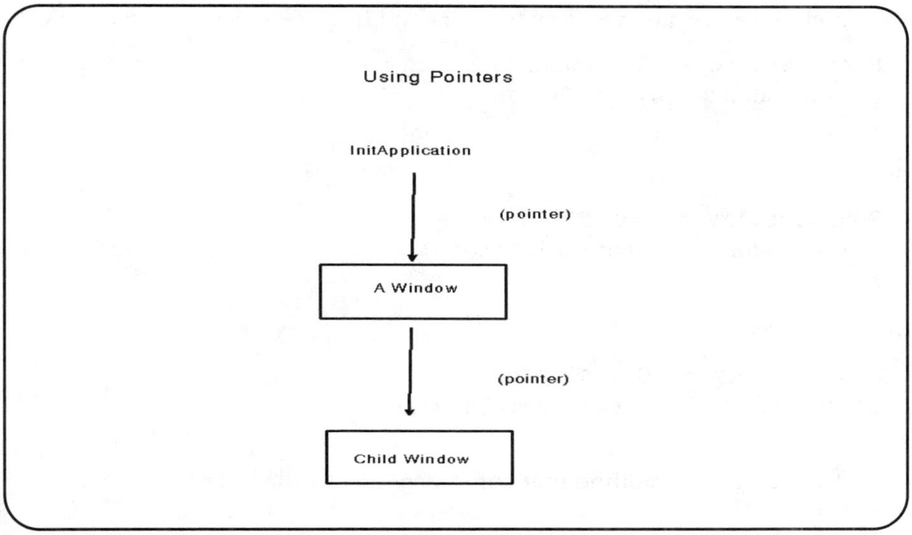

***Figure** 7.2. Using pointers.*

To designate between the `BasicInterface` and the `MDI Interface`, add "MDI" to MDI object names. A Basic MDI Application object looks like this:

```
MDIApplication = object(TApplication) { Derive an application object }
  FirstApplication : boolean;
  procedure InitMainWindow;  virtual; { Init a mainwindow }
  procedure InitApplication; virtual;
end;
```

The `MainMDIWindow` looks like this:

```
PMainMDIWindow = ^MainMDIWindow;
MainMDIWindow = object(TMDIWindow)
 function InitChild : PWindowsObject; virtual;
end;
```

There are two new things to notice:

1. You derive the `MainMDIWindow` from `TMDIWindow`.
2. You need to reimplement an `InitChild` method, which is responsible for constructing the specific kind of child window you want to attach to the `MainMDIWindow`.

A child can be any window type derived from TWindow. For example:

```
PChildWindow = ^ChildWindow;
ChildWindow = object(TWindow)
end;
```

or

```
PChildWindow = ^ChildWindow;
ChildWindow = object(MainWindow)
end;
```

or

```
PChildWindow = ^ChildWindow;
ChildWindow = object(ModelWindow)
end;
```

An InitChild method that constructed a ChildWindow might look like this:

```
function MainMDIWindow.InitChild : PWindowsObject;
begin
   InitChild := New(PChildWindow, Init(@Self, 'New child'));
end;
```

The InitChild method is not limited, however, to constructing a ChildWindow only; it can just as easily construct a TWindow or MainWindow directly:

```
function MainMDIWindow.InitChild : PWindowsObject;
begin
   InitChild := New(PMainWindow, Init(@Self, 'New child'));
end;
```

Several components (or features) are common to any MDI application. Every MDI application has a main window (called a frame window), and within the frame window an invisible window called the MDI client window, which holds MDI child windows. The client window manages (behind the scenes) its MDI child windows. In fact, TMDIWindow's methods mainly construct and manage child windows and process menu selections.

Each MDI frame window must have a menu that controls its child windows. Each child window is maintained in the frame window's ChildList (a linked list).

The frame window's menu is called a *child window menu*. Each time a child window is constructed and opened, it is appended to this menu automatically, and the currently selected child window is marked by a check.

Each child window can be maximized, minimized, tiled, and cascaded (features implemented for you already).

A few restrictions are placed on a child window:

1. It cannot have a menu; thus all its methods must be controlled by the frame window. This limitation is a good reason to use the `BasicInterface` if you need a multitasking system in which each window controls its own destiny.

2. The child window cannot extend outside the frame window's boundaries (`BasicInterface` child windows can).

Setting Up a Basic MDI Interface

It is simple enough to establish a Basic `MDI Interface`. It consists of an application object and an `MDI` Window (plus its menu). Actually, you have already seen the objects you need for a bare-bones interface. See listing 7.1 for the complete "first go" at the `MDI Interface`. Figure 7.3 shows the application created by this "first go."

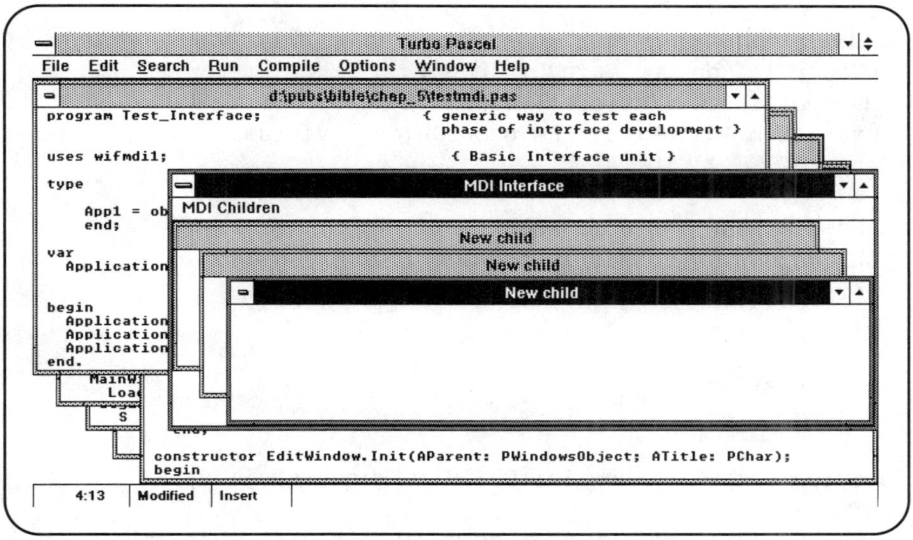

Figure 7.3. The application created by listing 7.1.

Listing 7.1. The first listing for the `MDI Interface`.

```
unit WIFmdi1;  { Creates a Basic MDI Windows application
                 interface derived from ObjectWindows;
                 ChildWindows are derived from TWindow object }
interface

uses
   WObjects,
   WinTypes,
   WinProcs,
   WIF5;

{$R WIFMdi1.RES }

type

  MDIApplication = object(TApplication) { Derive an application object
    FirstApplication : boolean;
    procedure InitMainWindow;  virtual; { Init a main window }
    procedure InitApplication; virtual;
  end;

  PMainMDIWindow = ^MainMDIWindow;
  MainMDIWindow = object(TMDIWindow)
   function InitChild : PWindowsObject; virtual;
  end;

  PChildWindow = ^ChildWindow;
  ChildWindow = object(TWindow)
  end;


implementation


function MainMDIWindow.InitChild : PWindowsObject;
begin
   InitChild := New(PChildWindow, Init(@Self, 'New child'));
end;
```

```
{ MDIApplication method implementation }

procedure MDIApplication.InitMainWindow;
begin
  if FirstApplication then
    MainWindow := New(PMainMDIWindow, Init('MDI Interface',
    LoadMenu(HInstance, 'MDIMenu1')))
  else
    MainWindow := New(PMainMDIWindow, Init('MDI Additional
      Instance',LoadMenu(HInstance, 'MDIMenu1')));
end;

procedure MDIApplication.InitApplication;
begin
   FirstApplication := True;
end;

end.
```

Look familiar? It should—it is a simplified version of the first version of the `BasicInterface`. It uses similar `InitApplication` and `InitMainWindow` methods. `InitMainWindow`, as in the `BasicInterface`, decides which window to construct and which menu to load. One minor difference between `MDIWindows` and `TWindows` is that the second parameter of the `LoadMenu` method must be a string.

A Model MDI

As written, a `ChildWindow` can be any kind of window derived from `TWindow`. For example, you could change one of the task models (windows objects) from Chapter 5, "Putting Pictures in Windows," to a child window and have a task window created each time you create a child. Listing 7.2 shows the code to handle it, and figure 7.4 shows the result. Note that the model window appears, but without its menu because child windows, regardless of type, are expected to be controlled by the frame window's child menu. The model, as it is designed, works when it is responding to the main menu's command messages, but not otherwise—a definite, and probably unwanted, variation on the model theme.

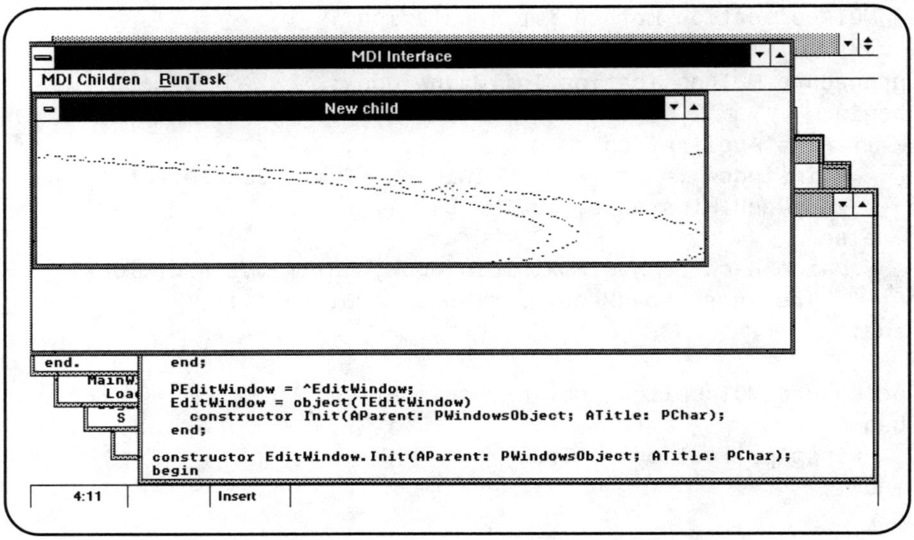

Figure 7.4. The result of listing 7.2.

Listing 7.2. Creating a task window for each child window.

```
unit WIFmdi3;  { Creates a Basic MDI Windows application
                 interface derived from ObjectWindows;
                 ChildWindows are derived from Model2 object }
interface

uses
   WObjects,
   WinTypes,
   WinProcs,
   WIF5,
   attract2;

{$R WIFMdi3.RES }

type

  MDIApplication = object(TApplication) { Derive an application object }
    FirstApplication : boolean;
    procedure InitMainWindow;  virtual; { Init a main window }
    procedure InitApplication; virtual;
  end;
```

```
  PMainMDIWindow = ^MainMDIWindow;
  MainMDIWindow = object(TMDIWindow)
   function InitChild : PWindowsObject; virtual;
  end;

  PChildWindow = ^ChildWindow;
  ChildWindow = object(Model2)
  end;


implementation

function MainMDIWindow.InitChild : PWindowsObject;
begin
   InitChild := New(PChildWindow, Init(@Self, 'New child'));
end;


{ MDIApplication method implementation }


procedure MDIApplication.InitMainWindow;
begin
  if FirstApplication then
    MainWindow := New(PMainMDIWindow, Init('MDI Interface',
    LoadMenu(HInstance, 'MDIMenu3')))
  else
  MainWindow := New(PMainMDIWindow, Init('MDI Additional Instance',
    LoadMenu(HInstance, 'MDIMenu3')));
end;

procedure MDIApplication.InitApplication;
begin
   FirstApplication := True;
end;

end.
```

MDI Message Processing

Message processing in MDI windows is similar to that in non-MDI windows. Each Windows command message (cm_) goes first to the child window currently selected. A child, therefore, gets the first chance to respond to the message. If it does not respond, the message goes to the MDI client window, and finally to the MDI frame window.

Each time you select an MDI child window, it becomes active and receives a Windows `wm_MDIActivate` message. You can, if you want, define a message-response method for this message (useful when you need to keep track of the active `ChildWindow`).

MDI child windows do not respond to command messages generated by the child window menu. That is a job for the frame window.

Editors

Before you get to the grand finale of this chapter, a multi-document text editor using the `MDI Interface`, you can implement a couple of simple editors to show you how easy it is to add powerful text-editing capability to a window.

ObjectWindows supplies two descendants of `TWindow`, which are specialized windows for text editing. `TEditWindow` is a text editor that enables you to edit text in a window: cut, copy, paste, and so on, to the clipboard, but does not allow you to read and write files. One of its descendants, `TFileWindow`, adds reading and writing to file capability.

These editors are ready to go and are useful right out of the box. To use an `Edit` window requires no more than a message to its `constructor` when you initialize an application's `MainWindow`.

The definition:

```
FileWindow = ^FileWindow;
FileWindow = object(TFileWindow)
  constructor Init(AParent: PWindowsObject; ATitle: PChar);
end;
```

The Implementation:

```
procedure Application.InitMainWindow;
begin
  MainWindow := New(PEditWindow, Init(nil, 'Edit Window Tester'));
end;
```

Simple, yes?

Listing 7.3 shows the complete code for generating the text editor shown in figure 7.5.

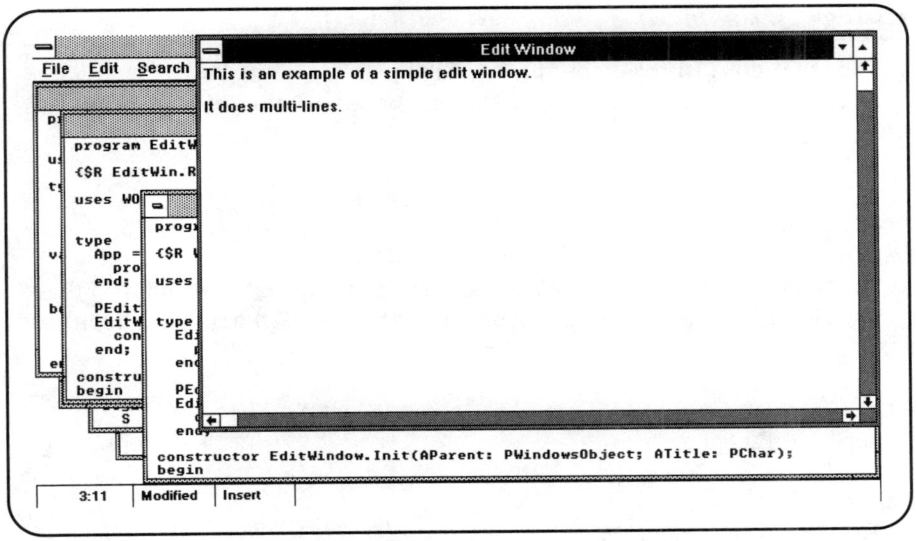

Figure 7.5. The text editor generated by listing 7.3.

Listing 7.3. Generating a text editor.

```
program EditWin;

{$R EditWin.RES}

uses WObjects, WinTypes, WinProcs, Strings, StdWnds;


type
  EditApp = object(TApplication)
    procedure InitMainWindow; virtual;
  end;

  PEditWindow = ^EditWindow;
  EditWindow = object(TEditWindow)
    constructor Init(AParent: PWindowsObject; ATitle: PChar);
  end;

constructor EditWindow.Init(AParent: PWindowsObject; ATitle: PChar);
begin
```

continues

Listing 7.3. continued

```
  TEditWindow.Init(AParent, ATitle);
  Attr.Menu := LoadMenu(HInstance, MakeIntResource(105));
end;


procedure EditApp.InitMainWindow;
begin
  MainWindow := New(PEditWindow, Init(nil, 'Edit Window'));
  HAccTable := LoadAccelerators(HInstance, MakeIntResource(100));
end;

var
  App : EditApp;

begin
  App.Init('EditWnd');
  App.Run;
  App.Done;
end.
```

Adding a `FileWindow` to an application is just as easy. Just derive the `EditWindow` from `TFileWindow` rather than from `TEditWindow`:

```
  EditWindow = ^EditWindow;
  EditWindow = object(TFileWindow)
    constructor Init(AParent: PWindowsObject; ATitle: PChar);
  end;

constructor EditWindow.Init(AParent: PWindowsObject; ATitle: PChar);
begin
  TFileWindow.Init(AParent, ATitle, nil);
  Attr.Menu := LoadMenu(HInstance, 'FileCommands');
end;
```

The `FileWindow` comes complete with a `FileDialog` for creating, opening, and saving files; complete clipboard connections including an Undo command, and a search and replace facility. The only "programming" required of you is creating a menu that contains the predefined IDs for file manipulation. All you need to add is a Search menu choice.

Note: The Turbo Pascal source code and resources are on the user disk in the back of this book. Chapter 8, "Resources and Control Objects," details resource creation.

Listing 7.4 shows the complete code for implementing the File window editor shown in figure 7.6.

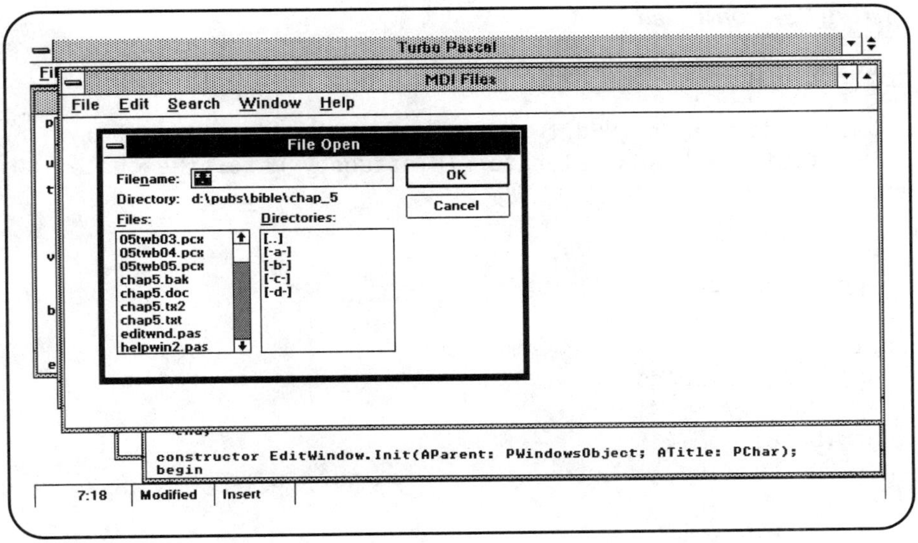

Figure 7.6. A file window editor.

Listing 7.4. Generating a file window editor.

```
program EditWin;

{$R EditWin.RES}

uses WObjects, WinTypes, WinProcs, Strings, StdWnds;


type
  EditApp = object(TApplication)
    procedure InitMainWindow; virtual;
  end;

  PEditWindow = ^EditWindow;
  EditWindow = object(TFileWindow)
    constructor Init(AParent: PWindowsObject; ATitle: PChar);
  end;

constructor EditWindow.Init(AParent: PWindowsObject; ATitle: PChar);
begin
  TEditWindow.Init(AParent, ATitle);
  Attr.Menu := LoadMenu(HInstance, MakeIntResource(105));
end;
```

continues

Listing 7.3. continued

```
procedure EditApp.InitMainWindow;
begin
  MainWindow := New(PEditWindow, Init(nil, 'Edit Window'));
  HAccTable := LoadAccelerators(HInstance, MakeIntResource(100));
end;

var
  App : EditApp;

begin
  App.Init('FileWnd');
  App.Run;
  App.Done;
end.
```

An MDI Editor

Now that you have created a FileWindow, you can use it as your MDI child window. It is just another window as far as the MDI application is concerned.

`TFileWindow` already has a rich set of methods for handling many of the menu command messages an editor needs to respond to, such as cut, copy, saving a file, and so on.

Table 7.1 lists the command-message response methods you use "as is," with no modification, in this example.

Table 7.1. *`FileWindow` methods.*

Method	*Responds to Command Message*
CMEditClear	cm_First + cm_EditClear
CMEditCopy	cm_First + cm_EditCopy
CMEditCut	cm_First + cm_EditCut
CMEditDelete	cm_First + cm_EditDelete
CMEditPaste	cm_First + cm_EditPaste
CMEditUndo	cm_First + cm_EditUndo
CMFileSave	cm_First + cm_FileSave
CMFileSaveAs	cm_First + cm_FileSaveAs

You need to modify the MDI MainWindow to handle the menu command messages to create and open files.

The new CMNewFile method needs to construct a new file editor. It looks like this:

```
procedure MDIFileWindow.CMNewFile(var Msg: TMessage);
begin
  Application^.MakeWindow(New(PFileEditor, Init(@Self, '')));
end;
```

The new CMOpenFile method needs to execute a file dialog and construct a new file editor. It looks like this:

```
procedure MDIFileWindow.CMOpenFile(var Msg: TMessage);
var
  FileName: array[0..fsPathName] of Char;
begin
  if Application^.ExecDialog(New(PFileDialog, Init(@Self,
    PChar(sd_FileOpen), StrCopy(FileName, '*.*')))) = id_Ok then
    Application^.MakeWindow(New(PFileEditor, Init(@Self, FileName)));
end;
```

It also would be convenient if menu items could be turned on and off, depending on whether a menu item is usable at the time. The easiest way to handle this enabling and disabling is to override MDIFileWindows' SetupWindow method to disable specific menu items. Then when a FileWindow is created, you enable the menu items.

The new SetupWindow method simply uses TMDIWindow's default SetupWindow (which has been called automatically if you have not overridden it) and then calls the EnableMenuItems method.

> **Note**: Whenever you override basic methods, such as SetupWindow, destructors, and so on, you often need to send a message explicitly to the ancestor's method to handle default processing. Sending a message to a method is simpler than rewriting the default code!

The new SetupWindow looks like this:

```
procedure MDIFileWindow.SetupWindow;
begin
  TMDIWindow.SetupWindow;
  EnableMenuItems(Disable);
end;
```

The `EnableMenuItems` implementation ensures that menu selections are available only when an editor is active. Its implementation is shown in the code for the entire MDI editor unit in listing 7.6 at the end of this chapter.

One other essential modification is to override the default `FileWindow` `destructor` to enable it to destroy all the editors created during an MDI session. The default `destructor` does not look automatically for the file editors you or your user might have created.

Fortunately, it is a simple matter to implement this new `destructor`, using the MDI `ForEach` method. A new `destructor` for `MDIFileWindow` looks like this:

```
destructor MDIFileWindow.Done;

   procedure DestroyEditors(AnEditor : PWindowsObject); far;
   begin
      PFileEditor(AnEditor)^.Done;
   end;
begin
   if (EditorCount) <> 0 then
   ForEach(@DestroyEditors);
   TMDIWindow.Done;
end;
```

There are also a few nifty features you can add to this editor to make it look even more similar to the Turbo Pascal for Windows ID. You can load an `Icon` for the `FileEditor` by modifying the `GetWindowClass` method:

```
procedure FileEditor.GetWindowClass(var AWndClass: TWndClass);
begin
  TFileWindow.GetWindowClass(AWndClass);
  AWndClass.hIcon := LoadIcon(HInstance, 'FILEICON');
end;
```

You also can save and restore states (Turbo Pascal for Windows style) by writing the window's current state and cursor position to a stream (in this case, a file) and reading it back. To save a state:

```
begin
  S := New(PBufStream, Init(DskFile, stCreate, 1024));
  PutChildren(S^);               { Handles the save }
  if S^.Status <> stOk then      { Status check }
  begin
    Dispose(S, Done);
    FileDelete(DskFile);
    MessageBox(HWindow, 'Unable to write desktop file.',
'Disk error',
```

```
    mb_Ok or mb_IconExclamation);
  end
  else Dispose(S, Done);
```

PutChildren, a TWindows object method, is the key to saving the state. It iterates through the window's child window list, writing the contents of each of the child windows to the stream.

To restore a state, use another TWindows object method, GetChildren, to do most of the work. TWindowsObject.GetChildren reads the stored contents' child windows from the stream, and puts them in the window's child window list.

Restore looks like this:

```
procedure MDIFileWindow.CMRestoreState(var Msg: TMessage);
var
  S: PStream;
  ErrorMsg: PChar;
begin
  ErrorMsg := nil;
  S := New(PBufStream, Init(DskFile, stOpenRead, 1024));
  if S^.Status <> stOk then          { Error checking }
    ErrorMsg := 'Unable to open desktop file.'
  else
  begin
    CloseChildren;
    GetChildren(S^);                 { Handles the restore }
    if S^.Status <> stOk then
    ErrorMsg := 'Error reading desktop file.';
    if LowMemory then                { More error checking }
    begin
    CloseChildren;
    ErrorMsg := 'Not enough memory to open file.'
    end
    else CreateChildren;
  end;
  if ErrorMsg <> nil then
    MessageBox(HWindow, ErrorMsg, 'Disk error', mb_Ok or
mb_IconExclamation);
end;
```

Finally, you can add a Help Window to the MDI FileEditor, using a HelpWnd unit like the one in listing 7.5 that uses a list box, buttons, and a control to implement a sample help window.

Listing 7.5. Creating a Help window.

```
unit HelpWind;

interface

uses Strings,
   WObjects,
   WinTypes,
   WinProcs;

const
  id_LB1 = 201;
  id_BN1 = 202;
  id_BN2 = 203;
  id_EC1 = 204;
  id_ST1 = 205;

type

  PHelpWindow = ^THelpWindow;
  THelpWindow = object(TWindow)
    LB1: PListBox;
    EC1: PEdit;
    constructor Init(AParent: PWindowsObject; ATitle: PChar);
    procedure SetupWindow; virtual;
    procedure IDLB1(var Msg: TMessage); virtual id_First + id_LB1;
    procedure IDBN1(var Msg: TMessage); virtual id_First + id_BN1;
    procedure IDBN2(var Msg: TMessage); virtual id_First + id_BN2;
    procedure FillEdit(SelStringPtr: PChar); virtual;
  end;

implementation

constructor THelpWindow.Init(AParent: PWindowsObject;
ATitle: PChar);
var
  TempStat : PStatic;
  TempBtn: PButton;
begin
  TWindow.Init(AParent, ATitle);
  DisableAutoCreate;
  Attr.Style := ws_PopupWindow or ws_Caption or ws_Visible;
  Attr.X := 100;
  Attr.Y := 100;
```

```
Attr.W := 300;
Attr.H := 300;
LB1 := New(PListBox, Init(@Self, id_LB1, 20, 20, 180, 80));
TempBtn := New(PButton, Init(@Self, id_BN1, 'Help', 220, 20, 60, 30, True));
TempBtn := New(PButton, Init(@Self, id_BN2, 'Cancel', 220, 70, 60, 30, False));
EC1 := New(PEdit, Init(@Self, id_EC1, '', 20, 180, 260, 90, 40, True));
EC1^.Attr.Style := EC1^.Attr.Style or ws_Border or ws_VScroll;
TempStat := New(PStatic, Init(@Self, id_ST1,'Help Information:',
                 20, 160, 160, 20, 0));
d;

ocedure THelpWindow.SetupWindow;
gin
TWindow.SetupWindow;
{ Fill the listbox }
LB1^.AddString('Help1');
LB1^.AddString('Help2');
LB1^.AddString('Help3');
LB1^.AddString('Help4');
LB1^.SetSelIndex(0);
d;

ocedure THelpWindow.IDLB1(var Msg: TMessage);
r
SelString: array[0..25] of Char;
gin
if Msg.LParamHi = lbn_DblClk then
begin
  LB1^.GetSelString(SelString, 25);
  FillEdit(SelString);
end;
d;

ocedure THelpWindow.IDBN1(var Msg: TMessage);
r
SelString: array[0..25] of Char;
gin
LB1^.GetSelString(SelString, 25);
FillEdit(SelString);
d;

ocedure THelpWindow.IDBN2(var Msg: TMessage);
gin
CloseWindow;
d;
```

continues

Listing 7.5. continued

```
procedure THelpWindow.FillEdit(SelStringPtr: PChar);
var
  TheString: PChar;
begin
  if StrComp(SelStringPtr, 'List Boxes') = 0 then
    TheString :=   'Help1.'
  else if StrComp(SelStringPtr, 'Buttons') = 0 then
    TheString :=   'Help2.'
  else if StrComp(SelStringPtr, 'Scroll Bars') = 0 then
    TheString :=   'Help3'
  else if StrComp(SelStringPtr, 'Edit Controls') = 0 then
    TheString :=   'Help4.';
  EC1^.SetText(TheString);
end;

end.
```

Figure 7.7 shows the complete MDI File Editor with several file editors open, and listing 7.6 shows the complete MDI File editor code that produced figure 7.7.

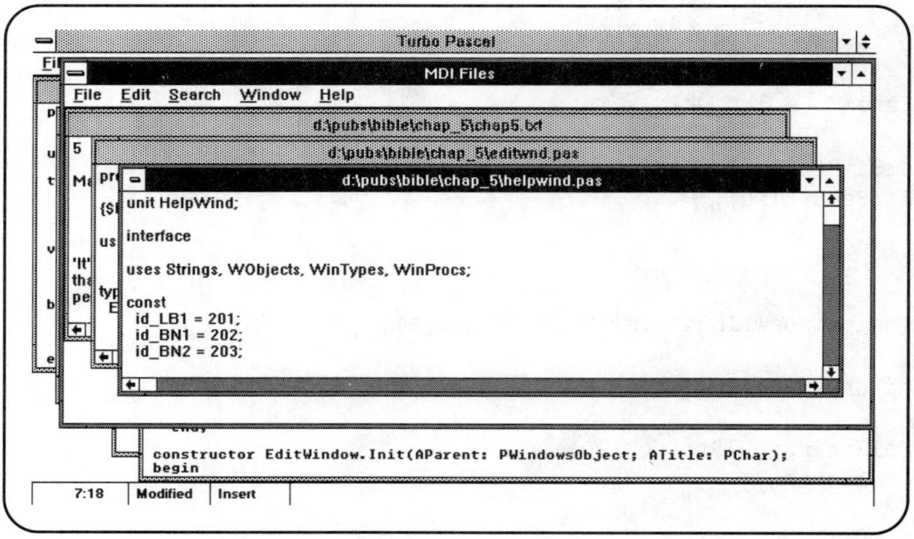

Figure 7.7. The MDI file editor.

MDI Wrap-up

That about wraps up the `MDI Interface` and the first stage of the introduction to developing Windows applications using Turbo Pascal for Windows. Chapter 8, "Resources and Control Objects," explains how to develop resources using the Whitewater Group's Resource Toolkit.

By now you should be getting the message that developing sophisticated applications for Windows is not a complicated, messy affair, but actually a pleasant one if you use Turbo Pascal for Windows. Windows development is not difficult if you use the OOP techniques outlined in these first seven chapters.

The complex part of Windows development is teaching an application to interact with Windows, and that interaction is already handled for you when you use ObjectWindows. You just need to make your applications respond to events and messages and use OOP techniques to derive your applications and windows. When you have learned to adjust your own thinking to OOP terms, application development for Windows is just as easy as application development for any other environment. In fact, application development for Windows is easier because the interface, including device drivers, I/O, and so forth, is already handled for you.

Developing one-window or many-window applications using Turbo Pascal for Windows is a piece of delicious cake—topping, your choice—really.

Listing 7.6. *Creating the complete MDI editor.*

```
unit mdi_ed2;                    { Adds File Editor to MDI }

{$R MDIed.RES}

interface

uses WObjects,
   WinTypes,
   WinProcs,
   WinDos,
   StdDlgs,
   StdWnds,
   Strings,
   HelpWind;

const
  cm_SaveState    = 200;
  cm_RestoreState = 201;
  cm_Help = 901;
```

continues

Listing 7.6. continued

```
const
  DskFile = 'MDI.DSK';

type

  { Declare MDIApp, a TApplication descendant }
  MDIApp = object(TApplication)
    procedure InitMainWindow; virtual;
    procedure InitInstance; virtual;
  end;

  { Declare MDIFileWindow, a TMDIWindow descendant }
  PMDIFileWindow = ^MDIFileWindow;
  MDIFileWindow = object(TMDIWindow)
    destructor Done; virtual;
    procedure SetupWindow; virtual;
    procedure CMNewFile(var Msg: TMessage);
    virtual cm_First + cm_MDIFileNew;
    procedure CMOpenFile(var Msg: TMessage);
    virtual cm_First + cm_MDIFileOpen;
    procedure CMSaveState(var Msg: TMessage);
    virtual cm_First + cm_SaveState;
    procedure CMRestoreState(var Msg: TMessage);
    virtual cm_First + cm_RestoreState;
    procedure CMHelp(var Msg: TMessage);
    virtual cm_First + cm_Help;
  end;


  { Declare TFileEditor, a TFileWindow descendant }
  PFileEditor = ^FileEditor;
  FileEditor = object(TFileWindow)
    constructor Init(AParent: PWindowsObject; AFileName: PChar);
    destructor Done; virtual;
    procedure GetWindowClass(var AWndClass: TWndClass);
virtual;
    function GetClassName: PChar; virtual;
  end;

const
  RFileEditor: TStreamRec = (
    ObjType: 1000;
    VmtLink: Ofs(TypeOf(TFileEditor)^);
    Load:    @TFileEditor.Load;
```

```
 Store:   @TFileEditor.Store);

FileEditor }

st
ditorCount: Integer = 0;

e
MenuState = (Enable, Disable);


lementation

cedure MDIFileWindow.CMHelp(var Msg: TMessage);

HelpWnd: PWindow;
gin
HelpWnd := New(PHelpWindow, Init(@Self, 'Help System'));
Application^.MakeWindow(HelpWnd);
d;

cedure EnableMenuItems(State: TMenuState);

cedure EnableCommand(Command: Word);

NewState: Word;
gin
NewState := mf_ByCommand;
if State = Enable then Inc(NewState, mf_Enabled)
else Inc(NewState, mf_Disabled + mf_Grayed);
EnableMenuItem(PWindow(Application^.MainWindow)^.Attr.Menu, Command, NewState);
d;

gin
EnableCommand(cm_FileSave);        { Response methods already built-in }
EnableCommand(cm_FileSaveAs);      { To TFileWindow }
EnableCommand(cm_ArrangeIcons);    { To TFileWindow }
EnableCommand(cm_TileChildren);
EnableCommand(cm_CascadeChildren);
EnableCommand(cm_CloseChildren);
EnableCommand(cm_EditCut);
EnableCommand(cm_EditCopy);
EnableCommand(cm_EditPaste);
EnableCommand(cm_EditDelete);
```

continues

Listing 7.6. continued

```
  EnableCommand(cm_EditClear);
  EnableCommand(cm_EditUndo);
  EnableCommand(cm_EditFind);
  EnableCommand(cm_EditReplace);
  EnableCommand(cm_EditFindNext);
end;

procedure IncEditors;
begin
  if EditorCount = 0 then EnableMenuItems(Enable); { New editor }
  Inc(EditorCount);
end;

procedure DecEditors;
begin
  Dec(EditorCount);
  if EditorCount = 0 then EnableMenuItems(Disable);
end;

constructor FileEditor.Init(AParent: PWindowsObject; AFileName:PChar);
begin
  TFileWindow.Init(AParent, '', AFileName);
  IncEditors;                    { Keep track of the number of editors }
end;

destructor FileEditor.Done;
begin
  TFileWindow.Done;              { Auto destruct using ancestor's Done }
  DecEditors;
end;

procedure FileEditor.GetWindowClass(var AWndClass: TWndClass);
begin
  TFileWindow.GetWindowClass(AWndClass);      { Optional icon }
  AWndClass.hIcon := LoadIcon(HInstance, 'FILEICON');
end;

function FileEditor.GetClassName: PChar;
begin
  GetClassName := 'FileEditor';
end;

procedure MDIFileWindow.CMNewFile(var Msg: TMessage);
```

```
begin
  Application^.MakeWindow(New(PFileEditor, Init(@Self, '')));
end;

destructor MDIFileWindow.Done;  { Destroy all editors }

   procedure DestroyEditors(AnEditor : PWindowsObject); far;
   begin
      PFileEditor(AnEditor)^.Done;
   end;
begin
   if (EditorCount) <> 0 then
   ForEach(@DestroyEditors);    { Use ForEach to destroy all editors }
   TMDIWindow.Done;
end;

procedure MDIFileWindow.SetupWindow;
begin
  TMDIWindow.SetupWindow;
  EnableMenuItems(Disable); { Menu items are not usable yet, so disable them }
end;

procedure MDIFileWindow.CMOpenFile(var Msg: TMessage);
var
  FileName: array[0..fsPathName] of Char;
begin
  if Application^.ExecDialog(New(PFileDialog, Init(@Self, PChar(sd_FileOpen),
    StrCopy(FileName, '*.*')))) = id_Ok then
    Application^.MakeWindow(New(PFileEditor, Init(@Self, FileName)));
end;

 { Save the position and contents of the windows to a desktop file. }
procedure MDIFileWindow.CMSaveState(var Msg: TMessage);
var
  S: PStream;

function FileDelete(Name: PChar): Integer; assembler;
asm
      PUSH  DS
      LDS   DX,Name
      MOV   AH,41H
      INT   21H
      JC @@1
      XOR   AX,AX
```

continues

Listing 7.6. continued

```
@@1:  NEG   AX
        POP   DS
end;

begin
  S := New(PBufStream, Init(DskFile, stCreate, 2048));
  PutChildren(S^);
  if S^.Status <> stOk then
  begin
    Dispose(S, Done);
    FileDelete(DskFile);
    MessageBox(HWindow, 'Unable to write desktop file.',
           'Disk error',  mb_Ok or mb_IconExclamation);
  end
  else Dispose(S, Done);
end;

{ Read windows positions and contents from a "desktop" file. }
procedure MDIFileWindow.CMRestoreState(var Msg: TMessage);
var
  S: PStream;
  ErrorMsg: PChar;
begin
  ErrorMsg := nil;
  S := New(PBufStream, Init(DskFile, stOpenRead, 1024));
  if S^.Status <> stOk then
    ErrorMsg := 'Unable to open desktop file.'
  else
  begin
    CloseChildren;
    GetChildren(S^);
    if S^.Status <> stOk then
    ErrorMsg := 'Error reading desktop file.';
    if LowMemory then
    begin
    CloseChildren;
    ErrorMsg := 'Not enough memory to open file.'
    end
    else CreateChildren;
  end;
  if ErrorMsg <> nil then
    MessageBox(HWindow, ErrorMsg, 'Disk error', mb_Ok or mb_IconExclamation);
end;
```

```
procedure MDIApp.InitMainWindow;
begin
  MainWindow := New(PMDIFileWindow, Init('MDI Files',
    LoadMenu(HInstance, 'Commands')));
  PMDIFileWindow(MainWindow)^.ChildMenuPos := 3;

     { Register types to be written to stream }
  RegisterType(RWindow);
  RegisterType(REdit);
  RegisterType(RFileEditor);
end;

procedure MDIApp.InitInstance;
begin
  TApplication.InitInstance;
  if Status = 0 then
     { Optional loading of accelerator table }
  begin
    HAccTable := LoadAccelerators(HInstance, 'FileCommands');
    if HAccTable = 0 then
    Status := em_InvalidWindow;
  end;
end;

end.
```

8

CHAPTER

RESOURCES AND CONTROL OBJECTS

Everyone agrees that the world is full of large objects. Sometimes the world is also full of large projects.

Andrei Codrescu

The previous seven chapters discussed object-oriented programming in general and its appropriateness to Windows application development in particular. The Turbo Pascal for Windows side of Windows application development was covered, using resources and control objects, but without detailing how you create and maintain resources and control objects.

Before you go a little deeper into resources and control objects, make sure that you understand the Pascal side of Windows application development. In general, it is a three-step process:

1. Deriving an application and a `MainWindow` (from the abstract objects in ObjectWindows).

2. Connecting the application and its `MainWindow` to resources.

3. Teaching the new application to respond to events and messages generated by Windows and resources, such as menus.

As it has been shown, OOP techniques simplify Windows application development by

- Encapsulating Windows' complexity in objects.
- Allowing you to derive new objects from existing ones (using inheritance).
- Allowing your applications to send general messages that another window or application responds to as it sees fit (using polymorphism).
- Making it easy for applications to use dynamic objects, collections, and streams, and thus allowing applications to mix and match objects, lists, and files of varying size and number.

The first part of this chapter shifts gears and explains how you create and maintain resources. The second part shows you several more ways to use the user interface devices called controls or control objects.

Resources

Resources are the menus, dialog boxes (or windows), bit maps, icons, keyboard accelerators, strings, and cursors that your Turbo Pascal for Windows applications use to establish a consistent, user-friendly interface.

You create resources outside of Turbo Pascal for Windows by

1. Using a resource editor to generate a linkable (binary) file.
2. Using a text editor to create a resource script file, which you "compile" or link into your executable (.EXE) file using the Microsoft Resource Compiler.

Resource code and Pascal code are stored in separate files (with RES and PAS extensions) and maintained as separate entities. This separation of entities is advantageous for several reasons:

- One resource, for example, can be used by more than one application.
- A resource or an application can be changed (and recompiled) without recompiling the other.
- Resources are, by default, *not loaded* into memory when the application starts. Rather, they are loaded when the application requests them. Figure 8.1 illustrates this concept.

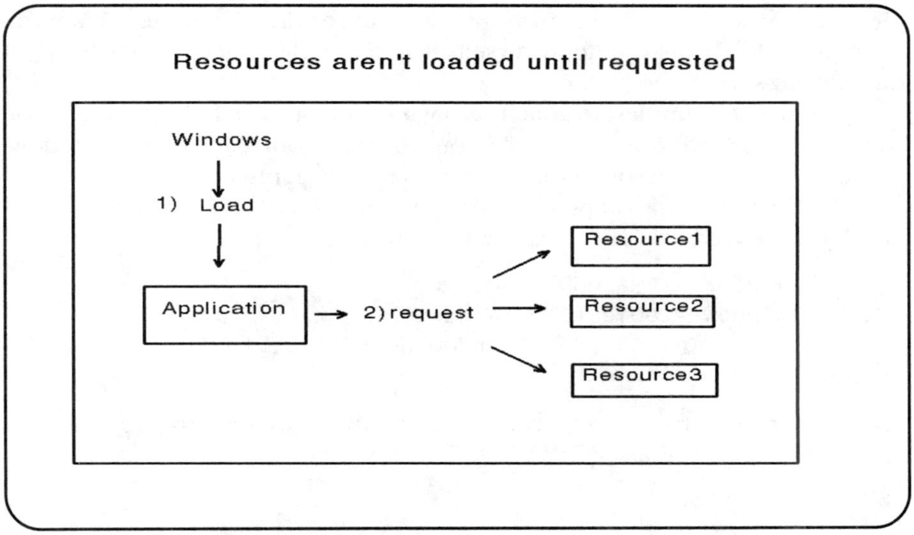

***Figure 8.1.** Resources are loaded when an application requests them.*

Resources are the specifications (expressed as data) for the corresponding interface elements (menus, dialogs, and so forth) that Windows constructs for your application. Resource data are stored in the EXE file, but not in the application's data segment, where you might expect them to be stored. Resource data and Pascal source code data do not compete for the same space.

You "connect" resources to the EXE file in one of the following ways:

1. Copying resources from a RES file into the compiled application's EXE file using the Whitewater Resource Toolkit (or another resource editor)
2. Adding the `{$R}` compiler directive to your `.PAS` file
3. Using the Microsoft Resource Compiler

The simplest alternative, used in the examples so far, is to use the `{$R}` compiler directive. This directive tells the compiler that you want to add the specified resource file to the end of the executable file. Note that you can compile Pascal source code that uses resources before you actually create the resources. Thus, you can write and test the Pascal or resource part of the application in either order.

If you use the `{$R}` directive to attach resources, however, it means that the resource and the Pascal source code are bound unless you unbind them by recompiling the Pascal source code. In other words, you cannot eliminate a resource specified by the `{$R}` directive without recompiling the Pascal source code. You can still add new resources by copying new resources into the EXE file, but you risk some confusion by mixing resources in this manner. When you compile code exclusively for yourself, it is probably easier to use the `{$R}` directive to specify resources.

For me, it is simplest to attach each window to its own resource file. If you want to change a window's resource, you edit the resource file for that window. A one-window, one-resource-file scenario reduces confusion.

For example, in Chapter 7, "Many Windows: A Multi-Document Interface," you derived a `MainMDIWindow` from `TMDIWindow`:

```
PMainMDIWindow = ^MainMDIWindow;
 MainMDIWindow = object(TMDIWindow)
     function InitChild : PWindowsObject; virtual;
 end;
```

and connected it to its resource, first using the {$R} directive to attach its resources to the EXE file:

```
{$R WIFMdi1.RES }
```

and then by attaching a menu resource (in MDIMainWindow.RES) to `MainMDIWindow`:

```
procedure MDIApplication.InitMainWindow;
begin
     if FirstApplication then
       MainWindow := New(PMainMDIWindow, Init('MDI Interface',
          LoadMenu(HInstance, 'MDIMenu1')))
     else
       MainWindow := New(PMainMDIWindow, Init('MDI Additional Instance',
          LoadMenu(HInstance, 'MDIMenu1')));
end;
```

The resource editor (the Whitewater Resource Toolkit) is usually preferred to create resources interactively. To have fun and to illuminate what a resource editor does for you behind the scenes, however, you will poke around a bit in a resource script file. Listing 8.1 shows a simple resource script file generated with the Whitewater Resource Toolkit (after creating the resource interactively) and the Turbo Pascal for Windows editor. The resource Scriptfile consists entirely of a menu resource specification. Later in this chapter, you learn easier ways to create resources using the Whitewater Resource Toolkit.

Listing 8.1. *A simple resource script file.*

```
106  MENU LOADONCALL MOVEABLE PURE DISCARDABLE
BEGIN
     POPUP "&File"
     BEGIN
          MenuItem  "&New", 101
          MenuItem  "&Open", 102
          MenuItem  "&Save", 103
          MenuItem  "Save&As", 104
     END
     MenuItem  "&WriteText", 501
     MenuItem  "&Help", 901
END
```

Each resource is a short block of information with a beginning and an end. The menu resource, for example, has a name:

```
EditMenu MENU
```

followed by a Pascal-like block of code:

```
BEGIN
     ....
END
```

which specifies menu items and their corresponding command messages:

```
MENUITEM "..." cm_F..
```

The specification for a dialog box might look like this in a .RC (script) file:

```
AboutBox DIALOG 30, 35, 150,100
CAPTION "A Dialog"
STYLE DS_MODALFRAME ¦ WS_CAPTION ¦ WS_SYSMENU
FONT 10, "Helv"
BEGIN
     CTEXT "A Dialog"          -1,  0,  20,  160,  10
     CTEXT "More text"         -1,  0,  28,  160,  10
     ICON  "An Icon"           -1,  8,   8,    0,   0
     DEFPUSHBUTTON "OK",    IDOK, 50,  45,   30,  14
END
```

Listing 8.2 shows a much more complex resource (.RC) file. Note that it includes not only menu and submenu resource specifications but also many other resources as well: dialogs, bit maps, strings, accelerators, and so on.

Listing 8.2. A complex resource file.

```
#include "rwpdemoc.pas"

men_Main MENU
BEGIN
     POPUP "&File"
     BEGIN
          MENUITEM "&New", cm_New
          MENUITEM "&Open...", cm_Open
          MENUITEM SEPARATOR
          MENUITEM "&Save", cm_Save
          MENUITEM "Save &as...", cm_SaveAs
          MENUITEM SEPARATOR
          MENUITEM "&Print...", cm_Print
          MENUITEM SEPARATOR
          MENUITEM "E&xit", cm_Exit
     END

     POPUP "&Edit"
     BEGIN
          MENUITEM "&Undo       Alt+Backspace", cm_Undo, GRAYED
          MENUITEM SEPARATOR
          MENUITEM "Cu&t        Shift+Del", cm_Cut, GRAYED
          MENUITEM "&Copy       Ctrl+Ins", cm_Copy, GRAYED
          MENUITEM "&Paste      Shift+Ins", cm_Paste, GRAYED
          MENUITEM SEPARATOR
          MENUITEM "Cl&ear               ", cm_Clear, GRAYED
          MENUITEM "D&elete", cm_Delete, GRAYED
     END

     POPUP "&View"
     BEGIN
          MENUITEM "&All", cm_All, GRAYED, CHECKED
          MENUITEM "&Some...", cm_Some, GRAYED
          MENUITEM SEPARATOR
          MENUITEM "&By...", cm_By, GRAYED
     END

     POPUP "&Options"
     BEGIN
          MENUITEM "&Directories...", cm_Directories
          MENUITEM SEPARATOR
          POPUP "&Environment"
          BEGIN
               MENUITEM "&Preferences...", cm_Preferences
```

```
                MENUITEM "&Mouse...", cm_Mouse
            END

            MENUITEM SEPARATOR
            MENUITEM "&Open...", cm_Options_Open
            MENUITEM "&Save", cm_Options_Save
            MENUITEM "Save &as...", cm_Options_SaveAs
        END

        POPUP "&Window"
        BEGIN
            MENUITEM "&Tile", cm_Tile
            MENUITEM "&Cascade", cm_Cascade
            MENUITEM "Arrange &icons", cm_ArrangeIcons
            MENUITEM "Close &all", cm_CloseAll, GRAYED
        END

     POPUP "&Help"
     BEGIN
         MENUITEM "&Index            Shift+F1", cm_Index, GRAYED
         MENUITEM "&Topic Search    Ctrl+F1", cm_Topic_Search, GRAYED
         MENUITEM "&Glossary", cm_Glossary, GRAYED
         MENUITEM "Using &Help", cm_Using_Help, GRAYED
         MENUITEM SEPARATOR
         MENUITEM "&About RWPDemo...", 145
     END

END

dlg_Open DIALOG 5, 17, 165, 149
CAPTION "Open"
STYLE WS_POPUP ¦ WS_CAPTION ¦ WS_SYSMENU
BEGIN
     LTEXT "File &name:", -1, 5, 3, 38, 12
     CONTROL "", 100, "COMBOBOX", CBS_DROPDOWN ¦ WS_VSCROLL
                   ¦ WS_GROUP ¦ WS_TABSTOP, 46, 2, 111, 44
     LTEXT "Path:", -1, 8, 18, 16, 8
     LTEXT "", 103, 29, 18, 127, 9, SS_LEFT ¦ WS_GROUP
     LTEXT "&Files:", -1, 12, 32, 16, 8
     LTEXT "&Directories", -1, 96, 33, 51, 9
     CONTROL "", 101, "LISTBOX", LBS_STANDARD, 6, 43, 70, 59
     CONTROL "", 102, "LISTBOX", LBS_STANDARD, 92, 43, 70, 59
     CONTROL "Options", -1, "button", BS_GROUPBOX ¦
               WS_GROUP, 8, 105, 150, 22
```

continues

Listing 8.2. continued

```
     CONTROL "&Text", 205, "BUTTON", BS_AUTORADIOBUTTON ¦
              WS_TABSTOP, 17, 113, 37, 12
     CONTROL "&Scribble", 206, "BUTTON", BS_AUTORADIOBUTTON ¦
              WS_TABSTOP, 68, 113, 36, 12
     CONTROL "&Graph", 207, "BUTTON", BS_AUTORADIOBUTTON ¦
              WS_TABSTOP, 118, 113, 35, 12
     DEFPUSHBUTTON "&OK", 1, 11, 130, 24, 14
     PUSHBUTTON "&Cancel", 2, 71, 130, 28, 14
     PUSHBUTTON "&Help", 210, 135, 130, 24, 14
END
dlg_SaveAs DIALOG 10, 18, 129, 147
CAPTION "Save As"
STYLE WS_POPUP ¦ WS_CAPTION ¦ WS_SYSMENU
BEGIN
     LTEXT "File &name:", -1, 8, 2, 38, 12
     CONTROL "", 100, "COMBOBOX", CBS_DROPDOWN ¦ WS_VSCROLL
              ¦ WS_GROUP ¦ WS_TABSTOP, 48, 2, 76, 38
     LTEXT "Path:", -1, 9, 19, 16, 8
     LTEXT "", 101, 29, 21, 92, 8
     LTEXT "&Directories", -1, 14, 30, 68, 9
     CONTROL "", 103, "LISTBOX", LBS_STANDARD, 11, 40, 70, 59
     DEFPUSHBUTTON "&OK", 1, 6, 127, 24, 14
     PUSHBUTTON "&Cancel", 2, 51, 127, 28, 14
     PUSHBUTTON "&Help", 210, 98, 127, 24, 14
END
dlg_Print DIALOG 36, 14, 163, 133
CAPTION "Print"
STYLE WS_POPUP ¦ WS_CAPTION ¦ WS_SYSMENU
BEGIN
     LTEXT "Copies:", -1, 5, 11, 28, 8
     LTEXT "", 211, 35, 12, 16, 8, WS_GROUP
     CONTROL "", -1, "static", SS_BLACKFRAME, 35, 10, 16, 10
     CONTROL "Pages", -1, "button", BS_GROUPBOX, 4, 24, 155, 30
     CONTROL "&All", 212, "BUTTON", BS_AUTORADIOBUTTON ¦
              WS_TABSTOP, 36, 29, 28, 12
     CONTROL "&Partial", 213, "BUTTON", BS_AUTORADIOBUTTON ¦
              WS_TABSTOP, 36, 41, 35, 8
     CONTROL "", 214, "static", SS_GRAYFRAME, 98, 41, 12, 8
     LTEXT "From:", -1, 75, 41, 19, 8
     LTEXT "To:", -1, 114, 41, 16, 8
     CONTROL "", 215, "static", SS_GRAYFRAME, 134, 41, 11, 8
     LTEXT "Printers", -1, 6, 61, 31, 8
     CONTROL "", 216, "LISTBOX", LBS_STANDARD, 3, 70, 143, 37
     DEFPUSHBUTTON "P&rint", 217, 5, 114, 24, 14
     PUSHBUTTON "Printer &setup...", 218, 37, 114, 51, 14
```

```
    PUSHBUTTON "&Cancel", 2, 97, 114, 27, 14
    PUSHBUTTON "&Help", 210, 133, 114, 24, 14
END

acc_Main ACCELERATORS
BEGIN
    VK_BACK, 24325, VIRTKEY, ALT
    VK_DELETE, 24320, VIRTKEY, SHIFT
    VK_INSERT, 24321, VIRTKEY, CONTROL
    VK_INSERT, 24322, VIRTKEY, SHIFT
    VK_F1, 141, VIRTKEY, SHIFT
    VK_F1, 142, VIRTKEY, CONTROL
END


dlg_About DIALOG 82, 19, 121, 86
CAPTION "About CUA"
STYLE WS_POPUP ¦ WS_CAPTION ¦ WS_SYSMENU
BEGIN
    LTEXT "Common User Access  Example", -1, 10, 5, 108, 11
    LTEXT "Copyright (c) 1990, Borland International", -1,
            26, 49, 70, 15
    DEFPUSHBUTTON "&OK", 1, 49, 69, 24, 14
    ICON "icon_1", -1, 53, 25, 16, 16
END



DIALOG_5 DIALOG 11, 18, 177, 79
CAPTION "Directories"
STYLE WS_POPUP ¦ WS_CAPTION ¦ WS_SYSMENU
BEGIN
    LTEXT "&Scribble Directory", -1, 9, 5, 66, 10, SS_LEFT
            ¦ WS_GROUP
    LTEXT "&Text Directory", -1, 9, 22, 64, 10, SS_LEFT ¦
            WS_GROUP
    LTEXT "&Graphics Directory", -1, 9, 40, 64, 8, SS_LEFT
            ¦ WS_GROUP
    CONTROL "", ID_ScribbleDirectory, "COMBOBOX",   CBS_DROPDOWN
            ¦ WS_VSCROLL ¦ WS_TABSTOP, 80, 4, 95, 32
    CONTROL "", id_TextDirectory, "COMBOBOX", CBS_DROPDOWN
            ¦ WS_VSCROLL ¦ WS_TABSTOP, 80, 22, 95, 32
    CONTROL "", id_GraphicDirectory, "COMBOBOX",
        CBS_DROPDOWN ¦ WS_VSCROLL ¦ WS_TABSTOP, 80, 40,
            95, 32
```

continues

Listing 8.2. continued

```
     DEFPUSHBUTTON "&OK", id_Ok, 16, 61, 24, 14
     PUSHBUTTON "&Cancel", id_Cancel, 68, 61, 26, 14
     PUSHBUTTON "&Help", id_Help, 122, 61, 24, 14
END
dlg_Preferences DIALOG 13, 21, 210, 88
CAPTION "Preferences"
STYLE WS_POPUP ¦ WS_CAPTION ¦ WS_SYSMENU
BEGIN
     CONTROL "Desktop file", -1, "button", BS_GROUPBOX, 5,
          7, 88, 52
     CONTROL "&None", 222, "BUTTON", BS_AUTORADIOBUTTON ¦
          WS_TABSTOP, 11, 17, 78, 11
     CONTROL "C&urrent directory", 223, "BUTTON",
          BS_AUTORADIOBUTTON ¦ WS_TABSTOP, 11, 28, 74, 13
     CONTROL "Conf&ig file directory", 224, "BUTTON",
          BS_AUTORADIOBUTTON ¦ WS_TABSTOP, 11, 41, 73, 12
     CONTROL "Autosave", -1, "button", BS_GROUPBOX, 97, 7,
          109, 52
     CONTROL "&Editor files", 225, "BUTTON", BS_AUTOCHECKBOX
          ¦ WS_TABSTOP, 102, 18, 91, 9
     CONTROL "&Environment", 226, "BUTTON", BS_AUTOCHECKBOX
          ¦ WS_TABSTOP, 102, 31, 88, 9
     CONTROL "&Desktop", 227, "BUTTON", BS_AUTOCHECKBOX ¦
          WS_TABSTOP, 102, 44, 60, 9
     DEFPUSHBUTTON "&OK", 1, 23, 67, 24, 14
     PUSHBUTTON "&Cancel", 2, 72, 67, 37, 14
     PUSHBUTTON "&Help", 210, 134, 67, 24, 14
END


dlg_Mouse DIALOG 14, 12, 190, 97
CAPTION "Mouse"
STYLE WS_POPUP ¦ WS_CAPTION ¦ WS_SYSMENU
BEGIN
     CONTROL "&Right mouse button", -1, "button",
          BS_GROUPBOX, 8, 5, 77, 59
     CONTROL "", 231, "scrollbar", SBS_HORZ, 95, 32, 86, 9
     LTEXT "Mouse Click", -1, 93, 11, 90, 9
     LTEXT "Fast", -1, 95, 22, 16, 8
     LTEXT "Slow", -1, 161, 22, 16, 8
     CONTROL "&Reverse mouse buttons", 232, "BUTTON",
          BS_AUTOCHECKBOX ¦ WS_TABSTOP, 97, 48, 90, 9
     CONTROL "&Nothing", 228, "BUTTON", BS_AUTORADIOBUTTON ¦
          WS_TABSTOP, 18, 19, 55, 12
```

```
    CONTROL "&Clear Window", 229, "BUTTON",
        BS_AUTORADIOBUTTON | WS_TABSTOP, 18, 33, 55, 12
    CONTROL "&Inverse Color", 230, "BUTTON",
        BS_AUTORADIOBUTTON | WS_TABSTOP, 18, 47, 55, 12
    DEFPUSHBUTTON "&Ok", 1, 11, 76, 24, 14
    PUSHBUTTON "&Cancel", 2, 64, 76, 30, 14
    PUSHBUTTON "&Help", 210, 123, 76, 24, 14
END


RCDATA_1 RCDATA
BEGIN
"\07\07Wake up!!\07\07\0"
, "\11Hello world"
, 25
0x05f
"\07"

END

CURSOR_1 CURSOR rwdemo.CUR


ico_RWPDemo ICON rwdemo.ICO


STRINGTABLE
BEGIN
    sth_FileNew, "Help on New"
    sth_FileOpen, "Help on Open"
    sth_FileSave, "Help on Save"
    sth_FileSaveAs, "Help on SaveAs"
    sth_FilePrint, "Help on Print"
    sth_FileExit, "Help on Exit"
    sth_File, "Help on File"
    sth_EditUndo, "Help on Undo"
    sth_EditCut, "Help on Cut"
    sth_EditCopy, "Help on Copy"
    sth_EditPaste, "Help on Paste"
    sth_EditClear, "Help on Clear"
    sth_EditDelete, "Help on Delete"
    sth_Edit, "Help on Edit"
    sth_ViewAll, "Help on View All"
    sth_ViewSome, "Help on View Some"
    sth_ViewBy, "Help on View By"
```

continues

Listing 8.2. continued

```
     sth_View, "Help on View"
     sth_OptionsDirectory, "Help on Directories"
     sth_OptionsEnvironment, "Help on Environment"
     sth_OptionsOpen, "Help on Options Open"
     sth_OptionsSave, "Help on Options Save"
     sth_OptionsSaveAs, "Help on Options Save As"
     sth_Option, "Help on Option"
     sth_EnvironmentPreferences, "Help on Preferences"
     sth_EnvironmentMouse, "Help on Mouse"
     sth_WindowTile, "Help on Window Tile"
     sth_WindowCascade, "Help on Window Cascade"
     sth_WindowArrange, "Help on Window Arrange"
     sth_WindowIcon, "Help on Window Icon"
     sth_WindowCloseAll, "Help on Window CloseAll"
     sth_Window, "Help on Window"
     sth_HelpIndex, "Help on Index"
     sth_HelpTopic, "Help on Topic"
     sth_HelpSearch, "Help on Search"
     sth_HelpGlossary, "Help on Glossary"
     sth_HelpUsing, "Help on Using Help"
     sth_HelpAbout, "Help on About"
     sth_Help, "Help on Help"
END

bmp_StatusLine BITMAP
BEGIN
'42 4D F6 02 00 00 00 00 00 00 76 00 00 00 28 00'
'00 00 40 00 00 00 14 00 00 00 01 00 04 00 00 00'
'00 00 80 02 00 00 00 00 00 00 00 00 00 00 00 00'
'00 00 00 00 00 00 00 00 00 00 00 00 80 00 00 80'
'00 00 00 80 80 00 80 00 00 00 80 00 80 00 80 80'
'00 00 80 80 80 00 C0 C0 C0 00 00 00 FF 00 00 FF'
'00 00 00 FF FF 00 FF 00 00 00 FF 00 FF 00 FF FF'
'00 00 FF FF FF 00 88 88 88 88 88 88 88 88 88 88'
'88 88 88 88 88 88 88 88 88 88 88 88 88 88 88 88'
'88 88 88 88 88 88 87 77 77 77 77 77 77 77 77 77'
'77 77 77 77 77 77 77 77 77 77 77 77 77 77 77 77'
'77 77 77 77 77 F8 87 88 88 88 88 88 88 88 88 88'
'88 88 88 88 88 88 88 88 88 88 88 88 88 88 88 88'
'88 88 88 88 88 F8 87 88 88 88 88 88 88 88 88 88'
'88 88 88 88 88 88 88 88 88 88 88 88 88 88 88 88'
'88 88 88 88 88 F8 87 88 88 88 88 88 88 88 88 88'
'88 88 88 88 88 88 88 88 88 88 88 88 88 88 88 88'
'88 88 88 88 88 F8 87 88 88 88 88 88 88 88 88 88'
'88 88 88 88 88 88 88 88 88 88 88 88 88 88 88 88'
```

```
'88 88 88 88 88 F8 87 88 88 88 88 88 88 88 88 88'
'88 88 88 88 88 88 88 88 88 88 88 88 88 88 88 88'
'88 88 88 88 88 F8 87 88 88 88 88 88 88 88 88 88'
'88 88 88 88 88 88 88 88 88 88 88 88 88 88 88 88'
'88 88 88 88 88 F8 87 88 88 88 88 88 88 88 88 88'
'88 88 88 88 88 88 88 88 88 88 88 88 88 88 88 88'
'88 88 88 88 88 F8 87 88 88 88 88 88 88 88 88 88'
'88 88 88 88 88 88 88 88 88 88 88 88 88 88 88 88'
'88 88 88 88 88 F8 87 88 88 88 88 88 88 88 88 88'
'88 88 88 88 88 88 88 88 88 88 88 88 88 88 88 88'
'88 88 88 88 88 F8 87 88 88 88 88 88 88 88 88 88'
'88 88 88 88 88 88 88 88 88 88 88 88 88 88 88 88'
'88 88 88 88 88 F8 87 88 88 88 88 88 88 88 88 88'
'88 88 88 88 88 88 88 88 88 88 88 88 88 88 88 88'
'88 88 88 88 88 F8 87 88 88 88 88 88 88 88 88 88'
'88 88 88 88 88 88 88 88 88 88 88 88 88 88 88 88'
'88 88 88 88 88 F8 87 88 88 88 88 88 88 88 88 88'
'88 88 88 88 88 88 88 88 88 88 88 88 88 88 88 88'
'88 88 88 88 88 F8 87 88 88 88 88 88 88 88 88 88'
'88 88 88 88 88 88 88 88 88 88 88 88 88 88 88 88'
'88 88 88 88 88 F8 87 88 88 88 88 88 88 88 88 88'
'88 88 88 88 88 88 88 88 88 88 88 88 88 88 88 88'
'88 88 88 88 88 F8 87 88 88 88 88 88 88 88 88 88'
'88 88 88 88 88 88 88 88 88 88 88 88 88 88 88 88'
'88 88 88 88 88 F8 8F FF FF FF FF FF FF FF FF FF'
'FF FF FF FF FF FF FF FF FF FF FF FF FF FF FF FF'
'FF FF FF FF FF F8 88 88 88 88 88 88 88 88 88 88'
'88 88 88 88 88 88 88 88 88 88 88 88 88 88 88 88'
'88 88 88 88 88 88'

END
```

Note: These bit maps must be developer-generated, either through the use of ASCII codes (the tedious way), or through the Whitewater Resource Toolkit (the easy way).

```
1 FONT rwdemo.FNT

dlg_FileNew DIALOG 37, 18, 130, 129
CAPTION "New"
STYLE DS_MODALFRAME | WS_POPUP | WS_CAPTION BEGIN
     CONTROL "Text", id_Text, "BUTTON", BS_AUTORADIOBUTTON |
          WS_TABSTOP, 39, 17, 41, 12
```

continues

Listing 8.2. continued

```
    CONTROL "Scribble", id_Scribble, "BUTTON",
        BS_AUTORADIOBUTTON ¦ WS_TABSTOP, 39, 39, 40, 12
    CONTROL "Graphics", id_Graphics, "BUTTON",
        BS_AUTORADIOBUTTON ¦ WS_TABSTOP, 39, 61, 41, 12
    CONTROL "", -1, "button", BS_GROUPBOX, 32, 8, 66, 74
    CONTROL "OK", id_OK, "BUTTON", BS_DEFPUSHBUTTON ¦
        WS_TABSTOP, 31, 98, 30, 14
    CONTROL "Cancel", id_Cancel, "BUTTON", BS_PUSHBUTTON ¦
        WS_TABSTOP, 71, 98, 31, 14
END

BITMAP_1 BITMAP
BEGIN
    '42 4D 16 01 00 00 00 00 00 00 76 00 00 00 28 00'
    '00 00 0A 00 00 00 14 00 00 00 01 00 04 00 00 00'
    '00 00 A0 00 00 00 00 00 00 00 00 00 00 00 00 00'
    '00 00 10 00 00 00 00 00 00 00 00 00 80 00 00 80'
    '00 00 00 80 80 00 80 00 00 00 80 00 80 00 80 80'
    '00 00 80 80 80 00 C0 C0 C0 00 00 00 FF 00 00 FF'
    '00 00 00 FF FF 00 FF 00 00 00 FF 00 FF 00 FF FF'
    '00 00 FF FF FF 00 88 88 88 88 88 08 88 00 77 7F'
    '87 77 77 00 00 00 88 8F 87 88 88 00 00 00 88 8F'
    '87 88 88 80 88 88 88 8F 87 88 88 44 00 04 88 8F'
    '87 88 88 00 00 00 88 8F 87 88 88 00 00 00 88 8F'
    '87 88 88 00 00 04 88 8F 87 88 88 00 10 00 88 8F'
    '87 88 88 00 00 40 88 8F 87 88 88 A0 82 02 88 8F'
    '87 88 88 00 00 00 88 8F 87 88 88 08 00 22 88 8F'
    '87 88 88 00 00 00 88 8F 87 88 88 00 00 00 88 8F'
    '87 88 88 00 00 00 88 8F 87 88 88 00 00 00 88 8F'
    '87 88 88 00 00 00 FF FF 8F FF FF 00 00 00 88 88'
    '88 88 88 00 00 00'
END
1000 MENU
BEGIN
    POPUP "Color"
    BEGIN
        MENUITEM "Red", 1
        MENUITEM "Green", 1
        MENUITEM "Blue", 1
    END

    POPUP "Width"
    BEGIN
        MENUITEM "Thin", 108
```

```
            MENUITEM "Normal", 1
            MENUITEM "Item", 1
        END

END

1001 MENU
BEGIN
        POPUP "Shape"
        BEGIN
            MENUITEM "Circle", 1
            MENUITEM "Rectangle", 1
        END

        POPUP "Color"
        BEGIN
            MENUITEM "Red", 1
            MENUITEM "Green", 1
            MENUITEM "White", 1
        END

END
```

Script files such as the ones in listing 8.1 and 8.2 have a .RC extension, are compiled with the Microsoft Resource Compiler, and then are appended to the Pascal application (usually using the `{$R}` directive). Your application is, of course, still responsible for attaching the resource to a window (in the Pascal for Windows code). For example, you load a menu already specified in a resource file by

```
ID 99:

constructor ATaskWindow.Init(AParent : PWindowsObject; ATitle : PChar);
begin
    TWindow.Init(AParent, ATitle); { Send message to ancestor's constructor }
    Attr.Menu  := LoadMenu(HInstance, PChar(99)); { 99 = menu ID }
end;
```

Resource Editors

Resource editors, such as the ones in the Whitewater Resource Toolkit (WRT), can generate script files (.RC) and linkable resource files (RES). Using the Whitewater Resource Toolkit, you usually want to generate RES files, the default. In that case, you select WRT's Save Menu item and specify a file.

To indicate that you want to generate a script file (.RC) rather than a resource file (RES), use the WRT's SaveAs menu item and select the .RC control button from the ensuing dialog window.

Notice that the dialogs, menus, keyboard accelerators, and so on, you use to interact with the Whitewater Resource Toolkit are similar to those you create for your applications. This is a beauty of the Windows interface: these resource editors are examples of the kinds of applications you can create using Windows development tools like Turbo Pascal for Windows and WRT. The way these (and other) applications use and interact with Windows resources is covered in Chapter 13, "Designing Windows Applications."

To give you a feel for using a resource editor, the Whitewater Resource Toolkit is used to create a dialog window and menu for an application.

Dialog Windows

A dialog box is a window made up of controls like those you see in figure 8.2.

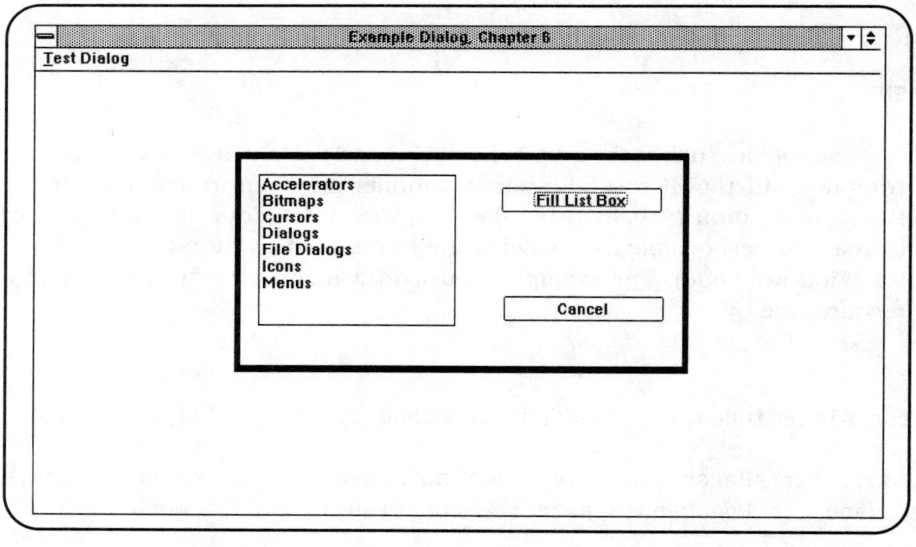

Figure 8.2. *A dialog box.*

Recall that controls are such items as list boxes, push buttons, edit fields, and so on. Each control is a child window that acts as an input device; in other words, it is an interactive component for communicating with a user. The dialog box (or window) is the parent window.

To create, edit, or design a dialog box, you start with a generic dialog box (with or without a caption). You move it around and change the type, content, and location of controls in the dialog box to create the specific dialog box you want.

The dialog box editor allows you to work with two palettes:

- Tools
- Alignment

Use the Tools palette to create a dialog box and its controls. Use the Alignment palette to align the controls within the dialog box.

By using the controls in a dialog box—that is, by clicking buttons, checking boxes, and selecting items from a list, a user can "control" an application. Controls enable a user to

1. Know which functions are available to him.
2. Alter the flow of an application (from object to object, from task to task, from function to function). Good use of dialog boxes (and its controls) can eliminate an application's mysteries and illuminate its purposes. The Apple Macintosh became popular in large part because it is so easy to use. Windows brings that ease of use to the PC.

Windows defines a set of messages that coordinate the exchange of information between an application and its controls. For example, list box "return" messages are prefixed by `lb_`. Combo box "return" messages are prefixed by `cb_`. Button "return" messages are prefixed by `bn_`, and so on.

In a dialog box (a window), messages go both ways: to the control and back from the control. To send a message—to add a string to a list box for example—you might do this:

```
procedure ADialog.AddStrings(var Msg: TMessage);
var
  Txt : PChar;
begin
  Txt := 'SomeText';
  SendDlgItemMsg(id_LB1, lb_AddString,0, LongInt(Txt));
end;
```

`SendDlgItemMsg` is a `TDialog` method. Thus, any dialog window you derive from `TDialog` automatically knows how to send dialog messages. `id_LB1` is a constant representing a list box ID. You use it to specify the control to receive the `SendDlgItemMsg`.

To get a result (of a user click, for example), your dialog window responds to a control notification message, which represents the user's action. Each control notification message includes a notification code (sent through `Msg.lParamHi`) that specifies the control's change of state.

Write a response method for any control notification message you want the dialog window or application to respond to. For example:

```
ADialog = object(TDialog)
  procedure HandleListBox1Msg(var Msg: TMessage); virtual
      id_First + id_BN1;
end;

procedure ADialog.HandleListBox1Msg(var Msg: TMessage);
begin
  case Msg.lParamHi of
    lbn_SelChange: { Handle selection here }
    lbn_DblClk:    { Handle a double click here }
  end;
end;
```

`lbn_` prefixed messages are generated when a user clicks in the list box. The `HandleListBox1Msg` method thus can be used to respond to the messages you want the list box to respond to. Notification messages you do not intercept are handled automatically (but without any response) by `TDialog` methods (which `ADialog` inherited).

A dialog is thus a two-way communication, sending messages to controls and responding to their notification messages. For example, create a dialog window that responds to a control (a button) by sending a message to another control (a list box). Listing 8.3 shows the complete code (which is covered in the following section), and figure 8.3 shows the displayed results.

Listing 8.3. *A dialog box example.*

```
program DialEx;              { Chapter 8, example dialog }

{$R EX_DIAL.RES}
uses WinTypes, WinProcs, WObjects;

const
  TheMenu      = 100;
  id_LB1       = 151;
  id_BN1       = 152;
  cm_DialogEx  = 101;    { Menu command message }

type
  PExDialog = ^ExDialog;
  ExDialog = object(TDialog)
    procedure IDBN1(var Msg: TMessage); virtual id_First + id_BN1;
    procedure IDLB1(var Msg: TMessage); virtual id_First + id_LB1;
  end;
```

```
  PDialogWindow = ^DialogWindow;
  DialogWindow = object(TWindow)
    constructor Init(AParent: PWindowsObject; ATitle: PChar);
    procedure CMDialogEx(var Msg: TMessage);
     virtual cm_First + cm_DialogEx;
  end;

  DlgApplication = object(TApplication)
    procedure InitMainWindow; virtual;
  end;

{ ExDialog }
procedure ExDialog.IDBN1(var Msg: TMessage);
var
  TextItem : PChar;
begin
  TextItem := 'Menus';
  SendDlgItemMsg(id_LB1, lb_AddString, 0, LongInt(TextItem));
  TextItem := 'Accelerators';
  SendDlgItemMsg(id_LB1, lb_AddString, 0, LongInt(TextItem));
  TextItem := 'Bitmaps';
  SendDlgItemMsg(id_LB1, lb_AddString, 0, LongInt(TextItem));
  TextItem := 'Cursors';
  SendDlgItemMsg(id_LB1, lb_AddString, 0, LongInt(TextItem));
  TextItem := 'Icons';
  SendDlgItemMsg(id_LB1, lb_AddString, 0, LongInt(TextItem));
  TextItem := 'Dialogs';
  SendDlgItemMsg(id_LB1, lb_AddString, 0, LongInt(TextItem));
  TextItem := 'File Dialogs';
  SendDlgItemMsg(id_LB1, lb_AddString, 0, LongInt(TextItem));
end;

procedure ExDialog.IDLB1(var Msg: TMessage);
var
  Idx : Integer;
  SelectedText: array[0..10] of Char;
begin
  if Msg.LParamHi = lbn_SelChange then
  begin
    Idx := SendDlgItemMsg(id_LB1, lb_GetCurSel, 0, LongInt(0));
    SendDlgItemMsg(id_LB1, lb_GetText, Idx, LongInt(@SelectedText));
    MessageBox(HWindow, SelectedText, 'List Box Notification', MB_OK);
  end;
end;
```

continues

Listing 8.3. continued

```
{ DialogWindow }
constructor DialogWindow.Init(AParent: PWindowsObject;
   ATitle: PChar);
begin
  TWindow.Init(AParent, ATitle);
  Attr.Menu := LoadMenu(Hinstance, MakeIntResource(TheMenu));
end;

procedure DialogWindow.CMDialogEx(var Msg: TMessage);
var
     Return : Integer;
begin
  Return := Application^.ExecDialog(New(PExDialog, Init(@Self,
   'EXDialog')));
  If Return = id_Cancel then
   MessageBox(HWindow, 'id_cancel', 'List Box Notification', MB_OK);
end;

{ DlgApplication }
procedure DlgApplication.InitMainWindow;
begin
  MainWindow := New(PDialogWindow, Init(nil, 'Example
                       Dialog, Chapter 8'));
end;

var
  MyApp: DlgApplication;
begin
  MyApp.Init('Example');
  MyApp.Run;
  MyApp.Done;
end.
```

Details

First, use the Whitewater Resource Toolkit to create a list box. Use the dialog editor to

1. First expand the size of the default dialog (which pops up whenever you open the dialog editor).

2. Select a list box from the control menu and, using the mouse, place it in the dialog window (see figure 8.4).

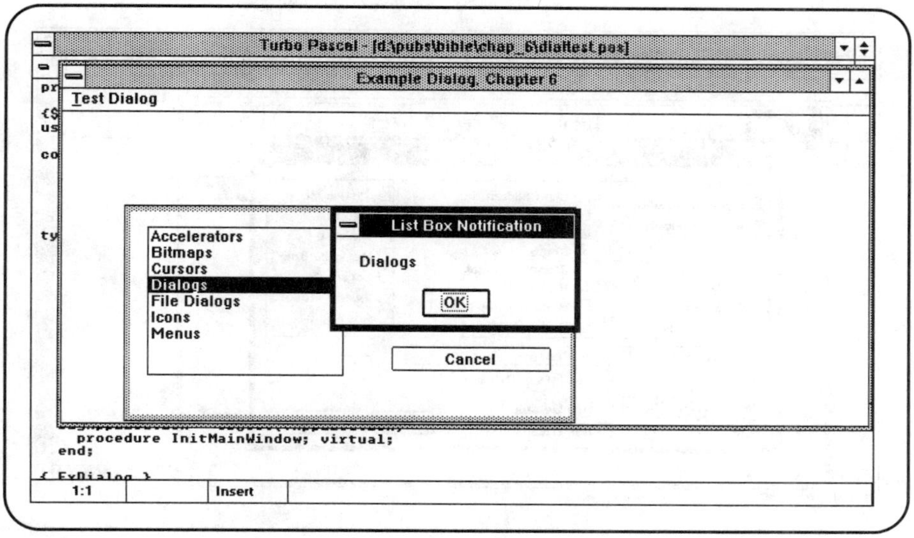

Figure 8.3. A dialog box example.

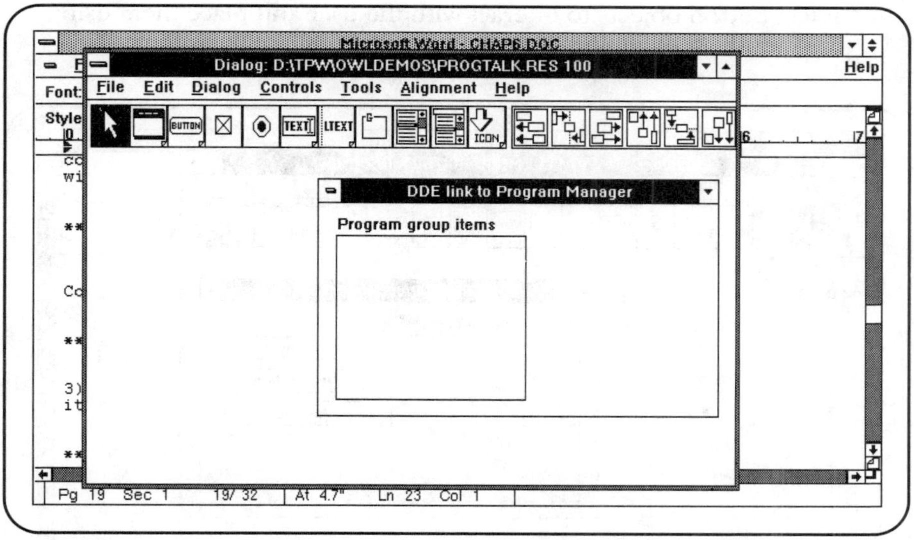

Figure 8.4. A list box from the control menu, placed into a dialog window.

3. Edit the attributes of the list box by clicking Controls/Attributes as shown in figure 8.5.

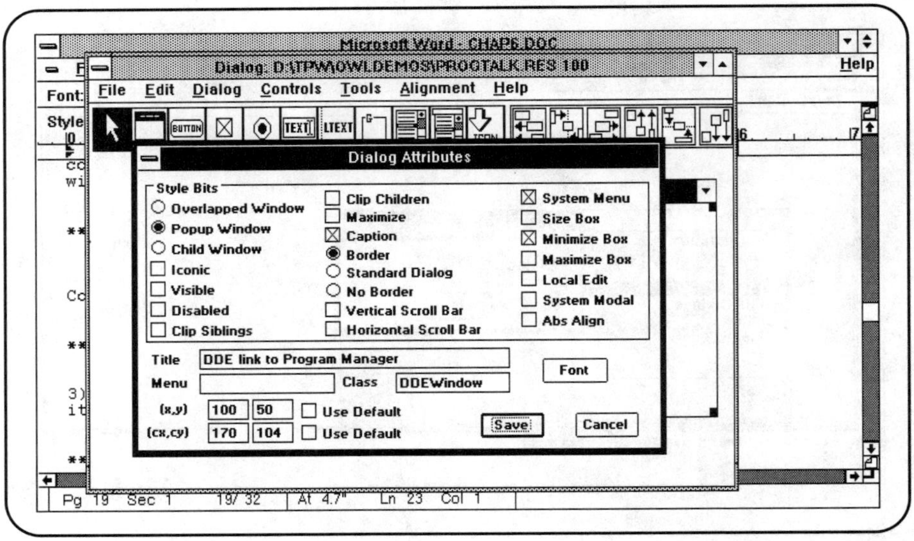

Figure 8.5. Controls/Attributes.

4. Select button objects to interact with the user and place them using the mouse (see figure 8.6).

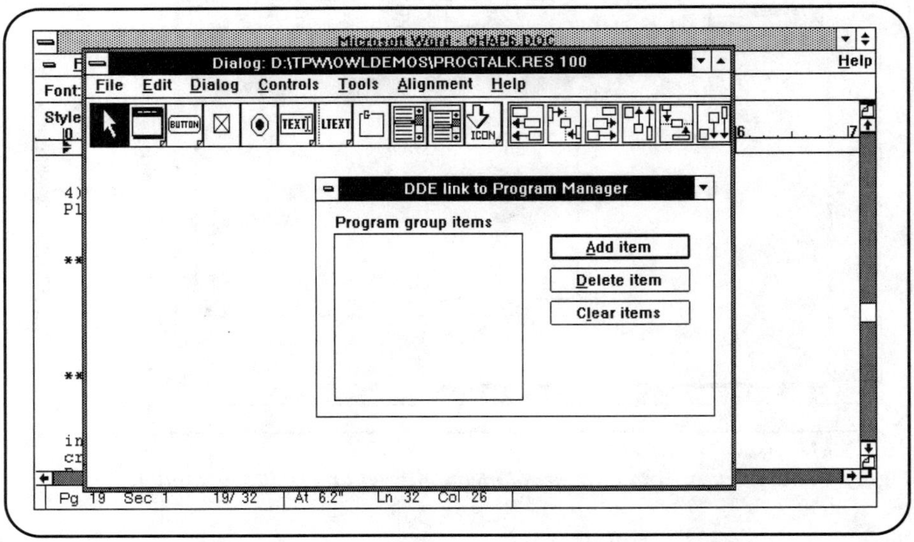

Figure 8.6. Button objects placed by using the mouse.

5. Select a button for completing the dialog and place it, as in figures 8.7 and 8.8.

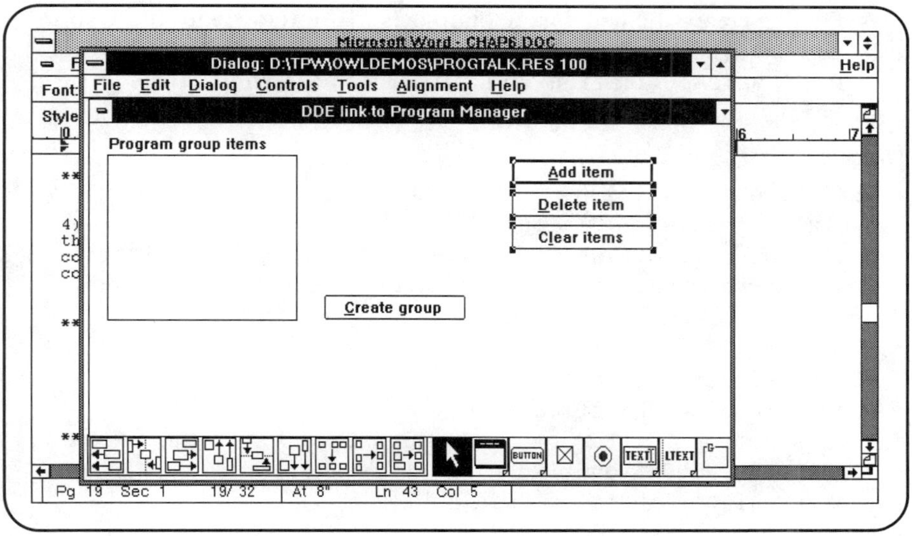

Figure 8.7. A button for completing the dialog.

6. Define notification codes.

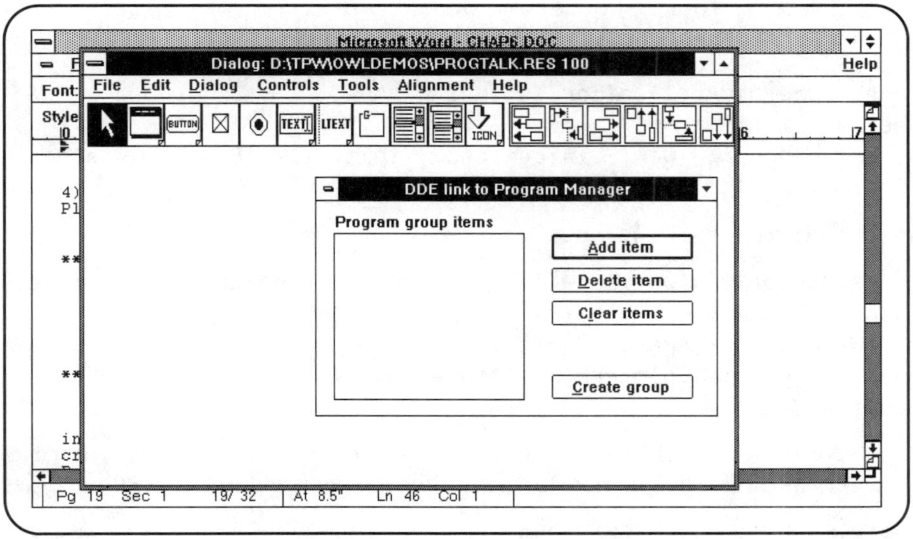

Figure 8.8. The new button in context.

7. Finally, create the usual gang of objects that interact with the resources you just created. As usual, create a new application object (deriving it from `BasicApplication`) and a `DlgWindow` (deriving it from `MainWindow`), and a `Dialog` to handle list box and button messages:

```
type
  PExDialog = ^ExDialog;
  ExDialog = object(TDialog)
    procedure IDBN1(var Msg: TMessage); virtual id_First + id_BN1;
    procedure IDLB1(var Msg: TMessage); virtual id_First + id_LB1;
  end;

  PDialogWindow = ^DialogWindow;
  DialogWindow = object(TWindow)
    constructor Init(AParent: PWindowsObject; ATitle: PChar);
    procedure CMDialogEx(var Msg: TMessage);
     virtual cm_First + cm_DialogEx;
  end;

  DlgApplication = object(TApplication)
    procedure InitMainWindow; virtual;
  end;
```

`InitMainWindow` should look familiar: construction of a type of window for the `DlgApplication`. In this case, a `DlgWindow`:

```
procedure DlgApplication.InitMainWindow;
begin
  MainWindow := New(PDialogWindow, Init(nil, 'Example Dialog, Chapter 6'
end;
```

Construct the `DlgWindow`:

```
constructor DialogWindow.Init(AParent: PWindowsObject; ATitle: PChar);
begin
  TWindow.Init(AParent, ATitle);
  Attr.Menu := LoadMenu(Hinstance, MakeIntResource(TheMenu));
end;
```

Note the use of `MakeIntResource`, a Windows function that typecasts integers into resource names. It is equivalent to typecasting into a `PChar` type:

```
Attr.Menu := LoadMenu(Hinstance, PChar(100));
```

which attaches the same menu to `DialogWindow`.

ExDialog is used only to interpret notification messages and has no fields. Because it is also a standard dialog, you do not need to define a new constructor. TDialog's constructor is called when DialogWindow sends an "execute dialog" message in response to the CMDialogEX menu command message:

```
procedure DialogWindow.CMDialogEx(var Msg: TMessage);
var
     Return : Integer;
begin
  Return := Application^.ExecDialog(New(PExDialog,
              Init(@Self, 'EXDialog')));
  If Return = id_Cancel then
    MessageBox(HWindow, 'id_cancel', 'List Box Notification', MB_OK);
```

Notice in this example that you take a quick look at the Return value of Application^.ExecDialog. Sometimes it is useful to check this result just in case Application^.ExecDialog fails. For example, if you specify the name of a dialog that can be executed, ExecDialog returns zero.

If the dialog cannot be executed (for example, if the dialog name is misspelled), ExecDialog returns a negative value corresponding to a predefined constant. To experiment with these error results, type some garbage into the dialog name field, and look at the result. For example, if you do not have a dialog resource named "NoDialog," type that name in the name field, where "ExDialog" is now. This process generates an error.

Define the method for responding to an AddString message:

```
{ ExDialog }
procedure ExDialog.IDBN1(var Msg: TMessage);
var
  TextItem : PChar;
begin
  TextItem := 'Menus';
  SendDlgItemMsg(id_LB1, lb_AddString, 0, LongInt(TextItem));
  TextItem := 'Accelerators';
  SendDlgItemMsg(id_LB1, lb_AddString, 0, LongInt(TextItem));
  TextItem := 'Bitmaps';
  SendDlgItemMsg(id_LB1, lb_AddString, 0, LongInt(TextItem));
  TextItem := 'Cursors';
  SendDlgItemMsg(id_LB1, lb_AddString, 0, LongInt(TextItem));
  TextItem := 'Icons';
  SendDlgItemMsg(id_LB1, lb_AddString, 0, LongInt(TextItem));
  TextItem := 'Dialogs';
  SendDlgItemMsg(id_LB1, lb_AddString, 0, LongInt(TextItem));
  TextItem := 'File Dialogs';
  SendDlgItemMsg(id_LB1, lb_AddString, 0, LongInt(TextItem));
end;
```

Here is a method for responding to a list-box notification message indicating that the user selected an item:

```
procedure ExDialog.IDLB1(var Msg: TMessage);
var
  Idx : Integer;
  SelectedText: array[0..10] of Char;
begin
  if Msg.LParamHi = lbn_SelChange then
  begin
    Idx := SendDlgItemMsg(id_LB1, lb_GetCurSel, 0, LongInt(0));
    SendDlgItemMsg(id_LB1, lb_GetText, Idx,
LongInt(@SelectedText));
    MessageBox(HWindow, SelectedText, 'List Box Notification',
MB_OK);
  end;
end;
```

Note that you can define dialogs in separate files specified by .DLG extensions. For example, the previous dialog's .DLG file looks like this:

```
EXDIALOG DIALOG DISCARDABLE LOADONCALL PURE MOVEABLE 30, 49,
188, 100
STYLE WS_POPUP ¦ WS_DLGFRAME
BEGIN
  CONTROL "Fill List Box" 152, "BUTTON", WS_CHILD ¦
     WS_VISIBLE ¦ WS_TABSTOP, 111, 13, 68, 12
  CONTROL "Cancel" 2, "BUTTON", WS_CHILD ¦ WS_VISIBLE ¦
     WS_TABSTOP, 112, 66, 68, 12
  CONTROL "LISTBOX" 151, "LISTBOX", WS_CHILD ¦ WS_VISIBLE ¦
     WS_BORDER ¦ WS_VSCROLL ¦ 0x3L, 8, 8, 83, 73
END
```

If you do maintain dialogs, menus, and so forth, in separate files, you can combine them whenever you need to by using the Whitewater Resource Toolkit Browser to copy resources between files. Do this by opening two browsers and using the Browser Copy command to copy resource specifications between files. Figure 8.9 illustrates this idea.

Note: The Whitewater Resource Toolkit is completely menu-driven. To add resources (controls, boxes, button, and so on), use your mouse to click the menu items, then drag them across the screen.

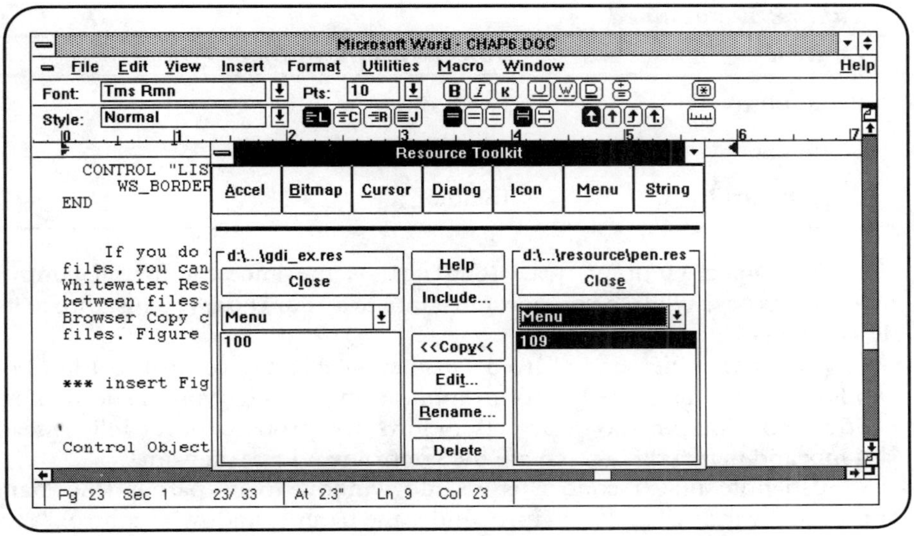

Figure 8.9. Using the Whitewater Resource Toolkit to copy resources between files.

Control Objects

Dialog boxes are composed of control objects, but control objects do not have to be part of a dialog. You might want to use control objects as stand-alone "windows."

ObjectWindows object types make it easy for you to incorporate any of ten controls in your own applications. These controls are listed in table 8.1.

Table 8.1. Controls to incorporate in your own applications.

Control	*ObjectWindows Object Type*
Check box	TCheckBox
Combo box	TComboBox
Edit control	TEdit
Group box	TGroupBox
List box	TListBox
MDI client	TMDIClient
Push button	TButton

continues

Table 8.1. continued

Control	*ObjectWindows Object Type*
Radio button	TRadioButton
Scroll bar	TScrollBar
Static control	TStatic

The ObjectWindows type, `TControl`, is the ancestor for all control objects. It is base type, so you never instantiate a `TControl`; you instantiate its descendents.

`TControl` is descended from `TWindow`. Thus, any control is a kind of window that can direct the flow of an application. Although you can derive new controls from the controls in ObjectWindows, you probably never will; instead you mix and match them to create the control window you want.

Also note that a control is a child window to its parent (the Main application window) and is, in turn, under the parent window's "control." It is the responsibility of the parent window to create the control (its child).

Derive a new kind of `MainWindow`, called a `TaskControlWindow`:

```
PTaskControlWindow = ^TaskControlWindow;
TaskControlWindow = object(MainWindow)
  constructor Init(AParent: PWindowsObject; ATitle: PChar);
end;
```

and add a radio button to it:

```
PTaskControlWindow = ^TaskControlWindow;
TaskControlWindow = object(MainWindow)
  Rad1: PRadioButton;
end;
```

In this example, the control (`Rad1`, a pointer to a `RadioButton`) is represented by a data field. Alternatively, it can be represented by a variable in its parent's constructor. For example:

```
constructor Init(AParent: PWindowsObject; ATitle: PChar);
var
     Rad1 : PRadioButton;

begin
     {....}
end;
```

Either way, the control is constructed by its parent's constructor.

Version 1:

```
constructor TaskControlWindow.Init(AParent: PWindowsObject; ATitle: PChar);
begin
  MainWindow.Init(AParent, ATitle);
  Rad1 := New(PRadioButton, Init(@Self, id_Rad1, 'Task 1',
    74, 64, 138, 24, Group1));
end;
```

Or (Version 2):

```
constructor TaskControlWindow.Init(AParent: PWindowsObject; ATitle: PChar);
var
   Rad1 : PRadioButton;
begin
  MainWindow.Init(AParent, ATitle);
  Rad1 := New(PRadioButton, Init(@Self, id_Rad1, 'Task 1',
    74, 64, 138, 24, Group1));
end;
```

You create other control objects similarly. For example, a list box:

```
constructor TaskControlWindow.Init(AParent: PWindowsObject; ATitle: PChar);
begin
  MainWindow.Init(AParent, ATitle);
  ListBox1 := New(PListBox, Init(@Self, id_LB1, 74, 64, 138, 24));
end;
```

or a combo box:

```
    constructor TaskControlWindow.Init(AParent: PWindowsObject;

ATitle: PChar);
begin
  MainWindow.Init(AParent, ATitle);
  ListBox1 := New(PComboBox, Init(@Self, id_CB1, 74, 64,
                 138, 24, cbs_DropList,40));
end;
```

Each control supported by an ObjectWindows object is a self-contained object with its own methods and data. Your application simply:

1. Constructs an object.
2. Sends it messages.
3. Processes the results.

Group Boxes

One way of using controls is to process them "as a group," by unifying them in a group box. A group box is a special kind of interface object that corresponds to the group box element in Windows. A good way to set up a group box is to create it as a stand-alone child window within another window's client area.

Create a group box that unifies a group of radio buttons. Each button enables a user to specify a task. In other words, the group box acts as a task controller. The user selects a task to execute by clicking a radio button. The application responds by iterating the task.

Recall the way you built the task manager in Chapters 5, 6, and 7 by deriving a new kind of main window (called `TaskWindow`), which responded to command messages (generated by a menu). The `TaskWindow` responded to a Run Task message by creating an instance of the window that contained the task.

The plan here is similar:

1. Derive a new window called `TaskControlWindow` from `MainWindow`.
2. Add controls to it: two radio buttons (to represent two tasks), a control box to unify the task buttons, and a method to maintain the group:

```
PTaskControlWindow = ^TaskControlWindow;
TaskControlWindow = object(MainWindow)
  TaskButton1,
  TaskButton2: PRadioButton;
  TaskGroup1: PGroupBox;
  constructor Init(AParent: PWindowsObject; ATitle: PChar);
  procedure HandleTaskGroup1Msg(var Msg: TMessage);
    virtual id_First + id_Group1;
end;
```

The `TaskControlWindow` constructor creates all the controls:

```
constructor TaskControlWindow.Init(AParent: PWindowsObject;
                    ATitle: PChar);
begin
  MainWindow.Init(AParent, ATitle);
  TaskGroup1 := New(PGroupBox, Init(@Self, id_Group1, 'Task
                    Box', 58, 52, 176, 108));
  TaskButton1 := New(PRadioButton, Init(@Self, id_Rad1,
                    'Task 1', 74, 64, 138, 24, Group1));
  TaskButton2 := New(PRadioButton, Init(@Self, id_Rad2,
                    'Task 2', 74, 84, 138, 24, Group1));
end;
```

The group handler decides how to interpret the button-state changes in the group:

```
procedure TaskControlWindow.HandleGroup1Msg(var Msg:
TMessage);
var
  TextBuff: array[0..20] of Char; { A button ID }
  Compare : integer;              { Int to record comparison }
  Task1 : PModel1;                { Pointer to a task }
  Task2 : PModel2;                { Pointer to a task }

begin
  if Rad1^.GetCheck <> 0            { User wants a task }
  then GetWindowText(Rad1^.HWindow, TextBuff,
SizeOf(TextBuff))
  else GetWindowText(Rad2^.HWindow, TextBuff,
SizeOf(TextBuff));

  Compare := StrComp(TextBuff,'Task 1');  { Which task ID is
it? }
  If Compare = 0  then                    { 0 = a match }
  begin
     Task1 := New(PModel1, Init(@Self, 'TimeSeries Model'));
     Application^.MakeWindow(Task1);
     Task1^.Iterate;                { Iterate the task }
  end
  else                              { Run the other task }
  begin
     Task2 := New(PModel2, Init(@Self, 'Henon Attractor'));
     Application^.MakeWindow(Task2);
     Task2^.Iterate;                { Iterate the task  }
  end;
end;
```

Listing 8.4 shows the complete `TaskControl` application, and figure 8.10 shows a screen display generated by the code in listing 8.4.

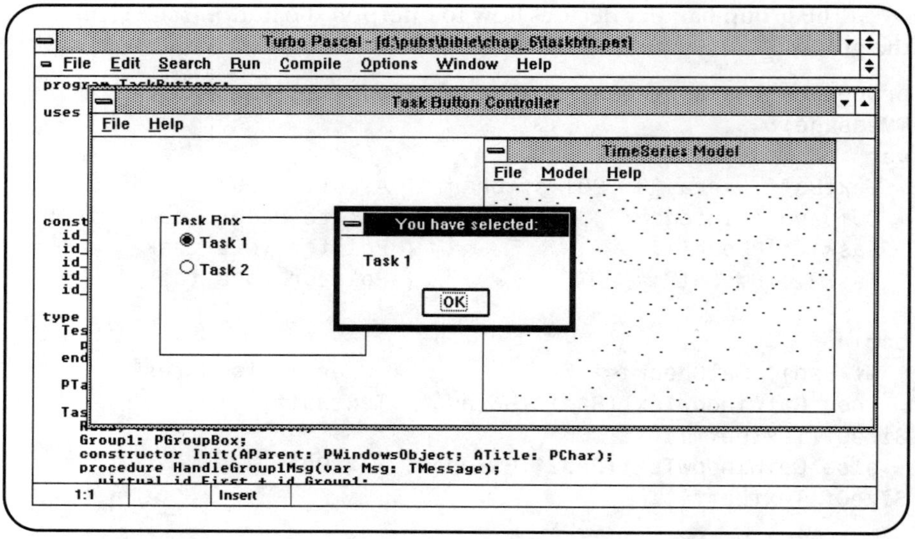

Figure 8.10. *Result of the* `TaskControl` *application.*

Listing 8.4. *The complete* `TaskControl` *application.*

```
program TaskButtons;

uses
    WObjects,
    WinTypes,
    WinProcs,
    Strings,
    wif5,        { Basic Interface }
    time1,       { Task 1 }
    attract2;    { Task 2 }

const
  id_Push1  = 101;
  id_Rad1   = 102;
  id_Rad2   = 103;
  id_Check1 = 104;
  id_Group1 = 105;

type
  TestApplication = object(TApplication)
    procedure InitMainWindow; virtual;
```

```
  end;

  PTaskControlWindow = ^TaskControlWindow;

  TaskControlWindow = object(MainWindow)
    Rad1, Rad2: PRadioButton;
    Group1: PGroupBox;
    constructor Init(AParent: PWindowsObject; ATitle: PChar);
    procedure HandleGroup1Msg(var Msg: TMessage);
      virtual id_First + id_Group1;
  end;

{ --------TaskControlWindow methods----------------- }

constructor TaskControlWindow.Init(AParent: PWindowsObject;
`                           ATitle: PChar);
begin
  MainWindow.Init(AParent, ATitle);
  Group1 := New(PGroupBox, Init(@Self, id_Group1, 'Task
             Box', 58, 52, 176, 108));
  Rad1 := New(PRadioButton, Init(@Self, id_Rad1, 'Task 1',
             74, 64, 138, 24, Group1));
  Rad2 := New(PRadioButton, Init(@Self, id_Rad2, 'Task 2',
             74, 84, 138, 24, Group1));
end;

procedure TaskControlWindow.HandleGroup1Msg(var Msg: TMessage);
var
  TextBuff: array[0..20] of Char;  { A button ID }
  Compare : integer;               { Int to record comparison }
  Task1 : PModel1;                 { Pointer to a task }
  Task2 : PModel2;                 { Pointer to a task }

begin
  if Rad1^.GetCheck <> 0
  then GetWindowText(Rad1^.HWindow, TextBuff, SizeOf(TextBuff))
  else GetWindowText(Rad2^.HWindow, TextBuff, SizeOf(TextBuff));

  Compare := StrComp(TextBuff,'Task 1');
  If Compare = 0  then
  begin
     Task1 := New(PModel1, Init(@Self, 'TimeSeries Model'));
     Application^.MakeWindow(Task1);
     Task1^.Iterate;               { Iterate the task }
```

continues

Listing 8.4. continued

```
end
else
begin
   Task2 := New(PModel2, Init(@Self, 'Henon Attractor'));
   Application^.MakeWindow(Task2);
   Task2^.Iterate;                      { Iterate the task }
end;

MessageBox(HWindow, TextBuff, 'You have selected:', MB_OK);
end;

{ ----------TestApplication Methods----------- }

procedure TestApplication.InitMainWindow;
begin
  MainWindow := New(PTaskControlWindow, Init(nil, 'Task
                        Button Controller'));
end;

var
  TestApp : TestApplication;

begin
  TestApp.Init('ButtTest');
  TestApp.Run;
  TestApp.Done;
end.
```

Using controls this way might seem similar to using a menu resource. It is, but controls are more flexible and more powerful than menus. Rather than a menu, the group can be made of pushbuttons, radio buttons, check boxes, and so on. Thus, you have interesting graphics possibilities, and some controls, such as an `EditControl`, for example, that allow you to easily manipulate data fields.

Controls in Combination

Review the `HelpWindow` from listing 7.5 in Chapter 7, "Many Windows: A Multi-Document Interface." The `HelpWindow` consisted of two control objects: a list box and an edit control, a constructor (to construct the `HelpWindow`), and several methods for handling the results from the control objects:

```
PHelpWindow = ^HelpWindow;
 HelpWindow = object(TWindow)
   LB1: PListBox;
   EC1: PEdit;
   constructor Init(AParent: PWindowsObject; ATitle: PChar);
   procedure SetupWindow; virtual;
   procedure IDLB1(var Msg: TMessage); virtual id_First + id_LB1;
   procedure IDBN1(var Msg: TMessage); virtual id_First + id_BN1;
   procedure IDBN2(var Msg: TMessage); virtual id_First + id_BN2;
   procedure FillEdit(SelStringPtr: PChar); virtual;
end;
```

All the control objects for HelpWindow are constructed when HelpWindow is constructed, using the New procedure:

```
constructor HelpWindow.Init(AParent: PWindowsObject; ATitle: PChar);
var
  TempStat : PStatic;
  TempBtn  : PButton;
begin
  TWindow.Init(AParent, ATitle);
  DisableAutoCreate;
  Attr.Style := ws_PopupWindow or ws_Caption or ws_Visible;
  Attr.X := 100;
  Attr.Y := 100;
  Attr.W := 300;
  Attr.H := 300;
  LB1 := New(PListBox, Init(@Self, id_LB1, 20, 20, 180, 80));
  TempBtn := New(PButton, Init(@Self, id_BN1, 'Help', 220,
             20, 60, 30, True));
  TempBtn := New(PButton, Init(@Self, id_BN2, 'Cancel', 220,
             70, 60, 30, False));
  EC1 := New(PEdit, Init(@Self, id_EC1, '', 20, 180, 260,
             90, 40, True));
  EC1^.Attr.Style := EC1^.Attr.Style or ws_Border or ws_VScroll;
  TempStat := New(PStatic, Init(@Self, id_ST1,'Help
             Information:', 20, 160, 160, 20, 0));
end;
```

You filled the list box by overriding TWindow's SetupWindow (in HelpWindow):

```
procedure HelpWindow.SetupWindow;
begin
  TWindow.SetupWindow;
```

```
  { Fill the listbox }
  LB1^.AddString('List Boxes');
  LB1^.AddString('Buttons');
  LB1^.AddString('Scroll Bars');
  LB1^.AddString('Edit Controls');
  LB1^.AddString('Static Controls');
  LB1^.AddString('Combo Boxes');
  LB1^.SetSelIndex(0);        { Set to beginning of list }
end;
```

You then specified various actions based on messages from buttons and lists. For example, list-box message 1:

```
procedure HelpWindow.IDLB1(var Msg: TMessage);
var
  SelString: array[0..25] of Char;
begin
  if Msg.LParamHi = lbn_DblClk then
  begin
    LB1^.GetSelString(SelString, 25);
    FillEdit(SelString);
  end;
end;
```

Button message 1:

```
procedure THelpWindow.IDBN1(var Msg: TMessage);
var
  SelString: array[0..25] of Char;
begin
  LB1^.GetSelString(SelString, 25);
  FillEdit(SelString);
end;
```

Bit Maps

You also can use a resource editor to create a bit map that can, in turn, be used for various purposes: for example, as a brush for filling figures, such as rectangles, ellipses, and so on.

Creating a bit map with the Whitewater Resource Toolkit is straightforward. You use the Bitmap editor and select tools to create the specific aspects of the bit map. You then save the bit map as a .BMP file, which you can load into your applications later. Figures 8.11, 8.12, and 8.13 show various aspects of a bit map being created with the Whitewater Resource Group's Bitmap editor packaged with Turbo Pascal for Windows.

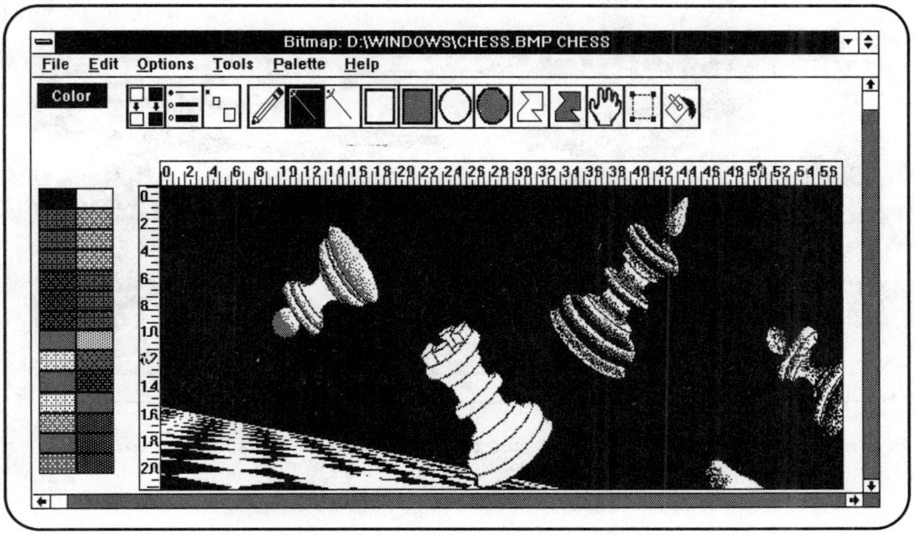

Figure 8.11. *One aspect of a bit map created with the Whitewater Resource Group's Bitmap editor.*

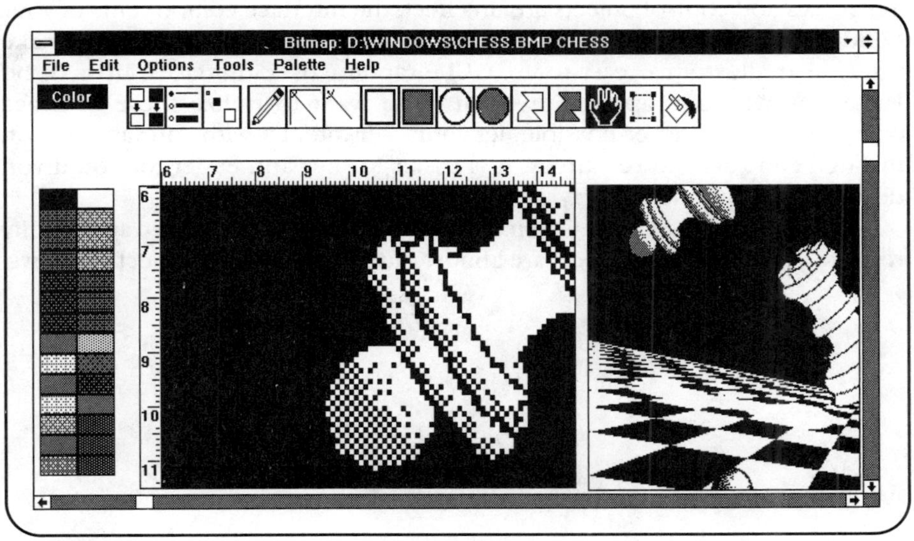

Figure 8.12. *Another aspect of a bit map.*

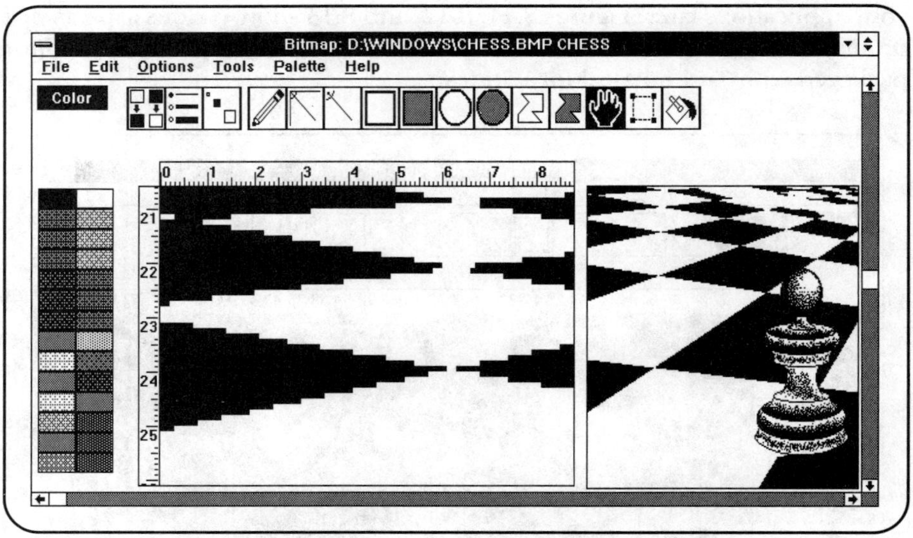

***Figure 8.13.** A third aspect of a bit map created with the WRG's Bitmap editor.*

Wrap-up

Resources and control objects are, in effect, the interface components of your Windows applications. They give your application the look and feel that make it a familiar, illustrative, easy-to-use GUI (graphical user interface). Most Turbo Pascal for Windows applications you write want to utilize these interface components. Whenever possible, let your user interact with your application through controls and resources. It is easier for her and easier for you if you develop applications this way.

Resource editors make it a snap for you to interactively design and modify resources, and control objects are almost plug-ins, thanks to ObjectWindows.

9

CHAPTER

MEMORY MATTERS

I have a good memory, though "good" is somewhat questionable, since there is a tendency to over-remember life rather than to look for new life to be lived.
Jim Harrison

Windows is a complex multitasking environment, with comparably complex memory-management capability. Because Windows allows applications to share memory, more applications can run effectively at the same time. For example, if you run multiple instances of an application, Windows uses the same code segments and resources for each instance. This multi-utilization of resources (icons, menus, dialogs, cursors, and so on) is an important advantage in separating resources from source code.

In addition, Windows can "move" memory you allocate for your application's code and data segments and resources, if you specify the memory as "moveable." Windows moves memory to create larger contiguous memory blocks. Code segments and resources also can be discarded to free memory (if you designate these segments and resources as "discardable"). One key result of Windows' memory management is that large applications can run simultaneously in a memory space much smaller than would be required without Windows. As an application developer, you want to take as much advantage of the Windows management system as you can.

Although memory management sounds daunting, it is not. If you use the hooks provided by Turbo Pascal for Windows, you can tap into this complex memory-management system. Essentially, you use a few built-in procedures such as `New`, `Dispose`, `GetMem`, `FreeMem`, and `MemAlloc` to allocate dynamic variables, and the Turbo Pascal for Windows compiler ensures that enough memory is in the Windows global heap to allocate the variables. (More on this in the next section).

The way you write applications is not affected much by the specific Windows mode you are using, but you should at least be aware of the modes available. The three modes (real, standard, and enhanced) are dependent on the amount of memory the system running Windows has.

Windows runs only in real mode on systems having less than 1M (megabyte) of RAM. In this mode, Windows runs in memory between 640K (kilobytes) and 1M. This is, of course, the most limiting mode primarily because Windows has less memory to use for swapping code segments, and so on. Windows can use EMS (Lotus-Intel-Microsoft Expanded Memory Specification) 4.0 in real mode. EMS specifies a standard scheme for accessing and using memory above 640K. Because this "extra memory" was not accounted for in early versions of DOS, applications dealt with this memory in any way they saw fit, until this specification was introduced. Windows requires that applications use memory in a similar, standardized way so that they can be swapped, for example, and are generally compatible.

Windows can run in either real or standard mode in systems with between 1M and 2M of memory. In standard mode, Windows can access as much as 16M of memory.

Finally, Windows can run in 386 enhanced mode on systems with at least 2M of memory. 386 enhanced mode is standard mode plus the ability to implement virtual memory, which, in effect, means that Windows can swap "pages" to disk in order to free additional memory. Page swapping is something you normally do not have to worry about when you develop Windows applications.

In general, Windows figures out the best mode for a system when it starts. All the examples in this book were compiled and run under Windows in both standard and 386 enhanced modes (Turbo Pascal for Windows requires one of these modes; it does not run in real mode).

Memory Management, Windows Style

Typically, when you write applications for DOS (but not Windows), memory is allocated at fixed (specific) locations. If you are using Turbo Pascal (for DOS) memory-allocation and deallocation procedures, this is handled automatically for you. You just use `New`, `Dispose`, and so on, and Turbo Pascal's memory-management system ensures enough memory to allocate space for a variable.

Windows, however, takes a more flexible approach to memory allocation. Memory blocks can be fixed, but also moved and discarded. By not forcing blocks of memory to be fixed, Windows can significantly improve memory use. For example, memory that is "moveable" can be "compacted" to create a larger block of free memory from smaller blocks of free memory, as illustrated in figure 9.1.

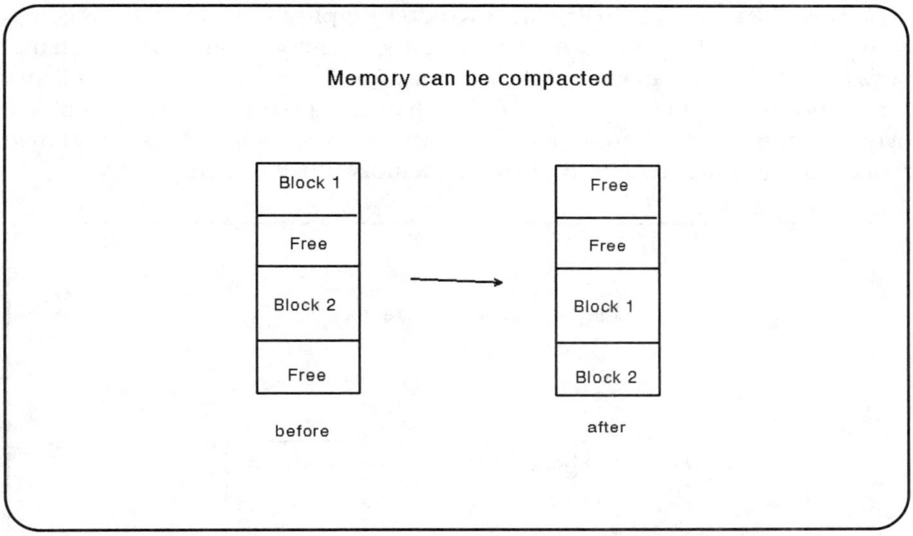

Figure 9.1. *Creating a larger block of free memory from smaller blocks of free memory.*

Another way Windows improves memory use is compaction through "discardable" memory blocks (see figure 9.2).

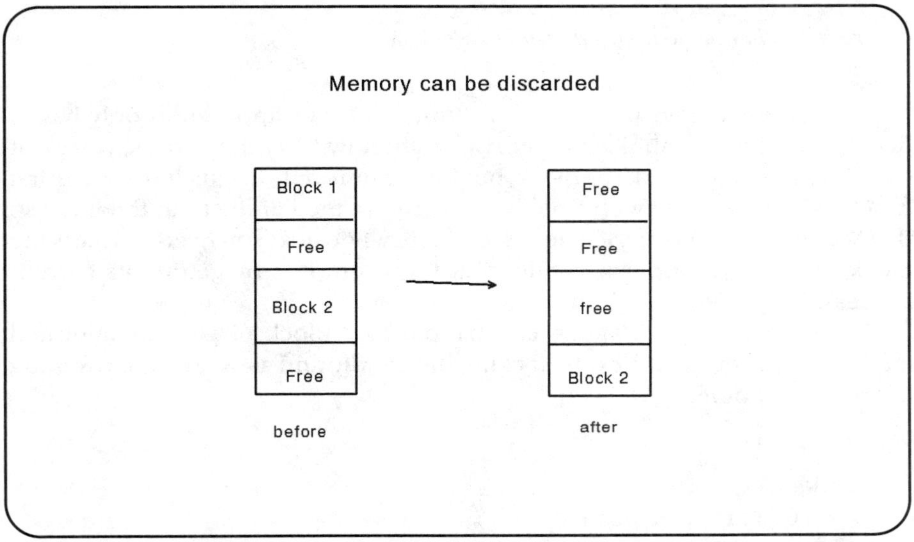

Figure 9.2. *Compacting through "discardable" memory blocks.*

How does your Turbo Pascal for Windows application know what is going on with memory? Easy. Most of the time, it does not even bother itself with the physical location of a memory block. It accesses memory through a handle to the memory block. In other words, rather than get a pointer to a memory block (a typical non-Windows approach), the application gets a handle (a name) that represents a pointer to a pointer to the memory block (see figure 9.3).

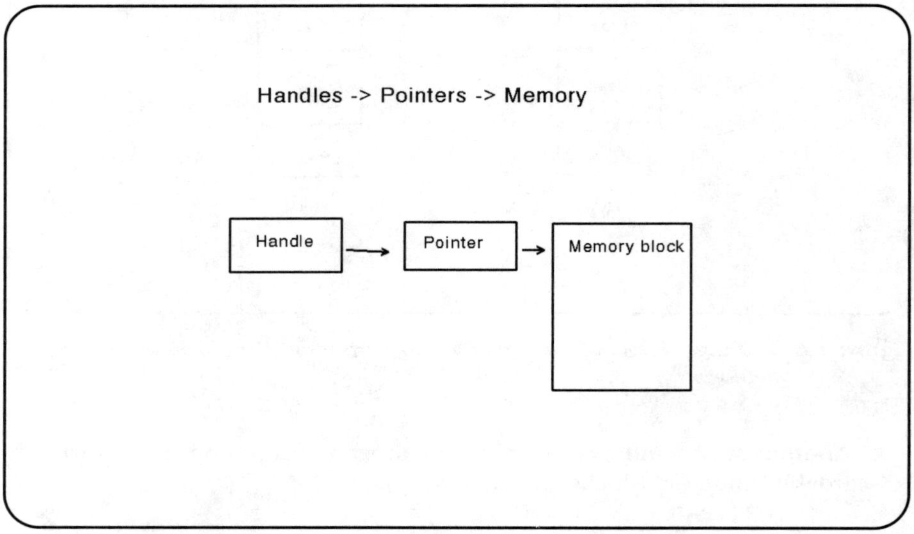

Figure 9.3. *A handle to access a memory block.*

To access memory managed by Windows, your application only has to determine where a chunk of memory is "right now." In other words, you must still obtain the address of the block, but for the time only in which you are using it. When you are done with a block, you give up the handle to it, freeing it so that Windows can move it if it needs to. Then, when next you need to access the block of memory, you ask Windows again where it is by getting its current address.

For example, if `GHandle` is a handle to a block of globally allocated memory, you get its address by locking the handle and assigning the resulting address to a pointer:

```
var

     GHandle : THandle;
     PtrGData: { A pointer }

begin
     GHandle := GlobalAlloc(gmem_Moveable, 50000); { Memory type and siz
```

```
    PtrGData:= GlobalLock(GHandle);
            {......}
end;
```

In this fragment, PtrGData "gets" the address of the memory block. By locking the block, you temporarily "fix" the block at some specific location so that Windows cannot move or discard it until you "unlock" the block using one of the Unlock procedures:

```
GlobalUnlock(GHandle);
```

or, if LHandle is a handle to a locally allocated memory block:

```
LocalUnlock(LHandle);
```

When the block has been unlocked, the pointer to the memory block (you just obtained) is no longer valid because Windows can again move or discard the memory. If you have to know where a block of memory is throughout the life of the application, allocate it as a fixed block:

```
GHandle := GlobalAlloc(gmem_fixed,10000);
```

This step "fixes" the block, preventing Windows from moving it about. In general, though, you do not want to fix memory blocks; instead you allocate them as moveable:

```
GHandle := GlobalAlloc(gmem_Moveable,2000);
```

or as movable and discardable:

```
GHandle := GlobalAlloc(gmem_Moveable or gmem_Discardable);
```

This line means that Windows can "discard" memory and "reload" it when it is needed again as well as move it—thus freeing up even more memory when necessary.

You no doubt have noticed the prefix global in most of the previous short examples. Deciding whether to allocate and use local or global memory blocks is an important issue, discussed in some detail in the next section.

Global and Local Memory

Your applications can allocate memory blocks in either of two areas: the global or the local heap.

The global heap is all the memory that Windows "claims" when you run it. The global heap is shared by Windows, Windows applications, and the "global" memory blocks allocated by Windows applications (like yours). Global memory is fantastically powerful because it is system-sized; it contains memory within and beyond your applications. A global memory block can be as large as 1M in Windows standard mode and 64M in 386 enhanced mode. A global memory block can be used to access the data in other programs.

The local heap is memory that is accessible only by a specific instance of your application. In other words, it is "private" to your application and just like the heap you were used to in Turbo Pascal (before Windows). The local heap is limited to whatever is left of the 64K data segment after your application has used some for a stack and its own global variables. The local heap is only 8K by default, but you can adjust its size using either the `$M` compiler directive or the Turbo Pascal for Window's IDE option/Compiler/MemorySize menus.

In addition, the maximum size of the local heap can depend on whether your application's data segment is fixed or movable. If it is fixed, the local heap is restricted to the size you allocated using the `$M` compiler directive (or the IDE) at compile time. If the data segment is moveable, your application can request a larger size than the one you specified at compile time. Sounds convenient, but there is a possible side effect: Windows might get a bit of extra memory for your application by moving the data segment, which in turn probably invalidates any far (or long) pointers to local data.

Whether you use local or global memory depends primarily on two factors:

1. How big a block you need
2. Whether the block is used for a local or global task

If you need only a little bit of memory (1K or less), then you probably want to use local memory because it is faster and does not require the 20 bytes of Windows overhead required to allocate a global memory block.

Global memory is your choice if you need a bigger block or to connect to system-wide resources, such as another application's data or the Clipboard—more on this in Chapter 11, "From Program to Program Using DDE (Dynamic Data Exchange)." Global memory is somewhat slower because it is accessed through Windows global memory handles, but it can be far larger.

Allocating Local Memory Blocks

Allocating local and global memory blocks is similar. The following segment shows how to allocate a moveable, local memory block of 256K:

```
var
  ALocalHandle : THandle;

begin
     ALocalHandle := LocalAlloc(lmem_Moveable,256);
     {.......}
end;
```

Allocate the local memory as either fixed, moveable, or moveable and discardable, using the Windows API function, `LocalAlloc`.

LocalAlloc returns a memory block identifier (a number) if it is successful and zero if it is not successful. This identifier is the handle to the memory block.

ALocalHandle is a THandle, already declared in ObjectWindows, which can be accessed by other functions needing to find the handle.

After you have asked to allocate the memory block, check to see whether the memory allocation has been successful. If the allocation was successful, LocalAlloc returns the handle to the memory block. If unsuccessful, it returns a zero:

```
if ALocalHandle <> 0 then
{....}
```

If the allocation has not been successful, bail out. If the allocation was successful, lock the memory block and get its address:

```
var
     APtrLocalData: { Pointer }

begin
     APtrLocalData := LocalLock(ALocalHandle);
     {......}
end;
```

If the lock is successful, LocalLock returns a pointer to the block (an address). If not, it returns nil. Check for success before moving on:

```
if APtrLocalData <> nil then
     { ..... }
```

If successful, process the data. When you are finished with the block, use the Windows API function LocalUnlock to unlock it, and either free or discard it so that Windows can recover the memory if necessary. Free the memory by freeing the handle:

```
LocalUnlock(ALocalHandle);
LocalFree(ALocalHandle):
```

or discard:

```
LocalUnlock(ALocalHandle);
LocalDiscard(ALocalHandle);
```

You must Unlock the block (which sets the Lock Count to zero) before you free or discard it. Otherwise, the free or discard operation fails because it automatically checks the Lock count to see whether it is zero. Zero indicates that the block can be freed or discarded.

Freeing a memory block removes its contents and invalidates the handle to the memory block by removing the handle from a table of valid local memory handles.

Discarding a memory block reallocates its size to zero, but does not remove the handle from the local memory handles table. You can reuse the handle, using the LocalRealloc procedure, and reallocate a new memory block of a different size:

```
var
     ALocalHandle: THandle;

begin
     { .... Previous allocation and use of block }
     LocalDiscard(ALocalHandle};
     ALocalHandle :=
     LocalReAlloc(ALocalHandle,512,lmem_Moveable);
     {.... more processing }
end;
```

You might want to reuse a memory block to save the unlocking- and new-handle allocation steps.

You also can find out how large a local block is by using LocalSize:

```
var
     ALocalHandle : THandle;
     MemoryBlockSize: Word;

begin
     ALocalHandle := LocalAlloc(lmem_Moveable,512);
     if ALocalHandle <> 0 then
          MemoryBlockSize := LocalSize(ALocalHandle);
end;
```

Notice again that you allocate and access the memory block indirectly through a handle to the memory block, not directly through a pointer. Because you are accessing memory indirectly (by handle), Windows can safely move memory blocks around and inform you where they are only when you need to know. Most of the time you do not know where a memory block is, and that is just fine. Thank you, Windows.

One way you can use a local memory block is simply to store a text buffer on the local heap. For example, you might want to store a large string for use by a single module, as the code in listing 9.1 illustrates. Note that a MessageBox is used to display the status and results of the local memory allocation, which occurs before the MainWindow is displayed. Also note that it is necessary to convert the displayed character into a string before using MessageBox to display it. Remember: Windows functions, such as MessageBox, that display strings require null-terminated strings.

Figure 9.4 shows a message box indicating that the local memory allocation has not occurred yet. Figure 9.5 shows the MessageBox displaying the first character in the locally allocated array of characters, after the allocation. Figure 9.6 shows the MainWindow displayed after the allocation.

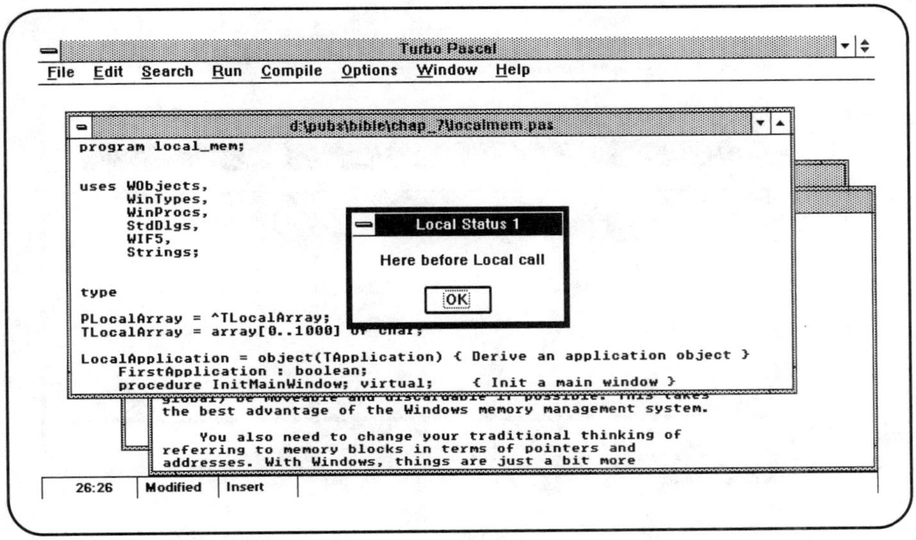

Figure 9.4. *A message box showing that the local memory allocation has not yet occurred.*

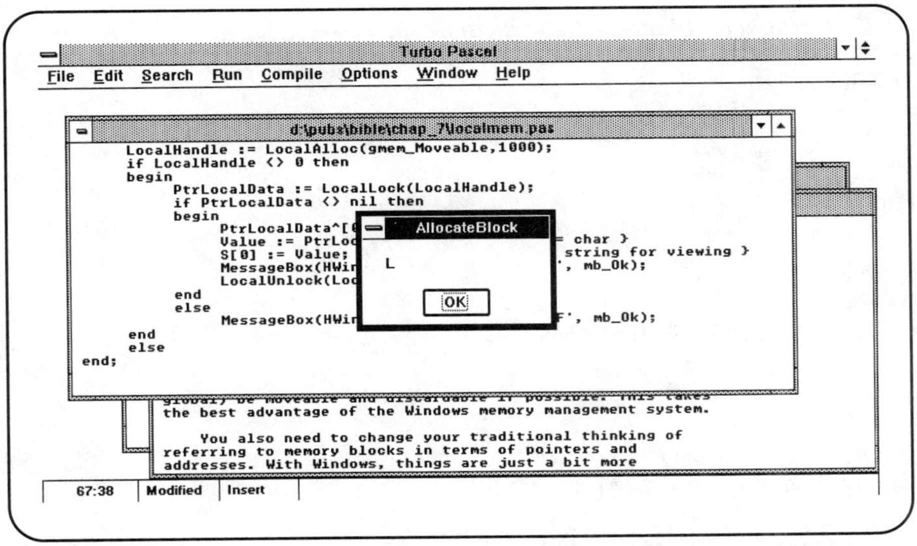

Figure 9.5. *A message box displaying the first character in the locally allocated array of characters (after allocation).*

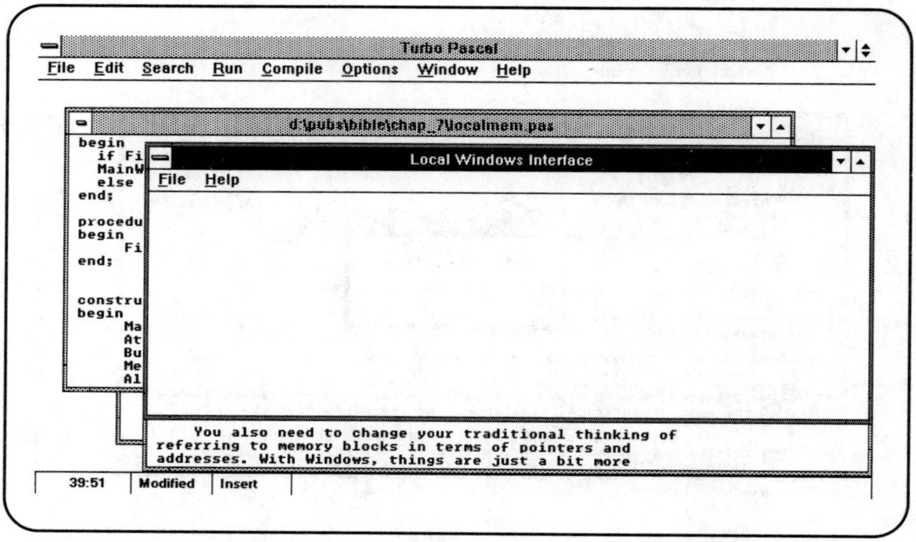

Figure 9.6. The `MainWindow` *displayed after allocation.*

Listing 9.1. Storing a text buffer on the local heap.

```
program local_mem;

uses
     WObjects,
     WinTypes,
     WinProcs,
     StdDlgs,
     Strings,
     WIF5;        { Basic Interface }

type

PLocalArray = ^TLocalArray;
TLocalArray = array[0..1000] of char;

LocalApplication = object(TApplication) { Derive an application object }
     FirstApplication : boolean;
     procedure InitMainWindow; virtual; { Init a main window }
     procedure InitApplication; virtual;
end;

PLocalWindow = ^LocalWindow;
```

```
LocalWindow = object(MainWindow)
     LocalHandle: THandle;
     PtrLocalData: PBigArray;
     Value: Char;
     S : array[0..9] of char;
     constructor Init(AParent : PWindowsObject; ATitle : PChar);
     procedure AllocateBlock;
end;


{ LocalApplication method implementation }

procedure LocalApplication.InitMainWindow;
begin
  if FirstApplication then
  MainWindow := New(PLocalWindow, Init(nil, 'Local Windows Interface'))
  else MainWindow := New(PLocalWindow, Init(nil,'Additional
               Instance of BI'));
end;

procedure LocalApplication.InitApplication;
begin
     FirstApplication := True;
end;

constructor LocalWindow.Init(AParent : PWindowsObject; ATitle : PChar);
begin
     MainWindow.Init(AParent, ATitle); { Send message to ancestor's constructor }
     Attr.Menu  := LoadMenu(HInstance, PChar(100)); { 100 = menu ID }
     ButtonDown := False;              { Set status flag }
     MessageBox(HWindow,' Here before Local call', 'Local
          Status 1', mb_Ok);
     AllocateBlock;                    { Allocate the block }
end;

procedure LocalWindow.AllocateBlock;
begin
     LocalHandle := LocalAlloc(gmem_Moveable,1000);
     if LocalHandle <> 0 then
     begin
          PtrLocalData := LocalLock(LocalHandle);
          if PtrLocalData <> nil then
          begin
```

continues

Listing 9.1. continued

```
                PtrLocalData^[0] := 'L';
                Value := PtrLocalData^[0];          { Value = char }
                S[0] := Value;  { Convert to a string for viewing }
                MessageBox(HWindow,S, 'AllocateBlock', mb_Ok);
                LocalUnlock(LocalHandle);
           end
           else
                MessageBox(HWindow,' Local Fail', 'LF', mb_Ok);
      end
      else
end;

var
  Application1: LocalApplication;  { An instance of BasicApplication }

                                   { Run Application1 }
begin
  Application1.Init('Local Interface');  { Init application instance }
  Application1.Run;                { Message loop }
  Application1.Done;               { Destroy application instance }
end.
```

Global Memory Blocks

Working with global memory blocks is similar. The following segment shows how to allocate a moveable, global memory block of 256K:

```
var
  AGlobalHandle : THandle;

begin
     AGlobalHandle := GlobalAlloc(gmem_Moveable,1024);
     {.......}
end;
```

Allocate the global memory as either fixed, moveable, or moveable or discardable, using the Windows API function `GlobalAlloc`.

`GlobalAlloc` returns a memory block identifier (a number) if it is successful and zero if not successful. This identifier is the handle to the memory block:

`AGlobalHandle` is a `THandle`, already declared in ObjectWindows, which can be accessed by other functions needing to find the handle.

After you have asked that the memory block be allocated, check to see whether the memory allocation has been successful. If the allocation was successful, `GlobalAlloc` returns the handle to the memory block. If unsuccessful, it returns a zero:

```
if AGlobalHandle <> 0 then
{....}
```

If the allocation has not been successful, bail out. If the allocation was successful, lock the memory block and get its address:

```
var
     APtrGlobalData: { Pointer }

begin
     APtrGlobalData := GlobalLock(AGlobalHandle);
     {......}
end;
```

If the lock is successful, `GlobalLock`, like `LocalLock`, returns a pointer to the block (an address). If not, it returns nil. Check for success before moving on:

```
if APtrGlobalData <> nil then
     { ..... }
```

If successful, process the data. When you are finished with the block, use the Windows API function `GlobalUnlock` to unlock it, and either free or discard it so that Windows can recover the memory if necessary. Free the memory by freeing the handle:

```
GlobalUnlock(AGlobalHandle);
GlobalFree(AGlobalHandle):
```

or discard:

```
GlobalUnlock(AGlobalHandle);
GlobalDiscard(AGlobalHandle);
```

Again, as with local memory allocation, you must unlock the block (setting the Lock Count to zero) before you free or discard it. Otherwise the free or discard operation fails because it automatically checks the Lock count to see whether it is zero.

Freeing a memory block removes its contents and invalidates the handle to the memory block by removing the handle from a table of valid global memory handles.

Discarding a global memory block reallocates its size to zero, but does not remove the handle from the global memory handles table. You can reuse the handle, using the `GlobalRealloc` procedure, and reallocate a new memory block of a different size:

```
var
     AGlobalHandle: THandle;

begin
     { .... Previous allocation and use of block }
     GlobalDiscard(AGlobalHandle};
     AGlobalHandle :=
     GlobalReAlloc(AGlobalHandle,512,gmem_Moveable);
     {.... more processing }
end;
```

You also can determine how large a global block is by using `GlobalSize`:

```
var
     AGlobalHandle : THandle;
     MemoryBlockSize: Word;

begin
     AGlobalHandle := GlobalAlloc(gmem_Moveable,1024);
     if AGlobalHandle <> 0 then
          MemoryBlockSize := GlobalSize(AGlobalHandle);
end;
```

Whenever you need to use a large block, use global memory. Listing 9.2 shows you how to create a large global buffer. Figure 9.7 shows a `MessageBox` displayed before the global allocation. Figure 9.8 shows the value of the first six characters of the global array. Figure 9.9 shows the `MainWindow` (`GlobalWindow`) displayed after the global allocation.

If the global allocation does not succeed, a `MessageBox` indicates the global failure. The user must acknowledge the failure, and then processing continues.

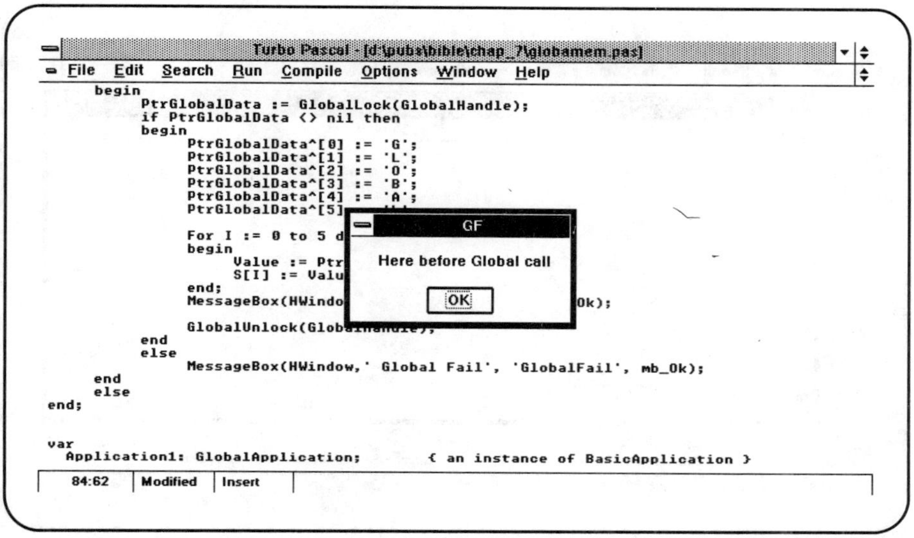

Figure 9.7. A message box showing that the global allocation has not occurred.

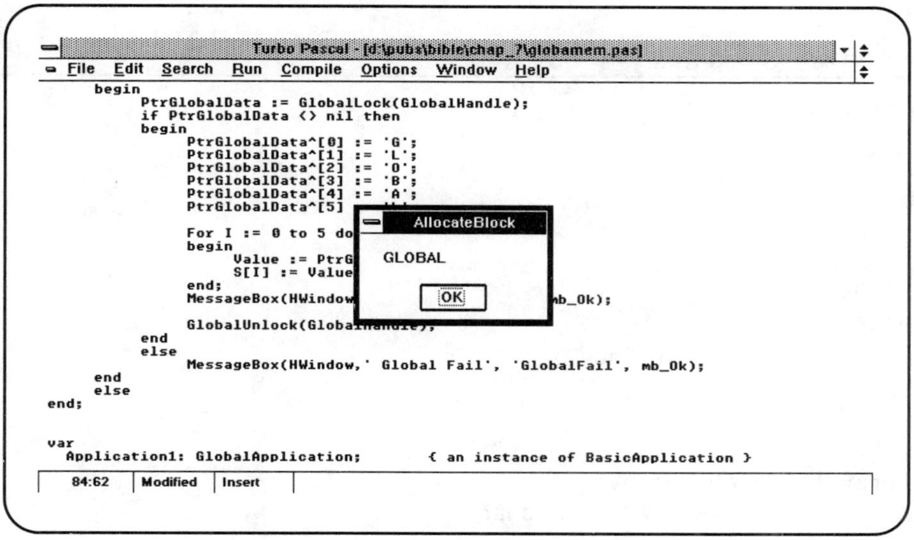

Figure 9.8. A message box displaying the first six characters in the globally allocated array after global allocation.

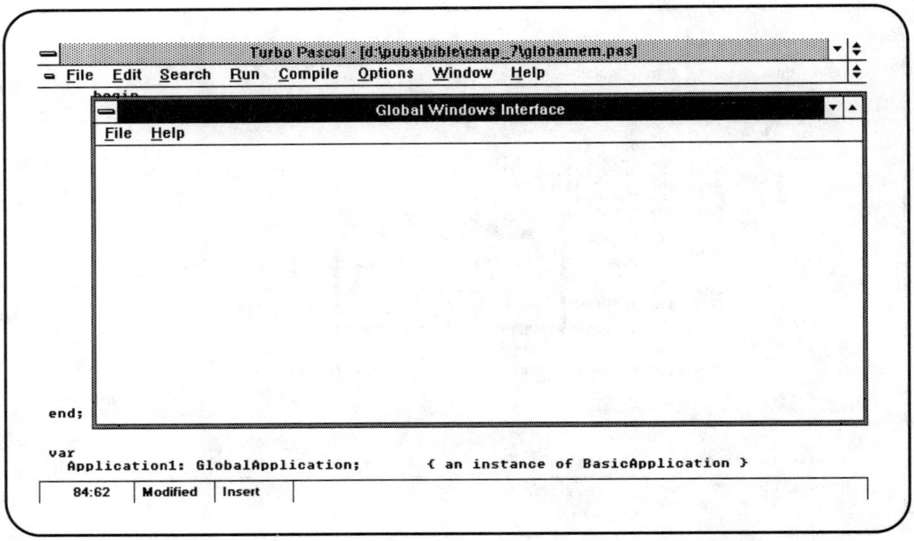

Figure 9.9. *The* `MainWindow` *(*`GlobalWindow`*) after the global allocation.*

Listing 9.2. *Creating a large global buffer.*

```
program glob_mem;

uses
     WObjects,
     WinTypes,
     WinProcs,
     StdDlgs,
     Strings,
     WIF5;   { Basic Interface }

type

PGlobalArray = ^TGlobalArray;
TGlobalArray = array[0..1024] of char;

GlobalApplication = object(TApplication) { Derive an application object }
    FirstApplication : boolean;
    procedure InitMainWindow; virtual;   { Init a main window }
    procedure InitApplication; virtual;
end;

PGlobalWindow = ^GlobalWindow;
```

```
GlobalWindow = object(MainWindow)
     GlobalHandle: THandle;
     PtrGlobalData: PGlobalArray;
     Value: Char;
     S : array[0..9] of char;
     constructor Init(AParent : PWindowsObject; ATitle : PChar);
     procedure AllocateBlock;
end;


{ BasicApplication method implementation }

procedure GlobalApplication.InitMainWindow;
begin
  if FirstApplication then
  MainWindow := New(PGlobalWindow, Init(nil, 'Global Windows Interface'))
  else MainWindow := New(PGlobalWindow, Init(nil,'Additional
                       Instance of GI'));
end;




procedure GlobalApplication.InitApplication;
begin
     FirstApplication := True;
end;

constructor GlobalWindow.Init(AParent : PWindowsObject; ATitle : PChar);
begin
     MainWindow.Init(AParent, ATitle); { Send message to ancestor's
                                          constructor }
     Attr.Menu  := LoadMenu(HInstance, PChar(100)); { 100 = menu ID }
     ButtonDown := False;               { Set status flag }
     MessageBox(HWindow,' Here before Global call', 'GF', mb_Ok);
     AllocateBlock;
end;

procedure GlobalWindow.AllocateBlock;
var
     I : integer;
begin
     GlobalHandle := GlobalAlloc(gmem_Moveable,1024);
     if GlobalHandle <> 0 then
```

continues

Listing 9.2. continued

```
    begin
        PtrGlobalData := GlobalLock(GlobalHandle);
        if PtrGlobalData <> nil then
        begin
            PtrGlobalData^[0] := 'G';
            PtrGlobalData^[1] := 'L';
            PtrGlobalData^[2] := 'O';
            PtrGlobalData^[3] := 'B';
            PtrGlobalData^[4] := 'A';
            PtrGlobalData^[5] := 'L';

            For I := 0 to 5 do
            begin
                Value := PtrGlobalData^[I];
                S[I] := Value;
            end;
            MessageBox(HWindow,S, 'AllocateBlock', mb_Ok);
            GlobalUnlock(GlobalHandle);
        end
        else
            MessageBox(HWindow,' Global Fail', 'GF', mb_Ok);
    end
    else
end;



var
  Application1: GlobalApplication; { An instance of BasicApplication }

                                   { Run Application1 }
begin
  Application1.Init('Global Interface'); { Init application instance }
  Application1.Run;                { Message loop }
  Application1.Done;               { Destroy application instance }
end.
```

Whether to use global or local memory depends both on the size of the memory block you are allocating and who needs to access it. In Chapter 11, you use global memory blocks to exchange data with the clipboard and other applications through DDE (Dynamic Data Exchange).

A Few Advanced Memory Matters

As a rule of thumb, when in doubt, allocate memory as moveable rather than fixed. A memory block should be allocated as fixed only if you must keep a memory block in a single location throughout the life of your application. If you fix a memory block, you sacrifice much of the sophistication of Windows' memory-management system.

There are a couple of notable variations on the fixer theme you might want to be aware of:

- All segments are moveable in standard (or 286 protected) mode because Windows can move segments without changing their addresses. Windows changes the base address in the segment descriptor table, not the segment address. Not so, of course, in real mode.
- Also, whenever your application gets a far pointer from Windows, the far pointer references a fixed data segment. For example, each time your application starts up, it gets a far pointer to a location in memory that holds a command-line argument for your application.

For a more in-depth discussion of how Windows manages code and data segments, check out Charles Petzold's excellent *Programming Windows*, a guide to programming Windows using C (Microsoft Press). Although Petzold's examples and attention are almost entirely C-oriented, he provides an incredible amount of useful and general information about Windows programming.

Direct Memory Access

Turbo Pascal for Windows has three predefined arrays (`Mem`, `MemW`, and `MemL`) that enable you to access memory directly. Using these arrays, you can change the values of a byte of memory. This book does not detail how to manipulate memory directly, because it is probably not a good idea to do so. By directly manipulating memory, you interfere with the Windows memory-management system and seriously jeopardize the life expectancy of your applications. Unless you have an outstanding reason for accessing memory directly, let Windows do it.

Data Segments

Each application running in Windows has its own 64K data segment. This data segment is the one pointed to by the data segment (DS) register. It consists of four parts:

1. A local heap (you specify size)
2. A stack (for local variables—the ones allocated in procedures and functions)
3. A stack data area for global variables and typed constants
4. A task header that identifies the segment

Each dynamic link library (DLL) running in Windows has its own 64K data segment as well, which consists of a task header and a local heap, but not a stack or stack data area. DLL procedures and functions use the stack of the application that called them.

Heap Errors

Something else you might want to think about are heap errors. If the Turbo Pascal for Windows heap manager cannot allocate the memory block you request (using `New` or `GetMem`), it generates a run-time error. A run-time error is probably not desirable for your application. More likely, you want your application to continue processing, even if it cannot allocate the memory block.

The solution is a `HeapError` variable. Use the `HeapError` variable to install a heap error function that is sent a message whenever the heap manager cannot allocate the memory block you request. The `HeapError` variable is a pointer to a function (in the system unit) with a header such as this:

```
function HeapFunc(Size: Word): Integer; far;
```

Install the `HeapFunc` by assigning its address to the `HeapError` variable:

```
HeapError := @HeapFunc;
```

`HeapFunc` is called automatically whenever a `New` or `GetMem` request fails. The `Size` parameter contains the size of the memory block that could not be allocated. The `HeapFunc` should return a zero, one, or two. A zero indicates a memory-allocation failure and causes a run-time error. A one indicates failure, but does not generate a run-time error. A two indicates success. To guarantee that your application does not crash after an unsuccessful memory-allocation attempt, have the `HeapFunc` return a one:

```
function HeapFunc(Size: Word): Integer; far;
begin
    HeapFunc := 1;
end;
```

When the `HeapFunc` returns a one, it forces `New` or `GetMem` to return a nil pointer rather than crash the program.

The `HeapError` variable also can be used to install a constructor-error-recovery system.

Code Segments

Each unit, library, or main program has its own code segment. Each of these code segments can be up to 64K in size, limited only by available memory.

Each code segment can be moveable or fixed, preloaded or demand-loaded, discardable or permanent. (The default attributes for a code segment are moveable, preloaded, and permanent. Unless you are doing some non-ordinary programming, you do not have to change these defaults. This mini-discussion is included just in case.)

If a code segment is moveable it can be moved by Windows to free memory blocks. If a code segment is fixed, Windows cannot move it. To make your application flexible for Windows, it should reside in moveable code segments.

If a code segment is preloaded, it is automatically loaded when you activate the application. If a code segment is demand-loaded, it is loaded only when a routine that resides in the segment is called.

If a code segment is discardable, it behaves much like an overlaid segment. Windows can temporarily discard it and free its memory when it needs to. Windows then reloads the segment when a procedure or function in the code segment is needed.

Reloading a segment is obviously more time-consuming. The trade-off: your application takes up less room and again is more flexible and can be moved around by Windows.

wm_Compacting

One other important matter you might want to inform your applications of is the `wm_Compacting` message. Windows broadcasts this message to all high-level windows when it begins to spend more than 12.5 percent of its time compacting memory.

Because compacting memory is obviously a time-consuming task for the Windows management system, it sends this message to indicate that it is spending too much time "managing" rather than running applications.

When an application receives this message, it should attempt to free as much memory as it can. Your application responds to this message the same way it responds to any Windows message: with a Windows message-response method. For example:

```
AnObjectInstance.WMCompacting(var Msg: TMessage);
begin
     { Handle compaction message by freeing memory here }
end;
```

Wrap-up

That discussion covers the general memory issues you need to know in order to write sensible Windows applications. Windows is a dynamic system in various ways, and object-oriented techniques can help you use and appreciate this dynamic quality.

In general, you should let Windows handle anything it can handle for you because (frankly) it is going to be better at it. You also can ease the process for Windows by letting the blocks of memory you allocate (whether local or global) be moveable and discardable, if possible. This takes the best advantage of the Windows memory-management system.

You also must change your traditional thinking when you refer to memory blocks in terms of pointers and addresses. With Windows, memory blocks are just a little more indirect. You get the address from a handle first because Windows has a built-in system for manipulating memory through handles. By using handles, other applications can "get a handle" on the memory that another application is using. This creates the useful possibility of exchanging data between applications, which you learn about in detail in Chapter 11.

10

CHAPTER

DISPLAY CONTEXTS AND DRAWING TOOLS

I wanted the audience to know that a computer was making the drawings. People would stand there for a long time watching the computer produce drawings. The pen would pause and people would say, "Gee, it's thinking of what to do next."

Aaron Cohen

Although you have already used the Graphics Device Interface in most of the previous chapters, this chapter spends a little time describing its features. To help the GDI make more sense, several examples of how you might use it to create complex graphics-oriented applications are covered.

The Windows GDI is a remarkable aspect of Windows because it allows you to write applications that display and manipulate graphics, independent of a specific display device. You can, for example, write applications that use the same code yet can be displayed in EGA, VGA, or Hercules modes.

Windows achieves device independence by using various device drivers that translate GDI function calls into commands that make sense to the specific output device being used. You write code as though the output device does not matter, which (in general) is how it is.

Handling a Display Context

A display context is the surface of an application window's client area, or more precisely, it *represents* the surface of an application window's client area. Any display context has attributes that represent colors, window position, drawing tools, and so on. (These attributes are set to default values by ObjectWindows, which is why you have not had to set any of these attributes in the examples so far.)

A display context uses a lot of memory, so Windows limits any Windows session to a total of five concurrent in-use display contexts. It is important, therefore, that your application release any display context it is using as soon as it no longer needs the display context. This action results in a repetitive, seemingly inefficient (but necessary) possessing and releasing of display contexts, and it does have a drawback. It means foremost that your application does not maintain control over a display context.

When an application releases a display context, it is giving it up to any other application that needs it. The new application can, in turn, manipulate its attributes. Each time an application releases a display context, the display context's attributes are reset to the defaults. Thus, your application must set any display context attributes for changing each time it receives a display context. In addition, your application must reselect any drawing tool (pen, brush, font) for use each time it receives a display context.

For example, derive a drawing window that resets a specific kind of pen (a drawing tool) each time it obtains a display context. In addition, let the user modify both the pen size (the width of the line it draws) and the pen style.

This example shows how to

- Obtain and release a display context.
- Use menu-command messages to invoke a dialog.
- Create, modify, and delete drawing tools.

Begin, as usual, by deriving an `Application` (object):

```
type
  DrawingApplication = object(BasicApplication)
    procedure InitMainWindow; virtual;
end;
```

and its `MainWindow` (a `DrawingWindow`):

```
type
  PDrawingWindow = ^DrawingWindow;
  DrawingWindow = object(MainWindow)
    DragDC: HDC;                  { A new display context }
    ThePen: HPen;                 { A drawing tool }
```

```
    PenSize: Integer;           { Pen variables }
    PenStyle: Integer;
  constructor Init(AParent: PWindowsObject; ATitle: PChar);
  destructor Done; virtual;
  function CanClose: Boolean; virtual;
                                { New mouse methods }
  procedure WMLButtonDown(var Msg: TMessage);
    virtual wm_First + wm_LButtonDown;
  procedure WMLButtonUp(var Msg: TMessage);
    virtual wm_First + wm_LButtonUp;
  procedure WMMouseMove(var Msg: TMessage);
    virtual wm_First + wm_MouseMove;
                                { Menu-response methods }
  procedure CMPenStyle(var Msg: TMessage);
    virtual cm_First + cm_PenStyle;
  procedure CMPenSize(var Msg: TMessage);
    virtual cm_First + cm_PenSize;
                                { Pen modifiers }
  procedure SetPenSize(NewSize: Integer);
  procedure SetPenStyle(NewStyle: Integer);
end;
```

The `CMPenSize` and `CMPenStyle` methods are menu-response methods, which respond to the menu commands `cm_PenSize` and `cm_PenStyle`. Declare these two commands in the `const` section:

```
const
     cm_PenStyle = 401;
     cm_PenSize  = 402;
```

These constants correspond to the menu items in the resource file, PEN.RES. Figure 10.1 shows the creation and testing of PEN.RES. Notice the matching constants.

When you construct the `DrawingWindow`:

1. Load the menu (PEN.RES) that contains the `PenSize` and `PenStyle` menu items.

2. Set the default pen size and style.

3. Create the pen, using `CreatePen`:

```
constructor DrawingWindow.Init(AParent: PWindowsObject;
ATitle: PChar);
begin
  TWindow.Init(AParent, ATitle);
  Attr.Menu := LoadMenu(HInstance, PChar(109));
```

```
    ButtonDown := False;
    PenSize := 1;           { Size increases with integer value }
    PenStyle := ps_DashDot; { Refers to a pen constant, an integer }
    ThePen := CreatePen(PenStyle, PenSize, 0);
  end;
```

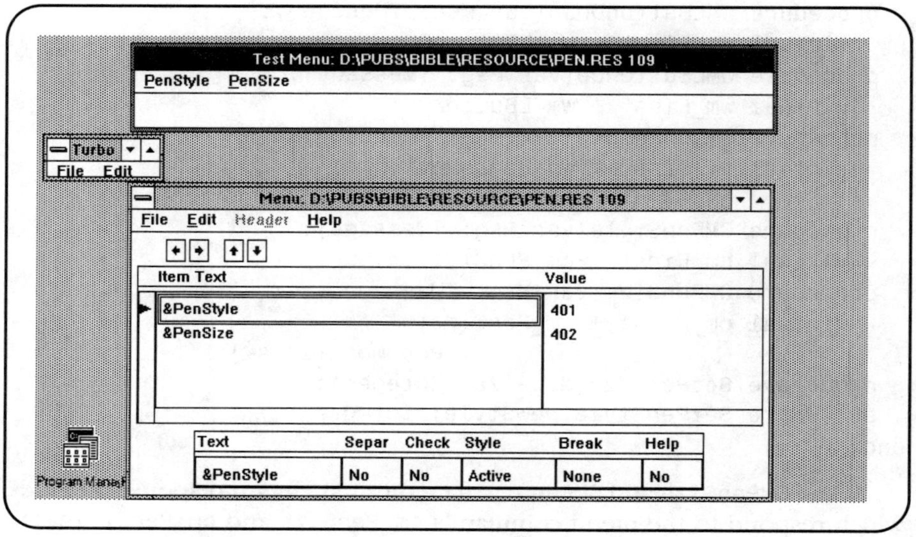

Figure 10.1. *Creation and testing of PEN.RES.*

Notice that the drawing tool (the pen) is not associated with a display context. You do not obtain a display context until you decide to use one. In this example, the user can draw in the window when she presses the left mouse button down:

```
procedure DrawingWindow.WMLButtonDown(var Msg: TMessage);
begin
  (* InvalidateRect(HWindow, nil, True); if you want the
             window cleared *)
  if not ButtonDown then
  begin
    ButtonDown := True;
    SetCapture(HWindow);
    DragDC := GetDC(HWindow);
    SelectObject(DragDC, ThePen);  { Select the pen created in Init }
    MoveTo(DragDC, Msg.LParamLo, Msg.LParamHi);       { Use the pen }
  end;
end;
```

She releases the display context when she is finished drawing:

```
procedure DrawingWindow.WMLButtonUp(var Msg: TMessage);
begin
  if ButtonDown then
  begin
    ButtonDown := False; ReleaseCapture;
    ReleaseDC(HWindow, DragDC);
  end;
end;
```

Notice that, although the display context has been released so that other applications can use their own display contexts, the `DrawingWindow` is still open, and you can still draw in the window. Each time you click the left mouse button, the application grabs a display context for you to use.

Now write the menu-response methods for modifying the pen's size and style. When the user selects the `PenSize` menu item, a dialog window appears that allows her to change the pen size:

```
procedure DrawingWindow.CMPenSize(var Msg: TMessage);
var
  InputText: array[0..5] of Char;
  NewSize, ErrorPos: Integer;
begin
  if not ButtonDown then
  begin
    Str(PenSize, InputText);
    if Application^.ExecDialog(New(PInputDialog,
      Init(@Self, 'Line Thickness', 'Input a new thickness:',
        InputText, SizeOf(InputText)))) = id_Ok then
    begin
      Val(InputText, NewSize, ErrorPos);
      if ErrorPos = 0 then SetPenSize(NewSize);
    end;
  end;
end;
```

A procedure for actually creating the new pen in the new size:

```
procedure DrawingWindow.SetPenSize(NewSize: Integer);
begin
  DeleteObject(ThePen);
  ThePen := CreatePen(PenStyle, NewSize, 0);
  PenSize := NewSize;
end;
```

The same goes for PenStyle. A response method that uses a dialog to allow the user to modify the pen's style is

```
procedure DrawingWindow.CMPenStyle(var Msg: TMessage);
var
  InputText: array[0..5] of Char;
  NewStyle, ErrorPos: Integer;
begin
  if not ButtonDown then
  begin
    Str(PenStyle, InputText);
    if Application^.ExecDialog(New(PInputDialog,
      Init(@Self, 'Pen Style', 'New Pen Style: 0 = solid
           1 = dash 2 = dot, and so on,
           InputText, SizeOf(InputText)))) = id_Ok then
    begin
      Val(InputText, NewStyle, ErrorPos);
      if ErrorPos = 0 then SetPenStyle(NewStyle);
    end;
  end;
end;
```

A SetPenStyle method to actually create the new pen is

```
procedure DrawingWindow.SetPenStyle(NewStyle: Integer);
begin
  DeleteObject(ThePen);
  ThePen := CreatePen(NewStyle, PenSize, 0);
  PenStyle := NewStyle;
end;
```

Notice that the DrawingWindow does not "own" a display context while the pen's size and style are modified. You do not need it to create and modify drawing tools (objects) that are used to draw on the display context. Also, notice that because the two variables PenStyle and PenSize maintain the status of the drawing tools, each time the DrawingWindow obtains a display context it uses the current settings for the pen. The pen (with its current values) is selected just after the display context is obtained:

```
DragDC := GetDC(HWindow);           { Get a display context }
SelectObject(DragDC, ThePen);       { Select the pen created in Init }
```

When you finish with the DrawingWindow (not the display context), delete the drawing tool (the pen) using DeleteObject:

```
destructor DrawingWindow.Done;
begin
  DeleteObject(ThePen);
  TWindow.Done;
end;
```

Because the drawing tool (object) is not part of the display context, it is not deleted automatically when the display context is released. Listing 10.1 shows the complete `Pen` modification example, and figure 10.2 shows the `DrawingWindow` created by this code.

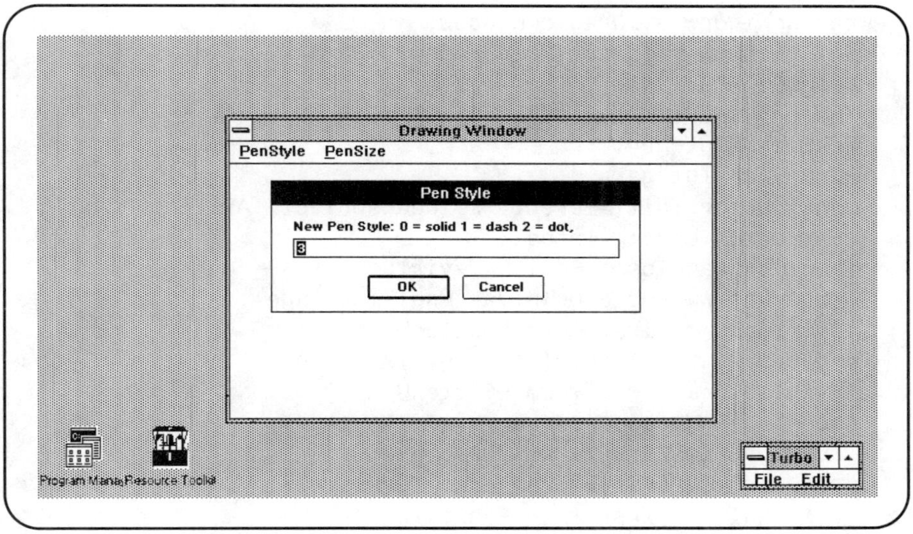

Figure 10.2. *The* `DrawingWindow` *created by listing 10.1.*

Listing 10.1. *The complete pen-modification example.*

```
program Pen;

uses
     Strings,
     WinTypes,
     WinProcs,
     WObjects,
     WIF5,      { Basic Interface }
     StdDlgs;

{$R Pen.Res }
```

continues

Listing 10.1. continued

```
const
     cm_PenStyle = 401;
     cm_PenSize  = 402;

type
  DrawingApplication = object(BasicApplication)
    procedure InitMainWindow; virtual;
  end;

  PDrawingWindow = ^DrawingWindow;
  DrawingWindow = object(MainWindow)
    DragDC: HDC;
    ThePen: HPen;
    PenSize: Integer;
    PenStyle: Integer;
    constructor Init(AParent: PWindowsObject; ATitle: PChar);
    destructor Done; virtual;
    function CanClose: Boolean; virtual;
    procedure WMLButtonDown(var Msg: TMessage);
      virtual wm_First + wm_LButtonDown;
    procedure WMLButtonUp(var Msg: TMessage);
      virtual wm_First + wm_LButtonUp;
    procedure WMMouseMove(var Msg: TMessage);
      virtual wm_First + wm_MouseMove;
    procedure CMPenStyle(var Msg: TMessage);
      virtual cm_First + cm_PenStyle;
    procedure CMPenSize(var Msg: TMessage);
      virtual cm_First + cm_PenSize;
    procedure SetPenSize(NewSize: Integer);
    procedure SetPenStyle(NewStyle: Integer);
  end;

{---------------------------------------------------}
{ DrawingWindow's method implementations:           }
{---------------------------------------------------}

constructor DrawingWindow.Init(AParent: PWindowsObject; ATitle: PChar);
begin
  TWindow.Init(AParent, ATitle);
  Attr.Menu := LoadMenu(HInstance, PChar(109));
  ButtonDown := False;
  PenSize := 1;
  PenStyle := ps_DashDot;
```

```
  ThePen := CreatePen(PenStyle, PenSize, 0);
end;

destructor DrawingWindow.Done;
begin
  DeleteObject(ThePen);
  TWindow.Done;
end;

procedure DrawingWindow.CMPenStyle(var Msg: TMessage);
var
  InputText: array[0..5] of Char;
  NewStyle, ErrorPos: Integer;
begin
  if not ButtonDown then
  begin
    Str(PenStyle, InputText);
    if Application^.ExecDialog(New(PInputDialog,
      Init(@Self, 'Pen Style', 'New Pen Style:
           0 = solid 1 = dash 2 = dot, etc.',
           InputText, SizeOf(InputText)))) = id_Ok then
    begin
      Val(InputText, NewStyle, ErrorPos);
      if ErrorPos = 0 then SetPenStyle(NewStyle);
    end;
  end;
end;

procedure DrawingWindow.SetPenStyle(NewStyle: Integer);
begin
  DeleteObject(ThePen);
  ThePen := CreatePen(NewStyle, PenSize, 0);
  PenStyle := NewStyle;
end;

function DrawingWindow.CanClose: Boolean;
var
  Reply: Integer;
begin
  CanClose := True;
```

continues

Listing 10.1. continued

```
  Reply := MessageBox(HWindow, 'Do you want to save?',
    'Drawing has changed', mb_YesNo or mb_IconQuestion);
  if Reply = id_Yes then CanClose := False;
end;

procedure DrawingWindow.WMLButtonDown(var Msg: TMessage);
begin
  (* InvalidateRect(HWindow, nil, True); *)
  if not ButtonDown then
  begin
    ButtonDown := True;
    SetCapture(HWindow);
    DragDC := GetDC(HWindow);
    SelectObject(DragDC, ThePen);
    MoveTo(DragDC, Msg.LParamLo, Msg.LParamHi);
  end;
end;

procedure DrawingWindow.WMMouseMove(var Msg: TMessage);
begin
  if ButtonDown then
    LineTo(DragDC, Integer(Msg.LParamLo), Integer(Msg.LParamHi));
end;

procedure DrawingWindow.WMLButtonUp(var Msg: TMessage);
begin
  if ButtonDown then
  begin
    ButtonDown := False;
    ReleaseCapture;
    ReleaseDC(HWindow, DragDC);
  end;
end;

procedure DrawingWindow.CMPenSize(var Msg: TMessage);
var
  InputText: array[0..5] of Char;
  NewSize, ErrorPos: Integer;
begin
  if not ButtonDown then
  begin
    Str(PenSize, InputText);
    if Application^.ExecDialog(New(PInputDialog,
```

```
      Init(@Self, 'Line Thickness', 'Input a new thickness:',
        InputText, SizeOf(InputText)))) = id_Ok then
    begin
      Val(InputText, NewSize, ErrorPos);
      if ErrorPos = 0 then SetPenSize(NewSize);
    end;
  end;
end;

procedure DrawingWindow.SetPenSize(NewSize: Integer);
begin
  DeleteObject(ThePen);
  ThePen := CreatePen(PenStyle, NewSize, 0);
  PenSize := NewSize;
end;

{---------------------------------------------------}
{ DrawingApplication's method implementations:      }
{---------------------------------------------------}

procedure DrawingApplication.InitMainWindow;
begin
  MainWindow := New(PDrawingWindow, Init(nil, 'Drawing Window'));
end;

{---------------------------------------------------}
{ Main program:                                     }
{---------------------------------------------------}

var
  App : DrawingApplication;

begin
  App.Init('DrawProgram');
  App.Run;
  App.Done;
end.
```

You also can think of a display context (DC) as a storage of the attributes that determine how Windows GDI functions operate in a window's client area. A display context "holds" 19 attributes (a mapping mode, pen, font, text color, and so on). Each time your application asks for a display context from Windows, Windows creates a new one with a default value for each attribute. You do not have to set each of the 19 attributes each time you receive a DC. Table 10.1 shows the device context attribute and its default.

Table 10.1. Device context attributes with their defaults.

DC Attribute	*Default*
Mapping mode	MM_TEXT
Window origin	0,0
Viewport origin	0,0
Window extents	1,1
Viewport extents	1,1
Pen	BLACK_PEN
Brush	WHITE_BRUSH
Font	SYSTEM_FONT
Bit map	—
Current pen position	0,0
Background mode	Opaque
Background color	White
Text color	Black
Drawing mode	R2_COPYPEN
Stretching mode	BLACK-ONWHITE
Polygon filling mode	Alternate
Intercharacter spacing	0
Brush origin	0,0
Clipping region	—

You can override any of the display context's default attributes if you want. Windows provides a function for setting or selecting each attribute and for getting the value of an attribute. For example, to set the mapping mode attribute:

```
var
    ADCHandle : HDC;
    AMapMode : Integer;
begin
    SetMapMode(ADCHandle, AMapMode);
    {...}
end;
```

To set the Windows origin:

```
var
     ADCHandle : HDC;
     X, Y : Integer;

begin
     SetWindowOrg(ADCHandle,X,Y);
     {......}
end;
```

To get the text color:

```
var
     TxtColor : LongInt;
     ADCHandle : HDC;
begin
     TxtColor := GetTextColor(ADCHandle);
     {....}
end;
```

Table 10.2 shows the functions to set or select each of the display context attributes.

Table 10.2. *Functions to set or select display context attributes.*

DC Attribute	***Set/Select***	***Get***
Mapping mode	SetMapMode	GetMapMode
Window origin	SetWindowOrg	GetWindowOrg
Viewport origin	SetViewportOrg	GetViewportOrg
Window extents	SetWindowExt	GetWindowExt
Viewport extents	SetViewportExt	GetViewportExt
Pen	SelectObject	SelectObject
Brush	SelectObject	SelectObject
Font	SelectObject	SelectObject
Bit map	SelectObject	SelectObject
Current pen position	MoveTo; LineTo	GetCurrentPosition
Background mode	SetBkMode	GetBkMode
Background color	SetBkColor	GetBkColor

continues

Table 10.2. continued

DC Attribute	***Set/Select***	***Get***
Text color	SetTextColor	GetTextColor
Drawing mode	SetROP2	GetROP2
Stretching mode	SetPolyFillMode	GetPolyFillMode
Polygon filling mode	SetPOlyFillMode	GetPolyFillMode
Intercharacter spacing	SetTextCharacterExtra	GetTextChar..
Brush origin	SetBrushOrg	GetBrushOrg
Clipping region	SelectClipRgn SelectObject	GetClipBox SelectObject

The surface of the display context itself is a bit map that corresponds to some specific device. Thus, any device context's bit map is specific to the current display context that represents the video adapter your application is using. This suggests the problem of making the device-context bit map usable by different adapters.

The solution is for your application to create device-independent bit maps using the following Windows GDI functions:

```
CreateCompatibleDC,
CreateCompatible Bitmap,
CreateDIBitmap.
```

For example:

```
procedure SomeWindow.SetupWindow;
var
  HandleDC: HDC;
begin
  TNoIconWindow.SetupWindow;
  HandleDC := GetDC(HWindow);
  ABitmap := CreateCompatibleBitmap(HandleDC, 80, 80);
  ABkgnd := CreateCompatibleBitmap(HandleDC, 1000, 1000);
  ReleaseDC(HWindow, HandleDC);
end;
```

Your application can decide whether drawings are clipped in the display context by modifying the clipping-region attribute in the display context. Usually, you want to use the default clipping region, the client area of the window.

Set the clipping region when you select an object:

```
SelectObject(ADCHandle,ARegionHandle);
```

or use `SelectClipRgn`:

```
SelectClipRgn(ADCHandle,ARegionHandle);
```

Mapping Modes

One of the attributes you might find useful to change is the mapping mode. Windows defines eight mapping modes (the default `MM_TEXT`, `MM_LOMETRIC`, and so on). Table 10.3 shows these mapping modes.

***Table 10.3.** Windows mapping modes.*

Mapping Mode	*Logical Unit*
MM_TEXT	pixel
MM_LOMETRIC	0.1 mm
MM_HIMETRIC	0.01 mm
MM_LOENGLISH	0.01 inch
MM_HIENGLISH	0.001 inch
MM_TWIPS	1/1440 inch
MM_ISOTROPIC	Arbitrary (x=y)
MM_ANISOTROPIC	Arbitrary (x<>y)

The default mapping mode is `MM_TEXT`, which moves `X` and `Y` values a pixel at a time. Its origin (0,0) is the upper-left corner of the window's client area. If you have difficulty understanding how a screen, window, and window's client areas differ, see figure 10.3.

In short, the screen is the entire display. The window is an entire window, including the caption bar, scroll bars, window frame, and any menu. The window client area is the part of a window excluding the caption bar, menu, and so forth.

Generally, when you use display contexts, you use the window client area (which is what is used in the examples). You should be aware, however, that there are Windows functions for converting coordinates between client area and screen, screen and window, and so on.

Assuming that you are working in the window's client area (the default), and assuming that you are working in MM_TEXT mapping mode (the default), you are using a pixel-based coordinate system beginning in the upper-left corner (see figure 10.4).

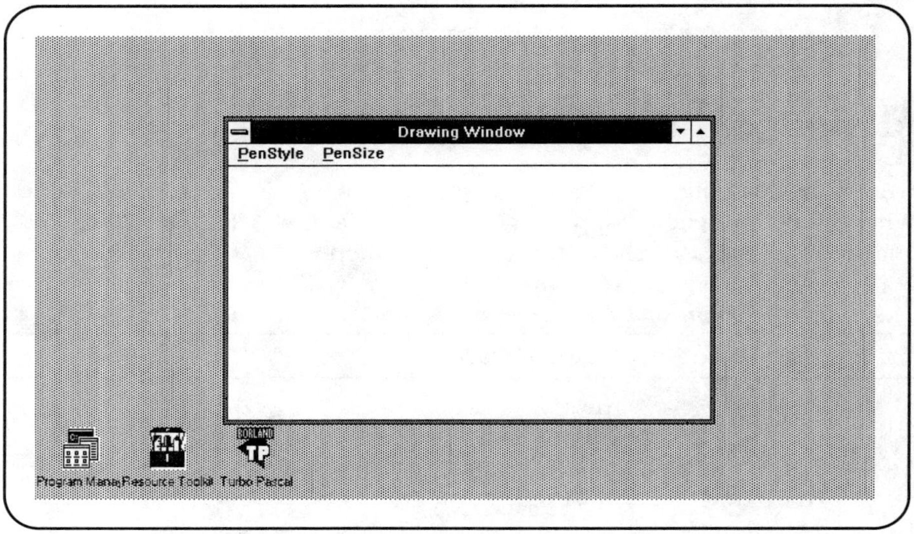

Figure 10.3. A screen, window, and window's client areas.

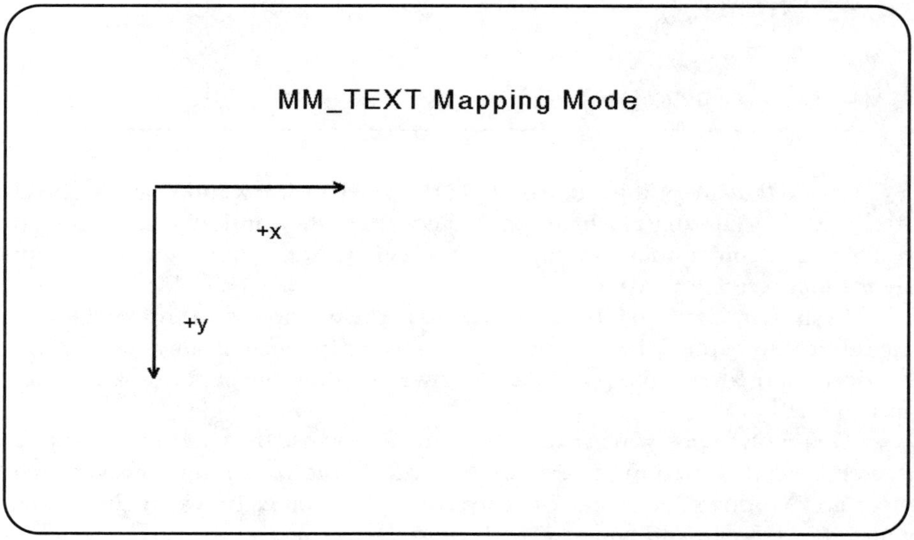

Figure 10.4. A pixel-based coordinate system beginning in the upper-left corner.

If you are used to working with mathematical coordinate systems, you might wonder why the origin is the upper-left corner. It is there because text flows from left to right, from top to bottom. Thus, additional text on a screen is shown by increasing X and Y (+X, +Y) coordinates—convenient for text, but backward for most mathematical coordinate systems.

If you need a more intuitive coordinate system for plotting graphs and others, however, you can change the mapping mode to one of five different modes that have their origin (0,0) in the lower-left corner. These lower-left mapping modes are sometimes called *metric mapping modes*. They are not pixel-based (like MM_TEXT); instead they increment their X and Y components by logical units (0.254mm, 0.1mm, and so forth). Figure 10.5 shows a metric mapping mode.

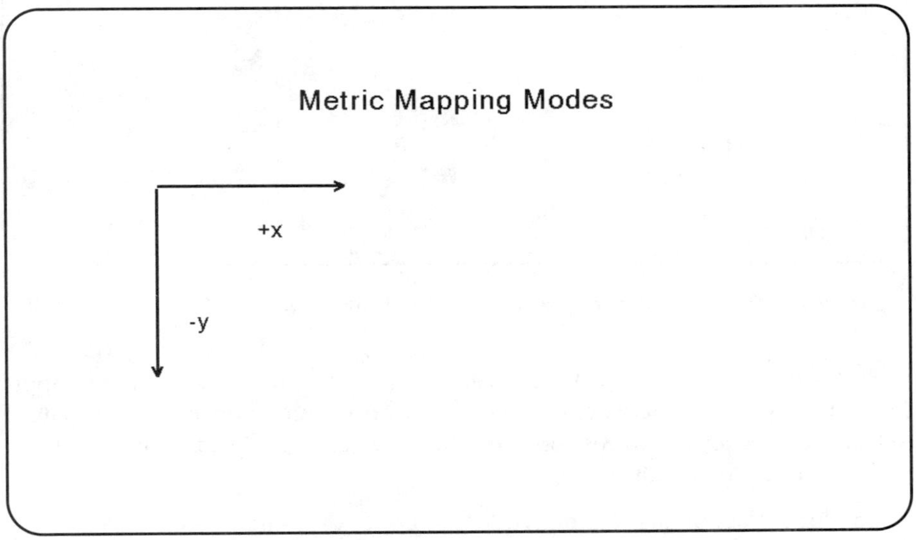

Figure 10.5. *A metric mapping mode.*

To set a MM_LOENGLISH metric mapping mode, for example, use SetMapMode:

```
SetMapMode(DC, MM_LOENGLISH)
```

Notice that if you use a metric mapping mode, anything you display in the client area must be located using negative values of Y. Not spiffy. You probably want to think in both positive X and Y. Fortunately, Windows offers a solution: you can change the "logical" origin of the client area using the Windows function SetViewportOrg and SelectClipRgn:

```
SetView(ADCHandle,ClientX/2,ClientY/2);
SelectClipRgn(ADCHandle,AClipregion);
```

which changes the coordinate system to look like figure 10.6.

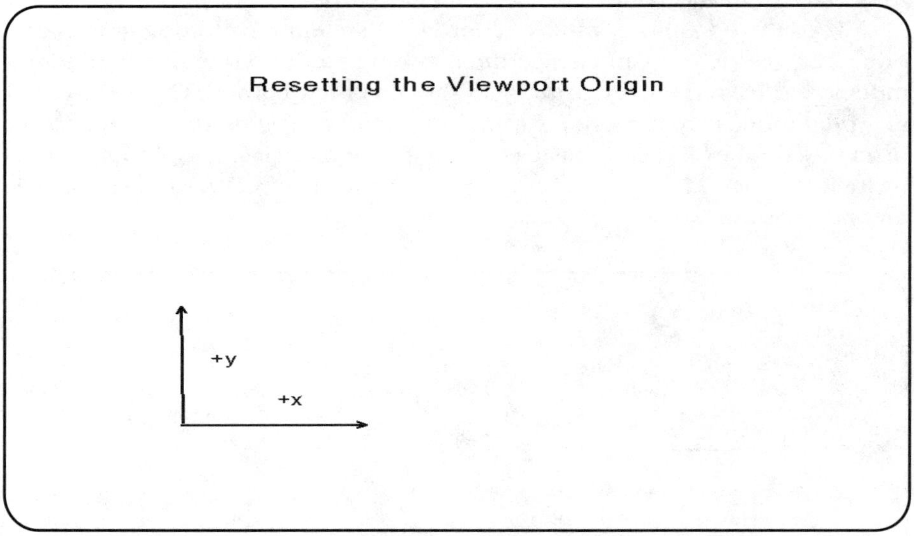

Figure 10.6. *The result of changing from the "logical" origin.*

Listing 10.2 shows a little application that shifts the origin from the upper-left to the upper-right corner of the client window in response to a menu item selection. The key menu-response methods are `CMUpperLeft`, which uses the default upper-left origin:

```
procedure MoveOriginWindow.CMUpperLeft(var Msg: TMessage);
begin
     DragDC := GetDC(HWindow);
     SetMapMode(DragDC,MM_TEXT);          { Use MM_TEXT mode }
     StrLCopy(S,'Hello',SizeOf(S) - 1);
     TextOut(DragDC,10,20,S,SizeOf(S));
     ReleaseDC(HWindow,DragDC);
end;
```

and `CMUpperRight`, which moves the origin to the upper-right corner of the client window:

```
procedure MoveOriginWindow.CMUpperRight(var Msg: TMessage);
begin
     DragDC := GetDC(HWindow);
     SetMapMode(DragDC,MM_TEXT);            { Set map mode }
```

```
    SetViewportOrg(DragDC,Attr.W,0);      { Shift origin }
    StrLCopy(S,'Hello',SizeOf(S) - 1);
    TextOut(DragDC,-60,20,S,SizeOf(S));  { Note -X coordinate }
    ReleaseDC(HWindow,DragDC);
end;
```

You do not have to explicitly set the MM_TEXT mapping mode because it is the default. It is done here for completeness.

Listing 10.2. *Setting the* MM_TEXT *mapping mode.*

```
program MoveOrigin;

uses
     Strings,
     WinTypes,
     WinProcs,
     WObjects;

{$R Pen.Res }{Pen resource is just used for convenience}

const
     cm_UpperLeft   = 401;
     cm_UpperRight  = 402;

type
  MoveOriginApplication = object(TApplication)
    procedure InitMainWindow; virtual;
  end;

  PMoveOriginWindow = ^MoveOriginWindow;
  MoveOriginWindow = object(TWindow)

    S : array[0..5] of Char;
    DragDC: HDC;
    constructor Init(AParent: PWindowsObject; ATitle: PChar);
    destructor Done; virtual;
    procedure CMUpperLeft(var Msg: TMessage);
      virtual cm_First + cm_UpperLeft;
    procedure CMUpperRight(var Msg: TMessage);
      virtual cm_First + cm_UpperRight;
  end;

{-----------------------------------------------------}
{ MoveOriginWindow's method implementations:          }
{-----------------------------------------------------}
```

continues

Listing 10.2. continued

```
constructor MoveOriginWindow.Init (AParent: PWindowsObject;
                                   ATitle: PChar);
begin
  TWindow.Init(AParent, ATitle);
  Attr.Menu := LoadMenu(HInstance, PChar(109));
  DisableAutoCreate;
  Attr.Style := ws_PopupWindow or ws_Caption or ws_Visible;

  Attr.X := 50;
  Attr.Y := 50;
  Attr.W := 200;
  Attr.H := 200;

end;

destructor MoveOriginWindow.Done;
begin
  TWindow.Done;
end;

procedure MoveOriginWindow.CMUpperLeft(var Msg: TMessage);
begin
     DragDC := GetDC(HWindow);
     SetMapMode(DragDC,MM_TEXT);              { Use MM_TEXT mode }
     StrLCopy(S,'Hello',SizeOf(S) - 1);
     TextOut(DragDC,10,20,S,SizeOf(S));
     ReleaseDC(HWindow,DragDC);
end;

procedure MoveOriginWindow.CMUpperRight(var Msg: TMessage);
begin
     DragDC := GetDC(HWindow);
     SetMapMode(DragDC,MM_TEXT);              { Set map mode }
     SetViewportOrg(DragDC,Attr.W,0);         { Shift origin }
     StrLCopy(S,'Hello',SizeOf(S) - 1);
     TextOut(DragDC,-60,20,S,SizeOf(S));      { Note -X coordinate }
     ReleaseDC(HWindow,DragDC);
end;


{-----------------------------------------------}
{ MoveOriginApplication's method implementations: }
{-----------------------------------------------}
```

```
procedure MoveOriginApplication.InitMainWindow;
begin
  MainWindow := New(PMoveOriginWindow, Init(nil, 'Origin
Window'));
end;

{-----------------------------------------------------}
{ Main program:                                       }
{-----------------------------------------------------}

var
  App : MoveOriginApplication;

begin
  App.Init('MoveOriginProgram');
  App.Run;
  App.Done;
end.
```

Figure 10.7 shows the resulting text display.

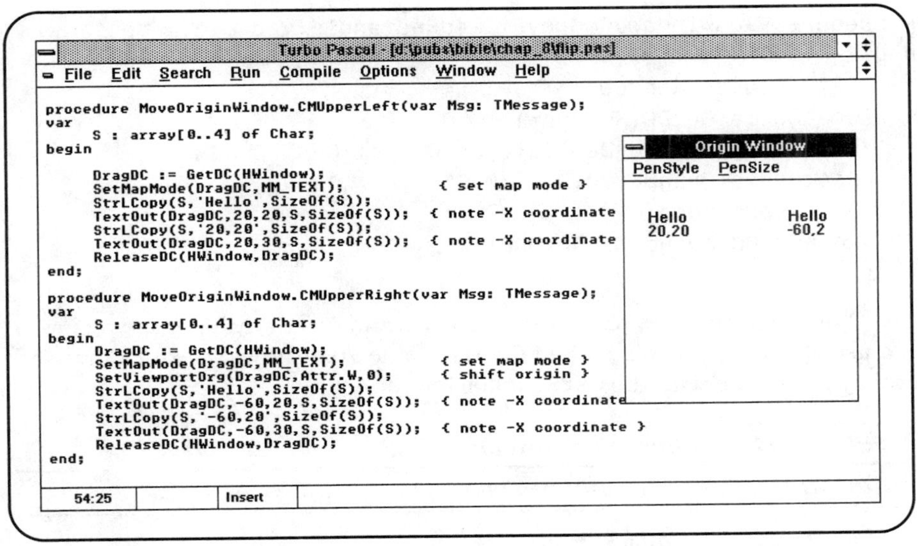

Figure 10.7. The result of listing 10.2.

Drawing Figures

Windows has a rich, built-in set of tools for drawing lines and various shapes; including lines, circles, ellipses, rectangles, round rectangles, chords, pies, polygons, and poly polygons.

You can draw these figures individually or in combination. To draw any figure, your application uses a pen, either the default pen (BLACK_PEN) or a custom pen that your application creates.

For example, the little example in listing 10.3 shows how to create an application that responds to user menu-item selections by drawing either a rectangle, a filled rectangle, or an ellipse in a DashDot pen style. It creates the pen, retrieves a display context, selects the pen, draws the figure, releases the display context, and deletes the object using menu-command message-response methods.

Notice that filling a rectangle is somewhat different than simply drawing the rectangle. The key difference lies in the drawing tool you use to produce the rectangle. When you draw a rectangle, you use a pen. When you draw and fill a rectangle, you use a brush that can be either a stock object (such as a GRAY_BRUSH) or a brush based on a bit map. The CMFilledRectangle method in listing 10.3 uses a stock brush:

```
procedure FigsWindow.CMGrayFilledRectangle(var Msg: TMessage);
begin
    SetCapture(HWindow);
    DragDC := GetDC(HWindow);
    SelectObject(DragDC, GetStockObject(GRAY_BRUSH));
    Rectangle(DragDC,20,20,200,200);
    ReleaseCapture;
    ReleaseDC(HWindow, DragDC);
end;
```

Windows provides seven stock brushes and three stock pens, which you can use effectively to create filled figures. Table 10.4 shows the stock drawing tools you can use with the GetStockObject function.

Table 10.4. Windows stock drawing tools.

Constant	*Brush/Pen Type*
Black_Brush	Black brush
DkGray_Brush	Dark gray brush
Gray_Brush	Gray brush
Hollow_Brush	Hollow brush
LtGray_Brush	Light gray brush

Constant	*Brush/Pen Type*
Null_Brush	Null brush
White_Brush	White brush
Black_Pen	Black pen
Null_Pen	Null pen
White_Pen	White pen

The following response method shows how to create and select a hatched brush, which is then used to fill a rectangle. Notice that the brush needs to be deleted when you are done with it:

```
procedure FigsWindow.CMHatchedRectangle(var Msg: TMessage);
begin
    SetCapture(HWindow);
    DragDC := GetDC(HWindow);
    TheBrush := CreateHatchBrush(hs_Vertical, RGB(0,255,0));
    SelectObject(DragDC,TheBrush);
    Rectangle(DragDC,20,20,200,200); DeleteObject(TheBrush);
    ReleaseCapture;
    ReleaseDC(HWindow, DragDC);
end;
```

Listing 10.3. *A figure-drawing and -filling program.*

```
program Figs;

uses
     Strings,
     WinTypes,
     WinProcs,
     WObjects,
     WIF5,     { Basic Interface }
     StdDlgs;


{$R FIGS.RES }


const
     cm_Rectangle             = 401;
     cm_Ellipse               = 402;
```

continues

Listing 10.3. continued

```
     cm_GrayFilledRectangle   = 403;
     cm_HatchedRectangle      = 404;

type
  FigsApplication = object(BasicApplication)
    procedure InitMainWindow; virtual;
  end;

  PFigsWindow = ^FigsWindow;
  FigsWindow = object(MainWindow)
    DragDC: HDC;
    TheBrush: HBrush;
    ThePen: HPen;
    PenSize: Integer;
    PenStyle: Integer;
    constructor Init(AParent: PWindowsObject; ATitle: PChar);
    destructor Done; virtual;
    procedure CMRectangle(var Msg: TMessage);
      virtual cm_First + cm_Rectangle;
    procedure CMGrayFilledRectangle(var Msg: TMessage);
      virtual cm_First + cm_GrayFilledRectangle;
    procedure CMHatchedRectangle(var Msg: TMessage);
      virtual cm_First + cm_HatchedRectangle;
    procedure CMEllipse(var Msg: TMessage);
      virtual cm_First + cm_Ellipse;
end;

{-----------------------------------------------}
{ FigsWindow's method implementations:          }
{-----------------------------------------------}

constructor FigsWindow.Init(AParent: PWindowsObject; ATitle: PChar);
begin
  TWindow.Init(AParent, ATitle);
  Attr.Menu := LoadMenu(HInstance, PChar(109));
  PenSize := 1;
  PenStyle := ps_DashDot;
  ThePen := CreatePen(PenStyle, PenSize, 0);
end;

destructor FigsWindow.Done;
begin
  DeleteObject(ThePen);
```

```
  TWindow.Done;
end;

procedure FigsWindow.CMRectangle(var Msg: TMessage);
begin
    SetCapture(HWindow);
    DragDC := GetDC(HWindow);
    SelectObject(DragDC, ThePen);
    Rectangle(DragDC,20,20,200,200);
    ReleaseCapture;
    ReleaseDC(HWindow, DragDC);
end;

procedure FigsWindow.CMGrayFilledRectangle(var Msg: TMessage);
begin
    SetCapture(HWindow);
    DragDC := GetDC(HWindow);
    SelectObject(DragDC, GetStockObject(GRAY_BRUSH));
    Rectangle(DragDC,20,20,200,200);
    ReleaseCapture;
    ReleaseDC(HWindow, DragDC);
end;

procedure FigsWindow.CMHatchedRectangle(var Msg: TMessage);
begin
    SetCapture(HWindow);
    DragDC := GetDC(HWindow);
    TheBrush := CreateHatchBrush(hs_Vertical, RGB(0,255,0));
    SelectObject(DragDC,TheBrush); Rectangle(DragDC,20,20,200,200);
    DeleteObject(TheBrush);
    ReleaseCapture;
    ReleaseDC(HWindow, DragDC);
end;

procedure FigsWindow.CMEllipse(var Msg: TMessage);
begin
    SetCapture(HWindow);
    DragDC := GetDC(HWindow);
    SelectObject(DragDC, ThePen);
    Ellipse(DragDC,20,20,200,200);
    ReleaseCapture;
    ReleaseDC(HWindow, DragDC);
end;
```

continues

Listing 10.3. continued

```
{-----------------------------------------------------}
{ FigsApplication's method implementations:           }
{-----------------------------------------------------}

procedure FigsApplication.InitMainWindow;
begin
  MainWindow := New(PFigsWindow, Init(nil, 'Drawing Window'));
end;

{-----------------------------------------------------}
{ Main program:                                       }
{-----------------------------------------------------}

var
  App : FigsApplication;

begin
  App.Init('FigsProgram');
  App.Run;
  App.Done;
end.
```

Figure 10.8, 10.9 and 10.10 show several of the shapes created by the display: a gray-filled rectangle, a gray-filled rectangle with an ellipse inside it, and a hatched rectangle.

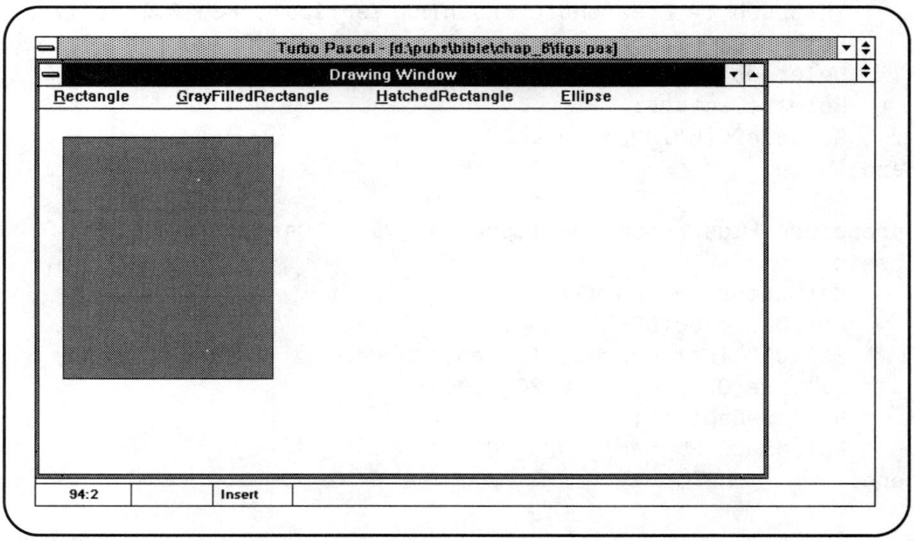

***Figure 10.8.** A gray-filled rectangle.*

A Stranger Graphics Function Demo

To illustrate how some of these functions work, use a menu to select various drawing functions (MoveToLineTo, Splotch, StrangeArcs, StrangePies, and RoundRect) that utilize many of the Windows primitive graphics functions for drawing lines, arcs, pies, and so on.

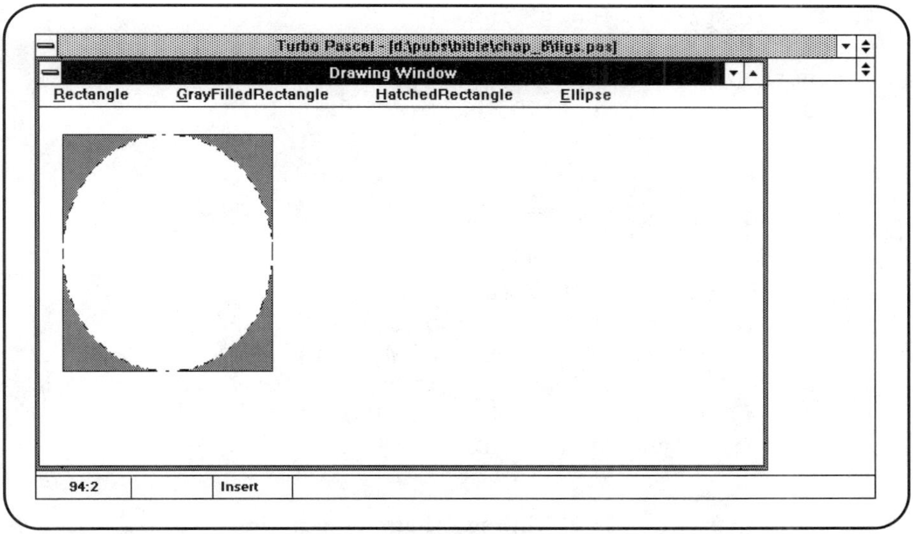

Figure 10.9. A gray-filled rectangle with an ellipse.

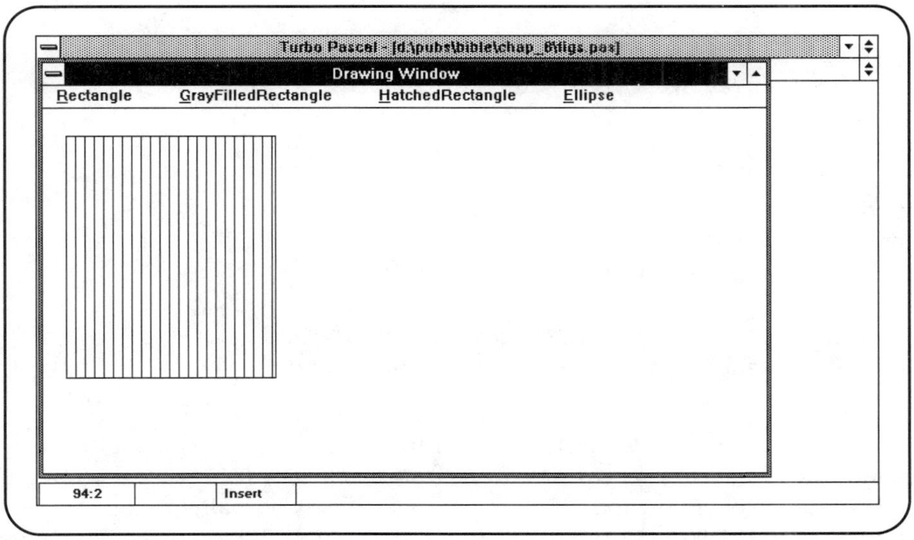

Figure 10.10. A hatched rectangle.

Each drawing function displays in its own window. By using one window per function, you can maintain many drawings simultaneously, switching between them. Each window constructs itself, maintains data fields specific to it, and has its own Paint procedure for updating its display.

The splotch window looks like this:

```
type
  PSplotchWindow = ^SplotchWindow;
  SplotchWindow = object(TWindow)
    Points: array[0..MaxPoints] of APoint;
    constructor Init(AParent: PWindowsObject; ATitle: PChar);
    procedure Paint(PaintDC: HDC; var PaintInfo:
          TPaintStruct); virtual;
  end;
```

A round rectangle window looks similar:

```
type
  PRRectangleWindow = ^RRectangleWindow;
  RRectangleWindow = object(TWindow)
    Points: array[0..MaxPoints] of APoint;
    constructor Init(AParent: PWindowsObject; ATitle: PChar);
  procedure Paint(PaintDC: HDC; var PaintInfo:
        TPaintStruct); virtual;
  end;
```

Notice that none of the windows that maintain drawings is the application's `MainWindow`. The application's `MainWindow`, as usual, is constructed at start-up by the `Application` (object):

```
type
  GDIExApp = object(TApplication)
    procedure InitMainWindow; virtual;
  end;


procedure GDIExApp.InitMainWindow;
begin
  { Create a main window of type TGDIWindow. }

  MainWindow := New(PGDIExWindow, Init('GDI Example',
     LoadMenu(HInstance,MakeIntResource(MenuID))));
end;
```

The `GDIExApp`'s `MainWindow`, in turn, maintains each of the drawing windows as a child window. Because the `MainWindow` (`GDIExWindow`) maintains a group of child windows, you can make it easy to maintain the children by deriving `GDIExWindow` from `TMDIWindow`, the base `MDI` Window (`TMDIWindow`), in ObjectWindows. Recall from Chapter 7, "Many Windows: A Multi-Document Interface," that a TMDIWindow already knows how to maintain child windows, which saves you tons of work.

GDIExWindow looks like this:

```
type
  PGDIExWindow = ^GDIExWindow;
  GDIExWindow = object(TMDIWindow)
    procedure CMStrangeArcs(var Msg: TMessage);
      virtual cm_First + cm_StrangeArcs;
    procedure CMStrangePies(var Msg: TMessage);
      virtual cm_First + cm_StrangePies;
    procedure CMRoundRect(var Msg: TMessage);
      virtual cm_First + cm_RoundRect;
    procedure CMMoveToLineTo(var Msg: TMessage);
      virtual cm_First + cm_MoveToLineTo;
    procedure CMSplotch(var Msg: TMessage);
      virtual cm_First + cm_Splotch;
    procedure CMQuit(var Msg: TMessage);
      virtual cm_First + cm_Quit;
    procedure WMDestroy(var Msg: TMessage);
      virtual wm_First + wm_Destroy;
end;
```

It consists mostly of message-response methods for handling Windows messages and menu-command messages, which indicate that the user has selected a drawing window for display.

Here are the corresponding menu-command message constants for GDIExWindow:

```
const
  MenuID            = 100; { Resource ID of the menu }
  cm_Quit           = 100; { File->Quit ID }
  cm_MoveToLineTo   = 201; { Shapes }
  cm_Splotch        = 202;
  cm_StrangeArcs    = 203;
  cm_StrangePies    = 204;
  cm_Roundrect      = 205;
```

These constants correspond to the menu items in the resource file, GDI_EX.RES. Figure 10.11 shows an aspect of the creation and testing of GDI_EX.RES.

Notice the matching constants.

In response to each menu item selection, the GDIExWindow menu-response method constructs the corresponding window.

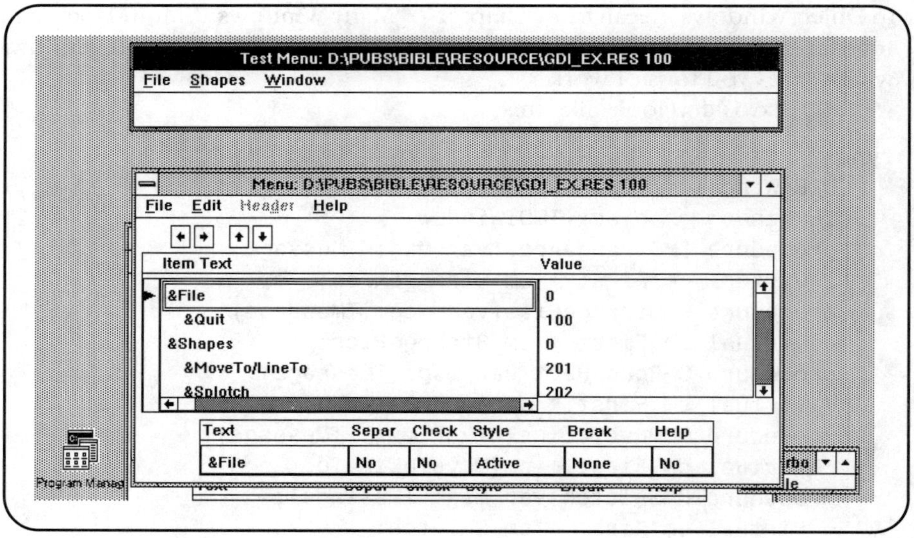

***Figure 10.11.** An aspect of the creation and testing of* `GDI_EX.RES`.

For example, a `SplotchWindow`:

```
procedure GDIExWindow.CMSplotch(var Msg: TMessage);
begin
  Application^.MakeWindow(New(PSplotchWindow, Init(@Self,
    'Splotch Window')));
end;
```

or a `RoundRectWindow`:

```
procedure GDIExWindow.CMRoundRect(var Msg: TMessage);
begin
  Application^.MakeWindow(New(PRRectangleWindow, Init(@Self,
    'Round Rectangle Window')));
end;
```

The same applies for the other drawing windows.

Listing 10.4 contains the complete code for the GDI example, and figures 10.12 and 10.13 show this `MDI` application running in different stages.

> **Note:** One particularly interesting and useful aspect of the MDI objects that compose the MDI interface is that MDI windows are repainted automatically when they are uncovered after being covered, unlike non-MDI windows (until you write Paint methods for redisplay).

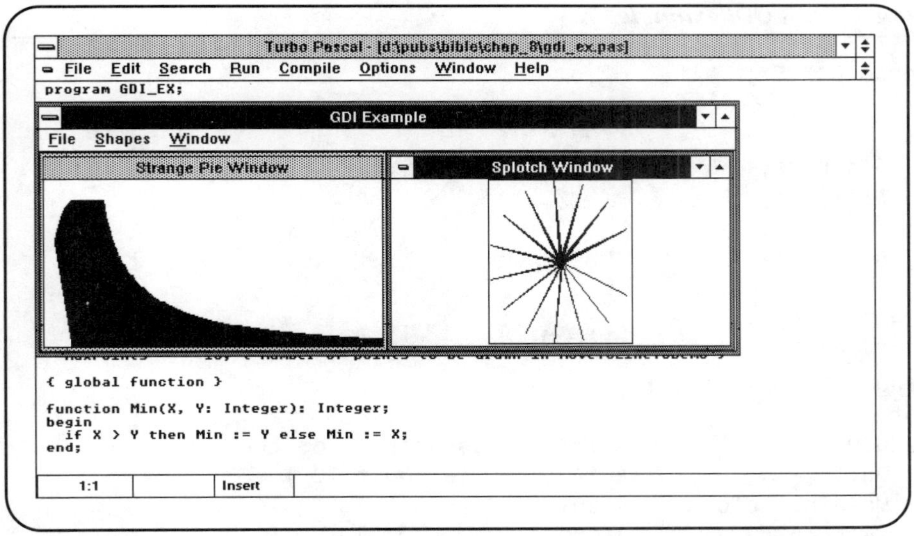

Figure 10.12. *One stage of running the MDI application of listing 10.4.*

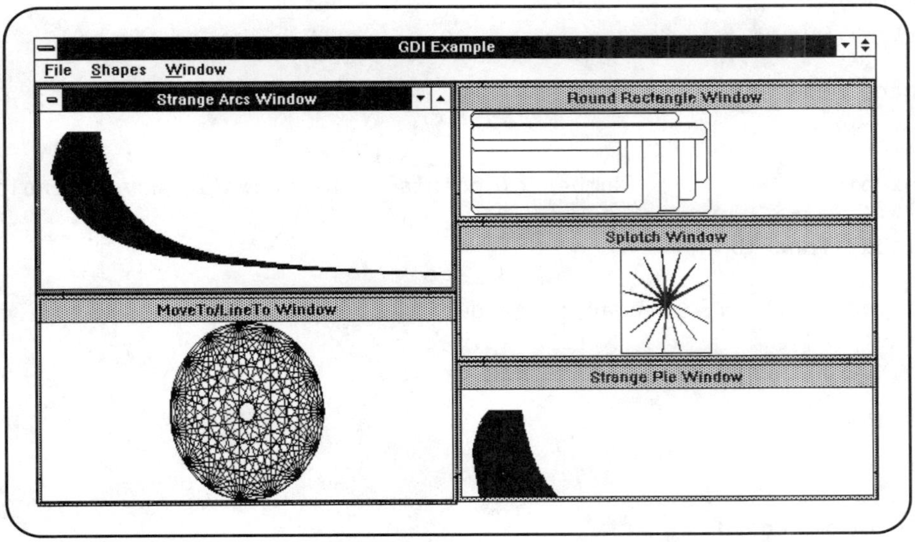

Figure 10.13. *Another stage during the MDI application execution.*

Listing 10.4. *A GDI example.*

```
program GDI_EX;

uses
     WinProcs,
     WinTypes,
     WObjects,
     Strings;

{$R GDI_EX.RES}

{ Menu bar constants }
const
  MenuID                = 100; { Resource ID of the menu }
  cm_Quit               = 100; { File->Quit ID }
  cm_MoveToLineTo       = 201; { Shapes }
  cm_Splotch            = 202;
  cm_StrangeArcs        = 203;
  cm_StrangePies        = 204;
  cm_Roundrect          = 205;


{ Shape constant }

const
  MaxPoints   =  15; { Number of points to be drawn in MoveToLineToDemo }

{ Global function }

function Min(X, Y: Integer): Integer;
begin
  if X > Y then Min := Y else Min := X;
end;


type
  APoint = record
    X, Y : Real;
  end;

{ NoIconWindow }

type
  PNoIconWindow = ^NoIconWindow;
```

```
  NoIconWindow = object(TWindow)
    procedure GetWindowClass(var AWndClass: TWndClass); virtual;
    function GetClassName: PChar;  virtual;
  end;

procedure NoIconWindow.GetWindowClass(var AWndClass: TWndClass);
begin
  TWindow.GetWindowClass(AWndClass);
  AWndClass.hbrBackground := GetStockObject(Black_Brush);
  AWndClass.hIcon := 0;
end;

{ No need to call the ancestor's method here, because you want to
  provide an entirely new window class name. }
function NoIconWindow.GetClassName: PChar;
begin
  GetClassName := 'NoIconWindow';
end;

{ Splotch window }

type
  PSplotchWindow = ^SplotchWindow;
  SplotchWindow = object(TWindow)
    Points: array[0..MaxPoints] of APoint;
    constructor Init(AParent: PWindowsObject; ATitle: PChar);
    procedure Paint(PaintDC: HDC; var PaintInfo: TPaintStruct); virtual;
  end;

constructor SplotchWindow.Init(AParent: PWindowsObject; ATitle: PChar);
var
  I: Integer;
  StepAngle: Integer;
  Radians: Real;
begin
  TWindow.Init(AParent, ATitle);
  StepAngle := 360 div MaxPoints;
  for I := 0 to MaxPoints - 1 do
  begin
    Radians := (StepAngle * I) * PI / 180;
    Points[I].x := Cos(Radians);
```

continues

Listing 10.4. continued

```
    Points[I].y := Sin(Radians);
  end;
end;

procedure SplotchWindow.Paint(PaintDC: HDC; var PaintInfo: TPaintStruct);
var
  TheRect: TRect;
  I, J: Integer;
  CenterX,
  CenterY: Integer;
  Radius,
  StepAngle: Word;
  Radians: real;
begin
  GetClientRect(HWindow,TheRect);   { Get the client window's coordinates }
  CenterX := TheRect.Right div 2;
  CenterY := TheRect.Bottom div 2;
  Radius := Min(CenterY, CenterX);

  Rectangle(PaintDC,CenterX - Radius, CenterY - Radius,
     CenterX + Radius, CenterY + Radius);

  for I := 0 to MaxPoints - 1 do
  begin
    for J := I + 1 to MaxPoints - 1 do
    begin
      MoveTo(PaintDC, CenterX + Round(Points[I].X / Radius *
          Radius), CenterY + Round(Points[I].Y / Radius *Radius));
      LineTo(PaintDC, CenterX + Round(Points[J].X * Radius),
          CenterY + Round(Points[J].Y * Radius));
    end;
  end;
end;

{ End splotch window }


{ Round rectangle window }

type
  PRRectangleWindow = ^RRectangleWindow;
  RRectangleWindow = object(TWindow)
    Points: array[0..MaxPoints] of APoint;
```

```
    constructor Init(AParent: PWindowsObject; ATitle: PChar);
    procedure Paint(PaintDC: HDC; var PaintInfo:
        TPaintStruct); virtual;
  end;

constructor RRectangleWindow.Init(AParent: PWindowsObject; ATitle: PChar);
var
  I: Integer;
  StepAngle: Integer;
  Radians: Real;
begin
  TWindow.Init(AParent, ATitle);
  StepAngle := 360 div MaxPoints;
  for I := 0 to MaxPoints - 1 do
  begin
    Radians := (StepAngle * I) * PI / 180;
    Points[I].x := Cos(Radians);
    Points[I].y := Sin(Radians);
  end;
end;

procedure RRectangleWindow.Paint(PaintDC: HDC;
  var PaintInfo: TPaintStruct);
var
  TheRect: TRect;
  I, J: Integer;
  CenterX,
  CenterY: Integer;
  Radius,
  StepAngle: Word;
  Radians: real;
begin
  GetClientRect(HWindow,TheRect);   { Get the client window's coordinates }
  CenterX := TheRect.Right div 2;
  CenterY := TheRect.Bottom div 2;
  Radius := Min(CenterY, CenterX);

  RoundRect(PaintDC,CenterX - Radius, CenterY - Radius,
     CenterX + Radius, CenterY + Radius,9,11);

  for I := 0 to MaxPoints - 1 do
  begin
    for J := I + 1 to MaxPoints - 1 do
```

continues

Listing 10.4. continued

```
    begin
      MoveTo(PaintDC, CenterX + Round(Points[I].X / Radius *
          Radius), CenterY + Round(Points[I].Y / Radius * Radius));
      RoundRect(PaintDC, CenterX + Round(Points[J].X *
          Radius), CenterY + Round(Points[J].Y *
          Radius),9,11,9,11);
    end;
  end;
end;
{ End round rectangle }

{ Strange arcs window }

type
  PStrangeArcsWindow = ^StrangeArcsWindow;
   StrangeArcsWindow = object(TWindow)
     procedure Paint(PaintDC: HDC; var PaintInfo:
      TPaintStruct); virtual;
  end;

procedure StrangeArcsWindow.Paint(PaintDC: HDC;
  var PaintInfo: TPaintStruct);

var
     X, EndX : integer;
begin
      For X := 1 to 400 do
      begin
          EndX := X + 50;
          Arc(PaintDC, X,15,EndX,250,50,0,0,0);
      end;
end;

{ End strange arcs }

{ Strange pie window }

type
  PStrangePiesWindow = ^StrangePiesWindow;
  StrangePiesWindow = object(TWindow)
    procedure Paint(PaintDC: HDC; var PaintInfo:
       TPaintStruct); virtual;
  end;
```

```
procedure StrangePiesWindow.Paint(PaintDC: HDC;
  var PaintInfo: TPaintStruct);

var
     X, EndX : integer;
begin
      For X := 1 to 400 do
      begin
          EndX := X + 50;
          Pie(PaintDC, X,15,EndX,250,50,0,0,0);
      end;
end;

{ End strange pies }



{ MoveToLineToWindow ---------------------------------- }


type
  PMoveToLineToWindow = ^MoveToLineToWindow;
  MoveToLineToWindow = object(TWindow)
    Points: array[0..MaxPoints] of APoint;
    constructor Init(AParent: PWindowsObject; ATitle: PChar);
    procedure Paint(PaintDC: HDC; var PaintInfo:
       TPaintStruct); virtual;
  end;

constructor MoveToLineToWindow.Init(AParent: PWindowsObject;
ATitle: PChar);
var
  I: Integer;
  StepAngle: Integer;
  Radians: Real;
begin
  TWindow.Init(AParent, ATitle);
  StepAngle := 360 div MaxPoints;
  for I := 0 to MaxPoints - 1 do
  begin
    Radians := (StepAngle * I) * PI / 180;
    Points[I].x := Cos(Radians);
    Points[I].y := Sin(Radians);
  end;
end;
```

continues

Listing 10.4. continued

```
procedure MoveToLinetoWindow.Paint(PaintDC: HDC;
  var PaintInfo: TPaintStruct);
var
  TheRect: TRect;
  I, J: Integer;
  CenterX,
  CenterY: Integer;
  Radius,
  StepAngle: Word;
  Radians: real;
begin
  GetClientRect(HWindow,TheRect);
  CenterX := TheRect.Right div 2;
  CenterY := TheRect.Bottom div 2;
  Radius := Min(CenterY, CenterX);
  Ellipse(PaintDC,CenterX - Radius, CenterY - Radius,
     CenterX + Radius, CenterY + Radius);
  for I := 0 to MaxPoints - 1 do
  begin
    for J := I + 1 to MaxPoints - 1 do
    begin
  MoveTo(PaintDC, CenterX + Round(Points[I].X * Radius),
         CenterY + Round(Points[I].Y * Radius));
  LineTo(PaintDC, CenterX + Round(Points[J].X * Radius),
         CenterY + Round(Points[J].Y * Radius));
    end;
  end;
end;

{ GDIExWindow ---------------------------------------- }

type
  PGDIExWindow = ^GDIExWindow;
  GDIExWindow = object(TMDIWindow)
    procedure CMStrangeArcs(var Msg: TMessage);
      virtual cm_First + cm_StrangeArcs;
    procedure CMStrangePies(var Msg: TMessage);
      virtual cm_First + cm_StrangePies;
    procedure CMRoundRect(var Msg: TMessage);
      virtual cm_First + cm_RoundRect;
    procedure CMMoveToLineTo(var Msg: TMessage);
      virtual cm_First + cm_MoveToLineTo;
```

```
    procedure CMSplotch(var Msg: TMessage);
      virtual cm_First + cm_Splotch;
    procedure CMQuit(var Msg: TMessage);
      virtual cm_First + cm_Quit;
    procedure WMDestroy(var Msg: TMessage);
     virtual wm_First + wm_Destroy;
  end;

procedure GDIExWindow.CMMoveToLineTo(var Msg: TMessage);
begin
  Application^.MakeWindow(New(PMoveToLineToWindow,
     Init(@Self, 'MoveTo/LineTo Window')));
end;

procedure GDIExWindow.CMSplotch(var Msg: TMessage);
begin
  Application^.MakeWindow(New(PSplotchWindow, Init(@Self,
    'Splotch Window')));
end;

procedure GDIExWindow.CMRoundRect(var Msg: TMessage);
begin
  Application^.MakeWindow(New(PRRectangleWindow, Init(@Self,
    'Round Rectangle Window')));
end;

procedure GDIExWindow.CMStrangeArcs(var Msg: TMessage);
begin
  Application^.MakeWindow(New(PStrangeArcsWindow,
     Init(@Self, 'Strange Arcs Window')));
end;

procedure GDIExWindow.CMStrangePies(var Msg: TMessage);
begin
  Application^.MakeWindow(New(PStrangePiesWindow,
     Init(@Self, 'Strange Pie Window')));
end;


procedure GDIExWindow.CMQuit(var Msg: TMessage);
begin
  CloseWindow;
end;
```

continues

Listing 10.4. continued

```
procedure GDIExWindow.WMDestroy(var Msg: TMessage);
begin
  TMDIWindow.WMDestroy(Msg);
end;

{ GDIExApp ------------------------------------------------ }

type
  GDIExApp = object(TApplication)
    procedure InitMainWindow; virtual;
  end;

procedure GDIExApp.InitMainWindow;
begin
  { Create a main window of type GDIExWindow. }
  MainWindow := New(PGDIExWindow,
    Init('GDI Example',
LoadMenu(HInstance,MakeIntResource(MenuID))));
end;

var
  ExApp: GDIExApp;

begin
  ExApp.Init('GDIExample');
  ExApp.Run;
  ExApp.Done;
end.
```

Wrap-up

The graphics possibilities with the Windows GDI are virtually endless (please excuse the pun). You can create drawings and shapes of almost every kind, and, with a bit of effort, create sophisticated graphics applications that utilize various fonts, icons, cursors, bit maps, and the like.

You can create this myriad of shapes on any device supported by Windows without writing code for a specific device. Although you might spend some time learning the ins and outs of Windows functions, you are more than compensated when you do not have to write device drivers or device-specific code. Windows is indeed the most universal interface to come down the DOS pike, and it becomes more useful and more powerful as you learn more about it.

For additional information about GDI definitions, functions, and the ObjectGraphics Toolbox (from the Whitewater Group), check the reference section in the second half of this book.

11

CHAPTER

FROM PROGRAM TO PROGRAM USING DDE (DYNAMIC DATA EXCHANGE)

As I look across my desk to the "computer museum" in the corner of my office, I can see the progress hardware has made in the past decade. We've gone from 64K Z80 CP/M machines like the Osborne I that ran Ron Cain's Small-C and Turbo Pascal 1.0 (and had room to spare!), to my new four-megabyte 386SX that runs Turbo C++ and Turbo Pascal 6.0. And I'm not at all surprised by the fact that the Osborne cost more than the 386.

Zack Urlocker

One of the most amazing and useful features of Microsoft Windows is its facility for letting applications share data. Windows accomplishes this data-sharing through a protocol called DDE (dynamic data exchange). Turbo Pascal for Windows compiles DDE between applications—those you write and even those you don't write yourself—readily accessible at a high level.

In general, to exchange data with other applications and programs through DDE, you have to learn:

- The Windows messages (`wm_prefixed`) that use DDE
- How to use global memory to buffer the data exchange

This chapter explains how DDE works with examples, including exchanges with the Clipboard and the Windows Program Manager. Although exchanges with the clipboard are not "technically" part of DDE because you do not send DDE messages to access the clipboard, the chapter lumps together the exchange of clipboard and DDE data. Call the lump something like "Windows global data exchange" because both the clipboard and DDE require the use of global memory buffers.

You also can "lump" DDE and DLL because they are conceptually similar. They differ significantly, however, in that DDE is the sharing of data between applications, and DLL is the sharing of code. Your applications share code by storing it in dynamic linkable libraries.

The capability to share data and code has many advantages and possibilities. Sharing reduces memory use (because a single copy, rather than two or more copies, of a segment of code or data saves space). Also, by sharing data in real time, your applications can save time and interact sensibly with each other. Applications using either the clipboard or DDE can respond to each other immediately, thus leading to a future of independently developed programs that depend on the output from each other.

This chapter focuses on data exchanges between Turbo Pascal for Windows applications and the clipboard and between applications using DDE. Chapter 12 covers DLL.

The Clipboard

The simplest way for your applications to exchange data is with the clipboard. Although you might think of the clipboard as the Clipboard program packaged with Windows, it isn't. The Clipboard is a clipboard viewer you use to display and manipulate the current contents of the clipboard. The clipboard, per se, is a functional Windows unit you use to exchange data between programs. It is, in fact, invisible unless you choose to "view" it.

When your applications are using the Open, Close, Write to, and Read commands from the clipboard, they are "conversing" with the clipboard unit—not the Clipboard program. If you want to see the actual exchange of data between your applications that use the clipboard, open the Clipboard program. Figure 11.1 shows a Clipboard program "view" of a data exchange between a Turbo Pascal for Windows application (details and code are described later in this section).

Many of the Windows applications are used to cut, copy, and paste data to and from the clipboard. The ObjectWindows' Edit control, `EditWindow`, and `FileWindow` objects, which you have already used, access the clipboard through these menu commands.

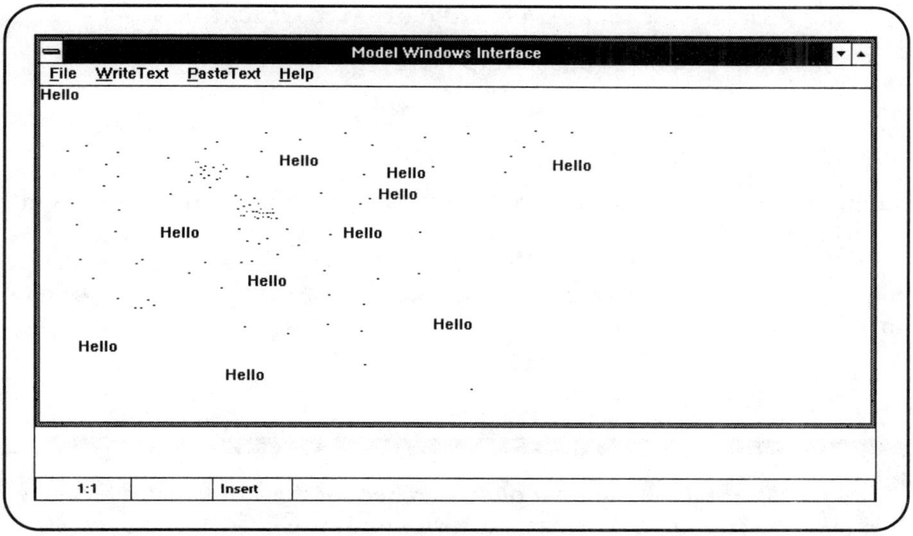

Figure 11.1. *"View" of a data exchange. "Hello" is pasted at various mouse locations.*

The Clipboard can accept a variety of data formats: text, bit maps, symbolic link formatted data, tiff format, and metafile picture format. Table 11.1 shows the clipboard format and the associated data.

Table 11.1. *Clipboard format and associated data.*

Format	***Format Explanation***
cf_Text	Null-terminated array of characters
cf_Bitmap	Windows' bit map format
cf_Sylk	Microsoft symbolic link format
cf_Tiff	Tag image file format
cf_MetafilePict	Windows metafile picture format

These clipboard formats are more or less industry standards, which many applications recognize. Thus, by using one or more of these formats to put data in the clipboard, you can send data to any application that can interact with the clipboard.

To place data in the Clipboard:

1. Open the clipboard (using the Windows function `OpenClipboard`).
2. Empty the clipboard (using `EmptyClipboard`).

3. Set a data handle to the clipboard (SetClipboardData).
4. Close the clipboard (CloseClipboard).

To open the clipboard, use

```
OpenClipboard(HWindow);
```

where HWindow is a window handle associated with the window that wants contact with the clipboard.

EmptyClipboard empties the clipboard and frees any handles to data in the clipboard, assigning ownership to the window (designated by HWindow) that opened the clipboard:

```
EmptyClipboard;
```

Note: All the information researched for this book that refers to the clipboard designates that you must use EmptyClipboard before you copy data to the clipboard. Various experiments suggest that emptying the clipboard isn't absolutely necessary. For example, if you omit EmptyClipboard from the code in listing 11.1, the data exchange between the Turbo Pascal for Windows application and the clipboard still works.

SetClipboardData requires two parameters: a cf_ clipboard constant that specifies the format of the data to be copied to the clipboard and a handle to a global memory block that contains the data to be copied. For example:

```
SetClipboardData(cf_Text,AStringGlobalHandle);
```

Recall from Chapter 9, "Memory Matters," that a global memory block is a special kind of system-wide memory shared by Windows applications. Your application can create these global memory blocks in the Windows global heap, and Windows can manage them. In general, an application does not have to use global memory blocks; usually it's a matter of choice (see Chapter 9 for a discussion of global versus local memory). Applications using the clipboard, however, must use global memory.

To add clipboard-access capability to a window, you derive a new window (called ClipWindow) from MainWindow and add a CopyText feature.

First, derive a new application:

```
  ClipApp = object(BasicApplication)   { ModelApp=a kind of
BasicApplication }
  procedure InitMainWindow; virtual; { Init a specific MainWindow }
end;
```

Next, add a new main window that can interact with the Clipboard:

```
PClipWindow = ^ClipWindow;
 ClipWindow = object(MainWindow)
  constructor Init(AParent : PWindowsObject; ATitle : PChar);
  procedure CMCopyText(var Msg: TMessage);
    virtual cm_First + cm_CopyText;
  function CopyText(Txt: PChar): boolean;
end;
```

ClipWindow has two key methods:

1. CMCopyText responds to the menu-command message (cm_CopyText).
2. CopyText actually handles the copying of text to the clipboard.
   cm_CopyText is a constant:

```
const
     cm_CopyText = 501;
```

is defined in the menu resource in WIF106:

```
{$R ....}
```

CMCopyText responds to the cm_CopyText message by copying a string ("Hello") to a null-terminated string (S). Recall that whenever you pass strings to Windows functions they must be a PChar type (a pointer to a null-terminated string). Then the string sends a message to CopyText and passes it to the string to copy to the clipboard:

```
procedure ClipWindow.CMCopyText(var Msg: TMessage);
var
      Stat : boolean;
      S : array[0..15] of char;
begin
      StrCopy(S,'Hello');
      Stat := CopyText(S);
end;
```

CopyText then sets a global memory handle, copies the string to global memory, opens and empties the clipboard, sets the clipboard data, and closes the clipboard:

```
function ClipWindow.CopyText(Txt: PChar): boolean;
var
      AStrGlobalHandle: THandle;
      AStrGlobalPtr: PChar;
```

```
begin
     CopyText := False;
     AStrGlobalHandle := GlobalAlloc(gmem_Moveable,StrLen(Txt) + 1);
      if AStrGlobalHandle <> 0 then
     begin
          AStrGlobalPtr := GlobalLock(AStrGlobalHandle);
          if AStrGlobalPtr <> nil then
          begin
               StrCopy(AStrGlobalPtr,Txt);
               GlobalUnlock(AStrGlobalHandle);
               OpenClipboard(HWindow);
               EmptyClipboard;
               SetClipboardData(cf_Text,AStrGlobalHandle);
               CloseClipboard;
               CopyText := True;
               GlobalFree(AStrGlobalHandle);
          end;

     end;

end;
```

Pasting from the Clipboard

Pasting text from the clipboard into your application is only slightly more complicated than copying text to the clipboard.

Listing 11.1. *Paste text.*

```
function ClipWindow.PasteText(TxtString: PChar;
     TxtSize:Integer): Integer;
var
     AStrGlobalHandle: THandle;
     AStrGlobalPtr: PChar;
     AStrGlobalSize : LongInt;

begin
     PasteText := -1;
     OpenClipboard(HWindow);
     IsClipboardFormatAvailable(cf_Text);
     AStrGlobalHandle := GetClipboardData(cf_Text);
     if AStrGlobalHandle <> 0 then
     begin
```

```
        AStrGlobalSize := GlobalSize(AStrGlobalHandle);
        AStrGlobalPtr  := GlobalLock(AStrGlobalHandle);
        if AStrGlobalPtr <> nil then
        begin
        if TxtSize < AStrGlobalSize then
             AStrGlobalSize := TxtSize;
        StrLCopy(TxtString,AStrGlobalPtr,AStrGlobalSize);
        GlobalUnlock(AStrGlobalHandle);
        PasteText := StrLen(TxtString);
        end;
      end;
      CloseClipboard;
end;
```

The example program in listing 11.2 copies text to the clipboard and allows the user to paste text from the clipboard to a specific location in the window. The location is determined by clicking the mouse.

Listing 11.2. *Pasting text from clipboard to the window.*

```
unit ClipWnd;

interface

uses
     WObjects,
     WinTypes,
     WinProcs,
     strings,
     WIF5;       { Basic Interface }

{$R wif106.res}

const
     cm_CopyText  = 501;
     cm_PasteText = 502;

type

ClipApp = object(BasicApplication)   { ModelApp=a kind of
                                       BasicApplication }
  procedure InitMainWindow; virtual; { Init a specific
                                       MainWindow }
end;
```

continues

Listing 11.2. continued

```
PClipWindow = ^ClipWindow;
 ClipWindow = object(MainWindow)
  Lo, Hi : Word;
  constructor Init(AParent : PWindowsObject; ATitle : PChar);
  procedure WMLButtonDown(var Msg: TMessage);
     virtual wm_First + wm_LButtonDown;
  procedure WMLButtonUp(var Msg: TMessage);
     virtual wm_First + wm_LButtonUp;
  procedure CMCopyText(var Msg: TMessage);
     virtual cm_First + cm_CopyText;
  procedure CMPasteText(var Msg: TMessage);
     virtual cm_First + cm_PasteText;
  function CopyText(Txt: PChar): boolean;
  function PasteText(TxtString: PChar; TxtSize: Integer):
     Integer;
end;


implementation


procedure ClipApp.InitMainWindow; { Init a model application window }
begin
  if FirstApplication then
  MainWindow := New(PClipWindow, Init(nil, 'Model Windows Interface'))
  else MainWindow := New(PClipWindow, Init(nil,'Additional
                         Instance of MI'));
end;

constructor ClipWindow.Init(AParent : PWindowsObject; ATitle: PChar);
begin
     TWindow.Init(AParent, ATitle); { Send message to ancestor's constructor
     Attr.Menu  := LoadMenu(HInstance, PChar(106)); { 99 = menu ID }
     ButtonDown := False;           { Set status flag }
end;


procedure ClipWindow.WMLButtonDown(var Msg: TMessage);
begin
     if not ButtonDown then
     begin
          ButtonDown := True;
          SetCapture(HWindow);
```

```
            DC := GetDC(HWindow);
        end;
end;

procedure ClipWindow.WMLButtonUp(var Msg: TMessage);
begin
        if ButtonDown then
        begin
            ButtonDown := False;
                { Determine mouse location }
            Lo := Msg.lParamLo;
            Hi := Msg.lParamHi;
            TextOut(DC,Lo,Hi,'.',1); { Put a dot at current mouse location }
            ReleaseCapture;
            ReleaseDC(HWindow,DC);
        end;
end;

procedure ClipWindow.CMCopyText(var Msg: TMessage);
var
        Stat : boolean;
        S : array[0..15] of char;
begin
        StrCopy(S,'Hello');
        Stat := CopyText(S);
end;


procedure ClipWindow.CMPasteText(var Msg: TMessage);
var
        Stat : integer;
        TxtStr: PChar;
        TxtSize: Integer;
        S : array[0..256] of Char;
begin
        New(TxtStr);
        TxtSize := 256;
        Stat := PasteText(TxtStr, TxtSize);
        DC := GetDC(HWindow);
        TextOut(DC,Lo,Hi,TxtStr,Stat); { Paste to mouse location }
        ReleaseDC(HWindow,DC);
end;
```

continues

Listing 11.2. continued

```
function ClipWindow.CopyText(Txt: PChar): boolean;
var
     AStrGlobalHandle: THandle;
     AStrGlobalPtr: PChar;

begin
     CopyText := False;
     AStrGlobalHandle := GlobalAlloc(gmem_Moveable,
StrLen(Txt) + 1);
     if AStrGlobalHandle <> 0 then
     begin
          AStrGlobalPtr := GlobalLock(AStrGlobalHandle);
          if AStrGlobalPtr <> nil then
          begin
               StrCopy(AStrGlobalPtr,Txt);
               GlobalUnlock(AStrGlobalHandle);
               OpenClipboard(HWindow);
               EmptyClipboard;
               SetClipboardData(cf_Text,AStrGlobalHandle);
               CloseClipboard;
               CopyText := True;
          end;

     end;

end;


function ClipWindow.PasteText(TxtString: PChar; TxtSize:
     Integer): Integer;
var
     AStrGlobalHandle: THandle;
     AStrGlobalPtr: PChar;
     AStrGlobalSize : LongInt;

begin
     PasteText := -1;
     OpenClipboard(HWindow);
     IsClipboardFormatAvailable(cf_Text);
     AStrGlobalHandle := GetClipboardData(cf_Text);
     if AStrGlobalHandle <> 0 then
     begin
       AStrGlobalSize := GlobalSize(AStrGlobalHandle);
```

```
      AStrGlobalPtr  := GlobalLock(AStrGlobalHandle);
      if AStrGlobalPtr <> nil then
      begin
      if TxtSize < AStrGlobalSize then
           AStrGlobalSize := TxtSize;
      StrLCopy(TxtString,AStrGlobalPtr,AStrGlobalSize);
      GlobalUnlock(AStrGlobalHandle);
      PasteText := StrLen(TxtString);
      end;
    end;
    CloseClipboard;
end;


end.  { Unit clipwnd }


program Test_Clip;    { A generic way to test each
                        phase of interface development }


uses
     WIF5,            { Basic Interface unit }
     clipwnd;         { Contains ClipApp    }

type

     App = object(ClipApp)
     end;

var
  Application: App;   { An instance of BasicApplication }
                      { Run Application1 }
begin
  Application.Init('ClipInterface');  { Init application instance }
  Application.Run;                    { Message loop }
  Application.Done;  { Destroy application instance }
end.
```

Sharing Data Between Applications

Dynamic data exchange (DDE) is a protocol that enables applications to share data. Applications share data by way of a "conversation" in which they "post" messages to each other. The two applications sharing data are called the *client* (who initiates the conversation by broadcasting a DDE message) and the *server* (who responds to the message).

DDE links between applications are either very cold, cold, hot, or warm, depending on the complexity of the link. A *very cold* link is simplest; a client broadcasts a WM_DDE_INITIATE message identifying the application and topic of interest. Any application (potential server) can respond to this message, and it is up to the client window to terminate all servers except the one it wants. (*Remember: use one window for each DDE link!*) After the unwanted servers are terminated, the client sends the data to the server.

A *cold* link is next simplest: a client broadcasts a WM_DDE_INITIATE message that identifies the application and the application topic it wants. Any potential server who can respond to this application topic responds to the client by sending a WM_DDE_ACK message.

When the client determines a link, it terminates any other acknowledgments of its broadcast message. It then requests the application with a WM_DDE_REQUEST message (if it wants data) or sends data to the server (if it wants to send data).

The client and the server can continue to "talk," either acknowledging the other's requests or not, until one of the linked applications posts a WM_DDE_TERMINATE message. Either the client or the server can post the terminate message.

A *hot* link is more sophisticated. After the applications have linked, a client posts a conditional message (WM_DDE_ADVISE), asking the server to inform the client when the value of a data field changes. That is when the client wants the data. This scenario allows the client to be updated regarding the status of a data field, a handy situation in particular if the application is processing in real time. For example, your application might want to recalculate a spreadsheet or database column each time a value changes and, in turn, act if the new calculated value exceeds a threshold.

During a hot link, a client can decide that it no longer wants data updates and "unadvise" the server by sending an "UNADVISE" message. An application also can maintain a hot and cold link simultaneously by requesting the data from some fields unconditionally and from others conditionally.

A *warm* link is a partly hot, partly cold link. In this scenario, the client makes its connection to a server, sends a WM_DDE_ADVISE message, but indicates with a flag containing the WM_DDE_ADVISE message that it wants to be informed only of changes in a data field; it doesn't want the data sent. If the client does decide that it wants the data, it requests it (WM_DDE_REQUEST). The client also can change this advise status by sending an "UNADVISE" message.

Atoms, and So On

Client and server applications identify data with character strings representing the application, topic in the application, and data in the application. These character strings are represented by "atoms," case-insensitive word values that refer to the character strings.

The atom character string is recorded in an atom table, which is stored in a shared data segment in a dynamic link library in Windows. You don't have to know the details of how this shared atom table works, but you do have to use it to establish a DDE link. Specifically, when the client application wants to initiate a DDE conversation, it adds the application, topic, and item names (if necessary) to the atom table:

```
ApplicationAtom := GlobalAddAtom('Application Name');
TopicAtom := GlobalAddAtom('Topic Name');
```

The DDE applications engaged in the conversation use the atom table to establish their link.

When your application has established the link, it deletes the names from the table:

```
GlobalDeleteAtom(ApplicationAtom);
GlobalDeleteAtom(TopicAtom);
```

The `wm_DDE_Initiate` message, which your application uses to establish a DDE conversation, is actually broadcast (or sent) to all top-level (or parent) windows. Any application can respond to this `DDE_Initiate` message, so it is up to the client application to terminate all these unwanted links. Your application handles this duty with a `WMDDE` message-response method, which posts a message to all unwanted respondees, terminating the link:

```
procedure TDDEWindow.WMDDEAck(var Msg: TMessage);
begin
  { .... }
  PostMessage(Msg.WParam, wm_DDE_Terminate, HWindow, 0);
    { .... }

end;
```

To initiate a DDE conversation, broadcast a message that identifies the application. In the next example, you establish a very cold link to the Program Manager, eventually using the link to create a program group that can, in turn, be used by any applications that access the Program Manager.

The `InitiateDDE` method looks like this:

```
procedure DDEWindow.InitiateDDE;
var
  AppAtom, TopicAtom: TAtom;              { Global atoms }
  lParam : Word;                          { Message parameter }
begin
  PostedMessage := wm_DDE_Initiate;       { Initiate DDE }
```

```
  AppAtom := GlobalAddAtom('PROGMAN');    { Specify server application }
  TopicAtom := GlobalAddAtom('PROGMAN'); { Specify server topic }
  SendMessage(HWnd(-1), wm_DDE_Initiate, HWindow,
    MakeLong(AppAtom, TopicAtom));
  GlobalDeleteAtom(AppAtom);                   { Done with global atoms }
  GlobalDeleteAtom(TopicAtom);
  PostedMessage := 0;
  if ServerWindow = 0 then        { DDE failed if ServerWindow = 0 }
     begin
        MessageBox(HWindow, 'Cannot establish DDE link to
          Program Manager.',
               'Error', mb_IconExclamation or mb_Ok);
        EndDDE;                { EndDDE if no successful DDE contact }
     end;
end;
```

Notice that you cancel the DDE link if the Program Manager is not available. A message is displayed indicating the lack of success, and EndDDE is called, like this:

```
procedure TDDEWindow.EndDDE;
var Msg :TMessage;
begin
     WMDestroy(Msg);
end;
```

WMDestroy sends messages to TerminateDDE and to TDlgWindow. WMDestroy destroys the additional dialog window you created:

```
procedure DDEWindow.WMDestroy(var Msg: TMessage);
begin
  TerminateDDE;
  TDlgWindow.WMDestroy(Msg);
end;
```

WMDDETerminate uses the Windows function TerminateDDE to break the DDE link, as such:

```
procedure TDDEWindow.WMDDETerminate(var Msg: TMessage);
begin
  if Msg.WParam = ServerWindow then TerminateDDE;
end;
```

Listing 11.3 shows the complete procedure of a unit and test program used for linking to the Program Manager and creating a program group. Figure 11.2 shows the dialog window in add-an-item-to-the-list mode created by the code. Figure 11.3 shows a group list. Figure 11.4 shows the Create Group mode. Figure 11.5 shows a group created using this code.

Listing 11.3. *Linking to the Program Manager.*

```
unit MakeGroup;

{ This unit based on BI's progtalk.pas }

interface

uses
     WinTypes,
     WinProcs,
     WObjects,
     Strings;

{$R MAKEGROU}
const
{ Resource IDs }
  id_DDEDialog    = 100;
  id_AddDialog    = 101;
  id_CreateDialog = 102;

{ DDE dialog item IDs }

  id_ListBox     = 100;
  id_AddItem     = 101;
  id_DeleteItem  = 102;
  id_ClearItems  = 103;
  id_CreateGroup = 104;

{ Add and Create dialog item IDs }

  id_InputLine = 100;

type
{ DDEDialog is the object type used to represent the Add
  Item and Create Group dialogs. }

  PDDEDialog = ^DDEDialog;
  DDEDialog = object(TDialog)
    Buffer: PChar;
```

continues

Listing 11.3. continued

```
    BufferSize: Word;
    constructor Init(AParent: PWindowsObject;
      AName, EditBuffer: PChar; EditBufferSize: Word);
    procedure SetupWindow; virtual;
    function CanClose: Boolean; virtual;
    procedure InputLine(var Msg: TMessage);
      virtual id_First + id_InputLine;
  end;

{ DDEWindow is the Application's MainWindow.
  It maintains a DDE conversation with the
  Program Manager, and allows a user to create
  program groups containing a user-specified
  list of program items. }

  PDDEWindow = ^DDEWindow;
  DDEWindow = object(TDlgWindow) { DDEWindow is a kind of TDlgWindow }
    ListBox: PListBox;           { List box for setting up group }
    ServerWindow: HWnd;          { The server's handle }
    ContactMessage: Word;
    constructor Init;
    procedure SetupWindow; virtual;
    function GetClassName: PChar; virtual;
    procedure InitiateDDE;       { DDE contact messages }
    procedure TerminateDDE;
    procedure EndDDE;

    procedure AddItem(var Msg: TMessage);  { Make group messages }
      virtual id_First + id_AddItem;
    procedure DeleteItem(var Msg: TMessage);
      virtual id_First + id_DeleteItem;
    procedure ClearItems(var Msg: TMessage);
      virtual id_First + id_ClearItems;
    procedure CreateGroup(var Msg: TMessage);
      virtual id_First + id_CreateGroup;
    procedure WMDDEAck(var Msg: TMessage); { Windows messages }
      virtual wm_First + wm_DDE_Ack;
    procedure WMDDETerminate(var Msg: TMessage);
      virtual wm_First + wm_DDE_Terminate;
    procedure WMDestroy(var Msg: TMessage);
      virtual wm_First + wm_Destroy;
  end;
```

```
{ DDEApp is the application object. It constructs
  a DDEWindow (its MainWindow) }

  DDEApp = object(TApplication)
     procedure InitMainWindow; virtual;
  end;


implementation


{ DDEDialog }

{ Input dialog constructor.
  Save the input buffer pointer and size
  for copying the contents of the EditControl }

constructor DDEDialog.Init(AParent: PWindowsObject;
  AName, EditBuffer: PChar; EditBufferSize: Word);
begin
  TDialog.Init(AParent, AName);
  Buffer := EditBuffer;
  BufferSize := EditBufferSize;
end;
{ SetupWindow is called right after the dialog is created.
  The Edit control is limited to the
  maximum length of the input buffer.
  Disable the Ok button by setting EnableWindow to false. }

procedure DDEDialog.SetupWindow;
begin
  SendDlgItemMessage(HWindow, id_InputLine, em_LimitText,
    BufferSize - 1, 0);
  EnableWindow(GetDlgItem(HWindow, id_Ok), False);
end;

{ Copy the contents of the edit control to the input buffer
  and return True, which allows the dialog to close. }

function DDEDialog.CanClose: Boolean;
begin
  GetDlgItemText(HWindow, id_InputLine, Buffer, BufferSize);
  CanClose := True;
end;
```

continues

Listing 11.3. continued

```
{ Edit control response method. Enable the Ok button
  if the edit control contains text, else
  disable the Ok button. }

procedure DDEDialog.InputLine(var Msg: TMessage);
begin
  if Msg.LParamHi = en_Change then
    EnableWindow(GetDlgItem(HWindow, id_Ok),
      SendMessage(Msg.LParamLo, wm_GetTextLength, 0, 0) <> 0);
end;

{ DDEWindow }

{ DDE window constructor. Create a TListBox object to
  represent the dialog's list box. Clear the DDE server
  window handle and the pending DDE message ID. }

constructor DDEWindow.Init;
begin
  TDlgWindow.Init(nil, PChar(id_DDEDialog));
  ListBox := New(PListBox, InitResource(@Self, id_ListBox));
  ServerWindow := 0;                  { No server yet. }
  ContactMessage := 0;
end;

{ SetupWindow is called right after the DDE window is
  created.  Initiate the DDE conversation. }


procedure DDEWindow.SetupWindow;
begin
  TDlgWindow.SetupWindow;
  InitiateDDE;
end;


{ Return window class name. This name corresponds to the
  class name specified for the DDE dialog in the resource
  file. }

function DDEWindow.GetClassName: PChar;
begin
  GetClassName := 'DDEWindow';
end;
```

```
{ Initiate a DDE conversation with the Program Manager.
  Bring up a message box if the Program Manager doesn't
  respond to the wm_DDE_Initiate message. }

procedure DDEWindow.InitiateDDE;
var
  AppAtom, TopicAtom: TAtom;
  lParam : Word;
begin
  ContactMessage := wm_DDE_Initiate;
  AppAtom := GlobalAddAtom('PROGMAN');
  TopicAtom := GlobalAddAtom('PROGMAN');

  lParam := AppAtom or (TopicAtom shl 16);

(* Either of the following SendMessage procedures works,
   but don't use both.

   SendMessage(HWnd(-1), wm_DDE_Initiate, HWindow,
   MakeLong(AppAtom, TopicAtom));
*)

  SendMessage(HWnd(-1), wm_DDE_Initiate,HWindow,lParam);

GlobalDeleteAtom(AppAtom);
GlobalDeleteAtom(TopicAtom);
ContactMessage := 0;
if ServerWindow = 0 then
  begin
     MessageBox(HWindow, 'Cannot establish DDE link to
                         Program Manager.',
       'Error', mb_IconExclamation or mb_Ok);
     EndDDE;                       { Bail out if no DDE }
     end;
end;


procedure DDEWindow.EndDDE;
var Msg :TMessage;
begin
     WMDestroy(Msg);
end;
```

continues

Listing 11.3. continued

```
{ Terminate the DDE conversation. Send the wm_DDE_Terminate
  message only if the server window still exists. }

procedure DDEWindow.TerminateDDE;
var
  W: HWnd;
begin
  W := ServerWindow;
  ServerWindow := 0;
  if IsWindow(W) then PostMessage(W, wm_DDE_Terminate, HWindow, 0);
end;

{ Add item button response method. Bring up the Add item
 dialog to input a program item string, and add that item to
 the list box. }

procedure DDEWindow.AddItem(var Msg: TMessage);
var
  Name: array[0..63] of Char;
begin
  if Application^.ExecDialog(New(PDDEDialog, Init(@Self,
    PChar(id_AddDialog), Name, SizeOf(Name)))) <> id_Cancel
     then ListBox^.AddString(Name); end;

{ Delete item button response method. Delete the currently
  selected item in the list box. }

procedure DDEWindow.DeleteItem(var Msg: TMessage);
begin
  ListBox^.DeleteString(ListBox^.GetSelIndex);
end;

{ Clear items button response method. Clear the list box. }

procedure DDEWindow.ClearItems(var Msg: TMessage);
begin
  ListBox^.ClearList;
end;

{ Create group button response method. Initiate the Create
  Group dialog to input the program group name. Then, if a DDE
  link has been established (ServerWindow <> 0) and there is
  no DDE message currently pending (ContactMessage = 0), build
```

```
  a list of Program Manager commands, and submit the commands
  using a wm_DDE_Execute message. To build the command list,
  first calculate the total length of the list, then allocate
  a global memory block of that size, and finally store the
  command list as a null-terminated string in the memory
  block. }

procedure DDEWindow.CreateGroup(var Msg: TMessage);
const
  sCreateGroup = '[CreateGroup(%s)]';
  sAddItem = '[AddItem(%s)]';
var
  Executed: Boolean;
  I, L: Integer;
  HCommands: THandle;
  PName, PCommands: PChar;
  Name: array[0..63] of Char;
begin
  if Application^.ExecDialog(New(PDDEDialog, Init(@Self,
    PChar(id_CreateDialog), Name, SizeOf(Name)))) <> id_Cancel then
  begin
    Executed := False;
    if (ServerWindow <> 0) and (ContactMessage = 0) then
    begin
      L := StrLen(Name) + (Length(sCreateGroup) - 1);
      for I := 0 to ListBox^.GetCount - 1 do
        Inc(L, ListBox^.GetStringLen(I) + (Length(sAddItem) - 2));
      HCommands := GlobalAlloc(gmem_Moveable or
         gmem_DDEShare, L);     { Must be DDEShare memory }
      if HCommands <> 0 then
      begin
        PName := Name;
        PCommands := GlobalLock(HCommands);
        WVSPrintF(PCommands, sCreateGroup, PName);
        for I := 0 to ListBox^.GetCount - 1 do
        begin
          ListBox^.GetString(Name, I);
          PCommands := StrEnd(PCommands);
          WVSPrintF(PCommands, sAddItem, PName);
        end;
        GlobalUnlock(HCommands);
        if PostMessage(ServerWindow, wm_DDE_Execute, HWindow,
            MakeLong(0, HCommands)) then
```

continues

Listing 11.3. continued

```
        begin
         ContactMessage := wm_DDE_Execute;
         Executed := True;
        end else GlobalFree(HCommands);
      end;
    end;
    if not Executed then
      MessageBox(HWindow, 'Program Manager DDE execute
          failed.', 'Error', mb_IconExclamation or mb_Ok);
  end;
end;

{ wm_DDE_Ack message response method. If the current DDE
  message is a wm_DDE_Initiate, store off the window handle of
  the window that responded. If more than one window responds,
  terminate all conversations but the first. If the current
  DDE message is a wm_DDE_Execute, free the command string
  memory block, focus the window, and clear the list box. }

procedure DDEWindow.WMDDEAck(var Msg: TMessage);
begin
  case ContactMessage of
    wm_DDE_Initiate:
      begin
        if ServerWindow = 0 then
          ServerWindow := Msg.WParam
        else
          PostMessage(Msg.WParam, wm_DDE_Terminate, HWindow, 0);
        GlobalDeleteAtom(Msg.LParamLo);
        GlobalDeleteAtom(Msg.LParamHi);
      end;
    wm_DDE_Execute:
      begin
        GlobalFree(Msg.LParamHi);
        ContactMessage := 0;
        SetFocus(HWindow);
        ListBox^.ClearList;
      end;
   end;
end;
```

```
{ wm_DDE_Terminate message response method. If the window
  signaling termination is the server window (the Program
  Manager), terminate the DDE conversation. Otherwise ignore
  the wm_DDE_Terminate. }

procedure DDEWindow.WMDDETerminate(var Msg: TMessage);
begin
  if Msg.WParam = ServerWindow then TerminateDDE;
end;

{ wm_Destroy message response method. Terminate the DDE link
  and call the inherited WMDestroy. }

procedure DDEWindow.WMDestroy(var Msg: TMessage);
begin
  TerminateDDE;
  TDlgWindow.WMDestroy(Msg);
end;

{ TDDEApp }

{ Create a DDE window as the application's main window. }

procedure DDEApp.InitMainWindow;
begin
  MainWindow := New(PDDEWindow, Init);
end;

end.


{ end MakeGrou unit }


program Test_Interface;  { A generic way to test each
                           phase of interface development }

uses
    WIF5,                { Basic Interface unit }
    makegrou;            { Contains DDEApp }
```

continues

Listing 11.3. continued

```
type

     App = object(DDEApp)
     end;

var
  Application: App;      { An instance of BasicApplication }

                         { Run Application1 }
begin
  Application.Init('BasicInterface');  { Init application instance }
  Application.Run;       { Message loop }
  Application.Done;      { Destroy application instance }
end.
```

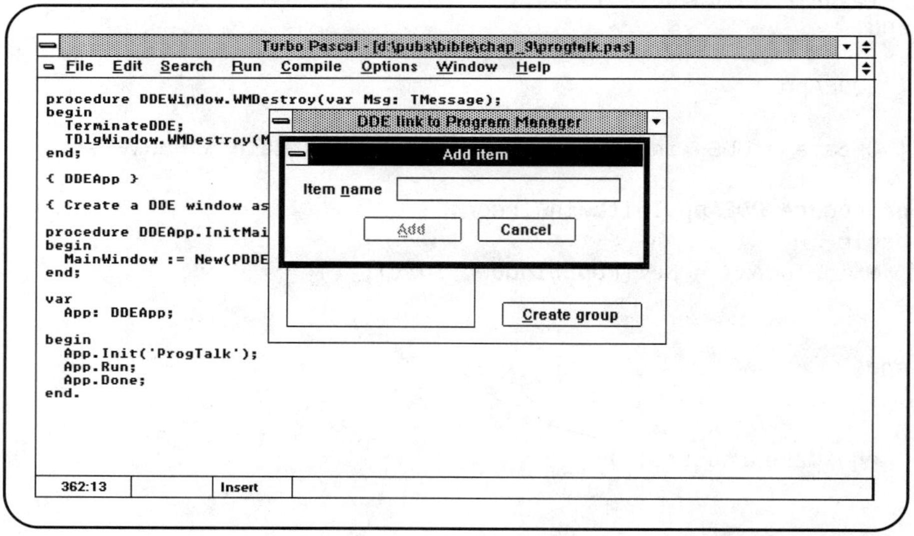

Figure 11.2. *The dialog window in add-an-item-to-the-list mode created by listing 11.3.*

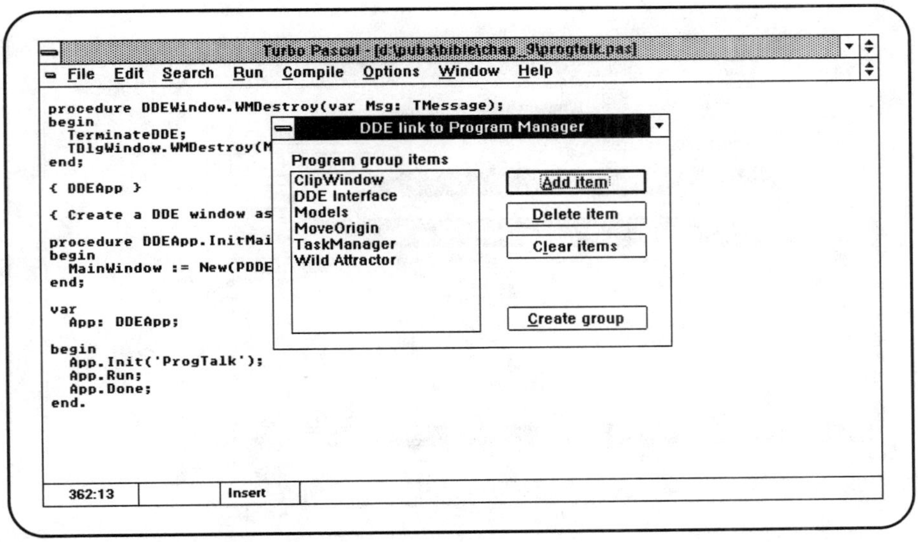

Figure 11.3. A group list.

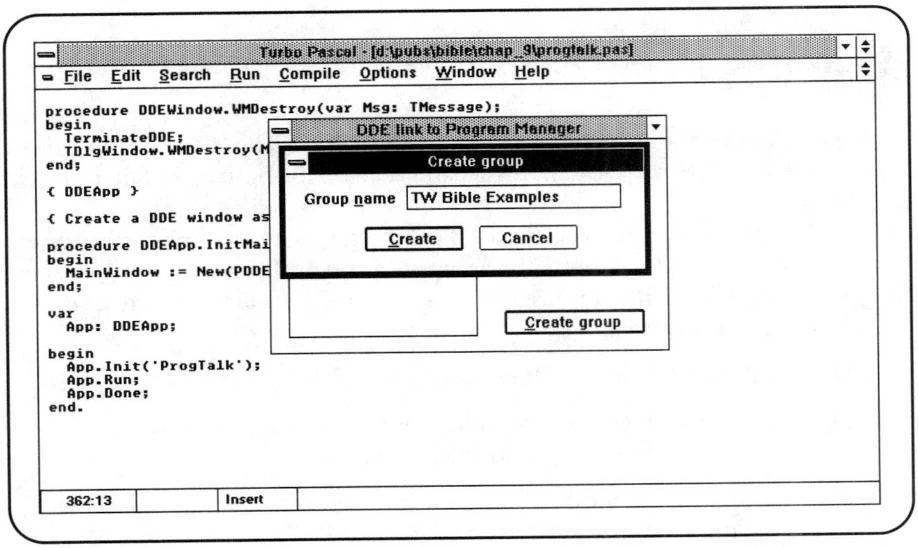

Figure 11.4. The Create Group mode.

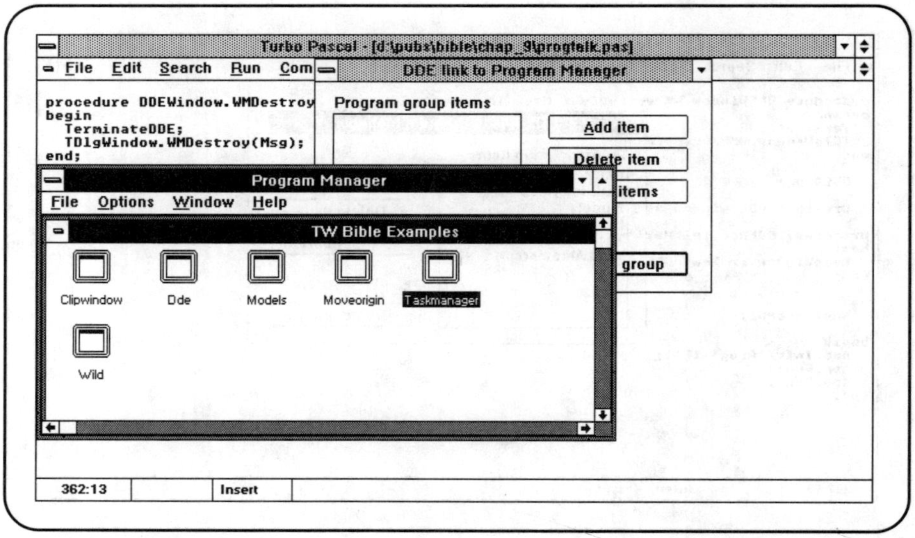

Figure 11.5. *A group created using listing 11.3.*

Wrap-up

DDE is one of the many features that makes Windows sing. If your application knows how to link to the DDE, it can act and react to the behavior of many other programs.

Although this chapter has focused on the application-clipboard connection and the very cold link between an application and the Program Manager, the possibilities for making more dramatic connections are virtually endless.

Your applications can

1. Modify the data fields in other programs.
2. Have their own data fields modified or behavior manipulated in response to the behavior of another program.
3. Directly command another program through the use of a program's MACRO language.

For example, you can access Microsoft Word, Excel, and other sophisticated programs through their MACRO languages.

For advanced information about DDE contacts, check the Reference section in Part III of this book.

12

CHAPTER

SHARING LIBRARIES: USING DLL (DYNAMIC LINK LIBRARIES)

When a child draws a tree, a green mass sits atop a brown trunk, as if the basic shape were like a Popsicle.

James Gleick

Dynamic link libraries are executable modules of code linked into an application at run-time. DLLs allow application developers to create and maintain independent application components. Similar to units in their modularity, DLLs are more powerful because they

1. Can be linked into an application at run-time.
2. Can be shared by many concurrently executing applications.
3. Can be written in a variety of languages, regardless of the language used to access the DLL.

Dynamically linked libraries (DLLs) permit several applications to share code and resources. These applications (also called *clients*) share a single copy of a procedure or function. The DLL file has to be present when the client application executes.

DLLs are similar to units, except the procedures and functions in units are linked into applications at link time (in other words, they are *statically linked*), and the procedures and functions in DLLs are accessible to the application at run-time (in other words, they are *dynamically linked*). The Windows program loader dynamically links the procedure and function calls in the application to their entry points in the DLLs, which then are used by the application.

DLLs are especially powerful because a Turbo Pascal for Windows application can use DLLs that were not written using Turbo Pascal for Windows, and applications written in other languages can use DLLs written with Turbo Pascal for Windows.

A DLL consists of indexed functions and procedures, and is a more or less straightforward aspect of Windows' application development. This chapter briefly shows you how to create and access a DLL in Turbo Pascal for Windows. For more extensive details about DLLs, see the Microsoft Software Developers Kit (SDK).

DLL Details

First, a few DLL rules:

- For an application to use a procedure or function contained in a DLL, the application must import the procedure or function using an external declaration.
- In imported procedures and functions, the external directive replaces the declaration and statement parts that otherwise would be present in the application.
- Imported procedures and functions behave similarly to normal ones, except they must use far calls (either a far procedure directive or a `{$F+}` compiler directive).

Turbo Pascal lets you import procedures and functions in DLLs in three different ways:

- By name
- By new name
- By ordinal

Although a DLL can have variables, you cannot import them into other modules. Any access to a DLL's variables must occur through a procedural interface.

For example, the following external declaration imports the function `GlobalAlloc` from the DLL called KERNEL (the Windows kernel):

```
function GlobalAlloc(Flags: Word; Bytes: Longint): THandle;
   far; external 'KERNEL' index 15;
```

Notice that the DLL name you specify after the external keyword and the new name you specify in a name clause do not have to be string literals. Any constant string expression will do. Also, the ordinal number specified in an index clause can be any constant integer expression. For example:

```
const
  ALib = 'ALIB';
  Ordinal = 8;


procedure ImportByName;     external ALib;
procedure ImportByNewName; external ALib name 'REALNAME';
procedure ImportByOrdinal; external ALib index Ordinal;
```

Using DLLs

Using a DLL is basically a two-step process:

1. Create the dynamic link library of functions and procedures, which includes an export procedure and function section.
2. Create the application that uses the library.

For example, designate a library with the library identifier:

```
library BitBtn;
```

or

```
library DLLStuff;
```

Any function you want to export in the library has to be specified by an export identifier. For example:

```
function BitButWinFn(HWindow: HWnd; Message: Word; wParam:
       Word; lParam: Longint): Longint; export;
```

And at the end of the library, you have to specify the functions that can be exported. For example:

```
exports
  BitButWinFn;
```

The application then uses the functions in the library more or less normally, with a couple of exceptions. First, the application has to load the library before it uses it. For example:

```
constructor ABitApp.Init(AName: PChar);
begin
  Lib := LoadLibrary(DLLName);
  if Lib < 32 then Status := em_DLLNotFound;
  TApplication.Init(AName);
end;
```

And it has to free the library when it is finished with it. For example:

```
destructor ABitApp.Done;
begin
  TApplication.Done;
  FreeLibrary(Lib);
end;
```

The example in listing 12.1 demonstrates a use of DLLs. In this example, an application imports custom controls from a DLL. Figure 12.1 shows the window and custom controls created by the code.

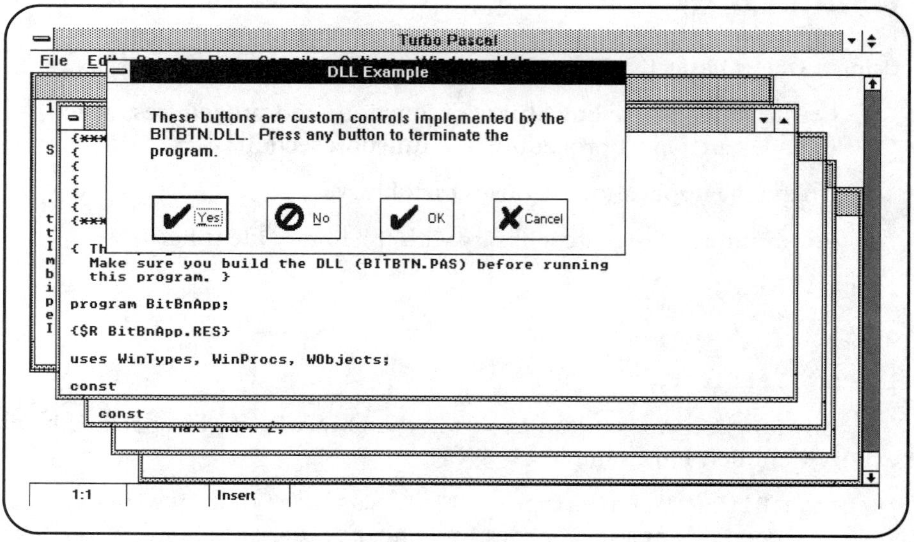

Figure 12.1. A window and its custom controls created by listing 12.1.

Listing 12.1. A dynamic link library (DLL) example.

```
{ A DLL library example that accesses
  Borland International's BitBtn.DLL. }


library ABitBtn;

uses
     WinTypes,
     WinProcs;

{$R ABITBTN.RES}

const
  ofState         = 0;
  ofDownBits      = 2;
  ofUpBits        = 4;
  ofFocUpBits     = 6;
  ofSize          = 8; { Amount of window extra bytes to use }

const
  bdBorderWidth = 1;

const
  bsDisabled      = $0001;
  bsFocus         = $0002;
  bsKeyDown       = $0004;
  bsMouseDown     = $0008;
  bsMouseUpDown   = $0010;
  bsDefault       = $0020;

function BitButtonWinFn(HWindow: HWnd; Message: Word;
  wParam: Word; lParam: Longint): Longint; export;

var
  DC: HDC;
  BitsNumber: Integer;
  Bitmap: TBitmap;
  Rect: TRect;
  Pt: TPoint;
  PS: TPaintStruct;
```

continues

Listing 12.1. continued

```
function Get(Ofs: Integer): Word;
begin
  Get := GetWindowWord(HWindow, Ofs);
end;

procedure SetWinWord(Ofs: Integer; Val: Word);
begin
  SetWindowWord(HWindow, Ofs, Val);
end;

function State: Word;
begin
  State := Get(ofState);
end;

function DownBits: Word;
begin
  DownBits := Get(ofDownBits);
end;

function UpBits: Word;
begin
  UpBits := Get(ofUpBits);
end;

function FocUpBits: Word;
begin
  FocUpBits := Get(ofFocUpBits);
end;

function GetState(AState: Word): Boolean;
begin
  GetState := (State and AState) = AState;
end;

procedure Paint(DC: HDC);
var
  MemDC: HDC;
  Bits, Oldbitmap: HBitmap;
  BorderBrush, OldBrush: HBrush;
  Frame: TRect;
  Height, Width: Integer;
```

```
begin
  if (State and (bsMouseDown + bsKeyDown) <> 0) and
      not GetState(bsMouseUpDown) then
    Bits := DownBits
  else
    if GetState(bsFocus) then Bits := FocUpBits
    else Bits := UpBits;

  { Draw a border }
  GetClientRect(HWindow, Frame);
  Height := Frame.bottom - Frame.top;
  Width := Frame.right - Frame.left;
  if GetState(bsDefault) then
    BorderBrush := GetStockObject(Black_Brush)
  else BorderBrush := GetStockObject(White_Brush);
  OldBrush := SelectObject(DC, BorderBrush);
  PatBlt(DC, Frame.left, Frame.top, Width, bdBorderWidth, PatCopy);
  PatBlt(DC, Frame.left, Frame.top, bdBorderWidth, Height, PatCopy);
  PatBlt(DC, Frame.left, Frame.bottom - bdBorderWidth, Width,
          bdBorderWidth, PatCopy);
  PatBlt(DC, Frame.right - bdBorderWidth, Frame.top,
          bdBorderWidth, Height, PatCopy);
  SelectObject(DC, OldBrush);

  { Draw a bit map }
  MemDC := CreateCompatibleDC(DC);
  OldBitmap := SelectObject(MemDC, Bits);
  GetObject(Bits, Sizeof(Bitmap), @Bitmap);
  BitBlt(DC, bdBorderWidth, bdBorderWidth, Bitmap.bmWidth,
          Bitmap.bmHeight, MemDC, 0, 0, srcCopy);
  SelectObject(MemDC, OldBitmap);
  DeleteDC(MemDC);
end;

procedure Repaint;
var
  DC: HDC;
begin
  DC := GetDC(HWindow);
  Paint(DC);
  ReleaseDC(HWindow, DC);
end;
```

continues

Listing 12.1. continued

```
procedure SetState(AState: Word; Enable: Boolean);
var
  OldState: Word;
begin
  OldState := State;
  if Enable then SetWinWord(ofState, State or AState)
  else SetWinWord(ofState, State and not AState);
  if State <> OldState then Repaint;
end;

function InMe(lPoint: Longint): Boolean;
var
  R: TRect;
  Point: TPoint absolute lPoint;
begin
  GetClientRect(HWindow, R);
  InflateRect(R, -bdBorderWidth, -bdBorderWidth);
  InMe := PtInRect(R, Point);
end;

procedure ButtonPressed;
begin
  SetState(bsMouseDown + bsMouseUpDown + bsKeyDown, False);
  SendMessage(GetParent(HWindow), wm_Command,
    GetDlgCtrlID(HWindow), Longint(HWindow));
end;

begin
  BitButtonWinFn := 0;
  case Message of                 { Message responses }
    wm_Create:
      begin
        DC := GetDC(0);
        if (GetSystemMetrics(sm_CYScreen) < 480) or
           (GetDeviceCaps(DC, numColors) < 16) then
          BitsNumber := 2000 + Get(gww_ID)
        else
          BitsNumber := 1000 + Get(gww_ID);
        ReleaseDC(0, DC);
        SetWinWord(ofUpBits, LoadBitmap(hInstance,
                        PChar(BitsNumber)));
```

```
      SetWinWord(ofDownBits, LoadBitmap(hInstance,
                      pChar(BitsNumber + 2000)));
      SetWinWord(ofFocUpBits, LoadBitmap(hInstance,
                      pChar(BitsNumber + 4000)));
      GetObject(DownBits, SizeOf(Bitmap), @Bitmap);
      GetWindowRect(HWindow, Rect);
      Pt.X := Rect.Left;
      Pt.Y := Rect.Top;
      ScreenToClient(PCreateStruct (lParam)^.hwndParent, Pt);
      MoveWindow(HWindow, Pt.X, Pt.Y,
      Bitmap.bmWidth + bdBorderWidth * 2,
      Bitmap.bmHeight + bdBorderWidth * 2, False);
      if (PCreateStruct(lParam)^.style and $1F) = bs_DefPushButton then
             SetState(bsDefault, True);
    end;
  wm_NCDestroy:
    begin
      BitButtonWinFn := DefWindowProc(HWindow, Message, wParam, lParam);
      DeleteObject(UpBits);
      DeleteObject(DownBits);
      DeleteObject(FocUpBits);
    end;
  wm_Paint:
    begin
      BeginPaint(HWindow, PS);
      Paint(PS.hDC);
      EndPaint(HWindow, PS);
    end;
  wm_EraseBkGnd:
    begin
    end;
  wm_Enable:
    SetState(bsDisabled, wParam <> 0);
  wm_SetFocus:
    SetState(bsFocus, True);
  wm_KillFocus:
    SetState(bsFocus, False);
  wm_KeyDown:
    if (wParam = $20) and not GetState(bsKeyDown) and
        not GetState(bsMouseDown) then
      SetState(bsKeyDown, True);
  wm_KeyUP:
    if (wParam = $20) and GetState(bsKeyDown) then
      ButtonPressed;
```

continues

Listing 12.1. continued

```
    wm_LButtonDblClk, wm_LButtonDown:
      if InMe(lParam) and not GetState(bsKeyDown) then
      begin
        if GetFocus <> HWindow then SetFocus(HWindow);
        SetState(bsMouseDown, True); SetCapture(HWindow);
      end;
    wm_MouseMove:
      if GetState(bsMouseDown) then
        SetState(bsMouseUpDown, not InMe(lParam));
    wm_LButtonUp:
      if GetState(bsMouseDown) then
      begin
        ReleaseCapture;
        if not GetState(bsMouseUpDown) then ButtonPressed
        else SetState(bsMouseDown + bsMouseUpDown, False);
      end;
    wm_GetDlgCode:
      if GetState(bsDefault) then
        BitButtonWinFn:= dlgc_DefPushButton
      else
        BitButtonWinFn := dlgc_UndefPushButton;
    bm_SetStyle:
      SetState(bsDefault, wParam = bs_DefPushButton);
  else
    BitButtonWinFn := DefWindowProc(HWindow, Message, wParam, lParam);
  end;
end;

exports                            { Export qualifier }
  BitButtonWinFn;

var
  Class: TWndClass;

begin
  with Class do
  begin
    lpszClassName := 'ABitButton';
    hCursor       := LoadCursor(0, idc_Arrow);
    lpszMenuName  := nil;
    style         := cs_HRedraw or cs_VRedraw or cs_DblClks
                          or cs_GlobalClass;
    lpfnWndProc   := TFarProc(@BitButtonWinFn);
```

```
    hInstance     := System.hInstance;
    hIcon         := 0;
    cbWndExtra    := ofSize;
    cbClsExtra    := 0;
    hbrBackground := 0;
  end;
  RegisterClass(Class);
end.

{ End DLL }


{ Main application uses the custom controls
  in the DLL: ABITBTN.PAS. }


program BitBnApp;

{$R BitBnApp.RES}

uses
      WinTypes,
      WinProcs,
      WObjects;

const
  DLLName = 'ABITBTN.DLL';              { The DLL }

const
  em_DLLNotFound = 1;

type
  PABitWindow = ^ABitWindow;
  ABitWindow = object(TDlgWindow)     { A dialog window }
        { Button response methods }
    procedure Yes(var Msg: TMessage);
      virtual id_First + id_Yes;
    procedure No(var Msg: TMessage);
      virtual id_First + id_No;
    procedure Ok(var Msg: TMessage);
      virtual id_First + id_OK;
    procedure Cancel(var Msg: TMessage);
       virtual id_First + id_Cancel;
  end;
```

continues

Listing 12.1. continued

```
  PABitApp = ^ABitApp;
  ABitApp = object(TApplication)
    Lib: THandle;                     { A library handle }
    constructor Init(AName: PChar);
    destructor Done; virtual;
    procedure InitMainWindow; virtual;
    procedure Error(ErrorCode: Integer); virtual;
  end;

{ ABitApp }

constructor ABitApp.Init(AName: PChar);
begin
  Lib := LoadLibrary(DLLName);      { Load the DLL }
  if Lib < 32 then Status := em_DLLNotFound;
  TApplication.Init(AName);
end;

destructor ABitApp.Done;
begin
  TApplication.Done;
  FreeLibrary(Lib);                 { Release the DLL }
end;

procedure ABitApp.InitMainWindow;
begin
  MainWindow := New(PABitWindow, Init(nil,
    MakeIntResource(100)));         { Use resource }
end;

procedure ABitApp.Error(ErrorCode: Integer);
begin
  case ErrorCode of
    em_DLLNotFound:
      MessageBox(0, DLLName + ' not found. ',
            'Fatal error', mb_Ok or mb_IconStop);
  else
    TApplication.Error(ErrorCode);
  end;
end;

{ ABitWindow methods }
```

```
procedure ABitWindow.Yes(var Msg: TMessage);
begin
  CloseWindow;
end;

procedure ABitWindow.No(var Msg: TMessage);
begin  { Cancel close }
end;

procedure ABitWindow.Ok(var Msg: TMessage);
begin
  CloseWindow;
end;

procedure ABitWindow.Cancel(var Msg: TMessage);
begin  { Cancel close }
end;

var
  App: ABitApp;

{ Main loop }

begin
  App.Init('Uses ABITBTN.DDL');
  App.Run;
  App.Done;
end.
```

13

CHAPTER

DESIGNING WINDOWS APPLICATIONS

My roads will not be exactly the same as yours, but, with our separate maps, we can each get from a particular place to another.

Douglas R. Hofstadter

Turbo Pascal for Windows offers application developers an exceptional way to design applications for Windows that can evolve as the needs of users evolve. If you build your Windows applications out of objects (using the ObjectWindows library):

1. Your application does not have to bother with the details of interacting with Windows at a low level.
2. Your application consists of easily modifiable objects.

The net result is easily modifiable and extendable Windows applications.

One important way of extending objects, as this book has shown, is through inheritance. When you want a new object similar to one that ObjectWindows (or your object library) already contains, you can derive a new object from the one you have, and create new behavior or override some existing behavior you must change.

Why is this important? Because problems and the needs of computer users change, and good applications always change in response to users. Windows is a general-purpose, flexible interface; user-friendly and (with the help of Turbo Pascal for Windows) developer-friendly.

This chapter reshapes the ideas discussed so far into a more or less general Windows design philosophy. This philosophy emphasizes two primary themes for designing efficient, expandable Windows applications:

1. Make new applications consistent with existing Windows applications. In other words, if you are going to use Windows as your user interface, take full advantage of it by using its strengths; for example, the consistency of its interface. IBM has published guidelines that address this issue, called the Common User Access (CUA), which this book uses as a basis.

2. Take advantage of object-oriented techniques that are flexible enough to let you extend and modify them as painlessly as possible. The object-oriented techniques built thoroughly into Turbo Pascal for Windows (that is, ObjectWindows) can save you an enormous amount of time and effort, as the previous 12 chapters have demonstrated.

The second part of this chapter describes more about discovering and extending objects as a primary step in application design.

Discussing consistency in the look and feel of applications and highlighting some of the important aspects of the Common User Access is a good way to start.

Common User Access

The Common User Access (CUA) is a set of guidelines that help you develop applications consistent with IBM's (and probably Microsoft's) ideas about how a Windows application should look and feel.

The CUA emphasizes two primary ideas:

1. Users should feel comfortable with an application and confident in the results of an action.

2. Users should control the flow of events.

Looking out for users' comfort and building their confidence is a big job. Making your application consistent with other Windows applications they might have used, and making it consistent with its own behavior can do the job. Each opening of a window should be less mysterious and more familiar. Similar tasks should run in similar-looking windows.

In addition, if possible, try to use metaphors with which the user is familiar. A classic example is a card-filing application on a computer that resembles a card-filing system used in businesses.

Also, avoid limiting users whenever you can. In other words, avoid restricting users' access to parts of an application. Users should be able to move anywhere they want when they want.

You can think of this process as event-flow. In other words, let the users control as much of the flow of the application as possible. This builds users' confidence and lets them overcome the all-too-typical fear of applications and thus, of the computer.

When you can, let users decide things for themselves using visual cues (icons, shapes, menus, lists, and so on). Encourage them to explore the application. Do not make them pay too dearly for mistakes. Provide an Undo, Backout, Feedback, and Help. The best application includes a context- and situation-sensitive Help system that provides not only general but also specific help.

Each application should have the standard appearance of a `MainWindow`, menu, and event-driven object-action cycle. Users' double or single mouse clicks should do similar things in applications. The same rule applies to the keyboard: if the applications you use already specify F1, Shift-F1, or Control-F1 to call up certain kinds of Help, consider using those keys yourself. Make the application feel as familiar as you can.

Use windows sparingly, but well. Do not make a window bigger than it has to be, and keep in mind that the `MainWindow` represents the application. When it is minimized the application virtually disappears.

When you can, notice the selection of an object visually. Show that an object has been selected or deselected. An excellent use of visual selection and deselection is the icon display used by many drawing applications to represent pens, brushes, and so on.

Do not restrict the mouse pointer. In other words, always make sure that it is free to move from window to window or from application to application. Use the keyboard selection cursor, and mark the input focus where input is occurring on the screen.

Make the menus' styles conform to the kind of menus typically used by applications such as the Program Manager. The Program Manager, by the way, is an excellent example to compare to your applications when you try to make them conform to the Common User Access.

CUA also recommends specific menu items for commonly used topics, such as File, Edit, View, Help, and so on. In addition, the CUA recommends specific keyboard accelerators for use with many commonly used topics. See the IBM CUA specification for more details.

Make dialog and file boxes, list viewers, entry windows, and others as consistent as possible. Do not mix too many elements in one application. Remember: you want your application to be as easy to know and use as possible.

Objects and Windows

Programs (that is, applications) become more powerful and more difficult to design and code almost daily, it seems. Was not there an early myth that software would eventually be easy to use, powerful, *and* easy to develop? (Ha, ha.)

Application ease of use and power might be keeping pace with each other, but ease of development is still desperately struggling to keep up. The Windows-OOP connection is a step in the right direction. Events and objects; objects and actions. Point, click, and an object responds to an event by carrying out an action. Windows is both powerful and easy to use. OOP also makes it easier to create and, in particular, to maintain applications.

Why is maintenance so important? Consider how one goes about designing an application.

Before object-oriented design, first-rate application developers primarily used something called "structured programming" or "structured design," a philosophy which advocates that you determine all the details of an application (in other words, its structure) before you begin coding it. Most developers, in fact, still use some structured philosophy as their design model.

You structure the application by breaking it into smaller structures of information, organized by levels of complexity. The most specific aspects of the structure are incorporated into larger, less specific structures.

In addition to "structuring" aspects of the application, you describe the application in terms of "data-flow diagrams." A *data-flow diagram* is a collection of blocks (the structured, usually functional, parts) and arrows. Each block represents a process for accepting, using, and often transforming data items, with arrows representing the flows from block to block. Figure 13.1 illustrates this scenario.

A complete system (or application) or subset of an application can be represented by a single block. Arranging an application into a hierarchy of data-flow diagrams is called *leveling* (because the application is organized into levels of complexity). The data-flow diagram modeling process leads to a complete set of diagrams that represent the system and its flow through various levels of complexity.

Using these structured blocks, you can view, use, or analyze an application from many perspectives—from overview (represented by a single diagram with a single block, and not much detail), to fine detail (represented by many different diagrams, each with multiple blocks).

After you have generated, checked, and agreed on the detailed data-flow diagrams, you often generate a hierarchical structure chart from them (see figure 13.2).

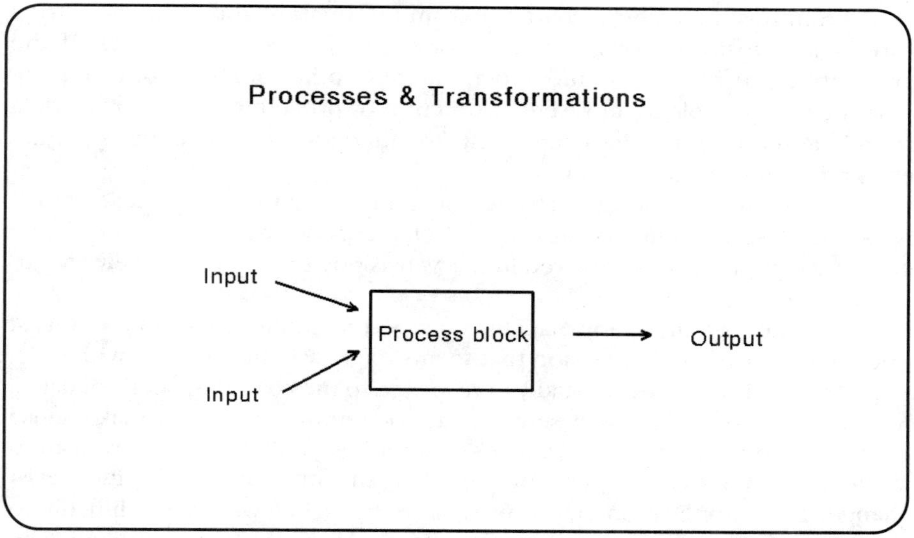

Figure 13.1. *A data-flow diagram.*

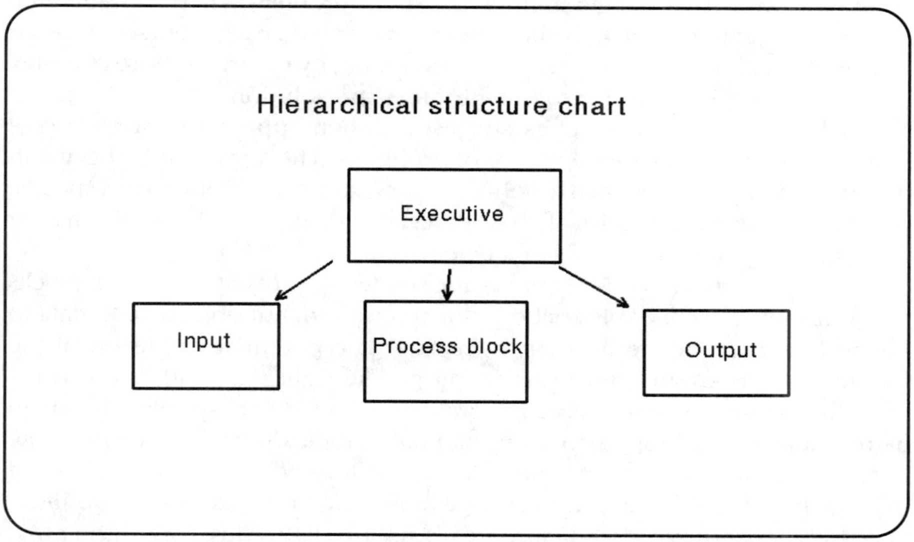

Figure 13.2. *A hierarchical structure chart.*

The hierarchical chart shows the flow of data in and out of the blocks. The blocks either transform the data or don't, and then return them (represented by the outgoing arrow). The chart shows how blocks interact with other blocks.

From this hierarchical chart and from information about the data structures and transformations, you can code the specific components of the application one block at a time, independent of other blocks. From a coding perspective, each block represents a function or procedure, and moving data from in and out of the block represents the function's or procedure's parameters and return values.

This structured design has been around a long time, and makes much sense because it seems to capture the elements of the application in one swoop. An application structured in this way is powerful and relatively easy to understand.

Yet, the structured approach is not a perfect design solution for at least one important reason—a reason that seems to grow in importance with time.

Applications change, usually in response to the changing needs of users. A structure that made much sense in the beginning might not make sense further down the line. Structured design supplies much-needed organization at the beginning of an application's life, but the structure itself might resist change. Most application developers have struggled with the "difficult to change" problem, even when their initial designs seemed correct or even exceptional.

The design of an application might be clear. It might be clear, in part, because it is based on a single solution to a single problem. A hard-coded single solution to a single problem is almost always clearer than a general-solution or a general-problem solution. The general solution, by nature, is more complex because it considers more than one problem and solution.

Object-oriented techniques suggest a design approach that addresses both the specific and general nature of problems. The approach is specific in that an object can be designed to solve specific aspects of a problem or a specific problem and yet be derivative of a base object that contains the general behavior for handling general problems of a type.

In an object-oriented design, the idea of the "flow of data" between blocks is diminished. Messages move about the application, but objects keep data to themselves and operate on their own data. The potential confusion of the wrong procedures and functions acting on the right data and vice versa is virtually eliminated. Methods can operate only on the data specified for them by the object definition. Also, the potential complexity that arises from the connections of blocks transforming data is diminished.

Objects have the notion of change built into them. Extension, modification, and a sense of general purpose are features in OOP. Thus, applications that use objects as the "structured blocks" can incorporate the notion of change in their "structures" from the beginning.

> **Note:** Object-oriented programming techniques do not attempt to eliminate structure; instead they attempt to incorporate change in structure. The best of both worlds? Perhaps.

Designing for Change

Object-oriented design anticipates the evolution of real-world systems and applications. Object-oriented Windows design utilizes the consistency of the Windows GUI. The interface remains similar although the application encapsulates its response to both the real world and Windows in modifiable objects. Any application of even modest complexity changes, so anticipating change is only natural.

In general, change comes in one of two forms: external or internal to the application. An external change is a change in the outside world that requires a change in the application's behavior, so the application can continue to accurately represent the outside world. Simple examples include:

1. Adding new printers or graphics terminals to an application's capability to communicate with devices.
2. Adding desktop publishing behavior to a word-processing application.

Structured design techniques, even without OOP, are expert at focusing on these kinds of changes. Notice that Windows already specializes in these kinds of problems for an application. Device-independence is a central tenet of Windows.

An internal change is a change in the way you (and subsequently the application) handle a problem. Nothing has to change in the outside world for you to have a better idea how an application works or handles the problem. This change is between you and the application, separate from the problem itself.

Your realization of a problem might simply arise from your using the application, from research, or (in very special cases) from a stroke of design genius. For example, you might rewrite a sort algorithm to increase its sorting speed when the number of items exceeds some threshold. You also might reorganize your code so that it makes more sense to another programmer. Finally, you might decide that an entirely different design approach is better.

You might discover (by reusing an application in a new situation) that a type you created for an application can be improved by redesigning it or by recomposing it into a different group of objects. Structured techniques (without OOP) implicitly assume that you have a complete understanding of the application and the world it represents before you begin coding it, and that the programmer or designer either does not make mistakes or learns from those mistakes. In short, structured techniques do not lend themselves well to internal changes.

Object-oriented programming languages such as Turbo Pascal for Windows attempt to offer the best of both worlds, with techniques for creating applications that can adapt easily to external or internal changes. If you're using OOP for your application design, you and your ideas can grow easily as the needs of the users of your application grows. You do not presume to know everything about the application and its "unknown" users before you begin to code. You cannot know everything about anything that is the least bit complex. Yet that is exactly what many application design philosophies have assumed all along.

Application projects do not usually become disasters during application development. Afterward, when the worlds, the users, or the designers' and programmers' understanding of the application changes, they can become disasters. Typically, applications do not evolve; they drift toward obsolescence as they become less and less appropriate for the new version of the problems they were supposed to solve. If applications are appropriately designed around objects, they have a good chance to survive.

For example, consider yourself and how you interact with the world. You begin by collecting the best information you can, and then you create (supposedly in your brain) a model of the world based on that information. (This process is happening, of course, at brain-wave speed. Then you behave based on the model.

Your model is no doubt flawed; more or less appropriate or good enough for you to survive (sounds imperfect, scary, but almost assuredly true). As you proceed through your life, you gain experience (external factors) and have new thoughts (internal factors) that lead you to change your carefully built, flawed model. You might even develop multiple models to represent the world's various aspects and complexities. Many of these models you regularly update in response to new technology, new programming techniques. For example, your perception of how a compiler works or the ways you communicate can lead you to change your model. Other models, perhaps less dependent on new techniques, might continue to work, and you might seldom (if ever) update them.

In this scenario, your life consists of modifying parts of your model (in response to new external and internal information), and not modifying other parts. You are continually learning from your model, and you change the model accordingly. Typically, if any model stops changing, chances are that it no longer is in step with the world. In one sense, a model is an indicator of learning and process.

An application is an expression of your current understanding of an external problem and your ability to represent it with its solutions. Thus, the design and the expression of the design are inexorably connected. The problem changes; your view of the problem changes; and your ability to design and develop an application changes.

A good design philosophy (whether for Windows or not) must support a view that anticipates change.

Here are a few ideas to keep in mind when you are designing applications:

1. Acknowledge that you cannot know everything about a problem or an application before you design it. Do not even try. Accept that there are some things about an application that you can learn only by designing and using it.

2. Try to get some form of the application working as soon as possible, and use each application forerunner to improve your understanding of the problem and application.

   Your early versions of the application might be only vague imitators of future—more perfect—versions. Let your applications reflect the evolution of your ideas. Refine and modify as you learn more. Object-oriented programming encourages change. Use objects to explore.

   An additional, and perhaps subtle, aspect of object-oriented design is that it encourages you not to spend too much time creating an application. It encourages you not to try to solve problems that never arise. Also, object-oriented design tends to isolate the effects of one part of a system from others so that changing one part of an application should not disrupt other parts.

3. Plan to change the design, not just the application, as you go. This does not mean "throw away parts recklessly," but rather "start some place reasonable, and let the design grow as you learn about the problem and the application." In other words, avoid static designs. Assume from the beginning that the application has to change.

4. Expect to make mistakes.

   The best way to find out whether you have made a mistake is to use the application. Chances are that your mistakes can be isolated in single objects, and thus you do not have to throw everything away at once. Instead, you modify the application, part by part, to reflect the evolution of your learning about the application and its users.

Object-Oriented Application Design

It would be so-o-o nice, but unfortunately so-o-o unexpected, if programmers and users had perfect knowledge about an application or the problem the application addresses. Unfortunately, this is seldom the case.

First, you probably cannot delude yourself into believing that you know everything about an application or problem. Second, the application you are developing and the techniques (the compilers, the languages, the hardware) you are using to design the application are evolving as well. You approximate, anticipate, speculate, and add new tools to your toolbox at every turn. Naturally, you want your applications to reflect your new power tools.

On the more personal side, you often make two convenient (and probably erroneous) approximations:

1. You, the designer, completely understand the problem before beginning the design.
2. Users read whatever information you give them before using the application, and thus know the application well before firing it up. (Demanding this kind of perfection from yourself, the application, or the users simply is not sensible.)

During development, object-oriented design encourages you to add, change, and delete objects at any time—whenever the mood moves you. It's assumed that, because every problem is in progress, every application addressing a problem is in progress; it's dynamic.

For example, suppose that you are designing an editor. You began (sensibly enough) by creating a `window_editor` type, which can process text through a buffer, move a cursor around in the buffer, find text, insert and delete text, and so on. As the application progresses (and the type definition develops), so does the need to test it. You decide that the simplest way to test the application is to write the text in the buffer to a file and read it back from the file to the buffer.

To make a `window_editor` file aware, you must give it some knowledge of inserting and retrieving text from files. The file has to understand how to open and close files, how to recognize the end of lines and the end of files, and so on.

You can add streams and whatever else you want to the editor. Then you should begin testing the features of the `file_editor`, one by one.

Several things occur. First, by using the application (as a file editor), you (the designer "turned" user) begin to see possibilities you had not imagined before. You might decide that more than one file can be opened at a time, that the files can exchange information, and that the size of the files is important. In short, the `file_editor` type is undergoing a "reuse test."

In a reuse test, you ask, "Does the application adapt easily to new situations?" If you decide that it does not, you begin modifying the type to make it more general. In this scenario, the application becomes too general and fails the "complexity test."

You have expanded the application too much; it is too complex. Suddenly, because you are running out of memory, you have to keep better tabs on memory use. Keeping tabs means that you have to change something else, which causes a few more problems that affect other parts of the application.

The `file_editor` type now is failing the "overambitious object test." It tries to do too much, and as a result cannot be reused. An evolved type, especially one that has survived several redesigns, often becomes too complex for further evolution. If the object begins to confuse you, it probably has a design problem. Check it out and redesign it, if you have to.

In this example, you discover the simple, tighter design that you should have created; a `text_buffer` type that can handle big chunks of text and keep track of the memory safety pool. For example, it checks for low memory conditions before it reads the entire file. You decide to make this low-level-memory awareness a part of the base file editor.

Now you derive a multiple file editor from this smarter, still single-file editor that can keep track of memory use. This type now can be used as a base type for other kinds of file editors.

The point of this hypothetical ramble is this: you design, experiment, and create every time you interact with the application or problem. Only in the simplest cases are you able to understand the problem completely and get the design right the first time.

A Tao of Windows

You might not know how to put a particular data field or method in a type. You might think that it takes years of experience to design types properly. To help dispel this myth and to keep you from wasting too much time on early design decisions, the book covers a relatively simple, but good beginning technique for describing the creation and development of types. This technique (based on the design philosophy recommended in *The Tao of Objects*, my first book) recognizes five stages of object design:

1. *Object discovery*. Try to determine which objects solve the problems your application addresses. Be more concerned with the boundaries and the gross interactions between objects than with how the objects work.

2. *Object construction*. As you start creating objects, you discover that you want data fields and methods to make the object work properly. You also might discover that you want other objects either as subjects

(object members of your object), or to work with some object in your application. An excellent technique during object creation is to develop test applications (mini-applications) for each type you create. As you write the test applications, you might uncover further type requirements.

3. *Application construction*. As you collect objects in the application, the needs of the application might require new behavior in existing objects, or entirely new objects.

4. *Application extension*. Application extension is an integral part of application development. Behavior is focused in objects. Objects change in order to change applications.

5. *Object reuse*. When you use old object types to build new applications, new needs bend and stretch the design of your old object types. If an old type does not fit easily into a new situation, it shows up in these prospective new applications, and you see the parts that have to be changed. The most useful objects are usually the "evolved" ones that have gone through several projects.

Notice that at each stage of application development you get new information to guide you through type design. Although it would be difficult and time-consuming to anticipate this information in a "pre-preemptive" design, it comes to you naturally as you pass through the appropriate stage. Although this style of OOP design uses a different philosophy than past structured methodologies, it is not a big deal to implement. (Many programmers tend to work this way regardless of what methodology they are supposed to be following.) As a guideline: don't force yourself to know everything at the beginning. Instead, allow yourself to learn as you go along.

Object Discovery

The first of the five stages, the icebreaker, deserves a closer look. What methods should you use to discover objects? Here are a few guidelines:

- Look for the "external factors" that are necessary for interactions between objects and the world outside the application. You might discover some data fields and methods at this point, but you mostly just discover the objects themselves.

- Find natural boundaries. If you think of something with boundaries in the world, chances are that it should be a boundary in an object as well. For example, the boundary between memory and disk is often reflected as a boundary in your application.

- Seek the behavior and data that are duplicated in the application. For example, a keyboard is a collection of buttons, so "button" is an obvious object. A simulation might consist of customers and bank tellers. A truck has four wheels, a spare, four doors, and so on.
- Flesh out the least common denominators of an application (its smallest units). For example, if you are manipulating text, the smallest unit is either a character, a word, a line, or a group of text with the same attributes; depending on how you intend to use the text.
- Try to imagine new situations in which you might use the type. Do you think it works there and adapts easily? For example, consider a bigger version of your application. Does it work?
- Separate the aspects of the application that change from those that probably will not change.
- Make a list of the data that your application has to know about. Look for data that seems to belong together. Collect these data elements into an object.
- Look for behavior you want to hide or data you want to protect from careless manipulation. This kind of behavior and data usually belongs inside an object.
- Look for the common interfaces between objects. Find out what objects have in common. Put common aspects into an abstract base type.
- Look for initialization and cleanup activities. These activities should be handled by constructors and destructors. Initialization and cleanup might help you discover types.

Star Wars and Dances: The Sequel

As an example, consider a video-store management application that was discussed in *The Tao of Objects*. Consider this version a sequel to that one, because there has been a long time to reconsider the problem and give it a new Windows face. If you have not read the book, don't worry, this chapter will bring you up to snuff.

The video-store management application tries to solve the problems inherent in setting up a user-driven video store. The video buff (that is, the user) comes into the store with a type of video in mind, but he does not know the title of any specific video.

Typically in this scenario, the user walks around the store and checks the various video boxes, which contain a three- or four-paragraph description of what the movie distributor wants the user to think. (*Movie Magic, Part 3* is a *Star Wars* clone, with overtones of *Lawrence of Arabia* and *Dances with Wolves* rolled into one fine picture. Every single reviewer, at least all the ones mentioned on the box, loved it.)

What the user unfortunately does not learn from the box is what the video is about, the level of violence, whether other folks have enjoyed the video, and not just what a few carefully selected, and carefully quoted, critics thought.

Now consider an alternative scenario. Suppose that the user can walk into a video store in which there are no shelves filled with video boxes. Instead, she steps up to a computer (or to a person operating a computer) and says, "Today I am in the mood for a movie with a romantic theme set in the near future, which my favorite reviewer liked, and which has no violence, and which has a social theme with moderate levels of nudity."

The computer then checks the user's file to see what she has viewed or liked in the past and retrieves the video titles that she has not checked out before, minus the ones that are already checked out. The computer numbers them corresponding to her personal profile.

She can get even more information about each of the titles; including the actors, directors, and so on; reviews of the videos; biographies of the people involved in making the movie; and even graphic descriptions (bit maps, and so on) depicting some aspect of the video. In other words, the user gets a more detailed view of the videos in the store based on the information users supply. (It might even be so much fun to play around with the video look-up system that video look-up becomes an arcade fad.)

When the user decides on a video, the clerk gets it from a stack (notice that the shelf space required for a store like this is smaller) and uses a bar-code reader to enter the number into the computer, which generates a receipt and does all the necessary bookkeeping.

Part of this is obviously an elaborate database system (which has to be easily updated at regular intervals, from various sources including the customers themselves). Part of it is the user interface, part the bar-code interface, and part the bookkeeping system. Try to describe this application using OOP.

First, make four lists that represent:

1. Data
2. Events
3. Behavior
4. Obvious objects

The data list consists of information the application has to know or remember. The event list consists of events that the application has to respond to. The behavior list is what the application has to do. The obvious-objects list includes anything that immediately springs to mind. For example, you know from the start you want to use a standard Windows application interface that uses menus and standard mouse clicks to select items from the menus.

Do not try to perfect these lists in the beginning; just write down what you can think of. Remember that the act of creating the application (not the creation of lists) ensures that the application is complete. The lists only act as "instigators" to help you discover the objects for your application. By looking at the lists, you see patterns that suggest objects. When you discover enough objects to describe the application without the lists, throw the lists away.

For some applications, the data list gives you the most information, and it is easiest to think of information for that list. Because Windows applications are primarily event-driven, you should anticipate events and responses to events in these lists.

How you define these lists depends on how you think about a problem. In general, however, it does not matter much how you order or assemble these lists, because all you are trying to do is discover the objects for your applications. Some of the items on the list might not even help you discover any objects, so you discard them mercifully.

Again, remember: it is OK to make mistakes, and it is OK to omit things you might want later. An object-oriented application allows you to easily modify the application when you discover inconsistencies. Because objects keep their data and behaviors to themselves, changes in the application tend to localize themselves—a major plus as the application evolves.

When you make the data list, group together data items that you are fairly sure should be an object. For example, a "person" object probably contains data fields for name, address, age, sex, membership number, and a list of videos this person has checked out. It might make sense to collect all these fields in an object.

Windows events are almost as obvious as data or behavior. A mouse, for example, generates an event that Windows routes to the correct window. A menu selection is an event, and so on. Because Windows applications depend so much on events such as the mouse and menus, it makes sense to always keep events in the forefront. Behavior should be responses to events.

For example, you can implement a context-sensitive help system depending on the application's current context (or state). Every time the user changes context (by making a selection from a menu, for example), the "help state context" changes. When the user asks for help, the type of help given depends on the state (that is, the context). Looking at a collection of events often helps you discover appropriate objects.

Remember that this is an process of iteration; an approach intended only to give you a framework— steps to follow to get you started. The framework might change as you sketch out the application, but in the end it is unimportant. Your goal is to determine what your objects should be and what you want. As you fill in the details, you discover new objects and new relationships between objects. That's fine; that is how it is supposed to work.

For example, the video-store application might begin with the following four lists:

```
Data List:


User
     Name
     Address
     User ID
     Video List (videos checked out in the past)
     User's Video Preference List


Video
     Name
     Quantity
     Price Structure
     Video Evaluation List


Rental Transaction
     Date
     User
     Video List


Business Report
     Date Range
     Data List
     Data Format
     Calculations



Event List:


User asks for some specific range of videos
```

```
User asks for further data on a specific video's Reviews
     Local opinions
     Box description/pictures
     Personnel: actors, directors, and so on.
     Theater runs and receipts

User checks out video(s).

User asks for computer-generated video selection based on
the user's profile.

User asks for best selling selection based on some level of
popularity.

User returns some or all checked out videos; possibly checks
out more.

User 'reviews' video just viewed.

New videos arrive.

New video data arrives.

Old videos are discarded/replaced.


Behavior List:


Create new user profile.

Create new video profile.

Create video request profile; combine with user profile and
search for appropriate videos.

Create management report.

Check out video.

Check in video.

Update profiles.
```

```
Obvious Objects:

Objects for connecting to Windows (use ObjectWindows for these)

Database (use collections)

Error Handler (use Error)

Time & Date (use System)

Menus (use ObjectWindows)

Dialogs (use ObjectWindows)

File Dialogs (use ObjectWindows)

Other controls, list boxes, buttons, and so on (use ObjectWindows)
```

Begin Discovering Objects

By this juncture, you might have glimpsed some objects; for example, in the Data List where some data obviously belongs together. In the video example, User, Video, Rental Transaction, Business Report, and so on, suggest objects.

Behavior usually requires more work. To help you visualize, you might want to put the behavior in a "block chart" as shown in figure 13.3.

Now consider an individual part and begin analyzing it for objects. Think about:

- What you want that part to produce. (Will the behavior lead to the production of an object; will the producer be an object?)
- What parts do you want to be portable, or at least retargetable (for example, user interface, other hardware, operating system interface)? Put these in an object.
- Does the block diagram suggest any new boundaries that might reveal new objects? For example, in a networking system, the network is a boundary. You might want to create "transaction objects" to send across the network.
- As you discover objects, consider what those objects have to know. Should they maintain this information themselves, or get it from another object? Take note of any object that gives information, even if it belongs in another part.

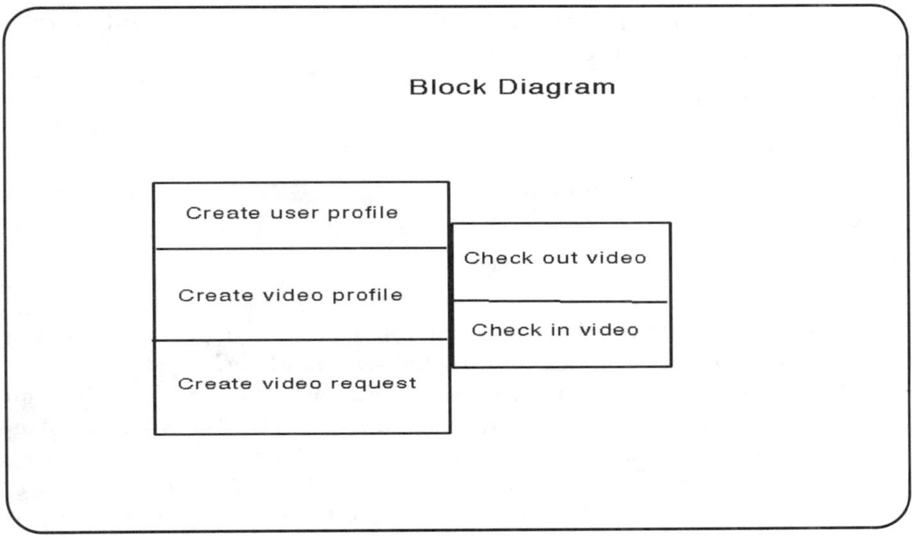

***Figure 13.3.** A block chart.*

You don't want your objects to become too complex. Just because you want a particular object does not mean that the object should be part of a single type rather than part of a type hierarchy.

If your objects are too complex, you will notice this problem during the object-creation phase. As you add and test functions, things seem to "go haywire" and "get out of hand." It becomes difficult to add new behavior because the type is managing too much itself. This is an indication that the type has to be factored into smaller sections and assembled through either inheritance or composition.

By factoring the type, you end up with several types, any of which is easier to implement because it is easier to think about.

Wrap-up

By now you should be thinking that designing Windows applications is both an art and a science. Creating applications, like art, requires much interpretation on the part of the designer and artist. Finding, creating, and recasting objects requires both artistic and engineering skills. On top of that, Windows *is* a GUI: ready-to-roll graphics.

You create your objects from the time you start thinking about them. Writing them is only the obvious phase of creation. You start with the type framework, and then add and test behavior. During application construction and extension, you may add more to the type.

Thus, object design occurs throughout the lifetime of an application in all five phases of application development:

1. Object discovery
2. Object creation
3. Application construction
4. Application extension
5. Object reuse

Users only pretend that they can force design to occur when it is convenient—in the first phases of a project—and not later.

That wraps up this part of the introductory study of Windows application development using the object-oriented techniques of Turbo Pascal for Windows. I hope that you have learned at least this small point: the sophisticated techniques in Turbo Pascal for Windows can help you create productive, creative, and flexible Windows applications that have the built-in capacity to evolve as the problems they attempt to solve inevitably evolve.

Object-oriented programming is both a method and a philosophy, and an important technique for developing event-driven Windows applications.

Windows and objects (Turbo Pascal style) are, some say, a dramatic one-two punch.

PART THREE

REFERENCES

A

REFERENCE

OBJECTWINDOWS OBJECTS

This reference chapter is an alphabetical listing of the ObjectWindows objects:

```
TApplication          TListBox
TBufStream            TMDIClient
TButton               TMDIWindow
TCheckBox             TObject
TCollection           TRadioButton
TComboBox             TScrollBar
TControl              TScroller
TDialog               TSortedCollection
TDlgWindow            TStatic
TDosStream            TStrCollection
TEdit                 TStream
TEmsStream            TWindow
TGroupBox             TWindowsObject
```

TApplication

`TApplication` is the base application object for all ObjectWindows applications. Each ObjectWindows application derives an application object type from `TApplication` in order to construct a specific main window for the application.

Fields

```
HAccTable
KBHandlerWnd
MainWindow
Name
Status
```

Methods

```
Init
CanClose
Error
ExecDialog
InitApplication
InitInstance
InitMainWindow
MakeWindow
MessageLoop
ProcessAccels
ProcessAppMsg
ProcessDlgMsg
ProcessMDIAccels
Run
SetKBHandler
ValidWindow
```

Fields

TApplication.HAccTable

`HAccTable: THandle;` (read/write)

`HAccTable` holds a handle to a Windows accelerator-table resource if you define one for the application.

TApplication.KBHandlerWnd

`KBHandlerWnd: PWindowsObject;` (read only)

`KBHandlerWnd` points to the currently active window if the window's keyboard handler mechanism is enabled. (The keyboard handler mechanism lets a window containing controls process keyboard input in dialog fashion. If the keyboard handler mechanism is disabled for the active window, `KBHandler` is nil.

TApplication.MainWindow

`MainWindow: PWindowsObject;` (read/write)

`MainWindow` points to the application's main window, which should be instantiated by your application type's `InitMainWindow` method.

TApplication.Name

`Name` holds the application's name.

TApplication.Status

`Status: Integer;`

`Status` indicates the current state of an application. If `Status` is greater than or equal to 0, then the application is operating successfully.

Methods

TApplication.Init

`constructor Init(AName: PChar);`

(Override: sometimes) Constructs the application object.

- Calls `TObject.Init`
- Sets the global variable `Application` to `@Self`
- Sets the `Name` field to `AName`
- Sets the `HAccTable` field and the `Status` field to 0
- Initializes the `MainWindow` and the `KBHandlerWnd` fields to nil

If the current instance is the first instance of an application, Init sends a message to InitApplication. If InitApplication succeeds, Init sends a message to InitInstance.

TApplication.CanClose

```
function CanClose: Boolean; virtual;
```

(Override: seldom) Returns True if it's OK for the application to close. By default, CanClose sends a message to the CanClose method of its main window and returns that method's return value. Rather than override TApplication.CanClose, override your application's main window's CanClose method.

TApplication.Error

```
procedure Error(ErrorCode: Integer); virtual;
```

(Override: sometimes) TApplication.Error processes the errors identified by the error value passed in ErrorCode. These errors are generated by the application object, a window, or a dialog object. ErrorCode can be an error you define or one of the following errors, which are detected and reported by ObjectWindows:

```
em_OutOfMemory
em_InvalidClient
em_InvalidChild
em_InvalidMainWindow
em_InvalidWindow
```

If there's an error, TApplication.Error displays the error code in a message box and asks the user whether it's OK to proceed. If not, application execution halts.

TApplication.ExecDialog

```
function ExecDialog(ADialog: PWindowsObject): Integer; virtual
```

(Override: never) After checking ValidWindow, ExecDialog executes the modal dialog object passed in ADialog by sending a message to the dialog object's Execute method.

If memory is low or the dialog cannot be executed, ExecDialog disposes of the object and returns a negative error status.

TApplication.InitApplication

```
procedure InitApplication; virtual;
```

(Override: sometimes) Handles initialization for the first instance of an application.

Because `TApplication.InitApplication` doesn't do anything, your application object type overrides `TApplication.InitApplication` if it needs to initialize any application-specific behavior.

TApplication.InitMainWindow

```
procedure InitMainWindow; virtual;
```

(Override: always) Your application always overrides `InitMainWindow` to construct a main window object.

For example:

```
procedure MyApplication.InitMainWindow;
begin
   MainWindow := New(PMainWindow, Init('Window Caption'));
end;
```

By default, `InitMainWindow` creates a `TWindow` object without a title.

TApplication.MakeWindow

```
function MakeWindow(AWindowsObject: PWindowsObject):
   PWindowsObject; virtual;
```

(Override: never) After checking the safety pool, `TApplication.MakeWindow` tries to create a window or modeless dialog element associated with the object passed in `AWindowsObject`. If memory is low, or if the window or dialog cannot be created, `MakeWindow` disposes of the object and returns nil. If successful, it returns `AWindowsObject`.

TApplication.MessageLoop

```
procedure MessageLoop; virtual;
```

(Override: never) Controls an application's general message loop that runs throughout the lifetime of the application. `TApplication.MessageLoop` sends a message to `ProcessAppMsg`, which handles the special messages required for modeless dialogs, accelerators, and MDI accelerators.

TApplication.ProcessAccels

```
function ProcessAccels(var Message: TMsg): Boolean; virtual;
```

(Override: sometimes) Handles special accelerator message processing. If an application doesn't use accelerator resources, you can improve performance by overriding this method to return False.

TApplication.ProcessAppMsg

```
function ProcessAppMsg(var Message: TMsg): Boolean; virtual;
```

(Override: sometimes) Checks for special processing for modeless dialog, accelerator, and MDI accelerator messages.

Sends messages to `ProcessDlgMsg`, `ProcessMDIAccels`, and `ProcessAccels`, and returns True if it encounters any of these special processing messages.

If your application doesn't create modeless dialogs, doesn't respond to accelerators, and isn't an MDI application, you can improve performance by overriding this method to return False.

TApplication.ProcessDlgMsg

```
function ProcessDlgMsg(var Message: TMsg): Boolean; virtual;
```

(Override: sometimes) Handles special modeless dialog and window message processing for keyboard input for controls.

If your application doesn't create modeless dialogs or windows with controls, you can improve performance by overriding this method to return False.

TApplication.ProcessMDIAccels

```
function ProcessMDIAccels(var Message: TMsg): Boolean; virtual;
```

Handles special accelerator message processing for MDI-compliant applications.

If your application isn't an MDI application, you can improve performance by overriding this method to return False.

TApplication.Run

```
procedure Run; virtual;
```

(Override: seldom) If an application initialization is successful, `Run` sets the application in motion by sending a message to `MessageLoop`.

TApplication.SetKBHandler

```
procedure SetKBHandler(AWindowsObject: PWindowsObject);
```

(Override: never) Activates keyboard handling by setting `KBHandlerWnd` to `AWindowsObject`.

TApplication.ValidWindow

```
function ValidWindow(AWindowsObject:
PWindowsObject):PWindowsObject;
```

Determines whether `AWindowsObject` is a valid object. If `AWindowsObject` is valid, `ValidWindow` returns a pointer to it. Otherwise, it returns nil.

`AWindowsObject` is invalid if

- Allocation of the object disturbed the safety pool
- The status field of `AWindowsObject` is nonzero

TBufStream

`TBufStream` implements a buffered version of `TDosStream`. Its additional fields specify the size and location of the buffer and the current and last positions within the buffer.

`TBufStream` overrides the eight methods of `TDosStream` and defines the abstract `TStreamFlush` method. The `TBufStream` constructor creates and opens a file by sending a message to `TDosStream.Init` (the constructor). Then it creates the buffer with `GetMem`.

`TBufStream` is more efficient than `TDosStream` when a large number of small data transfers occur on a stream; for example, if you're loading and storing objects using `TStream`.

`Get` and `TStream.Put` use `TBufStream` to improve performance.

Fields

```
Buffer
BufSize
BufPtr
BufEnd
```

Methods

`Init`
`Done`
`Flush`
`GetPos`
`GetSize`
`Read`
`Seek`
`Truncate`
`Write`

Fields

TBufStream.Buffer

`Buffer: Pointer;` (read only)

A pointer to the start of a stream's buffer.

TBufStream.BufSize

`BufSize: Word;` (read only)

Holds the buffer size in bytes.

TBufStream.BufPtr

`BufPtr: Word;` (read only)

An offset from the `Buffer` pointer that indicates the current position within the buffer.

TBufStream.BufEnd

`BufEnd: Word;` (read only)

If the buffer isn't full, `BufEnd` holds an offset from the `Buffer` pointer to the last used byte in the buffer.

Methods

TBufStream.Init

```
constructor Init(FileName: FNameStr; Mode, Size: Word);
```

Creates and opens a file with access `Mode` by calling `TDosStream.Init`. `Init` creates a buffer of `Size` bytes using `GetMem` and initializes the `Handle`, `Buffer`, and `BufSize` fields. Although buffer sizes usually range from 512 to 2,048 bytes, larger buffers are sometimes useful.

TBufStream.Done

```
destructor Done; virtual;
```

(Override: never) Closes and disposes of the file stream and flushes and disposes of its buffer.

TBufStream.Flush

```
procedure Flush; virtual;
```

(Override: never) If the stream is `stOK`, `Flush` flushes the calling file stream's buffer.

TBufStream.GetPos

```
function GetPos: Longint; virtual;
```

(Override: never) Returns the value of the calling stream's current position.

TBufStream.GetSize

```
function GetSize: Longint; virtual;
```

(Override: never) Flushes the buffer and then returns the total size in bytes of the calling stream.

TBufStream.Read

```
procedure Read(var Buf; Count: Word); virtual;
```

(Override: never) If `stOK`, reads `Count` bytes into the `Buf` buffer starting at the calling stream's current position. Note that `Buf` isn't the stream's buffer but an external buffer that holds the data read in from the stream.

TBufStream.Seek

```
procedure Seek(Pos: Longint); virtual;
```

(Override: never) Flushes the buffer and then resets the current position to `Pos` bytes from the start of the calling stream. The start of a stream is position 0.

TBufStream.Truncate

```
procedure Truncate; virtual;
```

(Override: never) Flushes the buffer and then deletes all data on the calling stream from the current position to the end. The current position is set to the new end of the stream.

TBufStream.Write

```
procedure Write(var Buf; Count: Word); virtual;
```

(Override: never) If `stOK`, writes `Count` bytes from the `Buf` buffer to the calling stream, starting at the current position. Note that `Buf` isn't the stream's buffer but an external buffer that holds the data being written to the stream. When `Write` is called, `Buf` points to the variable whose value is being written.

TButton

`TButton` is an interface object that corresponds to a push-button element in Windows.

You usually don't use `TButton` objects in dialog boxes (`TDialog`) or dialog windows (`TDlgWindow`). Rather, use them when you want to display a stand-alone button as a child window in another window's client area.

There are two types of push buttons:

- A regular button appears with a thin border.
- A default button appears with a thick border and represents the default action of the window.

Each window is allowed only one default push button.

Fields

None.

Methods

```
Init
InitResource
GetClassName
```

Methods

TButton.Init

```
constructor Init(AParent: PWindowsObject; AnId: Integer;
  AText: PChar; X,Y,W,H: Integer; IsDefault: Boolean);
```

Constructs a button object with the

- Passed parent window (`AParent`)
- Control ID (`AnId`)
- Associated text (`AText`)
- Position (`X`, `Y`) relative to the origin of the parent window's client area
- Width (`W`)
- Height (`H`)

Sends a message to `TControl.Init` and then adds `bs_DefPushButton` to the `Attr.Style` field if `IsDefault` is True. If not, it adds `bs_PushButton`.

TButton.InitResource

```
constructor InitResource(AParent: PWindowsObject, ResourceID: Word);
```

Constructs an ObjectWindows object that corresponds to a button element created by a dialog resource definition.

Sends messages to `TControl.InitResource` and `TWindowsObject`.

Because buttons have no data to transfer, you can use `DisableTransfer` to exclude the button from the transfer mechanism.

TButton.GetClassName

```
function GetClassName: PChar; virtual;
```

(Override: never) Returns the name of `TButton`'s window class, `Button`.

TCheckBox

TCheckBox is an interface object that corresponds to a check-box element in Windows. You usually don't use TCheckBox objects in dialog boxes (TDialog) or dialog windows (TDlgWindow). Rather, use them to display a stand-alone check box as a child window in another window's client area.

Check boxes have two states: checked and unchecked.

TCheckBox methods primarily manage the check box's state. Optionally, a check box can be part of a group (TGroupBox) that visually and functionally "groups" its controls.

Fields

Group

Methods

Init
InitResource
Load
BNClicked
Check
GetCheck
SetCheck
Store
Toggle
Transfer
Uncheck

Fields

TCheckBox.Group

Group: PGroupBox; (read only)

Group points to the TGroupBox control object that unifies the check box with other check boxes and radio buttons (TRadioButton).

Group is equal to nil if the check box isn't part of a group.

Methods

TCheckBox.Init

```
constructor Init(AParent: PWindowsObject; AnID: Integer; ATitle: PChar;
    X,Y,W,H: Integer; AGroup: PGroupBox);
```

(Override: sometimes) Constructs a check box object with the

- Passed parent window (AParent)
- Control ID (AnId)
- Associated text (ATitle)
- Position (X, Y) relative to the origin of the parent window's client area
- Width (W)
- Height (H)
- Associated group box (AGroup)

Init sets the check box's Attr.Style field to ws_Child or ws_Visible or ws_TabStop or bs_AutoCheckBox.

TCheckBox.InitResource

```
constructor InitResource(AParent: PWindowsObject; ResourceID: Word);
```

Associates a TCheckBox object with the resource named by ResourceID. It then enables the transfer mechanism by sending a message to EnableTransfer.

TCheckBox.Load

```
constructor Load(var S: TStream);
```

Constructs and loads a check box from the stream S by first sending a message to TButton.Load and then reading the additional field (Group) introduced by TCheckBox.

TCheckBox.BNClicked

```
procedure BNClicked(var Msg: TMessage); virtual nf_First + bn_Clicked;
```

(Override: sometimes) Automatically responds to the notification messages (which indicate that the check box was clicked) by toggling its state. If the check box's Group isn't nil, BNClicked notifies the TGroupBox by sending a message to its SelectionChanged method.

TCheckBox.Check

```
procedure Check; virtual;
```

(Override: seldom) Forces the check box into the checked state by sending a message to `SetCheck`.

TCheckBox.GetCheck

```
function GetCheck: Word; virtual;
```

(Override: seldom) Returns one of the following:

`bf_Unchecked (0)` if the check box is unchecked

`bf_Checked (1)` if the check box is checked

`bf_Grayed (2)` if the check box is grayed

TCheckBox.SetCheck

```
procedure SetCheck(CheckFlag: Word); virtual;
```

(Override: seldom) Forces the check box into the state specified by `CheckFlag`.

- If `CheckFlag` is 0, the state is unchecked.
- If `CheckFlag` is 1, the state is checked.
- If `CheckFlag` is 2, the state is grayed.

`SetCheck` also informs the check box's group that the selection has changed.

TCheckBox.Store

```
procedure Store(var S: TStream);
```

Stores the check box on the stream, `S`, by first sending a message to `TControl.Store` and then writing the additional field (`Group`) introduced by `TCheckBox`.

TCheckBox.Toggle

```
procedure Toggle; virtual;
```

(Override: seldom) Toggles the state of the check box by calling `Check` or `Uncheck`. For a 3-state check box, it toggles through all three states: unchecked, checked, and grayed.

TCheckBox.Transfer

```
function Transfer(DataPtr: Pointer; TransferFlag: Word): Word; virtual;
```

(Override: sometimes) Transfers the state of a check box in a `Word` type value to or from the memory location pointed to by `DataPtr`.

- If `TransferFlag` is `tf_GetData`, the check box's state data is transferred to the memory location.
- If `TransferFlag` is `tf_SetData`, the check box is set to the state indicated in the memory location.

Transfer returns the number of bytes stored in or retrieved from the memory location. If you pass `tf_SizeData`, `Transfer` returns the size of the transfer data.

TCheckBox.Uncheck

```
procedure Uncheck; virtual;
```

(Override: seldom) Forces the check box into the unchecked state by sending a message to `SetCheck`.

TCollection

`TCollection` is an abstract type for implementing a collection of items. The collection can contain various data types, including objects. Because it can include mixed data types, `TCollection` is a more general way of handling data than the traditional array, set, or list types.

`TCollection` objects size themselves dynamically at run-time and can be a base type for many specialized types, such as `TSortedCollection` and `TStrCollection`.

In addition to methods for adding and deleting items, `TCollection` offers several useful iterator routines that call a procedure or function for each item in the collection.

Fields

```
Count
Delta
Items
Limit
```

Methods

Init
Load
Done
AtDelete
AtFree
AtInsert
AtPut
At
Delete
DeleteAll
Error
FirstThat
ForEach
FreeAll
FreeItem
Free
GetItem
IndexOf
Insert
LastThat
Pack
PutItem
SetLimit
Store

Fields

TCollection.Count

`Count: Integer;` (read only)

The current number of items in the collection, up to (and including) `MaxCollectionSize`.

TCollection.Delta

`Delta: Integer;` (read only)

The number of items to increase the `Items` list by whenever the list becomes full. If `Delta` is 0, the collection cannot grow beyond the size set by `Limit`.

Increasing the size of a collection reduces performance. To minimize the number of times the collection increases its size, set the initial `Limit` to a value that accommodates all the items you might want to collect, and set `Delta` to a value that allows a reasonable amount of expansion.

TCollection.Items

`Items: PItemList;` (read only)

A pointer to an array of item pointers.

TCollection.Limit

`Limit: Integer;` (read only)

The currently allocated size (in elements) of the `Items` list.

Methods

TCollection.Init

```
constructor Init(ALimit, ADelta: Integer);
```

Creates a collection with `Limit` set to `ALimit` and `Delta` set to `ADelta`. The initial number of items is limited to `ALimit`, but the collection can grow in increments of `ADelta` until memory runs out or the number of items reaches `MaxCollectionSize`.

TCollection.Load

```
constructor Load(var S: TStream);
```

Creates and loads a collection from a stream. `Load` sends a message to `GetItem` for each item in the collection.

TCollection.Done

```
destructor Done; virtual;
```

(Override: often) Deletes and disposes of all items in a collection by sending a message to `FreeAll` and setting `Limit` to 0.

TCollection.AtDelete

```
procedure AtDelete(Index: Integer);
```

Deletes the item at the `Index`'th position and moves the ensuing items up by one position.

`Count` is decremented by 1, but the memory allocated to the collection (as specified by `Limit`) isn't reduced.

If `Index` is less than 0 or greater than or equal to `Count`, the `Error` method is sent a message with an argument of `coIndexError`.

TCollection.AtFree

```
procedure AtFree(Index: Integer);
```

Disposes of and deletes the item at the `Index`'th position.

TCollection.AtInsert

```
procedure AtInsert(Index: Integer; Item: Pointer);
```

Inserts `Item` at the `Index`'th position and moves the following items down by one position:

- If `Index` is less than 0 or greater than `Count`, the `Error` method is sent a message with an argument of `coIndexError` and the new Item isn't inserted.
- If `Count` is equal to `Limit` before the call to `AtInsert`, the allocated size of the collection is expanded by `Delta` items via a message sent to `SetLimit`.
- If the `SetLimit` call fails to expand the collection, the `Error` method is sent a message with an argument of `coOverflow`, and the new `Item` isn't inserted.

TCollection.AtPut

```
procedure AtPut(Index: Integer; Item: Pointer);
```

Replaces the item at `Index` position with the item specified by `Item`. If `Index` is less than 0 or greater than or equal to `Count`, the `Error` method is sent a message with an argument of `coIndexError`.

TCollection.At

```
function At(Index: Integer): Pointer;
```

Returns a pointer to the item indexed by `Index` in the collection. This method lets you manipulate a collection as though it were an indexed array. If `Index` is less than 0 or greater than or equal to `Count`, the `Error` method is sent a message with an argument of `coIndexError`, and a value of nil is returned.

TCollection.Delete

```
procedure Delete(Item: Pointer);
```

Deletes the item specified by `Item` from the collection. Equivalent to `AtDelete(IndexOf(Item))`.

TCollection.DeleteAll

```
procedure DeleteAll;
```

Deletes all items from the collection by setting `Count` to 0.

TCollection.Error

```
procedure Error(Code, Info: Integer); virtual;
```

(Override: sometimes) Receives a message whenever a collection error is encountered. By default, this method produces a run-time error of 212 - Code).

TCollection.FirstThat

```
function FirstThat(Test: Pointer): Pointer;
```

FirstThat applies a Boolean function (supplied by the function pointer Test) to each item in the collection until Test returns True. The result is the item pointer used when Test returned True, or nil if the Test function returned False for all items. Test must point to a far local function taking one Pointer parameter and returning a Boolean value. For example:

```
function Matches(Item: Pointer): Boolean; far;
```

The `Test` function cannot be a global function.

Assuming that `List` is a `TCollection`, the statement

```
P := List.FirstThat(@Matches);
```

corresponds to

```
I := 0;
while (I < List.Count) and not Matches(List.At(I)) do
  Inc(I);
if I < List.Count then P := List.At(I) else P := nil;
```

TCollection.ForEach

```
procedure ForEach(Action: Pointer);
```

`ForEach` applies an action (supplied by the procedure pointer `Action`) to each item in the collection. `Action` must point to a far local procedure taking one `Pointer` parameter; for example:

```
function PrintItem(Item: Pointer); far;
```

The `Action` procedure cannot be a global procedure.

Assuming that `List` is a `TCollection`, the statement

```
List.ForEach(@PrintItem);
```

corresponds to

```
for I := 0 to List.Count - 1 do PrintItem(List.At(I));
```

TCollection.FreeAll

```
procedure FreeAll;
```

Deletes and disposes of all items in the collection.

TCollection.FreeItem

```
procedure FreeItem(Item: Pointer); virtual;
```

(Override: sometimes) The `FreeItem` method must dispose of the `Item`. The default `FreeItem` assumes that `Item` is a pointer to a descendant of `TObject` and sends a message to the `Done` destructor:

```
if Item <> nil then Dispose(PObject(Item), Done);
```

`FreeItem` receives messages from `Free` and `FreeAll`, but should never be sent messages directly.

TCollection.Free

```
procedure Free(Item: Pointer);
```

Deletes and disposes of a specified `Item`. Equivalent to

```
Delete(Item);
FreeItem(Item);
```

TCollection.GetItem

```
function TCollection.GetItem(var S: TStream): Pointer; virtual;
```

(Override: sometimes) Sent a message by `Load` for each item in the collection.

You can override this method, but you shouldn't send it messages directly.

The default `GetItem` assumes that the items in the collection are descendants of `TObject` and sends a message to `TStream.Get` to load the item:

```
GetItem := S.Get;
```

TCollection.IndexOf

```
function IndexOf(Item: Pointer): Integer; virtual;
```

(Override: never) Returns the index of a specified `Item`. The converse operation of `At`. If `Item` isn't in the collection, `IndexOf` returns –1.

TCollection.Insert

```
procedure Insert(Item: Pointer); virtual;
```

(Override: never) Inserts `Item` into the collection and adjusts other indices if necessary. By default, insertions are made at the end of the collection by way of a message to

```
AtInsert(Count, Item);
```

TCollection.LastThat

```
function LastThat(Test: Pointer): Pointer;
```

`LastThat` applies a Boolean function (specified by the function pointer `Test`) to each item in the collection in reverse order until `Test` returns True.

The result is the item pointer used when `Test` returned True, or nil if the `Test` function returned False for all items.

Test must point to a far local function that takes a Pointer parameter and returns a Boolean; for example:

```
function Matches(Item: Pointer): Boolean; far;
```

The Test function cannot be a global function.

Assuming that List is a TCollection, the statement:

```
P := List.LastThat(@Matches);
```

corresponds to:

```
I := List.Count - 1;
while (I >= 0) and not Matches(List.At(I)) do Dec(I);
if I >= 0 then P := List.At(I) else P := nil;
```

TCollection.Pack

```
procedure Pack;
```

Deletes all nil pointers in the collection.

TCollection.PutItem

```
procedure PutItem(var S: TStream; Item: Pointer); virtual;
```

(Override: sometimes) PutItem receives a message from Store for each item in the collection. You can override this method, but you shouldn't send it a message directly.

The default PutItem assumes that the items in the collection are descendants of TObject, and thus sends a message to TStream.Put to store the item: S.Put(Item);

TCollection.SetLimit

```
procedure SetLimit(ALimit: Integer); virtual;
```

(Override: seldom) Expands or shrinks the collection by changing the allocated size to ALimit.

If ALimit is less than Count, ALimit is set to Count. If ALimit is greater than MaxCollectionSize, ALimit is set to MaxCollectionSize.

Then, if ALimit is different from the current Limit, a new Items array of ALimit elements is allocated. The old Items array then is copied into the new array, and the old array is disposed.

TCollection.Store

```
procedure Store(var S: TStream);
```

Stores the collection and all its items on the stream `S`. `Store` sends a message to `PutItem` for each item in the collection.

TComboBox

`TComboBox` is an interface object that corresponds to a combo box element in Windows. Usually you don't use `TComboBox` objects in dialog boxes (`TDialog`) or dialog windows (`TDlgWindow`). Rather, use a combo box object to display a stand-alone combo box as a child window in another window's client area. Combo box objects inherit most of their functionality from `TListBox`.

The three styles of combo boxes are

- Simple
- Drop down
- Drop down list

These styles are controlled by the Windows style constants `cbs_Simple`, `cbs_DropDown`, and `cbs_DropDownList`. These constants are passed to the `Init` constructor, which in turn tells Windows which type of combo box element to create.

Fields

```
TextLen
```

Methods

```
Init
InitResource
Load
GetClassName
GetMsgID (private)
HideList
SetUpWindow
ShowList
Store
Transfer
```

Fields

TComboBox.TextLen

`TextLen: Word;` (read only)

`TextLen` contains the length of the character buffer in the edit part of the combo box. The character buffer is equal to the number of bytes transferred by `Transfer`.

`TextLen` is set by `Init`.

Methods

TComboBox.Init

```
constructor Init(AParent: PWindowsObject; AnID: Integer;
   X,Y,W,H: Integer; CanDropList: Boolean; HasStaticControl:
   Boolean);
```

(Override: sometimes) Sends a message to `TListBox.Init` and constructs a combo box object with the following parameters:

- Passed parent window (`AParent`)
- Control ID (`AnId`)
- Position (`X`, `Y`) relative to the origin of the parent window's client area
- Width (`W`)
- Height (`H`)

Sets `TextLen` to `ATextLen`. Sets `Attr.Style` to (`Attr.Style and not lbs_Notify`) or `AStyle` or `cbs_Sort` or `ws_VScroll` or `ws_HScroll`.

TComboBox.InitResource

```
constructor InitResource(AParent: PWindowsObject;
  ResourceID: Integer; ATextLen: Word);
```

Associates a `TComboBox` object with the resource indicated by `ResourceID` with a maximum text length of `ATextLen-1`.

TComboBox.Load

```
constructor Load(var S: TStream);
```

Constructs and loads a combo box from the stream, `S`, by first sending a message to `TListBox.Load` and then reading the additional fields (`IsDropDown`, `IsList`) introduced by `TComboBox`.

TComboBox.GetClassName

```
function GetClassName: PChar; virtual;
```

(Override: never) Returns the name of `TComboBox`'s window class, `ComboBox`.

TComboBox.GetMsgID

```
function GetMsgID(AMsg : TMsgName): word; virtual;
```

Private method; used internally by `TComboBox`.

TComboBox.HideList

```
procedure HideList; virtual;
```

(Override: seldom) Hides the drop down list of a drop down or drop-down list combo box.

TComboBox.SetUpWindow

Handles some of the `TComboBox` window setup.

```
procedure SetUpWindow; virtual;
```

TComboBox.ShowList

```
procedure ShowList; virtual;
```

(Override: seldom) Displays the drop down list of a drop down or drop-down list combo box.

TComboBox.Store

```
procedure Store(var S: TStream);
```

Stores the combo box on the stream, `S`, by first sending a message to `TListBox.Store` and then writing the additional field (`TextLen`) introduced by `TComboBox`.

TComboBox.Transfer

```
function Transfer(DataPtr: Pointer; TransferFlag: Word);virtual;
```

Transfers data to or from the record pointed to by `DataPtr`.

The record should first be a pointer to a string collection that holds the entries of the combo box's list. Then an array of characters holding the currently selected entry is transferred.

- If `TransferFlag` is `tf_GetData`, the combo box's data is transferred to the `DataPtr` record. Transfer returns the size of the data transferred.
- If `TransferFlag` is `tf_SetData`, the data is transferred to the combo box from the record. Transfer returns the size of the data transferred.
- If `TransferFlag` is `tf_SizeData`, `Transfer` returns the size of the transfer data.

TControl

`TControl` is an abstract object type that unifies all control object types, such as `TScrollBar` and `TButton`. It's also the ancestor to `TMDIClient`, a specialized control for MDI-compliant applications.

You generally won't use control objects in dialog boxes (`TDialog`) or dialog windows (`TDlgWindow`), only as stand-alone controls in the client area of other windows.

Methods

```
Init
GetClassName
InitResource
Register
WMPaint
```

Methods

TControl.Init

```
constructor Init(AParent: PWindowsObject; AnId: Integer;
  ATitle: PChar; X,Y,W,H: Integer);
```

Constructs a control object with the following parameters:

- Associated parent window (`AParent`)
- Control ID (`AnId`)
- Associated text (`ATitle`)
- Position (X, Y) relative to the origin of the parent window's client area
- Width (W)
- Height (H)

Using these parameters, `Init` fills the control's `Attr` field inherited from `TWindow`.

By default, `Init` sets `Attr.Style` to `ws_Child` or `ws_Visible` or `ws_Group` or `ws_TabStop`; thus, all control objects are visible child windows.

TControl.GetClassName

```
function GetClassName: PChar; virtual;
```

(Override: always) Abstract method always overridden by descendant objects.

TControl.InitResource

```
constructor InitResource(AParent: PWindowsObject;
  ResourceID: Word);
```

Associates a control object with the control element in the resource specified by `ResourceID`.

Sends a message to `TWindow.InitResource` and `EnableTransfer` to enable the transfer mechanism.

TControl.Register

```
function Register: Boolean; virtual;
```

(Override: never) Returns True to indicate that `TControl` descendants use preregistered window classes.

TControl.WMPaint

```
procedure WMPaint(var Msg: TMessage); virtual; wm_First + wm_Paint;
```

(Override: seldom) Sends a message to `DefWndProc` enabling standard repainting of control objects.

TDialog

TDialog defines objects to serve as the modal and modeless dialog boxes used in Windows applications. A TDialog object has an associated dialog resource that describes the appearance and placement of its controls. Specify the dialog resource in the message to Init.

You can associate dialog box objects with either modal or modeless dialog elements by way of messages to Execute (for modal dialogs) or Create (for modeless dialogs). *Note:* When you create a modal dialog, you disable the operation of its parent window until the modal dialog is finished.

Fields

Attr
DialogProc
IsModal

Methods

Init
Load
Done
Cancel
Create
DefWndProc
EndDlg
Execute
GetItemHandle
Ok
SendDlgItemMsg
Store
WMClose
WMInitDialog
WMQueryEndSession

Fields

TDialog.Attr

```
Attr: TDialogAttr;
```

`Attr` holds the dialog box's creation attributes. `Attr` is defined as follows:

```
TDialogAttr = record
   Name: PChar;
   Param: Longint;
end;
```

The `Name` field contains the name or ID of the dialog resource. The `Param` field contains a parameter sent to the dialog procedure when the dialog is created.

TDialog.DialogProc

`DialogProc: TFarProc;` (read only)

`DialogProc` points to the procedure-instance address of the dialog function.

TDialog.IsModal

`IsModal: Boolean;` (read only)

`IsModal` is True if the dialog is modal and False if the dialog is modeless.

Methods

TDialog.Init

```
constructor Init(AParent: PWindowsObject; AName: PChar);
```

(Override: sometimes) Constructs the dialog object by sending a message to `TWindowsObject.Init`, passing it the parent window, `AParent`.

Next, `Init` sets the `Attr.Name` field to `AName`. `AName` can be the symbolic name of the dialog resource or an integer ID cast to type `PChar`.

`Init` also sends a message to `TWindowsObject.DisableAutoCreate` to prevent dialogs from being created and displayed automatically along with their parent windows.

TDialog.Load

```
constructor Load(var S: TStream);
```

Constructs and loads a dialog box from the stream, S, by first sending a message to TWindowsObject.Load and then reading the additional fields (Attr and IsModal) introduced by TDialog.

TDialog.Done

```
destructor Done; virtual;
```

(Override: sometimes) Disposes of the dialog box object. Sends a message to TWindowsObject.Done.

TDialog.Cancel

```
procedure Cancel(var Msg: TMessage); virtual; id_First + id_Cancel;
```

(Override: sometimes) Automatically responds to a dialog's Cancel button (when pressed) by sending a message to EndDlg with the value id_Cancel.

TDialog.Create

```
function Create: Boolean; virtual;
```

(Override: never) Creates a modeless dialog object's corresponding dialog element. Create returns True if the creation was successful. If unsuccessful, it sends a message to Error with the error code em_InvalidWindow.

TDialog.DefWndProc

```
procedure DefWndProc(var Msg: TMessage); virtual;
```

(Override: never) Forces Windows default-message processing by setting the result of the passed message equal to 0.

TDialog.EndDlg

```
procedure EndDlg(ARetValue: Integer); virtual;
```

(Override: never) Destroys modal and modeless dialog boxes. ARetValue is passed back as the return value from Execute for modal dialog boxes.

TDialog.Execute

```
function Execute: Integer; virtual;
```

(Override: never) Creates and displays a modal dialog object's corresponding dialog element. This method executes while the dialog box is on-screen, until its `EndDlg` method is sent a message.

Before the method finishes, it resets `HWindow` to 0. `Execute` returns the integer value returned by `EndDlg` if successful. If unsuccessful, `Execute` sends `Error` a message with the error code `em_InvalidWindow`.

TDialog.GetItemHandle

```
function GetItemHandle(DlgItemID: Integer): HWnd;
```

(Override: never) Returns the handle to the dialog's control identified by the passed ID, `DlgItemID`.

TDialog.Ok

```
procedure Ok(var Msg: TMessage); virtual; id_First + id_OK;
```

(Override: sometimes) Automatically responds to a dialog's OK button (when pressed) by sending messages to `CanClose` and `EndDlg` with the value `id_OK`. Also sends a message to `TransferData` to transfer data from the controls to the transfer buffer.

TDialog.SendDlgItemMsg

```
function SendDlgItemMsg(DlgItemID: Integer; AMsg, WParam: Word;
  LParam: Longint): Longint;
```

(Override: never) Sends a Windows control message, identified by `AMsg`, to the dialog's control identified by `DlgItemID`.

`WParam` and `LParam` become parameters in the Windows message. `SendDlgItemMsg` returns the value returned by the control or 0 if the control ID is invalid.

TDialog.Store

```
procedure Store(var S: TStream);
```

Stores the dialog box on the stream, `S`, by first sending a message to `TWindowsObject.Store` and then writing the additional fields (`Attr` and `IsModal`) introduced by `TDialog`.

TDialog.WMClose

```
procedure WMClose(var Msg: TMessage); virtual; wm_First + wm_Close;
```

If the dialog box is modal, `WMClose` sends a message to `EndDlg` to close the dialog box.

If the dialog box is modeless, `WMClose` sends a message to its `WMClose` method inherited from `TWindowsObject`.

TDialog.WMInitDialog

```
procedure WMInitDialog(var Msg: TMessage); virtual;
  wm_First + wm_InitDialog;
```

(Override: never) `WMInitDialog` automatically receives a message just before the dialog is displayed. It sends a message to `SetupWindow` to handle any initialization needed for the dialog or its controls.

TDialog.WMQueryEndSession

```
procedure WMQueryEndSession(var Msg : TMessage); virtual;
  wm_First + wm_QueryEndSession
```

This procedure ends the query session by first asking each application whether the query session should end. Uses the Windows API.

TDlgWindow

Dialog windows defined by `TDlgWindow` combine some of the characteristics of dialogs and some characteristics of windows.

A dialog window has an associated dialog resource that describes the appearance and position of its controls. It also has a window class that can specify icons and cursors.

To create and display dialog windows, use the modeless dialog `Create` methods. Don't use the `Execute` method.

Fields

None.

Methods

```
Init
Create
GetWindowClass
```

Methods

TDlgWindow.Init

```
constructor Init(AParent: PWindowsObject; AName: PChar);
```

Constructs a new `TDlgWindow` object by sending `TDialog.Init` a message.

`Init` also sends a message to `EnableAutoCreate` to ensure that the `TDlgWindow` object automatically is created and displayed along with its parent window.

TDlgWindow.Create

```
function Create: Boolean; virtual;
```

(Override: never) Registers the dialog window's class and sends a message to `TDialog.Create`.

`Create` returns True if successful.

TDlgWindow.GetWindowClass

```
procedure GetWindowClass(var AWndClass: TWndClass); virtual;
```

(Override: often) Defines the default window class record and passes it back in `AWndClass`. This window class specifies a standard icon and cursor.

Redefine `GetWindowClass` (and `GetClassName`) for any `TDlgWindow` descendants.

Also, make sure that your `GetWindowClass` method sends a message to `GetWindowClass` before modifying any `TWndClass` fields.

TDosStream

`TDosStream` is a specialized `TStream` implementing unbuffered DOS file streams. Its constructor, `Init`, lets you create or open a DOS file by specifying its name and access mode: either `stCreate`, `stOpenRead`, `stOpenWrite`, or `stOpen`.

`TDosStream` has one field new field, `Handle`, which represents the DOS file handle used to access an open file. Most applications use the buffered derivative of `TDosStream` called `TBufStream`. `TDosStream` overrides all the abstract methods of `TStream` except for `TStream.Flush`.

Fields

`Handle`

Methods

`Init`
`Done`
`GetPos`
`GetSize`
`Read`
`Seek`
`Truncate`
`Write`

Fields

TDosStream.Handle

`Handle: Word` (read only)

`Handle` is the DOS file handle used to access an open file stream.

Methods

TDosStream.Init

```
constructor Init(FileName: FNameStr; Mode: Word);
```

Creates a DOS file stream with `FileName` and access `Mode`. If successful, the `Handle` is set with the DOS file handle. Failure is indicated by a message to `Error` with an argument of `stInitError`.

The `Mode` argument must be set either: `stCreate`, `stOpenRead`, `stOpenWrite`, or `stOpen`.

TDosStream.Done

```
destructor Done; virtual;
```

(Override: never) Closes and disposes of the DOS file stream.

TDosStream.GetPos

```
function GetPos: Longint; virtual;
```

(Override: never) Returns the value of the calling stream's current position.

TDosStream.GetSize

```
function GetSize: Longint; virtual;
```

(Override: never) Returns the size in bytes of the calling stream.

TDosStream.Read

```
procedure Read(var Buf; Count: Word); virtual;
```

(Override: never) Reads `Count` bytes into the `Buf` buffer starting at the calling stream's current position.

TDosStream.Seek

```
procedure Seek(Pos: Longint); virtual;
```

(Override: never) Resets the current position to `Pos` bytes from the beginning of the calling stream.

TDosStream.Truncate

```
procedure Truncate; virtual;
```

(Override: never) Deletes all data on the calling stream from the current position to the end of the stream.

TDosStream.Write

```
procedure Write(var Buf; Count: Word); virtual;
```

Writes `Count` bytes from the `Buf` buffer to the calling stream, starting at the current position.

TEdit

TEdit is an interface object that corresponds to an edit control element in Windows.

You usually don't use TEdit objects in dialog boxes (TDialog) or dialog windows (TDlgWindow). Rather, you use them to display a stand-alone edit control as a child window in another window's client area.

There are two styles of edit control objects: single- and multiline. Multiline edit controls can use vertical scroll bars and allow the editing of multiple lines. Most of TEdit's methods manage the edit control's text.

TEdit includes several command-based message-response methods for responding automatically to Cut, Copy, Paste, Delete, Clear, and Undo menu selections from the edit control's parent window.

GetText and SetText are inherited from TEdit's ancestor, TStatic.

Fields

None.

Methods

Init
CanUndo
ClearModify
CMEditClear
CMEditCopy
CMEditCut
CMEditDelete
CMEditPaste
CMEditUndo
Copy
Cut
DeleteLine
DeleteSelection
DeleteSubText
GetClassName
GetLine
GetLineFromPos
GetLineIndex
GetLineLength
GetNumLines

```
GetSelection
GetSubText
Insert
IsModified
Paste
Scroll
Search
SetSelection
SetupWindow
Transfer
Undo
```

Methods

TEdit.Init

```
constructor Init(AParent: PWindowsObject; AnId: Integer;
  ATitle: PChar; X,Y,W,H: Integer; Multiline : Boolean);
```

(Override: sometimes) Constructs an edit control object with a parent window (`AParent`).

It fills its `Attr` fields with the following information:

- Passed control ID (`AnId`)
- Initial text (`ATitle`)
- Position (`X`, `Y`) relative to the origin of the parent window's client area
- Width (`W`)
- Height (`H`)

If `Multiline` is True, the edit control is a multiline edit control with horizontal and vertical scroll bars. In this case, the `Attr.Style` field includes the Windows style constants `es_Multiline`, `es_AutoVScroll`, `es_AutoHScroll`, `es_Left`, `ws_VScroll`, and `ws_HScroll`.

If `Multiline` is False, the edit control has a single line of text and a border (`ws_Border`), and is left-justified (`es_Left`).

TEdit.CanUndo

```
function CanUndo: Boolean; virtual;
```

(Override: seldom) Returns True if it's possible to undo the last edit.

TEdit.ClearModify

```
procedure ClearModify; virtual;
```

(Override: seldom) Resets the changes flag for the edit control.

TEdit.CMEditClear

```
procedure CMEditClear(var Msg: TMessage); virtual; cm_First + cm_EditClear
```

(Override: never) Automatically responds to a menu selection with a menu ID of `cm_EditClear` by sending a message to the `Clear` method.

TEdit.CMEditCopy

```
procedure CMEditCopy(var Msg: TMessage); virtual;
  cm_First + cm_EditCopy;
```

(Override: never) Automatically responds to a menu selection with a menu ID of `cm_EditCopy` by sending a message to the `Copy` method.

TEdit.CMEditCut

```
procedure CMEditCut(var Msg: TMessage); virtual;
  cm_First + cm_EditCut;
```

(Override: never) Automatically responds to a menu selection with a menu ID of `cm_EditCut` by sending a message to the `Cut` method.

TEdit.CMEditDelete

```
procedure CMEditDelete(var Msg: TMessage); virtual;
  cm_First + cm_EditDelete;
```

(Override: never) Automatically responds to a menu selection with a menu ID of `cm_EditDelete` by sending a message to the `DeleteSelection` method.

TEdit.CMEditPaste

```
procedure CMEditPaste(var Msg: TMessage); virtual;
  cm_First + cm_EditPaste;
```

(Override: never) Automatically responds to a menu selection with a menu ID of `cm_EditPaste` by sending a message to the `Paste` method.

TEdit.CMEditUndo

```
procedure CMEditUndo(var Msg: TMessage); virtual;
  cm_First + cm_EditUndo;
```

(Override: never) Automatically responds to a menu selection with a menu ID of cm_EditUndo by sending a message to the Undo method.

TEdit.Copy

```
procedure Copy; virtual;
```

(Override: seldom) Copies any currently selected text into the clipboard.

TEdit.Cut

```
procedure Cut; virtual;
```

(Override: seldom) Cuts (that is, copies and deletes) any currently selected text into the clipboard.

TEdit.DeleteLine

```
function DeleteLine(LineNumber: Integer): Boolean; virtual;
```

(Override: sometimes) Deletes the text in the line specified by LineNumber in a multiline edit control. DeleteLine doesn't delete the line break and has no effect on other lines.

DeleteLine returns True if successful.

TEdit.DeleteSelection

```
function DeleteSelection: Boolean; virtual;
```

(Override: seldom) Clears the currently selected text and returns False if no text is selected.

TEdit.DeleteSubText

```
function DeleteSubText(StartPos, EndPos: Integer): Boolean; virtual;
```

(Override: seldom) Deletes the text between the starting and ending positions specified by StartPos and EndPos.

The first character is at position 0, and the position numbers continue sequentially throughout all lines in a multiline edit control. Line breaks are counted as two characters. DeleteSubText returns True if successful.

TEdit.GetClassName

```
function GetClassName: PChar; virtual;
```

(Override: never) Returns the name of TEdit's window class, Edit.

TEdit.GetLine

```
function GetLine(ATextString: PChar; StrSize, LineNumber:
  Integer): Boolean; virtual;
```

(Override: seldom) Gets a multiline edit control's text from the line specified by LineNumber and returns it in ATextString.

StrSize indicates the number of characters to retrieve.

GetLine returns False if it's unable to retrieve the text or if the text is too long.

TEdit.GetLineFromPos

```
function GetLineFromPos(CharPos: Integer): Integer; virtual;
```

(Override: seldom) Returns from a multiline edit control the line number where the character position specified by CharPos occurs.

The position of the first character is 0 and the numbers continue sequentially throughout all the lines. Line breaks are counted as two characters.

TEdit.GetLineIndex

```
function GetLineIndex(LineNumber: Integer): Integer; virtual;
```

(Override: seldom) Returns from a multiline edit control the number of characters that appear before the line number specified by LineNumber. Line breaks are counted as two characters.

If the line doesn't exist, GetLineIndex returns the number of characters in the edit control.

TEdit.GetLineLength

```
function GetLineLength(LineNumber: Integer): Integer; virtual;
```

(Override: seldom) Returns from a multiline edit control the number of characters in the line specified by LineNumber. *Note:* Send GetLine a message before you send GetLineLength a message.

TEdit.GetNumLines

```
function GetNumLines: Integer; virtual;
```

(Override: seldom) Returns the number of lines that have been entered in a multiline edit control.

(Send `GetNumLines` a message before you send `GetLine` a message.)

TEdit.GetSelection

```
procedure GetSelection(var StartPos, EndPos: Integer); virtual;
```

(Override: seldom) Gets the starting and ending positions of the currently selected text and returns them in the `StartPos` and `EndPos` arguments. The first character is at position 0.

In a multiline edit control, the positions are counted sequentially through all lines, and line breaks are counted as two characters.

Use `GetSelection` with `GetSubText` to get the currently selected text.

TEdit.GetSubText

```
procedure GetSubText(ATextString: PChar; StartPos, EndPos: Integer); virtual;
```

(Override: seldom) Gets (in `ATextString`) the text in an edit control from the indices `StartPos` to `EndPos`.

The first character is at index 0.

In a multiline edit control, the characters are counted sequentially through all the lines, and line breaks are counted as two characters.

TEdit.Insert

```
procedure Insert(ATextString: PChar); virtual;
```

(Override: seldom) Inserts the text passed in `ATextString` into the edit control at the current text-insertion point, replacing any currently selected text.

`Insert` is similar to `Paste`, but doesn't affect the clipboard.

TEdit.IsModified

```
function IsModified: Boolean; virtual;
```

(Override: seldom) If the user has changed the text in the edit control, `IsModified` returns True.

TEdit.Paste

```
procedure Paste; virtual;
```

(Override: seldom) Inserts text from the clipboard into the edit control at the current insertion point.

TEdit.Scroll

```
procedure Scroll(HorizontalUnit, VerticalUnit: Integer); virtual;
```

(Override: seldom) Scrolls a multiline edit control horizontally and vertically by the numbers of characters specified by `HorizontalUnit` and `VerticalUnit`.

Positive values scroll to the right or down, and negative values scroll to the left or up.

TEdit.Search

```
procedure Search(StartPos: Integer; AText: PChar;
  CaseSensitive: Boolean): Integer;
```

`Search` searches the edit control's text (beginning with the character at `StartPos`) until it finds a match for `AText`.

- If the text is found, the matching text is selected, and `Search` returns the position of the start of the matched text.
- If `AText` isn't found, `Search` returns –1.

Pass –1 in `StartPos` to begin the search at the current position.

TEdit.SetSelection

```
function SetSelection(StartPos, EndPos: Integer): Boolean; virtual;
```

(Override: seldom) Forces selection of the text between the positions specified by `StartPos` and `EndPos`, but not including the character at `EndPos`.

The first character is at position 0, and the position numbers continue sequentially through all lines in a multiline edit control. Line breaks are counted as two characters.

TEdit.SetupWindow

```
procedure SetupWindow; virtual;
```

Limits the number of charcters that can be entered into the edit control by sending a message to `TStatic.SetupWindow`.

If the `TextLen` field is nonzero, the value `TextLen-1` is sent to Windows though an `em_LimitText` message.

TEdit.Transfer

```
function Transfer(DataPtr: Pointer; TransferFlag: Word): Word; virtual;
```

(Override: sometimes) Transfers `TextLen` characters of the current text of the edit control to or from the memory location pointed to by `DataPtr`.

- If `TransferFlag` is `tf_GetData`, the text is transferred to the memory location.
- If `TransferFlag` is `tf_SetData`, the edit control's text is set to the text at the memory location. Transfer returns `TextLen` (the number of bytes stored in or retrieved from the memory location).
- If `TransferFlag` is `tf_SizeData`, `Transfer` returns the size of the transfer data.

TEdit.Undo

```
procedure Undo; virtual;
```

(Override: seldom) Undoes the last edit.

TEmsStream

`TEmsStream` is a specialized `TStream` for implementing streams in EMS memory. `TEmsStream`'s new fields set up an EMS handle, a page count, stream size, and current position. `TEmsStream` overrides the six abstract methods of `TStream` and implements its own specialized constructor and destructor.

When you debug an application using EMS streams, the IDE cannot recover EMS memory allocated by applications if an application terminates prematurely or if you don't send a message to the (`Done`) destructor for an EMS stream. Only the `Done` method (or rebooting) can release the EMS pages owned by the stream.

Fields

```
Handle
PageCount
Size
Position
```

Methods

```
Init
Done
GetPos
GetSize
Read
Seek
Truncate
Write
```

Fields

TEmsStream.Handle

`Handle: Word;` (read only)

The EMS handle for the stream.

TEmsStream.PageCount

`PageCount: Word;` (read only)

The number of allocated pages for the stream: 16K per page.

TEmsStream.Size

`Size: Longint;` (read only)

The size of the stream in bytes.

TEmsStream.Position

`Position: Longint;` (read only)

The current position within the stream. The first position is 0.

Methods

TEmsStream.Init

```
constructor Init(MinSize: Longint);
```

Creates an EMS stream with the `MinSize` (in bytes). Sends a message to `Init` and then sets `Handle`, `Size` and `PageCount`. Sends a message to `Error` with an argument of `stInitError` if initialization fails.

TEmsStream.Done

```
destructor Done; virtual;
```

(Override: never) Disposes of the EMS stream and releases EMS pages used.

TEmsStream.GetPos

```
function GetPos: Longint; virtual;
```

(Override: never) Returns the value of the calling stream's current position.

TEmsStream.GetSize

```
function GetSize: Longint; virtual;
```

(Override: never) Returns the size of the calling stream.

TEmsStream.Read

```
procedure Read(var Buf; Count: Word); virtual;
```

(Override: never) Reads `Count` bytes into the `Buf` buffer starting at the calling stream's current position.

TEmsStream.Seek

```
procedure Seek(Pos: Longint); virtual;
```

(Override: never) Resets the current position to `Pos` bytes from the start of the calling stream.

TEmsStream.Truncate

```
procedure Truncate; virtual;
```

(Override: never) Deletes all data on the calling stream from the current position to the end. The current position is set to the new end of the stream.

TEmsStream.Write

```
procedure Write(var Buf; Count: Word); virtual;
```

(Override: never) Writes `Count` bytes from the `Buf` buffer to the calling stream, starting at the current position.

TGroupBox

`TGroupBox` is an interface object that corresponds to a group box element in Windows.

Normally, you don't use `TGroupBox` objects in dialog boxes (`TDialog`) or dialog windows (`TDlgWindow`). Rather, you use them when you want to display a stand-alone group box as a child window in another window's client area.

Group boxes unify a group of selection boxes (check boxes and radio buttons) and manage the states of their selection boxes.

Fields

```
NotifyParent
```

Methods

```
Init
Load
GetClassName
InitResource
SelectionChanged
Store
```

Fields

TGroupBox.NotifyParent

```
NotifyParent: Boolean; (read/write)
```

Indicates whether the parent will be notified when the state of the group box's selection boxes has changed.

Methods

TGroupBox.Init

```
constructor Init(AParent: PWindowsObject; AnID: Integer;
  AText: PChar; X,Y,W,H: Integer);
```

(Override: sometimes) Constructs a group box object with the following information:

- Passed parent window (`AParent`)
- Control ID (`AnId`)
- Associated text (`AText`)
- Position (`X`, `Y`) relative to the origin of the parent window's client area
- Width (`W`)
- Height (`H`)

Sends a message to `TControl.Init` and then adds the Windows style `bs_GroupBox` to the group box's `Attr.Style` field. Removes the style `ws_TabStop` from the group box's `Attr.Style` field. Sets `NotifyParent` to True. By default, the group box's parent is notified when the state of its selection boxes change.

TGroupBox.Load

```
constructor Load(var S: TStream);
```

Constructs and loads a group box from the stream, `S`, by sending a message to `TControl.Load` and reading the additional field (`NotifyParent`) introduced by `TGroupBox`.

TGroupBox.GetClassName

```
function GetClassName: PChar; virtual;
```

(Override: sometimes) Returns the name of `TGroupBox`'s window class, `Button`.

TGroupBox.InitResource

```
constructor InitResource(AParent: PWindowsObject; ResourceID: Word);
```

Subclasses the group box by constructing an ObjectWindows object to correspond to a group box element created by a dialog resource definition.

Sends a message to `TControl.InitResource` as well as `TWindowsObject.DisableTransfer` to exclude group boxes from the transfer mechanism because they have no data to be transferred.

TGroupBox.SelectionChanged

```
procedure SelectionChanged(ControlId: Integer); virtual;
```

(Override: sometimes) If `NotifyParent` is True, `SelectionChanged` notifies the parent window of the group box that one of its selections has changed by sending it a child-ID-based message. You can override this method to let the group box respond to its selections.

TGroupBox.Store

```
procedure Store(var S: TStream);
```

Stores the group box on the stream, `S`, by first sending a message to `TControl.Store` and then writing the additional field (`NotifyParent`) introduced by `TGroupBox`.

TListBox

`TListBox` is an interface object that corresponds to a list box element in Windows.

Usually, you don't use `TListBox` objects in dialog boxes (`TDialog`) or dialog windows (`TDlgWindow`). Rather, you display a stand-alone list box as a child window in another window's client area.

`TListBox`'s methods also serve object instances of its descendant, `TComboBox`.

Fields

None.

Methods

```
Init
AddString
ClearList
DeleteString
GetClassName
GetCount
GetMsgID
GetSelIndex
GetSelString
GetStringLen
GetString
InsertString
SetSelIndex
SetSelString
Transfer
```

Methods

TListBox.Init

```
constructor Init(AParent: PWindowsObject; AnId: Integer; X,Y, W,H: Integer);
```

(Override: sometimes) Constructs a list box object with the following parameters:

- Passed parent window (`AParent`)
- Control ID (`AnId`)
- Position (`X`, `Y`) relative to the origin of the parent window's client area
- Width (`W`)
- Height (`H`)

`Init` sends a message to `TControl.Init` and adds to the list box object's `Attr.Style` field the Windows style constant `lbs_Standard`, which supplies the scroll bar with the following

- A border (`ws_Border`)
- A vertical scroll bar (`ws_VScroll`)
- Automatic alphabetic sorting of list items (`lbs_Sort`)
- Parent window notification upon selection (`lbs_Notify`)

You can override these styles in a descendant class, or in the `Init` constructor of the list box's parent window object.

TListBox.AddString

```
function AddString(AString: PChar): Integer; virtual;
```

(Override: sometimes) Adds `AString` as a list item in the list box object, and returns the item's position index (starting at 0) or a negative value in case of an error.

List items are sorted automatically unless the style `lbs_Sort` is removed from the list box object's `Attr.Style` field before the list box is created.

TListBox.ClearList

```
procedure ClearList; virtual;
```

(Override: sometimes) Removes all (list) items from the list box.

TListBox.DeleteString

```
function DeleteString(Index: Integer): Integer; virtual;
```

(Override: sometimes) Removes the list item at the position index (starting at 0) passed in `Index`. `DeleteString` returns the number of remaining list items, or a negative value in case of an error.

TListBox.GetClassName

```
function GetClassName: PChar; virtual;
```

(Override: never) Returns the name of the `TListBox` window class, `ListBox`.

TListBox.GetCount

```
function GetCount: Integer; virtual;
```

(Override: seldom) Returns the number of list items in the list box, or a negative value in case of an error.

TListBox.GetMsgID

```
function GetMsgID(AMsg: TMsgName): virtual;
```

Translates list box messages for `TComboBox` objects. This method is *private* (not available to the programmer).

TListBox.SelIndex

```
function GetSelIndex: Integer; virtual;
```

(Override: seldom) Returns the position index (starting at 0) of the currently selected list item, or a negative value in case no item is selected.

TListBox.GetSelString

```
function GetSelString(AString: PChar; MaxChars: Integer):
  Integer; virtual;
```

(Override: seldom) Gets the currently selected list item (in `AString`), if it's shorter than `MaxChars`.

`GetSelString` returns the string length or a negative value in case of an error.

TListBox.GetStringLen

```
function GetStringLen(Index: Integer): Integer; virtual;
```

(Override: seldom) Returns the length of the list item (a string) at the position `Index`, or a negative value in case of an error.

TListBox.GetString

```
function GetString(AString: PChar; Index: Integer): Integer; virtual;
```

(Override: seldom) Gets in `AString` the list item at the position `Index`, and returns the string length or a negative value in case of an error.

TListBox.InsertString

```
function InsertString(AString: PChar; Index: Integer): Integer; virtual;
```

(Override: sometimes) Inserts `AString` as a list item in the list box at the position Index, and returns the item's position (starting at 0) or a negative value in case of an error. The list box items aren't resorted. If `Index` is –1, the string is added to the end of the list.

TListBox.SetSelIndex

```
function SetSelIndex(Index: Integer): Integer; virtual;
```

(Override: seldom) Forces selection of the list item at the position `Index`. If `Index` is –1, the list box is cleared of any selection.

`SetSelIndex` returns a negative number in case of an error.

TListBox.SetSelString

```
function SetSelString(AString: PChar; AIndex: Integer): Integer; virtual
```

(Override: seldom) Forces selection of the first list item matching `AString` that appears after the position index (beginning at 0) passed in `AIndex`.

If `AIndex` is –1, the entire list is searched from the beginning. `SetSelString` returns the position index of the newly selected item, or a negative value in case of an error.

TListBox.Transfer

```
function Transfer(DataPtr: Pointer; TransferFlag: Word): Word; virtual;
```

Transfers the list of entries and selected item(s) to or from the transfer record pointed to by `DataPtr`.

- If `TransferFlag` is `tf_GetData`, the list box's data is transferred to the memory location. The number of bytes transferred is returned.
- If `TransferFlag` is `tf_SetData`, the list box is loaded with the data from the memory location. The number of bytes transferred is returned.
- If `TransferFlag` is `tf_SizeData`, `Transfer` returns the size of the transfer data.

Depending on where the box allows multiple items to be selected, the transfer record varies. The first item transferred is always a pointer to a collection of strings.

- For single-selection list boxes, the pointer is followed by an integer index to the selected item.
- For multiple-selection list boxes, the collection is followed by a pointer to a `TMultiSelRec` record, which contains an array of integers, each indicating a selected item.

TMDIClient

Multiple Document Interface (MDI) client windows (represented by `TMDIClient`) are controls that manage the MDI child windows of an MDI application. `TMDIClient`'s methods manage MDI child windows.

Fields

ClientAttr

Methods

Init
Load
ArrangeIcons
CascadeChildren
GetClassName
Store
TileChildren

Fields

TMDIClient.ClientAttr

```
ClientAttr: TClientCreateStruct;
```

`ClientAttr` maintains a record of the MDI client window's attributes. The record (`TClientCreateStruct`) is defined as follows:

```
type
   PClientCreateStruct = ^TClientCreateStruct;
   TClientCreateStruct = record
      hWindowMenu: THandle;
      idFirstChild: Word;
  end;
```

Methods

TMDIClient.Init

```
constructor Init(AParent: PMDIWindow);
```

(Override: seldom) Constructs the MDI client window object with `AParent` as the parent window. `Init` sets the fields of `ClientAttr`. Then sends `TControl.Init` a message and adds the Windows style `ws_ClipChildren` to the window object's `Attr.Style` field.

`Init` also removes the client window from its parent's child window list so that the client window isn't treated like other child windows, such as list boxes and buttons.

TMDIClient.Load

```
constructor Load(var S: TStream);
```

Constructs and loads an MDI client window from the stream, `S`, by first sending `TControl.Load` a message and then reading the additional field (`ClientAttr`) introduced by `TMDIClient`.

TMDIClient.ArrangeIcons

```
procedure ArrangeIcons; virtual;
```

(Override: seldom) Arranges the minimized MDI child windows into a neat row at the bottom of the MDI client window.

TMDIClient.CascadeChildren

```
procedure CascadeChildren; virtual;
```

(Override: seldom) Sizes and arranges all of the nonminimized `MDI` child windows within the `MDI` client window.

TMDIClient.GetClassName

```
function GetClassName: PChar; virtual;
```

Returns `TControl`'s window class name, `MDIClient`.

TMDIClient.Store

```
procedure Store(var S: TStream);
```

Stores the MDI client window on the stream, `S`, by sending `TControl.Store` a message and then writing the additional field (`ClientAttr`) introduced by `TMDIClient`.

TMDIClient.TileChildren

```
procedure TileChildren; virtual;
```

(Override: seldom) Sizes and arranges all the nonminimized `MDI` child windows within the MDI client window using all available space without letting the windows overlap.

TMDIWindow

Multiple Document Interface (MDI) frame window (defined by `TMDIWindow`)—the main window of MDI-compliant applications.

`TMDIWindow` objects own a `TMDIClient` object and store it in the `ClientWnd` field. The child window menu presents manipulation options for the application's MDI child windows. This window is modified automatically to reflect all displayed MDI child windows.

Fields

```
ChildMenuPos
ClientWnd
```

Methods

```
Init
Load
Done
ArrangeIcons
CascadeChildren
CMCloseChildren
CMCreateChild
CMTileChildren
```

```
CreateChild
DefWndProc
GetClassName
GetClient
GetWindowClass
InitChild
InitClientWindow
SetupWindow
Store
TileChildren
```

Fields

TMDIWindow.ChildMenuPos

`ChildMenuPos: Integer; (read/write)`

`ChildMenuPos` specifies an index identifying the position of the child-window management menu. The index counts only top-level menu items. The top-left item is at position 0.

TMDIWindow.ClientWnd

`ClientWnd: PMDIClient; (read only)`

`ClientWnd` points to the MDI frame window's MDI client window, an object instance of `TMDIClient`.

Methods

TMDIWindow.Init

`constructor Init(ATitle: PChar; AMenu: HMenu);`

(Override: often) Constructs an MDI frame window object using the caption passed in `ATitle` and the menu passed in `AMenu`.

MDI frame windows must have menus. An MDI frame window has no parent window, and must be the main window of the application. By default, `Init` sets `ChildMenuPos` to 0, indicating that the child window menu is the top-left menu.

To modify `ChildMenuPos`, override `Init` in your descendant types. For example:

```
constructor NewMDIWindow.Init(ATitle: PChar; AMenu: HMenu);
begin
   TMDIWindow.Init(ATitle, AMenu);
   ChildMenuPos := 3;
end;
```

TMDIWindow.Load

```
constructor Load(var S: TStream);
```

Constructs and loads an MDI frame window from the stream, S, by calling `TWindow.Load` and then getting and reading the fields (`ClientWnd` and `ChildMenuPos`) defined by `TMDIWindow`.

TMDIWindow.Done

```
destructor Done; virtual;
```

(Override: sometimes) Disposes of the MDI client window object stored in `ClientWnd` before sending a message to `TWindow.Done` to dispose of the MDI frame window object.

TMDIWindow.ArrangeIcons

```
procedure ArrangeIcons;
```

(Override: seldom) Arranges the minimized MDI child windows into a neat row at the bottom of the MDI client window. Sends a message to `ClientWnd^.ArrangeIcons`.

TMDIWindow.CascadeChildren

```
procedure CascadeChildren;
```

(Override: seldom) Sizes and arranges all of the nonminimized MDI child windows within the MDI client window making them overlap. Displays the title bar of each one. Sends a message to `ClientWnd^.CascadeChildren`.

TMDIWindow.CMCloseChildren

```
procedure CMCloseChildren(var Msg: TMessage); virtual
  cm_First + cm_CloseChildren;
```

(Override: seldom) Responds to a menu selection with an ID of `cm_CloseChildren` by sending a message to `CloseChildren`.

TMDIWindow.CMCreateChild

```
procedure CMCreateChild(var Msg: TMessage); virtual
  cm_First + cm_CreateChild;
```

(Override: never) Responds to a menu selection with a menu ID of `cm_CreateChild` by sending a message to `CreateChild` to create a new child window.

TMDIWindow.CMTileChildren

```
procedure CMTileChildren(var Msg: TMessage); virtual
  cm_First + cm_TileChildren;
```

(Override: seldom) Responds to a menu selection with an ID of `cm_TileChildren` by sending a message to `TileChildren`.

TMDIWindow.CreateChild

```
function CreateChild: PWindowsObject; virtual;
```

Constructs and creates a new MDI child window by sending messages to `InitChild` and `MakeWindow`. You don't have to override `CreateChild` to handle descendant MDI child window types.

`CreateChild` returns a pointer to the new MDI child window.

TMDIWindow.DefWndProc

```
procedure DefWndProc(var Msg: TMessage); virtual;
```

Overrides `TWindow`'s default Windows message processing by sending a message to the Windows function `DefFrameProc` rather than `DefWindowProc`.

TMDIWindow.GetClassName

```
function GetClassName: PChar; virtual;
```

(Override: sometimes) Returns the name of `TMDIWindow`'s window class name, `TurboMDIWindow`.

TMDIWindow.GetClient

```
function GetClient: PMDIClient; virtual;
```

(Override: never) Returns a pointer to the MDI client window stored in `ClientWnd`.

TMDIWindow.GetWindowClass

```
procedure GetWindowClass(var AWndClass: TWndClass); virtual;
```

(Override: sometimes) Modifies the default window class record and sends it back in AWndClass. GetWindowClass sets the style field to 0 to remove the styles set by TWindow.GetWindowClass.

TMDIWindow.InitChild

```
function InitChild: PWindowsObject; virtual;
```

(Override: often) Constructs an MDI child window object (TWindow) with a default caption of "MDI Child" and returns a pointer to it.

If you define an MDI child window type descending from TWindow, override InitChild to construct a window using the new defined MDI child window type. For example:

```
function NewMDIWindow.InitChild: PWindowsObject;
begin
   InitChild := New(PNewMDIChild, Init(@Self, 'New MDI Child
Window'));
end;
```

TMDIWindow.InitClientWindow

```
procedure InitClientWindow; virtual;
```

(Override: sometimes) Constructs the MDI client window as a TMDIClient object and stores it in ClientWnd.

TMDIWindow.SetupWindow

```
procedure SetupWindow; virtual;
```

(Override: often) Constructs the MDI client window (ClientWnd) object's corresponding window element by sending a message to InitClientWindow. SetupWindow sends MakeWindow a message to create the MDI client window.

If you override SetupWindow in a descendant type, send a message to TMDIWindow.SetupWindow explicitly before implementing your application window's new behavior.

TMDIWindow.Store

```
procedure Store(var S: TStream);
```

Stores the MDI frame window on the stream, `S`, by sending a message to `TWindow.Store`. It then writes the additional fields (`ClientWnd` and `ChildMenuPos`) defined by `TMDIWindow`.

TMDIWindow.TileChildren

```
procedure TileChildren;
```

(Override: seldom) Sizes and arranges all the nonminimized MDI child windows within the MDI client window, using all available window space without overlapping the windows. Sends a message to `ClientWnd^.TileChildren`.

TObject

`TObject` is the starting point of the Object Windows object hierarchy. With the exception of `TPoint` and `TRect`, all ObjectWindows standard objects are derived (directly or indirectly) from `TObject`. Any object that uses ObjectWindows streams must trace its ancestry back to `TObject`.

Fields

None.

Methods

```
Init
Free
Done
```

Methods

TObject.Init

```
constructor Init;
```

Allocates space on the heap for an object.

Receives a message from all its descendant objects' constructors.

TObject.Free

```
procedure Free;
```

Disposes of the object and sends a message to the Done destructor.

TObject.Done

```
destructor Done; virtual;
```

Handles cleanup and disposal for dynamic objects.

TRadioButton

TRadioButton is an interface object that corresponds to a radio button element in Windows.

You normally don't use TRadioButton objects in dialog boxes (TDialog) or dialog windows (TDlgWindow). Instead, use them when you want to display a stand-alone radio button as a child window in another window's client area.

A radio button is in one of two states: checked or unchecked.

TRadioButton inherits its state-management methods from its ancestor, TCheckBox.

A check box can also be part of a group (TGroupBox), which visually and conceptually groups its controls.

Fields

None.

Methods

Init

Methods

TRadioButton.Init

```
constructor Init(AParent: PWindowsObject; AnID: Integer;
  ATitle: PChar; X,Y,W,H: Integer; AGroup: PGroupBox);
```

(Override: sometimes) Constructs a radio button object with the following arguments:

- Passed parent window (`AParent`)
- Control ID (`AnId`)
- Associated text (`ATitle`)
- Position (`X`, `Y`) relative to the origin of the parent window's client area
- Width (`W`)
- Height (`H`)
- Associated group box (`AGroup`)

Init sets the check box's `Attr.Style` field to `ws_Child` or `ws_Visible` or `bs_RadioButton`.

TScrollBar

`TScrollBar` objects represent stand-alone scroll bar controls. (*Note:* These do not include the scroll bars that are attached to windows.)

Scroll bars can be vertical (scrolling up and down) or horizontal (scrolling right and left). Most of `TScrollBar`'s methods manage the scroll bar's thumb position and range.

`TScrollBar` maintains a set of methods that respond automatically to the Windows scroll bar messages `wm_HScroll` and `wm_VScroll`.

The methods, such as `SBLineUp` and `SBPageDown`, are defined as notify-based methods. They automatically adjust the scroll bar's thumb position.

Fields

```
LineMagnitude
PageMagnitude
```

Methods

```
Init
Load
DeltaPos
GetClassName
GetPosition
GetRange
```

SBBottom
SBLineDown
SBLineUp
SBPageDown
SBPageUp
SBThumbPosition
SBThumbTrack
SBTop
SetPosition
SetRange
SetupWindow
Store
Transfer

Fields

TScrollBar.LineMagnitude

`LineMagnitude: Integer;` (read/write)

`LineMagnitude` is the number of range units to scroll the scroll bar when the user clicks on a scroll bar's arrows to request a small (that is, line) movement.

By default, `Init` sets `LineMagnitude` to 1. Also, by default, `SetupWindow` sets the scroll range from 0 to 100.

TScrollBar.PageMagnitude

`PageMagnitude: Integer;` (read/write)

`PageMagnitude` is the number of range units to scroll the scroll bar when the user requests a large (that is, page) movement by clicking in the scroll bar's scrolling area.

By default, `Init` sets `PageMagnitude` to 10. (By default, the scroll range is set to from 0 to 100.)

Methods

TScrollBar.Init

```
constructor Init(AParent: PWindowsObject; AnID: Integer;
  X,Y,W,H: Integer; IsHScrollBar: Boolean);
```

Constructs and initializes a `TScrollBar` object with the following information:

- Parent window (`AParent`)
- `AnID` as a control ID
- A position of (`X`, `Y`)
- A width of `W`
- A height of `H`

The scroll bar is horizontal (style `sbs_Horz`) if `IsHScrollBar` is True and vertical (style `sbs_Vert`) if `IsHScrollBar` is False.

If the requested height for a horizontal scroll bar or the requested width for a vertical scroll bar is 0, default values are set. `LineMagnitude` is initialized to 1 and `PageMagnitude` to 10.

TScrollBar.Load

```
constructor Load(var S: TStream);
```

Constructs and loads a scroll bar control from the stream, `S`, by first sending `TControl.Load` a message and then reading the additional fields (`LineMagnitude` and `PageMagnitude`) defined by `TScrollBar`.

TScrollBar.DeltaPos

```
function DeltaPos(Delta: Integer): Integer; virtual;
```

(Override: seldom) Changes the scroll bar's thumb position by the `Delta` value. It sends `SetPosition` a message.

A negative value moves the thumb up or left. The new thumb position is returned.

TScrollBar.GetClassName

```
function GetClassName: PChar; virtual;
```

(Override: never) Returns the name of `TScrollBar`'s window class, `Scrollbar`.

TScrollBar.GetPosition

```
function GetPosition: Integer; virtual;
```

(Override: seldom) Returns the scroll bar's current thumb position.

TScrollBar.GetRange

```
procedure GetRange(var LoVal, HiVal: Integer); virtual;
```

(Override: seldom) Gets the allowed range of scroll bar thumb positions in `LoVal` and `HiVal`.

TScrollBar.SBBottom

```
procedure SBBottom(var Msg: TMessage); virtual nf_First + sb_Bottom;
```

(Override: seldom) In response to a user request, `SBBottom` sets the thumb position to the highest allowable value.

This method receives a message in response to a scroll-based message carrying the code `sb_Bottom`. Sends a message to `SetPosition`.

TScrollBar.SBLineDown

```
procedure SBLineDown(var Msg: TMessage); virtual; nf_First + sb_LineDown;
```

(Override: seldom) Moves the thumb position down or right by `LineMagnitude`.

`SBLineDown` receives a message automatically in response to a scroll-based message carrying the code `sb_LineDown`. Sends `SetPosition` a message.

TScrollBar.SBLineUp

```
procedure SBLineUp(var Msg: TMessage); virtual; nf_First + sb_LineUp;
```

(Override: seldom) Moves the thumb position up or left by the `LineMagnitude`.

`sb_LineUp` receives a message automatically in response to a scroll-based message carrying the code `sb_LineUp`. Sends a message to `SetPosition`.

TScrollBar.SBPageDown

```
procedure SBPageDown(var Msg: TMessage); virtual; nf_First + sb_PageDown;
```

(Override: seldom) Moves the thumb position down or right by `PageMagnitude`.

`SBPageDown` receives a message automatically in response to a scroll-based message carrying the code `sb_PageDown`. Sends a message to `SetPosition`.

TScrollBar.SBPageUp

```
procedure SBPageUp(var Msg: TMessage); virtual; nf_First + sb_PageUp;
```

(Override: seldom) Moves the thumb position up or left by `PageMagnitude`.

`SBPageUp` receives a message automatically in response to a scroll-based message carrying the code `sb_PageUp`. Sends a message to `SetPosition`.

TScrollBar.SBThumbPosition

```
procedure SBThumbPosition(var Msg: TMessage); virtual;
  nf_First + sb_ThumbPosition;
```

(Override: seldom) Changes the thumb position to position chosen by the user and passed in a scroll-based message carrying the code `sb_ThumbPosition`. Sends `SetPosition` a message.

TScrollBar.SBThumbTrack

```
procedure SBThumbTrack(var Msg: TMessage); virtual; nf_First + sb_ThumbTrack;
```

(Override: sometimes) Changes the thumb position as the user drags the thumb. Sends a message to `SetPosition`.

`SBThumbTrack` receives a message in response to a scroll-based message carrying the code `sb_ThumbTrack`.

TScrollBar.SBTop

```
procedure SBTop(var Msg: TMessage); virtual; nf_First + sb_Top;
```

(Override: seldom) In response to a user request, `SBTop` sets the thumb position to the lowest allowable value.

`SBTop` receives a message in response to a scroll-based message carrying the code `sb_Top`. Sends a message to `SetPosition`.

TScrollBar.SetPosition

```
procedure SetPosition(ThumbPos: Integer); virtual;
```

(Override: sometimes) Sets the scroll bar's thumb position to `ThumbPos`.

- If `ThumbPos` is higher than the allowable range, the thumb position is set to the highest possibl value.
- If `ThumbPos` is lower than the allowable range, the thumb is set to the lowest possible value.

TScrollBar.SetRange

```
procedure SetRange(LoVal, HiVal: Integer); virtual;
```

(Override: seldom) Sets the scroll bar's allowable range of thumb positions from `LoVal` to `HiVal`.

TScrollBar.SetupWindow

```
procedure SetupWindow; virtual;
```

(Override: sometimes) Initializes the scroll bar's range from 0 to 100. To override this range, send a message to `SetRange`.

TScrollBar.Store

```
procedure Store(var S: TStream);
```

Stores the scroll bar control on the stream, `S`, by sending a message to `TControl.Store` and then writing the fields (`LineMagnitude` and `PageMagnitude`) defined by `TScrollBar`.

TScrollBar.Transfer

```
function Transfer(DataPtr: Pointer; TransferFlag: Word): Word; virtual;
```

(Override: sometimes) Transfers the scroll bar's range and current position to or from the memory location pointed to by `DataPtr`.

- If `TransferFlag` is `tf_GetData`, a transfer record holding the range and position is transferred to the memory location.
- If `TransferFlag` is `tf_SetData`, the transfer record at the memory location contains values that are used to set the range and position of the scroll bar.

In both cases, `Transfer` returns the number of bytes in the memory location.

The transfer record is defined as follows:

```
ScrollBarTransferRec = record
   LowValue: Integer;
   HighValue: Integer;
   Position: Integer;
end;
```

TScroller

`TScroller` objects are part of the `Scroller` field of `TWindow` and descendant objects.

A `TScroller` object adds an automatic window scrolling mechanism to a window.

Usually, you construct and manipulate `TScroller` objects from the methods of their owner window objects.

Fields

AutoMode
AutoOrg
HasHScrollBar
HasVScrollBar
TrackMode
Window
XLine
XPage
XPos
XRange
XUnit
YLine
YPage
YPos
YRange
YUnit

Methods

AutoScroll
BeginView
EndView
HScroll
Init
IsVisibleRect
Load
ScrollBy
ScrollTo
SetPageSize
SetRange
SetSBarRange
SetUnits
Store
VScroll
XRangeValue (private)
XScrollValue (private)
YRangeValue (private)
YScrollValue (private)

Fields

TScroller.AutoMode

`AutoMode: Boolean;` (read/write)

`AutoMode` is True if the scroller is in auto-scrolling mode. By default, `AutoMode` is True.

TScroller.AutoOrg

`AutoOrg: Boolean;`

`AutoOrg` controls the automatic adjustment of the origin of the display context used for painting the window.

- If `AutoOrg` is True (the default), the origin of the `Paint` method's display context is set to the origin of the scroller.
- If False, the display context's origin is (0,0) and `Paint` must read the scroll bar offsets to determine how to position objects on the display context.

TScroller.HasHScrollBar

`HasHScrollBar: Boolean;` (read/write)

If the owner window has a horizontal window scroll bar, `HasHScrollBar` is True.

TScroller.HasVScrollBar

`HasVScrollBar: Boolean;` (read/write)

If the owner window has a vertical window scroll bar, `HasVScrollBar` is False.

TScroller.TrackMode

`TrackMode: Boolean;` (read/write)

`TrackMode` is True if the scroller automatically tracks scroll-bar thumb movements by scrolling the window.

By default, `TrackMode` is True.

TScroller.Window

`Window: PWindow;` (read only)

Window points to the `TScroller`'s owner window.

TScroller.XLine

`XLine: Integer;` (read/write)

`XLine` is the number of `XUnit` units to scroll horizontally in response to a click on the scroll bar arrow.

The default is 1.

TScroller.XPage

`XPage: Integer;` (read/write)

`XPage` is the number of `XUnit` units to scroll horizontally in response to a click on the scroll bar's thumb area.

By default, `XPage` is equal to the current width of the window in `XUnit` units. Resizing the window updates this value.

TScroller.XPos

`XPos: Longint;` (read only)

`XPos` is the scroller's current horizontal position in terms of `XUnit` units.

TScroller.XRange

`XRange: Longint;` (read only)

`XRange` is the total number of horizontal `XUnit` units you can scroll a window.

Although you specify `XRange` values in the `Init` constructor, you can modify them later.

TScroller.XUnit

`XUnit: Integer;` (read only)

`XUnit` is the smallest number of device units (pixels) that the window can be scrolled horizontally.

Although you specify `XUnit` values in the `Init` constructor, you can modify them later.

TScroller.YLine

`YLine: Integer;` (read/write)

`YLine` is the number of `YUnit` units to scroll vertically in response to a click on the scroll bar arrow.

The default is 1.

TScroller.YPage

`YPage: Integer;` (read/write)

`YPage` is the number of `YUnit` units to scroll vertically in response to a click on the scroll bar's thumb area.

By default, `YPage` is equal to the current height of the window in `YUnit` units. Resizing the window updates this value.

TScroller.YPos

`YPos: Longint;` (read only)

YPos is the scroller's current vertical position in terms of YUnit units.

TScroller.YRange

`YRange: Longint;` (read only)

`YRange` is the total number of vertical `YUnit` units the window can be scrolled.

Although you specify `YRange` values in the Init constructor, you can modify them later.

TScroller.YUnit

`YUnit: Integer;` (read only)

`YUnit` is the smallest number of device units (pixels) that the window can be vertically scrolled.

Although you specify `YUnit` values in the `Init` constructor, you can modify them later.

Methods

TScroller.Init

```
constructor Init(TheWindow: PWindow; TheXUnit, TheYUnit: Integer;
  TheXRange, TheYRange: Longint);
```

Constructs a new TScroller object with TheWindow as the owner window, and TheXUnit, TheYUnit, TheXRange, and TheYRange fields using XUnit, YUnit, XRange and YRange.

Sets AutoMode and TrackMode to True and sets HasHScrollBar and HasVScrollBar, depending on the scroll bar attributes of the owner window.

TScroller.Load

```
constructor Load(var S: TStream);
```

Constructs and loads a scroller from the stream, S, by sending a message to TObject.Init and then reading the TScroller fields, with the exception of XPage, YPage, XPos, and YPos.

TScroller.AutoScroll

```
procedure AutoScroll; virtual;
```

(Override: sometimes) Depending on the position of the mouse cursor, performs auto-scrolling.

TScroller.BeginView

```
procedure BeginView(PaintDC: HDC; var PaintInfo: TPaintStruct); virtual;
```

(Override: sometimes) Sets the origin of the owner window's paint display context (PaintDC) according to the current scroller position.

TScroller.EndView

```
procedure EndView; virtual;
```

(Override: sometimes) Updates the position of the owner window's scroll bars synchronizing them with the position of the TScroller.

TScroller.HScroll

```
procedure HScroll(ScrollRequest: Word; ThumbPos: Integer); virtual;
```

(Override: never) Responds to horizontal scroll bar events by changing the position of the scroller and the horizontal scroll bar.

TScroller.IsVisibleRect

```
function IsVisibleRect(X, Y: Longint; XExt, YExt: Integer):
  Boolean; virtual;
```

(Override: seldom) Returns True if any part of the rectangle specified by the passed arguments is currently visible in the owner window.

TScroller.ScrollBy

```
procedure ScrollBy(Dx, Dy: Longint); virtual;
```

(Override: seldom) Scrolls by the amounts specified by `Dx` and `Dy`. Also updates the window's display.

TScroller.ScrollTo

```
procedure ScrollTo(X, Y: Longint); virtual;
```

(Override: sometimes) Scrolls to the position specified by `X` and `Y`. Also updates the window's display.

TScroller.SetPageSize

```
procedure SetPageSize; virtual;
```

(Override: sometimes) Sets the `XPage` and `YPage` fields to be the owner window's current width and height.

TScroller.SetRange

```
procedure SetRange(TheXRange, TheYRange: Longint); virtual;
```

(Override: never) Overrides the `XRange` and `YRange` values sent in the message to Init by setting them to `TheXRange` and `TheYRange`.

`SetRange` then sends a message to `SetSBarRange` to set the range of the owner window's scroll bars.

TScroller.SetSBarRange

```
procedure SetSBarRange; virtual;
```

(Override: never) Sets the range of the owner window's scroll bars by putting them in sync with the range of the `TScroller`.

TScroller.SetUnits

```
procedure SetUnits(TheXUnit, TheYUnit: Longint);virtual;
```

Sets the `XUnit` and `YUnit` fields to `TheXUnit` and `TheYUnit`.

TScroller.Store

```
procedure Store(var S: TStream);
```

Stores the scroller on the stream `S` by writing the `TScroller` fields, with the exception of `XPage`, `YPage`, `XPos` and `YPos`.

TScroller.VScroll

```
procedure VScroll(ScrollRequest: Word; ThumbPos: Integer); virtual;
```

(Override: never) Responds to vertical scroll bar events by changing the position of the scroller and the vertical scroll bar.

TScroller.XRangeValue

```
Function XRangeValue (AScrollUnit : Integer) : LongInt;
```

Private method; used internally by `TScroller` Object.

TScroller.XScrollValue

```
function XScrollValue(ARangeUnit : LongUnit) : Integer;
```

Private method; used internally by `TScroller` Object.

TScroller.YRangeValue

```
function YRangeValue(AScrollUnit : Integer): LongInt;
```

Private method; used internally by `TScroller` Object.

TScroller.YScrollValue

```
function YScrollValue(ARangeUnit : LongInt): Integer;
```

Private method; used internally by `TScroller` Object.

TSortedCollection

`TSortedCollection` is a descendant of `TCollection` for implementing collections sorted by key without duplicates.

Sorting is implied by a virtual `TSortedCollection.Compare` method that you override in order to define your own element-ordering behavior.

New items are inserted automatically in the order defined by the `Compare` method.

You can locate `Items` using the binary search method, `TSortedCollection.Search`.

You can also override the virtual `KeyOf` method that returns a pointer for `Compare` if `Compare` needs additional information.

Fields

`Duplicates`

Methods

`Init`
`Load`
`Compare`
`IndexOf`
`Insert`
`KeyOf`
`Search`
`Store`

Fields

TSortedCollection.Duplicates

```
Duplicates: Boolean;
```

The `Duplicates` field determines whether items with duplicates keys are accepted by the stream.

- If `Duplicates` is True, duplicate-key entries are inserted into the collection.
- If `Duplicates` is False, a new duplicate-key item replaces the existing item with that key.

  The default value is false.

Methods

TSortedCollection.Init

```
constructor Init(ALimit, ADelta: Integer);
```

Constructs the `TSortedCollection` based on `ALimit` and `ADelta`.

TSortedCollection.Load

```
constructor Load(var S: TStream);
```

Constructs and loads a sorted collection from the stream, `S`, by first sending a message to `TCollection.Load`. It then reads the `Duplicates` field.

TSortedCollection.Compare

```
function Compare(Key1, Key2: Pointer): Integer; virtual;
```

(Override: always) `Compare` is an abstract method that you must override in all descendant types.

`Compare` should compare the two key values and return one of the following results:

−1 if `Key1` < `Key2`
0 if `Key1` = `Key2`
1 if `Key1` > `Key2`

`Key1` and `Key2` are pointer values, extracted from their corresponding collection items by the `KeyOf` method. The `Search` method implements a binary search through the collection's items using `Compare` to compare the items.

TSortedCollection.IndexOf

```
function IndexOf(Item: Pointer): Integer; virtual;
```

(Override: never) `IndexOf` uses `TSortedCollection.Search` to find the index of `Item`. If `Item` isn't in the collection, `IndexOf` returns –1. For example:

```
if Search(KeyOf(Item), I) then IndexOf := I else IndexOf := -1;
```

TSortedCollection.Insert

```
procedure Insert(Item: Pointer); virtual;
```

(Override: never) If the target item isn't found in the sorted collection, it's inserted at the correct index position.

`Insert` sends a message to `Search` to determine whether the item exists, and if not, where to insert it. For example:

```
if not Search(KeyOf(Item), I) then AtInsert(I, Item);
```

TSortedCollection.KeyOf

```
function KeyOf(Item: Pointer): Pointer; virtual;
```

(Override: sometimes) If it gets an `Item` from the collection, `KeyOf` should return the corresponding key of the item. The default `KeyOf` returns `Item`.

Override `KeyOf` when the key of the item isn't the item itself.

TSortedCollection.Search

```
function Search(Key: Pointer; var Index: Integer): Boolean; virtual;
```

(Override: seldom) Returns True if `Item` (identified by `Key`) is found in the sorted collection.

If `Search` finds `Item`, `Index` is set to the found index; otherwise, `Index` is set to the index where the item would be placed if inserted.

TSortedCollection.Store

```
procedure Store(var S: TStream);
```

Stores the sorted collection and all its items on the stream, `S`, by sending `TCollection.Store` a message to write the collection. It then writes the `Duplicates` field to the stream.

TStatic

TStatic is an interface object that corresponds to a static control element in Windows. Usually, you don't use TStatic objects in dialog boxes (TDialog) or dialog windows (TDlgWindow). Instead, you use them to display a stand-alone static control as a child window in another window's client area.

Fields

TextLen

Methods

Init
InitResorce
Load
Clear
GetClassName
GetText
SetText
Store
Transfer

Fields

TStatic.TextLen

```
TextLen: Word;
```

TextLen holds the size of the text buffer for static controls.

Because of the null terminator at the end of the string, the number of characters that can be stored in the static control is one less than TextLen.

TextLen is also the number of bytes transferred by the Transfer method.

Methods

TStatic.Init

```
constructor Init(AParent: PWindowsObject; AnID: Integer;
  ATitle: PChar; X,Y,W,H: Integer);
```

(Override: seldom) Constructs a static control object with the following information:

- Parent window (AParent)
- Control ID (AnID)
- Text (ATitle)
- Position (X, Y) relative to the origin of the parent window's client area
- Width (W)
- Height (H)
- Text length (ATextLen)

The static control is left-justified because Init adds the Windows style ss_Left to the object's Attr.Style field. Init also removes the ws_TabStop style.

Init then sends a message to DisableTransfer to exclude TStatic objects from the transfer mechanism.

TStatic.InitResource

```
constructor InitResource(AParent: PWindowsObject; ResourceID,
  ATextLen: Word);
```

Associates a TStatic object with the static control resource specified by ResourceID and sets the TextLen field to ATextLen.

Sends a message to TControl.InitResource to construct and associate the object with its static control resource.

TStatic.Load

```
constructor Load(var S: TStream);
```

Constructs and loads a static control from the stream, S, by sending a message to TControl.Load and then reading the TextLen field.

TStatic.Clear

```
procedure Clear; virtual;
```

(Override: seldom) Clears the static control's text.

TStatic.GetText

```
function GetText(ATextString: PChar; MaxChars: Integer): Integer; virtu
```

(Override: seldom) Gets the static control's text and stores it in `ATextString`. `MaxChars` specifies the maximum size of `ATextString`. `GetText` returns the size of the retrieved string.

TStatic.SetText

```
procedure SetText(ATextString: PChar); virtual;
```

(Override: seldom) Sets the static control's text to the string passed in `ATextString`.

TStatic.Store

```
procedure Store(var S: TStream);
```

Stores the static control on the stream, `S`, by sending a message to `TControl.Store` and then writing the `TextLen` field.

TStatic.Transfer

```
function Transfer(DataPtr: Pointer; TransferFlag: Word): Word;
virtual;
```

(Override: sometimes) Transfers `TextLen` characters of the current text of the static control to or from the memory location pointer to by `DataPtr`.

- If `TransferFlag` is `tf_GetData`, the text is transferred to the memory location.
- If `TransferFlag` is `tf_SetData`, the static control's text is set to the text at the memory location. `Transfer` returns `TextLen` (the number of bytes stored in or retrieved from the memory location).
- If `TransferFlag` is `tf_SizeData`, `Transfer` returns the size of the transfer data.

TStrCollection

`TStrCollection` is a descendant of `TSortedCollection` for implementing a sorted list of ASCII strings.

Override the Compare method to provide conventional lexicographic ASCII string ordering. You can override Compare to allow for other orderings, such as those for non-English character sets.

Fields

None.

Methods

Compare
FreeItem
GetItem
PutItem

Methods

TStrCollection.Compare

```
function Compare(Key1, Key2: Pointer): Integer; virtual;
```

(Override: sometimes) Compares the strings Key1^ and Key2^ as follows:

Return −1 if Key1 < Key2
Return 0 if Key1 = Key2
Return +1 if Key1 > Key2

TStrCollection.FreeItem

```
procedure FreeItem(Item: Pointer); virtual;
```

(Override: seldom) Removes the string Item^ from the sorted collection and disposes of the string.

TStrCollection.GetItem

```
function GetItem(var S: TStream): Pointer; virtual;
```

(Override: seldom) By default, reads a string from the TStream by sending S.ReadStr a message.

TStrCollection.PutItem

```
procedure PutItem(var S: TStream; Item: Pointer); virtual;
```

(Override: seldom) By default, writes the string `Item^` on to the `TStream` by sending `S.WriteStr` a message.

TStream

`TStream` is an abstract object that handles polymorphic I/O to and from a storage device.

To create your own derived stream objects, override the virtual methods: `GetPos`, `GetSize`, `Read`, `Seek`, `Truncate`, and `Write`.

For example, ObjectWindows overrides these methods to derive `TDosStream` and `TEmsStream`.

For buffered derived streams, you must also override `Flush`.

Fields

`ErrorInfo`
`Status`

Methods

`CopyFrom`
`Error`
`Flush`
`Get`
`GetPos`
`GetSize`
`Init`
`Put`
`Read`
`ReadStr`
`Reset`
`Seek`
`StrRead`
`StrWrite`
`Truncate`
`Write`
`WriteStr`

Fields

TStream.ErrorInfo

`ErrorInfo: Integer;` (read/write)

`ErrorInfo` contains additional information when `Status` isn't `stOk`:

Status Values	*Error Information*
stError	DOS or EMS error code; if available
stInitError	DOS or EMS error code; if available
stReadError	DOS or EMS error code; if available
stWriteError	DOS or EMS error code; if available
stGetError	object type ID of unregistered object type
stPutError	VMT data segment offset of unregistered object type

TStream.Status

`Status: Integer;` (read/write)

Indicates the current status of the stream using the following error codes:

TStream error codes:	
stOk	No error
stError	Access error
stInitError	Cannot initialize stream
stReadError	Read beyond end of stream
stWriteError	Cannot expand stream
stGetError	Get of unregistered object type
stPutError	Put of unregistered object type

If `Status` isn't `stOk`, all operations on the stream are suspended until `Reset` is sent a message.

Methods

TStream.CopyFrom

```
procedure CopyFrom(var S: TStream; Count: Longint);
```

Copy `Count` bytes from stream, `S`, to the calling stream object. For example:

```
{Create a copy of entire stream}
ANewStream := New(TEmsStream, Init(AnOldStream^.GetSize));
AnOldStream^.Seek(0);
ANewStream^.CopyFrom(AnOldStream, AnOldStream^.GetSize);
```

TStream.Error

```
procedure Error(Code, Info: Integer); virtual;
```

(Override: sometimes) Receives a message whenever a stream error occurs. The default `Error` stores `Code` and `Info` in the `Status` and `ErrorInfo` fields. Then, if the global variable `StreamError` isn't nil, it sends a message to the procedure pointed to by `StreamError`.

After an error has occurred, all stream operations on the stream are suspended until a message is sent to `Reset`.

TStream.Flush

```
procedure Flush; virtual;
```

(Override: sometimes) An abstract method you must override if your descendant implements a buffer. This method can flush any buffers by clearing the read buffer, by writing the write buffer, or both.

The default `Flush` doesn't do anything.

TStream.Get

```
function Get: PObject;
```

Reads an object from the stream. The object must have been written previously to the stream by `Put`.

- `Get` first reads an object type ID (a `word`) from the stream.
- Then it finds the corresponding object type by comparing the ID to the `ObjType` field of all registered object types.
- Finally, it sends the `Load` constructor of that object type a message to create and load the object.

If the object type ID read from the stream is 0, `Get` returns a nil pointer. If the object type ID hasn't been registered (using `RegisterType`), `Get` sends a message to `Error` and returns a nil pointer. Otherwise, `Get` returns a pointer to the newly created object.

TStream.GetPos

```
function GetPos: Longint; virtual;
```

(Override: always) Returns the value of the calling stream's current position. You must override this abstract method.

TStream.GetSize

```
function GetSize: Longint; virtual;
```

(Override: always) Returns the total size of the calling stream. You must override this abstract method.

TStream.Init

```
constructor Init;
```

Creates a `TStream`.

TStream.Put

```
procedure Put(P: PObject);
```

Writes an object to the stream. You can later read the object from the stream using `Get`.

- First `Put` finds the type-registration record of the object by comparing the object's VMT offset to the `VmtLink` field of all registered object types (see the `TStreamRec` type).
- Then it writes the object type ID (the `ObjType` field of the registration record) to the stream.
- Finally it sends a message to the `Store` method of that object type in order to write the object.

If the `P` argument sent to `Put` is nil, `Put` writes a word containing 0 to the stream. If the object type of `P` hasn't been registered (using `RegisterType`), `Put` sends a message to `Error` and doesn't write anything to the stream.

TStream.Read

```
procedure Read(var Buf; Count: Word); virtual;
```

(Override: always) You must override this abstract method in all descendant types.

`Read` should read `Count` bytes from the stream into `Buf` and advance the current position of the stream by `Count` bytes.

If an error occurs, `Read` should send `Error` a message, and fill `Buf` with `Count` bytes of 0.

TStream.ReadStr

```
function ReadStr: PString;
```

Reads a string from the current position of the calling stream, returning a `PString` pointer. `ReadStr` sends a message to `GetMem` to allocate `(Length+1)` bytes for the string.

TStream.Reset

```
procedure Reset;
```

Resets any stream error condition by setting `Status` and `ErrorInfo` to 0. This method lets you continue stream processing following an error condition that you've corrected.

TStream.Seek

```
procedure Seek(Pos: Longint); virtual;
```

(Override: always) You must override this abstract method in all descendants.

`Seek` sets the current position to `Pos` bytes from the start of the calling stream. The beginning of a stream is position 0.

TStream.StrRead

```
function StrRead: PChar;
```

Reads a null-terminated string from the stream by first reading the length of the string and then reading that number of characters. Returns a pointer to the null-terminated string read.

TStream.StrWrite

```
function StrWrite(P: PChar);
```

Writes the null-terminated string, `P`, to the stream by first writing the length of the string and then writing the number of characters.

TStream.Truncate

```
procedure Truncate; virtual;
```

(Override: always) You must override this abstract method in all descendants.

`Truncate` deletes all data on the calling stream from the current position to the end.

TStream.Write

```
procedure Write(var Buf; Count: Word); virtual;
```

(Override: always) You must override this abstract method in all descendant types.

`Write` should write `Count` bytes from `Buf` onto the stream and advance the current position of the stream by `Count` bytes.

If an error occurs, `Write` should send `Error` a message.

TStream.WriteStr

```
procedure WriteStr(P: PString);
```

Writes the string `P^` to the calling stream, beginning at the current position.

TWindow

`TWindow` defines fundamental behavior for all window and control objects.

Object instances of `TWindow` are empty generic windows, which can define menus, cursors, and icons.

Fields

```
Attr
DefaultProc
FocusChildHandle
Scroller
```

Methods

```
Init
InitResource
Load
Done
Create
DefWndProc
GetID
GetWindowClass
Paint
SetCaption
SetupWindow
Store
WMActivate
WMCreate
WMHScroll
WMLButtonDown
WMMove
WMPaint
WMSize
WMVScroll
```

Fields

TWindow Attr

```
Attr: TWindowAttr;
```

`Attr` holds a `TWindowAttr` record, which defines a window's creation attributes.

These attributes include:

- The window's associated text, style, extended style, position, and size
- The window handle
- The control ID

These attributes traditionally are set to defaults in the object's `Init` constructor, but can be overridden in a descendant type's `Init` constructor.

Here's the record definition for `TWindowAttr`:

```
TWindowAttr = record
   Title: PChar;
   Style: Longint;
   ExStyle: Longint;
   X, Y, W, H: Integer;
   Param: Pointer;
   case Integer of
    0: (Menu: HMenu);   { window menu's handle or... }
    1: (Id: Integer);   { control's child identifier }
end;
```

TWindow.DefaultProc

`DefaultProc: TFarProc;` (read only)

`DefaultProc` holds the address of the default window procedure, which defines the Windows default processing for Windows messages.

TWindow.FocusChildHandle

`FocusChildHandle: THandle;` (read only)

`FocusChildHandle` stores the Windows handle to the window's child window that had the focus the last time the window was activated.

TWindow.Scroller

`Scroller: PScroller;` (read/write)

`Scroller` holds a pointer to a `TScroller` object, which is the window's scroller, if it has a scroller. You should construct a scroller in the window's `Init` constructor.

Methods

TWindow.Init

`constructor Init(AParent: PWindowsObject; ATitle: PChar);`

(Override: often) Constructs a window object with the parent window sent in `AParent` and the associated text (caption for windows) sent in `ATitle`. `AParent` should be nil for main windows because they have no parent.

The object's Attr.Style field is set to ws_OverlappedWindow unless the window is an MDI child window, when the Attr.Style field is set to ws_ClipSiblings.

The position and extent fields in the Attr record are set to defaults suitable for overlapped and pop-up windows. You can override Init in your descendant types as long as you first explicitly sent Init a message. Then you can reset the Attr fields.

By default, Scroller is set to nil.

TWindow.InitResource

```
constructor InitResource(AParent: PWindowsObject; ResourceID: Word);
```

Constructs an ObjectWindows object that is associated with an interface element (usually a control) created by a resource definition.

Sends a message to TWindowsObject.Init.

TWindow.Load

```
constructor Load(var S: TStream);
```

Constructs and loads a window from the stream, S, by first sending TWindowsObject.Load a message. Then it reads and gets the additional fields (Attr and Scroller) created by TWindow.

TWindow.Done

```
destructor Done; virtual;
```

(Override: often) Disposes of the TScroller object in Scroller, if any, before sending a message to TWindowsObject.Done to dispose of the object.

TWindow.Create

```
function Create: Boolean; virtual;
```

Creates the window object's corresponding interface element unless the object was constructed with InitResource. If the object was created with InitResource, the interface element already exists.

Create first sends a message to Register to register the window class if it's not already registered.

`Create` then creates the window and sends a message to `SetupWindow`, which you can define to initialize the newly created window.

If successful, `Create` returns True. If unsuccessful, it returns False and calls `Error`.

TWindow.DefWndProc

```
procedure DefWndProc(var Msg: TMessage); virtual;
```

(Override: never) Sends a message to the window's default procedure, which handles default processing for incoming Windows messages. It stores the result of this message in the `Result` field of the message record, `Msg`.

TWindow.GetID

```
function GetId: Integer; virtual;
```

(Override: seldom) Returns the window identifier, such as a control ID.

TWindow.GetWindowClass

```
procedure GetWindowClass(var AWndClass: TWndClass);virtual;
```

(Override: often) Fills a window class record, passed in `AWndClass`, with default values for its registration attributes.

The registration attributes and default values are shown in the following table:

Attribute	*Default Value*
Style field	cs_HRedraw or cs_VRedraw
Icon	Generic icon
Cursor	Stock arrow cursor
Background	Color system's window background color

Retrieve the name of the class to be registered by sending a message to `GetClassName`.

TWindow.Paint

```
procedure Paint(PaintDC: HDC; var PaintInfo: TPaintStruct);
virtual;
```

(Override: often) Acts as a placeholder for descendant types that define Paint methods. Paint receives a message automatically in response to a request (wm_Paint) from Windows to redisplay the window's contents.

Use PaintDC as the display context because it's obtained before the message is sent to Paint, and released after Paint. The PaintInfo paint structure sent contains information about the paint request.

TWindow.SetCaption

```
procedure SetCaption (ATitle : PChar);
```

Sets a TWindow caption.

TWindow.SetupWindow

```
procedure SetupWindow; virtual;
```

(Override: often) Sets up the newly created window. If the window is an MDI child window, SetupWindow sends a message to SetFocus to give the new window the focus. If the window has a scroller object, SetupWindow sends a message to SetSBarRange to set the range of its scroll bars.

TWindow.Store

```
procedure Store(var S: TStream);
```

Stores the window on the stream, S, by sending a message to TWindowsObject.Store and then writing and putting the additional fields (Attr and Scroller) introduced by TWindow.

TWindow.WMActivate

```
procedure WMActivate(var Msg: TMessage); virtual
  wm_First + wm_Activate;
```

(Override: sometimes) For windows that intercept keyboard messages for its controls, WMActivate responds to the window that loses and receives the focus by saving the handle of the child control that currently has the focus in FocusChildHandle and restoring the focus.

TWindow.WMCreate

```
procedure WMCreate(var Msg: TMessage); virtual; wm_First + wm_Create;
```

Responds to the `wm_Create` message by sending messages first to `Setup` Window and then `DefWndProc`. Because window creation is handled differently under ObjectWindows than under Windows, the `wm_Create` message needs to be trapped and used to set up window object attributes.

TWindow.WMHScroll

```
procedure WMHScroll(var Msg: TMessage); virtual;
  wm_First + wm_HScroll;
```

(Sometimes) For windows with scrollers, `WMHScroll` responds to horizontal-window scroll bar events by sending messages to the scroller's `HScroll` method and `DefWndProc`.

TWindow.WMLButtonDown

```
procedure WMLButtonDown(var Msg: TMessage); virtual;
  wm_First + wm_LButtonDown;
```

(Override: sometimes) For windows with auto-scrolling scrollers, `WMLButtonDown` responds to a left mouse-button click by capturing all future mouse input until the mouse button is released. It also instructs Windows to send `wm_Timer` messages while the mouse button is down.

If you plan to override this method to process mouse clicks, but still plan to use auto-scrolling, be sure to send a message to this method from your `WMLButtonDown` method.

TWindow.WMMove

```
procedure WMMove(var Msg: TMsg); virtual; wm_First + wm_Move;
```

Updates `Attr.X` and `Attr.Y` when the `wm_Move` message is received.

If the window is iconic or zoomed, the message is ignored.

TWindow.WMPaint

```
procedure WMPaint(var Msg: TMessage); virtual; wm_First + wm_Paint;
```

(Override: seldom) Responds to the Windows `wm_Paint` message by sending a message to the window object's `Paint` method. If the window has a scroller, `WMPaint` sends a message to `BeginView` before sending messages to `Paint` and `EndView` after sending `Paint` a message.

TWindow.WMSize

```
procedure WMSize(var Msg: TMessage); virtual; wm_First +
wm_Size;
```

(Override: sometimes) For windows with scrollers, `WMSize` responds to a window-sizing event by sending a message to `SetPageSize` to adjust in response to the new window size.

TWindow.WMVScroll

```
procedure WMVScroll(var Msg: TMessage); virtual; wm_First +
wm_VScroll;
```

(Override: sometimes) For windows with scrollers, `WMVScroll` responds to vertical-window scroll bar events by sending messages to the scroller's `VScroll` method and `DefWndProc`.

B

REFERENCE

ObjectWindows Constants

bf_XXXX Constants

Buttons, check boxes, and radio-button objects use `bf_` constants to define their three possible states.

ObjectWindows defines the following button-flag constants:

Constant	*Value*	*Meaning*
bf_Unchecked	0	Item is unchecked
bf_Checked	1	Item is checked
bf_Grayed	2	Item is grayed

cm_XXXX Constants

ObjectWindows contains several constants that define the ranges of command-message constants:

Constant	*Value*	*Meaning*
cm_First	$A000	Beginning of command messages
cm_Count	$6000	Number of command messages
cm_Internal	$FF00	Beginning of command messages reserved for internal use.
cm_Reserved		cm_Internal – cm_First

ObjectWindows defines `cm_` constants for three standard menus; File, Edit, and Window:

Constant	*Value*	*Menu Equivalent*
cm_Reserved	cm_Internal – cm_First;	None
cm_EditCut	cm_Reserved + 0	Edit | Cut
cm_EditCopy	cm_Reserved + 1	Edit | Copy
cm_EditPaste	cm_Reserved + 2	Edit | Paste
cm_EditDelete	cm_Reserved + 3	Edit | Delete
cm_EditClear	cm_Reserved + 4	Edit | Clear
cm_EditUndo	cm_Reserved + 5	Edit | Undo
cm_EditFind	cm_Reserved + 6	Search | Find
cm_EditReplace	cm_Reserved + 7	Search | Replace
cm_EditFindNext	cm_Reserved + 8	Search | Search Again
cm_FileNew	cm_Reserved + 9	File | New
cm_FileOpen	cm_Reserved + 10	File | Open
cm_MDIFileNew	cm_Reserved + 11	File | New
cm_MDIFileOpen	cm_Reserved + 12	File | Open
cm_FileSave	cm_Reserved + 13	File | Save
cm_FileSaveAs	cm_Reserved + 14	File | Save As
cm_ArrangeIcons	cm_Reserved + 15	Window | Arrange Icons
cm_TileChildren	cm_Reserved + 16	Window | Tile
cm_CascadeChildren	cm_Reserved + 17	Window | Cascade
cm_CloseChildren	cm_Reserved + 18	Window | Close All
cm_CreateChild	cm_Reserved + 19	Window | Open
cm_Exit	cm_Reserved + 20	File | Exit

coXXXX Constants

coXXXX constants are sent as the Code parameter to the TCollection.Error method when a TCollection object detects an error during an operation.

ObjectWindows defines the following standard error codes for all ObjectWindows collections:

Error Code	*Value*	*Meaning*	*Error Origin*
coIndexError	–1	Index out of range	The Info parameter passed to the Error method contains the invalid index.
coOverflow	–2	Collection overflow	SetLimit failed to expand the collection to the requested size.

The Info parameter passed to the Error method contains the requested size.

em_XXXX Constants

Several standard error conditions are flagged by ObjectWindows constants starting with em_.

ObjectWindows defines the following error flags:

Constant	*Value*	*Meaning*
em_OutOfMemory	–2	A memory allocation used the safety pool.
em_InvalidClient	–3	An MDI client window could not be created.
em_InvalidChild	–4	One or more of the window's children is not valid.
em_InvalidWindow	–1	Window is invalid because Create did not succeed.
em_InvalidMainWindow	–5	Main window could not be created.

id_XXXX Constants

ObjectWindows has several constants that define the ranges of child ID messages:

Constant	*Value*	*Meaning*
id_First	$8000	Start of child ID messages
id_Count	$1000	Number of child ID messages
id_Reserved	$8F00	Reserved for internal use
id_InternalOffset	id_Internal – id_First;	Internal offset
id_FirstMDIChild	id_InternalOffset + 1	Base for child ID numbers
id_MDIClient	id_InternalOffset + 2	Child ID number of the MDI client window

nf_XXXX Constants

ObjectWindows has several constants that define the ranges of notification messages:

Constant	*Value*	*Meaning*
nf_First	$9000	Beginning of notification messages
nf_Count	$1000	Number of notification messages
nf_Internal	$9F00	Beginning of notification messages reserved for internal use

stXXXX Constants

Two sets of constants begin with `st`. These are used by the ObjectWindows streams system.

`TDosStream` and `TBufStream` use the following stream-access-mode constants to determine the file-access mode for a file that is opened for an ObjectWindows stream:

Constant	*Value*	*Meaning*
stCreate	$3C00	Create new file
stOpenRead	$3D00	Open a file for reading only
stOpenWrite	$3D01	Open a file for writing only
stOpen	$3D02	Open a file for reading and writing

The following values are returned by `TStream.Error` in the `TStream.ErrorInfo` field when a stream error occurs:

Error Code	*Value*	*Meaning*
stOk	0	No error
stError	–1	Access error
stInitError	–2	Cannot initialize the stream
stReadError	–3	Read beyond end of stream
stWriteError	–4	Cannot expand the stream
stGetError	–5	Get unregistered object type
stPutError	–6	Put unregistered object type

tf_XXXX Constants

The Transfer method uses flag constants beginning with `tf_`. ObjectWindows defines the following transfer function constants:

Constant	*Value*	*Meaning*
tf_SizeData	0	Determine the size of data transferred by the object
tf_GetData	1	Get data from the object
tf_SetData	2	Send data to set the value of the object

wb_XXXX Constants

The Flags field in `TWindowsObject` is a bit-mapped field. You can access these bits with constants beginning with `wb_`.

ObjectWindows defines the following values:

Constant	*Value*	*Meaning If Set*
wb_KeyboardHandler	$01	Window handles key events like a dialog.
wb_FromResource	$02	Dialog was loaded from a resource.
wb_AutoCreate	$04	Window is created when parent window is created.
wb_MDIChild	$08	Window is an MDI child window.
wb_Transfer	$10	Window participates in the Transfer mechanism. By default, this bit is set by InitResource and cleared by Init.

wm_XXXX Constants

ObjectWindows has several constants related to standard Windows messages. These define the ranges of messages that are reserved for Windows.

ObjectWindows defines the following window message constants:

Constant	*Value*	*Meaning*
wm_First	$0000	Beginning of Windows messages
wm_Count	$8000	Number of Windows messages

C

REFERENCE

OBJECTWINDOWS PROCEDURES AND FUNCTIONS

ObjectWindows has a number of procedures and functions that are separate from the ObjectWindows objects. These procedures and functions are defined in this reference chapter.

`Abstract`	procedure
`AllocMultiSel`	function
`DisposeStr`	procedure
`FreeMultiSel`	procedure
`GetObjectPtr`	function
`LongDiv`	function
`LongMul`	function
`LowMemory`	function
`MemAlloc`	function
`NewStr`	function
`RegisterType`	procedure
`RegisterWObjects`	procedure
`RestoreMemory`	procedure

Abstract

Calling this procedure terminates the program with run-time error 211.

```
procedure Abstract;
```

Use the `Abstract` procedure when you implement abstract object types to ensure that descendant types override virtual ancestor behavior.

AllocMultiSel

Allocates a `TMultiSelRec` with `Count` selections and sufficient space in the `Selections` field to hold `Count` selections (0..`Count-1`).

```
function AllocMultiSel(Count: Integer): PMultiSelRec;
```

Returns nil if there is not enough memory to allocate the entire record.

DisposeStr

A memory-management procedure; destroys the string pointed to by P.

```
procedure DisposeStr(P: PString);
```

FreeMultiSel

Frees a `TMultiSelRec` record allocated by `AllocMultiSel`.

```
procedure FreeMultiSel(P: PMultiSelRec);
```

GetObjectPtr

A memory-management function. Returns a pointer to the Windows object specified by HWindow.

```
function GetObjectPtr(HWindow: HWnd): PWindowsObject;
```

LongDiv

An optimized inline assembly-coded function for handling integer division. Returns the integer value X/Y.

```
function LongDiv(X: Longint; Y: Integer): Integer;
   inline($59/$58/$5A/$F7/$F9);
```

LongMul

An optimized, in-line assembly-coded multiplication function. Returns the long integer value X * Y.

```
function longmul(X, Y: Integer): Longint;
   inline($5A/$58/$f7/$EA);
```

LowMemory

If a memory allocation uses memory in the safety pool at the end of the heap, LowMemory returns True.

The safety pool size is determined by the SafetyPoolSize variable.

Resources and applications that use much memory (such as complex dialog boxes) should be programmed to check LowMemory to ensure that their memory demand does not exceed available memory.

```
function LowMemory: Boolean;
```

MemAlloc

Allocates Size bytes of memory on the heap and returns a pointer to the allocated block. If the requested block cannot be allocated, MemAlloc returns nil.

```
function MemAlloc(Size: Word): Pointer;
```

MemAlloc does not allow the allocation to use the safety pool. You can dispose of a block allocated by MemAlloc using the standard procedure FreeMem.

NewStr

A memory-management function. Creates space for a new string and returns a pointer to it.

```
function Newstr(S: String): PString;
```

RegisterType

If an ObjectWindows type is used in stream input and output, you must register the object type using this method.

```
procedure RegisterType(var S: TStreamRec);
```

Standard object types are preregistered with `ObjType` values in the reserved range 0..99.

`RegisterType` creates an entry in a linked list of `TStreamRec` records.

RegisterWObjects

A stream procedure used to register WObjects.

```
procedure RegisterWObjects;
```

RestoreMemory

A memory-management procedure. Re-establishes the memory state that existed before an attempt to execute another program (using WinExec).

```
procedure RestoreMemory;
```

D

REFERENCE

OBJECTWINDOWS RECORDS

LongRec
PtrRec
TDialogAttr
TMessage
TMultiSelRec
TScrollBarTransferRec
TStreamRec
TWindowAttr
WordRec

LongRec

LongRec is a record type for handling double-word-length variables.

```
LongRec = record
     Lo, Hi: Word;
end;
```

PtrRec

`PtrRec` holds the offset and segment values of a pointer.

```
PtrRec = record
     Ofs, Seg: Word;
end;
```

TDialogAttr

`TDialogAttr` holds attribute values for `TDialog` objects.

```
TDialogAttr = record
     Name: PChar;
     Param: Longint;
end;
```

TMessage

The message-processing loop in `TApplication` stores Windows message information in `TMessage` records. This information is passed to the appropriate message-response method.

```
TMessage = record
    Receiver: HWnd;
    Message: Word;
    case Integer of
      0: (WParam: Word;
          LParam: Longint;
          Result: Longint);
      1:  (WParamLo: Byte;
          WParamHi: Byte;
          LParamLo: Word;
          LParamHi: Word;
          ResultLo: Word;
          ResultHi: Word);
    end;
```

TMultiSelRec

TMultiSelRec holds a list of selected items for transfer to or from a multiple-selection list box.

```
TMultiSelRec = record
   Count: Integer;
   Selections: array[0..0] of Integer;
end;
```

- Count indicates the number of selected items.
- Selections is an open-ended array of integers.

Using AllocMultiSel, you can allocate a record with enough selection items to accommodate all list-box items.

TScrollBarTransferRec

Before you can load or store objects on a TStream, you must register any ObjectWindows object types using a TStreamRec.

```
{ TScrollBar transfer record }
  TScrollBarTransferRec = record
    LowValue: Integer;
    HighValue: Integer;
    Position: Integer;
end;
```

TStreamRec

The RegisterType procedure registers an object type by setting a TStreamRec record for it.

```
TStreamRec = record
   ObjType: Word;
   VmtLink: Word;
   Load: Pointer;
   Store: Pointer;
   Next: Word;
end;
```

The fields in the stream-registration record are defined as follows:

Field	*Contents*
ObjType	Unique numerical ID for the object type
VmtLink	Link to the object type's virtual-method table entry
Load	Pointer to the object type's Load constructor
Store	Pointer to the object type's `Store` method
Next	Pointer to the next `TStreamRec`

ObjectWindows reserves object-type `ID`s (ObjType) with values from 0 to 999 for its own use. You can define your own object-type `ID`s in the range 1,000 to 65,535.

By convention, a `TStreamRec` for a `Txxxx` object type is called `Rxxxx`. For example, the `TStreamRec` for a `TCalculator` type is called `RCalculator`:

```
type
   TCalculator = object(TDialog)
     constructor Load(var S: TStream);
     procedure Store(var S: TStream);
     ...
   end;

const
   RCalculator: TStreamRec = (
     ObjType: 2099;
     VmtLink: Ofs(TypeOf(TCalculator)^);
     Load: @TCalculator.Load;
     Store: @TCalculator.Store);
begin
   RegisterType(RCalculator);
   ...
end;
```

TWindowAttr

`TWindow` objects define their attributes in `TWindowAttr` records.

```
TWindowAttr = record
   Title: PChar;
   Style: Longint;
   ExStyle: Longint;
   X, Y, W, H: Integer;
```

```
  Param: Pointer;
  case Integer of
    0: (Menu: HMenu);      { window menu's handle or... }
    1: (Id: Integer);      { control's child identifier }
 end;
```

WordRec

WordRec is a utility record that lets you access the Lo and Hi bytes of a word.

```
WordRec = record
  Lo, Hi: Byte;
end;
```

E

REFERENCE

THE WINCRT UNIT

The Turbo Pascal for Windows `WinCrt` unit implements a terminal-like text screen in a window. If your application uses `WinCrt`, it does not have to contain any Windows-specific code. This unit is useful for reimplementing existing Turbo Pascal text-based applications in Windows, without adding much extra code.

To use the `WinCrt` unit, include it in your application's uses clause:

```
uses WinCrt;
```

Table E.1. *`WinCrt` procedures and functions.*

Procedure or Function	***Value***
AssignCrt	Associates a text file with the CRT window
ClrEol	Clears all characters from the current cursor position to the end of the line
ClrScr	Clears the screen and returns cursor to the upper-left corner of the screen
CursorTo	Moves the cursor to the specified coordinates in a virtual screen
DoneWinCrt	Destroys the CRT window

continues

Table E.1. continued

Procedure or Function	*Value*
GotoXY	Moves the cursor to the specified coordinates in a virtual screen
InitWinCrt	Creates the CRT window
KeyPressed	Returns True when the user presses a key
ReadBuf	Inputs one line from the CRT window
ReadKey	Reads one character from the keyboard
ScrollTo	Scrolls the CRT window to a specific screen location
TrackCursor	Scrolls the CRT window to keep cursor visible
WhereX	Returns the X coordinate of the current cursor location
WhereY	Returns the Y coordinate of the current cursor location
WriteBuf	Writes a block of characters to the CRT window
WriteChar	Writes one character to the CRT window

AssignCrt

Associates a text file with the CRT window.

```
procedure AssignCrt(var F: Text);
```

For example:

```
program sample;
uses
    WinCrt;

var
  AScreenFile: Text;

begin
  AssignCRT(AScreenFile);
```

```
  Rewrite(AScreenFile);
  Writeln(AScreenFile,'AScreenFile to screen.');
  Close(AScreenFile);
end.
```

ClrEol

Clears all the characters from the cursor position to the end of the line without moving the cursor.

```
procedure ClrEol;
```

For example:

```
program sample;
uses
     WinCrt;

begin
  Writeln('String here.');
  Writeln('Press a key...');
  Readln;
  CursorTo(16,10);
  ClrEol;
end.
```

ClrScr

Clears the screen and returns the cursor to the upper-left corner of the screen.

```
procedure ClrScr;
```

For example:

```
program sample;
uses
     WinCrt;

begin
  Writeln('Hi. Press a key...');
  Readln;
  ClrScr;
end.
```

CursorTo

Moves the cursor to the specified coordinates in a virtual screen.

```
procedure CursorTo(X, Y: Integer);
```

The upper-left corner of the CRT window is represented by the coordinates 0,0. `CursorTo` sets the `Cursor` variable to (X,Y). For example:

```
program sample;
uses
     WinCrt;

begin
  CursorTo(18,15);
  Writeln('18/15 coordinates.');
end.
```

DoneWinCrt

Destroys any existing CRT.

```
procedure DoneWinCrt;
```

Calling `DoneWinCrt` before an application terminates prevents the CRT window from entering an inactive state. For example:

```
program sample;
uses
     WinCrt;

begin
  Writeln('This is a CRT window.');
  Writeln('Return.');
  Readln;
  DoneWinCRT;
  Writeln('This is another CRT window.');
end.
```

GotoXY

Moves the cursor to the specified coordinates with a virtual screen.

```
procedure GotoXY(X, Y: Integer);
```

The upper-left corner of the virtual screen corresponds to the coordinates 1,1.

Use `CursorTo` rather than `GotoXY` when you develop new Windows applications. `GotoXY` is available strictly for compatibility with the Crt unit of DOS-based Turbo Pascal. For example:

```
program sample;
uses
     WinCrt;

begin
  GotoXY(20,20);
  Writeln('Hi');
end.
```

InitWinCrt

Creates the CRT window.

```
procedure InitWinCrt;
```

If you use `Read`, `Readln`, `Write`, or `Writeln` in a file that has been assigned to the CRT, `InitWinCrt` is called automatically for you. For example:

```
program sample;
uses
     Strings,
     WinCrt,
     WinDOS;

begin
  StrCopy(WindowTitle,'CRT Window created by InitWinCRT.');
  InitWinCRT;
end.
```

KeyPressed

Decides whether the user has pressed a key.

```
function KeyPressed: Boolean;
```

Use `ReadKey` to read the key.

Return	*Value*
True	If a key has been pressed
False	If a key has not been pressed

For example:

```
program sample;
uses
     WinCrt;

begin
  repeat
     Write('A continuous string');
  until KeyPressed;
end.
```

ReadBuf

Inputs a line from the CRT window.

```
function ReadBuf(Buffer: PChar; Count: Word): Word;
```

`Buffer` points to a line buffer that has space for `Count` number of characters. `Count` holds the number of characters to read in the buffer.

Up to `Count - 2` characters can be inserted. An end-of-line marker (a #13 followed by a #10) is automatically appended to the line when the user presses Enter (Return). The command returns the number of characters read, including the end-of-line or end-of-file marker. For example:

```
program sample;
uses
     WinCrt;

var
```

```
  Chars: PChar;

begin
  GetMem(Chars, 20);
  Chars := #20#0#0#0#0#0#0#0#0#0#0#0#0#0#0#0#0#0#0#0;
  Writeln('Enter a phrase:');
  ReadBuf(Chars, 20);
  Writeln(' You entered: '); Writeln(Chars);
end.
```

ReadKey

Reads a character from the keyboard.

```
function ReadKey: Char;
```

The character is not echoed on the screen. For example:

```
program sample;
uses
     WinCrt;

var
  AChar: Char;

begin
  Writeln('Press a key');
  AChar := Readkey;
  Writeln(' You pressed ', AChar, '.');
end.
```

ScrollTo

Scrolls the CRT window to display the virtual screen location specified by X,Y in the upper-left corner.

```
procedure ScrollTo(X, Y: Integer);
```

The upper-left corner of the virtual screen corresponds to the coordinates 0,0. For example:

```
program sample;
uses
     WinCrt;

begin
  GotoXY(10,20);
  Writeln('Hi');
  Writeln('Enter a line and Return.');
  Readln;
  ScrollTo(0,8);
end.
```

TrackCursor

Scrolls the CRT window if necessary to make the cursor visible.

```
procedure TrackCursor;
```

For example:

```
program sample;
uses
     WinCrt;

var
  I: integer;

begin
  for I := 1 to 20 do
    Write('CursoR');
  TrackCursor;
  Readln;
end.
```

WhereX

Returns the X coordinate of the current cursor position.

```
function WhereX: Integer;
```

For example:

```
program sample;
uses
     WinCrt;

begin
  Writeln(WhereX, 'WhereX.');
end.
```

WhereY

Returns the Y coordinate of the current cursor position.

```
function WhereY: Integer;
```

For example:

```
program sample;
uses
     WinCrt;

begin
     Writeln(WhereY, 'WhereY.');
end.
```

WriteBuf

Writes a specified block of characters to the CRT window.

```
procedure WriteBuf(Buffer: PChar; Count: Word);
```

`Buffer` points to the first character in the block. `Count` holds the number of characters to write to the buffer.

If `AutoTracking` is on, the CRT window scrolls to make certain that the cursor is visible after writing the block of characters. For example:

```
program sample;
uses
     WinCrt;

var
  ABuffer: PChar;

begin
  GetMem(ABuffer, 100);
  ABuffer := 'WriteBuf';
  WriteBuf(ABuffer, 100);
end.
```

WriteChar

Writes one character to the CRT window.

```
procedure WriteChar(Ch: Char);
```

For example:

```
program sample;
uses
     WinCrt;

begin
  WriteChar('F');
end.
```

F

REFERENCE

A WINCRT EXAMPLE

The following application implements a minibrowser that traces a hierarchy of objects in either Turbo Pascal or C++. It was originally written in Turbo Pascal for DOS, but required almost no changes to be compiled with Turbo Pascal for Windows and run as a Windows application.

The main addition to this version is the `WinCrt` unit, which implements a text window in Windows for the application's output. The application is far from complete and could use many additions to be useful as a browser, but it illustrates how a typical Turbo Pascal DOS-based (and object-oriented) application can be run (with little modification) in Windows. It uses object-oriented techniques, but not the ObjectWindows library.

The application consists of a main module and two units (nodes2 and cell list), which are printed here.

This minibrowser module reconstructs an object hierarchy from either Pascal or C++ source code. The reconstruction problem can be dissected into several smaller problems:

- Getting a "key" object from a user
- Searching a specified project's files for keywords that reconstruct a hierarchy for that "key" object
- Displaying the results or allowing a user to edit the files containing objects in the hierarchy

A user specifies an object she wants to know about. The minibrowser then reads a project file (to learn the files for use in building a hierarchy). It then reconstructs either a C++ or Turbo Pascal hierarchy, depending on the language you specify at run-time. The methods `Init_files` and `Init_Types` handle file- and hierarchy-type initialization.

The minibrowser (through the `Hierarchy` object) then searches the files specified in the project file, first for base types—"objects" or "classes"—(through the base method), and then for derived types (through the derived method). If it finds a derived type, it determines its ancestor (through the ancestor method) and then recursively backtracks to its ancestor, adding the object name to a list as it goes. It then searches forward again for base and derived types. If it finds a base type, the search is over, and it sends a message to `BackTrack` to display the constructed hierarchy. Depending on whether you want to display or edit, it then sends a message to the appropriate object—`DisplayStr` or `Editor`.

Each part of the minibrowser is implemented as an "object," so you can easily modify and extend the big object (the minibrowser module) without changing its overall design by reimplementing selective objects. For example, the `Editor` object in the main module obtains file, line, and position information. To extend this module, add a method that passes this information to your editor of choice. One line of code (and an editor library) does the trick.

```
unit nodes2; { Contains abstract cell and cell-list types }

interface

uses
     CRT,
     DOS,
     cellist;
type

AnyTypePtr = ^AnyType;
AnyType = object(Node)
  constructor init;
  destructor done; virtual;
  procedure DSAction; virtual;      { Type Action  }
  procedure BTAction; virtual;      { Type Action  }
  procedure EditAction; virtual;    { Type Action  }
end;

AnyTypeListPtr = ^AnyTypeList;
AnyTypeList = object(List)
  constructor init;
  destructor Done; virtual;
```

```
procedure GetNodes; virtual;       { Process AnyTypeList }
end;

implementation
{ constructors }
constructor AnyType.init;      begin end;  { abstract }
constructor AnyTypeList.Init;  begin end;  { abstract }

{ destructors }

destructor AnyType.done;       begin end;  { abstract }
destructor AnyTypeList.Done;   begin end;  { abstract }

{ methods }

procedure AnyType.DSAction;     begin end; { abstract }
procedure AnyType.BTAction;     begin end; { abstract }
procedure AnyType.EditAction;   begin end; { abstract }
procedure AnyTypeList.GetNodes; begin end; { abstract }

end. { unit nodes2 }

unit cellist; { Contains base, node, and list types }

{$S-}
interface

type

{ Abstract base object type }
  BasePtr = ^Base;
  Base = object
    destructor Done; virtual;
  end;

{ Abstract linked list node type }
  NodePtr = ^Node;
  Node = object(Base)
    Next: NodePtr;
  end;

{ Simplified Linked list type }
  ListPtr = ^List;
  List = object(base)
```

```
    Last: NodePtr;
    procedure Append(N: NodePtr);
    procedure Clear;
    function First: NodePtr;
    function Next(N: NodePtr): NodePtr;
 end;

implementation
{ destructor }
destructor  Base.Done; begin end;
{ List methods }
procedure List.Append(N: NodePtr);
begin
  if Last = nil then Last := N
  else N^.Next := Last^.Next;
  Last^.Next := N;
  Last := N;
end;

procedure List.Clear;
begin  Last := nil; end;

function List.First: NodePtr;
begin
  if Last = nil then First := nil
  else First := Last^.Next;
end;

function List.Next(N: NodePtr): NodePtr;
begin
  if N = Last then Next := nil
  else Next := N^.Next;
end;

end. { Unit cell list }

{ Main module }

program browser;            { Contains specific browser }
uses
     WINCRT,                { Key unit needed for Windows }
     nodes2,
     cellist;
```

```
type

StringPtr = ^String;

BrowserListPtr = ^BrowserList;
BrowserList = object(AnyTypeList)
  constructor init;
  destructor done; virtual;
  procedure GetNodes; virtual;
end;

DisplayStrPtr = ^DisplayStr;
DisplayStr = object(AnyType)
  Value: StringPtr;
  constructor Init(V: String);
  destructor Done; virtual;
  procedure DSAction; virtual;     { Process a StrCell }
end;

BackTrackPtr = ^BackTrack;
BackTrack = object(AnyType)
  Value: StringPtr;
  constructor Init(V: String);
  destructor Done; virtual;
  procedure BTAction; virtual;     { Process a BTCell }
end;

EditPtr = ^Editor;
Editor = object(AnyType)
  FileName : String;
  Line     : String;
  LineNo   : word;
  Position : word;
  constructor Init(F: string; L: string; Ln: word; P: word);
  destructor Done; virtual;
  procedure EditAction; virtual;   { Edit }
end;

TextFile = object(base)
  F          : Text;
  FileName   : String;
  Line       : String;
  Buf        : array[0..8191] of char; { Buffer for faster I/O }
```

```
  LineNo    : word;
  Position  : word;
  function open_file: boolean;
end;

HierarchyPtr = ^hierarchy;
Hierarchy = object(TextFile)
  Recurse : boolean;
  Method : String;
  Language_type : char;
  End_type, Base_type, Derived_type       : string[30];
  Object_type, Search_type, Ancestor_type : String[30];
  function base       : boolean;   { Looks for base types }
  function derived    : boolean;   { Looks for derived types }
  function ancestor   : boolean;   { Looks for ancestors }
  constructor     init;
  destructor      done; virtual;
  procedure init_types;   { Sets types for C++ or Pascal }
  procedure init_files;   { Sets files for C++ or Pascal }
  procedure construct;             { Flow controller }
  procedure Reconstruct;  { Calls construct and simplifies recursion}
  procedure update_backtrack_list; { Keeps track of types }
  procedure find_methods;          { Finds methods }
end;

var                         { Globals }
  Display, Edit : boolean;
  H      : HierarchyPtr;
  L      : BrowserListPtr;
  P      : AnyTypePtr;

{ Constructors }

constructor DisplayStr.Init(V: String);
begin
  GetMem(Value, Length(V) + 1);
  Value^ := V;
end;

constructor BackTrack.Init(V: String);
begin
  GetMem(Value, Length(V) + 1);
  Value^ := V;
end;
```

```
constructor Editor.Init(F: string; L: string; Ln: word; P: word);
begin
  FileName := F;
  Line     := L;
  LineNo   := Ln;
  Position := P;
end;

constructor Hierarchy.init;   begin end;
constructor BrowserList.init; begin end;

{destructors }

destructor Editor.Done; begin end;

destructor DisplayStr.Done;
begin  FreeMem(Value, Length(Value^) + 1); end;

destructor BackTrack.Done;
begin  FreeMem(Value, Length(Value^) + 1); end;

destructor  Hierarchy.done;   begin end;
destructor  BrowserList.done; begin end;

{ Methods }


procedure DisplayStr.DSAction;
var
  Ch : char;
begin
  writeln(Value^);
  Ch := readkey;
end;

procedure BackTrack.BTAction;      { Show the object hierarchy }
begin  writeln(Value^); end;

procedure Editor.EditAction;
var Ch : char;
begin
  writeln(#13, #10,'File      = ',FileName);
```

```
  writeln('Line      = ',Line);
  writeln('LineNumber= ',LineNo);
  writeln('Position  = ',Position);
  { Call editor here and pass it appropriate information. }
end;

procedure hierarchy.init_types;
begin
  case Language_type of
  'p': begin                        { Pascal }
         Base_type := ' = object';
         Derived_type := ' = object(';
         End_type := 'end';
       end;
  'c': begin                        { C++ }
         Base_type := 'class ';
         Derived_type := ' :';
         End_type := '}';
       end;
  end; { case }
end;

procedure hierarchy.init_files;
begin
  case Language_type of
  'p': FileName := 'cltest2.pas';  { Pascal }
  'c': FileName := 'cltest.cpp';   { C++ }
  end;  { case }
{ Add functions here to read a project's files }
end;

procedure hierarchy.find_methods;
var
  NextLine     : string;
  TempPosition : word;
begin
  Method := '';
  NextLine := Line;
  TempPosition := 0;
  While (TempPosition = 0) do
  begin
    TempPosition := Pos(End_type,NextLine);
    Method := Method + NextLine + #13 + #10;
    readln(F,NextLine);
```

```
  end;
  L^.Append(New(DisplayStrPtr,Init(Method)));

L^.Append(New(EditPtr,Init(FileName,Line,LineNo,Position)));
end;

function hierarchy.base: boolean;
begin
  LineNo := 1;
  case Language_type of
  'p': Search_type := Object_type + Base_type;
  'c': Search_type := Base_type + Object_type;
  end; { case }
  while not eof(F) do
  begin
    readln(F,Line);
    Position := Pos(Search_type,Line);
    If (Position > 0) then
    begin
      Position := Pos(Derived_type,Line);
      If (Position = 0) then
        begin
          find_methods;
          base := true;
          exit;
        end;
    end;
    inc(LineNo);
  end;
  base := false;
end;

function hierarchy.derived: boolean;
begin
  case Language_type of
  'p': Search_type := Object_type + Derived_type;
  'c': Search_type := Base_type + Object_type + Derived_type;
  end; { case }
  LineNo := 1;
  while not eof(F) do
  begin
    readln(F,Line);
    Position := Pos(Search_type,Line);
    If (Position > 0) then
```

```
    begin
      If ancestor then
      begin
        find_methods;
        derived := true;
        exit;
      end;
    end;
    inc(LineNo);
  end;
  derived := false;
end;

function hierarchy.ancestor: boolean;
var
  T_Ancestor_type : string[30];
  I,J,L : integer;
begin
    Ancestor_type := '';
    T_Ancestor_type := '';
    I := Length(Line);              { Start at the end of the line }
    while (Line[I] = #32) do        { Space }
    dec(I);
    while (Line[I] = ')') do        { Empty in C++ }
    dec(I);
    case Language_type of
    'c':
      while (Line[I] <> #32) do     { Space }
      begin
        T_Ancestor_type := T_Ancestor_type + Line[I];
        dec(I);
      end;
    'p':
      while (Line[I] <> '(') do
      begin
        T_Ancestor_type := T_Ancestor_type + Line[I];
        dec(I);
      end;
    end; { case }

      L := Length(T_Ancestor_type);
      for I := L downto 1 do        { Reverse the list }
         Ancestor_type := Ancestor_type + T_Ancestor_type[I];
end;
```

```
procedure hierarchy.update_backtrack_list;
begin
  L^.Append(New(BackTrackPtr, Init(Object_type)));
end;

function TextFile.open_file: boolean;
begin
  {$I-}                     { Test for I/O error }
  assign(F,FileName);
  Reset(f);
  {$I+}
  Open_file := (IOResult = 0);
end;

procedure hierarchy.Reconstruct;
var
    Count : integer;

begin
  Count := 1;
  Recurse := true;          { Still more ancestors }
  While Count < 10 do
  While Recurse do          { Recursively backtrack for ancestors }
  begin
    construct;
    inc(Count);
  end;
end;

procedure hierarchy.construct;
begin
  If Open_file then         { If open successful }
  begin
    SetTextBuf(F,buf);
    update_backtrack_list;
    Close(F);
    If Open_file then
      If Derived then       { If derived class, find its ancestor }
      begin
          Object_type := ancestor_type;    { Set up for backtrack }
          Close(F);
          Recurse := true;         { Still more ancestors }
      end
    ELSE
```

```
      Close(F);
      IF Open_file then
      If Base then            { If base type, you are done. }
      begin
        Close(F);
        Recurse := false;     { No more ancestors }
      end;
    end;
  end;

  procedure display_mode;
  var Ch : char;
  begin
    write('e-Edit or d-display ');   { Display/edit option }
    Ch := Readkey;
    writeln;
    If Ch = 'e' then Edit := true
    Else Display := true;
  end;

  procedure BrowserList.GetNodes;   { Process the browser list }
  begin
    P  := AnyTypePtr(First);        { Set pointer to first node }
    while P <> nil do
    begin
      P^.BTAction;
      P := AnyTypePtr(Next(P));
    end;

    If Display = true then          { Is it displaying ? }
    begin
      P  := AnyTypePtr(First);
      while P <> nil do
      begin
        P^.DSAction;
        P := AnyTypePtr(Next(P));
      end;
    end;

    If Edit = true then             { Editing ? }
    begin
      P  := AnyTypePtr(First);
      while P <> nil do
      begin
```

```
      P^.EditAction;
      P := AnyTypePtr(Next(P));
    end;
  end;
end;

{ main }

begin
  Clrscr;
  Edit := false;           { Initializations }
  Display := false;
  New(L,init);             { Initialize a new browser list }
  L^.clear;
  New(H,init);             { Initialize a new hierarchy list }
  write('Enter Language — p or c : ');
  readln(H^.Language_type);
  write('Enter Object: ');
  readln(H^.Object_type);
  writeln;
  H^.Init_files;
  H^.Init_types;
  H^.ReConstruct;
  display_mode;            { Set display or edit }
  L^.GetNodes;             { Process the browser list }
  Dispose(L,Done);         { Clean up }
  Dispose(H,Done);

end. { main }
```

G

REFERENCE

THE STRINGS UNIT

The Strings unit supports a class of character strings terminated by a null byte, called *null-terminated strings*. The Windows Application Programming Interface (API) requires this format.

Null-terminated strings differ from typical Turbo Pascal strings, whose length is determined by a length byte.

A Turbo Pascal string is limited to 255 characters. The size of a null-terminated string is limited by the data segment (64K).

The Strings unit has many functions and procedures for manipulating null-terminated strings and for converting null-terminated strings to Turbo Pascal strings. Table G.1 lists the functions and procedures in the strings unit.

Table G.1. *Strings unit functions.*

Function Name	***Description***
StrCat	Appends a copy of one string to the end of another and returns the concatenated string
StrComp	Compares two strings
StrCopy	Copies one string to another
StrDispose	Disposes of a previously allocated string
StrECopy	Copies one string to another and returns a pointer to the end of the resulting string

continues

Table G.1. continued

Function Name	*Description*
StrEnd	Returns a pointer to the end of a string
StrIComp	Compares two strings without case sensitivity
StrLCat	Appends characters from a string to the end of another and returns the concatenated string
StrLComp	Copies characters from one string to another
StrLCopy	Compares two strings, up to a maximum length
StrLen	Returns the number of characters in `Str`
StrLIComp	Compares two strings, up to a maximum length, without case sensitivity
StrLower	Converts a string to lowercase
StrMove	Copies characters from one string to another
StrNew	Allocates a string on the heap
StrPas	Converts a null-terminated string to a Pascal style string
StrPCopy	Copies a Pascal style string to a null-terminated string
StrPos	Returns a pointer to the first occurrence of a string in another string
StrRScan	Returns a pointer to the first occurrence of a string in another string
StrScan	Returns a pointer to the first occurrence of a character in a string
StrUpper	Converts a string to uppercase

StrCat

Appends a copy of one string to the end of another string and returns the concatenated string.

```
function StrCat(Test, Source: PChar): PChar;
```

StrCat does not check the string length. The destination buffer must have space for at least StrLen(Test) + StrLen(Source) + 1 characters. For example:

```
program Sample;
uses
    Strings,
    WinCrt;

const
  Windows: PChar = 'Windows';
  Bible  : PChar = 'Bible';
var
  S: array[0..15] of Char;
begin
  StrCopy(S, Windows);
  StrCat(S, ' ');
  StrCat(S, Bible);
  Writeln(S);
end.
```

StrComp

Compares two strings.

```
function StrComp(Str1, Str2 : PChar): Integer;
```

Return Values:
<0 if Str1 < Str2
=0 if Str1 = Str2
>0 if Str1 > Str2

For example:

```
program Sample;
uses
     Strings,
     WinCrt;

var
  C: Integer;
  Result: PChar;
  S1, S2: array[0..79] of Char;
begin
```

```
  Readln(S1);
  Readln(S2);
  C := StrComp(S1, S2);
  if C < 0 then Result := ' is less than ' else
    if C > 0 then Result := ' is greater than ' else
      Result := ' is equal to ';
  Writeln(S1, Result, S2);
end.
```

StrCopy

Copies one string to another.

```
function StrCopy(Test, Source: PChar): PChar;
```

`StrCopy` does not check the string length. The destination buffer must have room for at least `StrLen(Source) + 1` characters. For example:

```
program Sample;
uses
     Strings,
     WinCrt;

var
  S: array[0..15] of Char;
begin
  StrCopy(S, 'Windows Bible');
  Writeln(S);
end.
```

StrDispose

Disposes of a string on a heap.

```
function StrDispose(Str: PChar);
```

`StrDispose` disposes of a string that was previously allocated with `StrNew`. If `Str` is nil, `StrDispose` does not do anything. For example:

```
program Sample;
uses
     Strings,
     WinCrt;
```

```
var
  P: PChar;
  S: array[0..79] of Char;
begin
  Readln(S);
  P := StrNew(S);
  Writeln(P);
  StrDispose(P);
end.
```

StrECopy

Copies one string to another string and returns a pointer to the end of the new string.

```
function StrECopy(Test, Source: Pchar): PChar;
```

StrECopy does not check the string length. The destination buffer must have space for at least StrLen(Source) + 1 characters. For example:

```
program Sample;
uses
     Strings,
     WinCrt;

const
  Windows: PChar = 'Windows';
  Bible  : PChar = 'Bible';
var
  S: array[0..15] of Char;
begin
  StrECopy(StrECopy(StrECopy(S, Windows), ' '), Bible);
  Writeln(S);
end.
```

StrEnd

Returns a pointer to the end of a string.

```
function StrEnd(Str: PChar): Pchar;
```

For example:

```
program Sample;
uses
     Strings,
     WinCrt;

var
  S: array[0..79] of Char;
begin
  Readln(S);
  Writeln('String length is ', StrEnd(S) - S);
end.
```

StrIComp

Compares two strings without case sensitivity.

```
function StrIComp(Str1, Str2:PChar): Integer;
```

For example:

```
program Sample;
uses
     Strings,
     WinCrt;

var
  Result: PChar;
  S1, S2: array[0..79] of Char;
begin
  Readln(S1);
  Readln(S2);
  if StrLComp(S1, S2, 8) = 0 then
    Result := 'equal'
  else
    Result := 'not equal';
  Writeln('The first eight characters are ', Result);
end.
```

StrLCat

Appends characters from one string to the end of another string and returns the concatenated string.

```
function StrLCat(Test, Source: PChar; MaxLen: Word): PChar;
```

For example:

```
program Sample;
uses
     Strings,
     WinCrt;

var
  S: array[0..9] of Char;
begin
  StrLCopy(S, 'This', SizeOf(S) - 1)
  StrLCat(S, ' ', SizeOf(S) - 1);
  StrLCat(S, 'String', SizeOf(S) - 1);
  Writeln(S);
end.
```

StrLComp

Compares two strings, up to a maximum length.

```
function StrLComp(Str1, Str2: PChar; MaxLen: Word): Integer;
```

For example:

```
program Sample;
uses
     Strings,
     WinCrt;

var
  Result: PChar;
  S1, S2: array[0..79] of Char;
begin
  Readln(S1);
  Readln(S2);
  if StrLComp(S1, S2, 8) = 0 then
    Result := 'equal'
  else
    Result := 'not equal';
  Writeln('The first eight characters are ', Result);
end.
```

StrLCopy

Copies characters from one string to another string.

```
function StrLCopy(Test, Source: PChar; MaxLen: Word): PChar;
```

For example:

```
program Sample;
uses
     Strings,
     WinCrt;

var
  S: array[0..9] of Char;
begin
  StrLCopy(S, 'A string', SizeOf(S) - 1);
  Writeln(S);
end.
```

StrLen

Returns the number of characters in `Str`.

```
function StrLen(Str: PChar): Word;
```

For example:

```
program Sample;
uses
     Strings,
     WinCrt;

var
  S: array[0..79] of Char;
begin
  Readln(S);
  Writeln('String length is ', StrLen(S));
end.
```

StrLIComp

Compares two strings, up to a maximum length, without case sensitivity.

```
function StrLIComp(Str1, Str2: PChar; MaxLen: Word): Integer;
```

For example:

```
program Sample;
uses
     Strings,
     WinCrt;

var
  C: Integer;
  Result: PChar;
  S1, S2: array[0..79] of Char;
begin
  Readln(S1);
  Readln(S2);
  C := StrComp(S1, S2);
  if C < 0 then Result := ' is less than ' else
    if C > 0 then Result := ' is greater than ' else
      Result := ' is equal to ';
  Writeln(S1, Result, S2);
end.
```

StrLower

Converts a string to lowercase.

```
function StrLower(Str: PChar): PChar;
```

For example:

```
program Sample;
uses
     Strings,
     WinCrt;

var
  S: array[0..79] of Char;
begin
  Readln(S);
  Writeln(StrUpper(S)); Writeln(StrLower(S));
end.
```

StrMove

Copies characters from one string to another string.

```
function StrMove(Test, Source: PChar; Count: Word): PChar;
```

For example:

```
program Sample;
uses
     Strings,
     WinCrt;

{ Allocate a string on the heap }

function StrNew(S: PChar): PChar;
var
  L: Word;
  P: PChar;
begin
  if (S = nil) or (S^ = #0) then StrNew := nil else
  begin
    L := StrLen(S) + 1;
    GetMem(P, L);
    StrNew := StrMove(P, S, L);
  end;
end;
{ Dispose the string allocated on the heap }
procedure StrDispose(S: PChar);
begin
  if S <> nil then FreeMem(S, StrLen(S) + 1);
end;
```

StrNew

Allocates a string on the heap.

```
function StrNew(Str: PChar): PChar;;
```

`StrNew` allocates a copy of `Str` on the heap. If `Str` is nil or points to an empty string, `StrNew` returns nil and does not allocate space on the heap for the string. Otherwise, `StrNew` makes a duplicate of `Str`, determining the space needed by a call to the `GetMem` standard procedure. It returns a pointer to the duplicated string. The allocated space is `StrLen(Str) + 1` bytes long.

For example:

```
program Sample;
uses
     Strings,
     WinCrt;

function StrNew(S: PChar): PChar;
var
  L: Word;
  P: PChar;
begin
  if (S = nil) or (S^ = #0) then StrNew := nil else
  begin
    L := StrLen(S) + 1;
    GetMem(P, L);
    StrNew := StrMove(P, S, L);
  end;
end;
```

StrPas

Converts a null-terminated string to a Turbo Pascal string. For example:

```
program Sample;
uses
     Strings,
     WinCrt;

function StrPas(Str: PChar): PChar;

uses Strings, WinCrt;

var
  A: array[0..79] of Char;
  S: string[79];
begin
  Readln(A);
  S := StrPas(A);
  Writeln(S);
end.
```

StrPCopy

Copies a Turbo Pascal string to a null-terminated string.

```
function StrPCopy(Test: PChar; Source: String);
```

StrPCopy does not check the string length. The destination buffer must have space for at least Length(Source) + 1 characters. For example:

```
program Sample;
uses
     Strings,
     WinCrt;

var
  A: array[0..79] of Char;
  S: string[79];
begin
  Readln(S);
  StrPCopy(A, S);
  Writeln(A);
end.
```

StrPos

Returns a pointer to the first occurrence of a string in another string.

```
function StrPos(Str1, Str2: PChar): PChar;
```

Return Value:
0 if Str2 does not occur in Str1. For example:

```
program Sample;
uses
     Strings,
     WinCrt;

var
  P: PChar;
  S, SubStr: array[0..79] of Char;
begin
  Readln(S);
  Readln(SubStr);
```

```
  P := StrPos(S, SubStr);
  if P = nil then
    Writeln('String not found');
  else
    Writeln('String found at index ', P - S);
end.
```

StrRScan

Returns a pointer to the first occurrence of a string in another string.

```
function StrRScan(Str: PChar; Chr: Char): PChar;
```

Return Value:
0 if `Chr` does not occur in `Str`. For example:

```
program Sample;
uses
     Strings,
     WinCrt;

{Return a pointer to the name part of a full path name }

function NamePart(FileName: PChar): PChar;
var
  P: PChar;
begin
  P := StrRScan(FileName, '\');
  if P = nil then
  begin
    P := StrRScan(FileName, ':');
    if P = nil then P := FileName;
  end;
  NamePart := P;
end;
```

StrScan

Returns a pointer to the first occurrence of a character in a string.

```
function StrScan(Str: PChar; Chr: Char): PChar;
```

Return Value:
0 if `Chr` does not occur in `Str`. For example:

```
program Sample;
uses
     Strings,
     WinCrt;

{ Return true if file name has wild cards in it }

function HasWildcards(FileName: PChar): Boolean; begin
  HasWildcards := (StrScan(FileName, '*') <> nil) or
    (StrScan(FileName, '?') <> nil);
end;
```

StrUpper

Converts a string to uppercase.

```
function StrUpper(Str: PChar): PChar;
```

For example:

```
Program sample;
uses
     Strings,
     WinCrt;

var
  S: array[0..79] of Char;
begin
  Readln(S);
  Writeln(StrUpper(S));
  Writeln(StrLower(S));
end.
```

H

REFERENCE

THE TURBO PASCAL FOR WINDOWS SYSTEM UNIT

The System unit (SYSTEM.TPU) is the Turbo Pascal run-time library. It implements low-level, run-time support routines for all built-in features, such as file I/O, string-handling, floating point, and dynamic memory allocation.

Because all units and programs automatically use the System unit, you never need to refer to it in a `Uses` clause. Table H.1 lists the System unit's variables and constants. Table H.2 is an alphabetical index of all the procedures and functions in the System unit.

Table H.1. *System unit variables and typed constants.*

Variables (Uninitialized)		
Variable	***Type***	***Description***
Input	Text	Input standard file
Output	Text	Output standard file

continues

Table H.1. continued

Constants (Initialized Variables)			
Variable	***Type***	***Value***	***Description***
CmdLine	PChar	nil	Command line pointer
CmdShow	Integer	0	`CmdShow` parameters for `CreateWindow`
ErrorAddr	Pointer	nil	Run-time error address
ExitCode	Integer	0	Exit code
ExitProc	Pointer	nil	Exit procedure
FileMode	Byte	2	File open mode
HeapBlock	Word	8192	Heap block size
HeapError	Word	nil	Heap error function
HeapLimit	Word	1024	Heap small block limit
HeapList	Word	0	Heap segment list
HInstance	Word	0	Handle of this instance
HPrevInst	Word	0	Handle of previous instance
InOutRes	Integer	0	I/O result buffer
PrefixSeg	Word	0	Program segment prefix (PSP)
RandSeed	LongInt	0	Random seed

***Table H.2.** System procedures and functions.*

Procedure/Function	***Type***	***Use***
Abs	Func	Returns the absolute value of the argument
Addr	Func	Returns the address of a specified object
Append	Proc	Opens an existing file for appending
ArcTan	Func	Returns the arctangent of the argument

Procedure/Function	***Type***	***Use***
Assign	Proc	Assigns the name of an external file to a file variable
BlockRead	Proc	Reads one or more records into a variable
BlockWrite	Proc	Writes one or more records from a variable
Chr	Func	Returns a character with a specified ordinal number
Close	Proc	Closes an open file
Concat	Func	Concatenates a sequence of strings
Copy	Func	Returns a substring of a string
Cos	Func	Returns the cosine of the argument (x is an angle, in radians)
CSeg	Func	Returns the current value of the CS register
Dec	Proc	Closes an open file
Delete	Proc	Deletes a substring from a string
Dispose	Proc	Disposes a dynamic variable
DSeg	Func	Returns the current value of the DS register
Eof	Func	Returns the end-of-file status
Eoln	Func	Returns the end-of-line status of a text file
Erase	Proc	Erases an external file
Exit	Proc	Exits immediately from the current block
Exp	Func	Returns the exponential of the argument

continues

Table H.2. continued

Procedure/Function	*Type*	*Use*
FilePos	Func	Returns the current file position of a file
FileSize	Func	Returns the current size of a file
FillChar	Proc	Fills a specified number (count) of contiguous bytes with a specified value (can be type `Byte` or `Char`)
Flush	Proc	Flushes the buffer of a text file open for output
Frac	Func	Returns the fractional part of the argument
FreeMem	Proc	Disposes a dynamic variable of a specified size
GetDir	Proc	Returns the current directory of specified drive
GetMem	Proc	Creates a dynamic variable of the specified size and puts the address of the block in a pointer variable
Halt	Proc	Stops program execution and returns to the operating system
Hi	Func	Returns the high-order byte of the argument
Inc	Proc	Increments a variable
Insert	Proc	Inserts a substring into a string
Int	Func	Returns the integer part of the argument
IOResult	Func	Returns the status of the last I/O operation performed
Length	Func	Returns the dynamic length of a string
Ln	Func	Returns the natural logarithm of the argument

Procedure/Function	*Type*	*Use*
Lo	Func	Returns the low-order byte of the argument
MaxAvail	Func	Returns the size of the largest contiguous free block in the heap
MemAvail	Func	Returns the amount of all free memory in the heap
MkDir	Proc	Creates a subdirectory
Move	Proc	Copies bytes from source to destination
New	Proc	Creates a new dynamic variable and sets a pointer variable to point to it
Odd	Func	Tests whether the argument is an odd number
Ofs	Func	Tests whether the argument is an odd number
Ord	Func	Returns the ordinal number of an ordinal-type value
ParamCount	Func	Returns the number of parameters passed to the program on the command line
ParamStr	Func	Returns a specified command-line parameter
Pi	Func	Returns the value of pi
Pos	Func	Searches for a substring in a string
Pred	Func	Returns the predecessor of the argument
Ptr	Func	Converts a segment base and an offset address to a pointer-type value
Random	Func	Returns a random number

continues

Table H.2. continued

Procedure/Function	***Type***	***Use***
Randomize	Proc	Initializes the built-in random number generator with a random value (obtained from the system clock)
Read	Proc	For typed files, reads a file component into a variable. For text files, reads one or more values into one or more variables
Readln	Proc	Executes the Read procedure, then skips to the next line of the file
Rename	Proc	Renames an external file
Reset	Proc	Opens an existing file
Rewrite	Proc	Creates and opens a new file
Round	Func	Rounds a real-type value to an integer-type value
RunError	Proc	Halts program execution
ScrollTo	Proc	Scrolls the CRT window to show virtual screen location
Seek	Proc	Moves the current position of a file to a specified component
SeekEof	Func	Returns the end-of-file status of a file
SeekEoln	Func	Returns the end-of-line status of a file
Seg	Func	Returns the segment of a specified object
SetTextBuf	Proc	Assigns an I/O buffer to a text file
Sin	Func	Returns the sine of the argument

Procedure/Function	*Type*	*Use*
SizeOf	Func	Returns the number of bytes occupied by the argument
SPtr	Func	Retruns the current value of the SP register
Sqr	Func	Returns the square of the argument
Sqrt	Func	Returns the square root of the argument
SSeg	Func	Returns the current value of the SS register
Str	Proc	Converts a numeric value to a string
Succ	Func	Returns the successor of the argument
Swap	Func	Swaps the high- and low-order bytes of the argument
Trunc	Func	Truncates a real-type value to an integer-type value
Truncate	Proc	Truncates the file at the current file position
UpCase	Func	Converts a character to uppercase
Val	Proc	Converts a string value to its numeric representation
Write	Proc	For typed files, writes a variable into a file component; for text files, writes one or more values to the file
Writeln	Proc	Executes the `Write` procedure, then outputs an end-of-line marker to the file

I

REFERENCE

THE TURBO PASCAL FOR WINDOWS WINDOS UNIT

Constants

WinDos Constants include the following:

- Flag constants
- File-mode constants
- File-attribute constants
- File-name component string lengths
- FileSplit return flags

Flag Constants

The Flag constants test individual flag bits in the Flags register after a call to Intr or MsDos. They include the following:

Constant	*Value*
fCarry	$0001
fParity	$0004
fAuxiliary	$0010
fZero	$0040
fSign	$0080
fOverflow	$0800

File-mode Constants

File-handling procedures use `fmXXXX` constants when disk files are opened and closed.

The mode fields of Turbo Pascal for Windows' variables contain one of the following values:

Constant	*Value*
fmClosed	$D7B0
fmInput	$D7B1
fmOutput	$D7B2
fmInOut	$D7B3

File-attribute Constants

The `faXXXX` constants test, set, and clear file-attribute bits in conjunction with the `GetFAttr`, `SetFAttr`, `FindFirst`, and `FindNext` procedures.

The `faXXXX` constants are additive. The `faAnyFile` constant is the sum of all attributes. The `faXXXX` constants can be any of the following:

Constant	*Value*
faReadOnly	$01
faHidden	$02
faSysFile	$04
faVolumeID	$08
faDirectory	$10
faArchive	$20
faAnyFile	$3F

File-name Component String Length Constants

The fsXXXX constants are the maximum file-name component string lengths used by the FileSearch and FileExpand functions. They can be any of the following:

Constant	*Value*
fsPathName	79
fsDirectory	67
fsFileName	8
fsExtension	4

FileSplit Return Flag Constants

The FileSplit function uses the fcXXXX constants. The returned value is a combination of the fcDirectory, fcFileName, and the fcExtension bit masks. The value indicates which components were in the path.

If the name or extension contains any wild-card characters (* or ?), the fcWildcards flag is set. Possible constant values are

Constant	*Value*
fcExtension	$0001
fcFileName	$0002
fcDirectory	$0004
fcWildcards	$0008

Types

Types in the WinDos unit:

- File record
- TRegisters
- TDateTime
- TSearchRec

File Record Type

The record definitions used internally by Turbo Pascal for Windows are also declared in the WinDos unit.

`TFileRec` is used for both typed and untyped files.

`TTextRec` is used internally by any variable of the predefined Turbo Pascal file type, text.

The records look like the following:

```
type

{ Typed and untyped files }

    TFileRec = record
    Handle: Word;
    Mode: Word;
    RecSize: Word;
    Private: array[1..26] of Byte;
    UserData: array[1..16] of Byte;
    Name: array[0..79] of Char;
  end;


{ Textfile record }

  PTextBuf = ^TTextBuf;
  TTextBuf = array[0..127] of Char;
  TTextRec = record
    Handle: Word;
    Mode: Word;
    BufSize: Word;
    Private: Word;
    BufPos: Word;
    BufEnd: Word;
    BufPtr: ^TTextBuf;
    OpenFunc: Pointer;
    InOutFunc: Pointer;
    FlushFunc: Pointer;
    CloseFunc: Pointer;
    UserData: array[1..16] of Byte;
    Name: array[0..79] of Char;
    Buffer: TTextBuf;
  end;
```

TRegisters Type

The Intr and MsDos procedures use variables of type TRegisters to specify the input register contents and examine the output register contents of a software interrupt.

TRegisters looks like this:

```
type
  TRegisters = record
    case Integer of
    0: (AX,BX,CX,DX,BP,SI,DI,DS,ES,Flags: Word);
    1: (AL,AH,BL,BH,CL,CH,DL,DH: Byte);
  end;
```

Note: A variant record is used to map the 8-bit registers on top of their 16-bit equivalents.

TDateTime Type

Variables of TDateTime type are used with the UnpackTime and PackTime procedures to examine and construct 4-byte, packed date-and-time values for the GetFTime, SetFTime, FindFirst, and FindNext procedures.

TDateTime looks like the following:

```
type
  TDateTime = record
    Year,Month,Day,Hour,Min,Sec: Word;
  end;
```

The valid ranges of its fields are

Year	1980..2099
Month	1..12
Day	1..31
Hour	0..23
Min	0..59
Sec	0..59

TSearchRec Type

The FindFirst and FindNext procedures use variables of type TSearchRec to scan directories.

TSearchRec looks like the following:

```
type
  TSearchRec = record
    Fill: array[1..21] of Byte;
    Attr: Byte;
    Time: Longint;
    Size: Longint;
    Name: array[0..12] of Char;
  end;
```

The information for each file found by one of these procedures is reported in a TSearchRec.

Attr contains the file's attributes (constructed from file-attribute constants).

Time contains its packed date and time.

Size contains its size in bytes.

Name contains its name.

Fill is reserved by DOS and should not be modified.

An Index of WinDos Procedures and Functions by Function (or Category)

Date and Time Procedures

GetDate	procedure
GetFTime	procedure
GetTime	procedure
PackTime	procedure
SetDate	procedure
SetFTime	procedure
SetTime	procedure
UnpackTime	procedure

Directory-handling Procedures and Functions

CreateDir	procedure
GetCurDir	function
RemoveDir	procedure
SetCurDir	procedure
Disk status	function
DiskFree	function
DiskSize	function

Environment-handling Functions

GetArgCount	function
GetArgStr	function
GetEnvVar	function

File-handling Procedures and Functions

FileExpand	function
FileSearch	function
FileSplit	function
FindFirst	procedure
FindNext	procedure
GetFAttr	procedure
SetFAttr	procedure

Interrupt Support Procedures

GetIntVec	procedure
Intr	procedure
MsDos	procedure
SetIntVec	procedure

Miscellaneous Procedures and Functions

DosVersion	function
GetCBreak	procedure
GetVerify	procedure
SetCBreak	procedure
SetVerify	procedure

DosError Variable

`DosError` is used by many of the procedures and functions in the `WinDos` unit to report errors. It looks like this:

```
var DosError: Integer;
```

The values stored in `DosError` are DOS error codes.

A value of 0 indicates no error; other possible error codes are as follows:

Error Code	*Meaning*
2	File not found
3	Path not found
5	Access denied
6	Invalid handle
8	Not enough memory
10	Invalid environment
11	Invalid format
18	No more files

Date and Time Procedures

Turbo Pascal for Windows supplies a complete set of date and time procedures. These include:

```
GetDate
GetFTime
GetTime
PackTime
SetDate
SetFTime
SetTime
UnpackTime
```

GetDate

Returns the current date in the operating system.

```
procedure GetDate(var Year, Month, Day, DayOfWeek: Word);
```

GetFTime

Returns the date and time a file was last written.

```
procedure GetFTime(var F; var Time: Longint);
```

`F` must be a file variable (typed, untyped, or text file) that has been assigned and opened. The time returned in `Time` can be unpacked through a call to `UnpackTime`.

GetTime

Returns the current time in the operating system.

```
procedure GetTime(var Hour, Minute, Second, Sec100: Word);
```

For example:

```
uses
    WinDos,
    WinCrt;


var
  H, M, S, Hund : Word;
function LeadingZero(W : Word) : String;
 var
   S : String;
begin
  Str(W:0,S);
  if Length(S) = 1 then
    S := '0' + S;
    LeadingZero := S;
end;
begin
  GetTime(H,M,S,Hund);
  Writeln('It's  ',LeadingZero(H),':',
LeadingZero(M),':',LeadingZero(S),
           '.',LeadingZero(Hund));
end.
```

PackTime

Converts a `TDateTime` record.

```
procedure PackTime(var T: DateTime; var Time: Longint);
```

Converts the record into a 4-byte, packed date-and-time `Longint` used by `SetFTime`. For example:

```
uses
   WinDos,
   WinCrt;


var
  F: text;
  H, M, S, Hund : Word; { For GetTime}
  Ftime : Longint;      { For Get/SetFTime}
```

```
  Dt : TDateTime;       { For Pack/UnpackTime}
function LeadingZero(W : Word) : String;
var
  S : String;
begin
  Str(W:0,S);
  if Length(S) = 1 then
    S := '0' + S;
  LeadingZero := S;
end;
begin
  Assign(F, 'File.txt');
  GetTime(H,M,S,Hund);
  Rewrite(F);               { Create a new file }
  GetFTime(F,Ftime);        { Get the creation time }
  Writeln('File created @ ',LeadingZero(H),
          ':',LeadingZero(M),':',
          LeadingZero(S));
  UnpackTime(Ftime,Dt);
  with Dt do
    begin
      Writeln('File timestamp = ',
              LeadingZero(Hour),':',
              LeadingZero(Min),':',
              LeadingZero(Sec));
      Hour := 0;
      Min := 10;
      Sec := 0;
      PackTime(Dt,Ftime);
      Writeln('Setting file timestamp ', 'to 12:10 AM');
      Reset(F); { Reopen file for reading }
                { Else close will update time }
      SetFTime(F,Ftime);
    end;
  Close(F);                   { Close file }
end.
```

SetDate

Sets the current date in the operating system.

```
procedure SetDate(Year, Month, Day: Word);
```

For example:

```
uses
    WinDos;

begin
  { Set the system date to 5/8/58 }
  SetDate(1958,5,8);
end.
```

SetFTime

Sets the date and time a file was last written.

```
procedure SetFTime(var F; Time: Longint);
```

Any errors are reported in `DosError`. The only error code is 6, an Invalid File Handle. *Note:* `F` must be open.

SetTime

Sets the current time in the operating system.

```
procedure SetTime(Hour, Minute, Second, Sec100: Word);
```

For example:

```
uses
    WinDos;

begin
  { Set system clock to 12:01 AM }
  SetTime(0,1,0,0);
end.
```

UnpackTime

Converts a `Longint` to a record.

```
procedure UnpackTime(Time: Longint; var DT: TDateTime);
```

Converts a 4-byte, packed date-and-time `Longint` returned by `GetFTime`, `FindFirst`, or `FindNext` into an unpacked `DateTime` record.

Directory-handling Procedures and Functions

Turbo Pascal for Windows supplies a complete set of directory-handling procedures and functions:

```
CreateDir
GetCurDir
RemoveDir
SetCurDir
DiskFree
DiskSize
```

CreateDir

Creates a new subdirectory.

```
procedure CreateDir(Dir: PChar)
```

Executes the same functions as `MkDir`, but uses a Turbo Pascal style string rather than a null-terminated string. For example:

```
uses
    WinCrt,
    WinDOS;

const
  Create: PChar = 'C:\MyDir';
  CDrive: Byte = 3;

begin
  CreateDir(ADir);
  Writeln('Creating new directory @ ', ADir,'.');
end.
```

GetCurDir

Returns the current directory of a specified drive.

```
function GetCurDir(Dir: PChar; Drive: Byte): PChar;
```

The following values represent their respective drives. This procedure continues until all drives have a name:

0 = Default drive
1 = Drive A
2 = Drive B
3 = Drive C

For example:

```
uses
    WinCrt,
    WinDOS;

const
  CDrive:Byte = 3;

var
  CurDir: PChar;

begin
  GetMem(CurDir, 80);
  GetCurDir(CurDir, CDrive);
  Writeln('Current directory = ', CurDir,'.');
end.
```

RemoveDir

Removes an empty subdirectory.

```
procedure Remove(Dir: PChar);
```

For example:

```
uses
    WinCrt,
    WinDos;

const
  Remove: PChar = 'C:\OldDir';
  CDrive: Byte = 3;

begin
  RemoveDir(ADir);
  Writeln('Directory removed @ ', ADir,'.');
end.
```

SetCurDir

Changes the current directory to the specified path.

```
procedure SetCurDir(Dir: PChar)
```

If `Dir` specifies a drive letter, the drive is also changed. For example:

```
uses
    WinCrt,
```

```
    WinDOS;

const
  ChangeTo: PChar = 'C:\';
  CDrive: Byte = 3;

var
  CurDir: PChar;

begin
  GetMem(CurDir, 80);
  SetCurDir(ChangeTo);
  GetCurDir(CurDir, CDrive);
  Writeln('Current directory = ', CurDir,'.');
end.
```

DiskFree

Returns the number of free bytes on a disk drive. If the drive number is invalid, it returns –1; otherwise it returns the number of kilobytes (K) free.

```
function DiskFree(Drive: Byte): Longint;
```

where

0 = Default drive
1 = Drive A
2 = Drive B
3 = Drive C

and so on.

For example:

```
uses
    WinDos,
    WinCrt;

begin
  Writeln(DiskFree(0) div 1024, 'K free ');
end.
```

DiskSize

Returns the total size, in bytes, of specified disk drive.

```
function DiskSize(Drive: Byte): Longint;
```

where

0 = Default drive
1 = Drive A
2 = Drive B
3 = Drive C

and so on. DiskSize returns the value –1 if the drive number is invalid. For example:

```
uses
    WinDos,
    WinCrt;

begin
  Writeln(DiskSize(0) div 1024, 'K ');
end.
```

Environment-handling Functions

Turbo Pascal for Windows supplies a complete set of environment-handling functions:

```
GetArgCount
GetArgStr
GetEnvVar
```

GetArgCount

Returns the number of parameters passed to the application by the command line.

```
function GetArgCount: Integer
```

For example:

```
uses
    WinCrt,
    WinDOS;

var
  ArgCount:  Integer;

begin
  ArgCount := GetArgCount;
  Writeln('There were ', ArgCount,' arguments on the command line');
end.
```

GetArgStr

Returns the command-line parameter specified by Index.

```
function GetArgStr(Test: PChar; Index: Integer; MaxLen: Word): PChar;
```

The return value depends on the parameter:

Parameter	*Return Value*
Index < 0 or > GetArGCount	Empty string
Index = 0	File name of current module; `Test` = returned value

For example:

```
uses
    WinCrt,
    WinDos;

var
  ArgN: PChar;

begin
  GetMem(ArgN, 20);
  GetArgStr(ArgN, 1, 19);
  Writeln('The 1st argument was ''', ArgN, '''.');
end.
```

GetEnvVar

Returns a pointer to the value of a specified environment variable.

```
function GetEnvVar(VarName: PChar): PChar;
```

Returns value 0 if the specified environment variable does not exist. For example:

```
uses
    WinCrt,
    WinDos;

var
  EnvironVar: PChar;

begin
  GetMem(EnvironVar, 255);
```

```
  EnvironmentVar := GetEnvVar('Path');
  Writeln('The current path is: ');
  Writeln(EnvironVar);
end.
```

File-handling Procedures and Functions

Turbo Pascal for Windows supplies a complete set of file-handling procedures and functions:

```
FileExpand
FileSearch
FileSplit
FindFirst
FindNext
GetFAttr
SetFAttr
```

FileExpand

Expands a file name into a fully qualified file name.

```
function FileExpand(Test, Name: PChar): PChar;
```

For example:

```
uses
    WinCrt,
    WinDOS;

const
  MyFile: PChar = 'File.txt';

var
  Location: PChar;

begin
  GetMem(Location, 80);
  FileExpand(Location, MyFile);
  Writeln(MyFile, ' is @ ', Location, '.');
end.
```

FileSearch

Searches for a file.

```
function FileSearch(Test, Name, List: PChar): PChar;
```

Searches in a list of directories (DirList). The directories in DirList must be separated by semicolons. For example:

```
uses
    WinCrt,
    WinDos;

var
  S: array[0..fsPathName] of Char;
begin
  FileSearch(S, 'Turbo.Exe', GetEnvVar('Path'));
  if S[0] = #0 then
    Writeln('Turbo.Exe wasn't found')
  else
    Writeln('Found as ', FileExpand(S, S));
end.
```

FileSplit

Splits a file name into its three components.

```
function FileSplit(Path, Dir, Name, Ext: PChar): Word;
```

For example:

```
uses
    Strings,
    WinCrt,
    WinDos;

var
  Path: array[0..fsPathName] of Char;
  Dir: array[0..fsDirectory] of Char;
  Name: array[0..fsFileName] of Char;
  Ext: array[0..fsExtension] of Char;
begin
  Write('Filename (Work.pas): ');
  Readln(Path);
  FileSplit(Path, Dir, Name, Ext);
  if Name[0] = #0 then StrCopy(Name, 'Work');
```

```
  if Ext[0] = #0 then StrCopy(Ext, '.PAS');
  StrECopy(StrECopy(StrECopy(Path, Dir), Name), Ext);
  Writeln('New name = ', Path);
end.
```

FindFirst

Searches the specified directory for the matching file.

```
procedure FindFirst(Path: PChar; Attr: Word; var F: TSearchRec);
```

For example:

```
uses
   WinDos,
   WinCrt;

var
  DirInfo: TSearchRec;
begin
  FindFirst('*.PAS', Archive, DirInfo);
  while DosError = 0 do
  begin
    Writeln(DirInfo.Name);
    FindNext(DirInfo);
  end;
end.
```

FindNext

Finds the next entry that matches the name and attributes specified in an earlier call to `FindFirst`.

```
procedure FindNext(var F: TSearchRec);
```

Errors are reported in `DosError`. The only possible error code is 18: no more files. For example:

```
uses
    WinDos,
    WinCrt;

var
  DirInfo: TSearchRec;
begin
```

```
  FindFirst('*.PAS', Archive, DirInfo);
  while DosError = 0 do
  begin
    Writeln(DirInfo.Name);
    FindNext(DirInfo);
  end;
end.
```

GetFAttr

Returns the attributes of a file.

```
procedure GetFAttr(var F; var Attr: Word);
```

F must be a file variable (typed, untyped, or text file) that has been assigned but has not been opened. For example:

```
uses
    WinDos,
    WinCrt;

var
  F: file;
  Attr: Word;
begin
  { Get file name from command line }
  Assign(F, ParamStr(1));
  GetFAttr(F, Attr);
  Writeln(ParamStr(1));
  if DosError <> 0 then
    Writeln('DOS error code = ', DosError)
  else
  begin
    Write('Attribute = ', Attr);
    { Determine file attribute type
       using the flags in the WinDos unit }
    if Attr and faReadOnly <> 0 then
      Writeln('Read only file');
    if Attr and faHidden <> 0 then Writeln('Hidden file');
    if Attr and faSysFile <> 0 then Writeln('System file');
    if Attr and faVolumeID <> 0 then Writeln('Volume ID');
    if Attr and faDirectory <> 0 then Writeln('Directory name');
    if Attr and faArchive <> 0 then Writeln('Archive (normal file)');
  end; { else }
end.
```

SetFAttr

Sets the attributes of a file.

```
procedure SetFAttr(var F; Attr: Word);
```

Errors are reported in `DosError`. The possible error codes are:

3 (Invalid path)
5 (File access denied)

Note: The file cannot be open. For example:

```
uses
    WinDos;

var
  F: file;
begin
  Assign(F, 'C:\Myfile.txt');
  SetFAttr(F, faHidden);
  Readln;
  SetFAttr(F, faArchive);
end.
```

Interrupt Support Procedures

Turbo Pascal for Windows supplies a complete set of interrupt support procedures:

```
GetIntVec
Intr
MsDos
SetIntVec
```

GetIntVec

Returns the address stored in a specified interrupt vector.

```
procedure GetIntVec(IntNo: Byte; var Vector: Pointer);
```

For example:

```
uses
    WinDos,
    WinCrt;

var
  Int1 : Pointer;
{$F+}
procedure TimerHandler; interrupt;
  begin
    { Timer ISR }
  end;
{$F-}
begin
  GetIntVec($1C,Int1);
  SetIntVec($1C,Addr(TimerHandler));
  Writeln('Press a key to exit');
  repeat until Keypressed;
       SetIntVec($01C,Int1);
end.
```

Intr

Executes a specified software interrupt.

```
procedure Intr(IntNo: Byte; var Regs: TRegisters);
```

where

`IntNo` is the software interrupt number (0...255).

`TRegisters` is a record defined in DOS.

> **Note:** Do not use software interrupts that
>
> 1. Depend on specific values in `SP` or `SS` for entry
> 2. Modify `SP` or `SS` on exit.

For example:

```
uses
    WinCrt,
    WinDos;

var
```

```
  Date,
  Year,
  Month,
  Day   : String;
  Regs  : TRegisters;

begin
  Regs.ah := $2a;
  with Regs do
  intr($21,Regs);
  with Regs do
    begin
      Str(cx,Year);
      Str(dh,Month);
      Str(dl,Day);
    end;
  Date := Month+'/'+Day+'/'+Year;
  writeln('Date = ', Date);
end.
```

MsDos

Executes a DOS function call.

```
procedure MsDos(var Regs: TRegisters);
```

Remember not to use software interrupts that either depend on specific values in SP or SS for entry or that modify SP or SS on exit. For example:

```
uses
    WinCrt,
    WinDos;

var
  Date,
  Year,
  Month,
  Day   : String;
  Regs  : TRegisters;

begin
  Regs.ah := $2a;
  with Regs do
  msdos(Regs);
  with Regs do
```

```
    begin
      Str(cx,Year);
      Str(dh,Month);
      Str(dl,Day);
    end;
  Date := Month+'/'+Day+'/'+Year;
  Writeln('Date = ', Date);
end.
```

SetIntVec

Sets a specified interrupt vector to a specified address.

```
procedure SetIntVec(IntNo: Byte; Vector: Pointer);
```

Miscellaneous Procedures and Functions

Turbo Pascal for Windows supplies several miscellaneous procedures and functions:

```
DosVersion
GetCBreak
GetVerify
SetCBreak
SetVerify
```

DosVersion

Returns the DOS version number.

```
function DosVersion: Word;
```

The result's low byte is the major version number, and the high byte is the minor version number. For example:

```
uses
    WinDos;

var
  Ver: Word;
begin
  Ver := DosVersion;
  Writeln('DOS version = ', Lo(Ver), '.', Hi(Ver));
end.
```

GetCBreak

Returns the state of Ctrl-Break checking in DOS.

```
procedure GetCBreak(var Break: Boolean);
```

For example:

```
uses
    WinDos,
    WinCrt;

const
  OffOn : array [Boolean] of String[3] =
    ('off','on');
var
  cb : Boolean;
begin
  GetCBreak(cb);
  Writeln('Control-Break checking is ', OffOn[cb]);
  cb := not(cb);
  Writeln('Turning Control-Break checking ', OffOn[cb]);
  SetCBreak(cb);
end.
```

GetVerify

Returns the state of the verify flag in DOS.

```
procedure GetVerify(var Verify: Boolean);
```

For example:

```
uses
    WinDos,
    WinCrt;

const
  OffOn : array [Boolean] of String[3] =     ('off','on');
var
  Boo : Boolean;
```

```
begin
  GetVerify(Boo);
  Writeln('Write verify = ', OffOn[Boo]);
  Boo := not(Boo);
  Writeln('Turning write verify ', OffOn[Boo]);
  SetVerify(Boo);
 end.
```

SetCBreak

Sets the state of Ctrl-Break checking in DOS.

```
procedure SetCBreak(Break: Boolean);
```

SetVerify

Sets the state of the verify flag in DOS.

```
procedure SetVerify(Verify: Boolean);
```

J

REFERENCE

DEBUGGING TURBO PASCAL FOR WINDOWS APPLICATIONS

The Turbo Pascal for Windows Debugger is a powerful tool for debugging Windows applications. It goes a major step or two further than the built-in debugging capabilities of the Turbo Pascal for Windows compiler. The Turbo Pascal for Windows compiler's bug-detecting power focuses on making sure that your application code makes syntactic sense. If you have an unknown identifier or have omitted a necessary semicolon, it'll find it. But it cannot guarantee more than correct syntax. Your code can survive compiler bug-detection and still crash miserably (at run-time). Run-time errors are the domain of another class of bug detectors, "debuggers."

Debuggers help you isolate and correct mistakes that usually are not due to errors in syntax. This is a broad and complex group of errors that you can make in the logic of your code, by not accounting for the full range of possible actions of your code, and so on. Debugging, in this realm, is an imperfect "art" at best, and debugging Windows applications is more imperfect yet. The key, I think, to debugging Windows applications lies in isolating the more likely error-prone areas of your code.

A few simple development tactics will help:

1. Code in small fragments. Use object-oriented techniques to keep data and the behavior for manipulating data in objects.

2. Develop objects, units, or other structural blocks one at a time. Make sure that an object or a block works before moving on to other objects or blocks, particularly if these objects and blocks are interrelated.

3. Reduce the number of procedures, functions, and so on that can manipulate data. If you don't use objects, use local variables.

These tactics will help, but they probably won't eliminate all your bugs. When you discover a bug in your Windows application, call on Turbo Debugger for Windows. In effect, it slows down the execution of an application and lets you examine its specific aspects. You can examine the stack, variable values, CPU registers, Windows messages, and so on.

Turbo Debugger gives you seven main ways to explore:

1. Tracing (executing an application one line at a time).

2. Back tracing (stepping backward through the application code a line at a time, and reversing the execution).

3. Stepping (executing the application code one line at a time but "stepping over" any calls to procedures or functions). This way, the procedure or function is executed as a block and any values are returned, but you don't "trace" through the procedure or function a line at a time.

4. Viewing (opening a window for viewing the states of various components of the application). These components are the application's variables, breakpoints you set, the stack, a Turbo Debugger log, a data file, a source file, CPU code, memory, registers, numeric processor information, object hierarchies, the application's execution history, and the application's output.

5. Inspecting data structures (such as arrays).

6. Changing (manipulating the application by replacing the current value of a variable with a new value that you specify).

7. Watching application variables (tracking the changing values of variables you specify).

All the Turbo Debugger for Windows features are available in pull-down menus.

The simplest way to use Turbo Debugger for Windows is load the application you want to debug into a Turbo Pascal for Windows edit window, and then select Debugger from the Turbo Pascal for Windows Run/Debugger menu. Make sure, though, that you select Options/Linker/Debug info in EXE before you run Turbo Debugger.

The specifics of how you debug your application depend on the kind of application and possible error. In general, you don't want to trace through an entire Windows application. Instead, try to isolate the error as best you can and set breakpoints in likely troubled areas. (I know, I know; if you know where the error is, you probably don't need the debugger—yes and no.) If you're developing the application object by object or block by block, you can at least reduce the bug to that area. Set a breakpoint and then trace through the application from the breakpoint.

In many situations, making sure that a procedure, function, or method gets called, or monitoring a variable's values, can locate the bug. I usually start any debug session by setting breakpoints and adding the variables within those breakpoints using Add Watch. Then I step or trace through the code.

If you get a run-time error that typically looks like this:

```
Runtime error 204 at 0002:018
```

note the address (you probably will want to write it down), and use the Find Error command on the Turbo Pascal for Windows Search menu to locate the error in your source code.

The Find Error dialog box appears. Enter the address of the error in the Error Address box. Turbo Pascal for Windows then recompiles your code and stops when it reaches the address you specify, highlighting the statement that caused the error.

Then, fix the error (in the edit window) and recompile. Repeat the process if you have to.

K

REFERENCE

TURBO PASCAL FOR WINDOWS ERROR MESSAGES

Turbo Pascal for Windows generates two kinds of error messages: compiler error messages and run-time error messages.

If you're using the IDE to compile your source code and a compiler error occurs, Turbo Pascal for Windows makes the Edit window active and moves the cursor to the location where it detected the error in your source code.

If the error occurs when you're using the command-line compiler, Turbo Pascal for Windows displays the error message and number and the offending source line. A caret (^) in the displayed source line indicates the error's location.

If your application generates an error at run-time, it will terminate, and the following message is displayed:

```
Runtime error <num> at <xxxx:yyyy>
```

where:

- `num` is the run-time error number
- `xxxx:yyyy` is the run-time error address

Compiler Error Messages

Compiler error messages are numbered from 1 to 168. The following error messages are currently implemented in Turbo Pascal for Windows 1.0.

Note: Not all numbers have a corresponding error message.

Error Number	*Error Message*
1	Out of memory
2	Identifier expected
3	Unknown identifier
4	Duplicate identifier
5	Syntax error
6	Error in real constant
7	Error in integer constant
8	String constant exceeds line
9	Too many nested files
10	Unexpected end of file
11	Line too long
12	Type identifier expected
13	Too many open files
14	Invalid file name
15	File not found
16	Disk full
17	Invalid compiler directive
18	Too many files
19	Undefined type in pointer definition
20	Variable identifier expected
21	Error in type
22	Structure too large

Error Number	*Error Message*
23	Set base type out of range
24	File components may not be files or objects
25	Invalid string length
26	Type mismatch
27	Invalid subrange base type
28	Lower bound > than upper bound
29	Ordinal type expected
30	Integer constant expected
31	Constant expected
32	Integer or real constant expected
33	Pointer type identifier expected
34	Invalid function result type
35	Label identifier expected
36	BEGIN expected
37	END expected
38	Integer expression expected
39	Ordinal expression expected
40	Boolean expression expected
41	Operand types do not match operator
42	Error in expression
43	Illegal assignment
44	Field identifier expected
45	Object file too large
46	Undefined external
47	Invalid object file record
48	Code segment too large
49	Data segment too large
50	DO expected

continues

Error Number	*Error Message*
51	Invalid PUBLIC definition
52	Invalid EXTRN definition
53	Too many EXTRN definitions
54	OF expected
55	INTERFACE expected
56	Invalid relocatable reference
57	THEN expected
58	TO or DOWNTO expected
59	Undefined forward
61	Invalid typecast
62	Division by zero
63	Invalid file type
64	Cannot read or write variables of this type
65	Pointer variable expected
66	String variable expected
67	String expression expected
68	Circular unit reference
69	Unit name mismatch
70	Unit version mismatch
72	Unit file format error
73	IMPLEMENTATION expected
74	Constant and case types don't match
75	Record variable expected
76	Constant out of range
77	File variable expected
78	Pointer expression expected
79	Integer or real expression expected
80	Label not within current block
81	Label already defined

Error Number	*Error Message*
82	Undefined label in preceding statement part
83	Invalid @ argument
84	UNIT expected
85	";" expected
86	":" expected
87	"," expected
88	"(" expected
89	")" expected
90	"=" expected
91	":=" expected
92	"[" or "(." expected
93	"]" or ".)" expected
94	"." expected
95	".." expected
96	Too many variables
97	Invalid FOR control variable
98	Integer variable expected
99	File and procedure types are not allowed here
100	String length mismatch
101	Invalid ordering of fields
102	String constant expected
103	Integer or real variable expected
104	Ordinal variable expected
105	INLINE error
106	Character expression expected
112	CASE constant out of range
113	Error in statement
114	Cannot call an interrupt procedure

continues

Error Number	*Error Message*
116	Must be in 8087 mode to compile
117	Target address not found
118	Include files are not allowed here
120	NIL expected
121	Invalid qualifier
122	Invalid variable reference
123	Too many symbols
124	Statement part too large
126	Files must be var parameters
127	Too many conditional symbols
128	Misplaced conditional directive
129	ENDIF directive missing
130	Error in initial conditional defines
131	Header does not match previous definition
132	Critical disk error
133	Cannot evaluate this expression
136	Invalid indirect reference
137	Structured variables are not allowed here
140	Invalid floating-point operation
142	Procedure or function variable expected
143	Invalid procedure or function reference
146	File access denied
147	Object type expected
148	Local object types are not allowed
149	VIRTUAL expected
150	Method identifier expected
151	Virtual constructors are not allowed
152	Constructor identifier expected

Error Number	*Error Message*
153	Destructor identifier expected
154	Fail only allowed within constructors
155	Invalid combination of opcode and operands
156	Memory reference expected
157	Cannot add or subtract relocatable symbols
158	Invalid register combination
159	286/287 instructions are not enabled
160	Invalid symbol reference
161	Code generation error
162	ASM expected
163	Duplicate dynamic method index
164	Duplicate resource identifier
165	Duplicate or invalid export index
166	Procedure or function identifier expected
167	Cannot export this symbol
168	Duplicate export name

The following section provides more detailed explanations of the compiler error messages. When possible, suggestions for correcting the errors are supplied.

Compiler error 1: Out of memory

This error occurs when the compiler runs out of memory.
To solve this problem, you might:

- Try to increase the amount of available memory in Windows.
- Set Options/Linker/Link buffer to disk.
- If you're not using the IDE and are using the command-line compiler, use the /L option to place the link buffer on disk.

If none of these solutions helps, your application (or unit) might be too large to compile in the amount of memory available on your system. Try dividing the application or unit that won't compile into two or more smaller units.

Compiler error 2: Identifier expected

The compiler expected an identifier at this point. One possibility is that you're trying to redeclare a reserved word. Another possibility is the existence of misplaced syntax preceding the location of the error.

Compiler error 3: Unknown identifier

Most likely, this identifier hasn't been declared or isn't visible within the current scope.

Compiler error 4: Duplicate identifier

The identifier is already being used within the current block. You're either actually duplicating the identifier or possibly misspelling one of the duplicated identifiers.

Compiler error 5: Syntax error

The compiler detected an illegal character.

Compiler error 6: Error in real constant

You should specify a real constant in the following form:

```
const

RealConst = 3.5688855;
```

Compiler error 7: Error in integer constant

You should specify an integer constant in the following form:

```
const

IntConst = 380;
```

Note: Whole real numbers greater than the maximum integer allowed must be followed by a decimal point and a zero.

For example:

```
84,245,567,797.0
```

Compiler error 8: String constant exceeds line

You possibly omitted the closing quote in a string constant or mistyped it.

Compiler error 9: Too many nested files

The compiler permits a maximum of 15 nested source-code files. One possibile source of error is an excessive number of nested Include files.

Compiler error 10: Unexpected end of file

This error is generated when:

- Your source code file ends before the final `End` of the main statement part. In this case, the `begins` and `ends` are probably unbalanced.
- An Include file ends in the middle of a statement part. Every statement part must be contained in one file.
- You didn't close a comment.

Compiler error 11: Line too long

The maximum length of a line is 126 characters.

Compiler error 12: Type identifier expected

The identifier doesn't denote a type correctly.

Compiler error 13: Too many open files

This error usually means that:

1. You haven't specified a `FILES` number in your CONFIG.SYS file.
2. You have specified too few files in your CONFIG.SYS.

Increase the number of files in your CONFIG.SYS to 20 or more using the `FILES` statement:

```
FILES = 30;
```

Compiler error 14: Invalid file name

The file name is invalid or specifies a nonexistent path.

Compiler error 15: File not found

The file couldn't be located in the current directory or in any of the search directories you've specified in the Directories path.

Compiler error 16: Disk full

Delete files, use a new disk, and so on, to free up some additional disk space.

Compiler error 17: Invalid compiler directive

Usually, one of the following problems exists:

- The compiler directive letter is unknown.
- One of the compiler-directive parameters is invalid.
- You're using a global compiler directive when compilation of the application's main body has begun.

Compiler error 18: Too many files

You're using too many files when you compile the program or unit. One solution is to combine Include files or units.

Compiler error 19: Undefined type in pointer definition

When you declared the pointer type, you referenced a type that hasn't been declared.

Compiler error 20: Variable identifier expected

The identifier doesn't denote a variable correctly.

Compiler error 21: Error in type

The symbol you're using cannot begin a `type` definition.

Compiler error 22: Structure too large

In Turbo Pascal for Windows, structured types must be no larger than 65520 bytes (64K).

Compiler error 23: Set base type out of range

The base type of a set must be a subrange between 0 and 255 or an enumerated type with fewer than 257 possible values.

Compiler error 24: File components may not be files or objects

The component type of a file type cannot be an object type or a file type, nor can it be any structured type within an object type or file type.

Compiler error 25: Invalid string length

The maximum length of a string must be in the range 1..255.

Compiler error 26: Type mismatch

Usually, this error results from one of the following:

- Incompatible types of the variable and the expression in an assignment statement.
- Incompatible types of the actual and formal parameter in a call to a procedure or function.
- An expression type that's incompatible with the index type in array indexing.
- Incompatible types of operands in an expression.

Compiler error 27: Invalid subrange base type

Ordinal types are the only valid base types.

Compiler error 28: Lower bound > than upper bound

When you declared the subrange type, you specified a lower bound greater than the upper bound.

Compiler error 29: Ordinal type expected

Pointer, real, string, and structured types aren't allowed in this situation.

Compiler error 30: Integer constant expected

Only an integer constant is permitted in this situation.

Compiler error 31: Constant expected

Only a constant is permitted in this situation.

Compiler error 32: Integer or real constant expected

Only a numeric constant is permitted in this situation.

Compiler error 33: Pointer type identifier expected

The identifier doesn't denote a type properly.

Compiler error 34: Invalid function result type

Valid function result types can be only simple types, string types, and pointer types.

Compiler error 35: Label identifier expected

The identifier doesn't denote a label properly.

Compiler error 36: BEGIN expected

A `begin` was expected at this point, or there's an error in the block structure of the unit or program.

```
Begin
    ...
    ...
End
```

The `begin...end` block constitutes a construct, which is a compound statement. The `begin` and `end` reserved words act as statement brackets. For example:

```
{ Compound statement used within an "if" statement }

if First < Last then
begin
  Temp := First;
  First := Last;
  Last := Temp;
end;
```

Compiler error 37: END expected

An `end` was expected here, or there's an error in the block structure of the unit or program.

Use `end` with:

- `begin` to form compound statements
- `case` to form case statements
- `record` to declare record types
- `object` to declare object types
- `asm` to call the inline assembler

For example:

```
{ with "begin" to form compound statement }

if First < Last then
begin
  Temp := First;
  First := Last;
  Last := Temp;
end;

{ with "case" statement }
```

```
case Ch of
  'A'..'Z', 'a'..'z':  WriteLn('Letter');
  '0'..'9':            WriteLn('Digit');
  '+', '-', '*', '/':  WriteLn('Operator');
else
  WriteLn('Special character');
end;

{ with record type definitions }

type
  Class  = (Num, Dat, Str);
  Date   = record
    D, M, Y: Integer;
  end;
  Facts = record
    Name: string[10];
    case Kind: Class of
      Num: (N: real);
      Dat: (D: Date);
      Str: (S: string);
  end;

{ with object type definitions }

type
  LocationPtr = ^Location;
  Location = object
    X, Y: Integer;
    procedure Init(PX, PY: Integer);
    function GetX: Integer;
    function GetY: Integer;
  end;

{ with asm }
asm
  mov ax,1
  mov cx, 100

end;
```

Compiler error 38: Integer expression expected

An `Integer` type was expected.

Compiler error 39: Ordinal expression expected

The expression must be of an ordinal type.

Compiler error 40: Boolean expression expected

The expression must be of type `Boolean`.

Compiler error 41: Operand types do not match operator

The operator cannot be used on operands of this type; for example, `'C' div '6'`.

Compiler error 42: Error in expression

This symbol cannot participate in this expression. Possibly, you've omitted an operator between two operands.

Compiler error 43: Illegal assignment

You cannot assign values to files and untyped variables. You can assign values to a function identifier only within the statement part of the function.

Compiler error 44: Field identifier expected

The identifier doesn't denote a field in the record variable.

Compiler error 45: Object file too large

Turbo Pascal for Windows cannot link in OBJ files larger than 64K.

Compiler error 46: Undefined external

The external procedure or function doesn't have a matching `PUBLIC` definition in an object file. Check to make sure that you've specified all object files in `$L` file-name directives, and verify that you've correctly spelled the procedure or function identifier in the .ASM file.

The `$L` (Link Object File) directive instructs the compiler to link the named file with the program or unit being compiled. Use the `$L` directive to link in code written in assembly language for subprograms declared to be external.

Compiler error 47: Invalid object file record

The OBJ file contains an invalid object record.

Compiler error 48: Code segment too large

The maximum size of a program's or unit's code is 65520 bytes (64K). To break a code segment correctly, do the following:

- If you're compiling a program, reconstruct the program by moving some of its procedures or functions into a unit.
- If you're compiling a unit, divide it into two or more units.

Compiler error 49: Data segment too large

The maximum size of a program's data segment is 65520 bytes (64K), including the data declared by the used units. If you need more global data than this, declare the larger structures as pointers, and allocate them dynamically using the `New` procedure.

The `New` procedure creates a new dynamic variable and specifies a pointer variable to point to it. For example:

```
New(P, Init(326, 243));
```

Compiler error 50: DO expected

The reserved word `do` hasn't been used correctly.
`do` (a reserved word) is used in `while`, `for`, and `with` statements. For example:

```
while Ch = ' ' do Ch := GetChar;
for Ch := 1 to 100 do Ch := GetChar;
with Date[C] do month := 1;
```

Compiler error 51: Invalid PUBLIC definition

This error can occur if:

- Two or more `PUBLIC` directives in assembly language code define the same identifier.
- The OBJ file defines `PUBLIC` symbols that aren't in the `CODE` segment.

Compiler error 52: Invalid EXTRN definition

This error can occur if:

- The identifier was referred to through an `EXTRN` directive in assembly language, but wasn't declared in the Turbo Pascal for Windows program or unit, nor in the interface part of any of the used units.
- The identifier denotes an absolute variable.
- The identifier denotes an inline procedure or function.

Compiler error 53: Too many EXTRN definitions

Turbo Pascal for Windows doesn't allow .OBJ files with more than 256 `EXTRN` definitions.

Compiler error 54: OF expected

You haven't used the reserved word `of` correctly.
`of` is used in array, set, and file type declarations, and in `case` statements. For example:

```
{ array declaration }

type
  InList   = array[1..650]     of Integer;
  CharData = array['A'..'Z']   of Byte;
  Matrix   = array[0..5, 0..5] of real;

{ Set types }

type
  Day = (Sun, Mon, Tue, Wed, Thu, Fri, Sat);
  CharSet = set of Char;
  Digits = set of 0..9;
  Days = set of Day;

{ File type declarations }
type
  Person = record
     FirstName: string[15];
     LastName : string[25];
     Address  : string[35];
  end;
```

```
    PersonFile = file of Person;
    NumberFile = file of Integer;
    SwapFile = file;

  {case statement }

  case Ch of
     'A'..'Z', 'a'..'z':  WriteLn('Letter');
     '0'..'9':            WriteLn('Digit');
     '+', '-', '*', '/':  WriteLn('Operator');
  else
    WriteLn('Special character');
  end;
```

Compiler error 55: INTERFACE expected

You haven't used the reserved word `interface` correctly.

The interface section of a unit is the public part. It determines which components are visible and accessible to any program (or other unit) using that unit.

The interface section begins with the reserved word `interface`, which appears after the unit header, and ends with the reserved word `implementation`.

In the unit interface, you declare constants, data types, variables, procedures, and functions.

The "bodies" of the public procedures and functions are in the implem entation section.

A `uses` clause can appear in the interface section. (If a `uses` clause is present, `uses` must immediately follow the reserved word `interface`).

Compiler error 56: Invalid relocatable reference

This error can occur if:

- The OBJ file contains data and relocatable references in segments other than CODE. For example, you might be trying to declare initialized variables in the DATA segment.
- The OBJ file contains byte-sized references to relocatable symbols. This error can occur if you use the `HIGH` and `LOW` operators with relocatable symbols, or if you refer to relocatable symbols in `DB` directives.
- An operand refers to a relocatable symbol that you didn't define in the `CODE` or `DATA` segments.
- An operand refers to an `EXTRN` procedure or function with an offset.

Compiler error 57: THEN expected

You haven't used the reserved word then correctly. For example:

```
{ 'if-then' statements }

if (I < Min) or (I > Max) then I := 0;

if ParamCount <> 2 then
begin
  WriteLn('Bad command line');
  Halt(1);
end
else
begin
  ReadFile(ParamStr(1));
  WriteFile(ParamStr(2));

end;
```

Compiler error 58: TO or DOWNTO expected

You haven't used the reserved word to or downto correctly. For example:

```
{ for ... to, for ... downto }

for I := 1 to ParamCount do
  WriteLn(ParamStr(I);

for I := 1 to 21 do
  for J := 1 to 21 do
  begin
    X := 0;
    for K := 1 to 21 do
      X := X + Mat1[I, K] * Mat2[K, J];
    Mat[I, J] := X;

  end;
```

Compiler error 59: Undefined forward

This error might occur if:

- You declared the procedure or function in the interface part of a unit, but didn't define it in the implementation part.
- You declared the procedure or function forward but didn't define it.

Compiler error 61: Invalid typecast

This error might occur if:

- In a variable typecast, the sizes of the variable reference and the destination type differ.
- You're attempting to typecast an expression where only a variable reference is allowed.

Compiler error 62: Division by zero

The preceding operand attempts to divide by zero.

Compiler error 63: Invalid file type

The file-handling procedure doesn't support the given file's type. For example, you might have made a call to `Readln` with a typed file or to `Seek` with a text file.

Compiler error 64: Cannot read or write variables of this type

`Read` and `Readln` can input the following variable types:

```
Char
Integer
real
string
```

`Write` and `Writeln` can output the following variable types:

```
Char
Integer
real
string
Boolean
```

Compiler error 65: Pointer variable expected

This variable must be of a pointer type.

A pointer type variable contains the memory address of a dynamic variable of a specified base type.

Compiler error 66: String variable expected

This variable must be of a string type.

Compiler error 67: String expression expected

This expression must be of a string type.

Compiler error 68: Circular unit reference

Two units cannot `use` each other in their interface parts.

Compiler error 69: Unit name mismatch

The name of the unit found in the TPU file doesn't match the name specified in the `uses` clause. Or, the name of the unit file name doesn't match the name of the unit in the unit header within the file.

Compiler error 70: Unit version mismatch

One or more of the units used by this unit have been changed since this unit was compiled. Use Compile/Make or Compile/Build to automatically recompile the units that have changed.

The Compile/Make command creates an EXE file according to the following rules:

- If a primary file has been named in the `Primary File` dialog box, that file is compiled. Otherwise, the file in the active edit window is compiled. Turbo Pascal checks all files that the file being compiled depends on to see whether they exist and that they are current.
- If the source file for a given unit has been modified since the TPU (object code) file was created, that unit is recompiled.
- If the interface for a given unit has been changed, all other units that depend on it are recompiled.
- If a unit links in an OBJ file (external routines), and the OBJ file is newer than the unit's TPU file, the unit is recompiled.
- If a unit contains an Include file and the Include file is newer than that unit's TPU file, the unit is recompiled.
- If the source to a unit (TPU file) cannot be located, that unit is not compiled, but used as is.

This option is identical to Compile/Build except that it's conditional. (Build rebuilds all files regardless of whether they're out of date.)

The Compile/Build command rebuilds all the components of your program regardless of whether they're current.

This option is identical to Compile/Make except that it is unconditional. (Make rebuilds only those files that aren't current.)

The Compile/Build command recompiles all the files included in the primary file.

If you abort a Build command by pressing Ctrl-Break or get errors that stop the build, you can pick up where it left off by choosing Compile/Make.

Compiler error 72: Unit file format error

The TPU file is invalid. Check to ensure that it's a TPU file.

Compiler error 73: IMPLEMENTATION expected

Either the reserved word `implementation` doesn't appear correctly or you've used it improperly.

The `implementation` part of the unit is where you find the bodies of the procedures and functions declared in the interface part of the unit.

Compiler error 74: Constant and case types don't match

The type of the `case` constant is incompatible with the `case` statement's selector expression.

Compiler error 75: Record variable expected

This variable must be of a record type.

A record contains a number of components, or fields, that can be of different types. For example:

```
{ Record Type Definitions }

type
  Class  = (Num, Dat, Str);
  Date   = record
      D, M, Y: Integer;
  end;
  Facts = record
    Name: string[10];
```

```
    case Kind: Class of
      Num: (N: real);
      Dat: (D: Date);
      Str: (S: string);
end;
```

Compiler error 76: Constant out of range

You're probably trying to do one of the following:

- Index an array with an out-of-range constant.
- Assign an out-of-range constant to a variable.
- Pass an out-of-range constant as a parameter to a procedure or function.

Compiler error 77: File variable expected

This variable must be of a file type.

A file type consists of a linear sequence of components of the component type, which can be any type except a file type. If the word `of` and the component type are omitted, the `type` denotes an untyped file. The predefined file type `Text` signifies a file containing characters organized into lines. For example:

```
{ File type declarations }

type
  Person = record
    FirstName: string[15];
    LastName : string[25];
    Address  : string[35];
  end;
  PersonFile = file of Person;
  NumberFile = file of Integer;
  SwapFile = file;
```

Compiler error 78: Pointer expression expected

This expression must be of a pointer type. A pointer type variable contains the memory address of a dynamic variable of a specified base type.

Compiler error 79: Integer or real expression expected

This expression must be of either an `Integer` or `Real` type.

Compiler error 80: Label not within current block

A `goto` statement cannot reference a label outside the current block.

Compiler error 81: Label already defined

The label already marks a statement.

Compiler error 82: Undefined label in preceding statement part

You declared and referenced the label in a statement part, but you never defined it.

Compiler error 83: Invalid @ argument

Valid arguments are variable references and procedure or function identifiers.

Compiler error 84: UNIT expected

The reserved word `unit` doesn't appear where it should. Units are the basis of modular programming in Turbo Pascal for Windows. You use units to create libraries and to divide large programs into logically related modules.

Compiler error 85: ";" expected

A semicolon was expected.

Compiler error 86: ":" expected

A colon was expected.

Compiler error 87: "," expected

A comma was expected.

Compiler error 88: "(" expected

An opening parenthesis was expected.

Compiler error 89: ")" expected

A closing parenthesis was expected.

Compiler error 90: "=" expected

An equal sign was expected.

Compiler error 91: ":=" expected

An assignment operator was expected.

Compiler error 92: "[" or "(." expected

A left bracket was expected.

Compiler error 93: "]" or ".)" expected

A right bracket was expected.

Compiler error 94: "." expected

A period was expected.

Compiler error 95: ".." expected

A subrange was expected.

A subrange type is a range of values from an ordinal type called the host type. The definition of a subrange type specifies the least and the largest value in the subrange. Both constants must be of the same ordinal type, and the first constant must be less than or equal to the second constant. For example:

```
  0..99
-128..127
```

Compiler error 96: Too many variables

Global
The total size of the global variables declared within a program or unit cannot exceed 64K.

Local
The total size of the local variables declared within a procedure or function cannot exceed 64K.

Compiler error 97: Invalid FOR control variable

The `for` statement control variable must be a simple variable defined in the declaration part of the current subprogram. For example:

```
{for ... to, for ... downto }

for I := 1 to ParamCount do
  WriteLn(ParamStr(I);

for I := 1 to 10 do
  for J := 1 to 10 do
  begin
    X := 0;
    for K := 1 to 10 do
      X := X + Mat1[I, K] * Mat2[K, J];
    Mat[I, J] := X;

  end;
```

Compiler error 98: Integer variable expected

This variable must be of an `Integer` type.

Compiler error 99: File and procedure types are not allowed here

A typed constant cannot be of a file type.

Compiler error 100: String length mismatch

The length of the string constant doesn't match the number of components in the character array.

Compiler error 101: Invalid ordering of fields

The fields of a record-type constant must be written in the order of declaration.

Compiler error 102: String constant expected

A string constant doesn't appear where it should.

In inline assembler statements, string constants must be enclosed in single or double quotes.

Two consecutive quotes of the same type as the enclosing quotes count as only one character.

String constants of any length are allowed in `DB` directives, and cause allocation of a sequence of bytes containing the ASCII values of the characters in the string.

When not in a `DB` directive, a string constant can be no longer than four characters, and denotes a numeric value that can participate in an expression.

The numeric value of a string constant is calculated as:

```
+ Ord(Ch1)

+ Ord(Ch2) shl 8

+ Ord(Ch3) shl 16

+ Ord(Ch4) shl 24
```

where

- `Ch1` is the rightmost (last) character
- `Ch4` is the leftmost (first) character

If the string is shorter than four characters, the leftmost (first) character or characters are assumed to be 0 (zero).

Here are some examples of string constants and their corresponding numeric values:

String Constant	*Numeric Value*
'a'	00000061H
'ba'	00006261H
'cba'	636261H
'dcba'	64636261H
'a'	00006120H
'a'	20202061H
'a'*2	000000E2H
'a'-'A'	00000020H
Not 'a'	FFFFFF9EH

Compiler error 103: Integer or real variable expected

This variable must be of an `Integer` or `Real` type.

Compiler error 104: Ordinal variable expected

This variable must be of an ordinal type.

Turbo Pascal has nine predefined ordinal types. Five of these integer types denote a specific subset of the whole numbers, as shown in the following:

Type	*Range*	*Size*
Shortint	128..127	8-bit
Integer	–32768..32767	16-bit
Longint	–2147483648..2147483647	32-bit
Byte	0.255	8-bit
Word	0.65535	16-bit

The other four predefined ordinal types are the booleans (`Boolean`, `WordBool`, `LongBool`), and `Char`.

Two other classes of user-defined ordinal types are enumerated types and subrange types.

Compiler error 105: INLINE error

The < operator isn't permitted in conjunction with relocatable references to variables.

These references are always word-sized.

Compiler error 106: Character expression expected

This expression must be of a `Char` type.

Compiler error 112: CASE constant out of range

For `Integer` type `case` statements, the constants must be within the range –32768..32767.

Compiler error 113: Error in statement

This symbol cannot start a statement.

Compiler error 114: Cannot call an interrupt procedure

You cannot directly call an interrupt procedure.

The interrupt directive allows you to declare `interrupt` procedures.

An `interrupt` procedure looks like this:

```
procedure IntProc(Flags, CS, IP, AX, BX,
  CX, DX, SI, DI, DS, ES, BP: Word); interrupt;
```

The registers are passed as pseudo-parameters so that you can use and modify them in the code of the interrupt procedure.

Compiler error 116: Must be in 80x87 mode to compile

This construct can be compiled only in the `{$N+}` state.

Operations on the 80x87 `Real` types (`Single`, `Double`, `Extended`, and `Comp`) are not allowed in the `{$N-}` state.

Compiler error 117: Target address not found

The Search/Find Error command couldn't locate a statement that corresponds to the specified address.

Compiler error 118: Include files are not allowed here

Every statement part must be contained entirely in one file.

Compiler error 120: NIL expected

Typed constants of pointer types can be initialized only to the value `nil`.

Compiler error 121: Invalid qualifier

You're probaby trying to do one of the following:

- Index a variable that is not an array.
- Specify fields in a variable that is not a record.
- Dereference a variable that is not a pointer.

Compiler error 122: Invalid variable reference

This construct follows the syntax of a variable reference, but it doesn't denote a memory location.

You're probably calling a pointer function, but forgetting to dereference the result.

Compiler error 123: Too many symbols

The program or unit declares more than 64K of symbols.

If you're compiling with `{$D+}`, try turning it off. (*Note:* This step prevents you from finding run-time errors in that module.)

You can also try moving some declarations into a separate unit.

Compiler error 124: Statement part too large

Turbo Pascal limits the size of a statement part to about 24K.

If you encounter this error, move sections of the statement part into one or more procedures.

Compiler error 126: Files must be var parameters

You're probably trying to declare a file-type value parameter.

File-type parameters must be `var` parameters.

Compiler error 127: Too many conditional symbols

There isn't enough room to define further conditional symbols.

Try to eliminate some symbols, or shorten some of the symbolic names.

Compiler error 128: Misplaced conditional directive

The compiler encountered an `{$ELSE}` or `{$ENDIF}` directive without a matching `{$IFDEF}`, `{$IFNDEF}`, or `{$IFOPT}` directive.

Compiler error 129: ENDIF directive missing

The source file ended within a conditional compilation construct.

Turbo Pascal requires an equal number of `{$IFxxx}`s and `{$ENDIF}`s in a source file.

Compiler error 130: Error in initial conditional defines

The initial conditional symbols specified in Options/Compiler/Conditional Defines (or in a `/D` directive) are invalid.

Turbo Pascal for Windows expects zero or more identifiers separated by blanks, commas, or semicolons.

Compiler error 131: Header does not match previous definition

The procedure or function header specified in an interface part or `FORWARD` declaration doesn't match this header.

Compiler error 132: Critical disk error

A critical error occurred during compilation (for example, a Drive Not Ready error).

Compiler error 133: Cannot evaluate this expression

You might be trying to use a nonsupported feature in a constant expression or in a debug expression.

For example, you might be attempting to use the `Sin` function in a `const` declaration, or attempting to call a user-defined function in a debug expression.

Compiler error 136: Invalid indirect reference

The statement attempts to make an invalid indirect reference.

For example, you might be using an absolute variable whose base variable is not known in the current module, or using an inline routine that references a variable not known in the current module.

Compiler error 137: Structured variables are not allowed here

You might be trying to perform a nonsupported operation on a structured variable.

For example, you might be trying to multiply two records.

Compiler error 140: Invalid floating-point operation

An operation on two real type values produced an overflow or a division by zero.

Compiler error 142: Procedure or function variable expected

In this context, the address operator (@) can be used only with a procedure or function variable.

Compiler error 143: Invalid procedure or function reference

You're probably trying to call a procedure in an expression.

A procedure or a function must be compiled in the `{$F+}` state, and cannot be declared with inline or interrupt if it is to be assigned to a procedure variable.

Compiler error 146: File access denied

The file couldn't be opened or created. The program might be trying to write to a read-only file.

Compiler error 147: Object type expected

The identifier doesn't denote an object type.

Compiler error 148: Local object types are not allowed

Object types can be defined only in the outermost scope of a program or unit.

Object type definitions within procedures and functions are not allowed.

Compiler error 149: VIRTUAL expected

The keyword `virtual` is missing.

`virtual` is a procedure directive. A `virtual` method is a method whose call is linked to its code at run-time, by a process called late binding. For example:

```
procedure Method(<parameter list>); virtual;
```

Declaring a method as `virtual` makes it possible for methods with the same name to be implemented in different ways up and down a hierarchy of object types.

Compiler error 150: Method identifier expected

The identifier doesn't denote a method.

Compiler error 151: Virtual constructors are not allowed

A constructor method must be static.

Compiler error 152: Constructor identifier expected

The identifier doesn't denote a constructor.

Compiler error 153: Destructor identifier expected

The identifier doesn't denote a destructor.

Compiler error 154: Fail only allowed within constructors

The `Fail` standard procedure can be used only within constructors.

Compiler error 155: Invalid combination of opcode and operands

The assembler opcode doesn't accept this combination of operands. Possible causes are

- Too many or too few operands for this assembler opcode; for example, `INC AX,BX` or `MOV AX`.
- The number of operands is correct, but their types or order don't match the opcode; for example, `DEC 1`, `MOV AX,CL` or `MOV 1,AX`.

Compiler error 156: Memory reference expected

The assembler operand isn't a memory reference, which is required here.

Most likely, you've omitted the square brackets around an index register operand; for example, `MOV AX,BX+SI` rather than `MOV AX,[BX+SI]`.

Compiler error 157: Cannot add or subtract relocatable symbols

The only arithmetic operation that can be performed on a relocatable symbol in an assembler operand is addition or subtraction of a constant.

Variables, procedures, functions, and labels are relocatable symbols. Assuming that `Var` is variable and `Const` is a constant, then the instructions `MOV AX,Const+Const` and `MOV AX,Var+Const` are valid, but `MOV AX,Var+Var` is not.

Compiler error 158: Invalid register combination

Valid index-register combinations are `[BX]`, `[BP]`, `[SI]`, `[DI]`, `[BX+SI]`, `[BX+DI]`, `[BP+SI]`, and `[BP+DI]`. Other index-register combinations, such as `[AX]`, `[BP+BX]`, and `[SI+DX]`, are not allowed.

Local variables are always allocated on the stack and accessed by way of the BP register. The assembler automatically adds `[BP]` in references to such variables; therefore, a construct like `Local[BX]` (where `Local` is a local variable) appears valid, but it's not, because the final operand would become `Local[BP+BX]`.

Compiler error 159: 286/287 instructions are not enabled

Use a {$G+} compiler directive to enable 286/287 opcodes, but notice that the resulting code cannot be run on 8086- and 8088-based machines.

Compiler error 160: Invalid symbol reference

This symbol cannot be accessed in an assembler operand. Possible causes are

- You're trying to access a standard procedure, a standard function, or the `Mem`, `MemW`, `MemL`, `Port`, or `PortW` special arrays in an assembler operand.
- You're trying to access a string, floating-point, or set constant in an assembler operand.
- You're trying to access an inline procedure or function in an assembler operand.
- You're trying to access the `@Result` special symbol outside a function.
- You're trying to generate a short JMP instruction that jumps to something other than a label.

Compiler error 161: Code generation error

The preceding statement part contains a LOOPNE, LOOPE, LOOP, or JCXZ instruction that cannot reach its target label.

Compiler error 162: ASM expected

The compiler expects an `asm` reserved word at this location.

Compiler error 163: Duplicate dynamic method index

This dynamic method index has been used already by another method.

Compiler error 164: Duplicate resource identifier

This resource file contains a resource with a name or ID that has been used already by another resource.

Compiler error 165: Duplicate or invalid export index

The ordinal number specified in the index cause is not within the range 1..32767, or has been used already by another exported routine.

Compiler error 166: Procedure or function identifier expected

The exports clause allows only procedures and functions to be exported.

Compiler error 167: Cannot export this symbol

A procedure or function cannot be exported unless it was declared with the export function.

Compiler error 168: Duplicate export name

The name specified in the name clause has been used already by another exported routine.

Run-time Error Messages

Error Number	*Error Message*
1	Invalid function number
2	File not found
3	Path not found
4	Too many open files
5	File access denied
6	Invalid file handle
12	Invalid file access code
15	Invalid drive number
16	Cannot remove current directory
17	Cannot rename across drives
100	Disk read error

Error Number	*Error Message*
101	Disk write error
102	File not assigned
103	File not open
104	File not open for input
105	File not open for output
106	Invalid numeric format
200	Division by zero
201	Range check error
202	Stack overflow error
203	Heap overflow error
204	Invalid pointer operation
205	Floating point overflow
206	Floating point underflow
207	Invalid floating point operation
210	Object not initialized
211	Call to abstract method
212	Stream registration error
213	Collection index out of range
214	Collection overflow error

Run-time error 1: Invalid function number

You tried to call a nonexistent DOS function.

Run-time error 2: File not found

The routines `Reset`, `Append`, `Rename`, and `Erase` report this error if the name assigned to the file variable doesn't specify an existing file.

Run-time error 3: Path not found

The routines `Reset`, `Append`, `Rewrite`, `Rename`, and `Erase` report this error if the name assigned to the file variable is invalid or specifies a non-existent subdirectory.

The routines `ChDir`, `MkDir`, and `RmDir` report this error if the path is invalid or if it specifies a non-existent subdirectory.

Run-time error 4: Too many open files

The routines `Reset`, `Rewrite`, and `Append` report this error if the program has too many open files.

DOS never allows more than 15 open files per process.

If you get this error with less than 15 open files, the CONFIG.SYS file might not include a `FILES=xx` entry (or `xx` might specify too few files).

Increase the number `xx` to some suitable value, between 20 and 30.

Run-time error 5: File access denied

Reported By	*When Problem Occurs*
Reset	FileMode allows writing, and the name assigned to the file variable specifies a directory or a read-only file.
Append	FileMode allows writing, and the name assigned to the file variable specifies a directory or a read-only file.
Rewrite	The directory is full, or the name assigned to the file variable specifies a directory or an existing read-only file.
Rename	The name assigned to the file variable specifies a directory, or the new name specifies an existing file.
Erase	The name assigned to the file variable specifies a directory or a read-only file.
MkDir	A file with the same name exists in the parent directory, or there is no room in the parent directory, or the path specifies a device.
RmDir	The directory isn't empty, or the path doesn't specify a directory, or the path specifies the root directory.

Reported By	*When Problem Occurs*
Read	(On a typed or untyped file): The file is not open for reading.
BlockRead	(On a typed or untyped file): The file is not open for reading.
Write	(On a typed or untyped file): The file is not open for writing.
BlockWrite	(On a typed or untyped file): The file is not open for writing.

Run-time error 6: Invalid file handle

This error is reported if an invalid file handle is passed to a DOS system call.

This error should never occur; if it does, you know that the file variable is somehow trashed.

Run-time error 12: Invalid file access code

`Reset` and `Append` report this error (on a typed or untyped file) if the value of FileMode is invalid.

Run-time error 15: Invalid drive number

`GetDir` and `ChDir` report this error if the drive number is invalid.

Run-time error 16: Cannot remove current directory

`RmDir` reports this error if the path specifies the current directory.

Run-time error 17: Cannot rename across drives

`Rename` reports this error if both names are not on the same drive.

Run-time error 100: Disk read error

`Read` reports this error on a typed file if you attempt to read past the end of the file.

Run-time error 101: Disk write error

`Close`, `Write`, `Writeln`, and `Flush` report this error if the disk becomes full.

Run-time error 102: File not assigned

`Reset`, `Rewrite`, `Append`, `Rename`, and `Erase` report this error if the file variable has not been assigned a name through a call to `Assign`.

Run-time error 103: File not open

The following procedures (or functions) report this error if the file isn't open:

```
BlockRead
BlockWrite
Close
Eof
FilePos
FileSize
Flush
Read
Seek
Write
```

Run-time error 104: File not open for input

The following procedures (or functions) report this error on a text file if the file isn't open for input:

```
Eof
Eoln
Read
ReadLn
SeekEof
SeekEoln
```

Run-time error 105: File not open for output

This error occurs if you try to use standard input and output functions such as `Readln` and `Writeln` without the `Uses WinCRT;` statement.

To correct this error, just add `Uses WinCRT;` to your program.

Run-time error 106: Invalid numeric format

`Read` and `Readln` report this error if a numeric value read from a text file doesn't conform to the proper numeric format.

Run-time error 200: Division by zero

The program attempted to divide a number by 0 during a `/`, `mod`, or `div` operation.

Run-time error 201: Range check error

This error is reported by statements compiled in the {$R+} state, when one of the following situations arises:

- The index of an array was out of range.
- The program attempted to assign an out-of-range value to a variable.
- The program attempted to pass an out-of-range value as a parameter to a procedure or function.

Run-time error 202: Stack overflow error

An application reports this error on entry to a procedure or function compiled in the {$S+} state when there isn't enough stack space to allocate the subprogram's local variables.

Increase the size of the stack with the `$M` compiler directive.

The Stack Overflow error can also be caused by infinite recursion, or by an assembly language procedure that doesn't maintain the stack properly.

Run-time error 203: Heap overflow error

`New` and `GetMem` report this error when there isn't enough free space in the heap to allocate a block of the requested size.

Run-time error 204: Invalid pointer operation

`Dispose` and `FreeMem` report this error if the pointer is nil or if it points to a location outside the heap.

Run-time error 205: Floating point overflow

A floating-point operation produced a number too large for Turbo Pascal (or the numeric coprocessor, if there is one) to handle.

Run-time error 206: Floating point underflow

A floating-point operation produced an underflow.

This error is reported only if you are using a numeric coprocessor with a control word that unmasks underflow exceptions.

By default, an underflow causes a result of zero to be returned.

Run-time error 207: Invalid floating point operation

One of the following floating-point errors occurred:

- The real value passed to `Trunc` or `Round` could not be converted to an integer within the `Longint` range (–2147483648 to 2147483647).
- The argument passed to the `Sqrt` function was negative.
- The argument passed to the `Ln` function was 0 or negative.
- An 80x87 stack overflow occurred.

Run-time error 210: Object not initialized

With range-checking on, you made a call to an object's `virtual` method, before the object had been initialized by way of a constructor call.

Run-time error 211: Call to abstract method

This error is generated by the `Abstract` procedure in the `WObjects` unit.

It indicates that your program tried to execute an abstract `virtual` method.

Run-time error 212: Stream registration error

This error is generated by the `RegisterType` procedure in the `WObjects` unit.

It indicates that one of the following errors has occurred:

- The stream registration record does not reside in the data segment.
- The `ObjType` field of the stream registration record is 0.

- The type has already been registered.
- Another type with the same `ObjType` value already exists.

Run-time error 213: Collection index out of range

The index passed to a `TCollection` method is out of range.

Run-time error 214: Collection overflow error

This error is reported by a `TCollection` if an attempt is made to add an element when the collection cannot be expanded.

L

REFERENCE

WINDOW MANAGER INTERFACE PROCEDURES AND FUNCTIONS

Alphabetical listing of Windows Manager Interface procedures and functions:

```
Caret                      Input
Clipboard                  Menu
Cursor                     Message
Dialog-Box                 Painting
Display and Movement       Property
Error                      Scrolling
Hardware                   System
Hook                       Window-Creation
Information
```

Caret Procedures and Functions

```
CreateCaret                HideCaret
DestroyCaret               SetCaretBlinkTime
GetCaretBlinkTime          SetCaretPos
GetCaretPos                ShowCaret
```

CreateCaret

```
procedure CreateCaret(Wnd: HWnd; ABitmap: HBitmap; Width,
Height: Integer);
```

Creates a new shape for the system caret.

Parameters	*Description*
Wnd	Owning window of the new caret
ABitmap	Bitmap that defines the caret; if 0 caret is black; if 1 caret is gray
Width	Caret width (in logical units)
Height	Caret height (in logical units)

DestroyCaret

```
procedure DestroyCaret;
```

Destroys the current caret, frees it from the owning window, and removes it from the screen (if it is currently visible).

GetCaretBlinkTime

```
function GetCaretBlinkTime: Word;
```

Gets caret blink (time between flashes of the caret).

Return Value:
Blink rate (in milliseconds).

GetCaretPos

```
procedure GetCaretPos(var Point: TPoint);
```

Gets the current caret position (in client coordinates).

Parameter	*Description*
Point	Receiving `TPoint` structure

HideCaret

```
procedure HideCaret(Wnd: HWnd);
```

Nondestructively removes the caret from the display screen.

Parameter	*Description*
Wnd	Owning window of caret or 0 if owning window is in current task

SetCaretBlinkTime

```
procedure SetCaretBlinkTime(MSeconds: Word);
```

Sets the elapsed time between caret flashes.

Parameter	*Description*
MSeconds	Blink rate (in milliseconds)

SetCaretPos

```
procedure SetCaretPos(X, Y: Integer);
```

Moves the caret to the specified (X, Y) position.

Parameter	*Description*
X, Y	New position (in logical coordinates)

ShowCaret

```
procedure ShowCaret(Wnd: HWnd);
```

Shows a caret that is owned by `Wnd` on the display.

Parameter	*Description*
Wnd	Window identifier or 0 for a window in the current task.

Clipboard Procedures and Functions

```
ChangeClipboardChain
CloseClipboard
EmptyClipboard
EnumClipboardFormats
GetClipboardData
GetClipboardFormatName
GetClipboardOwner
GetClipboardViewer
GetPriorityClipboardFormat
IsClipboardFormatAvailable
OpenClipboard
RegisterClipboardFormat
SetClipboardData
SetClipboardViewer
```

ChangeClipboardChain

```
function ChangeClipboardChain(Wnd, WndNext: HWnd): Bool;
```

Removes `Wnd` from the chain of clipboard viewers and replaces it with `WndNext`.

Parameters	*Description*
Wnd	Window to be removed from chain
WndNext	Window that follows `Wnd` in the clipboard-viewer chain.

Return Value:
Nonzero if the window is found and removed.

CloseClipboard

```
function CloseClipboard: Bool;
```

Closes the clipboard to allow the clipboard to be accessed by other applications.

Return Value:
Nonzero if clipboard is closed; else 0.

EmptyClipboard

```
function EmptyClipboard: Bool;
```

Empties the clipboard and frees handles to data in the clipboard. Ownership is assigned to the window that has the clipboard open.

Return Value:
Nonzero if the clipboard is emptied; 0 if error.

EnumClipboardFormats

```
function EnumClipboardFormats(Format: Word): Word;
```

Enumerates list of available clipboard formats.

Parameter	*Description*
Format	Known format or 0 for first format in list; the formats are specified by the `cf_Clipboard` formats.

Return Value:
Next known clipboard format; 0 if end of format list or if clipboard closed.

GetClipboardData

```
function GetClipboardData(Format: Word): THandle;
```

Gets clipboard data in a specified format. The clipboard controls the returned memory block.

Parameter	*Description*
Format	Clipboard data format; one of the `cf_ Clipboard` formats' constants

Return Value:
Memory block containing clipboard data; 0 if error.

GetClipboardFormatName

```
function GetClipboardFormatName(Format: Word; FormatName: PChar;
  MaxCount: Integer): Integer;
```

Gets a registered format name from the clipboard.

Parameters	*Description*
Format	Clipboard format; one of the `cf_ Clipboard` formats' constants
FormatName	Receiving buffer
MaxCount	Size of buffer

Return Value:
Actual length of copied string; 0 if invalid format requested.

GetClipboardOwner

```
function GetClipboardOwner: HWnd;
```

Gets the window that currently owns the clipboard.

Return Value:
Owning window; 0 if no owner.

GetClipboardViewer

```
function GetClipboardViewer: HWnd;
```

Gets the first window in the clipboard-viewer chain.

Return Value:
Window currently responsible for displaying the clipboard; 0 if no viewer.

GetPriorityClipboardFormat

```
function GetPriorityClipboardFormat(var PriorityList;
  Count: Integer): Integer;
```

Gets the first clipboard format in `PriorityList` for which data exists.

Parameters	*Description*
PriorityList	Integer array containing clipboard formats in priority order; the formats are `cf_ Clipboard` formats
Count	Size of `PriorityList`

Return Value:
Highest priority format in list: –1 if no match; 0 if there's no data in the clipboard.

IsClipboardFormatAvailable

```
function IsClipboardFormatAvailable(Format: Word): Bool;
```

Determines whether data in the specified format is in the clipboard.

Parameter	*Description*
Format	Registered clipboard format; one of the `cf_Clipboard` formats' constants

Return Value:
Nonzero if data available in `Format`; else 0.

OpenClipboard

```
function OpenClipboard(Wnd: HWnd): Bool;
```

Opens the clipboard for exclusive use by an application.

Parameter	*Description*
Wnd	Window identifier

Return Value:
Nonzero if successful; 0 if `Clipboard` already opened by another application.

RegisterClipboardFormat

```
function RegisterClipboardFormat(FormatName: PChar): Word;
```

Registers a clipboard format, incrementing the format's reference count if it had been previously registered.

Parameter	*Description*
FormatName	Format name (null-terminated)

Return Value:
Registered format identifier ($C000 to $FFFF) if successful; else 0.

SetClipboardData

```
function SetClipboardData(Format: Word; Mem: THandle): THandle;
```

Sets a data handle to the clipboard in `Format`. Usually the data handle is freed before the function returns.

Parameters	*Description*
Format	One of the `cf_ Clipboard` formats' constants
Mem	Handle to global memory block containing data in `format` or 0 for `wm_RenderFormat` message

Return Value:
Data identifier assigned by `Clipboard`.

SetClipboardViewer

```
function SetClipboardViewer(Wnd: HWnd): HWnd;
```

Adds a window to the chain of windows to be notified by a `wm_DrawClipboard` message whenever the clipboard changes.

Parameter	*Description*
Wnd	Window identifier

Return Value:
Next window in clipboard-viewer chain.

Cursor Procedures and Functions

```
ClipCursor
CreateCursor
DestroyCursor
GetCursorPos
LoadCursor
SetCursor
SetCursorPos
ShowCursor
```

ClipCursor

```
procedure ClipCursor(Rect: LPRect);
```

Keeps cursor within `Rect`. If `Rect` is nil the cursor is unbounded.

Parameter	*Description*
Rect	Bounding `TRect` in screen coordinates

CreateCursor

```
function CreateCursor(Instance: THandle; Xhotspot, Yhotspot,
   Width, Height: Integer; ANDBitPlane, XORBitPlane: Pointer): HCursor
```

Creates a cursor.

Parameters	Description
Instance	Module instance creating the cursor
Xhotspot, Yhotspot	Position of cursor hotspot
Width	Cursor width (in pixels)
Height	Cursor height (in pixels)
ANDBitPlane	Array of bytes containing `AND` mask
XORBitPlane	Array of bytes containing `XOR` mask

Return Value:
Cursor identifier if successful; else 0.

DestroyCursor

```
function DestroyCursor(Cursor: HCursor): Bool;
```

Destroys cursor and frees associated memory.

Parameter	Description
Cursor	Cursor identifier

Return Value:
Nonzero if successful; else 0.

GetCursorPos

```
procedure GetCursorPos(var Point: TPoint);
```

Gets the screen coordinates of the cursor's current position.

Parameter	Description
Point	Receiving `TPoint` structure

LoadCursor

```
function LoadCursor(Instance: THandle; CursorName: PChar): HCursor;
```

Loads the named cursor resource.

Parameters	Description
Instance	Module instance whose executable file contains the cursor or 0 for predefined cursor
CursorName	String (null-terminated) or integer ID name or a predefined cursor, specified with one of the `idc_ Standard` cursor IDs' constants.

Return Value:
Cursor identifier if successful; 0 if cursor is not found; undefined if not a cursor resource.

SetCursor

```
function SetCursor(Cursor: HCursor): HCursor;
```

Sets the cursor shape to the specified cursor resource.

Parameter	Description
Cursor	Cursor resource identifier (previously returned by `LoadCursor`)

Return Value:
Previous cursor shape; 0 if no previous cursor.

SetCursorPos

```
procedure SetCursorPos(X, Y: Integer);
```

Moves the cursor to the specified screen coordinates. The position is adjusted if it lies outside the `ClipCursor` rectangle.

Parameter	Description
X, Y	New position (in screen coordinates) of the cursor

ShowCursor

```
function ShowCursor(Show: Bool): Integer;
```

Shows the cursor if its display count (initially set to 0) is greater than or equal to 0. Otherwise the cursor is hidden.

Parameter	*Description*
Show	Nonzero to increment display count or 0 to decrement display count

Return Value:
New display count.

Dialog-Box Procedures and Functions

```
CheckDlgButton
CheckRadioButton
CreateDialog
CreateDialogIndirect
CreateDialogIndirectParam
CreateDialogParam
DefDlgProc
DialogBox
DialogBoxIndirect
DialogBoxIndirectParam
DialogBoxParam
DlgDirList
DlgDirListComboBox
DlgDirSelect
DlgDirSelectComboBox
EndDialog
GetDialogBaseUnits
GetDlgCtrlID
GetDlgItem
GetDlgItemInt
GetDlgItemText
GetNextDlgGroupItem
GetNextDlgTabItem
IsDialogMessage
IsDlgButtonChecked
MapDialogRect
SendDlgItemMessage
SetDlgItemInt
SetDlgItemText
```

CheckDlgButton

```
procedure CheckDlgButton(Dlg: HWnd; IDButton: Integer;
  Check: Word);
```

Places or removes a check mark from a button control or changes the state of a 3-button control.

Parameters	*Description*
Dlg	Dialog box that contains the button
IDButton	Button control to be modified
Check	Removed(0), checked(1), grayed(2)

CheckRadioButton

```
procedure CheckRadioButton(Dlg: HWnd; IDFirstButton,
  IDLastButton, IDCheckButton: Integer);
```

Checks `IDCheckButton` and removes the check mark from the group of radio buttons specified by `IDFirstButton` and `IDLastButton`.

Parameters	*Description*
Dlg	Dialog box
IDFirstButton	ID of first radio button in group
IDLastButton	ID of last radio button in group
IDCheckButton	ID of radio button to check

CreateDialog

```
function (Instance: THandle; TemplateName: PChar; WndParent: HWnd;
  DialogFunc: TFarProc): HWnd;
```

Creates a modeless dialog box defined by `TemplateName` dialog box resource.

Parameters	*Description*
Instance	Module instance whose executable file contains the dialog box resource
TemplateName	Dialog box resource name (null-terminated)
WndParent	Parent window of the dialog box
DialogFunc	Dialog function procedure-instance address or nil if class defined

Return Value:
Dialog box window handle if successful; else 0.

CreateDialogIndirect

```
function CreateDialogIndirect(Instance: THandle;
  DialogTemplate: PChar; Parent: HWnd; DialogFunc: TFarProc): HWnd;
```

Creates a modeless dialog box defined by dialog template.

Parameters	*Description*
Instance	Module instance
DialogTemplate	Structure containing dialog box template
WndParent	Owning window of the dialog box
DialogFunc	Dialog callback function procedure-instance address

Return Value:
Dialog box window handle if successful; else 0.

CreateDialogIndirectParam

```
function CreateDialogIndirectParam(Instance: THandle;
  var DialogTemplate; WndParent: HWnd; DialogFunc: TFarProc;
  InitParam: Longint): HWnd;
```

Creates the modeless dialog box defined by dialog template. It differs from `CreateDialogIndirect` because it allows you to pass a parameter, `InitParam`, to the callback function.

Parameters	*Description*
Instance	Module instance
DialogTemplate	Structure containing dialog box template
WndParent	Owning window of the dialog box
DialogFunc	Dialog function procedure-instance address, or nil if class defined
InitParam	Value passed to dialog function (`lParam` of `wm_InitDialog` message) when the dialog box is created

Return Value:
Dialog box window handle if successful; else 0.

CreateDialogParam

```
function CreateDialogParam(Instance: THandle; TemplateName: PChar;
  WndParent: HWnd; DialogFunc: TFarProc; InitParam:
  Longint): HWnd;
```

Creates a modeless dialog box defined by `TemplateName`.

Parameter	***Description***
Instance	Module instance whose executable file contains the dialog box template
TemplateName	Dialog box template name (null-terminated)
Parent	Owning window of the dialog box
DialogFunc	Dialog function procedure-instance address, or nil if class defined
InitParam	Value passed to dialog function (`lParam` of `wm_Init Dialog` message) when the dialog box is created

Return Value:
Dialog box window handle if successful; else 0.

DefDlgProc

```
function DefDlgProc(Dlg: HWnd; Msg, wParam: Word;
  lParam: Longint): Longint;
```

Supplies default processing for dialogs with a private window class.

Parameters	***Description***
Dlg	Dialog box identifier
Msg	Message number
wParam	Message-dependent information
lParam	Message-dependent information

Return Value:
Result of the message processing.

DialogBox

```
function DialogBox(Instance: THandle; TemplateName: PChar;
  WndParent: HWnd; DialogFunc: TFarProc): Integer;
```

Creates a modal dialog box defined by `TemplateName` and sends `wm_InitDialog` before displaying the dialog.

Parameters	*Description*
Instance	Module instance whose executable file contains the dialog box template
TemplateName	Dialog box template name (null-terminated)
WndParent	Owning window
DialogFunc	Dialog callback function procedure-instance address

Return Value:
`EndDialog nResult` parameter; –1 if dialog could not be created.

DialogBoxIndirect

```
function DialogBoxIndirect(Instance, DialogTemplate:THandle;
  WndParent: HWnd; DialogFunc: TFarProc): Integer;
```

Creates the modal dialog box defined by dialog template, and sends `wm_InitDialog` before displaying the dialog.

Parameters	*Description*
Instance	Module instance whose executable file contains the dialog box template
DialogTemplate	Global memory block containing dialog template structure
WndParent	Owning window
DialogFunc	Dialog callback function procedure-instance address

Return Value:
`EndDialog nResult` parameter; –1 if dialog could not be created.

continues

DialogBoxIndirectParam

```
function DialogBoxIndirectParam(Instance, DialogTemplate: THandle;
  WndParent: HWnd; DialogFunc: TFarProc; InitParam: Longint): Integer;
```

Creates the modal dialog box defined by dialog template and sends `wm_InitDialog` before displaying the dialog. Also, `DialogBoxIndirectPAram` allows you to send an initial parameter to the callback function.

Parameters	*Description*
Instance	Module instance whose executable file contains the dialog box template
DialogTemplate	Global memory block containing dialog template structure
WndParent	Owning window
DialogFunc	Dialog function procedure-instance address
InitParam	Passed in `lParam` of `wm_InitDialog` message

Return Value:

`EndDialog nResult` parameter; –1 if dialog could not be created.

DialogBoxParam

```
function DialogBoxParam(Instance: THandle; TemplateName: PChar;
  Parent: HWnd; DialogFunc: TFarProc; InitParam: Longint): Integer;
```

Creates the modal dialog box defined by `TemplateName` and sends `wm_InitDialog` before displaying the dialog. Also allows you to send an initial parameter to the callback function.

Parameters	*Description*
Instance	Module instance whose executable file contains the dialog box template
TemplateName	Dialog box template name (null-terminated)
Parent	Owning window
DialogFunc	Dialog function procedure-instance address
InitParam	Passed in `lParam` of `wm_InitDialog` message

Return Value:

`EndDialog nResult` parameter; –1 if dialog could not be created.

DlgDirList

```
function DlgDirList(Dlg: HWnd; PathSpec: PChar; IDListBox,
  IDStaticPath: Integer; Filetype: Word): Integer;
```

Fills `IDListBox` with a file or directory listing that matches the path name specified by `PathSpec`.

Parameter	***Description***
Dlg	Dialog box containing `IDListBox`
PathSpec	Path name string (null-terminated)
IDListBox	List-box control ID
IDStaticPath	Static-text control ID to display current drive and directory
Filetype	$0000 (read/write), $0001 (read-only), $0002 (hidden), $0004 (system), $0010 (subdirectories), $0020 (archives), $2000 (`lb_Dir`), $4000(drives), $8000 (exclusive)

Return Value:
Nonzero if listing made; 0 if invalid search path.

DlgDirListComboBox

```
function DlgDirListComboBox(Dlg: HWnd; PathSpec: PChar;
  IDComboBox, IDStaticPath: Integer; Filetype: Word): Integer;
```

Fills `IDComboBox` with a file or directory listing that matches the path name specified by `PathSpec`.

Parameters	***Description***
Dlg	Dialog box containing `IDComboBox`
PathSpec	Path name string (null-terminated)
IDComboBox	Combo box control ID
IDStaticPath	Static-text control ID to display current drive and directory
Filetype	$0000 (read/write), $0001 (read-only), $0002 (hidden), $0004 (system), $0010 (subdirectories), $0020 (archives), $2000 (`lb_Dir`), $4000(drives), $8000 (exclusive)

Return Value:
Nonzero if listing made; 0 if invalid search path.

DlgDirSelect

```
function DlgDirSelect(Dlg: HWnd; Str: PChar; IDListBox: Integer): Bool
```

Gets current list-box selection and fills `Str`.

Parameter	***Description***
Dlg	Dialog box containing `IDListBox`
Str	Path name buffer
IDListBox	List-box control ID

Return Value:
Nonzero if current selection is a directory; else 0.

DlgDirSelectComboBox

```
function DlgDirSelectComboBox(Dlg: HWnd; Str: PChar;
  IDComboBox: Integer): Bool;
```

Gets current combo box selection, from a simple combo box (`cbs_Simple`) only, and fills `Str`.

Parameters	***Description***
Dlg	Dialog box containing `IDComboBox`
Str	Path name buffer
IDComboBox	Combo box control ID

Return Value:
Nonzero if current selection is a directory; else 0.

DlgDirSelect

```
function DlgDirSelect(Dlg: HWnd; Str: PChar; IDListBox: Integer): Bool
```

Gets current list-box selection and fills `Str`.

Parameters	***Description***
Dlg	Dialog box containing `IDListBox`
Str	Path name buffer
IDListBox	List-box control ID

Return Value:
Nonzero if current selection is a directory; else 0.

DlgDirSelectComboBox

```
function DlgDirSelectComboBox(Dlg: HWnd; Str: PChar;
  IDComboBox: Integer): Bool;
```

Gets current combo box selection, from a simple combo box (`cbs_Simple`) only, and fills `Str`.

Parameters	*Description*
Dlg	Dialog box containing `IDComboBox`
Str	Path name buffer
IDComboBox	Combo box control ID

Return Value:
Nonzero if current selection is a directory; else 0.

EndDialog

```
procedure EndDialog(Dlg: HWnd; Result: Integer);
```

Terminates a modal dialog box. The value specified by `Result` is returned to the creating `DialogBox` function.

Parameters	*Description*
Dlg	Dialog to be destroyed
Result	Return value

GetDialogBaseUnits

```
function GetDialogBaseUnits: Longint;
```

Gets dialog base units. The base width represents the average system font width. The dialog unit is 1/4 and 1/8 the returned base width and height unit, respectively.

Return Value:
Height (in pixels), base unit in high word; width (in pixels), base unit in low word.

GetDlgCtrlID

```
function GetDlgCtrlID(Wnd: HWnd): Integer;
```

Gets a control window's ID value.

Parameter	*Description*
Wnd	Control identifier

Return Value:
Control's numeric identifier; 0 if error.

GetDlgItem

```
function GetDlgItem(Dlg: HWnd; IDDlgItem: Integer): HWnd;
```

Gets a control handle contained in the specified dialog box.

Parameters	*Description*
Dlg	Dialog box containing the control
IDDlgItem	Control ID

Return Value:
Control identifier; 0 if the specified control doesn't exist.

GetDlgItemInt

```
function GetDlgItemInt(Dlg: HWnd; IDDlgItem: Integer;
  Translate: LPBool; Signed: Bool): Word;
```

Translates a control's text, in a dialog box, into an integer value. Preceding spaces are stripped.

Parameter	*Description*
Dlg	Dialog box identifier
IDDlgItem	Item ID
Translate	Returned Boolean value; 0 if translation error

Return Value:
Translated value.

GetDlgItemText

```
function GetDlgItemText(Dlg: HWnd; IDDlgItem: Integer;
  Str: PChar; MaxCount: Integer): Integer;
```

Gets a control's text.

Parameters	*Description*
Dlg	Dialog box identifier
IDDlgItem	Item ID
Str	Buffer to receive text
MaxCount	Size of buffer

Return Value:
Number of characters copied.

GetNextDlgGroupItem

```
function GetNextDlgGroupItem(Dlg: HWnd; Ctrl: HWnd;
  Previous: Bool): HWnd;
```

Gets the next or previous `ws_Group` style control from `Ctrl`. The search is cyclical.

Parameters	*Description*
Dlg	Dialog box identifier
Ctrl	Search start control identifier
Previous	Zero to search for previous control or nonzero to search for next

Return Value:
Control identifier.

GetNextDlgTabItem

```
function GetNextDlgTabItem(Dlg: HWnd; Ctrl: HWnd; Previous: Bool): HWnd;
```

Gets the next or previous `ws_TabStop` style control from `Ctrl`. The search is cyclical.

Parameters	Description
Dlg	Dialog box identifier
Ctrl	Search start control identifier
Previous	Zero to search for previous control or nonzero to search for next

Return Value:
Control identifier.

IsDialogMessage

```
function IsDialogMessage(Dlg: HWnd; var Msg: TMsg): Bool;
```

Determines and processes messages for modeless dialog boxes, converting keyboard messages into command messages.

Parameters	Description
Dlgs	Dialog box identifier
Msg	`TMsg` structure

Return Value:
Nonzero if `Msg` processed (`TranslateMessage` and `DispatchMessage` shouldn't be sent messages); else 0.

IsDlgButtonChecked

```
function IsDlgButtonChecked(Dlg: HWnd; IDButton: Integer): Word;
```

Determines whether button control is checked.

Parameters	Description
Dlg	Dialog box identifier
IDButton	Button control ID

Return Value:
Nonzero if checked; else 0. For 3-state button: grayed (2), checked (1), or 0.

MapDialogRect

```
procedure MapDialogRect(Dlg: HWnd; var Rect: TRect);
```

Converts dialog box units in `Rect` to screen units.

Parameters	*Description*
Dlg	Dialog box identifier
Rect	TRect structure

SendDlgItemMessage

```
function SendDlgItemMessage(Dlg: HWnd; IDDlgItem: Integer;
  Msg, wParam: Word; lParam: Longint): Longint;
```

Sends a message to a dialog box control specified by `IDDlgItem`. The function returns after the message is processed.

Parameters	*Description*
Dlg	Dialog box identifier
IDDlgItem	Integer ID of destination dialog item
Msg	Message type
wParam	Additional message information
lParam	Additional message information

Return Value:
Value returned by control's window function; 0 if invalid `IDDlgItem`.

SetDlgItemInt

```
procedure SetDlgItemInt(Dlg: HWnd; IDDlgItem: Integer;
  Value: Word; Signed: Bool);
```

Sets the text of a dialog box control to the converted string value specified by `Value`.

Parameters	*Description*
Dlg	Dialog box identifier
IDDlgItem	Control's integer ID
Value	Set value
Signed	Nonzero if Value is signed

SetDlgItemText

```
procedure SetDlgItemText(Dlg: HWnd; IDDlgItem: Integer; Str: PChar);
```

Sets the caption or text of a dialog box control to the value specified by `Str`.

Parameters	*Description*
Dlg	Dialog box identifier
IDDlgItem	Control's integer ID
Str	String (null-terminated)

Display and Movement Procedures and Functions

```
ArrangeIconicWindows
BeginDeferWindowPos
BringWindowToTop
CloseWindow
DeferWindowPos
EndDeferWindowPos
GetClientRect
GetWindowRect
GetWindowText
GetWindowTextLength
IsIconic
IsWindowVisible
IsZoomed
MoveWindow
OpenIcon
SetWindowPos
SetWindowText
ShowOwnedPopups
ShowWindow
```

ArrangeIconicWindows

```
function ArrangeIconicWindows(Wnd: HWnd): Word;
```

Arranges icons in an `MDI` client window or icons on the desktop window.

Parameters	*Description*
Wnd	Parent window identifier

Return Value:
Height of one row of icons; 0 if no icons.

BeginDeferWindowPos

```
function BeginDeferWindowPos(NumWindows: Integer): THandle;
```

Allocates memory for multiple window-position data structure.

Parameters	*Description*
NumWindows	Initial number of windows with position information that needs to be stored.

Return Value:
Window-position structure identifier.

BringWindowToTop

```
procedure BringWindowToTop(Wnd: HWnd);
```

Activates and brings `Wnd` to top of a stack of overlapping windows.

Parameters	*Description*
Wnd	Pop-up or child window

CloseWindow

```
procedure CloseWindow(Wnd: HWnd);
```

Minimizes `Wnd`. Icons for overlapped windows are moved into the icon area of the screen.

Parameters	*Description*
Wnd	Window to be minimized

DeferWindowPos

```
function DeferWindowPos(WinPosInfo: THandle;
  Wnd, WndInsertAfter: HWnd; X, Y, cX, cY: Integer;
  Flags: Word): THandle;
```

Updates `WinPosInfo` for the window identified by `Wnd`.

Parameters	*Description*
WinPosInfo	Multiple window-position data structure identifier
Wnd	Update information is stored regarding this window
WndInsertAfter	`Wnd` is inserted after this window
X, Y	Windows upper-left corner position
cX	Window's new width
cY	Window's new height
Flags	One of the `swp_ Set` window position flags

Return Value:
Updated multiple window-position data structure.

EndDeferWindowPos

```
procedure EndDeferWindowPos(WinPosInfo: THandle);
```

In a single screen-refresh cycle, `EndDeferWindowPos` updtaes the size and position of one or more windows.

Parameters	*Description*
WinPosInfo	Multiple window data structure containing update information for multiple windows

GetClientRect

```
procedure GetClientRect(Wnd: HWnd; var Rect: TRect);
```

Gets a window's client coordinates.

Parameters	*Description*
Wnd	Window identifier
Rect	`TRect` to receive client coordinates

GetWindowRect

```
procedure GetWindowRect(Wnd: HWnd; var Rect: TRect);
```

Gets the dimensions of a window's bounding rectangle into `Rect` (in screen coordinates).

Parameters	*Description*
Wnd	Window identifier
Rect	Receiving `TRect` structure

GetWindowText

```
function GetWindowText(Wnd: HWnd; Str: PChar;
  MaxCount: Integer): Integer;
```

Copies window's caption or a control's text into `Str`.

Parameters	*Description*
Wnd	Window or control identifier
Str	Receiving string buffer
MaxCount	Size of Str

Return Value:
Number of bytes copied; 0 if no text.

GetWindowTextLength

```
function GetWindowTextLength(Wnd: HWnd): Integer;
```

Gets a window's caption or a control's text length.

Parameters	*Description*
Wnd	Window or control identifier

Return Value:
Text length.

IsIconic

```
function IsIconic(Wnd: HWnd): Bool;
```

Determines whether a window is iconic (minimized).

Parameters	Description
Wnd	Window identifier

Return Value:
Nonzero if minimized; else 0.

IsWindowVisible

```
function IsWindowVisible(Wnd: HWnd): Bool;
```

Determines whether `ShowWindow` has made a window visible.

Parameters	Description
Wnd	Window identifier

Return Value:
Nonzero if window exists on-screen (even if it is covered); else 0.

IsZoomed

```
function IsZoomed(Wnd: HWnd): Bool;
```

Determines whether a window is maximized.

Parameters	Description
Wnd	Window identifier

Return Value:
Nonzero if maximized; else 0.

MoveWindow

```
procedure MoveWindow(Wnd: HWnd; X, Y, Width, Height: Integer;
  Repaint: Bool);
```

Sends a `wm_Size` message to a window. `Width` and `Height` values passed with `wm_Size` are those of the client area.

Parameters	Description
Wnd	Pop-up or child window identifier
X, Y	New upper-left corner of window
Width	New window width
Height	New window height
Repaint	Nonzero to repaint window after moving

OpenIcon

```
function OpenIcon(Wnd: HWnd): Bool;
```

Restores a minimized window to its original size and position.

Parameters	*Description*
Wnd	Window identifier

Return Value:
Nonzero if successful; else 0.

SetWindowPos

```
procedure SetWindowPos(Wnd, WndInsertAfter: HWnd;
  X, Y, cx, cy: Integer; Flags: Word);
```

Changes the size, position, and ordering of a window.

Parameters	*Description*
Wnd	Window identifier
WndInsertAfter	Preceding window in window manager's list
X, Y	Upper-left corner
cx	New window width
cy	New window height
Flags	One of the `swp_` Set window-position flags

SetWindowText

```
procedure SetWindowText(Wnd: HWnd; Str: PChar);
```

Sets the caption title for a window or text of a control with `Str`.

Parameters	*Description*
Wnd	Window or control identifier
Str	String (null-terminated)

ShowOwnedPopups

```
procedure ShowOwnedPopups(Wnd: HWnd; Show: Bool);
```

Shows or hides, as specified by `Show`, all pop-up windows associated with the specified window.

Parameters	Description
Wnd	Window identifier
Show	Nonzero to show all hidden pop ups or 0 to hide all visible pop-ups

ShowWindow

```
function ShowWindow(Wnd: HWnd; CmdShow: Integer): Bool;
```

Shows or hides a window specified by `CmdShow`.

Parameters	Description
Wnd	Window identifier
CmdShow	One of the `sw_ Show` window constants

Return Value:
Nonzero if window was previously visible; 0 if window was previously hidden.

Error Procedures and Functions

```
FlashWindow
MessageBeep
MessageBox
```

FlashWindow

```
function FlashWindow(Wnd: HWnd; Invert: Bool): Bool;
```

Flashes a window or icon and inverts an open window's active status.

Parameters	Description
Wnd	Window to be flashed
Invert	Nonzero to flash or 0 to return to original state (ignored for icons)

Return Value:
Nonzero if window was active previous to call; else 0.

MessageBeep

```
procedure MessageBeep(BeepType: Word);
```

Beeps the system speaker.

Parameters	*Description*
BeepType	Set to 0

MessageBox

```
function MessageBox(Parent: HWnd; Txt, Caption: PChar;
  TextType: Word): Integer;
```

Creates and displays a dialog box containing the specified message and caption and any predefined icons and push-button as specified by `TextType`.

Parameters	*Description*
Parent	Owning window of message box
Txt	Message to display (null-terminated)
Caption	Dialog-box caption (null-terminated) or nil for "Error"
TextType	One or a combination of the `mb_` Message box flags' constants

Return Value:
One of the ID dialog-box command `ID`s if successful; 0 if there's not enough memory to create and display message box.

Hardware Procedures and Functions

```
EnableHardwareInput
GetAsyncKeyState
GetInputState
GetKeyboardState
GetKeyNameText
GetKeyState
GetKBCodePage
OemKeyScan
SetKeyboardState
MapVirtualKey
VkKeyScan
```

EnableHardwareInput

```
function EnableHardwareInput(EnableInput: Bool): Bool;
```

Disables mouse and keyboard input, saving or discarding input as specified by `EnableInput`.

Parameters	*Description*
EnableInput	Nonzero to save input; 0 to discard input

Return Value:
Nonzero (the default) if input was previously enabled; else 0.

GetAsyncKeyState

```
function GetAsyncKeyState(Key: Integer): Integer;
```

Determines the state of a virtual key.

Parameters	*Description*
Key	Virtual-key code

Return Value:
`Key` is down if high-order bit is 1.

GetInputState

```
function GetInputState: Bool;
```

Determines whether the system queue currently contains mouse, keyboard, or timer events.

Return Value:
Nonzero if input detected; else 0.

GetKeyboardState

```
procedure GetKeyboardState(var KeyState: Byte);
```

Copies the virtual keyboard key-set status into `KeyState`. If high bit of byte is 1, key is down. If low bit is 1, key was pressed odd number of times since system start-up.

Parameters	*Description*
KeyState	256-byte character array

GetKeyNameText

```
function GetKeyNameText(lParam: Longint; Buffer: PChar;
  Size: Integer): Integer;
```

Gets key name string for keys longer than a single character.

Parameters	*Description*
lParam	Long parameter to wm_KeyDown message
Buffer	Receiving buffer
Size	Size of buffer

Return Value:
Number of bytes copied.

GetKeyState

```
function GetKeyState(VirtKey: Integer): Integer;
```

Determines whether the state of a virtual key is up, down, or toggled.

Parameters	*Description*
VirtKey	Virtual key

Return Value:
Key is down if high-order bit is 1; Key is toggled if low-order bit is 1.

GetKBCodePage

```
function GetKBCodePage: Integer;
```

Gets the currently loaded OEM or ANSI table.
Return Value: Current code page:

(437) USA
(850) International
(860) Portugal
(861) Iceland
(863) French Canadian
(865) Norway/Denmark

OemKeyScan

```
function OemKeyScan(OemChar: Word): Longint;
```

Maps `OemChar` into OEM (IBM character set) scan codes. The OEM character set is the IBM character set.

Parameters	*Description*
OemChar	OEM ASCII character code (0 to $0FF)

Return Value:
Scan code and shift state (bit 2 Ctrl key, bit 1 Shift key pressed) in low- and high-order word, respectively, if successful; else –1 in low- and high-order word.

SetKeyboardState

```
procedure SetKeyboardState(var KeyState: Byte);
```

Copies `KeyState` into Windows keyboard-state table.

Parameters	*Description*
KeyState	Array of 255 bytes containing key states

MapVirtualKey

```
function MapVirtualKey(Code, MapType: Word): Word;
```

Maps a virtual-key or scan code for a key to its corresponding scan code, virtual-key code, or ASCII value as specified by `MapType`.

Parameters	*Description*
Code	Virtual-key or scan code for a key determined by `MapType` value
MapType	(0) virtual-key code, (1) scan code, (2) virtual-key code

Return Value:
`MapType` values: 0 returns scan code; 1 returns virtual-key code; 2 returns unshifted ASCII value.

VkKeyScan

```
function VkKeyScan(AChar: Word): Word;
```

Translates `AChar` into its corresponding virtual-key code and shift state.

Parameters	*Description*
AChar	ANSI character to find corresponding virtual-key code

Return Value:
Virtual-key code in the low-order byte; the following shift states in the high-order byte:

(0) No shift
(1) Shifted
(2) Control char
(6) Control+Alt
(7) Shift+Control-Alt
or (3), (4), or (5), which aren't used for characters

If there's an error, both bytes are –1.

Hook Procedures and Functions

```
CallMsgFilter
DefHookProc
SetWindowsHook
UnhookWindowsHook
```

CallMsgFilter

```
function CallMsgFilter(var Msg: TMsg; Code: Integer): Bool;
```

Sends `Msg` to the current message filter function.

Parameters	*Description*
Msg	`TMsg` containing message to be filtered
Code	Filter function code

Return Value:
0 if message should be processed; else nonzero.

DefHookProc

```
function DefHookProc(Code: Integer; wParam: Word; lParam: Longint;
  NextHook: TFarProc): Longint;
```

Calls next function in chain of hook (message filter) functions.

Parameters	Description
Code	Determines how message is processed
wParam	Message word parameter
lParams	Message long parameter
NextHook	TFarProc to next hook function

Return Value:
A value depending on code.

SetWindowsHook

```
function SetWindowsHook(FilterType: Integer;
  FilterFunc: TFarProc): TFarProc;
```

Installs a filter function in the chain of filter functions specified by `FilterType`. The filter function is passed a `Code`, `wParam`, and `lParam`, which have values that are filter-type-dependent.

Parameters	Description
FilterType	One of the `wh_` Windows hook codes
FilterFunc	Filter function's procedure-instance address

Return Value:
Procedure-instance address of previously installed filter function; nil if no previous filter.

UnhookWindowsHook

```
function UnhookWindowsHook(Hook: Integer; HookFunc: TFarProc): Bool;
```

Removes a hook function from the chain of hook functions specified by `Hook`.

Parameters	Description
Hook	One of `wh_ Windows` hook codes
HookFunc	`Hook` function's procedure-instance address

Return Value:
Nonzero if successful; else 0.

Information Procedures and Functions

```
AnyPopup
ChildWindowFromPoint
EnumChildWindows
EnumTaskWindows
EnumWindows
FindWindow
GetNextWindow
GetParent
GetTopWindow
GetWindow
GetWindowTask
IsChild
IsWindow
SetParent
WindowFromPoint
```

AnyPopup

```
function AnyPopup: Bool;
```

Decides whether a pop-up window is on the screen.

Return Value:
Nonzero if pop-up window exists; else 0.

ChildWindowFromPoint

```
function ChildWindowFromPoint(WndParent: HWnd; APoint: TPoint): HWnd;
```

Determines which child window owned by `WndParent` contains `APoint`.

Parameters	***Description***
WndParent	Parent window
APoint	`TPoint` structure of client coordinates to be tested

Return Value:
Child window that contains the point; 0 if point lies outside the parent window; `WndParent` if the point is not contained in any child window.

EnumChildWindows

```
function EnumChildWindows(WndParent: HWnd; EnumFunc: TFarProc;
  lParam: Longint): Bool;
```

Enumerates child windows of given parent, passing the child handle and `lParam` to the callback. Enumeration ends if the `callback` returns 0 or the last child is enumerated.

Parameters	*Description*
WndParent	Parent window of child windows to enumerate
EnumFunc	`Callback` function's procedure-instance address
lParam	Value passed to `callback` function

Return Value:
Nonzero if all child windows have been enumerated; else 0.

EnumTaskWindows

```
function EnumTaskWindows(Task: THandle; EnumFunc: TFarProc;
  lParam: Longint): Bool;
```

Enumerates all windows in a task, passing the window handle and `lParam` to the `callback`. Enumeration ends if the `callback` returns 0 or all windows are enumerated.

Parameters	*Description*
Task	Task identifier
EnumFunc	`Callback` function's procedure-instance address
lParam	Value passed to `callback`

Return Value:
Nonzero if all windows are enumerated; else 0.

EnumWindows

```
function EnumWindows(EnumFunc: TFarProc; lParam: Longint): Bool;
```

Enumerates all parent windows on the screen passing the window handle and `lParam` to the `callback`. Enumeration ends if the `callback` returns 0 or all windows are enumerated.

Parameters	Description
EnumFunc	`Callback` function's procedure-instance address
lParam	Value passed to `callback`

Return Value:
Nonzero if all windows are enumerated; else 0.

FindWindow

```
function FindWindow(ClassName, WindowName: PChar): HWnd;
```

Finds a top-level parent window with matching `ClassName` and `WindowName` does not search child windows.

Parameters	Description
ClassName	Window's class name (null-terminated or nil for all)
WindowName	Window's text caption or 0 for all

Return Value:
Window handle; 0 if no window.

GetNextWindow

```
function GetNextWindow(Wnd: HWnd; Flag: Word): HWnd;
```

Gets next or previous window from `Wnd`, if top-level window searches for next top-level window or if child window searches for next child window.

Parameters	Description
Wnd	Window identifier
Flag	One of the `gw_ Get` window constants: `gw_HWndNext` or `gw_HWndPrev`

Return Value:
Window identifier.

GetParent

```
function GetParent(Wnd: HWnd): HWnd;
```

Gets a window's parent window handle.

Parameters	Description
Wnd	Window identifier

Return Value:
Parent window identifier; 0 if no parent window.

GetTopWindow

```
function GetTopWindow(Wnd: HWnd): HWnd;
```

Gets a window's top-level child window.

Parameters	Description
Wnd	Parent window identifier

Return Value:
Child window identifier; 0 if no child window.

GetWindow

```
function GetWindow(Wnd: HWnd; Cmd: Word): HWnd;
```

Gets the window with the relationship specified in `Cmd` to the window specified in `Wnd`.

Parameters	Description
Wnd	Original window
Cmd	One of the `gw_` Get window constants

Return Value:
Window identifier; 0 if window is not found or if invalid `Cmd`.

GetWindowTask

```
function GetWindowTask(Wnd: HWnd): THandle;
```

Gets a window's application task identifier.

Parameters	Description
Wnd	Window identifier

Return Value:
Task identifier.

IsChild

```
function IsChild(Parent, Wnd: HWnd): Bool;
```

Determines whether `Wnd` is a child window of `Parent`.

Parameters	*Description*
Parent	Window identifier
Wnd	Test window

Return Value:
Nonzero if child window; else 0.

IsWindow

```
function IsWindow(Wnd: HWnd): Bool;
```

Determines whether `Wnd` is a valid window.

Parameters	*Description*
Wnd	Window identifier

Return Value:
Nonzero if valid; else 0.

SetParent

```
function SetParent(WndChild, WndNewParent: HWnd): HWnd;
```

Changes the parent of a child window to `WndNewParent`.

Parameters	*Description*
WndChild	Child window identifier
WndNewParent	Parent window identifier

Return Value:
Previous parent window.

WindowFromPoint

```
function WindowFromPoint(Point: TPoint): HWnd;
```

Decides which window contains the specified point.

Parameters	Description
Point	`TPoint` to be checked (in screen coordinates)

Return Value:
Window identifier; 0 if there's no window at specified point.

Input Procedures and Functions

```
EnableWindow
GetActiveWindow
GetCapture
GetCurrentTime
GetDoubleClickTime
GetFocus
GetTickCount
IsWindowEnabled
KillTimer
ReleaseCapture
SetActiveWindow
SetCapture
SetDoubleClickTime
SetFocus
SetSysModalWindow
SetTimer
SwapMouseButton
```

EnableWindow

```
function EnableWindow(Wnd: HWnd; Enable: Bool): Bool;
```

Enables or disables mouse and keyboard input to a window or control.

Parameters	Description
Wnd	Window to be enabled or disabled
Enable	Nonzero to enable; 0 to disable

Return Value:
Nonzero if successful; else 0.

GetActiveWindow

```
function GetActiveWindow: HWnd;
```

Gets the handle of the window that has the current input focus.

Return Value:
Active window identifier.

GetCapture

```
function GetCapture: HWnd;
```

Gets the window that is currently receiving all mouse input.

Return Value:
Window that has the mouse capture; 0 if no window.

GetCurrentTime

```
function GetCurrentTime: Longint;
```

Gets the elapsed time since the system was rebooted.

Return Value:
Current time (in milliseconds).

GetDoubleClickTime

```
function GetDoubleClickTime: Word;
```

Gets the maximum time between a series of two mouse clicks (that is, a double-click).

Return Value:
Current double-click time (in milliseconds)

GetFocus

```
function GetFocus: HWnd;
```

Gets the window that currently has the input focus.

Return Value:
Window identifier if successful; else 0.

GetTickCount

```
function GetTickCount: Longint;
```

Gets the elapsed time since the system started.

Return Value:
Elapsed time (in milliseconds).

IsWindowEnabled

```
function IsWindowEnabled(Wnd: HWnd): Bool;
```

Determines whether a window is enabled for mouse and keyboard input.

Parameters	***Description***
Wnd	Window identifier

Return Value:
Nonzero if enabled; else 0.

KillTimer

```
function KillTimer(Wnd: HWnd; IDEvent: Integer): Bool;
```

Kills a timer event; removes any associated `wm_Timer` messages from the message queue.

Parameters	***Description***
Wnd	Window identifier
IDEvent	Timer event ID

Return Value:
Nonzero if successful; 0 if invalid `IDEvent`.

ReleaseCapture

```
procedure ReleaseCapture;
```

Releases mouse capture; restores normal input processing.

SetActiveWindow

```
function SetActiveWindow(Wnd: HWnd): HWnd;
```

Activates a top-level window.

Parameters	*Description*
Wnd	Window identifier

Return Value:
Previously active window.

SetCapture

```
function SetCapture(Wnd: HWnd): HWnd;
```

Causes all cursor input to be sent to `Wnd` regardless of the position of the mouse.

Parameters	*Description*
Wnd	Window identifier

Return Value:
Previous window that received all mouse input; 0 if there's no corresponding window.

SetDoubleClickTime

```
procedure SetDoubleClickTime(Count: Word);
```

Sets maximum elapsed time allowed between the first and second clicks of a mouse double click.

Parameters	*Description*
Count	Milliseconds between double clicks, or 0 to use default (500) value.

SetFocus

```
function SetFocus(Wnd: HWnd): HWnd;
```

Assigns input focus to a window and directs all keyboard input to the window.

Parameters	Description
Wnd	Window identifier or 0 to ignore keystrokes

Return Value:
Previous window having input focus; 0 if there's no corresponding window.

SetSysModalWindow

```
function SetSysModalWindow(Wnd: HWnd): HWnd;
```

Makes a `Wnd` a system-modal window. The system-modal state is terminated when the window is destroyed.

Parameters	Description
Wnd	Window identifier

Return Value:
Previous system-modal window.

SetTimer

```
function SetTimer(Wnd: HWnd; IDEvent: Integer; Elapse: Word;
  TimerFunc: TFarProc): Word;
```

Creates a system timer, causing a `wm_Timer` message to be sent to an application at the interval specified by `Elapse`.

Parameters	Description
Wnd	Window identifier or 0 if there's no associated window
IDEvent	Nonzero timer-event identifier or ignored if `Wnd` is 0
Elapse	Number of milliseconds between timer events
TimerFunc	`Callback` function's procedure-instance address or nil to place `wm_Timer` messages in application queue

Return Value:
`IDEvent` if `Wnd` is not 0, indicating a new timer event; 0 if error.

SwapMouseButton

```
function SwapMouseButton(Swap: Bool): Bool;
```

Reverses or restores the meaning of the left and right mouse button specified by `Swap`.

Parameters	*Description*
Swap	Nonzero to swap button meanings or 0 to restore original meanings

Return Value:
Nonzero if meanings reversed; else 0.

Menu Procedures and Functions

```
AppendMenu
CheckMenuItem
CreateMenu
CreatePopupMenu
DeleteMenu
DestroyMenu
DrawMenuBar
EnableMenuItem
GetMenu
GetMenuCheckMarkDimensions
GetMenuItemCount
GetMenuItemID
GetMenuState
GetMenuString
GetSubMenu
GetSystemMenu
HiliteMenuItem
InsertMenu
LoadMenuIndirect
ModifyMenu
RemoveMenu
SetMenu
SetMenuItemBitmaps
TrackPopupMenu
```

AppendMenu

```
function AppendMenu(Menu: HMenu; Flags, IDNewItem: Word;
  NewItem: PChar): Bool;
```

Appends a new item (with a state specified by `Flags`) to the end of a menu.

Parameters	Description
Menu	Menu to be changed

Flags	One or a combination of the following `mf_ Menu` flags' constants:
	`mf_Bitmap`
	`mf_Checked`
	`mf_Disabled`
	`mf_Enabled`
	`mf_Grayed`
	`mf_MenuBarBreak`
	`mf_MenuBreak`
	`mf_OwnerDraw`
	`mf_Popup`
	`mf_Separator`
	`mf_String`
	`mf_Unchecked`

IDNewItem	Command ID or menu handle if pop-up menu.
NewItem	New menu string, or when using a bit map as an item, the low-order word holds a handle to the bit map.

Return Value:
Nonzero if successful; else 0.

CheckMenuItem

```
function CheckMenuItem(Menu: HMenu; IDCheckItem, Check: Word): Bool;
```

Places or removes a check mark from menu items in a pop-up menu.

Parameters	Description
Menu	Pop-up menu
IDCheckItem	Menu item to be checked

Check	How item should be checked and how its position is specified; any combination of the following
	`mf_ Menu` flags:
	`mf_ByCommand`
	`mf_ByPosition`
	`mf_Checked`
	`mf_Unchecked`

Return Value:
Previous state of `Item`; –1 if the menu item does not exist.

CreateMenu

```
function CreateMenu: HMenu;
```

Creates an empty menu.

Return Value:
Menu identifier if successful; else 0.

CreatePopupMenu

```
function CreatePopupMenu: HMenu;
```

Creates an empty pop-up menu.

Return Value:
Menu identifier if successful; else 0.

DeleteMenu

```
function DeleteMenu(Menu: HMenu; Position, Flags: Word): Bool;
```

Deletes an item from `Menu`. If the item is a pop-up, its handle is destroyed, and the memory it used is freed.

Parameters	***Description***
Menu	Menu identifier
Position	Position or command ID

Flags	One of the `mf_` Menu flags' constants:
	`mf_ByPosition`
	`mf_ByCommand`

Return Value:
Nonzero if successful; else 0.

DestroyMenu

```
function DestroyMenu(Menu: HMenu): Bool;
```

Destroys `Menu` and frees associated memory.

Parameters	Description
Menu	Menu identifier

Return Value:
Nonzero if successful; else 0.

DrawMenuBar

```
procedure DrawMenuBar(Wnd: HWnd);
```

Redraws a window's menu bar. Used if the menu bar changes after the window is created.

Parameters	Description
Wnd	Window identifier

EnableMenuItem

```
function EnableMenuItem(Menu: HMenu; IDEnableItem, Enable: Word): Bool
```

Enables, disables, or grays a menu item specified by `Enable`.

Parameters	Description
Menu	Menu identifier
IDEnableItem	ID or position of menu item or pop-up to be checked
Enable	A combination of the `mf_ Menu` flags' constants: `mf_Command` or `mf_ByPosition` with `mf_Disabled`, `mf_Enabled`, or `mf_Grayed`

Return Value:
Previous state of menu item; –1 if menu item doesn't exist.

GetMenu

```
function GetMenu(Wnd: HWnd): HMenu;
```

Gets a window's menu handle.

Parameters	Description
Wnd	Owning window of menu

Return Value:
Menu identifier; 0 if there's no menu; undefined if `Wnd` is a child window.

GetMenuCheckMarkDimensions

```
function GetMenuCheckMarkDimensions: Longint;
```

Gets the dimensions of the default check mark bitmap displayed next to checked menu items.

Return Value:
Height (in pixels) in the high-order word; width (in pixels) in the low-order word.

GetMenuItemCount

```
function GetMenuItemCount(Menu: HMenu): Word;
```

Gets the number of top-level menus and the menu items in a specified menu.

Parameters	*Description*
Menu	The menu identifier

Return Value:
The number of menu items, if successful; –1 if unsuccessful.

GetMenuItemID

```
function GetMenuItemID(Menu: HMenu; Pos: Integer): Word;
```

Gets the menu item's numeric ID located at the specified position in the menu.

Parameters	*Description*
Menu	Pop-up menu identifier
Pos	`Item` position, starting at 0, in menu

Return Value:
`Item` ID if successful; 0 if item is a pop-up; –1 if error.

GetMenuState

```
function GetMenuState(Menu: HMenu; ID, Flags: Word): Word;
```

Gets state information for a specified menu item.

Parameters	Description
Menu	Menu or pop-up menu identifier
ID	Menu item ID

Flags	One of the `mf_ Menu` flags' constants:
	`mf_ByPosition`
	`mf_ByCommand`

Return Value:
Flags mask of the following `mf_ Menu` flags values:

```
mf_Checked
mf_Disabled
mf_Enabled
mf_MenuBarBreak
mf_MenuBreak
mf_Separator
mf_Unchecked
```

If pop-up, the high-order byte contains the number of items; –1 if `ID` is invalid.

GetMenuString

```
function GetMenuString(Menu: HMenu; IDItem: Word; Str: PChar;
  MaxCount: Integer; Flag: Word): Integer;
```

Copies a menu item's label into `Str`. The copied label is null-terminated.

Parameters	Description
Menu	Menu identifier
IDItem	Menu item ID
Str	Receiving buffer
MaxCount	Size of the buffer

Flag	One of the `mf_ Menu` flags' constants:
	`mf_ByPosition`
	`mf_ByCommand`

Return Value:
Number of bytes copied.

GetSubMenu

```
function GetSubMenu(Menu: HMenu; Pos: Integer): HMenu;
```

Gets a pop-up menu's handle.

Parameters	*Description*
Menu	Menu identifier
Pos	Position of pop-up menu in `Menu`

Return Value:
Pop-up menu identifier; 0, if no pop-up menu exists at `Pos`.

GetSystemMenu

```
function GetSystemMenu(Wnd: HWnd; Revert: Bool): HMenu;
```

Gets a window's system menu for copying and changing.

Parameters	*Description*
Wnd	Window identifier

`Revert` 0 to return handle to a copy of the system menu or nonzero to return handle to original system menu.

Return Value:
System menu identifier; 0 if `Revert` is nonzero and the system menu has not been changed.

HiliteMenuItem

```
function HiliteMenuItem(Wnd: HWnd; Menu: HMenu;
  IDHilite, Hilite: Word): Bool;
```

Highlights or removes highlighting from a top-level menu item.

Parameters	*Description*
Wnd	Window identifier
Menu	Top-level menu identifier
IDHilite	Integer ID or position of menu item
Hilite	A combination of the `mf_` Menu flags, `mf_ByCommand` or `mf_ByPosition` with `mf_Hilite` or `mf_Unhilite`

Return Value:
Nonzero if successful; else 0.

InsertMenu

```
function InsertMenu(Menu:HMenu; Position, Flags, IDNewItem: Word;
  NewItem: PChar): Bool;
```

Inserts new menu item with a state specified by `Flags`.

Parameters	*Description*
Menu	Menu identifier
Position	Command ID or position of menu item to insert new menu item after or –1 to append to end

Flags	One of the `mf_` Menu flags, `mf_ByCommand` or `mf_ByPosition` combined with any of the following:
	`mf_Bitmap`
	`mf_String`
	`mf_OwnerDraw`
	`mf_Separator`
	`mf_Popup`
	`mf_MenuBarBreak`
	`mf_MenuBreak`
	`mf_Checked`
	`mf_Unchecked`

IDNewItem	New menu item command ID or menu handle if pop-up
NewItem	New menu item contents

Return Value:
Nonzero if successful; else 0.

LoadMenuIndirect

```
function LoadMenuIndirect(var MenuTemplate): HMenu;
```

Loads the menu defined by `MenuTemplate`.

Parameters	*Description*
MenuTemplate	Array of `TMenuItemTemplate` structures

Return Value:
`Menu` identifier if successful.

ModifyMenu

```
function ModifyMenu(Menu: HMenu; Position, Flags, IDNewItem: Word;
  NewItem: PChar): Bool;
```

Changes an existing menu item that has a new state that is specified by `Flags`.

Parameters	*Description*
Menu	Menu identifier
Position	Command ID or position of menu item

Flags	Combination of `mf_ByCommand` or `mf_ByPosition` with one of the following `mf_ Menu` flags' constants:
	`mf_Disabled`
	`mf_Enabled`
	`mf_Grayed`
	`mf_Bitmap`
	`mf_String`
	`mf_OwnerDraw`
	`mf_Separator`
	`mf_Popup`
	`mf_MenuBarBreak`
	`mf_MenuBreak`
	`mf_Checked`
	`mf_Unchecked`

IDNewItem	Command ID or menu handle, if flags set to `mf_Popup`, of modified menu item
NewItem	`String` (`mf_String`), `HBitmap` (`mf_Bitmap`), or application supplied data (`mf_OwnerDraw`)

Return Value:
Nonzero if successful; else 0.

RemoveMenu

```
function RemoveMenu(Menu: HMenu; Position, Flags: Word): Bool;
```

Nondestructively removes a menu item and an associated pop-up from the specified menu. You can use the pop-up in ensuing operations.

Parameters	Description
Menu	Menu identifier
Position	Command ID or position of menu item
Flags	One of the `mf_` Menu flags, `mf_ByCommand` or `mf_ByPosition` specifying the nature of the `Position` argument.

Return Value:
Nonzero if successful; else 0.

SetMenu

```
function SetMenu(Wnd: HWnd; Menu: HMenu): Bool;
```

Sets and redraws a window's menu to the menu specified by `Menu`. The previous menu is not destroyed.

Parameters	Description
Wnd	Window identifier
Menu	New menu or 0 to remove current menu

Return Value:
Nonzero if successful; else 0.

SetMenuItemBitmaps

```
function SetMenuItemBitmaps(Menu: HMenu; Position, Flags: Word;
  BitmapUnchecked, BitmapChecked: HBitmap): Bool;
```

Associates two bitmaps with a menu item. One is displayed when the item is checked and the other when the item is unchecked.

Parameters	Description
Menu	Menu identifier
Position	Command ID or position of menu item
Flags	One of the `mf_` Menu flags' constants, `mf_ByCommand` or `mf_ByPosition`
BitmapUnchecked	`HBitmap` to be displayed when item not checked or 0 to display nothing

Parameters	Description
BitmapChecked	HBitmap to be displayed when item checked or 0 to display nothing; if BitmapUnchecked and BitmapChecked are 0, Windows uses default check mark

Return Value:
Nonzero if successful; else 0.

TrackPopupMenu

```
function TrackPopupMenu(Menu: HMenu; Flags: Word; x, y, cx: Integer;
  Wnd: HWnd; var Rect: TRect): Bool;
```

Displays a floating pop-up menu and tracks item selection. Floating pop-up menus can appear anywhere on the screen.

Parameters	Description
Menu	Pop-up menu identifier
Flags	Set to 0, not used
x, y	Upper-left position (in screen coordinates) of menu
cx	Menu width (in screen units) or 0 for default
Wnd	Owning window of the pop-up menu, to receive wm_Command messages
Rect	TRect defining mouse area where menu remains visible if the user releases the mouse button

Return Value:
Nonzero if successful; else 0.

Message Procedures and Functions

```
CallWindowProc
DispatchMessage
GetMessage
GetMessagePos
GetMessageTime
InSendMessage
PeekMessage
PostAppMessage
```

```
PostMessage
PostQuitMessage
ReplyMessage
SendMessage
SetMessageQueue
TranslateAccelerator
TranslateMDISysAccel
TranslateMessage
WaitMessage
```

CallWindowProc

```
function CallWindowProc(PrevWndProc: TFarProc; Wnd: HWnd;
  Msg, wParam: Word; lParam: Longint): Longint;
```

Sends a message to `PrevWndProc`. Enables window subclassing by allowing messages to be intercepted before they are sent to the window function of the class.

Parameters	*Description*
PrevWndProc	Procedure-instance address of the previous window function
Wnd	Window that receives the message
Msg	Message identifier
wParam	Additional message-dependent information
lParam	Additional message-dependent information

Return Value:
Value from `call` to `PrevWndProc`.

DispatchMessage

```
function DispatchMessage(var Msg: TMsg): Longint;
```

Passes the message in `Msg` to the window's window function.

Parameters	*Description*
Msg	`TMsg` structure

Return Value:
A value returned from the window function.

GetMessage

```
function GetMessage(var Msg: TMsg; Wnd: HWnd; MsgFilterMin,
  MsgFilterMax: Word): Bool;
```

Gets a message (within the filter range) from the application's message queue. Yields control to other applications if there are no messages pending, or `wm_Paint`, or `wm_Timer` is the next message.

Parameters	*Description*
Msg	Receiving `TMsg` structure
Wnd	Message destination window or 0 for all windows in applications
MsgFilterMin	0 for no filtering or `wm_KeyFirst` for keyboard only or `wm_MouseFirst` for mouse only
MsgFilterMax	0 for no filtering or `wm_KeyLast` for keyboard only or `wm_MouseLast` for mouse only

Return Value:
Nonzero if not a `wm_Quit` message; else 0.

GetMessagePos

```
function GetMessagePos: Longint;
```

Gets the cursor position for the previous message obtained from `GetMessage`.

Return Value:
X-coordinates in low word;
Y-coordinates in high word.

GetMessageTime

```
function GetMessageTime: Longint;
```

Gets the time that has elapsed since a system reboot for the last message obtained from `GetMessage`.

Return Value:
Message time (in milliseconds).

InSendMessage

```
function InSendMessage: Bool;
```

Decides whether the message being processed by the current window function was sent through `SendMessage`.

Return Value:
Nonzero if the message was sent by `SendMessage`; else 0.

PeekMessage

```
function PeekMessage(var Msg: TMsg; Wnd: HWnd;
  MsgFilterMin, MsgFilterMax, RemoveMsg: Word): Bool;
```

Checks the application queue for a message and copies it to `Msg`. If there are no messages, the function returns immediately, giving control to Windows.

Parameters	*Description*
Msg	Receiving `TMsg` structure
Wnd	Messages destination window or 0 for any window in application or –1 for messages posted by `PostAppMessage` function.
MsgFilterMin	Lowest message ID to examine, or 0 for no limit
MsgFilterMax	Highest message ID to examine, or 0 for no limit
RemoveMsg	One or more of the `pm_ Peek` message options

Return Value:
Nonzero if message available; else 0.

PostAppMessage

```
function PostAppMessage(Task: THandle; Msg, wParam: Word;
  lParam: Longint): Bool;
```

Posts a message to an application. The `Wnd` of the message is set to 0.

Parameters	*Description*
Task	Application to receive message
Msg	Message type
wParam	Additional message information
lParam	Additional message information

Return Value:
Nonzero if successful; else 0.

PostMessage

```
function PostMessage(Wnd: HWnd; Msg, wParam: Word;
  lParam: Longint): Bool;
```

Posts a message to an application window.

Parameters	*Description*
Wnd	Window to receive message or $FFFF for all overlapped or pop-up windows
Msg	Message type
wParam	Additional message information
lParam	Additional message information

Return Value:
Nonzero if successful; else 0.

PostQuitMessage

```
procedure PostQuitMessage(ExitCode: Integer);
```

Posts a `wm_Quit` message usually in response to a `wm_Destroy` message.

Parameters	*Description*
ExitCode	Application exit code (`wParam` of `wm_Quit` message)

ReplyMessage

```
procedure ReplyMessage(Reply: Longint);
```

Replies to a message sent by a `SendMessagecall`, allowing both the requester of the `SendMessage` and `ReplyMessage` to continue processing.

Parameters	*Description*
Reply	Message-dependent return result

SendMessage

```
function SendMessage(Wnd: HWnd; Msg, wParam: Word;
  lParam: Longint): Longint;
```

Sends a message to the window function of a specified window. The function doesn't return until the message is processed.

Parameters	Description
Wnd	Window to receive message or $FFFF to send to all pop-up windows in system
Msg	Message type
wParam	Additional message information
lParam	Additional message information

Return Value:
Value returned by the receiving window function.

SetMessageQueue

```
function SetMessageQueue(Msg: Integer): Bool;
```

Creates a new application message queue of a specified size. The old queue is deleted.

Parameters	Description
Msg	Size of queue

Return Value:
Nonzero if successful; else 0.

TranslateAccelerator

```
function TranslateAccelerator(Wnd: HWnd; AccTable: THandle;
  var Msg: TMsg): Integer;
```

Translates any keyboard accelerators (`wm_KeyUp` and `wm_KeyDown`) into menu command messages, `wm_Command` and `wm_SysCommand`, which then are sent directly to the window.

Parameters	*Description*
Wnd	Window identifier
AccTable	Accelerator table identifier (returned by LoadAccelerators)
Msg	TMsg information retrieved from GetMessage or PeekMessage

Return Value:
Nonzero if translation occurred; else 0.

TranslateMDISysAccel

```
function TranslateMDISysAccel(Wnd: HWnd; var Msg: TMsg): Bool;
```

Translates any keyboard accelerators for MDI child window system-menu wm_SysCommand messages. These messages then are sent directly to the window.

Parameters	*Description*
Wnd	MDI client parent window
Msg	TMsg information retrieved from GetMessage or PeekMessage

Return Value:
Nonzero if translation occurred; else 0.

TranslateMessage

```
function TranslateMessage(var Msg: TMsg): Bool;
```

Translates wm_KeyDown/wm_KeyUp combinations to wm_Charor wm_DeadChar, and wm_SysKeyDown/wm_SysKeyUp combinations to wm_SysChar or wm_SysDeadChar. Also posts the character message to the application queue.

Parameters	*Description*
Msg	TMsg information retrieved from GetMessage or PeekMessage

Return Value:
Nonzero if translation occurred; else 0.

WaitMessage

```
procedure WaitMessage;
```

Yields control to other applications and does not return until a message appears in the application queue.

Painting Procedures and Functions

```
BeginPaint
DrawFocusRect
DrawIcon
DrawText
EndPaint
ExcludeUpdateRgn
FillRect
FrameRect
GetDC
GetUpdateRect
GetUpdateRgn
GetWindowDC
GrayString
InvalidateRect
InvalidateRgn
InvertRect
ReleaseDC
UpdateWindow
ValidateRect
ValidateRgn
```

BeginPaint

```
function BeginPaint(Wnd: HWnd; var Paint: TPaintStruct): HDC;
```

Prepares a window for painting in response to a `wm_Paint` message. Fills `Paint` with the required information in order to paint.

Parameters	*Description*
Wnd	Window to be repainted
Paint	`TPaintStruct` to receive painting information

Return Value:
Device context identifier.

DrawFocusRect

```
procedure DrawFocusRect(DC: HDC; var Rect: TRect);
```

Does XOR to draw a focus style rectangle.

Parameters	*Description*
DC	Device context identifier
Rect	TRect to be drawn

DrawIcon

```
function DrawIcon(DC: HDC; X, Y: Integer; Icon: HIcon): Bool;
```

Draws an icon.

Parameters	*Description*
DC	Device context identifier
X, Y	Upper-left corner of the icon
Icon	Icon to be drawn

Return Value:
Nonzero if successful; else 0.

DrawText

```
function DrawText(DC: HDC; Str: PChar; Count: Integer;
  var Rect: TRect; Format: Word): Integer;
```

Draws formatted text whose formatting is specified by Format. The text is clipped to the bounding rectangle, unless specified by dt_NoClip.

Parameters	*Description*
DC	Device-context identifier
Str	String to be drawn; if Count is –1, must be null-terminated
Count	Number of bytes in string
Rect	Bounding TRect of the text
Format	One or more of the dt_ Text drawing formatting flags

Return Value:
Text height.

EndPaint

```
procedure EndPaint(Wnd: HWnd; var Paint: TPaintStruct);
```

Denotes end of painting in `Wnd`.

Parameters	*Description*
Wnd	Repainted window
Paint	`TPaintStruct` retrieved from `BeginPaint` function

ExcludeUpdateRgn

```
function ExcludeUpdateRgn(DC: HDC; Wnd: HWnd): Integer;
```

Excludes a window's updated region from a clipping region, thus preventing drawing outside the valid areas of the window.

Parameters	*Description*
DC	Device context identifier
Wnd	Window being updated

Return Value:
One of the `Region` flags' constants.

FillRect

```
function FillRect(DC: HDC; var Rect: TRect; Brush: HBrush): Integer;
```

Fills a rectangle, using `Brush` up to the right and bottom borders.

Parameters	*Description*
DC	Device context identifier
Rect	`TRect` to be filled
Brush	Fill brush

Return Value:
Not used.

FrameRect

```
procedure FrameRect(DC: HDC; var Rect: TRect; Brush: HBrush): Integer;
```

Draws a border one logical unit wide around a rectangle.

Parameters	*Description*
DC	Device context identifier
Rect	`TRect` defining corners of the rectangle
Brush	Framing brush

GetDC

```
function GetDC(Wnd: HWnd): HDC;
```

Gets a display context for use by GDI functions in a window's client area.

Parameters	*Description*
Wnd	Window identifier

Return Value:
Display context identifier; 0 if error.

GetUpdateRect

```
function GetUpdateRect(Wnd: HWnd; var Rect: TRect;
  Erase: Bool): Bool;
```

Gets the smallest enclosing rectangle of a window's update region.

Parameters	*Description*
Wnd	Window identifier
Rect	Receiving `TRect` structure
Erase	Nonzero to erase update region background

Return Value:
Nonzero if non-empty update region; else 0.

GetUpdateRgn

```
function GetUpdateRgn(Wnd: HWnd; Rgn: HRgn; Erase: Bool): Integer;
```

Copies into `Rgn` a window's update region.

Parameters	*Description*
Wnd	Window identifier
Rgn	Receiving update region
Erase	Nonzero if background should be erased and child windows redrawn

Return Value:
One of the `Region` flags' constants.

GetWindowDC

```
function GetWindowDC(Wnd: HWnd): HDC;
```

Gets a display context usually used for painting nonclient areas of a window.

Parameters	*Description*
Wnd	Window identifier

Return Value:
Display context identifier; 0 if there's an error.

GrayString

```
function GrayString(DC: HDC; Brush: HBrush; OutputFunc: TFarProc;
  Data: Longint; Count, X, Y, Width, Height: Integer): Bool;
```

Draws gray text (using the currently selected font) by sending a message to `OutputFunc` that contains `DC` (with a bit map of `Height` and `Width` size), `Data`, and `Count`.

Parameters	*Description*
DC	Device context identifier
Brush	`HBrush` used for graying
OutputFunc	Draw function procedure-instance address or nil to use `TextOut`
Data	Data to pass to `OutputFunc` or string if `OutputFunc` is 0

Parameters	*Description*
Count	Size of `Data` or 0 and `Data` is a string to calculate length, or –1 and `OutputFunc` returns 0 and image is displayed but not shown
X,Y	Starting logical position of enclosing rectangle
Width	Width (in logical units) of enclosing rectangle, or 0 and `Data` is a string to calculate width
Height	Height (in logical units) of enclosing rectangle, or 0 and `Data` is a string to calculate height

Return Value:
Nonzero if successful; 0 if the output function returned 0 or if insufficient memory to create the bit map.

InvalidateRect

```
procedure InvalidateRect(Wnd: HWnd; Rect: LPRect; Erase: Bool);
```

Invalidates a window's client area by adding `Rect` to the window's update region.

Parameters	*Description*
Wnd	Window identifier
Rect	`TRect` to be added to update region or nil for the entire client area
Erase	Nonzero for `BeginPaint` to erase background

InvalidateRgn

```
procedure InvalidateRgn(Wnd: HWnd; Rgn: HRgn; Erase: Bool);
```

Invalidates a window's client area by adding `Rgn` to the window's update region.

Parameters	*Description*
Wnd	Window identifier
Rgn	Region identifier (in client coordinates)
Erase	Nonzero for `BeginPaint` to erase background

InvertRect

```
procedure InvertRect(DC: HDC; var Rect: TRect);
```

Inverts the colors of the rectangle specified by `Rect`.

Parameters	Description
DC	Device context identifier
Rect	`TRect` structure (in logical coordinates)

ReleaseDC

```
function ReleaseDC(Wnd: HWnd; DC: HDC): Integer;
```

Releases a common or window device context, thus making it available to other applications.

Parameters	Description
Wnd	Window identifier
DC	Device context identifier

Return Value:
1 if device context released; else 0.

UpdateWindow

```
procedure UpdateWindow(Wnd: HWnd);
```

Sends a `wm_Paint` message directly to a window's `window` function if the update region of the window is not empty.

Parameters	Description
Wnd	Window identifier

ValidateRect

```
procedure ValidateRect(Wnd: HWnd; Rect: LPRect);
```

Validates the client area by removing `Rect` from the window's update region.

Parameters	Description
Wnd	Window identifier
Rect	`TRect` (in client coordinates) to be removed from update region or nil for entire client area

ValidateRgn

```
procedure ValidateRgn(Wnd: HWnd; Rgn: HRgn);
```

Validates the client area by removing the region specified by Rgn from the window's update region.

Parameters	*Description*
Wnd	Window identifier
Rgn	Region identifier (in client coordinates)

Property Procedures and Functions

```
EnumProps
GetProp
RemoveProp
SetProp
```

EnumProps

```
function EnumProps(Wnd: HWnd; EnumFunc: TFarProc): Integer;
```

Enumerates a window's property list sending Wnd, nDummy, PSTR, and hData to the callback. Enumeration ends if the callback returns 0 or if all properties are enumerated.

Parameters	*Description*
Wnd	Window identifier
EnumFunc	Callback function's procedure-instance address

Return Value:
Previous value returned by callback; –1 if window has no properties.

GetProp

```
function GetProp(Wnd: HWnd; Str: PChar): THandle;
```

Gets the associated data handle from a window's property list.

Parameters	Description
Wnd	Window identifier
Str	String (null-terminated) or atom

Return Value:
Data handle if property list contains `Str`; else 0.

RemoveProp

```
function RemoveProp(Wnd: HWnd; Str: PChar): THandle;
```

Removes an entry (specified by `Str`) from a window's property list. An application is responsible for freeing the returned data handle.

Parameters	Description
Wnd	Window identifier
Str	String (null-terminated) or an atom

Return Value:
Data handle to string; 0 if the string is not found.

SetProp

```
function SetProp(Wnd: HWnd; Str: PChar; Data: THandle): Bool;
```

Adds or changes an entry (specified by `Str`) to a window's property list.

Parameters	Description
Wnd	Window identifier
Str	String (null-terminated) or atom value created by calling `AddAtom`
Data	Associated property data handle

Return Value:
Nonzero if added; else 0.

Scrolling Procedures and Functions

```
GetScrollPos
GetScrollRange
ScrollDC
ScrollWindow
```

```
SetScrollPos
SetScrollRange
ShowScrollBar
```

GetScrollPos

```
function GetScrollPos(Wnd: HWnd; Bar: Integer): Integer;
```

Gets the current position of a scroll-bar thumb relative to the current scrolling range.

Parameters	*Description*
Wnd	Window containing scroll bar
Bar	One of the `sb_ Scroll` bar constants

Return Value:
Current scroll-bar thumb position.

GetScrollRange

```
procedure GetScrollRange(Wnd: HWnd; Bar: Integer;
  var MinPos, MaxPos: Integer);
```

Gets a scroll bar's minimum and maximum positions.

Parameters	*Description*
Wnd	Window containing scroll bar
Bar	One of the `sb_ Scroll` bar constants
MinPos	Integer to receive minimum position
MaxPos	Integer to receive maximum position

ScrollDC

```
function ScrollDC(DC: HDC; dx, dy: Integer; var Scroll, Clip: TRect;
  UpdateRgn: HRgn; UpdateRect: LPRect): Bool;
```

Scrolls a rectangle of bits by `dx` and `dy` units.

Parameters	Description
DC	Device context identifier
dx	Horizontal scroll units
dy	Vertical scroll units
Scroll	`TRect` containing scrolling rectangle `Clip TRect` containing clipping rectangle
UpdateRgn	`ScrollDC` region uncovered by the scrolling process; if nil, update region is not computed
UpdateRect	Receiving `TRect` containing the bounding rectangle of the scroll update region; if nil, update rectangle is not computed

Return Value:
Nonzero if successful; else 0.

ScrollWindow

```
procedure ScrollWindow(Wnd: HWnd; XAmount, YAmount: Integer;
  Rect, ClipRect: LPRect);
```

Scrolls a window's client area by `XAmount` and `YAmount`. The uncovered area is combined with the window's update regions

Parameters	Description
Wnd	Window identifier
XAmount	Device units to scroll in x-direction
YAmount	Device units to scroll in y-direction
Rect	Client area `TRect` to be scrolled or nil for the entire client area
ClipRect	Clipping `TRect` to be scrolled or nil for the entire window

SetScrollPos

```
function SetScrollPos(Wnd: HWnd; Bar, Pos: Integer; Redraw:
Bool): Integer;
```

Sets a scroll bar's thumb to `Pos`.

> **Note:** The scroll bar's "thumb" is the "Scroll Box" in a scroll bar that indicates your position in a file. Thus, you can set the "thumb" to any position.

Parameters	*Description*
Wnd	Window identifier or scroll-bar control identifier if `Bar` is set to `sb_Ctl`
Bar	One of the `sb_ Scroll` bar constants
Pos	New position
Redraw	Nonzero to redraw scroll bar

Return Value:
Previous position of scroll bar thumb.

SetScrollRange

```
procedure SetScrollRange(Wnd: HWnd; Bar, MinPos, MaxPos: Integer;
  Redraw: Bool);
```

Sets a scroll bar's minimum and maximum position values.

Parameters	*Description*
Wnd	Window identifier or scroll bar control identifier if `Bar` is set to `sb_Ctl`
Bar	One of the `sb_ Scroll` bar constants
MinPos	Minimum scrolling position
MaxPos	Maximum scrolling position or 0 and `MinPos` set to 0 to hide the scroll bar
Redraw	Nonzero to redraw the scroll bar

ShowScrollBar

```
procedure ShowScrollBar(Wnd: HWnd; Bar: Word; Show: Bool);
```

Shows or hides a scroll bar as specified by `Show`.

Parameters	*Description*
Wnd	Window identifier or scroll bar control if `Bar` is set to `sb_Ctl`
Bar	One of the `sb_ Scroll` bar constants
Show	Nonzero to show the scroll bar or 0 to hide it

System Procedures and Functions

```
GetCurrentTime
GetSysColor
GetSystemMetrics
SetSysColors
```

GetCurrentTime

```
function GetCurrentTime: Longint;
```

Gets the elapsed time since the system was rebooted.

Return Value:
Current time (in milliseconds).

GetSysColor

```
function GetSysColor(Index: Integer): Longint;
```

Gets a Windows display element's current color.

Parameters	*Description*
Index	Display element

Return Value:
RGB color value.

GetSystemMetrics

```
function GetSystemMetrics(Index: Integer): Integer;
```

Gets the system metrics, such as mouse status, pixel width, and height of various display elements, and Windows debug version.

Parameters	*Description*
Index	One of the `sm_` System metrics codes' constants

Return Value:
The requested system metric value.

SetSysColors

```
procedure SetSysColors(Changes: Integer; var SysColor;
  var ColorValues);
```

Sets the system colors for the display elements specified in `SysColor`.

Parameters	*Description*
Change	Number of system colors to change
SysColor	Integer array whose indexes are `color_ System` color codes
ColorValues	`Longint` array containing corresponding RGB color value for each color index in `SysColor`

Window-Creation Procedures and Functions

```
AdjustWindowRect
AdjustWindowRectEx
CreateWindow
CreateWindowEx
DefDlgProc
DefFrameProc
DefMDIChildProc
DefWindowProc
DestroyWindow
GetClassInfo
GetClassLong
GetClassName
GetClassWord
GetLastActivePopup
GetWindowLong
GetWindowWord
RegisterClass
SetClassLong
SetClassWord
```

```
SetWindowLong
SetWindowWord
UnregisterClass
```

AdjustWindowRect

```
procedure AdjustWindowRect(var Rect: TRect; Style: Longint;
  Menu: Bool);
```

Computes the size a window rectangle requires based on `Rect` size.

Parameters	*Description*
Rect	`TRect` containing client rectangle coordinates to be converted
Style	Window styles of the window with a client rectangle that is to be converted
Menu	Nonzero if window has a menu

AdjustWindowRectEx

```
procedure AdjustWindowRectEx(var Rect: TRect; Style: Longint;
  Menu: Bool; ExStyle: Longint);
```

Computes the size of a window rectangle with extended style based on `Rect` size. Assumes a single row menu, if there's a menu.

Parameters	*Description*
Rect	`TRect` structure containing client rectangle coordinates to be converted
Style	Window styles of the window whose client rectangle will be converted
Menu	Nonzero if the window has a menu
ExStyle	Extended style of the window being created

CreateWindow

```
function CreateWindow(ClassName, WindowName: PChar; Style: Longint;
  X, Y, Width, Height: Integer; WndParent: HWnd; Menu: HMenu;
  Instance: THandle; Param: Pointer): HWnd;
```

Creates a pop-up, overlapped, or child window.

Parameters	*Description*
ClassName	Window class name (null-terminated) or a predefined control-class name
WindowName	Window caption or name (null-terminated)
Style	One or a combination of window or control style constants: bs_ Button styles cbs_ Combo box styles ds_ Dialog styles es_ Edit control styles lbs_ List box styles sbs_ Scroll bar styles ss_ Static control styles ws_ Window styles
X, Y	Starting window position or cw_UseDefault
Width	Starting window width (in device units)
Height	Starting window height (in device units)
WndParent	Owner window
Menu	Menu or child-window identifier
Instance	Associated module instance
Param	Value passed in TCreateStruct in lParam of the wm_Create message; this must be a pointer to a TClientCreateStruct for MDI client window creation

Return Value:
Window identifier if successful; else 0.

CreateWindowEx

```
function CreateWindowEx(ExStyle: Longint; ClassName, WindowName: PChar;
  Style: Longint; X, Y, Width, Height: Integer; WndParent: HWnd;
  Menu: HMenu; Instance: THandle; Param: Pointer): HWnd;
```

Creates a pop-up, overlapped, or child window with an extended style.

Parameters	Description
ExStyle	One of the ws_ex_ Extended window styles' constants
ClassName	Window class name (null-terminated) or a predefined control-class name
WindowName	Window caption or name (null-terminated)
Style	One or a combination of window or control style constants: bs_ Button styles cbs_ Combo box styles ds_ Dialog styles es_ Edit control styles lbs_ List box styles sbs_ Scroll bar styles ss_ Static control styles ws_ Window styles
X, Y	Starting window position or cw_UseDefault
Width	Starting window width (in device units)
Height	Starting window height (in device units)
WndParent	Owner window
Menu	Menu or child-window identifier
Instance	Associated module instance
Param	Value passed in TCreateStruct in lParam of the wm_Create message, must be a pointer to a TClientCreateStruct for MDI client window creation

Return Value:
Window identifier if successful; else 0.

DefDlgProc

```
function DefDlgProc(Dlg: HWnd; Msg, wParam: Word;
  lParam: Longint): Longint;
```

Handles default processing for dialogs with a private window class.

Parameters	Description
Dlg	Dialog box identifier
Msg	Message number

Parameters	*Description*
wParam	Message-dependent information
lParam	Message-dependent information

Return Value:
Result of the message processing.

DefFrameProc

```
function DefFrameProc(Wnd, MDIClient: HWnd; Msg, wParam: Word;
  lParam: Longint): Longint;
```

Handles default message processing for `MDI` frame windows.

Parameters	*Description*
Wnd	`MDI` frame window
MDIClient	`MDI` client window
Msg	Message number
wParam	Message-dependent information
lParam	Message-dependent information

Return Value:
Result of message processing.

DefMDIChildProc

```
function DefMDIChildProc(Wnd: HWnd; Msg, wParam: Word;
  lParam: Longint): Longint;
```

Handles default message processing for `MDI` child windows.

Parameters	*Description*
Wnd	`MDI` child window
Msg	Message number
wParam	Message-dependent information
lParam	Message-dependent information

Return Value:
Result of the message processing.

DefWindowProc

```
function DefWindowProc(Wnd: HWnd; Msg, wParam: Word;
  lParam: Longint): Longint;
```

Handles default message processing for any messages not explicitly handled by an application.

Parameters	*Description*
Wnd	Window identifier
Msg	Message number
wParam	Message-dependent information
lParam	Message-dependent information

Return Value:
Result of the message processing.

DestroyWindow

```
function DestroyWindow(Wnd: HWnd): Bool;
```

Destroys a window or a modeless dialog box and any of its associated child windows.

Parameters	*Description*
Wnd	Window identifier

Return Value:
Nonzero if successful; else 0.

GetClassInfo

```
function GetClassInfo(Instance: THandle; ClassInfo: PChar;
  var WndClass: TWndClass): Bool;
```

Gets class information for the specified class. `TWndClass` fields: `lpszClassName`, `lpszMenuName`, and `hInstance` are not returned.

Parameters	*Description*
Instance	Application instance that created the class or 0 for a predefined Windows class `ClassName` Class name (null-terminated) or ID
WndClass	`TWndClass` to receive class information

Return Value:
Nonzero if successful; 0 if matching class is not found.

GetClassLong

```
function GetClassLong(Wnd: HWnd; Index: Integer): Longint;
```

Gets the long value at Index from a window's `TWndClass` structure. Positive byte offsets (from 0) to access extra class bytes.

Parameters	*Description*
Wnd	Window identifier
Index	Byte offset or the constant `gcl_WndProc`

Return Value:
Value retrieved.

GetClassName

```
function GetClassName(Wnd: HWnd; ClassName: PChar;
  MaxCount: Integer): Integer;
```

Gets a window's class name.

Parameters	*Description*
Wnd	Window identifier
ClassName	Buffer to receive class name
MaxCount	Size of buffer

Return Value:
Number of characters copied; 0 if there's an error.

GetClassWord

```
function GetClassWord(Wnd: HWnd, Index: Integer): Word;
```

Gets the word value at `Index` from a window's `TWndClass` structure. Positive byte offsets (from 0) to access extra class bytes.

Parameters	*Description*
Wnd	Window identifier
Index	Byte offset or one of the `gcw_ Class` field offsets' constants

Return Value:
Value retrieved.

GetLastActivePopup

```
function GetLastActivePopup(WndOwner: HWnd): HWnd;
```

Gets the most recently active pop-up window.

Parameters	*Description*
WndOwner	Owning parent window of pop-up.

Return Value:
Pop-up window identifier; `WndOwner`.

GetWindowLong

```
function GetWindowLong(Wnd: HWnd; Index: Integer): Longint;
```

Gets information about a window or a window's extra byte values.

Parameters	*Description*
Wnd	Window identifier
Index	Byte `oTbffset` or one of the `gwl_ Window` field offsets

Return Value:
Specified window information.

GetWindowWord

```
function GetWindowWord(Wnd: HWnd; Index: Integer): Word;
```

Gets information about a window or window-class extra byte values.

Parameters	Description
Wnd	Window identifier
Index	Positive byte offset or one of the gww_ Window field offsets' constants

Return Value:
Word value.

RegisterClass

```
function RegisterClass(var WndClass: TWndClass): Bool;
```

Registers a window class whose attributes are specified by `WndClass`.

Parameters	Description
WndClass	`TWndClass` structure

Return Value:
Nonzero if class registered; else 0.

SetClassLong

```
function SetClassLong(Wnd: HWnd; Index: Integer;
  NewLong: Longint): Longint;
```

Replaces the long value specified by Index in the window's `TWndClass` structure.

Parameters	Description
Wnd	Window identifier
Index	One of the `gcl_ Class` field offsets or positive byte offset to set extra 4-byte values
NewLong	Replacement value

Return Value:
Previous value.

SetClassWord

```
function SetClassWord(Wnd: HWnd; Index: Integer; NewWord: Word): Word;
```

Replaces the word value specified by `Index` in the window's `TWndClass` structure.

Parameters	*Description*
Wnd	Window identifier
Index	One of the `gcw_ Class` field offsetsor positive byte offset to set extra 2-byte value
NewWord	Replacement value

Return Value:
Previous value.

SetWindowLong

```
function SetWindowLong(Wnd: HWnd; Index: Integer;
  NewLong: Longint): Longint;
```

Replaces an attribute of a window's window-class structure with a new value.

Parameters	*Description*
Wnd	Window identifier
Index	One of the `gwl_ Window` field offsets or positive byte offset to access extra 4-byte values
NewLong	Replacement value

Return Value:
Previous value.

SetWindowWord

```
function SetWindowWord(Wnd: HWnd; Index: Integer;
  NewWord: Word): Word;
```

Changes the value of an attribute (specified by `Index`) in a window's window-class structure.

Parameters	Description
Wnd	Window identifier
Index	One of the `gww_ Window` field offsets or positive byte offset to access extra 2-byte values
NewWord	Replacement value

Return Value:
Previous value.

UnregisterClass

```
function UnregisterClass(ClassName: PChar; Instance: THandle): Bool;
```

Deletes a window class from the window-class table and frees any associated memory.

Parameters	Description
ClassName	Class name (null-terminated) of a previously registered class
Instance	Module instance that created the class

Return Value:
Nonzero if successful; 0 if invalid `ClassName`.

M

REFERENCE

SYSTEM SERVICES INTERFACE PROCEDURES AND FUNCTIONS

Alphabetical listing of System Services Interface procedures and functions:

Application-Execution	Operating-System Interrupt
Atom-Management	Resource-Management
Communication	Segment
File I/O	Sound
Initialization-File	String-Manipulation
Memory-Management	Task
Module-Management	Utility Macros

Application-Execution Functions

LoadModule
WinExec
WinHelp

LoadModule

```
function LoadModule(ModuleName: PChar; ParameterBlock: Pointer): THand
```

Loads and runs a Windows application.

Parameters	*Description*
ModuleName	Application file name (null-terminated)
ParameterBlock	Four field structure
EnvSeg	`Word`, environment segment address or 0 for Windows environment
CmdLine	`Longint`, command line
CmdShow	`Longint`, two `Word`-length structure, first word set to 2, second set to `CmdShow` of `ShowWindow`
Reserved	`Longint`, must be 0

Return Value:
Library module instance identifier (value greater than 32) if successful. If not, its value is less than 32, and one of the following:

(0) no memory
(5) attempt to link task
(6) multiple data segments
(10) invalid Windows version
(11) invalid EXE file
(12) OS/2 app
(13) DOS 4.0 app
(14) invalid EXE type
(15) not protect mode

WinExec

```
function WinExec(CmdLine: PChar; CmdShow: Word): Word;
```

Executes an application specified by `CmdLine`.

Parameters	*Description*
CmdLine	Command line to execute the application (null-terminated)
CmdShow	Specifies how an application window is initially displayed

Return Value:
Value greater than 32 if successful; otherwise it returns one of the following:

(0) no memory
(5) attempted to dynamically link to a task
(6) library has multiple data segments
(10) Windows version incorrect
(11) invalid EXE file
(12) OS/2 application
(13) DOS 4.0 application
(14) unknown EXE type
(15) not a protected-mode application

WinHelp

```
function WinHelp(Wnd: HWnd; HelpFile: PChar; Command: Word;
  Data: Longint): Bool;
```

Invokes Windows help engine with a command specified by `Command`.

Parameters	*Description*
Wnd	Window identifier
HelpFile	Name (null-terminated) of help file including path, if needed
Command	One of the `help_` Help commands
Data	Context identifier number if `Command` set to `help_Context` or help topic keyword (null-terminated) if `Command` set to `help_Key`

Return Value:
Nonzero if successful; else 0

Atom-Management Procedures and Functions

```
AddAtom
DeleteAtom
FindAtom
```

```
GetAtomHandle
GetAtomName
GlobalAddAtom
GlobalDeleteAtom
GlobalFindAtom
GlobalGetAtomName
InitAtomTable
MakeIntAtom
```

AddAtom

```
function AddAtom(Str: PChar): Atom;
```

Adds `Str` to the atom table. A reference count is maintained for each unique string instance.

Parameters	*Description*
Str	Null-terminated character string

Return Value:
Unique atom identifier if successful; else –1.

DeleteAtom

```
function DeleteAtom(AnAtom: Atom): Atom;
```

Deletes an atom. If the `Atom`'s reference count is zero, the associated string is removed from the atom table.

Parameters	*Description*
AnAtom	Atom identifier

Return Value:
Zero if successful; else `Atom`.

FindAtom

```
function FindAtom(Str: PChar): Atom;
```

Searches the atom table for the atom associated with `Str`.

Parameters	*Description*
Str	Search string (null-terminated)

Return Value:
Atom associated with `Str`; 0 if atom isn't found in table.

GetAtomHandle

```
function GetAtomHandle(AnAtom: Atom): THandle;
```

Gets the string that corresponds to a specified atom.

Parameters	***Description***
AnAtom	Atom identifier

Return Value:
Local memory handle to atom string; 0 if the atom does not exist.

GetAtomName

```
function GetAtomName(AnAtom: Atom; Buffer: PChar; Size: Integer): Word;
```

Copies the associated atom string into `Buffer`.

Parameters	***Description***
AnAtom	Atom identifier
Buffer	Buffer to receive atom string
Size	Buffer size (in bytes)

Return Value:
Number of bytes copied into `Buffer`; 0 if an invalid atom was specified.

GlobalAddAtom

```
function GlobalAddAtom(Str: PChar): Atom;
```

Adds `Str` to the atom table, thus creating a new global atom.

Parameters	***Description***
Str	String (null-terminated)

Return Value:
Newly created atom; 0 if error.

GlobalDeleteAtom

```
function GlobalDeleteAtom(AnAtom: Atom): Atom;
```

Decreases a global atom's reference count by one, deleting the atom and its associated string from the atom table if the reference count becomes 0.

Parameters	*Description*
AnAtom	Atom identifier

Return Value:
Zero if successful; else `AnAtom`.

GlobalFindAtom

```
function GlobalFindAtom(Str: PChar): Atom;
```

Gets the global atom associated with `Str`.

Parameters	*Description*
Str	Search string (null-terminated)

Return Value:
Global atom; 0 if `Str` is not in the table.

GlobalGetAtomName

```
function GlobalGetAtomName(AnAtom: Atom; Buffer: PChar; Size: Integer): W
```

Copies the string associated with `AnAtom` into `Buffer`.

Parameters	*Description*
AnAtom	Atom identifier
Buffer	Receive buffer
Size	Size of Buffer

Return Value:
Number of bytes copied; 0 if `AnAtom` is not valid.

InitAtomTable

```
function InitAtomTable(Size: Integer): Bool;
```

Initializes the atom hash table and sets its size. Default is 37.

Parameters	*Description*
Size	Number of table entries in atom hash table (should be a prime)

Return Value:
Nonzero if successful; else 0.

MakeIntAtom (type)

```
MakeIntAtom = PStr;
```

Use `MakeIntAtom` for typecasting integer numbers into atoms. This is equivalent to typecasting into the Turbo Pascal type `PChar`.

Communication Procedures and Functions

```
BuildCommDCB
ClearCommBreak
CloseComm
EscapeCommFunction
FlushComm
GetCommError
GetCommEventMask
GetCommState
OpenComm
ReadComm
SetCommBreak
SetCommEventMask
SetCommState
TransmitCommChar
UngetCommChar
WriteComm
```

BuildCommDCB

```
function BuildCommDCB(Def: PChar; var DCB: TDCB): Integer;
```

Translates `Def` into appropriate device-control block codes that are copied into `DCB`.

Parameters	*Description*
Def	DOS MODE command line (null-terminated) of device-control information
DCB	Receiving `TDCB` structure

Return Value:
Zero if `Def` is translated; else negative.

ClearCommBreak

```
function ClearCommBreak(Cid: Integer): Integer;
```

Restores character transmission and places the line in a non-break state.

Parameters	*Description*
Cid	Communication device to be restored

Return Value:
Zero, if successful; negative if `Cid` is not a valid device.

CloseComm

```
function CloseComm(Cid: Integer): Integer;
```

Closes `Cid`, flushing the output queue. Frees any memory used for transmit and receive queues.

Parameters	*Description*
Cid	Communications device

Return Value:
Zero if device is closed; negative if error.

EscapeCommFunction

```
function EscapeCommFunction(Cid, Func: Integer): Integer;
```

Executes the extended function specified by `Func` on a communications device.

Parameters	*Description*
Cid	Communications device
Func	One of the `EscapeComm` constants

Return Value:
Zero if successful; negative if `ab` invalid function code was specified.

FlushComm

```
function FlushComm(Cid, Queue: Integer): Integer;
```

Flushes a communication device's transmit or receive queue.

Parameters	*Description*
Cid	Communications device to be flushed
Queue	Zero to flush transmit queue or 1 to flush receive queue

Return Value:
Nonzero if successful; else 0.

GetCommError

```
function GetCommError(Cid: Integer; var Stat: TComStat): Integer;
```

Clears a device communications error.

Parameters	*Description*
Cid	Communications device
Stat	`TComStat` to receive device status information or nil

Return Value:
One of the `ce_ Comm` error flags' constants.

GetCommEventMask

```
function GetCommEventMask(Cid, EvtMask: Integer): Word;
```

Gets a device's current event mask, then clears it.

Parameters	*Description*
Cid	Communications device
EvtMask	Events to be enabled

Return Value:
Current event mask value.

GetCommState

```
function GetCommState(Cid: Integer; var DCB: TDCB): Integer;
```

Gets a device's device control block.

Parameters	*Description*
Cid	Communications device
DCB	`TDCB` to receive the current device control block

Return Value:
Zero if successful; else negative.

OpenComm

```
function OpenComm(ComName: PChar; InQueue, OutQueue: Word): Integer;
```

Opens a communications device. The device is initialized to a default configuration. Transmit and receive queues are allocated.

Parameters	*Description*
ComName	String containing COMn or LPTn, where n is an integer
InQueue	Receive queue size or ignored for LPT ports
OutQueue	Transmit queue size or ignored for LPT ports

Return Value:
`Cid` handle if successful; else negative error value (one of the `ie_ Open` communication error flags).

ReadComm

```
function ReadComm(Cid: Integer; Buf: PChar, Size: Integer): Integer;
```

Reads `Cid` and copies up to `Size` characters into `Buf`.

Parameters	Description
Cid	Communications device
Buf	Receiving buffer
Size	Size of Buffer

Return Value:
Number of characters read; 0 if no characters are in the receive queue; negative if error.

SetCommBreak

```
function SetCommBreak(Cid: Integer): Integer;
```

Suspends character transmission and places the device's transmission line in a break state.

Parameters	Description
Cid	Communications device

Return Value:
Zero if successful; negative if invalid `Cid`.

SetCommEventMask

```
function SetCommEventMask(Cid: Integer; EvtMask: Word): PWord;
```

Activates and gets the current state of a device's event mask.

Parameters	Description
Cid	Communications device
EvtMask	Any combination of `ev_ Comm` event constants

Return Value:
Pointer to an event mask; each set bit indicates an occurrence of the event.

SetCommState

```
function SetCommState(var DCB: TDCB): Integer;
```

Reinitializes a communications device specified by the `Id` field of `DCB` to the state specified by `DCB`. Transmit and receive queues are not affected.

Parameters	***Description***
DCB	`TDCB` structure

Return Value:
Zero if successful; else negative.

TransmitCommChar

```
function TransmitCommChar(Cid: Integer; AChar: Char): Integer;
```

Puts `AChar` at the head of the communication device's transmit queue for immediate transmission.

Parameters	***Description***
Cid	Communications device
AChar	Character to transmit

Return Value:
Zero if successful; negative if transmission is not possible because the previous character has not been sent.

UngetCommChar

```
function UngetCommChar(Cid: Integer; AChar: Char): Integer;
```

Puts `AChar` back into communication device's receiving queue.

Parameters	***Description***
Cid	Communications device
AChar	Character to `Unget`

Return Value:
Zero if successful; else negative.

WriteComm

```
function WriteComm(Cid: Integer; Buf: PChar; Size: Integer): Integer;
```

Outputs the buffer specified by `Buf` to a communications device.

Parameters	*Description*
Cid	Communications device
Buf	Buffer containing characters to be written
Size	Number of characters to output

Return Value:
Number of characters written; negative if error has an absolute value that equals the number of characters written before the error occurred.

File I/O Procedures and Functions

```
GetDriveType
GetSystemDirectory
GetTempDrive
GetTempFileName
GetWindowsDirectory
_lclose
_lcreat
_llseek
_lopen
_lread
_lwrite
OpenFile
SetHandleCount
```

GetDriveType

```
function GetDriveType(Drive: Integer): Word;
```

Decides whether `Drive` is removeable, fixed, or remote.

Parameters	*Description*
Drive	Drive to check (A is 0, B is 1, and so on.)

Return Value:
One of the `drive_ Drive` types constants; 0 if drive cannot be determined; 1 if drive does not exist.

GetSystemDirectory

```
procedure GetSystemDirectory(Buffer: PChar; Size: Word);
```

Gets the Windows system subdirectory path name.

Parameters	*Description*
Buffer	Receiving buffer
Size	Size of Buffer (at least 144 characters)

GetTempDrive

```
function GetTempDrive(DriveLetter: Char): Char;
```

Gets the disk drive that has the optimal access time for temporary file operations.

Parameters	*Description*
DriveLetter	Disk drive letter or 0 to return current drive

Return Value:
Disk drive letter.

GetTempFileName

```
function GetTempFileName(DriveLetter: Char; PrefixString: PChar;
  Unique: Word; TempFileName: PChar): Integer;
```

Derives a unique temporary file name with a path name of either the root directory or the directory specified by the `TEMP` environment variable.

Parameters	*Description*
DriveLetter	Suggested drive or `tf_ForceDrive` bit-or-ed with suggested drive or 0 for default drive
PrefixString	`File name` three character prefix (null-terminated)

Parameters	*Description*
Unique	Base file-name numeric value, or 0 for system-derived value
TempFileName	Receiving path-name buffer (at least 144 bytes long)

Return Value:
File name's numeric value.

GetWindowsDirectory

```
function GetWindowsDirectory(Buffer: PChar; Size: Word): Word;
```

Gets the Windows directory path name.

Parameters	*Description*
Buffer	Receiving path name buffer
Size	Size of Buffer (should be at least 144 bytes long)

Return Value:
Length of the string copied into `Buffer`.

_lclose

```
function _lclose(FileHandle: Integer): Integer;
```

Closes a specified file.

Parameters	*Description*
FileHandle	DOS file handle

Return Value:
Zero if successful; else –1.

_lcreat

```
function _lcreat(PathName: PChar; Attribute: Integer):Integer;
```

Opens the specified file.

Parameters	*Description*
Path name	The DOS path name of the file to be opened
Attribute	One of: (0) read or write, (1) read only, (2) hidden, or (3) system file

Return Value:
DOS file handle if successful; else –1.

_llseek

```
function _llseek(FileHandle: Integer; Offset: Longint;
  Origin: Integer): Longint;
```

Positions the pointer in an open file.

Parameters	*Description*
FileHandle	DOS file handle
Offset	Number of bytes to move the pointer
Origin	Specifies the starting point and direction of the move: (0) forward from the beginning, (1) from the current position, or (2) back from the end of the file

Return Value:
The new offset of the pointer; –1 if unsuccessful.

_lopen

```
function _lopen(PathName: PChar; ReadWrite: Integer): Integer;
```

Opens a file.

Parameters	*Description*
Path name	String specifying the path and file name

ReadWrite	Specifies the read and write access; one of the following `of_ Open` file constants:
	`of_Read`
	`of_ReadWrite`
	`of_Write`

Return Value:
The DOS file handle if successful; else –1.

_lread

```
function _lread(FileHandle: Integer; Buffer: PChar;
  Bytes: Integer): Word;
```

Read bytes from an open file.

Parameters	*Description*
FileHandle	The DOS file handle
Buffer	Receiving buffer
Bytes	The number of bytes to read

Return Value:
The number of bytes read, if successful; –1 if not; 0 if at the end of file.

_lwrite

```
function _lwrite(FileHandle: Integer; Buffer: PChar;
  Bytes: Integer): Word;
```

Writes data from `Buffer` into the specified file.

Parameters	*Description*
FileHandle	DOS file handle
Buffer	Holds the data to be written
Bytes	The number of bytes to be written

Return Value:
The number of bytes written to the file, if successful; else –1.

OpenFile

```
function OpenFile(FileName: PChar; var ReOpenBuff: TOFStruct;
  Style: Word): Integer;
```

Creates, opens, reopens, or deletes a file.

Parameters	*Description*
File Name	The specified file name
ReOpenBuff	Receives information about file when opened
Style	Specifies the action; one of the `of_ Open` file constants

Return Value:
DOS file handle if successful; else –1.

SetHandleCount

```
function SetHandleCount(Number: Word): Word;
```

Changes the number of file handles available to a task to the value specified by `Number`.

Parameters	***Description***
Number	Number of required file handles (maximum of 255)

Return Value:
Number of file handles available.

Initialization-File Procedures and Functions

```
GetPrivateProfileInt
GetPrivateProfileString
GetProfileInt
GetProfileString
WritePrivateProfileString
WriteProfileString
```

GetPrivateProfileInt

```
function GetPrivateProfileInt(ApplicationName, KeyName: PChar;
  Default: Integer; FileName: PChar): Word;
```

Gets an integer key value from a specified initialization file.

Parameters	***Description***
ApplicationName	Application heading name in `FileName`
KeyName	`Key` name in `FileName`
Default	Default value if `KeyName` not found
File Name	Initialization file name in Windows directory

Return Value:
`Key` value; 0 if negative or if `Key` value isn't an integer.

GetPrivateProfileString

```
function GetPrivateProfileString(ApplicationName, KeyName, Default,
  ReturnedString: PChar; Size: Integer; FileName: PChar): Integer;
```

Gets a string key value from a specified initialization file.

Parameters	*Description*
ApplicationName	Application heading name in `FileName`
KeyName	Key name in `FileName` or nil to obtain list of key names
Default	Default value if `KeyName` not found
ReturnedString	Receiving buffer
Size	Size of Buffer
File Name	Initialization file name in Windows directory

Return Value:
Number of characters copied.

GetProfileInt

```
function GetProfileInt(AppName, KeyName: PChar; Default: Integer): Word;
```

Gets an integer key value from Windows WIN.INI file.

Parameters	*Description*
AppName	Application heading name
KeyName	Search key name
Default	Default value if `KeyName` is not found

Return Value:
Key value; 0 if negative or if key value isn't an integer.

GetProfileString

```
function GetProfileString(AppName, KeyName, Default,
  ReturnedString: PChar; Size: Integer): Integer;
```

Gets a string key value from Windows WIN.INI file

Parameters	*Description*
AppName	Application heading name
KeyName	Search key name or nil to obtain all key names associated with `AppName`
Default	Default value if `KeyName` not found
ReturnedString	Receiving buffer
Size	Size of Buffer

Return Value:
Number of characters copied.

WritePrivateProfileString

```
function WritePrivateProfileString(ApplicationName,
  KeyName, Str, FileName: PChar): Bool;
```

Searches `FileName` for a specified application heading and key name; then replaces the `Key` name with `Str`.

Parameters	*Description*
ApplicationName	Application heading name
KeyName	Key name appearing under the application heading name or nil to delete entire section
Str	New key name string or nil to delete key name
File name	Initialization file name (null-terminated)

Return Value:
Nonzero if successful; else 0.

WriteProfileString

```
function WriteProfileString(ApplicationName, KeyName, Str: PChar): Bool
```

Searches WIN.INI for the specified application heading and key name; then replaces the key name with `Str`.

Parameters	*Description*
ApplicationName	Application heading
KeyName	Key name appearing under the application heading name, or nil to delete entire application section
Str	New key name value or nil to delete key name

Return Value:
Nonzero if successful; else 0.

Memory-Management Procedures and Functions

```
DefineHandleTable
GetFreeSpace
GetWinFlags
GlobalAlloc
GlobalCompact
GlobalDiscard
GlobalDosAlloc
GlobalDosFree
GlobalFlags
GlobalFree
GlobalHandle
GlobalLock
GlobalLRUNewest
GlobalLRUOldest
GlobalNotify
GlobalReAlloc
GlobalSize
GlobalUnlock
GlobalUnwire
GlobalWire
LimitEMSPages
LocalAlloc
LocalCompact
LocalDiscard
LocalFlags
LocalFree
LocalHandle
```

```
LocalInit
LocalLock
LocalReAlloc
LocalShrink
LocalSize
LocalUnlock
LockData
LockSegment
SetSwapAreaSize
SwitchStackBack
SwitchStackTo
UnlockData
UnLockSegment
```

DefineHandleTable

```
function DefineHandleTable(Offset: Word): Bool;
```

Creates a private handle table in the default data segment. The table holds the addresses of locked global memory objects, returned by `GlobalLock`. If these memory objects are moved, Windows updates their addresses when running in real mode. Addresses aren't updated in protected modes (Standard and 386-Enhanced).

The handle table consists of two Word-type values followed by an array of addresses.

- The first word is the number of entries in the table, which must be initialized before the call to `DefineHandleTable`.
- The second is the number of entries to set to 0 when Windows updates its list of least recently used memory. Either word can be changed at any time.

The addresses in the rest of the table are returned by `GlobalLock`.

Parameters	***Description***
Offset	The offset of the table from the beginning of the data segment. A value of 0 indicates that Windows should no longer update the table

Return Value:
Zero if successful; else nonzero.

GetFreeSpace

```
function GetFreeSpace(Flag: Word): Longint;
```

Gets the amount of free memory in the global heap.

Parameters	*Description*
Flag	The constant gmem_Not_Banked to scan below bank line or 0 to scan above; ignored for non-EMS systems

Return Value:
Memory available (in bytes).

GetWinFlags

```
function GetWinFlags: Longint;
```

Gets the memory-configuration flags in effect during the current Windows session.

Return Value:
Flag mask specifying the current memory configuration; can include one of the following wf_ Windows memory configuration flags:

```
wf_CPU286
wf_CPU386
wf_PMode
wf_SmallFrame
wf_Win286
wf_Win386
```

GlobalAlloc

```
function GlobalAlloc(Flags: Word; Bytes: Longint): THandle;
```

Allocates requested amount of memory, at minimum, from the global heap.

Parameters	*Description*
Flags	Flag mask; one or more of the gmem_ Global memory flags constants
Bytes	Number of bytes to allocate

Return Value:
Allocated global memory identifier; 0 if error.

GlobalCompact

```
function GlobalCompact(MinFree: Longint): Longint;
```

Compacts global memory and, when necessary and possible, removes discardable segments to create a `MinFree` size block.

Parameters	*Description*
MinFree	Desired free bytes or 0 to return largest free segment, if all discardable segments are removed

Return Value:
Size of largest free block.

GlobalDiscard

```
function GlobalDiscard(Mem: THandle): THandle;
```

Discards the specified global memory block if the block is discardable and unlocked.

Parameters	*Description*
Mem	The handle of the global memory block to discard

Return Value:
Handle of the block if successfully discarded; else 0.

GlobalDosAlloc

```
function GlobalDosAlloc(Bytes: LongInt): Longint;
```

Allocates global memory in the first megabyte of linear address space that can be accessed by DOS.

Avoid using this function, if possible, because low memory is a scarce system resource.

Parameters	*Description*
Bytes	The number of bytes to allocate

Return Value:
Zero if memory could not be allocated; else, the value is a paragraph-segment value in the high-order word and a selector in the low-order word.

In Real mode, the paragraph-segment value can be used to access the allocated memory. In protected mode, the selector should not be used.

GlobalDosFree

```
function GlobalDosFree(Selector: Word): Word;
```

Frees a block of memory allocated by `GlobalDosAlloc`.

Parameters	*Description*
Selector	The selector of the memory to free

Return Value:
Zero if successful; else `Selector`.

GlobalFlags

```
function GlobalFlags(Mem: THandle): Word;
```

Gets information about `Mem`.

Parameters	*Description*
Mem	Global memory block identifier

Return Value:
In high byte: `em_Ddeshare`, `gmem_Discardable`, `gmem_Discarded`, or `gmem_Not_Banked`. In low byte: lock reference-count.

GlobalFree

```
function GlobalFree(Mem: THandle): THandle;
```

Frees an unlocked global memory block and invalidates its handle.

Parameters	*Description*
Mem	Global memory block identifier

Return Value:
Zero if successful; else `Mem`.

GlobalHandle

```
function GlobalHandle(Mem: Word): Longint;
```

Gets the handle of a global memory object with the specified segment address.

Parameters	*Description*
Mem	Segment address

Return Value:
Handle and segment address in low- and high-word, respectively; 0 if `Handle` doesn't exist.

GlobalLock

```
function GlobalLock(Mem: THandle): Pointer;
```

Increments the reference count of a global memory block and returns a pointer to it.

Parameters	*Description*
Mem	Global memory block identifier

Return Value:
Memory block address if successful; else nil.

GlobalLRUNewest

```
function GlobalLRUNewest(Mem: THandle): THandle;
```

Reduces the chance a global memory object will be discarded by moving it into the newest, least recently used memory position.

Parameters	*Description*
Mem	Global memory object identifier

Return Value:
Zero if invalid `Mem`.

GlobalLRUOldest

```
function GlobalLRUOldest(Mem: THandle): THandle;
```

Increases the chance a global memory object will be discarded by moving it into the oldest, least recently used memory position.

Parameters	*Description*
Mem	Global memory object identifier

Return Value:
Zero if invalid `Mem`.

GlobalNotify

```
procedure GlobalNotify(NotifyProc: TFarProc);
```

Calls `NotifyProc` passing the handle of the global memory block to be discarded. If `NotifyProc` returns nonzero, the block is discarded.

Parameters	*Description*
NotifyProc	Notification callback procedure's instance-address

GlobalReAlloc

```
function GlobalReAlloc(Mem: THandle; Bytes: Longint;
  Flags: Word): THandle;
```

Reallocates a global memory block to `Bytes` size.

Parameters	*Description*
Mem	Global memory block identifier
Bytes	New size of `Mem`

Flags	One or more of the following `gmem_` Global memory flags:
	`gmem_Discardable`
	`gmem_Notify`
	`gmem_Moveable`
	`gmem_NoCompact`
	`gmem_NoDiscard`
	`gmem_ZeroInit`

Return Value:
Reallocated global memory block identifier; 0 if error.

GlobalSize

```
function GlobalSize(Mem: THandle): Longint;
```

Gets the current size of a global memory block.

Parameters	Description
Mem	Global memory block identifier

Return Value:
Size (in bytes); 0 if `Mem` is invalid or discarded.

GlobalUnlock

```
function GlobalUnlock(Mem: THandle): Bool;
```

Unlocks a global memory block locked by `GlobalLock`. If the block's lock reference-count reaches 0, the block is subject to moving or discarding.

Parameters	Description
Mem	Global memory block identifier

Return Value:
Zero if lock reference-count decrements to 0; else nonzero.

GlobalUnWire

```
function GlobalUnWire(Mem: THandle): Bool;
```

Unlocks a memory segment previously locked by `GlobalWire`.

Parameters	Description
Mem	Segment identifier

Return Value:
Nonzero if segment unlocked; else 0.

GlobalWire

```
function GlobalWire(Mem: THandle): PChar;
```

Moves a segment, which must be locked for a long period, into low memory and locks it.

Parameters	*Description*
Mem	Segment identifier

Return Value:
New segment location if successful; else nil.

LimitEmsPages

```
procedure LimitEmsPages(Kbytes: Longint);
```

Limits amount of expanded memory (in K) that Windows assigns to an application when running under expanded memory configuration.

Parameters	*Description*
Kbytes	Number of kilobytes of expanded memory assigned

LocalAlloc

```
function LocalAlloc(Flags, Bytes: Word): THandle;
```

Allocates a local memory block from the local heap. The true size might be larger than the specified size.

Parameters	*Description*

Flags	One or more of the following `lmem_` Local memory flags constants:
	`lmem_Discardable`
	`lmem_Fixed`
	`lmem_Modify`
	`lmem_Moveable`
	`lmem_Nocompact`
	`lmem_Nodiscard`
	`lmem_Zeroinit`

Bytes	Size (in bytes) of block to allocate

Return Value:
Local memory block identifier if successful; else 0.

LocalCompact

```
function LocalCompact(MinFree: Word): Word;
```

Generates a free block of at least `MinFree` size. If necessary, the function moves or discards unlocked blocks.

Parameters	Description
MinFree	Number of desired free bytes, or 0 to return largest contiguous block

Return Value:
Size (in bytes) of largest block.

LocalDiscard

```
function LocalDiscard(Mem: THandle): THandle;
```

Discards the specified local memory block, leaving its handle valid, meaning the handle can be reused by calling `LocalReAlloc`.

Parameters	Description
Mem	The handle of the local memory block

Return Value:
Zero if successful; else `Mem`.

LocalFlags

```
function LocalFlags(Mem: THandle): Word;
```

Gets information about a memory block.

Parameters	Description
Mem	Local memory block identifier

Return Value:
In high byte: `lmem_Discardable` or `lmem_Discarded`
In low byte: lock count

LocalFree

```
function LocalFree(Mem: THandle): THandle;
```

Frees a local memory block and invalidates its handle.

Parameters	*Description*
Mem	Local memory block identifier

Return Value:
Zero if successful; else `Mem`.

LocalHandle

```
function LocalHandle(Mem: Word): THandle;
```

Gets the handle of a local memory object at a specified address.

Parameters	*Description*
Mem	Local memory object address

Return Value:
Local memory object identifier.

LocalInit

```
function LocalIni(Segment, Start, End: Word): Bool;
```

Initializes a local heap and calls `GlobalLock` to lock the segment.

Parameters	*Description*
Segment	Segment address of local heap
Start	Offset address to start of local heap
End	Offset address to end of local heap

Return Value:
Nonzero if initialized; else 0.

LocalLock

```
function LocalLock(Mem: THandle): Pointer;
```

Locks `Mem` and increments its lock count. The block cannot be moved or discarded.

Parameters	*Description*
Mem	Local memory block identifier

Return Value:
Pointer to block if successful; else nil.

LocalReAlloc

```
function LocalReAlloc(Mem: THandle; Bytes, Flags: Word): THandle;
```

Changes the size or attributes, as specified by `Flags`, of a local memory block.

Parameters	*Description*
Mem	Local memory block identifier
Bytes	New size (in bytes) of block

Flags	One or more of the `lmem_` Local memory flags:
	`lmem_Discardable`
	`lmem_Modify`
	`lmem_Moveable`
	`lmem_NoCompact`
	`lmem_NoDiscard`
	`lmem_ZeroInit`

Return Value:
Local memory block identifier if successful; else 0.

LocalShrink

```
function LocalShrink(Seg: THandle; Size: Word): Word;
```

Reduces the local heap to the specified size whose value must be greater than the minimum size specified in the application's module-definition file.

Parameters	*Description*
Seg	Segment containing local heap, or 0 for current data segment
Size	Desired size (in bytes),

Return Value:
Size after shrinkage.

LocalSize

```
function LocalSize(Mem: THandle): Word;
```

Gets the size of a local memory block.

Parameters	*Description*
Mem	Local memory block identifier

Return Value:
Size (in bytes) of block; 0 if invalid `Mem`.

LocalUnlock

```
function LocalUnlock(Mem: THandle): Bool;
```

Unlocks a local memory block by decrementing its lock count.

Parameters	*Description*
Mem	Local memory block identifier

Return Value:
Zero if lock count decremented to 0 (making the block subject to moving or discarding); else nonzero.

LockData

```
function LockData(Dummy: Integer): THandle;
```

Locks the current moveable data segment in memory.

Parameters	*Description*
Dummy	Not used; set to 0

Return Value:
Identifier for the locked data segment if successful; else 0.

LockSegment

```
function LockSegment(Segment: Word): THandle;
```

Locks a segment (except protected-mode, non-discardable segments) and increments its lock reference-count.

Parameters	Description
Segment	Segment address or –1 for current segment

Return Value:
Pointer to segment; nil if error or discarded.

SetSwapAreaSize

```
function SetSwapAreaSize(Size: Word): Longint;
```

Increases the amount of memory (up to one-half of remaining space after Windows is loaded) an application can use for its code segments.

Parameters	Description
Size	Number of 16-byte paragraphs

Return Value:
Number of paragraphs obtained in low-order word; maximum size available in high-order word.

SwitchStackBack

```
procedure SwitchStackBack;
```

Restores the current task's stack to its data segment preserving the contents of `AX:DX` registers.

UnlockData

```
function UnlockData(Dummy: Integer): THandle;
```

Unlocks the current, moveable data segment.

Parameters	Description
Dummy	Not used; set to 0

Return Value:
Identifier for the unlocked segment; else 0.

UnlockSegment

```
function UnlockSegment(Segment: Word): THandle;
```

Unlocks a segment specified by `Segment`.

Parameters	*Description*
Segment	Segment address or –1 to unlock current data segment

Return Value:
Zero if reference count was decremented to 0; else nonzero.

Module-Management Procedures and Functions

```
FreeLibrary
FreeModule
FreeProcInstance
GetCodeHandle
GetInstanceData
GetModuleFileName
GetModuleHandle
GetModuleUsage
GetProcAddress
GetVersion
LoadLibrary
MakeProcInstance
```

FreeLibrary

```
procedure FreeLibrary(LibModule: THandle);
```

Invalidates `LibModule` and frees any associated memory if the module is no longer referenced.

Parameters	*Description*
LibModule	Loaded library module

FreeModule

```
function FreeModule(Module: THandle): Bool;
```

Invalidates `Module` and frees any associated memory if the module is no longer referenced.

Parameters	*Description*
Module	Loaded module identifier

Return Value:
Not used.

FreeProcInstance

```
procedure FreeProcInstance(Proc: TFarProc);
```

Frees a function's procedure-instance address.

Parameters	*Description*
Proc	Function's procedure-instance address (to be freed)

GetCodeHandle

```
function GetCodeHandle(Proc: TFarProc): THandle;
```

Gets the code segment that contains the specified function and loads the segment, if necessary.

Parameters	*Description*
Proc	Function's procedure-instance address

Return Value:
Code segment that contains the function.

GetInstanceData

```
function GetInstanceData(Instance: THandle; Data, Count: Word): Intege
```

Copies a previous instance data into `Data`.

Parameters	Description
Instance	Previous application's instance identifier
Data	Receiving buffer
Count	Size of Buffer

Return Value:
Number of bytes copied.

GetModuleFileName

```
function GetModuleFileName(Module: THandle; FileName: PChar;
  Size: Integer): Integer;
```

Gets the full path name (null-terminated) of the executable file for the specified module.

Parameters	Description
Module	Module identifier
File name	Receiving buffer
Size	Size of Buffer

Return Value:
Number of bytes copied.

GetModuleHandle

```
function GetModuleHandle(ModuleName: PChar): THandle;
```

Gets a module's handle.

Parameters	Description
ModuleName	Module name (null-terminated)

Return Value:
Module identifier if successful; else 0.

GetModuleUsage

```
function GetModuleUsage(Module: THandle): Integer;
```

Gets a module's reference count.

Parameters	*Description*
Module	Module identifier

Return Value:
Reference count.

GetProcAddress

```
function GetProcAddress(Module: THandle; ProcName: PChar): TFarProc;
```

Gets the address of an exported library function.

Parameters	*Description*
Module	Library module
ProcName	Function name (null-terminated) or ordinal name

Return Value:
Function's entry point if successful; else 0.

GetVersion

```
function GetVersion: Word;
```

Gets Window's current version number.

Return Value:
Minor version number in high-order byte;
Major version number in low-order byte.

LoadLibrary

```
function LoadLibrary(LibFileName: PChar): THandle;
```

Loads the library module.

Parameters	*Description*
LibFileName	Library file name (null-terminated).

Return Value:
Library module instance identifier (value greater than 32) if successful. If not, its value is less than 32 and one of the following:

(0) no memory
(5) attempt to link task
(6) multiple data segments
(10) invalid Windows version
(11) invalid EXE file
(12) OS/2 app
(13) DOS 4.0 app
(14) Invalid EXE type
(15) not protect mode

MakeProcInstance

```
function MakeProcInstance(Proc: TFarProc; Instance: THandle): TFarProc;
```

Creates a procedure-instance address for the specified exported function.

Parameters	***Description***
Proc	Exported function `TFarProc` address
Instance	Module instance identifier

Return Value:
Function procedure-instance address if successful; else 0.

Operating-System Interrupt Procedures and Functions

`DOS3Call`
`NetBIOSCall`

DOS3Call

```
procedure DOS3Call;
```

Calls the DOS interrupt function `21h`.

`DOS3Call` should be used only in assembly language routines, as the registers for the `INT 21h` call must be set. Under Windows, `DOS3Call` works somewhat faster than a direct call to the software interrupt.

NetBIOSCall

```
procedure NetBIOSCall;
```

Calls the NETBIOS interrupt `5Ch`. Use this call instead of a direct call to the `5Ch` software interrupt for future compatibility.

You should call `NetBIOSCall` only in assembly language routines because the CPU registers must be set for the interrupt call.

Resource-Management Procedures and Functions

```
AccessResource
AllocResource
FindResource
FreeResource
LoadAccelerators
LoadBitmap
LoadCursor
LoadIcon
LoadMenu
LoadResource
LoadString
LockResource
SetResourceHandler
SizeofResource
UnlockResource
```

AccessResource

```
function AccessResource(Instance, ResInfo: THandle): Integer;
```

Opens and positions the resource file to the beginning of a resource. Be sure to close the file after reading the resource.

Parameters	*Description*
Instance	Instance module whose executable file contains the resource
ResInfo	Desired resource, created by calling the `FindResource` function

Return Value:
DOS file handle; –1 if the resource is not found.

AllocResource

```
function AllocResource(Instance, ResInfo: THandle;
  Size: Longint): THandle;
```

Allocates uninitialized memory for `ResInfo`.

Parameters	***Description***
Instance	Module instance of executable file containing the resource
ResInfo	Desired resource
Size	Size in bytes to allocate for the resource; ignored if 0

Return Value:
Allocated global memory block.

FindResource

```
function FindResource(Instance: THandle; Name, ResType: PChar): THandle;
```

Locates a resource in a resource file.

Parameters	***Description***
Instance	Module instance whose executable file contains the resource
Name	Resource name either a null-terminated string or an integer `ID`
ResType	One of the `rt_ Resource` types constants, a null-terminated string, or an integer `ID`

Return Value:
Resource identifier; 0 if the resource isn't found.

FreeResource

```
function FreeResource(ResData: THandle): Bool;
```

Invalidates `ResData` and frees associated memory if the resource is no longer referenced.

Parameters	Description
ResData	Resource data identifier

Return Value:
Zero if successful; else nonzero.

LoadAccelerators

```
function LoadAccelerators(Instance: THandle; TableName: PChar): THandle
```

Loads an accelerator table from an executable file.

Parameters	Description
Instance	Module instance whose executable file contains the accelerator table
TableName	Accelerator table name (null-terminated) or integer ID

Return Value:
Accelerator table identifier if successful; else 0.

LoadBitmap

```
function LoadBitmap(Instance: THandle; BitmapName: PChar): HBitmap;
```

Loads a bit map resource.

Parameters	Description
Instance	Module instance whose executable file contains the bit map, or 0 for predefined bit map
BitmapName	String (null-terminated) or integer ID specifying the bit map, or a predefined bit map, specified by an obm_ Predefined bit maps constant

Return Value:
Bit map identifier if successful; else 0.

LoadCursor

```
function LoadCursor(Instance: THandle; CursorName: PChar): HCursor;
```

Loads a cursor resource.

Parameters	*Description*
Instance	Module instance whose executable file contains the cursor, or 0 for predefined cursor
CursorName	String (null-terminated) or integer `ID` name or a predefined cursor, specified with one of the `idc_ Standard` cursor IDs constants

Return Value:
Cursor identifier if successful; 0 if cursor isn't found; undefined if not a cursor resource.

LoadIcon

```
function LoadIcon(Instance: THandle; IconName: PChar): HIcon;
```

Loads an icon resource.

Parameters	*Description*
Instance	Module instance whose executable file contains the icon, or 0 for predefined icon
IconName	String or integer `ID` name or predefined icon, specified with one of the `idi_ Standard` icon IDs

Return Value:
Icon identifier if successful; else 0.

LoadMenu

```
function LoadMenu(Instance: THandle; MenuName: PChar): HMenu;
```

Loads a menu resource.

Parameters	Description
Instance	Module instance whose executable file contains the menu
MenuName	String (null-terminated) or integer ID name of menu

Return Value:
Menu identifier if successful; else 0.

LoadResource

```
function LoadResource(Instance, ResInfo: THandle): THandle;
```

Allocates memory for and loads a resource.

Parameters	Description
Instance	Module instance whose executable file contains the resource
ResInfo	Resource identifier (returned by `FindResource`)

Return Value:
Resource identifier if successful; else 0.

LoadString

```
function LoadString(Instance: THandle; ID: Word; Buffer: PChar;
  BufferMax: Integer): Integer;
```

Loads a string resource and copies it into `Buffer` appending a null-character.

Parameters	Description
Instance	Module instance whose executable file contains the string
ID	`Integer ID` of string
Buffer	Receiving buffer
BufferMax	Size of Buffer

Return Value:
Number of bytes copied; 0 if the string does not exist.

LockResource

```
function LockResource(ResData: THandle): Pointer;
```

Gets the address of a loaded resource and increments its reference-count. The resource can no longer be moved or discarded.

Parameters	*Description*
ResData	Resource identifier returned from `LoadResource`

Return Value:
Pointer to loaded resource; else nil.

SetResourceHandler

```
function SetResourceHandler(Instance: THandle; ResType: Pointer;
  LoadFunc: TFarProc): TFarProc;
```

Sets up a callback, which is called by Windows when a resource is being locked (that is, `LockResource`). The callback is passed a `Mem` to the stored resource, `Instance`, and `ResInfo` (from `FindResource`).

Parameters	*Description*
Instance	Module instance whose executable file contains the resource
ResType	Pointer to short integer specifying a resource type
LoadFunc	`Callback` function's procedure-instance address

Return Value:
Pointer to callback function.

SizeofResource

```
function SizeofResource(Instance, ResInfo: THandle): Word;
```

Gets the size of a resource.

Parameters	*Description*
Instance	Module instance whose executable file contains the resource.
ResInfo	Selected resource, returned by `FindResource`.

Return Value:
Size (in bytes) of resource; 0 if the resource isn't found.

UnlockResource

```
function UnlockResource(RezData: THandle): Bool;
```

Unlocks the `RezData` resource and decrements its reference counter.

Parameters	*Description*
RezData	Global memory block `Identifier`.

Return Value:
Zero if the reference counter is 0; else nonzero.

Segment Procedures and Functions

```
AllocDStoCSAlias
AllocSelector
ChangeSelector
DefineHandleTable
FreeSelector
GetCodeInfo
GlobalFix
GlobalPageLock
GlobalPageUnlock
GlobalUnfix
LockSegment
UnlockSegment
```

AllocDStoCSAlias

```
function AllocDStoCSAlias(Selector: Word): Word;
```

Maps `Selector` to a code-segment selector.

Parameters	Description
Selector	Data-segment selector

Return Value:
Corresponding code-segment selector if successful; else 0.

AllocSelector

```
function AllocSelector(Selector: Word): Word;
```

Allocates a new selector, which is an exact copy of `Selector`. If `Selector` is nil, `AllocSelector` allocates a new, uninitialized selector.

`AllocSelector` and related functions are not aften used; avoid using these functions, if possible.

Parameters	Description
Selector	Selector to be copied

Return Value:
A selector if successful; else 0.

ChangeSelector

```
function ChangeSelector(DestSelector, SourceSelector: Word): Word;
```

Changes the attributes of a selector from code to data or vice versa. The value of the selector is not affected.

Usually, you should change the selector only if absolutely necessary. The converted selector should be used immediately, because there's no way to keep the source and destination selectors synchronized.

Parameters	Description
DestSelector	The selector that receives the converted selector must have been previously allocated with `AllocSelector`
SourceSelector	The selector to be converted

Return Value:
Converted selector; else 0 (indicating failure).

DefineHandleTable

```
function DefineHandleTable(Offset: Word): Bool;
```

Creates a private handle table in the default data segment. The table holds the addresses of locked global memory objects, as returned by `GlobalLock`. If the memory objects are moved, Windows updates these addresses when running in real mode. Addresses aren't updated in protected modes (Standard and 386 Enhanced).

The handle table consists of two `Word`-type values followed by an array of addresses.

- The first word is the number of entries in the table, which must be initialized before the call to `DefineHandleTable`.
- The second is the number of entries to set to zero when Windows updates its list of least recently used memory. Either word can be changed at any time.

The addresses in the rest of the table are returned by `GlobalLock`.

Parameters	*Description*
Offset	The offset of the table from the beginning of the data segment. A value of 0 indicates that Windows should no longer update the table

Return Value:s
Nonzero if successful; 0 if successful.

FreeSelector

```
function FreeSelector(Selector: Word): Word;
```

Frees and invalidates a selector allocated by `AllocSelector` or `AllocDStoCSAlias`.

Parameters	*Description*
Selector	The selector to free

Return Value:
Zero if successful; else `Selector`.

GetCodeInfo

```
procedure GetCodeInfo(Proc: TFarProc; SegInfo Pointer);
```

Gets information about the code segment that contains `Proc`.

Parameters	*Description*
Proc	Function address or module handle and segment number.
SegInfo	Any array of four 32-bit values.

GlobalFix

```
procedure GlobalFix(Mem: THandle);
```

Fixes a global memory block in memory and increases its lock reference count by one.

Parameters	*Description*
Mem	Global memory block identifier

GlobalPageLock

```
function GlobalPageLock(Selector: THandle): Word;
```

Increments a memory block's page-lock count.

Parameters	*Description*
Selector	Memory selector

Return Value:
Incremented page-lock count if successful; else 0.

GlobalPageUnlock

```
function GlobalPageUnlock(Selector: THandle): Word;
```

Decrements a memory block's page-lock count. If count reaches 0, the page can be moved or swapped to disk.

Parameters	Description
Selector	Memory selector

Return Value:
Decremented page-lock count if successful; else 0.

GlobalUnfix

```
function GlobalUnfix(Mem: THandle): Bool;
```

Unlocks a global memory block locked by `GlobalFix`. If the block's lock reference-count reaches 0, the block can be moved or discarded.

Parameters	Description
Mem	Global memory block identifier

Return Value:
Zero if lock reference-count decrements to 0; else nonzero.

LockSegment

```
function LockSegment(Segment: Word): THandle;
```

Locks a segment (except protected-mode, non-discardable segments) and increments its lock reference-count.

Parameters	Description
Segment	Segment address or –1 for current segment

Return Value:
Pointer to `Segment`; nil if error or if segment is discarded.

UnlockSegment

```
function UnlockSegment(Segment: Word): THandle;
```

Unlocks a segment specified by `Segment`.

Parameters	Description
Segment	Segment address, or –1 to unlock current data segment

Return Value:
Zero if reference count was decremented to 0; else nonzero.

Sound Procedures and Functions

```
CloseSound
CountVoiceNotes
GetThresholdEvent
GetThresholdStatus
OpenSound
SetSoundNoise
SetVoiceAccent
SetVoiceEnvelope
SetVoiceNote
SetVoiceQueueSize
SetVoiceSound
SetVoiceThreshold
StartSound
StopSound
SyncAllVoices
WaitSoundState
```

CloseSound

```
procedure CloseSound;
```

Flushes all voice queues, frees any allocated buffers, and closes the play device.

CountVoiceNotes

```
function CountVoiceNotes(Voice: Integer): Integer;
```

Counts the number of notes in `Voice`.

Parameters	***Description***
Voice	Voice queue

Return Value:
Number of notes.

GetThresholdEvent

```
function GetThresholdEvent: LPInteger;
```

Gets a recent threshold event.

Return Value:
Pointer to threshold event.

GetThresholdStatus

```
function GetThresholdStatus: Integer;
```

Gets a threshold event status where each set bit represents a voice-queue level that is currently below threshold.

Return Value:
Current threshold event status flags.

OpenSound

```
function OpenSound: Integer;
```

Opens the play device for exclusive use by the application.

Return Value:
Number of available `s_Sound` voices; `s_SerDVNA` if in use; `s_SerOFM` if insufficient memory.

SetSoundNoise

```
function SetSoundNoise(Source, Duration: Integer): Integer;
```

Sets a noise source and duration values for the play device.

Parameters	***Description***
Source	Any one of the `SetSoundNoise` constants
Duration	Noise duration (in clock ticks)

Return Value:
Zero if successful; `s_SerDSR` if an invalid `Source`.

SetVoiceAccent

```
function SetVoiceAccent(Voice, Tempo, Volume, Mode,
  Pitch: Integer): Integer;
```

Replaces the envelope in a voice queue.

Parameters	Description
Voice	A voice queue (starting from one)
Tempo	Quarter notes played per minute (default, 120)
Volume	Volume level (0 to 255)
Mode	One of the `SetVoiceAccent` sound constants
Pitch	Pitch of played notes (0 to 83)

Return Value:
Zero if successful; else one of these negative constants:

```
s_SerDMD
s_SerDTP
s_SerDVL
s_SerQFUL
```

SetVoiceEnvelope

```
function SetVoiceEnvelope(Voice, Shape, RepeatCount: Integer): Integer;
```

Places a voice envelope in the voice queue and replaces the existing voice envelope.

Parameters	Description
Voice	A voice queue
Shape	OEM wave-shape table index
RepeatCount	Number of repetitions of wave-shape per note

Return Value:
Zero if successful; else one of these negative constants:

```
s_SerQFUL
s_SerDSH
```

SetVoiceNote

```
function SetVoiceNote(Voice, Value, Length, Cdots: Integer): Integer;
```

Places a note on a voice queue with the specified qualities.

Parameters	Description
Voice	A voice queue
Value	A note (one of 84) or 0 for rest
Length	Reciprocal of note duration
Cdots	Note duration in dots: `(Length *(Cdots *3/2))`

Return Value:
Zero if successful; else one of these negative constants:

```
s_SerDCC
s_SerDLN
s_SerBDNT
s_SerQFUL
```

SetVoiceQueueSize

```
function SetVoiceQueueSize(Voice, Bytes: Integer): Integer;
```

Sets the size of non-playing voice queue. The default is 192 bytes or approximately 32 notes.

Parameters	Description
Voice	A voice queue
Bytes	Size (in bytes) of voice queue

Return Value:
Zero if successful; else one of the following negative constants:

```
s_SerMACT
s_SerOFM
```

SetVoiceSound

```
function SetVoiceSound(Voice: Longint; Frequency: Longint;
  Duration: Integer): Integer;
```

Places the sound frequency and duration on a voice queue.

Parameters	Description
Voice	A voice queue
Frequency	Hertz and fractional frequency in high- and low-order words
Duration	Sound duration (in clock ticks)

Return Value:
Zero if successful; else one of the following negative constants:

```
s_SerDDR
s_SerDFQ
s_SerDVL
s_SerQFUL
```

SetVoiceThreshold

```
function SetVoiceThreshold(Voice, Notes: Integer): Integer;
```

Sets the threshold level for a voice queue. If the number of notes in queue drop below the threshold, the threshold flag is set.

Parameters	*Description*
Voice	A voice queue
Notes	Number of notes specifying the threshold level

Return Value:
Zero if successful; 1 if Note is out of range.

StartSound

```
function StartSound: Integer;
```

Non-destructively plays the voice queue.

Return Value:
Not used.

StopSound

```
function StopSound: Integer;
```

Stops playing all voice queues, flushes queue contents, and turns off voice sound drivers.

Return Value:
Not used.

SyncAllVoices

```
function SyncAllVoices: Integer;
```

Places a sync mark in all voice queues.

Return Value:
Zero if successful; `s_SerQFUL` if the voice queue is full.

WaitSoundState

```
function WaitSoundState(State: Integer): Integer;
```

Waits for the play driver to enter the state specified by `State`.

Parameters	***Description***
State	One of the `WaitSoundState` constants

Return Value:
Zero if successful; `s_SerDST` if an invalid `State`.

String-Manipulation Procedures and Functions

```
AnsiLower
AnsiLowerBuff
AnsiNext
AnsiPrev
AnsiToOem
AnsiToOemBuff
AnsiUpper
AnsiUpperBuff
IsCharAlpha
IsCharAlphaNumeric
IsCharLower
IsCharUpper
lstrcat
lstrcmp
lstrcmpi
lstrcpy
lstrlen
```

```
OemToAnsi
OemToAnsiBuff
ToAscii
wvsprintf
```

AnsiLower

```
function AnsiLower(Str: PChar): PChar;
```

Uses the language driver to convert `Str` to lowercase.

Parameters	*Description*
Str	Null-terminated string or a single character (in low-order byte)

Return Value:
Converted string or character.

AnsiLowerBuff

```
function AnsiLowerBuff(Str: PChar; Length: Word): Word;
```

Uses the language driver to convert `Str` to lowercase.

Parameters	*Description*
Str	Buffer of characters
Length	Number of characters in buffer; if 0, length is 64K (65,536)

Return Value:
Length of the converted string.

AnsiNext

```
function AnsiNext(CurrentChar: PChar): PChar;
```

Iterates through strings whose characters are two or more bytes long.

Parameters	*Description*
CurrentChar	Null-terminated string

Return Value:
Pointer to next character in string.

AnsiPrev

```
function AnsiPrev(Start, CurrentChar: PChar): PChar;
```

Iterates backward through strings whose characters are two or more bytes long.

Parameters	*Description*
Start	Beginning of string (null-terminated)
CurrentChar	Points to a character in the string

Return Value:
Pointer to previous character in the string.

AnsiToOem

```
function AnsiToOem(AnsiStr, OemStr: PChar): Integer;
```

Translates `AnsiStr` to OEM-defined character set. Length can be greater than 64K.

Parameters	*Description*
AnsiStr	String (null-terminated) of ANSI characters
OemStr	Location where translated string is to be copied, can be same as `AnsiStr`

Return Value:
Always –1.

AnsiToOemBuff

```
procedure AnsiToOemBuff(AnsiStr, OemStr: PChar; Length: Integer);
```

Translates `AnsiStr` to OEM-defined character set.

Parameters	*Description*
AnsiStr	Buffer of ANSI characters
OemStr	Location where translated string is to be copied, can be same as `AnsiStr`
Length	Size of `AnsiStr`, if 0, the length is 64K

AnsiUpper

```
function AnsiUpper(Str: PChar): PChar;
```

Uses the language driver to convert `Str` to uppercase.

Parameters	*Description*
Str	String (null-terminated) or a single character (in low-order byte)

Return Value:
Converted string or character.

AnsiUpperBuff

```
function AnsiUpperBuff(Str: PChar; Length: Word): Word;
```

Uses the language driver to convert `Str` to uppercase.

Parameters	*Description*
Str	Buffer of characters
Length	Size of `Str`; if 0, length is 64K

Return Value:
Length of the converted string.

IsCharAlpha

```
function IsCharAlpha(AChar: Char): Bool;
```

Uses the language driver and the current language to determine if `AChar` is alphabetical.

Parameters	*Description*
AChar	Test character

Return Value:
Nonzero if alphabetical; else 0.

IsCharAlphaNumeric

```
function IsCharAlphaNumeric(AChar: Char): Bool;
```

Uses the language driver and the current language to determine if `AChar` is alphanumeric.

Parameters	*Description*
AChar	Test character

Return Value:
Nonzero if alphanumeric; else 0.

IsCharLower

```
function IsCharLower(AChar: Char): Bool;
```

Uses the language driver and the current language to determine if `AChar` is lowercase.

Parameters	*Description*
AChar	Test character

Return Value:
Nonzero if lowercase; else 0.

IsCharUpper

```
function IsCharUpper(AChar: Char): Bool;
```

Uses the language driver and the current language to determine if `AChar` is uppercase.

Parameters	*Description*
AChar	Test character

Return Value:
Nonzero if uppercase; else 0.

lstrcat

```
function lstrcat(Str1, Str2: PChar): PChar;
```

Concatenates `Str2` to `Str1`.

Parameters	*Description*
Str1	First string (null-terminated)
Str2	Second string (null-terminated)

Return Value:
`Str1` if successful; else 0.

lstrcmp

```
function lstrcmp(Str1, Str2: PChar): Integer;
```

Does case-sensitive, lexicographical comparison of two strings based on the currently selected language. Uppercase characters evaluate lower than lowercase characters.

Parameters	*Description*
Str1	First string (null-terminated)
Str2	Second string (null-terminated)

Return Value:
Less than 0 if `Str1` < `Str2`; 0 if `Str1` = `Str2`; Greater than 0 if `Str1` > `Str2`.

lstrcmpi

```
function lstrcmpi(Str1, Str2: PChar): Integer;
```

Does case-insensitive, lexicographical comparison of two strings based on the currently selected language.

Parameters	*Description*
Str1	First string (null-terminated)
Str2	Second string (null-terminated)

Return Value:
Less than 0 if `Str1` < `Str2`; 0 if `Str1` = `Str2`; Greater than 0 if `Str1` > `Str2`.

lstrcpy

```
function lstrcpy(Str1, Str2: PChar): PChar;
```

Copies `Str2` to `Str1` (including null).

Parameters	Description
Str1	First string (null-terminated)
Str2	Second string (null-terminated)

Return Value:
Pointer to `Str1` if successful; else 0.

lstrlen

```
function lstrlen(Str: PChar): Integer;
```

Calculates length (not including null) of `Str`.

Parameters	Description
Str	String (null-terminated)

Return Value:
Length (in bytes) of `Str`.

OemToAnsi

```
function OemToAnsi(OemStr, AnsiStr: PChar): Bool;
```

Translates `OemStr` to ANSI character set.

Parameters	Description
OemStr	String of OEM characters (null-terminated)
AnsiStr	Receive buffer or `OemStr` to translate in place

Return Value:
Always –1 (False).

OemToAnsiBuff

```
procedure OemToAnsiBuff(OemStr, AnsiStr: PChar; Length: Integer);
```

Translates `OemStr` to ANSI character set.

Parameters	Description
OemStr	Buffer of OEM characters
AnsiStr	Receive buffer or `OemStr` to translate in place
Length	Size of OemStr

ToAscii

```
function ToAscii(VirtKey, ScanCode: Word; KeyState: PChar;
  CharBuff: Pointer; Flags: Word): Integer;
```

Translates `VirtKey` and the current keyboard state into corresponding ANSI characters.

Parameters	Description
VirtKey	Virtual-key code
ScanCode	Raw key scan code, high bit set if key up
KeyState	Array of 256 Bytes containing the state of each key, high bit set if key up
CharBuff	Pointer to a 32-bit receiving buffer
Flags	Not used

Return Value:
(2) accent and dead key copied to `CharBuff`,
(1) one ANSI character copied to `CharBuff`,
(0) translation is not possible with current keyboard state.

wvsprintf

```
function wvsprintf(Output, Format, ArgList: PChar): Integer;
```

Formats and stores a series of characters in a buffer.

Parameters	Description
Output	Buffer to receive formatted characters
Format	Format control string
ArgList	An array of arguments to the format control string

Return Value:
If successful, the number of characters in `Output`, (not counting 0).

If not successful, the number of characters returned is less than the length of `Format`.

Task Procedures and Functions

```
Catch
ExitWindows
GetCurrentPDB
GetCurrentTask
GetDOSEnvironment
GetNumTasks
SetErrorMode
Throw
Yield
```

Catch

```
function Catch(var CatchBuf: TCatchBuf): Integer;
```

Copies the state of all systems registers and the instruction pointer into `CatchBuf`.

Parameters	*Description*
CatchBuf	`TCatchBuf` to copy execution environment state

Return Value:
Zero if the environment is copied.

ExitWindows

```
function ExitWindows(Reserved: DWord; ReturnCode: Word): Bool;
```

Initiates standard Windows shutdown procedure. All applications must agree to terminate for Windows to exit. Calls DOS `Integer 21H function 4CH`.

Parameters	*Description*
Reserved	Set to 0
ReturnCode	Value passed to DOS (AL)

Return Value:
Zero if one or more applications refuse to terminate.

GetCurrentPDB

```
function GetCurrentPDB: Word;
```

Gets the current DOS Program Data Base (PDB — and also known as the Program Segment Prefix).

Return Value:
Current PDB paragraph address or selector.

GetCurrentTask

```
function GetCurrentTask :THandle;
```

Gets the handle of the currently executing task.

Return Value:
Task identifier if successful; else 0.

GetDOSEnvironment

```
function GetDOSEnvironment: PChar;
```

Gets the current task's DOS environment string.

Return Value:
Task's environment string.

GetNumTasks

```
function GetNumTasks: Word;
```

Gets the number of tasks that are currently executing in the system.

Return Value:
Number of currently executing tasks.

SetErrorMode

```
function SetErrorMode(Mode: Word): Bool;
```

Specifies whether Windows displays an error box on DOS `INT 24H` errors. If not, Windows fails the original `INT 21H` call, allowing the application to handle the error.

Parameters	*Description*
Mode	(0) Windows displays error box, (1) Windows fails to the application

Return Value:
Nonzero if set; else 0.

Throw

```
procedure Throw(var CatchBuf: TCatchBuf; ThrowBack: Integer);
```

Restores an application's execution environment. Execution continues at the `Catch` function that originally saved the environment to `CatchBuf`.

Parameters	*Description*
CatchBuf	`TCatchBuf` containing the execution environment
ThrowBack	Value returned to `Catch` function

Yield

```
function Yield: Bool;
```

Halts the current task and starts a waiting task.

Return Value:
Not used.

Utility Macros and Functions

```
GetNearestPaletteIndex
HiByte
HiWord
```

```
LoByte
LoWord
MakeIntAtom
MakeIntResource
MakeLong
MakePoint
MulDiv
PaletteRGB
RGB
```

GetNearestPaletteIndex

```
function GetNearestPaletteIndex(Palette: HPalette;
  Color: TColorRef): Word;
```

Gets the closest matching color in a logical-palette to `Color`.

Parameters	*Description*
Palette	Logical palette identifier
Color	`TColorRef` to be matched

Return Value:
Logical-palette entry index.

HiByte

```
function HiByte(A: Word): Byte;

inline(
     $5A/          { POP AX     }
     $8A/$C4/      { MOV AL,AH }

     $32/$E4);     { XOR AH,AH }
```

Extracts the high-order byte from a 16-bit integer value.

Parameters	*Description*
A	The 16-bit integer

Return Value:
The high-order byte.

HiWord

```
function HiWord(AnInteger: Longint): Word;
```

Extracts the high-order word from a 32-bit integer value.

Parameters	*Description*
AnInteger	The 32-bit integer

Return Value:
The high-order word.

LoByte

```
function LoByte(A: Word): Byte;

      inline(
            $5A/        { POP AX    }
            $32/$E4);   { XOR AH,AH }
```

Extracts the low-order byte from a 16-bit integer value.

Parameters	*Description*
A	The 16-bit integer

Return Value:
The low-order byte.

LoWord

```
function LoWord(AnInteger: Longint): Word;
```

Extracts the low-order word from a 32-bit integer value.

Parameters	*Description*
AnInteger	The 32-bit integer

Return Value:
The low-order word.

MakeIntAtom (type)

```
MakeIntAtom = PStr;
```

Use `MakeIntAtom` for typecasting integer numbers into atoms. It's equivalent to typecasting into the Turbo Pascal type `PChar`.

MakeIntResource (type)

```
MakeIntResource = PStr;
```

Use `MakeIntResource` for typecasting integer numbers into resource names. It's equivalent to typecasting into the Turbo Pascal type `PChar`.

MakeLong

```
function MakeLong(Low, High: Word): Longint;
```

Concatenates two word values into one unsigned long value.

Parameters	*Description*
Low	The low-order word of the new unsigned long
High	The high-order word of the new unsigned long

Return Value:
The resulting unsigned `Longint`.

MakePoint (type)

```
MakePoint = TPoint;
```

Use `MakePoint` for typecasting long integer numbers into `TPoint` records.

MulDiv

```
function MulDiv(Number, Numerator, Denominator: Integer): Integer;
```

Multiplies `Numerator` by `Number` and divides the result by `Denominator`, rounding to the nearest integer.

Parameters	Description
Number	A number
Numerator	Another number
Denominator	Another number

Return Value:
Result value; 32,767, or –32,767 if overflow or if Denominator is 0.

PaletteRGB

```
function PaletteRGB(Red, Green, Blue: Byte): Longint;
```

Produces a palette-relative RGB color value from three primary color values ranging from 0 to 255. The return value has two in the high-order byte.

Parameters	Description
Red	The red intensity value
Green	The green intensity value
Blue	The blue intensity value

Return Value:
The resulting RGB color.

RGB

```
function RGB(Red, Green, Blue: Byte): Longint;
```

Produces an RGB color value from three primary color values ranging from 0 to 255.

Parameters	Description
Red	The red intensity value
Green	The green intensity value
Blue	The blue intensity value

Return Value:
The resulting RGB color.

N

REFERENCE

GDI (GRAPHICS DEVICE INTERFACE) PROCEDURES AND FUNCTIONS

The Graphics Device Interface (GDI) built into Windows gives Windows applications a full range of functions for displaying and manipulating graphics.

The GDI uses device drivers to translate function calls into commands that can be used by output devices. In particular, GDI functions give your application drawing capabilities that are independent of the display device used:

```
Bitmap                            Font
Clipping                          Line-drawing
Color palette                     Mapping
Coordinate translation            Metafile
Device context                    Printer-control
Device-independent bitmap         Rectangle
Drawing-attribute                 Region
Drawing-tool                      Shape-drawing
Environment                       Text-drawing
Escape
```

Bitmap Procedures and Functions

A bitmap is the surface of a display context. Because a bitmap represents the memory configuration of a device, it is dependent on the device being addressed.

GDI supplies techniques for addressing the device-dependence problem, including device-independent bitmaps:

```
BitBlt
CreateBitmap
CreateBitmapIndirect
CreateCompatibleBitmap
CreateDiscardableBitmap
ExtFloodFill
FloodFill
GetBitmapBits
GetBitmapDimension
GetPixel
LoadBitmap
PatBlt
SetBitmapBits
SetBitmapDimension
SetPixel
StretchBlt
```

BitBlt

Copies a bitmap from `SrcDC` to `DestDC`, and handles the specified raster operation.

```
function BitBlt(DestDC: HDC; X, Y, Width, Height: Integer;
  SrcDC: HDC; XSrc, YSrc: Integer; Rop: Longint): Bool;
```

Parameter	*Description*
DestDC	Device context to receive the bitmap
X, Y	Upper-left corner of the destination rectangle
Width	Width of the destination rectangle and source bitmap
Height	Height of the destination rectangle and source bitmap
SSrcDC	Device context to copy bitmap from, or 0 for raster operation on `DestDC` only
XSrc, YSrc	Upper-left corner of `SrcDC`

Parameter	Description
Rop	One of the Ternary raster operations' constants for copying from source to destination

Return Value:
Nonzero if bitmap is drawn; else 0.

CreateBitmap

Creates a device-dependent memory bitmap.

```
function CreateBitmap(Width, Height: Integer; Planes,BitCount: Byte;
  Bits: Pointer): HBitmap;
```

Parameter	Description
Width	Width (in pixels) of the bitmap
Height	Height (in pixels) of the bitmap
Planes	Number of color planes in the bitmap
BitCount	Number of color bits per display pixel
Bits	Short-integer array containing initial bitmap values; if nil the new bitmap is left uninitialized

Return Value:
Bitmap identifier if successful; else 0.

CreateBitmapIndirect

Creates `Bitmap`.

```
function CreateBitmapIndirect(var Bitmap: TBitmap): HBitmap;
```

Parameter	Description
Bitmap	`TBitmap` structure

Return Value:
Bitmap identifier if successful; else 0

CreateCompatibleBitmap

Creates a bitmap compatible with DC.

```
function CreateCompatibleBitmap(DC: HDC; Width, Height: Integer): HBitmap;
```

Parameter	Description
DC	Device context
Width	Bitmap width (in bits)
Height	Bitmap height (in bits)

Return Value:
Bitmap identifier if successful; else 0.

CreateDiscardableBitmap

Creates a discardable bitmap compatible with `DC`.

```
function CreateDiscardableBitmap(DC: HDC; Width, Height: Integer): HBi
```

Parameter	Description
DC	Device context
Width	Bitmap width (in bits)
Height	Bitmap height (in bits)

Return Value:
Bitmap identifier if successful; else 0.

ExtFloodFill

Fills an area of a raster display surface in the manner specified by `FillType`. Uses the current brush.

```
function ExtFloodFill(DC: HDC; X, Y: Integer; Color: TColorRef;
  FillType: Word): Bool;
```

Parameter	Description
DC	Device context identifier
X, Y	Fill begin point
Color	`TColorRef` of boundary or area to be filled
FillType	One of the Flood fill style flags' constants

Return Value:
Nonzero if successful; else 0.

FloodFill

Fills the display area with the current brush bounded by `Color`.

```
function FloodFill(DC: HDC; X, Y: Integer; Color: TColorRef): Bool;
```

Parameter	*Description*
DC	Device context identifier
X, Y	Position to begin filling
Color	Boundary color, a `TColorRef`

Return Value:
Nonzero if successful; else 0.

GetBitmapBits

Copies the bits of a bitmap into `Bits`.

```
function GetBitmapBits(Bitmap: HBitmap; Count: Longint;
  Bits: Pointer): Longint;
```

Parameter	*Description*
Bitmap	Bitmap identifier
Count	Number of bytes to copy
Bits	Byte array conforming to a structure in which horizontal scan lines are multiples of 16 bits

Return Value:
Number of bytes in the bitmap; 0 if error.

GetBitmapDimension

Gets the height and width of a bitmap.

```
function GetBitmapDimension(Bitmap: HBitmap): Longint;
```

Parameter	*Description*
Bitmap	Bitmap identifier

Return Value:
Height (in tenths of millimeters) in high word; width (in tenths of millimeters) in low word; 0 if the dimensions haven't been used.

GetPixel

Gets the RGB color at the specified point.

```
function GetPixel(DC: HDC; X, Y; Integer): Longint;
```

Parameter	Description
DC	Device context identifier
X, Y	Point to be examined

Return Value:
RGB color value; –1 if point is not in clipping region.

LoadBitmap

Loads the bitmap resource.

```
function LoadBitmap(Instance: THandle; BitmapName: PChar): HBitmap;
```

Parameter	Description
Instance	Module instance whose executable file contains the bitmap or 0 for predefined bitmap
BitmapName	String (null-terminated) or integer `ID` specifying the bitmap, or a predefined bitmap, specified by an `obm_ Predefined` bitmaps constant

Return Value:
Bitmap identifier if successful; else 0.

PatBlt

Creates a bit pattern, using `Rop`, the selected brush, and the pattern already on the device.

```
function PatBlt(DC: HDC; X, Y, Width, Height: Integer; Rop: Longint):
```

Parameter	Description
DC	Device context identifier
X, Y	Upper-left corner of rectangle
Width	Width (in logical units) of rectangle
Height	Height (in logical units) of rectangle

Rop	One of the following `Ternary` raster operations:
	`PatCopy`
	`PatInvert`
	`DSTInvert`
	`Blackness`
	`Whiteness`

Return Value:
Nonzero if the bit pattern is drawn; else 0.

SetBitmapBits

Sets the bits of `Bitmap` to the bit values in `Bits`.

```
function SetBitmapBits(Bitmap: HBitmap; Count: Longint;
  Bits: Pointer): Longint;
```

Parameter	*Description*
Bitmap	`HBitmap` to set
Count	Size (in bytes) of `Bits`
Bits	Byte array of bitmap bits

Return Value:
Number of bytes used to set bitmap bits; 0 if error.

SetBitmapDimension

Sets a bitmap's height and width in 0.1-millimeter units.

```
function SetBitmapDimension(ABitmap: HBitmap; X, Y: Integer): Longint;
```

Parameter	*Description*
Bitmap	Bitmap identifier
X	Bitmap width (in 0.1-millimeter units)
Y	Bitmap height (in 0.1-millimeter units)

Return Value:
Height of previous dimensions in high-order word; width of previous dimensions in low-order word.

SetPixel

Paints the pixel at the specified point.

```
function SetPixel(DC: HDC; X, Y: Integer; Color: TColorRef): Longint;
```

Parameter	*Description*
DC	Device context
X, Y	Logical coordinates of point
Color	`TColorRef` specifying the color to paint the point

Return Value:
`TColorRef` used to paint; –1 if the point is outside the *clipping region*.

StretchBlt

Moves a bitmap (stretching or compressing it if required) from a source rectangle to a destination rectangle. The source and destination are combined as specified by `Rop`.

```
function StretchBlt(DestDC: HDC; X, Y, Width, Height: Integer;
  SrcDC: HDC; XSrc, YSrc, SrcWidth, SrcHeight: Integer; Rop: Longint): Bool;
```

Parameter	*Description*
DestDC	Receiving device context
X, Y	Upper-left corner of destination rectangle
Width	Destination rectangle width (in logical units)
Height	Destination rectangle height (in logical units)
SrcDC	Source bitmap device context
XSrc, YSrc	Upper-left corner of source rectangle
SrcWidth	Source rectangle width (in logical units)
SrcHeight	Source rectangle height (in logical units)
Rop	`Ternary` raster operations to be performed

Return Value:
Nonzero if bitmap is drawn; else 0.

Clipping Procedures and Functions

Every display context has a clipping region attribute to prevent drawing outside an intended area. The default clipping region (the window's client area) is good enough for most applications. Applications that create special visual effects might need to change the clipping region.

```
ExcludeClipRect
GetClipBox
IntersectClipRect
OffsetClipRgn
PtVisible
RectVisible
SelectClipRgn
```

ExcludeClipRect

Creates a new clipping region that consists of the region minus the specified rectangle.

```
function ExcludeClipRect(DC: HDC; X1, Y1, X2, Y2: Integer): Integer;
```

Parameter	Description
DC	Device context
X1, Y1	Upper-left corner of the rectangle
X2, Y2	Lower-right corner of the rectangle

Return Value:
One of the Region flags' constants.

GetClipBox

Gets the tightest bounding rectangle around the current clipping boundary.

```
function GetClipBox(DC: HDC; var Rect: TRect): Integer;
```

Parameter	Description
DC	Device context
Rect	Receiving `TRect` structure

Return Value:
One of the `Region` flags' constants.

IntersectClipRect

Creates a new clipping region from the intersection of the region and the specified rectangle.

```
function IntersectClipRect(DC: HDC; X1, Y1, X2, Y2: Integer): Integer;
```

Parameter	Description
DC	Device context
X1, Y1	Upper-left corner of rectangle
X2, Y2	Lower-right corner of rectangle

Return Value:
One of the `Region` flags.

OffsetClipRgn

Moves the device's clipping region according to the specified `X` and `Y` offsets.

```
function OffsetClipRgn(DC: HDC; X, Y: Integer): Integer;
```

Parameter	*Description*
DC	Device context
X	Logical units to move left or right
Y	Logical units to move up or down

Return Value:
One of the `Region` flags' constants.

PtVisible

Determines whether a point lies within the specified device's clipping region.

```
function PtVisible(DC: HDC; X, Y: Integer): Bool;
```

Parameter	*Description*
DC	Device context
X,Y	A point

Return Value:
If the point lies within the clipping region of `DC`, nonzero; else 0.

RectVisible

Decides whether any part of `Rect` lies within the specified device-context clipping region.

```
function RectVisible(DC: HDC; var Rect: TRect): Bool;
```

Parameter	*Description*
DC	Device context
Rect	`TRect` structure

Return Value:
Nonzero if in the clipping region; else 0.

SelectClipRgn

Uses a copy of `Rgn` as the current clipping region for the device context.

```
function SelectClipRgn(DC: HDC; Rgn: HRgn): Integer;
```

Parameter	*Description*
DC	Device context
Rgn	Selected region

Return Value:
One of the `Region` flags' constants.

Color Palette Procedures and Functions

Although some display devices can show many colors, they can show only a few at one time. The system palette is a group of colors currently available on the device for simultaneous display.

Windows gives your application some control over the colors in the device's system palette. If your applications use only simple colors, you don't need to use a palette directly.

```
AnimatePalette
CreatePalette
GetNearestPaletteIndex
GetPaletteEntries
GetSystemPaletteEntries
GetSystemPaletteUse
RealizePalette
SelectPalette
SetPaletteEntries
SetSystemPaletteUse
UpdateColors
```

Modifying the system palette affects everything drawn on the screen, including the colors of other applications. In other words, one application can cause all the other applications to appear with incorrect colors.

The Windows palette manager solves this problem by mediating among applications that change the system palette. Windows supplies each application with a logical palette (a group of colors for a specific application).

The palette manager maps the requested colors from the logical palette to the colors available in the system palette.

- If the requested color isn't listed in the system palette, the palette manager can add the color to the system palette.
- If the logical palette specifies more colors than the system palette can handle, the additional colors are matched to the closest available color in the system palette.

Windows reserves 20 permanent colors in the system palette to generally preserve the color scheme of Windows and all Windows applications.

AnimatePalette

Replaces entries in `Palette` between `StartIndex` and `NumEntries` with `PaletteColors`.

```
procedure AnimatePalette(Palette: HPalette; StartIndex: Word;
  NumEntries: Word; var PaletteColors);
```

Parameter	Description
Palette	The logical palette
StartIndex	The first entry in palette to be animated
NumEntries	The number of entries in palette to be animated
PaletteColors	An array of `TPaletteEntry` structures

CreatePalette

Creates a logical color palette.

```
function CreatePalette(var LogPalette: TLogPalette): HPalette;
```

Parameter	Description
LogPalette	`TLogPalette` containing color information about the logical palette

Return Value:
Logical palette identifier if successful; else 0.

GetNearestPaletteIndex

Gets the closest matching color in a logical palette to `Color`.

```
function GetNearestPaletteIndex(Palette: HPalette; Color: TColorRef): W
```

Parameter	Description
Palette	Logical palette identifier
Color	`TColorRef` to be matched

Return Value:
Logical-palette entry index.

GetPaletteEntries

Gets the specified range of palette entries and copies the palette range to `PaletteEntries`.

```
function GetPaletteEntries(Palette: HPalette; StartIndex,
  NumEntries: Word; var PaletteEntries): Word;
```

Parameter	Description
Palette	Logical palette identifier
StartIndex	First entry
NumEntries	Number of entries
PaletteEntries	TPaletteEntry array to receive the palette entries

Return Value:
Number of entries retrieved; 0 if error.

GetSystemPaletteEntries

Gets a range of palette entries from the system palette.

```
function GetSystemPaletteEntries(DC: HDC; StartIndex, NumEntries: Word;
  var PaletteEntries: TPaletteEntry): Word;
```

Parameter	Description
DC	Device context
StartIndex	First entry to retrieve
NumEntries	Number of entries to retrieve
PaletteEntries	Receiving TPaletteEntry array

Return Value:
Number of entries retrieved; 0 if error.

GetSystemPaletteUse

Decides whether an application has full access to the system palette.

```
function GetSystemPaletteUse(DC: HDC): Word;
```

Parameter	Description
DC	Device context

Return Value:
One of the syspal_ system palette flags.

RealizePalette

Maps the selected logical palette to entries in the system palette.

```
function RealizePalette(DC: HDC): Word;
```

Parameter	Description
DC	Device context

Return Value:
Number of entries in logical palette mapped to different system palettes since last `RealizePalette`.

SelectPalette

Selects `Palette` as the device context's selected palette object, which then is used by GDI to control displayed colors.

```
function SelectPalette(DC: HDC; Palette: HPalette;
  ForceBackground: Bool): HPalette;
```

Parameter	Description
DC	Device context
Palette	Logical palette to select
ForceBackground	If nonzero then background palette; or if 0, foreground palette when window has the input focus

Return Value:
Replaced logical palette if successful; else 0.

SetPaletteEntries

Sets logical palette entries in the specified range to the values in `PaletteEntries`.

```
function SetPaletteEntries(Palette: HPalette; StartIndex,
  NumEntries: Word; var PaletteEntries): Word;
```

Parameter	Description
Palette	Logical palette identifier
StartIndex	First entry to set
NumEntries	Number of entries to set
PaletteEntries	Array of `TPaletteEntry` structure

Return Value:
Number of entries set; 0 if error.

SetSystemPaletteUse

Allows an application to use the full system palette.

```
function SetSystemPaletteUse(DC: HDC; Usage: Word): Word;
```

Parameter	*Description*
DC	Device context
Usage	One of the `syspal_` system palette flags

Return Value:
Previous system palette usage.

UpdateColors

Updates the client area by matching the current colors of the client area pixel-by-pixel with the system palette.

```
function UpdateColors(DC: HDC): Integer;
```

Parameter	*Description*
DC	Device context

Return Value:
Not used.

Coordinate-Translation Procedures and Functions

Sometimes you might want to translate between the logical coordinates (you draw with them) and physical bitmap coordinates (to which the current mapping mode translates logical coordinates). GDI supplies the following functions to handle coordinate translations:

```
ChildWindowFromPoint
ClientToScreen
DPtoLP
LPtoDP
ScreenToClient
WindowFromPoint
```

ChildWindowFromPoint

Decides which child window owned by `WndParent` contains `APoint`.

```
function ChildWindowFromPoint(WndParent: HWnd; APoint: TPoint): HWnd;
```

Parameter	Description
WndParent	Parent window
APoint	`TPoint` structure of client coordinates to be tested

Return Value:
Child window that contains the point; 0 if point lies outside the parent window; `WndParent` if point isn't contained within any child window.

ClientToScreen

Converts client coordinates in `APoint` to screen coordinates.

```
procedure ClientToScreen(Wnd: HWnd; var Point: TPoint);
```

Parameter	Description
Wnd	Window containing client area
APoint	`TPoint` containing client coordinates

DPtoLP

Converts device points to logical points.

```
function DPtoLP(DC: HDC; var Points; Count: Integer): Bool;
```

Parameter	Description
DC	Device context
Points	Array of `TPoint` structures
Count	Number of points in `Points`

Return Value:
Nonzero if all points are converted; else 0.

LPtoDP

Converts logical points in `Points`, in the current mapping mode, to device points.

```
function LPtoDP(DC: HDC; var Points; Count: Integer): Bool;
```

Parameter	Description
DC	Device context
Points	Array of `TPoint` structures
Count	Size of `Points`

Return Value:
Nonzero if all points converted; else 0.

ScreenToClient

Converts and replaces the screen-coordinate values in `Point` with the client coordinates of the specified window.

```
procedure ScreenToClient(Wnd: HWnd; var Point);
```

Parameter	*Description*
Wnd	Window identifier
Point	`TPoint` structure

WindowFromPoint

Decides which window contains the specified point.

```
function WindowFromPoint(Point: TPoint): HWnd;
```

Parameter	*Description*
Point	`TPoint` to be checked (in screen coordinates)

Return Value:
Window identifier; 0 if no window is at the specified point.

Device-Context Procedures and Functions

A device context represents the device driver, output device, and (sometimes) the communications port. Your application's graphic functions relate to a specific device.

```
CreateCompatibleDC
CreateDC
CreateIC
DeleteDC
GetDCOrg
RestoreDC
SaveDC
```

CreateCompatibleDC

Creates a memory device context compatible with `DC`.

```
function CreateCompatibleDC(DC: HDC): HDC;
```

Parameter	Description
DC	Device context; if 0, a memory device context is created

Return Value:
New memory device context if successful; else 0.

CreateDC

Creates a device context for `DriverName` device.

```
function CreateDC(DriverName, DeviceName, Output: PChar;
  InitData: Pointer): HDC;
```

Parameter	Description
DriverName	DOS file name (without extension and null-terminated) of the device driver
DeviceName	Name of specific device to be supported (null-terminated)
Output	Output DOS file or device name (null-terminated)
InitData	DEVMODE structure containing device-specific initialization data

Return Value:
Device context identifier if successful; else 0.

CreateIC

Creates an information context for the device.

```
function CreateIC(DriverName, DeviceName, Output, InitData: PChar): HDC;
```

Parameter	Description
DriverName	Device-driver DOS file name (no extension and null-terminated)
DeviceName	Specific device name (null-terminated)
Output	Output DOS file or device name (null-terminated)
InitData	Device-specific initialization data; nil for default initialization

Return Value:
Information context identifier if successful; else 0.

DeleteDC

Deletes the device context. Notifies the device and releases all storage and systems resources if `DC` is the last device context for the device.

```
function DeleteDC(DC: HDC): Bool;
```

Parameter	*Description*
DC	Device context

Return Value:
Nonzero if successful; else 0.

GetDCOrg

Gets a device's final translation origin (in screen coordinates), which is the offset used by Windows to translate device coordinates to client coordinates.

```
function GetDCOrg(DC: HDC): Longint;
```

Parameter	*Description*
DC	Device context

Return Value:
X-coordinate in the low word; Y-coordinate in the high word.

RestoreDC

Restores a device context to the state specified by `SaveDC` (a previous state) from the context stack. State information is deleted if `SaveDC` isn't at the top of the stack.

```
function RestoreDC(DC: HDC; SaveDC: Integer): Bool;
```

Parameter	*Description*
DC	Device context
SaveDC	Returns value of a previous `SaveDC` call or –1 for most recently saved device context

Return Value:
Nonzero if restored; else 0.

SaveDC

Saves the current state of DC on the context stack.

```
function SaveDC(DC: HDC): Integer;
```

Parameter	*Description*
DC	Device context identifier

Return Value:
Saved device context if successful; else 0.

Device-Independent Bitmap Procedures and Functions

Because bitmaps represent the memory configuration of a specific device, they're dependent on the device that's addressed. Thus, bitmaps saved from one device might be incompatible with another device. GDI supplies device-independent (DI) bitmaps to help you through this problem. Use the following routines for DI bitmaps:

```
CreateDIBitmap
GetDIBits
SetDIBits
SetDIBitsToDevice
StretchDIBits
```

CreateDIBitmap

Creates a device-specific memory bitmap from a device-independent bitmap described by `InfoHeader` and `InitInfo`.

```
function CreateDIBitmap(DC: HDC; var InfoHeader: TBitmapInfoHeader;
  Usage: Longint; InitBits: PChar; var InitInfo: TBitmapInfo;
  Usage: Word): HBitmap;
```

Parameter	*Description*
DC	Device context
InfoHeader	`TBitmapInfoHeader` that describes bitmap size and format
Usage	If `cbm_Init` the bitmap is initialized according to `InitBits` and `InitInfo`

Parameter	*Description*
InitBits	Byte array containing initial bitmap values, format dependent on `biBitCount` field of `InitInfo`
InitInfo	`TBitmapInfo` structure that describes dimensions and color format
Usage	One of the `DIB_ Color` table identifiers' constants

Return Value:
Bitmap identifier if successful; else 0.

GetDIBits

Copies a bitmap, in device independent format, to `Bits`.

```
function GetDIBits(DC: HDC; Bitmap: THandle; StartScan, NumScans: Word;
  Bits: Pointer; var BitInfo: TBitmapInfo; Usage: Word): Integer;
```

Parameter	*Description*
DC	Device context
Bitmap	Source bitmap
StartScan	First scan line
NumScans	Number of lines to copy
Bits	Buffer to receive bitmap or nil to fill `BitsInfo`
BitInfo	`TBitmapInfo` containing color format and dimension of bitmap
Usage	Indicates the source of colors; one of the `Dib_ Color` table identifiers' constants

Return Value:
Number of scan lines copied; 0 if error.

SetDIBits

Sets a bitmap's bits to the values of a device-independent bitmap (`DIB`) specification.

```
function SetDIBits(DC: HDC; Bitmap: THandle; StartScan, NumScans: Word;
  Bits: Pointer; var BitsInfo: TBitmapInfo; Usage: Word): Integer;
```

Parameter	Description
DC	Device context
Bitmap	Bitmap identifier
StartScan	Scan line number corresponding to first scan line in `Bits`
NumScans	Number of scan lines in `Bits`
Bits	Array of bytes containing the `DIB` bits whose format is specified by the `biBitCount` field of `BitsInfo`
BitsInfo	`TBitmapInfo` containing `DIB` information
Usage	Describes contents of `bmiColors` fields of `BitsInfo`; either one of the `DIB_ Color` table identifiers

Return Value:
Number of scan lines copied if successful; else 0.

SetDIBitsToDevice

Sets the bits on a device surface directly from a device-independent bitmap (`DIB`).

```
function SetDIBitsToDevice(DC: HDC; DestX, DestY, Width, Height, SrcX,
  SrcY, StartScan, NumScans: Word; Bits: Pointer;
  var BitsInfo:TBitmapInfo; Usage: Word): Integer;
```

Parameter	Description
DC	Device context
DestX, DestY	Device destination rectangle origin
Width	`DIB` rectangle x-extent
Height	`DIB` rectangle y-extent
SrcX, SrcY	`DIB` source position
StartScan	`DIB` scan line number corresponding to first scan line in `Bits`
NumScans	`DIB` scan lines in `Bits`
Bits	Array of bytes containing the `DIB` bits whose format is specified by the `biBitCount` field of `BitsInfo`
BitsInfo	`TBitmapInfo` containing `DIB` information
Usage	Describes contents of `bmiColors` fields of `BitsInfo`; either one of `DIB_ Color` table identifiers

Return Value:
Number of scan lines set.

StretchDIBits

Moves a device-independent bitmap (stretching or compressing the bitmap if required) from a source rectangle to a destination rectangle. The source and destination are combined as specified by `Rop`.

```
function StretchDIBits(DC: HDC; DestX, DestY, DestWidth, DestHeight,
  SrcX, SrcY, SrcWidth, SrcHeight: Word; Bits: Pointer; var BitsInfo:
  TBitmapInfo; Usage: Word; Rop: DWord): Integer;
```

Parameter	*Description*
DC	Receiving device context
DestX, DestY	Destination rectangle origin (in logical units)
DestWidth	Destination rectangle x-extent (in logical units)
DestHeight	Destination rectangle y-extent (in logical units)
SrcX, SrcY	Source rectangle origin (in pixels) in the `DIB`
SrcWidth	Source rectangle width (in pixels)
SrcHeight	Source rectangle height (in pixels)
Bits	Byte array containing `DIB` bits
Usage	`DIB_RGB_Colors` specifies whether the `BitsInfo.bmiColors` field contains RGB values or `DIB_Pal_Colors` specifies indexes to currently realized logical palette

Return Value:
Number of scan lines copied.

Drawing-Attribute Procedures and Functions

Windows applications write to a logical entity called a display context (a virtual surface with associated attributes). The display context manages the display of graphics on the screen.

You don't control the display context attributes. You can, however, adjust certain drawing attributes, including background color and mode, foreground color for text, drawing (color-combining) mode, bitmap-stretching mode, and polygon-filling mode.

You can also modify the drawing tools you use to change the attributes of displayed graphics. The attributes of these tools dictate the appearance of graphics drawn with GDI functions.

```
GetBkColor
GetBkMode
GetPolyFillMode
GetROP2
```

```
GetStretchBltMode
GetTextColor
SetBkColor
SetBkMode
SetPolyFillMode
SetROP2
SetStretchBltMode
SetTextColor
```

GetBkColor

Gets the current device background color.

```
function GetBkColor(DC: HDC): Longint;
```

Parameter	*Description*
DC	Device context

Return Value:
RGB color value.

GetBkMode

Gets the current device background mode, used for text, hatched brushes, and nonsolid line-pen styles.

```
function GetBkMode(DC: HDC): Integer;
```

Parameter	*Description*
DC	Device context

Return Value:
One of the `Background` modes' constants.

GetPolyFillMode

Gets the current polygon filling mode.

```
function GetPolyFillMode(DC: HDC): Integer;
```

Parameter	*Description*
DC	Device context

Return Value:
Polygon filling mode; one of the `PolyFill` modes' constants.

GetROP2

Gets the current drawing mode.

```
function GetROP2(DC: HDC): Integer;
```

Parameter	*Description*
DC	Raster device context

Return Value:
Drawing mode; one of the `r2_ Binary` raster operations' constants.

GetStretchBltMode

Gets the current stretching mode.

```
function GetStretchBltMode(DC: HDC): Integer;
```

Parameter	*Description*
DC	Device context

Return Value:
One of the `StretchBlt` modes' constants.

GetTextColor

Gets the current foreground color used to draw characters.

```
function GetTextColor(DC: HDC): Longint;
```

Parameter	*Description*
DC	Device context

Return Value:
RGB color value.

SetBkColor

Sets the current background to `Color` or the nearest physical color supported by the device.

```
function SetBkColor(DC: HDC; Color: TColorRef): Longint;
```

Parameter	Description
DC	Device context
Color	New background `TColorRef`

Return Value:
Previous RGB background color if successful; else $80,000,000.

SetBkMode

Sets the background mode that specifies whether the GDI should remove existing background colors before drawing text, hatched brushes, or using nonsolid pen styles.

```
function SetBkMode(DC: HDC; BkMode: Integer): Integer;
```

Parameter	Description
DC	Device context
BkMode	One of the `Background` modes' constants

Return Value:
Previous mode if successful; else 0.

SetPolyFillMode

Sets the polygon filling mode used by GDI functions that use the polygon algorithm for computing interior points.

```
function SetPolyFillMode(DC: HDC; PolyFillMode: Integer): Integer;
```

Parameter	Description
DC	Device context
PolyFillMode	One of the `PolyFill` modes' constants

Return Value:
Previous filling mode if successful; else 0.

SetROP2

Sets the current drawing mode to the value specified by `DrawMode`. This mode specifies how object interiors and pens are combined with colors already on the display surface.

```
function SetROP2(DC: HDC; DrawMode: Integer): Integer;
```

Parameter	*Description*
DC	Device context
DrawMode	Any one of the `r2_ Binary` raster operations' constants

Return Value:
Previous drawing mode.

SetStretchBltMode

Sets the stretching mode used by `StretchMode` to contract a bitmap.

```
function SetStretchBltMode(DC: HDC; StretchMode: Integer): Integer;
```

Parameter	*Description*
DC	Device context
StretchMode	One of the `StretchBlt` modes' constants

Return Value:
Previous stretching mode.

SetTextColor

Sets the text color or nearest device-supported color used by `TextOut` and `ExtTextOut` to draw a character's face. `SetTextColor` is used also by the GDI to convert bitmaps from monochrome to color and vice versa.

```
function SetTextColor(DC: HDC; Color: TColorRef): Longint;
```

Parameter	*Description*
DC	Device context
Color	Text `TColorRef`

Return Value:
Previous text RGB color value.

Drawing Tool Procedures and Functions

The display context manages the screen display of graphics. To display graphics in other ways, you can change the drawing tools used to render the graphics:

- Pens dictate the appearance of drawn lines.
- Brushes dictate the appearance of filled shapes.

- Fonts dictate the appearance of drawn text.

To assign the attributes of a drawing tool, a Windows application selects a logical or stock tool in a display context.

- Your application creates a logical tool by filling the fields of a particular record (`TLogPen`, `TLogBrush`, or `TLogFont`).
- A stock tool is an existing, Windows-defined tool representing the most common attribute choices.

Logical Tools
`DeleteObject`
`GetBrushOrg`
`GetObject`
`SelectObject`
`SetBrushOrg`
`UnrealizeObject`
`CreateBrushIndirect`
`CreateDIBPatternBrush`
`CreateHatchBrush`
`CreatePatternBrush`
`CreateSolidBrush`
`EnumObjects`
`CreatePen`
`CreatePenIndirect`
`CreateFont`
`CreateFontIndirect`

Stock Tools
`GetStockObject`

DeleteObject

Deletes `Handle` from memory and frees all associated system resources.

```
function DeleteObject(Handle: THandle): Bool;
```

Parameter	*Description*
Handle	Handle to a logical pen, brush, font, bitmap, region, or palette

Return Value:
Nonzero if deleted; 0 if `Handle` isn't valid or currently selected in a device context.

GetBrushOrg

Gets the current device brush origin.

```
function GetBrushOrg(DC: HDC): Longint;
```

Parameter	Description
DC	Device context

Return Value:
X-coordinates in low word; Y-coordinates in high word.

GetObject

Fills a buffer with data that defines a logical object and returns the number of entries for logical palettes.

```
function GetObject(hObject: THandle; Count: Integer;
  ObjectPtr: Pointer): Integer;
```

Parameter	Description
hObject	Object
Count	Number of bytes to copy to `ObjectPtr`
ObjectPtr	Receiving buffer; `TLogPen`, `TLogBrush`, `TLogFont`, `TBitmap`, or an integer

Return Value:
Number of bytes copied; 0 if error.

SelectObject

Selects a logical object for `DC`. Only one object can be selected at one time, and it should be deleted when it's no longer being used.

```
function SelectObject(DC: HDC; hObject: THandle): THandle;
```

Parameter	Description
DC	Device context
hObject	One of the following: bitmap, brush, font, pen, or region

Return Value:
Object being replaced or nonzero if metafile `DC`; 0 if error.

SetBrushOrg

Sets the origin of the selected brush. The brush shouldn't be a stock object.

```
function SetBrushOrg(DC: HDC; X, Y: Integer): Longint;
```

Parameter	*Description*
DC	Device context
X,Y	New origin (in device units), ranging from 0 to 7

Return Value:
Previous origin where X-coordinate is in low-order word; Y-coordinate is in high-order word.

UnrealizeObject

Resets the origin the next time selected if `hObject` is a brush or to realize the palette if `hObject` is a logical palette.

```
function UnrealizeObject(hObject: HBrush): Bool;
```

Parameter	*Description*
hObject	Object to be reset

Return Value:
Nonzero if successful; else 0.

CreateBrushIndirect

Creates a logical brush defined by `LogBrush`.

```
function CreateBrushIndirect(var LogBrush: TLogBrush): HBrush;
```

Parameter	*Description*
LogBrush	`TLogBrush` structure

Return Value:
Logical brush identifier if successful; else 0.

CreateDIBPatternBrush

Creates a logical brush from the device-independent bitmap defined by `PackedDIB`.

```
function CreateDIBPatternBrush(PackedDIB: THandle;
  Usage: Word): HBitmap;
```

Parameter	*Description*
PackedDIB	Global memory containing `TBitmapInfo` structure plus array of pixels
Usage	One of the `DIB_ Color` table identifiers' constants

Return Value:
Logical brush identifier if successful; else 0.

CreateHatchBrush

Creates a logical brush with a specified hatch style.

```
function CreateHatchBrush(Index: Integer; Color: TColorRef): HBrush;
```

Parameter	*Description*
Index	One of the `hs_ Hatch` styles' constants
Color	`TColorRef` that specifies the color of the hatches

Return Value:
Logical brush identifier if successful; else 0.

CreatePatternBrush

Creates a logical brush with a `Bitmap` pattern.

```
function CreatePatternBrush(Bitmap: HBitmap): HBrush;
```

Parameter	*Description*
Bitmap	`HBitmap` bitmap

Return Value:
Logical brush identifier if successful; else 0.

CreateSolidBrush

Creates a logical brush.

```
function CreateSolidBrush(Color: TColorRef): HBrush;
```

Parameter	*Description*
Color	Brush `TColorRef`

Return Value:
Logical brush identifier if successful; else 0.

EnumObjects

Enumerates the object types currently available on a device by passing TLogPen or TLogBrushand data to the callback. Enumeration ends if the callback returns 0 or all objects are enumerated.

```
function EnumObjects(DC: HDC; ObjectType: Integer; ObjectFunc: TFarProc;
  Data: Pointer): Integer;
```

Parameter	*Description*
DC	Device context
ObjectType	Can be one of the obj_ GDI object type constants: obj_Brush or obj_Pen
ObjectFunc	Callback function's procedure-instance address
Data	Data passed to callback

Return Value:
Last value returned by callback.

CreatePen

Creates a logical pen.

```
function CreatePen(PenStyle, Width: Integer; Color: TColorRef): HPen;
```

Parameter	*Description*
PenStyle	One of the ps_ Pen styles' constants
Width	Pen width (in logical units)
Color	Pen TColorRef

Return Value:
Logical pen identifier if successful; else 0.

CreatePenIndirect

Creates a logical pen defined by LogPen.

```
function CreatePenIndirect(var LogPen: TLogPen): HPen;
```

Parameter	*Description*
LogPen	TLogPen structure

Return Value:
Logical pen identifier if successful; else 0.

CreateFont

Creates a logical font selected from GDI's pool of physical fonts according to specified characteristics.

```
function CreateFont(Height, Width, Escapement, Orientation,
  Weight:Integer; Italic, Underline, StrikeOut, CharSet,
  OutputPrecision,ClipPrecision, Quality, PitchAndFamily: Byte;
  FaceName: PChar): HFont;
```

Parameter	***Description***
Height	Font height (in logical units)
Width	Average font width (in logical units)
Escapement	Line angle (in tenths of degrees)
Orientation	Character baseline angle (in tenths of degrees)
Weight	Font weight (0 to 1000); or use a `fw_` Font weight flag such as `fw_Normal` or `fw_Bold`
Italic	Font is italic
Underline	Font is underlined
StrikeOut	Font is struck out
CharSet	One of the Font character set flags' constants
OutputPrecision	One of the `out_` Font output precision flags' constants
ClipPrecision	One of the `clip_` Font clipping precision flags' constants
Quality	One of the Font output quality flags' constants
PitchAndFamily	One of the Font pitch flags' constants combined with one of the `ff_` Font family flags
Facename	Font typeface name (null-terminated)

Return Value:
Logical font identifier if successful; else 0.

CreateFontIndirect

Creates a logical font selected from the GDI's pool of physical fonts according to the characteristics in `ALogFont`.

```
function CreateFontIndirect(var LogFont: TLogFont): HFont;
```

Parameter	***Description***
ALogFont	`TLogFont` structure

Return Value:
Logical font identifier if successful; else 0.

GetStockObject

Gets a handle to a predefined stock pen, brush, or font.

```
function GetStockObject(Index: Integer): THandle;
```

Parameter	Description
Index	One of the `Stock` logical objects' constants

Return Value:
Selected logical object identifier if successful; else 0.

Environment Procedures and Functions

```
GetEnvironment
SetEnvironment
Escape
```

GetEnvironment

Gets the current environment for the device attached to the system port.

```
function GetEnvironment(PortName, Environ: PChar;
  MaxCount: Word): Integer;
```

Parameter	Description
PortName	Port name (null-terminated)
Environ	Buffer to receive environment (first field must contain device name) or nil to return required size
MaxCount	Size of buffer

Return Value:
Number of bytes copied; 0 if environment cannot be found.

SetEnvironment

Creates or replaces a device's environment.

```
function SetEnvironment(PortName, Environ: PChar; Count: Word): Intege
```

Parameter	*Description*
PortName	System port name (null-terminated)
Environ	Buffer containing new environment
Count	Number of bytes in `Environ` to copy or 0 to delete current environment

Return Value:
Number of bytes copied; 0 if error; –1 if environment is deleted.

Escape

Allows access to device-specific facilities not supported by the GDI.

```
function Escape(DC: HDC; Escape, Count: Integer; InData,
  OutData: Pointer): Integer;
```

Parameter	*Description*
DC	Device context
Count	Bytes of data in `InData`
InData	The input data structure
OutData	Structure to receive `Escape` output data or nil for no output data

Return Value:
A positive number if successful; 0 if escape isn't implemented; negative if error; if error, may be one of the `sp_ Spooler` error codes.

Font Procedures and Functions

A font is a subset of a particular typeface. Font procedures and functions create, remove, select, and get information about fonts.

```
AddFontResource
CreateFont
CreateFontIndirect
EnumFonts
GetCharWidth
RemoveFontResource
SetMapperFlags
```

AddFontResource

Adds font resource from `FileName` font-resource file to the system font table.

```
function AddFontResource(FileName: PChar): Integer;
```

Parameter	*Description*
FileName	Handle to loaded module or null-terminated string

Return Value:
Number of fonts added; 0 if no fonts were added.

CreateFont

Creates a logical font selected from GDI's pool of physical fonts according to the specified characteristics.

```
function CreateFont(Height, Width, Escapement, Orientation, Weight: Integer;
  Italic, Underline, StrikeOut, CharSet, OutputPrecision, ClipPrecision,
  Quality, PitchAndFamily: Byte; FaceName: PChar): HFont;
```

Parameter	*Description*
Height	Font height (in logical units)
Width	Average font width (in logical units)
Escapement	Line angle (in tenths of degrees)
Orientation	Character baseline angle (in tenths of degrees)
Weight	Font weight (0 to 1000); or use a `fw_` font weight flag such as `fw_Normal` or `fw_Bold`
Italic	Font is italic
Underline	Font is underlined
StrikeOut	Font is struck out
CharSet	One of the font character set flags' constants
OutputPrecision	One of the `out_` font output precision flags' constants
ClipPrecision	One of the `clip_` font clipping precision flags' constants
Quality	One of the font output quality flags' constants
PitchAndFamily	One of the font pitch flags' constants combined with one of the `ff_` font family flags
Facename	font typeface name (null-terminated)

Return Value:
Logical font identifier if successful; else 0.

CreateFontIndirect

Creates a logical font selected from GDI's pool of physical fonts according to the characteristics in `ALogFont`.

```
function CreateFontIndirect(var LogFont: TLogFont): HFont;
```

Parameter	*Description*
ALogFont	`TLogFont` structure

Return Value:
Logical font identifier if successful; else 0.

EnumFonts

Enumerates available fonts having the specified typeface on a device. The `callback` is passed `TLogFont`, `TTextMetric`, `FontType`, and `Data`. Enumeration ends if the `callback` returns 0 or when all fonts are enumerated.

```
function EnumFonts(DC: HDC; FaceName: PChar; FontFunc:
TFarProc; Data: Pointer): Integer;
```

Parameter	*Description*
DC	Device context
FaceName	Typeface name (null-terminated) or nil to randomly select one font for each available typeface
FontFunc	`Callback` function's procedure-instance address
Data	Data passed to the `callback` function

Return Value:
Last value returned by the `callback`.

GetCharWidth

Gets individual character widths for a group of consecutive characters.

```
function GetCharWidth(DC: HDC; FirstChar, LastChar: Word;
  var Buffer): Bool;
```

Parameter	*Description*
DC	Device context
FirstChar	First character in consecutive character group
LastChar	Last character in consecutive character group
Buffer	Receiving integer array for width values

Return Value:
Nonzero if successful; else 0.

RemoveFontResource

Removes a font from Windows' font table. The font isn't removed until all outstanding references to the resource are deleted.

```
function RemoveFontResourc(FileName: PChar): Bool;
```

Parameter	*Description*
FileName	Font-resource file name (null-terminated) or module-instance handle

Return Value:
Nonzero if successful; else 0.

SetMapperFlags

Changes the font-mapper algorithm as specified by `Flag`.

```
function SetMapperFlags(DC: HDC; Flag: Longint): Longint;
```

Parameter	*Description*
DC	Device context
Flag	If first bit set to 1, only fonts whose X- and Y-aspects exactly match the device are selected

Return Value:
Previous font-mapper flag.

Line-Drawing Procedures and Functions

Line-drawing procedures and functions use the specified display context's current pen for drawing.

```
Arc
LineDDA
LineTo
MoveTo
Polyline
```

Arc

Draws an elliptical arc centered in the bounding rectangle.

```
function Arc(DC: HDC; X1, Y1, X2, Y2, X3, Y3, X4, Y4: Integer): Bool;
```

Parameter	Description
DC	Device context
X1, Y1	Upper-left corner of bounding rectangle
X2, Y2	Lower-right corner of bounding rectangle
X3, Y3	Arc's starting point
X4, Y4	Arc's end point

Return Value:
Nonzero if the arc is drawn; else 0. The bounding rectangle cannot be taller or wider than 32,767 units (that is, an integer value).

LineDDA

Computes all successive points in a line and calls `LineFunc` passing `X` and `Y` of the point and `Data`.

```
procedure LineDDA(X1, Y1, X2, Y2: Integer; LineFunc: TFarProc;
  Data: Pointer);
```

Parameter	Description
X1, Y1	First point in line
X2, Y2	Last point in line
LineFunc	`Callback` function procedure-instance address
Data	Data passed to `LineFunc`

LineTo

Draws a line, using selected pen, from the current position up to the specified endpoint.

```
function LineTo(DC: HDC; X, Y: Integer): Bool;
```

Parameter	Description
DC	Device context
X, Y	Endpoint of the line

Return Value:
Nonzero if drawn; else 0.

MoveTo

Moves the current position to the specified point.

```
function MoveTo(DC: HDC; X, Y: Integer): Longint;
```

Parameter	Description
DC	Device context
X, Y	New position

Return Value:
X-coordinates of previous position in low-order word; Y-coordinates of previous position in high-order word.

Polyline

Draws a set of line segments using a selected pen, where each subsequent point is specified by `Points`.

```
function Polyline(DC: HDC; var Points; Count: Integer): Bool;
```

Parameter	Description
DC	Device context
Points	Array of `TPoint` structures
Count	Size of `Points`

Return Value:
Nonzero if successful; else 0.

Mapping Procedures and Functions

Mapping modes describe the relative size, position, and orientation of logical coordinates versus device coordinates:

```
GetMapMode
GetViewportExt
GetViewportOrg
GetWindowExt
GetWindowOrg
OffsetViewportOrg
OffsetWindowOrg
ScaleViewportExt
ScaleWindowExt
SetMapMode
SetViewportExt
SetViewportOrg
SetWindowExt
SetWindowOrg
```

GetMapMode

Gets the current mapping mode.

```
function GetMapMode(DC: HDC): Integer;
```

Parameter	*Description*
DC	Device context

Return Value:
An mm_ Mapping modes' constant.

GetViewportExt

Gets the viewport extents of a device context.

```
function GetViewportExt(DC: HDC): Longint;
```

Parameter	*Description*
DC	Device context

Return Value:
X-extents (in device units) in low-order word; Y-extents (in device units) in high-order word.

GetViewportOrg

Gets the viewport origin of a device context.

```
function GetViewportOrg(DC: HDC): Longint;
```

Parameter	*Description*
DC	Device context

Return Value:
X-coordinate (in device units) in low-order word; Y-coordinate (in device units) in high-order word.

GetWindowExt

Gets a window's extents.

```
function GetWindowExt(DC: HDC): Longint;
```

Parameter	Description
DC	Device context

Return Value:
X-extents (in device units) in low-order word; Y-extents (in device units) in high-order word.

GetWindowOrg

Gets a window's origin.

```
function GetWindowOrg(DC: HDC): Longint;
```

Parameter	Description
DC	Device context

Return Value:
X-coordinates (in logical coordinates) in low word; Y-coordinates (in logical coordinates) in high word.

OffsetViewportOrg

Changes a viewport origin by summing the current origin with the specified `X` and `Y` values.

```
function OffsetViewportOrg(DC: HDC; X, Y: Integer): Longint;
```

Parameter	Description
DC	Device context
X	X-coordinate origin offset
Y	Y-coordinate origin offset

Return Value:
Y-coordinates of previous origin in high-order word; X-coordinates of previous origin in low-order word.

OffsetWindowOrg

Changes a window's origin by summing the current origin with the specified `X` and `Y` values.

```
function OffsetWindowOrg(DC: HDC; X, Y: Integer): Longint;
```

Parameter	Description
DC	Device context
X	X-coordinate (in logical units) origin offset
Y	Y-coordinate (in logical units) origin offset

Return Value:
Y-coordinates of previous origin in high-order word; X-coordinates of previous origin in low-order word.

ScaleViewportExt

Changes the current viewport extents.

```
function ScaleViewportExt(DC: HDC; Xnum, Xdenom, Ynum, Ydenom:
  Integer): Longint;
```

Parameter	Description
DC	Device context
Xnum	Value to multiply current X-extent
Xdenom	Value to divide current X-extent
Ynum	Value to multiply current Y-extent
Ydenom	Value to divide current Y-extent

Return Value:
Previous Y-extent in high-order word; previous X-extent in low-order word.

ScaleWindowExt

Changes the current window extents.

```
function ScaleWindowExt(DC: HDC; Xnum, Xdenom, Ynum, Ydenom:
  Integer): Longint;
```

Parameter	Description
Xnum	Value to multiply current X-extent
Xdenom	Value to divide current X-extent
Ynum	Value to multiply current Y-extent
Ydenom	Value to divide current Y-extent

Return Value:
Previous Y-extent in high-order word; previous X-extent in low-order word.

SetMapMode

Sets the device-context mapping mode that defines logical-to-device units' transformations for GDI and X- and Y-axis orientation.

```
function SetMapMode(DC: HDC; MapMode: Integer): Integer;
```

Parameter	*Description*
DC	Device context
MapMode	One of the `mm_ Mapping` modes' constants

Return Value:
Previous mapping mode.

SetViewportExt

Sets a viewport's X- and Y-extents, which defines how the GDI stretches or compresses logical units to fit device units.

```
function SetViewportExt(DC: HDC; X, Y: Integer): Longint;
```

Parameter	*Description*
DC	Device context
X, Y	New viewport extents (in device units)

Return Value:
Previous X-extent in low-order words; previous Yextents in high-order words.

SetViewportOrg

Sets a viewport's origin to define how the GDI maps logical coordinates to points in device coordinates.

```
function SetViewportOrg(DC: HDC; X, Y: Integer): Longint;
```

Parameter	*Description*
DC	Device context
X, Y	New viewport origin (in device units)

Return Value:
X-coordinates of previous origin in low-order word; Y-coordinates of previous origin in high-order word.

SetWindowExt

Sets a window's X- and Y-extents. This, along with the viewport extents, defines how GDI stretches or compresses logical units to fit device units.

```
function SetWindowExt(DC: HDC; X, Y: Integer): Longint;
```

Parameter	*Description*
DC	Device context
X, Y	Window extents

Return Value:
Previous Xextents in low-order words; previous Yextents in high-order words; 0 if error.

SetWindowOrg

Sets a window's origin within the viewport of the specified device context.

```
function SetWindowOrg(DC: HDC; X, Y: Integer): Longint;
```

Parameter	*Description*
DC	Device context
X, Y	New window origin

Return Value:
Previous X-coordinate in low-order word; previous Y-coordinate in high-order word.

Metafile Procedures and Functions

A metafile is a set of GDI commands for creating text or graphics images. Metafile functions create, close, copy, delete, play, retrieve, and get information about metafiles.

```
CloseMetaFile
CopyMetaFile
CreateMetaFile
DeleteMetaFile
EnumMetaFile
GetMetaFile
GetMetaFileBits
PlayMetaFile
PlayMetaFileRecord
SetMetaFileBits
```

CloseMetaFile

Closes DC and creates a metafile handle that can be used to play the metafile.

```
function CloseMetaFile(DC: THandle): THandle;
```

Parameter	*Description*
DC	Metafile device context

Return Value:
Metafile identifier if successful; else 0.

CopyMetaFile

Copies `SrcMetaFile` to the file FileName.

```
function CopyMetaFile(SrcMetaFile: THandle; FileName: PChar): THandle;
```

Parameter	*Description*
SrcMetaFile	Source metafile
FileName	Metafile name (null-terminated) or 0 to copy to a memory metafile

Return Value:
New metafile identifier.

CreateMetaFile

Creates a metafile device context.

```
function CreateMetaFile(FileName: PChar): THandle;
```

Parameter	*Description*
FileName	Metafile name (null-terminated) or nil to specify a memory metafile

Return Value:
Metafile device context identifier if successful; else 0.

DeleteMetaFile

Invalidates a metafile handle and frees its associated system resources. The metafile isn't deleted.

```
function DeleteMetaFile(MF: THandle): Bool;
```

Parameter	Description
MF	Metafile identifier

Return Value:
Nonzero if successful; 0 if MF isn't a valid handle.

EnumMetaFile

Enumerates GDI calls in a metafile passing the following information:

- DC
- A pointer to the metafile's object handles table
- A pointer to a record in the metafile
- The number of objects with associated handles in the table
- `ClientData` to the `callback`

```
function EnumMetaFile(DC: HDC; MF: THandle; CallbackFunc:
  TFarProc; ClientData: LPByte): Bool;
```

Enumeration ends if the `callback` returns 0 or if all GDI calls are enumerated.

Parameter	Description
DC	Device context associated with metafile
MF	Metafile identifier
CallbackFunc	`Callback` function's procedure-instance address
ClientData	Data passed to `callback`

Return Value:
Nonzero if all GDI calls in metafile are enumerated; else 0.

GetMetaFile

Creates a handle for the named metafile.

```
function GetMetaFile(FileName: PChar): THandle;
```

Parameter	Description
FileName	Metafile DOS file name (null-terminated)

Return Value:
Metafile identifier if successful; else 0.

GetMetaFileBits

Gets a read-only global memory block containing the metafile as a collection of bits. Used to determine size and save as metafile.

```
function GetMetaFileBits(MF: THandle): THandle;
```

Parameter	Description
MF	Memory metafile identifier, becomes invalid after call

Return Value:
Global memory block if successful; else 0.

PlayMetaFile

Plays the contents of a metafile on the specified device.

```
function PlayMetaFile(DC: HDC; MF: THandle): Bool;
```

Parameter	Description
DC	Device context
MF	Metafile identifier

Return Value:
Nonzero if successful; else 0.

PlayMetaFileRecord

Executes the GDI function call contained in a metafile record.

```
procedure PlayMetaFileRecord(DC: HDC; var HandleTable: THandleTable;
  var MetaRecord: TMetaRecord; Handles: Word);
```

Parameter	Description
DC	Device context
HandleTable	`THandleTable` used for metafile playback
MetaRecord	`TMetaRecord` of metafile to play
Handles	Size of `HandleTable`

SetMetaFileBits

Creates a memory metafile from the data specified by `Mem`.

```
function SetMetaFileBits(Mem: THandle): THandle;
```

Parameter	*Description*
Mem	Global memory block containing metafile data previously created by `GetMetaFileBits`

Return Value:
Memory metafile identifier if successful; else 0.

Printer-Control Procedures and Functions

Device capabilities

Device capabilities' constants are associated with specific capabilities of a device context. They are used in the `GetDeviceCaps` function:

Constant	*Meaning*
AspectX	Relative pixel width
AspectXY	Diagonal pixel length
AspectY	Relative pixel height
BitsPixel	Number of bits per pixel
ClipCaps	Clipping capabilities; returns a `cp_` clipping capabilities' constant
ColorRes	Color resolution in bits per pixel
CurveCaps	Curve capabilities; returns a `cc_` curve capabilities' constant
DriverVersion	Device driver version; for example, $100 is 1.0
HorzRes	Horizontal width in pixels
HorzSize	Horizontal size in millimeters
LineCaps	Line capabilities; returns a `lc_` line capabilities' constant
LogPixelsX	Number of pixels per horizontal inch
LogPixelsY	Number of pixels per vertical inch
NumBrushes	Number of brushes the device has
NumColors	Number of colors the device supports
NumFonts	Number of fonts the device has
NumMarkers	Number of markers the device has
NumPens	Number of pens the device has
NumReserved	Number of reserved entries in palette
PDeviceSize	Size required for device descriptor
Planes	Number of color planes
PolygonalCaps	Polygonal capabilities; returns a `pc_` polygonal capabilities' constant

Constant	*Meaning*
RasterCaps	Raster capabilities; returns a `rc_` raster capabilities' constant
SizePalette	Number of entries in physical palette
Technology	Device classification; returns a `dt_` device technology constant
TextCaps	Text capabilities; returns a `tc_` text capabilities' constant
VertRes	Vertical width in pixels
VertSize	Vertical size in millimeters

Rectangle Procedures and Functions

A rectangle is defined by the Windows data structure, `TRect`. Rectangle functions modify and get information about rectangles:

```
CopyRect
EqualRect
InflateRect
IntersectRect
OffsetRect
PtInRect
SetRectEmpty
UnionRect
```

CopyRect

Copies `SourceRect` to `DestRect`.

```
procedure CopyRect(var DestRect, SourceRect: TRect);
```

Parameter	*Description*
DestRect	`TRect` structure
SourceRect	`TRect` structure

EqualRect

Compares the upper-left and lower-right corners of two rectangles.

```
function EqualRect(var Rect1, Rect2: TRect): Bool;
```

Parameter	Description
Rect1, Rect2	Rectangles to be compared

Return Value:
Nonzero if equal; else 0.

InflateRect

Changes the width and height of Rect. Adds X to left and right ends and Y to top and bottom of rectangle.

```
procedure InflateRect(var Rect: TRect; X, Y: Integer);
```

Parameter	Description
Rect	TRect structure
X	Positive or negative value to change rectangle width
Y	Positive or negative value to change rectangle height

IntersectRect

Finds the intersection of two rectangles.

```
function IntersectRect(var DestRect, Src1Rect, Src2Rect:
  TRect): Integer;
```

Parameter	Description
DestRect	TRect structure representing the resulting rectangle
Src1Rect	TRect structure representing a source rectangle
Src2Rect	TRect structure representing a source rectangle

Return Value:
If intersection isn't empty, nonzero; 0 if intersection is empty.

OffsetRect

Adjusts a rectangle's coordinates by the specified X and Y offsets

```
procedure OffsetRect(var Rect: TRect; X, Y: Integer);
```

Parameter	Description
Rect	TRect structure
X	Units to move left or right
Y	Units to move up or down

PtInRect

Decides whether a point lies within, or on the left or top side, of a rectangle.

```
function PtInRect(var Rect: TRect; Point: TPoint): Bool;
```

Parameter	*Description*
Rect	`TRect` structure
Point	`TPoint` structure

Return Value:
Nonzero if `Point` lies within `Rect`; else 0.

SetRectEmpty

Sets all `Rect` coordinates to 0.

```
procedure SetRectEmpty(var Rect: TRect);
```

Parameter	*Description*
Rect	Receiving `TRect` structure

UnionRect

Creates a union of two rectangles and stores the result in `DestRect`.

```
function UnionRect(var DestRect, Src1Rect, Src2Rect: LPRect):
  Integer;
```

Parameter	*Description*
DestRect	Result `TRect` structure
Src1Rect	Source `TRect` structure 1
Src2Rect	Source `TRect` structure 2

Return Value:
Nonzero if union isn't empty; 0 if empty.

Region Procedures and Functions

A region is an area (a polygon or an ellipse) in a window. Regions can be filled with graphical output.

Region procedures and functions create, modify, and get information about regions:

```
CombineRgn
CreateEllipticRgn
CreateEllipticRgnIndirect
CreatePolygonRgn
CreatePolyPolygonRgn
CreateRectRgn
CreateRectRgnIndirect
CreateRoundRectRgn
EqualRgn
FillRgn
FrameRgn
GetRgnBox
InvertRgn
OffsetRgn
PaintRgn
PtInRegion
RectInRegion
SetRectRgn
```

CombineRgn

Combines regions `SrcRgn1` with `SrcRgn2` and puts the result in `DestRgn`. `CombineMode` specifies the method used to combine the regions.

```
function CombineRgn(DestRgn, SrcRgn1, SrcRgn2: HRgn;
  CombineMode: Integer): Integer;
```

Parameter	*Description*
DestRgn	Region to be replaced with new region
SrcRgn1	An existing region
SrcRgn2	An existing region
CombineMode	One of the `rgn_ Combine` region flags

Return Value:
One of the `Region` flags' constants.

CreateEllipticRgn

Creates an elliptical region bounded by the specified rectangle.

```
function CreateEllipticRgn(X1, Y1, X2, Y2: Integer): HRgn;
```

Parameter	Description
X1, Y1	Upper-left corner of bounding rectangle
X2, Y2	Lower-right corner of bounding rectangle

Return Value:
New region identifier if successful; else 0.

CreateEllipticRgnIndirect

Creates an elliptical region bounded by the rectangle specified in `ARect`.

```
function CreateEllipticRgnIndirect(var Rect: TRect): HRgn;
```

Parameter	Description
ARect	`TRect` containing upper-left and lower-right corners of the bounding rectangle

Return Value:
New region identifier if successful; else 0.

CreatePolygonRgn

Creates a polygon region.

```
function CreatePolygonRgn(var Points; Count, PolyFillMode:
  Integer): HRgn;
```

Parameter	Description
Points	`TPoint` array containing vertices of the polygon
Count	Number of points in `Points`
PolyFillMode	Mode for filling the region; use one of the `PolyFill` modes' constants

Return Value:
New region identifier if successful; else 0.

CreatePolyPolygonRgn

Creates a region consisting of a series of possibly overlapping closed polygons.

```
function CreatePolyPolygonRgn(var Points; var PolyCounts;
  Counts, PolyFillMode: Integer): HRgn;
```

Parameter	Description
Points	TPoint array containing vertices of the polygons
PolyCounts	Integer array where each corresponding element specifies the number of points for each polygon in Points
Count	Size of PolyCounts
PolyFillMode	One of the PolyFill modes

Return Value:
Region identifier if successful; else 0.

CreateRectRgn

Creates a rectangular region bounded by the specified rectangle.

```
function CreateRectRgn(X1, Y1, X2, Y2: Integer): HRgn;
```

Parameters	Description
X1, Y1	Upper-left corner of bounding rectangle
X2, Y2	Lower-right corner of bounding rectangle

Return Value:
Region identifier if successful; else 0.

CreateRectRgnIndirect

Creates a rectangular region bounded by ARect.

```
function CreateRectRgnIndirect(var Rect: TRect): HRgn;
```

Parameter	Description
ARect	TRect containing upper-left and lower-right corners of the region

CreateRoundRectRgn

Creates a rectangular region with rounded corners bounded by the specified region.

```
function CreateRoundRectRgn(X1, Y1, X2, Y2, X3, Y3: Integer): HRgn;
```

Parameter	Description
X1, Y1	Upper-left corner of region
X2, Y2	Lower-right corner of region
X3	Ellipse width for rounded corners
Y3	Ellipse height for rounded corners

Return Value:
Region identifier if successful; else 0.

EqualRgn

Compares two regions.

```
function EqualRgn(SrcRgn1, SrcRgn2: HRgn): Bool;
```

Parameter	Description
SrcRgn1, SrcRgn2	Regions to be compared

Return Value:
Nonzero if equal; else 0.

FillRgn

Fills a region using `Brush`.

```
function FillRgn(DC: HDC; Rgn: HRgn; Brush: HBrush): Bool;
```

Parameter	Description
DC	Device context
Rgn	Region to be filled
Brush	Fill brush

Return Value:
Nonzero if successful; else 0.

FrameRgn

Draws a border around a region.

```
function FrameRgn(DC: HDC; Rgn: HRgn; Brush: HBrush; Width,
  Height: Integer): Bool;
```

Parameter	Description
DC	Device context
Rgn	Region to be closed
Brush	Framing brush
Width	Border width in vertical brush strokes (logical units)
Height	Border height in horizontal brush strokes (logical units)

Return Value:
Nonzero if successful; else 0.

GetRgnBox

Gets a region's bounding rectangle.

```
function GetRgnBox(Rgn: HRgn; var Rect: TRect): Integer;
```

Parameter	Description
Rgn	Region identifier
Rect	Receiving `TRect`

Return Value:
Regions type, one of the `Region` flags:

```
ComplexRegion
NullRegion
SimpleRegion;
```

0 if invalid region.

InvertRgn

Inverts the colors of the region specified by `Rgn`.

```
function InvertRgn(DC: HDC; Rgn: HRgn): Bool;
```

Parameter	Description
DC	Device context
Rgn	Region identifier (in device units)

Return Value:
Nonzero if successful; else 0.

OffsetRgn

Moves a region by the specified `X` and `Y` offsets.

```
function OffsetRgn(Rgn: HRgn; X, Y: Integer): Integer;
```

Parameter	*Description*
Rgn	Region identifier
X	Units to move left or right
Y	Units to move up or down

Return Value:
One of the `Region` flags' constants.

PaintRgn

Fills a region with the current brush.

```
function PaintRgn(DC: HDC; Rgn: HRgn): Bool;
```

Parameter	*Description*
DC	Device context
Rgn	Fill region

Return Value:
Nonzero if successful; else 0.

PtInRegion

Decides whether a point lies within a region.

```
function PtInRegion(Rgn: HRgn; X, Y: Integer): Bool;
```

Parameter	*Description*
Rgn	Region identifier
X, Y	A point

Return Value:
Nonzero if the point lies within `Rgn`; else 0.

RectInRegion

Decides whether any part of `Rect` lies within a region.

```
function RectInRegion(Region: HRgn; var Rect: TRect): Bool;
```

Parameter	*Description*
Region	`HRgn` region identifier
Rect	`TRect` structure

Return Value:
Nonzero if within region boundaries; else 0.

SetRectRgn

Uses the space allocated for `Rgn` to create a rectangular region with a specified size.

```
procedure SetRectRgn(Rgn: HRgn; X1, Y1, X2, Y2: Integer);
```

Parameter	*Description*
Rgn	Region identifier
X1, Y1	Upper-left corner of rectangle region
X2, Y2	Lower-left corner of rectangle region

Shape-Drawing Procedures and Functions

Shape-drawing functions use a specified display context's pen to draw the perimeter and the display context's current brush to fill the interior. They do not, however, affect the current position. The shape-drawing procedures and functions are as follows:

```
Chord
DrawFocusRect
Ellipse
Pie
Polygon
PolyPolygon
Rectangle
RoundRect
```

Chord

Draws a chord bounded by the intersection of an ellipse centered in the bounding rectangle and a line segment.

```
function Chord(DC: HDC; X1, Y1, X2, Y2, X3, Y3, X4, Y4: Integer): Bool
```

Parameter	Description
DC	Device context
X1, Y1	Upper-left corner of bounding rectangle
X2, Y2	Lower-right corner of bounding rectangle
X3, Y3	One end of the line segment
X4, Y4	One end of the line segment

Return Value:
Nonzero if the chord is drawn; else 0.

DrawFocusRect

Performs `XOR` to draw a focus style rectangle.

```
procedure DrawFocusRect(DC: HDC; var Rect: TRect);
```

Parameter	Description
DC	Device context
Rect	`TRect` to be drawn

Ellipse

Draws an ellipse centered in the bounding rectangle, whose border is drawn with the current pen and filled with the current brush.

```
function Ellipse(DC: HDC; X1, Y1, X2, Y2: Integer): Bool;
```

Parameter	Description
DC	Device context
X1, Y1	Upper-left corner of the bounding rectangle
X2, Y2	Lower-left corner of the bounding rectangle

Return Value:
Nonzero if the ellipse was drawn; else 0.

Pie

Draws a pie-shaped wedge using the current pen and filled with the current brush, centered in the bounding rectangle.

```
function Pie(DC: HDC; X1, Y1, X2, Y2, X3, Y3, X4, Y4: Integer): Bool;
```

Parameter	*Description*
DC	Device context
X1, Y1	Upper-left corner of bounding rectangle
X2, Y2	Lower-left corner of bounding rectangle
X3, Y3	Starting point of arc
X4, Y4	Endpoint of arc

Return Value:
Nonzero if drawn; else 0.

Polygon

Draws a polygon using the current polygon-filling mode, whose vertices are specified by `Points`. If necessary, the polygon is closed.

```
function Polygon(DC: HDC; var Points; Count: Integer): Bool;
```

Parameter	*Description*
DC	Device context
Points	Array of `TPoint` structures
Count	Size of `Points`

Return Value:
Nonzero if successful; else 0.

PolyPolygon

Draws a series of possibly overlapping polygons using the current polygon-filling mode, whose vertices are specified by `Points`. The polygons are not closed automatically.

```
function PolyPolygon(DC: HDC; var Points; var PolyCounts;
  Count: Integer): Bool;
```

Parameter	Description
DC	Device context
Points	Array of `TPoint` structures
PolyCounts	Array of integers in which each number specifies the number of vertices for each polygon in `Points`
Count	Size of `PolyCounts`

Return Value:
Nonzero if drawn; else 0.

Rectangle

Draws a rectangle using the current pen and fills its interior with the current brush.

```
function Rectangle(DC: HDC; X1, Y1, X2, Y2: Integer): Bool;
```

Parameter	Description
DC	Device context
X1, Y1	Upper-left corner of rectangle
X2, Y2	Lower-right corner of rectangle

Return Value:
Nonzero if rectangle drawn; else 0.

RoundRect

Draws a rectangle with rounded corners using the current pen and filled using the current brush.

```
function RoundRect(DC: HDC; X1, Y1, X2, Y2, X3, Y3: Integer):
Bool;
```

Parameter	Description
DC	Device context
X1, Y1	Upper-left corner of rectangle
X2, Y2	Lower-right corner of rectangle
X3	Ellipse width used to draw rounded corners
Y3	Ellipse height used to draw rounded corners

Return Value:
Nonzero if drawn; else 0.

Text-Drawing Procedures and Functions

Text-drawing functions use the display context's current font to draw.

```
ExtTextOut
GetTabbedTextExtent
GetTextAlign
GetTextExtent
GetTextFace
GetTextMetrics
SetTextAlign
SetTextJustification
TabbedTextOut
TextOut
```

ExtTextOut

Writes a string (using the current font) within `Rect`.

```
function ExtTextOut(DC: HDC; X, Y: Integer; Options: Word; Rect: LPRect;
  Str: PChar; Count: Word; Dx: LPInteger): Bool;
```

Parameter	*Description*
DC	Device context
X, Y	Origin of first character cell
Options	Can be a combination of `eto_ ExtTextOut` options
ARect	`TRect` or nil
Str	String to write
Count	Number of characters in string
Dx	Array of values specifying distance between adjacent cells or 0 for default spacing

Return Value:
Nonzero if string is drawn; else 0.

GetTabbedTextExtent

Computes the height and width (in pixels) of `Str` using the current font. Tabs are expanded as specified.

```
function GetTabbedTextExtent(DC: HDC; Str: PChar; Count, TabPositions:
  Integer; var TabStopPositions): Longint;
```

Parameter	Description
DC	Device context
Str	Line of text
Count	Number of characters in `Str`
TabPositions	Number of tab-stop positions in `TabStopPositions` or 0 and tabs are expanded eight average character widths
TabStopPositions	Integer array containing increasing order of tabstop positions (in pixels)

Return Value:
Height in high-order word; width in low-order word.

GetTextAlign

Gets text-alignment flags.

```
function GetTextAlign(DC: HDC): Word;
```

Parameter	Description
DC	Device context

Return Value:
Combination of `ta_` text alignment options flags

GetTextExtent

Calculates the dimensions of `Str` based on the current font.

```
function GetTextExtent(DC: HDC; Str: PChar; Count: Integer): Longint;
```

Parameter	Description
DC	Device context
Str	Line of text
Count	Number of characters in `Str`

Return Value:
Height (in logical units) in high word; width (in logical units) in low word.

GetTextFace

Copies current font's typeface name to `Facename`.

```
function GetTextFace(DC: HDC; Count: Integer; Facename: PChar): Intege
```

Parameter	Description
DC	Device context
Count	Size of Facename
Facename	Receiving buffer

Return Value:
Number of bytes copied.

GetTextMetrics

Gets the metrics of the current font.

```
function GetTextMetrics(DC: HDC; var Metrics: TTextMetric): Bool;
```

Parameter	Description
DC	Device context
Metrics	Receiving TTextMetric structure

Return Value:
Nonzero if successful; else 0.

SetTextAlign

Sets text-alignment flags used by TextOut and ExtTextOut for positioning text in relationship to its bounding rectangle.

```
function SetTextAlign(DC: HDC; Flags: Word): Word;
```

Parameter	Description
DC	Device or display context
Flags	A combination of the ta_ Text alignment options' constants

Return Value:
Previous horizontal alignment in low-order byte; previous vertical alignment in high-order byte.

SetTextJustification

Defines justification parameters used by the GDI to justify a line of text.

```
function SetTextJustification(DC: HDC; BreakExtra, BreakCount:
  Integer): Integer;
```

Parameter	Description
DC	Device context
BreakExtra	Extra line space (in logical units) to be added
BreakCount	Number of break characters (usually space character) in line

Return Value:
1 if successful; else 0.

TabbedTextOut

Draws a line of text with tabs expanded as specified in `TabStopPositions`, using the current font.

```
function TabbedTextOut(DC: HDC; X, Y: Integer; Str: PChar; Count,
  TabPositions: Integer; var TabStopPositions; TabOrigin:
  Integer): Longint;
```

Parameter	Description
DC	Device context
X, Y	String starting point
Str	String to be drawn
Count	Size (in characters) of `Str`
TabPositions	Number of tab-stop positions in `TabStopPositions` or 0 if tab-stops are expanded eight average character widths
TabStopPositions	Integer array containing ascending tab-stop positions (in pixels)
TabOrigin	Starting position (in logical units) from which tabs are expanded

Return Value:
Not used.

TextOut

Draws a line of text using the current font.

```
function TextOut(DC: HDC; X, Y: Integer; Str: PChar; Count: Integer):
```

Parameter	Description
DC	Device context
X, Y	String starting point
Str	String to be drawn
Count	Size (in characters) of `Str`

Return Value:
Nonzero if drawn; else 0.

O

REFERENCE

OBJECTGRAPHICS (A WHITEWATER GROUP GRAPHICS TOOLKIT)

ObjectGraphics is a library of object types that you can use to handle most of the details of graphics manipulation in your Turbo Pascal for Windows applications.

ObjectGraphics is designed to be used along with ObjectWindows, which defines the object types for handling the details of window management for Turbo Pascal for Windows applications.

ObjectGraphics contains many useful graphics objects that you can more or less plug into your Turbo Pascal for Windows applications. These graphic objects include the following:

Graphics Object	*Use*
TBezier	Displayed as a curve and defined by a polynomial approximation
TChooser	Used to select other graphics objects from a picture; drawn as a rectangular shape
TCurve	Drawn using control points

continues

Graphics Object	*Use*
TEllipse	A simple elliptical graphics object
TEllipticalArc	Drawn as an elliptical arc
TGBitmap	Implements the platform-specific data and functions for creating and using bitmaps
TGPrinter	Provides an abstract protocol for printing ObjectGraphics graphic objects
TGraphic	A formal class which defines behavior which can be inherited by its descendants
TGScroller	A customized scroller
TGWindow	A customized window
TIcon	Handles platform-independent manipulation of icons
TLabel	Implements simple attributed text
TLine	A simple graphics object which owns a pen, but not a brush
TLogBitmap	A formal type which defines the platform-independent data and behaviors for bitmaps
TPicture	A collection of graphics objects
TPie	A pie-shaped graphics object
TPolygon	A graphics object with a polygonal shape
TPolyLine	A graphics object drawn as a group of connected line segments
TPolyMark	A group of graphics markers used to mark the corners or vertices of other graphics
TPolyShape	A formal class which defines behavior which its descendants can inherit
TPort	Defines most of the platform-dependent behavior used in ObjectGraphics applications
TRectangle	A simple graphics object
TRegion	Used to describe a complex area of the display
TRichText	A collection of `TLabels`
TRoundRect	A rectangle with round corners

Graphics Object	*Use*
TShape	A formal type defining behavior which can be inherited by its descendants. `TShape` descendants draw themselves by outlining (framing) with a `TPen` object and then filling with a `TBrush` object
TSubPicture	A collection of graphics objects. It differs from a `TPicture` only by not assumming ownership of its member objects. Thus, it doesn't dispose its member objects in its destructor
TBrush	A logical graphics brush, used to fill `TShape` objects. Brushes bundle diverse attributes of shape interiors
TColor	Used to specify a color attribute; its physical representation is dependent upon the color model used by the platform
TPoint	Holds and manipulates X and Y-coordinates
TGraphSpace	Determines how a conceptual world is mapped to the physical display device
TIndexColor	Used to specify a color attribute, based on an index into a color palette
TLogPort	A formal type which defines behavior which can be inherited by its descendants
TMathRect	Used for mathematical manipulation of coordinates defining a rectangular area
TMemoryStream	A `TStream` descendant which reads and writes to memory, rather than to the disk or to EMS
TPen	A logical drawing pen which bundles diverse attributes of a line
TPointColl	A collection of points
TSystemColor	A color object whose color is based on a color specified by the user as an environment option
TTextPen	A logical text drawing tool

ObjectGraphics objects are used similarly to ObjectWindows objects. For example, the following short application uses ObjectGraphics and ObjectWindows to create a picture window:

```
program APicture;

uses
        OGL1,                    { ObjectGraphics units }
        OGL2,                    { ''     ''            }
        OGL3,                    { ''     ''            }
        WObjects,                { ObjectWindows units  }
        WinTypes,                { ''     ''            }
        WinProcs;                { ''     ''            }

type

  APictureApp = object(TApplication)
    procedure InitMainWindow; virtual;
  end;

  PPictureWindow = ^APictureWindow;

  APictureWindow  = object(TGWindow)  { a customized window }
   constructor Init(AParent: PWindowsObject; ATitle: PChar);
   procedure BeginDrag(MousePt: PGPoint; KeyStates: Word); virtual;
  end;

constructor APictureWindow.Init(AParent: PWindowsObject; ATitle: PChar
 var
   Rect1, Rect2, Rect3: PRectangle;
   BrushColor: PColor;
 begin
   AGWindow.Init(AParent, ATitle);
   Rect1 := New(PRectangle, Init(30, 30, 100, 100, tc_Tools));
   BrushColor := New(PColor, Init(ps_Red));
   Rect1^.Brush^.SetColor(BrushColor);
   Picture^.Add(Rect1);
   Rect2 := New(PRectangle, Init(50, 50, 120, 120, tc_Tools));
   BrushColor^.SetPrimary(ps_Green);
   Rect2^.Brush^.SetColor(BrushColor);
   Picture^.Add(Rect2);
   Rect3 := New(PRectangle, Init(70, 70, 140, 140, tc_Tools));
   BrushColor^.SetPrimary(ps_Blue);
   Rect3^.Brush^.SetColor(BrushColor);
   Picture^.Add(Rect3);
   Dispose(BrushColor, Done);
 end;
```

```
procedure APictureWindow.BeginDrag(MousePt: PGPoint; KeyStates:Word);

var
  SelGraphic: PGraphic;
begin
  SelGraphic := Picture^.ThatContains(MousePt);
  if SelGraphic <> nil then
  begin
    Picture^.BringFront(SelGraphic);

    {SelGraphic^.Invalidate(Port);}
    Port^.Associate(@Self);
    SelGraphic^.Draw(Port);
    Port^.Dissociate;
  end;
end;

procedure APictureApp.InitMainWindow;
begin
  MainWindow := New(PPictureWindow, Init(nil, Application^.Name));
end;

var
  PictureApp: APictureApp;

begin
  PictureApp.Init('This Picture');
  PictureApp.Run;
  PictureApp.Done;
end.
```

For more information about ObjectGraphics, write to:

> The Whitewater Group
> 1800 Ridge Avenue
> Evanston, Illinois 60201

P

REFERENCE

NOTES FOR MANAGING A PROJECT

Turbo Pascal for Windows has a built-in IDE (integrated development environment) that makes it very easy to develop large programming projects.

In particular, try to make good use of the configuration (CFG) file and its corresponding desktop (DSK) file. These files enable you to set up a project's files and have them automatically compiled (as a project) and loaded (as a project) each time you start Turbo Pascal for Windows.

Because Turbo Pascal for Windows remembers where you are in each of these files (using the desktop file), you can work on many files at once without keeping track (yourself) of where you are.

Your current environment (including compiler, linker, editor, and other preferences) are saved for you each time you close Turbo Pascal for Windows.

In writing this book, I made each chapter a project and each new window development a unit, and I used the Make compile option to compile code. The Make option can save you much organizational time because it automatically performs several checks on your files:

1. It compares the date and time of the TPU file for each unit used by the main program in the project with the unit's corresponding PAS file. If the PAS file has changed, Make recompiles it, creating a new (updated) TPU file (unit).

2. It checks to see whether you've changed the interface part of a modified unit. If so, Make recompiles all units using this unit.
3. It checks to see whether you've changed any Include or OBJ files used by any units. If a TPU is older than any of the Include or OBJ files Make links in, it recompiles the unit.

Q

REFERENCE

GLOSSARY

abstract type—A specific kind of base type designed to be used strictly as a basis for other types. It has no instances, and thus can be used only to derive new types. It specifies an interface for all types derived from it. Use an abstract type to group common code. For example, if you have several different collection types, they can all inherit from a single abstract type. Also known as *formal class* in some languages.

accelerator—An accelerator is a "mini-macro" created with a key (or combination of keys) for making menu selections. For example, you can define an accelerator (such as Shift-Delete) to replace a menu selection (such as Edit-Cut).

access specifier—A keyword that controls access to data members and methods within user-defined types. Turbo Pascal for Windows has one: `private`. See the individual definitions for `private`.

ancestor—The type that a descendant type inherits from.

atom—In the DDE protocol, a word value that represents a character string. An atom is not case-sensitive.

base type—Defines a common interface to a group of descendant types. It generalizes the intended uses for a hierarchy of types. In other words, it describes the range of messages that an object of a type can handle. A base type can also be called an *ancestor*.

behavior—Another name for a method declared within a type.

binding (early)—Resolving a method call at compile-time. See binding (late).

binding (late)—Resolving a method call at run-time. When you resolve a method call, you insert the code to determine the address (or another reference) of the method definition at the point where the method is sent a message.

bitmap—A bitmap is a picture, or more specifically, the data representing a picture.

browser—A software tool for inspecting object hierarchies.

built-in type—A type (such as `double`, `char`, and so on) included (or built) in a language. The compiler already knows how to handle it, and doesn't have to learn about it each time it encounters an instance of one.

chaos—Stochastic (or random) behavior occurring in a deterministic system.

characteristic—Another name for data declared within a type.

clipping region — A polygonal or elliptical shape in which any drawing on a display context's virtual surface can appear. The window's client area is the default clipping region.

composition—Including user-defined object types as parts of other object types, rather than derivation (inheritance).

constants — ObjectWindows defines numerous constants to represent command messages; button, check box, and radio button states; errors; child ID, notification, and streams messages; transfer flags; bitmapped fields; and Windows messages.

The use of constants improves program readability and makes it easier for a program to change, if it needs to, in response to changes in subsequent versions of Windows. See ObjectWindows constants in Reference B, "ObjectWindows Constants," for more information and a detailed list of constants.

constructor—A special kind of method that initializes a type.

A constructor can have any legal name not already in use, though often the identifier Init is used:

```
Plant = object
  constructor Setup;  { constructor }
end;
```

In Turbo Pascal for Windows, you must explicitly define and call (send a message to) a constructor. A user-defined type can have any number of constructors, but they can't be virtual because the virtual-method mechanism depends on the constructor to set up the link to the VMT (virtual method table).

controls—User interface devices. ObjectWindows supports the following controls:

- Check boxes
- Combo boxes
- Edit controls
- Group boxes
- List boxes
- `MDI` clients
- Push buttons
- Radio buttons
- Scroll bars
- Static controls

cursor—The shape on the screen that represents the position for the next input. In text-based applications, a cursor is either a block or a line, or something in between. In Windows applications, however, a cursor is a 32-by-32 pixel bitmap. A Windows cursor, therefore, can be one of many different shapes, and is a bitmap.

data hiding—Removing some data from public view. Also known as *data abstraction*.

data members—Characteristics of a type.

DDE (dynamic data exchange)—Microsoft Windows protocol for letting applications share data.

derivation—Another name for inheritance.

descendant—A type that inherits the characteristics and behaviors of another type.

destructor—A special type of method that performs cleanup for a user-defined object type.

In Turbo Pascal for Windows, a destructor can have any legal name not already in use:

```
Bridge = object
  constructor Create;  { constructor }
  destructor Remove; { destructor   }
end;
```

In Turbo Pascal for Windows, destructors can be static or virtual, and a type can have more than one destructor. A destructor can be inherited just like other methods.

dialog box—An input screen (or window) for letting a user enter information in your application. Can be bare-bones or contain other Windows graphical elements (called *controls*).

The resource data associated with a dialog box specifies the dialog box's size, screen location, and text labels.

display context—The surface of the window, which you must specify in order to display text or graphics in a window.

dispose—Procedure for de-allocating objects allocated on the heap:

```
Dispose(ShapePointer);
```

Alternatively (and preferably), you should call the destructor inside the Dispose call by using the following extended syntax to clean up an object:

```
PtrSomeObject = ^SomeObject;
SomeObject = object
  constructor Init;
  destructor Done;
end;

var
  P : PtrSomeObject;

Dispose(P, Done); { call the destructor to clean up properly }
```

DLL (dynamic link libraries)—A library of indexed functions and procedures. Executable modules of code linked into an application at run-time.

DLLs allow programmers to develop and maintain independent program components. Similar to units in their modularity, they are more powerful because they can be

1. Linked into an application at run-time
2. Shared by many concurrently executing programs
3. Written in a variety of languages, regardless of the language used to access the DLL

dynamic binding — Another name for *late binding*. See binding (late).

dynamic method table (DMT) — A method table new to Turbo Pascal for Windows for dispatching late-bound methods. Whereas the VMT (virtual method table) encodes a pointer for all late-bound methods in an object type, the VMT encodes only the methods that were overridden in the object type. If a descendant type overrides only a few virtual methods, a DMT uses less space than a VMT. See VMT.

dynamic variable—A variable allocated on the heap and manipulated with pointers.

dynamic variable allocation—Creating and destroying variables at run-time rather than at compile-time. See binding (late).

encapsulation—Combining data (characteristics) with the methods (behaviors) for manipulating it; organizing code into user-defined types.

event—An occurrence that affects a program from the outside world. Some examples are keystrokes, mouse-button clicks, a character from a serial port, and occurrences triggered by the system software (DOS, BIOS), such as a "timer tick."

GDI—See Windows GDI.

Global and local memory—Your applications can allocate memory blocks in either of two areas: the global or the local heap.

The global heap is all the memory that Windows "claims" when you run it. The global heap is shared by Windows, Windows applications, and the "global" memory blocks allocated by Windows applications. Global memory is powerful because it's system-sized: memory within and beyond your applications. A global memory block can be as large as 1M in Windows standard mode and 64M in 386-enhanced mode. A global memory block can be used to access the data in other programs.

The local heap is memory accessible only by a specific instance of your application. In other words, it's "private" to your application and just like the heap you've been used to in Turbo Pascal (before Windows). It's limited to whatever's left of the 64K data segment after your application's used some of it for a stack and its own global variables. The local heap is only 8K by default, but you can adjust its size using either the $M compiler directive or by way of the Turbo Pascal for Window's IDE option/Compiler/MemorySize menus.

GUI (graphical user interface)—Windows is a graphical user interface (GUI). Everything—text, dots, fills, and pictures—is treated by Windows not as ASCII characters (DOS-style) but as pixels turned on and off in a display context (the Windows name for a painting surface).

handle—A name; represents a pointer to a pointer to a memory block.

heap—The free memory available to an application. The global heap contains memory available to all applications. The local heap contains memory available only to a specific application.

hierarchy—A group of types derived from a base type. Turbo Pascal for Windows implements single inheritance. Although an ancestor can have many descendants, and a descendant can have many ancestors, a descendant can have only one immediate ancestor. See the following illustration.

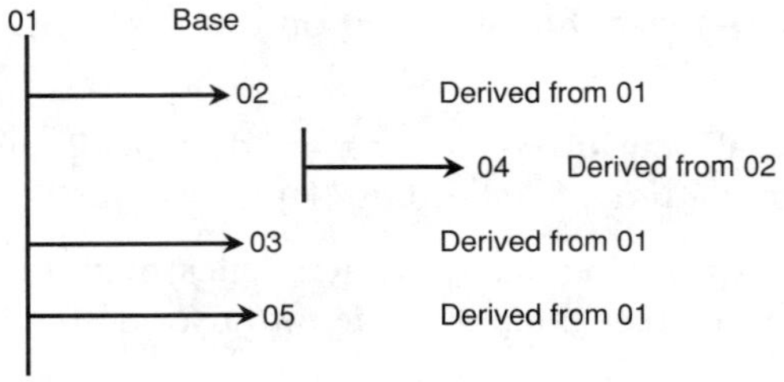

icon—An icon is the graphical screen element that represents your application program's state. You select an icon from the program manager's window to run programs, for example. An icon, too, is a bitmap.

implementation—Describes how an object type behaves. You can compile, but not link, code with just the interface description. Therefore, you can create different implementations later and link them in then, without recompiling the rest of the project. By separating the interface from the implementation, you isolate bugs and make experimentation easier.

inheritance—Organizing user-defined types into hierarchies. Note that Turbo Pascal for Windows implements single inheritance. In other words, a descendant can have only one immediate ancestor, as shown in the following illustration.

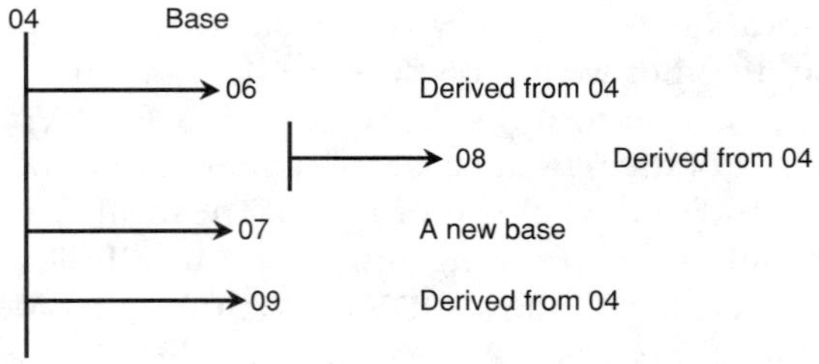

initialization—Setting a variable or instance of a type to a specific value.

instance—A variable of a type.

interface—In Turbo Pascal for Windows, the object definition.

The interface says, "Here's what a type looks like, and here are its behaviors." But it doesn't specify how the type behaves. That's left to the implementation, which defines the type's specific behavior. The interface describes what a type does. The implementation describes how the type works.

list box—A list box is a sort of window (it's defined by a rectangle on the screen) that shows the user a list of information. This information can be integers, strings, and so on. The user can click on a list item, and the selected item can be transferred into another variable or can trigger other messages and actions.

local memory—See global and local memory.

MDI (multiple document interface)—ObjectWindows supports the Windows `Multi-document interface` (MDI) standard, which allows an application or task to work simultaneously with many open documents. Think of these documents usually as text, database, or spreadsheet files.

Several components (or features) are common to any MDI application. Every MDI application has a main window (called a frame window), and within the frame window an invisible window called the MDI client window, which holds MDI child windows. The client window manages (behind the scenes) its MDI child windows. TMDIWindow's methods primarily construct and manage child windows and process menu selections.

The `MDI` frame window is the `Main` Window of the `multi-document interface` (`MDI`).

menu—Displays application options and allows the user to make selections. The menu's resource identifies the order and number of these options.

message—The name of a method passed to an instance of an object type. When you send a message to an instance of an object, you call one of its methods. To send a message to an instance of an object, you specify the object and the method you want to invoke. For example, if `SomeType` is an instance of an object and `Init` is a method, then the following sends an `Init` message to the object:

```
SomeType.Init;
```

method—In Turbo Pascal for Windows, a procedure or function declared within an object, used to access the data within the object.

model—A mathematical representation of some aspect of the world.

new—A procedure for allocating space for a type on the heap and initializing the object in one operation. New is invoked with two parameters: a pointer name and a constructor call:

```
new(ArcPointer,Init(35,24,35));
```

object—An instance of an object type; a record that can inherit, consisting of data and methods.

override—Reimplement, redefine. Used to describe the reimplementation of methods by object types.

pixel—A dot; the smallest displayable element of a computer screen.

pointer —Contains the address of (that is, points to) a variable. In Turbo Pascal for Windows, designated by ^:

```
IntPointer : ^Integer;
```

polymorphic collections—The ObjectWindows `TCollection` object is an abstract type for "collecting" data.

`TCollection` objects can size themselves dynamically at run-time, and they can be polymorphic. Thus, a collection can grow as you want it to, without your changing any code. And because it's polymorphic, you can put any kind of object (and even nonobjects) in it. You can even mix the object types within a single collection!

Because a collection uses untyped pointers, it doesn't need to know anything about the objects it's given to process. It just stores them and gives them back.

polymorphic type—A type not known until run-time.

polymorphism—Single interface, many implementations. Specifically, calling a `virtual` method for a variable whose precise type isn't known at compile-time. The behavior is established at run-time by way of late binding.

private—Any members following `private` can be accessed only by functions within the same unit.

resource—Another name for the graphical elements that compose your Windows application. Because resources (cursor shape, menus, icons, and so on) are similar in all your applications, it makes sense to store them in files outside your source code and link them with your source code when you need them. This process makes them easy to modify without affecting your application code.

Resources are data characterized by the following types:

- Accelerators
- Bitmaps
- Cursors
- Icons
- Dialog boxes
- Menus
- Strings

scope—The lifetime and accessibility of a variable. Defines which parts of a program can access specific variables. For example, a variable declared within a function is (by default) local, and can be accessed only by code within the function.

scope (global)—Accessible by code within the program or application.

scope (local)—Accessible only by code within the function or procedure.

static method—A method resolved by the compiler at compile-time (see early binding).

static instance—An instance of an object type named in the `var` declaration (in Turbo Pascal for Windows) and allocated in the data segment and on the stack.

strange attractor—In phase space, an attractor is a point or limit cycle in a dynamic system, which draws or attracts a system. In other words, as the system changes state, it can reach equilibrium (settle down) to a point or a cycle.

A strange attractor is an attractor that's "broken up" or fragmented in phase space. It represents a system whose order, when plotted in a time-series, isn't obvious, but shows itself in a shape (an order) in phase space.

stream—A stream is a collection of objects on its way to some device: a file, port, EMS, and so on.

strings—(null-terminated and Turbo Pascal); the Windows API requires that strings be null-terminated, the format used by C. In other words, a string is represented as a sequence of characters terminated by a NULL (#0). Turbo Pascal for Windows stores null-terminated strings as arrays of characters.

```
type
  NTstring = array[0..79] of Char;
```

A null-terminated string in Turbo Pascal for Windows can be as long as 65,535 characters (a limitation imposed by DOS and Windows).

Turbo Pascal stores its standard strings in the `string` type: a length byte followed by a sequence of as many as 255 characters.

```
type
  TPstring = string[80];
```

Because Windows doesn't recognize Turbo Pascal strings, your application must either use null-terminated strings exclusively or convert any Pascal strings to null-terminated before passing them to Windows (to display, for example).

The strings unit supplied by Turbo Pascal for Windows provides the conversion functions and a complete manipulation package for handling null-terminated strings. See *strings* in the reference section for details.

strings (resource)—Text displayed by application menus, dialog boxes, error messages, and so on. Strings don't have to be specified as resources, but maintaining them as resources helps keep your specific application code and its visual aspects separate.

structured programming—Combines two ideas:

1. *Structured program flow*. In other words, the flow of control of a program is determined by the syntax of the program code.
2. *Invariants*. Assertions that hold every time control reaches them.

type—Tells the range of values (or states) a variable can assume and the operators that you can apply to it. Everything you can know about a "class of objects" that a variable or instance can represent.

For example, an integer type is a number within the range –32768...32767 and is represented by a signed 16-bit format. A byte is a number within the range 0...255 and is represented by an ungrouped 8-bit format.

type extensibility—The ability to add functionality to code. You derive new types (through inheritance) and add or modify behaviors and characteristics to suit your needs.

unit—In Turbo Pascal for Windows, a collection of constants, data types, variables, procedures, and functions that are separately compiled.

If data members in a type are declared after the keyword, `private`, any function, method, or procedure within a unit can access it, but no functions, methods, or procedures outside the unit can.

virtual method—A method resolved by the compiler at run-time. (See late binding.)

In Turbo Pascal for Windows, you declare a `virtual` method by adding the keyword, `virtual`, after the method:

```
procedure Show; virtual;
```

user-defined type—A single structure containing the characteristics and behaviors for the type. In Turbo Pascal for Windows, we call it an *object*. The compiler treats this type the way it treats a built-in type.

VMT (virtual method table)—In Turbo Pascal for Windows, each type (object) has a VMT that contains information about the type, including its size and a pointer to the code implementing each of its virtual methods. When an instance of a type sends a message to a constructor, the constructor automatically establishes a link to the VMT.

Each type has one VMT. Each instance of a type links to the type VMT. *Important*: You must not send a message to a virtual method before sending a message to its constructor! Turbo Pascal allows you to use the `{$R+}` switch to check for the proper construction of an instance of a type sending a message to an object type. If the instance hasn't been properly initialized (via a constructor), a range-check error occurs.

WinCrt—A Turbo Pascal for Windows unit that implements a terminal-like text screen in a window. If your applications use `WinCrt`, they don't have to contain any Windows-specific code. This unit is useful for reimplementing existing Turbo Pascal text-based applications in Windows without adding a lot of extra code.

Windows Graphics Device Interface (GDI)—The Windows GDI allows you to write applications that display and manipulate graphics independent of a specific display device. You can, for example, write applications that use the same code, yet can be displayed in EGA, VGA, or Hercules modes.

Windows achieves device independence by using various device drivers that translate GDI function calls into commands that make sense to the specific output device being used. So, you write code as though the output device doesn't matter, which (in general) is how it is.

WinProcs, WinTypes—Two of the three units packaged with Turbo Pascal for Windows, which establish the interface between your applications and Windows. `WinTypes` and `WinProcs` define the Turbo Pascal for Windows function types and processes for sending messages directly to the Windows API.

If your application sends messages to the Windows API only through ObjectWindows, it doesn't need to include the WinTypes and WinProcs units.

WObjects—One of the three units packaged with Turbo Pascal for Windows that establish the interface between your applications and Windows. `WObjects` is the ObjectWindows object library.

with—Turbo Pascal for Windows keyword. You can access a type's data members by using a dot (`AType.Member`) or a `with` statement:

```
with AType do
begin
  X:= 2;
  Y:= 3;
  Z:= 4;
end;
```

R

REFERENCE

REFERENCES, RESOURCES, AND NOTES

Here are a few of the books I think you should know about, if you want more information about object-oriented programming, Turbo Pascal, Windows, modeling, chaos theory, and other topics I've touched on in this book. This list is only a sample of the many works available on these subjects, but it reflects the books I have on my shelf. Most of these have in some way contributed to my understanding of "tough" computing topics.

Abraham, Ralph; Christopher Shaw. *Dynamics—4 Volumes*. Santa Cruz, California: Aerial Press, 1984-1989. A great introduction and study of dynamics using pictures. If you want to really "get a feel" for chaos theory, check out this one. Starts with periodic behavior and works toward the harder stuff: chaotic and bifurcation behavior. Great personalized drawings.

Casti, John L. *Alternate Realities: Mathematical Models of Nature and Man*. New York: John Wiley and Sons, 1989. A thorough mathematical discussion of modeling. Chapters on formal representation, cellular automata; catastrophe theory, chaos, and the relationship of modeling to the way we view the world.

Cheney, Ward; David Kincaid. *Numerical Mathematics and Computing*. Monterey, California: Brooks/Cole Publishing, 1980, 1985. If you're writing code that uses numbers, you should have at least one good numerical computing book at hand. This is the one I go back to time and again, and I used it several times while writing *Turbo Pascal for Windows Bible*. Fascinating information about the truth (and not-so truth) of numerical processing by computer. Don't use numbers without it.

Eckel, Bruce. *Using C++*. Berkeley, California: Osborne McGraw-Hill, 1989. Although the subject of *Turbo Pascal for Windows Bible* is object-oriented programming for Windows, Turbo Pascal-style, you can learn a lot about OOP from C++. This one is my favorite C++ programming guides: 600 pages of code, descriptions, and ideas about OOP. It precedes the Turbo C++ compiler, so examples are developed around Zortech's C++ compiler. You can easily apply the examples to any C++, however, and you can use Bruce's ideas if you're programming in Turbo Pascal. Goes into many advanced topics. A good book to explore and study if you want to get to the heart of object-oriented programming.

Entsminger, Gary. *Tao of Objects*. Redwood City, California: M&T Books, 1990. My first book. A gentle introduction to object-oriented programming using Turbo Pascal and C++ examples. Predates Turbo Pascal for Windows, but useful for Turbo Pascal programmers who want an uncluttered introduction to OOP.

Gleick, James. *Chaos: Making a New Science*. New York: Viking Press, 1987. A great introduction to chaos theory. Very easy, fun reading. Focuses as much on the people who "rediscovered" chaos as it does on the theory itself. Anyone interested in chaos should start here.

Hofstadter, Douglas; Daniel Dennett. *The Mind's I*. New York: Bantam Books, 1981. Like all of Hofstadter's books, this one really gets your brain working. A collection of stories and essays about self-reflection, self-consciousness, recursion, machines with souls, scientific speculations, and other mind-stretching stuff.

Meyer, Bertrand. *Object-oriented Software Construction*. Englewood Cliffs, New Jersey: Prentice-Hall, 1988. A good discussion about the issues and principles relating to software design using object-oriented techniques. Outlines the path that leads to object-orientedness and, generally attempts to convince you to program with objects. The second half of the book, unfortunately for Turbo Pascalers, focuses entirely on Meyer's language, "Eiffel," making it less useful than it could have been. Worth a look, though, because of the extensive study of design.

O'Brien, Tim. *Turbo Pascal, The Complete Reference*. Berkeley, California: Borland/Osborne McGraw-Hill, 1989. A good reference for Turbo Pascal. Includes a good introductory chapter on object-oriented programming Turbo Pascal-style.

Petzold, Charles. *Windows Programming*, 2nd Edition. Redmond, Washington: Microsoft Press, 1990. This is the classic work on Windows programming. A first class "Windows Bible" C-style. If you want the nitty-gritty details of how a C programmer attacks C, or if you want to know as much as possible about Windows programming, get this book. I found it very useful in writing Turbo Pascal for Windows code.

Sethi, Ravi. *Programming Languages: Concepts and Constructs*. Reading, MA: Addison-Wesley, 1989. Excellent study of the development, design, and content of modern programming languages. In particular, several fine chapters on object-oriented programming. Good discussions of Modula-2, C++, and Smalltalk. Chapters on encapsulation, inheritance, functional programming, logic programming, and several tough, advanced chapters on interpreters and lambda calculus. Highly recommended for studying the development of programming languages. Should give you a good idea of the problems that language developers encounter.

Stewart, Ian. *Does God Play Dice? The Mathematics of Chaos*. New York: Basil Blackwell, 1989. In-depth study of the mathematics of chaos, turbulence, and strange attractors. Good combination of history, mathematics, and philosophy. Inspired discussions of logistic mapping, Lorenz & Henon attractors, and fractals.

Swan, Tom. *Mastering Turbo Pascal 6*. Carmel, Indiana: Hayden Books, 1991. Latest version of Tom's fine series on Turbo Pascal. A good reference with a lot of code and information about OOP.

Turbo Power Software. Scotts Valley, California: *Object Professional User's Manual*, 1990. Three volumes of object-oriented discussion Turbo Pascal-style. Accompanies the fine Turbo Power object library for Turbo Pascal 5.5 (and later). Complete source code for the library is included, so this package (manuals and code) makes an excellent in-depth resource for ideas about object-oriented programming. Full of good code and coding ideas for Turbo Pascal programmers.

Vasey, Phil, et al. *Prolog++ Programming Reference Manual*. London: Logic Programming Associates Ltd., 1990. One of those rare creatures: a programming manual that really shines. In addition to showing you how to program in Prolog++, the object-oriented version of Prolog, it compares object-oriented languages and discusses the key features of OOP. Available from Quintus Computer Systems in Mountain View, California.

Yourdon, E.N.; L.L. Constantine. *Structured Design*. Englewood Cliffs, New Jersey: Prentice-Hall, 1979. A classic work on structured methodology by the gurus of the field.

Quotation Acknowledgments

SAMS gratefully acknowledges permission from the following sources to reprint material in their control:

In the Introduction, Ice 9 Publishing for lyrics from "Box of Rain" by Robert Hunter. From the album *American Beauty* by The Grateful Dead. New York: Warner Bros., Inc, 1970.

In Chapter 1, Microsoft Press for lines from *Programming Windows*, 2nd Edition by Charles Petzold. Redmond, Washington: Microsoft Press, 1990.

In Chapter 2, Que Corporation for lines from *Using Borland C++* by Lee Atkinson and Mark Atkinson. Carmel, Indiana: Que Corporation, 1991.

In Chapter 3, M&T Books for lines from *The Tao of Objects* by Gary Entsminger. Redwood City, California: M&T Books, 1990.

In Chapter 4, Osborne-McGraw Hill for lines from *Windows Programming* by William H. Murray, III and Chris H. Pappas. Berkeley, California: Osborne-McGraw Hill: 1990.

In Chapter 5, Microsoft Press for lines from *Programming Windows*, 2nd ed. by Charles Petzold. Redmond, Washington: Microsoft Press, 1990.

In Chapter 6, Prentice-Hall for lines from *Object-oriented Software Construction* by Bertrand Meyer. Englewood Cliffs, New Jersey: Prentice-Hall, 1988.

In Chapter 7, Vintage Books (Random House) for lines from *Gödel, Escher, Bach: An Eternal Golden Braid* by Douglas Hofstadter. New York: Vintage Books, 1979.

In Chapter 8, Addison-Wesley Publishing Co. for lines from *Raised by Puppets only to be Killed by Research* by Andrei Codrescu. Reading, Massachusetts, Addison-Wesley, 1989.

In Chapter 9, Clark City Press for lines from *Just Before Dark* by Jim Harrison. Livingston, Montana: Clark City Press, 1991.

In Chapter 10, W.H. Freeman & Co. for lines from *Aaron's Code* by Pamela McCorduck. New York: W.H. Freeman & Co., 1991.

In Chapter 11, M&T Books for lines from *The Tao of Objects* by Gary Entsminger. Redwood City, California: M&T Books, 1990.

In Chapter 12, Viking Penguin for lines from *Nature's Chaos* by Eliot Porter and James Gleick. New York: Viking Penguin, 1990.

In Chapter 13, Vintage Books (Random House) for lines from *Gödel, Escher, Bach: An Eternal Golden Braid* by Douglas Hofstadter. New York: Vintage Books, 1979.

S

REFERENCE

ASCII CODE CHARACTER SET

ASCII Dec	Value Hex	ASCII Character	ASCII Dec	Value Hex	ASCII Character
000	00	null	019	13	!!
001	01	☺	020	14	¶
002	02	☻	021	15	§
003	03	♥	022	16	▬
004	04	♦	023	17	↨
005	05	♣	024	18	↑
006	06	♠	025	19	↓
007	07	●	026	1A	→
008	08	◘	027	1B	←
009	09	○	028	1C	FS
010	0A	■	029	1D	GS
011	0B	♂	030	1E	RS
012	0C	♀	031	1F	US
013	0D	♪	032	20	SP
014	0E	♪♪	033	21	!
015	0F	☼	034	22	"
016	10	►	035	23	#
017	11	◄	036	24	$
018	12	↕	037	25	%

ASCII	***Value***		***ASCII***	***Value***	
Dec	***Hex***	***ASCII Character***	***Dec***	***Hex***	***ASCII Character***
038	26	&	079	4F	O
039	27	'	080	50	P
040	28	(	081	51	Q
041	29	)	082	52	R
042	2A	*	083	53	S
043	2B	+	084	54	T
044	2C	,	085	55	U
045	2D	-	086	56	V
046	2E	.	087	57	W
047	2F	/	088	58	X
048	30	0	089	59	Y
049	31	1	090	5A	Z
050	32	2	091	5B	[
051	33	3	092	5C	\
052	34	4	093	5D	]
053	35	5	094	5E	^
054	36	6	095	5F	_
055	37	7	096	60	`
056	38	8	097	61	a
057	39	9	098	62	b
058	3A	:	099	63	c
059	3B	;	100	64	d
060	3C	<	101	65	e
061	3D	=	102	66	f
062	3E	>	103	67	g
063	3F	?	104	68	h
064	40	@	105	69	i
065	41	A	106	6A	j
066	42	B	107	6B	k
067	43	C	108	6C	l
068	44	D	109	6D	m
069	45	E	110	6E	n
070	46	F	111	6F	o
071	47	G	112	70	p
072	48	H	113	71	q
073	49	I	114	72	r
074	4A	J	115	73	s
075	4B	K	116	74	t
076	4C	L	117	75	u
077	4D	M	118	76	v
078	4E	N	119	77	w

ASCII Value Dec	Hex	ASCII Character	ASCII Value Dec	Hex	ASCII Character
120	78	x	161	A1	í
121	79	y	162	A2	ó
122	7A	z	163	A3	ú
123	7B	{	164	A4	ñ
124	7C	¦	165	A5	Ñ
125	7D	}	166	A6	ª
126	7E	~	167	A7	º
127	7F	DEL	168	A8	¿
128	80	Ç	169	A9	⌐
129	81	ü	170	AA	¬
130	82	é	171	AB	½
131	83	â	172	AC	¼
132	84	ä	173	AD	¡
133	85	à	174	AE	«
134	86	å	175	AF	»
135	87	ç	176	B0	░
136	88	ê	177	B1	▒
137	89	ë	178	B2	▓
138	8A	è	179	B3	│
139	8B	ï	180	B4	┤
140	8C	î	181	B5	╡
141	8D	ì	182	B6	╢
142	8E	Ä	183	B7	╖
143	8F	Å	184	B8	╕
144	90	É	185	B9	╣
145	91	æ	186	BA	║
146	92	Æ	187	BB	╗
147	93	ô	188	BC	╝
148	94	ö	189	BD	╜
149	95	ò	190	BE	╛
150	96	û	191	BF	┐
151	97	ù	192	C0	└
152	98	ÿ	193	C1	┴
153	99	Ö	194	C2	┬
154	9A	Ü	195	C3	├
155	9B	¢	196	C4	─
156	9C	£	197	C5	┼
157	9D	¥	198	C6	╞
158	9E	Pt	199	C7	╟
159	9F	*f*	200	C8	╚
160	A0	á	201	C9	╔

ASCII Value *Dec*	*Hex*	*ASCII Character*	*ASCII Value* *Dec*	*Hex*	*ASCII Character*
202	CA	╩	229	E5	σ
203	CB	╦	230	E6	µ
204	CC	╠	231	E7	τ
205	CD	═	232	E8	Φ
206	CE	╬	233	E9	θ
207	CF	╧	234	EA	Ω
208	D0	╨	235	EB	δ
209	D1	╤	236	EC	∞
210	D2	╥	237	ED	ø
211	D3	╙	238	EE	∈
212	D4	╘	239	EF	∩
213	D5	╒	240	F0	≡
214	D6	╓	241	F1	±
215	D7	╫	242	F2	≥
216	D8	╪	243	F3	≤
217	D9	┘	244	F4	⌠
218	DA	┌	245	F5	⌡
219	DB	█	246	F6	÷
220	DC	▄	247	F7	≈
221	DD	▌	248	F8	°
222	DE	▐	249	F9	•
223	DF	▀	250	FA	·
224	E0	α	251	FB	√
225	E1	β	252	FC	η
226	E2	Γ	253	FD	²
227	E3	π	254	FE	■
228	E4	Σ	255	FF	

Index

A

B

C

D

E

F

G

H

I

K

L

M

N

O

P

Q

R

U

X–Z

IF YOUR COMPUTER USES 3 1/2-INCH DISKS

Though many personal computers use 5 1/4-inch disks to store information, some newer computers use 3 1/2-inch disks. If your computer requires 3 1/2-inch disks, return this form to SAMS to obtain (free of charge) a 3 1/2-inch disk to use with this book.

Simply complete the information on this form and mail this page to:

Turbo Pascal® for Windows™ Bible
Disk Exchange

SAMS
11711 N. College Avenue, Suite 140
Carmel, IN 46032

Name: ______________________________

Address: ______________________________

City: ______________ State: __________ ZIP: __________

Phone: ______________________________